Learn Microsoft® Excel 2002 VBA Programming with XML and ASP

Julitta Korol

Wordware Publishing, Inc.

Library of Congress Cataloging-in-Publication Data

Korol, Julitta.
    Learn Microsoft Excel 2002 VBA programming with XML and ASP / by Julitta Korol.
        p.   cm.
    Includes index.
    ISBN 1-55622-761-2 (pb.)
    1. Microsoft Excel (Computer file)   2.   Microsoft Visual Basic for Windows.
    3. Active server pages.   4. Electronic spreadsheets.   5. Computer software--
    Development.   6. XML (Document markup language)   I. Title.
    HF5548.4.M523 K686 2002
    005.369--dc21   2002152725
                                                           CIP

ISBN 1-55622-761-2
10 9 8 7 6 5 4 3 2 1
0301

All inquiries for volume purchases of this book should be addressed to Wordware Publishing,
Inc., at the above address. Telephone inquiries may be made by calling:

(972) 423-0090

Dedication

To my mother and my mother-in-law, Genowefa Malinowska and Alfreda Korol. They have always been against the long hours and long nights it takes to write technical books. My life may not have been very comfortable during the past 10 years (I certainly could have slept more and relaxed more, and tried all the other highly recommended things); however, the decade that I've dedicated to writing so that others can benefit may be that special mission I was born to complete. Hey, you never know.

Contents

Acknowledgments xiii
Introduction xv

Chapter 1 Introduction to Spreadsheet Automation 1
Understanding Macros 2
    Common Uses for Macros 2
    Planning a Macro 3
    Recording a Macro 5
    Running the Macro 8
    Modifying the Macro 8
    Adding Comments 12
    Analyzing the Macro Code 13
    Cleaning Up the Macro Code 14
    Testing the Modified Macro 15
    Two Levels of Macro Execution 16
    Improving Your Macro 17
    Renaming the Macro 20
    Other Methods of Running Macros 20
    Saving Macros 26
    Printing Macros 27
    Storing Macros in the Personal Macro Workbook 27
    Opening Workbooks Containing Macros 29
The Visual Basic Editor Window 31
    Understanding the Project Explorer Window 31
    Understanding the Properties Window 32
    Understanding the Code Window 33
    Other Windows in the Visual Basic Editor Window 35
What's Next 36

Chapter 2 First Steps in Visual Basic for Applications 37
Understanding Instructions, Modules, and Procedures 38
    Assigning a Name to the VBA Project 39
    Renaming the Module 40
    Calling a Procedure from Another Project 41
Understanding Objects, Properties, and Methods 43
    Learning about Objects, Properties, and Methods 45
Syntax Versus Grammar 48
    Breaking Up Long VBA Statements 51
    Understanding VBA Errors 51

In Search of Help. 54
On-the-fly Syntax and Programming Assistance 55
Using the Object Browser. 60
Using the VBA Object Library 66
Locating Procedures with the Object Browser 68
Using the Immediate Window. 68
Obtaining Information in the Immediate Window 71
Learning about Objects 72
Doing Things with Spreadsheet Cells. 73
Using the Range Property 73
Using the Cells Property 73
Using the Offset Property 75
Other Methods of Selecting Cells 77
Selecting Rows and Columns 77
Obtaining Information about the Worksheet 78
Entering Data in a Worksheet 78
Returning Information Entered in a Worksheet. 78
Finding Out about Cell Formatting 79
Moving, Copying, and Deleting Cells 80
Doing Things with Workbooks and Worksheets 80
Doing Things with Windows. 82
Managing the Excel Application 83
What's Next. 83

Chapter 3   Understanding Variables, Data Types, and Constants 85
Saving Results of VBA Statements 86
What Are Variables? 86
Data Types. 87
How to Create Variables 88
How to Declare Variables 89
Specifying the Data Type of a Variable 92
Assigning Values to Variables 94
Forcing Declaration of Variables 98
Understanding the Scope of Variables 99
Procedure-Level (Local) Variables 100
Module-Level Variables 100
Project-Level Variables. 102
Lifetime of Variables 102
Understanding and Using Static Variables. 102
Declaring and Using Object Variables 104
Using Specific Object Variables. 106
Finding a Variable Definition. 106
Using Constants in VBA Procedures 107
Built-in Constants 108
What's Next. 110

Chapter 4 **VBA Procedures: Subroutines and Functions** **111**

About Function Procedures 112

Creating a Function Procedure 112

Executing a Function Procedure 115

Passing Arguments 118

Specifying Argument Types 120

Passing Arguments by Reference and by Value 122

Using Optional Arguments 123

Locating Built-in Functions 125

Using the MsgBox Function 127

Using the InputBox Function 134

Using the InputBox Method 138

Using Master Procedures and Subprocedures 142

What's Next 145

Chapter 5 **Decision Making with VBA** **147**

Relational and Logical Operators 148

If…Then Statement 149

Decisions Based on More Than One Condition 152

The If…Then…Else Statement 154

The If…Then…ElseIf Statement 158

Nested If…Then… Statements 160

Select Case Statement 161

Using Is with the Case Clause 163

Specifying a Range of Values in a Case Clause 164

Specifying Multiple Expressions in a Case Clause 165

What's Next 166

Chapter 6 **Repeating Actions in VBA** **167**

Do Loops: Do…While and Do…Until 168

Watching a Procedure Execute 173

While…Wend Loop 174

For…Next Loop 174

For Each…Next Loop 177

Exiting Loops Early 178

Nested Loops 179

What's Next 180

Chapter 7 **Managing Lists and Tables of Data with VBA** **181**

Understanding Arrays 182

Declaring Arrays 184

Array Upper and Lower Bounds 185

Using Arrays in VBA Procedures 185

Arrays and Looping Statements 187

Using a Two-Dimensional Array 189

Static and Dynamic Arrays 190

Array Functions 193

The Array Function 193

The IsArray Function. 194
The Erase Function. 195
The LBound and UBound Functions 195
Errors in Arrays 196
Parameter Arrays 198
What's Next. 199

Chapter 8 Manipulating Files and Folders with VBA 201
Manipulating Files and Folders 202
Finding Out the Name of the Active Folder (the CurDir Function) 202
Changing the Name of a File or Folder (the Name Function) 203
Checking the Existence of a File or Folder (the Dir Function) 204
Finding Out the Date and Time the File Was Modified
(the FileDateTime Function) 207
Finding Out the Size of a File (the FileLen Function) 207
Returning and Setting File Attributes (the GetAttr
and SetAttr Functions). 208
Changing the Default Folder or Drive (the ChDir and
ChDrive Statements) 210
Creating and Deleting Folders (the MkDir and RmDir Statements) . . . 211
Copying Files (the FileCopy Statement) 212
Deleting Files (the Kill Statement). 214
Writing to and Reading from Files (Input/Output) 215
File Access Types 215
Working with Sequential Files 215
Working with Random Access Files 224
Working with Binary Files 230
Modern Methods of Working with Files and Folders 232
Finding Information about Files with the WSH 234
Properties of the File Object 239
Properties of the Folder Object. 240
Properties of the Drive Object 241
Creating a Text File Using WSH 242
Performing Other Operations with WSH 244
What's Next. 247

Chapter 9 Controlling Other Applications with VBA 249
Launching Applications 250
Moving between Applications 254
Controlling Another Application. 255
Other Methods of Controlling Applications 258
Understanding Automation. 258
Understanding Linking and Embedding 258
Linking and Embedding with VBA 260
COM and Automation 261
Understanding Binding 261
Late Binding 261
Early Binding 262

Establishing a Reference to an Object Library 263
Creating Automation Objects 265
 Using the CreateObject Function 265
 Creating a New Word Document Using Automation. 266
 Using the GetObject Function 267
 Opening an Existing Word Document 268
 Using the New Keyword 269
 Using Automation to Access Microsoft Outlook 270
What's Next 271

Chapter 10 Dialog Boxes and Custom Forms. 273
Excel Dialog Boxes 274
File Open and File Save As Dialog Boxes 277
GetOpenFilename and GetSaveAsFilename Methods 281
Creating Forms. 283
 Tools for Creating User Forms 285
 Placing Controls on a Form. 290
Sample Application 1: Info Survey. 290
 Adding Buttons, Check Boxes, and Other Controls to a Form 292
 Changing Control Names. 296
 Setting Other Control Properties 297
 Preparing a Worksheet to Store Custom Form Data. 298
 Displaying a Custom Form 300
 Setting the Tab Order. 300
 Understanding Form and Control Events 301
 Writing VBA Procedures to Respond to Form and Control Events 303
 Writing a Procedure to Initialize the Form 304
 Writing a Procedure to Populate the List Box Control. 306
 Writing a Procedure to Control Option Buttons 306
 Writing Procedures to Synchronize the Text Box with the Spin Button. . 308
 Writing a Procedure that Closes the User Form 308
 Transferring Form Data to the Worksheet 309
 Using the Info Survey Application 310
Sample Application 2: Students and Exams 310
 Using MultiPage and TabStrip Controls 311
 Writing VBA Procedures for the Students and Exams Custom Form . . . 314
 Using the Students and Exams Custom Form 318
What's Next 322

Chapter 11 Custom Collections and Class Modules 323
Working with Collections 324
 Declaring a Custom Collection. 326
 Adding Objects to a Custom Collection 326
 Removing Objects from a Custom Collection 328
Insert: Module or Class Module? 329
 Creating Custom Objects. 329
Creating a Class 330
 Variable Declarations 330

Defining the Properties for the Class 331
Creating the Property Get Procedures. 332
Creating the Property Let Procedures 333
Creating the Class Methods 334
Creating an Instance of a Class. 335
Event Procedures in the Class Module 336
Creating the User Interface 337
Watching the Execution of Your VBA Procedures 346
What's Next... 349

Chapter 12 Creating Custom Menus and Toolbars with VBA 351
Toolbars 352
Using the CommandBar Object 353
Creating a Custom Toolbar 354
Deleting a Custom Toolbar 357
Using the CommandBar Properties 357
Working with CommandBar Controls 357
Working with Menus. 364
Menu Programming 365
Creating a Submenu 368
Modifying a Built-in Shortcut Menu 370
Creating a Shortcut Menu 371
What's Next... 374

Chapter 13 Debugging VBA Procedures and Handling Errors. 375
Testing VBA Procedures. 376
Stopping a Procedure 376
Using Breakpoints 378
Using the Immediate Window in Break Mode 381
Using the Stop Statement 383
Adding a Watch Expression. 384
Using Quick Watch 387
Using the Locals Window and the Call Stack Dialog Box 388
Stepping through VBA Procedures 390
Stepping through a Procedure 391
Stepping Over a Procedure. 392
Setting the Next Statement 393
Showing the Next Statement. 394
Stopping and Resetting VBA Procedures 394
Understanding and Using Conditional Compilation 394
Navigating with Bookmarks 397
Trapping Errors 398
What's Next... 403

Chapter 14 Event Programming in Microsoft Excel 2002. 405
Introduction to Event Procedures 406
Enabling and Disabling Events 408
Event Sequences. 409

Worksheet Events 409
Workbook Events 415
Chart Events. 427
    Embedded Chart Events 431
Events Recognized by the Application Object. 432
Query Table Events 436
What's Next... 438

Chapter 15 Using Excel with Microsoft Access. 439
Object Libraries 440
    Setting Up References to Object Libraries. 442
Connecting to Microsoft Access. 443
    Using Automation to Connect to a Microsoft Access Database 443
    Using DAO to Connect to a Microsoft Access Database. 447
    Using ADO to Connect to a Microsoft Access Database. 448
Performing Microsoft Access Tasks from Excel 449
    Creating a New Microsoft Access Database 450
    Opening a Microsoft Access Form 451
    Opening a Microsoft Access Report 454
    Running a Microsoft Access Query 455
    Calling a Microsoft Access Function 459
Retrieving Microsoft Access Data into an Excel Worksheet 459
    Retrieving Data with the GetRows Method 459
    Retrieving Data with the CopyFromRecordset Method 461
    Retrieving Data with the TransferSpreadsheet Method 463
    Using the OpenDatabase Method 464
    Creating a Text File from Microsoft Access Data 466
    Creating a Query Table from Microsoft Access Data 468
Using Microsoft Access Data in Excel. 470
    Creating an Embedded Chart from Microsoft Access Data 470
Transferring the Excel Spreadsheet to an Access Database 472
Linking an Excel Spreadsheet to a Microsoft Access Database. 472
Importing an Excel Spreadsheet to a Microsoft Access Database 474
Placing Excel Data in an Access Table. 474
What's Next... 476

Chapter 16 Excel and the Internet 477
Creating Hyperlinks Using VBA. 478
Creating and Publishing HTML Files Using VBA. 482
    Web Server — Storing and Opening Workbooks 488
Web Queries 488
    Creating and Running Web Queries with VBA. 490
    Web Queries with Parameters 493
    Dynamic Web Queries 497
    Refreshing Data. 499
Excel and Active Server Pages 499
    Creating an ASP Script 501
    Installing Internet Information Services (IIS) or Personal Web Server . . 504

Creating a Virtual Directory 505
Running Your First ASP Script 508
Generating a Tab-delimited File on the Web Server 509
Creating an Excel File from User Input 514
Printing Excel Data to an Internet Browser
    using the GetString Method 523
Creating Charts in ASP. 525
What's Next... 530

Chapter 17 XML and Excel 2002 . . . . **531**
What is XML? 532
XML Support in Excel 2002 533
Creating XML Spreadsheet Files with VBA. 534
Viewing the XML Source File in Notepad. 536
Well-Formed XML Documents 539
Viewing the XML Source File in Internet Explorer. 540
Building XML Files Outside of Microsoft Excel 2002. 542
The XML Flattener 543
Formatting XML Data with Stylesheets. 545
Linking an XML Document to a Stylesheet 550
Viewing XML Documents Formatted with Stylesheets. 550
Using an XSLT Template 553
XML Data Islands 555
    Using VBScript to Transform the Contents of XML Data Islands 557
Saving a Range of Cells as an XML Document 559
The XML Document Object Model 561
    Transform XML into HTML with an XSL Stylesheet Programmatically . 563
    Using VBScript and XML DOM to Transform XML Documents 566
    Working with XML Document Nodes 567
    Retrieving Information from Element Nodes 569
XML via ADO 573
    Saving an ADO Recordset as XML to Disk 573
    Two Types of XML Files 574
    Applying an XSL Stylesheet 576
    Transforming Attribute-Based XML Data into an HTML Table. 578
    Loading an ADO Recordset 580
    Saving the ADO Recordset to XML in Memory 581
    Saving the ADO Recordset into the XML DOMDocument Object 584
XML and ASP 586
Posting Excel XML Data to a Web Server. 591
What's Next... 613

Appendix A—Programming PivotTables and PivotCharts 615
Appendix B—Programming Special Features 643
Appendix C—Introduction to Using and Programming Smart Tags 661
Appendix D—Microsoft Office XP Web Components. 675
Index 698

Acknowledgments

I would like to express my grateful appreciation to all the people involved in the creation of this book. Special thanks go to Wordware Publishing, Inc. editors Beth Kohler and Heather Hill for their help, comments, and thorough review of this book. It was a pleasure to work with you ladies. Your queries were so skillfully put together that I've decided to bind them for future reference.

Many thanks to Wes Beckwith for all his efforts and patience in coordinating this project.

To Witold Sikorski of Mikom Publishing, Warsaw, Poland, a big thank you for introducing me to Jim Hill of Wordware Publishing, Plano, Texas. Needless to say, if these two hadn't met several years ago at a book fair in Frankfurt, Germany, I would have never become a bilingual author.

A special thanks goes to Terrence Joubert for taking the time to review several chapters from the previous version of this book (*Learn Microsoft Excel 2000 VBA Programming*) and for his list of suggestions to include in this new release. Due to time constraints and the size of the book, I could not implement all of his great suggestions. I am looking forward to Terrence's book, *ADO .NET Programming*, also from Wordware Publishing.

Thanks to the readers of the previous version of this book for their praise and criticism. I'm happy to hear that so many of you have found the book very useful in self-teaching Excel VBA programming. I apologize to those of you who have found some subjects missing or not adequately covered. I have tried to do a better job this time; however, please keep in mind this book isn't a know-it-all reference but a step-by-step manual. To take you through the subjects in an easy-to-follow manner I had to make choices as to what goes in and what's not covered.

To my close friends, Ludmila Larmor, Jolanta and Dariusz Partyka, and Mariola Weyna for their encouragement and support.

Finally, I'd like to thank my husband, Paul, simply for being my husband and sharing with me the same fields of interest. Paul has been gaining experience with the .NET technology while I was busy writing.

Introduction

This book shows you what's doable with Microsoft Excel 2002 beyond the standard user interface. If you ever wanted to open a new worksheet without using the menu or create a fully automated custom form to gather data and store the results in a spreadsheet, you've got to learn some programming. This book shows you how to become more productive by delegating many time-consuming and repetitive tasks to Excel. Using Excel's built-in language, VBA (Visual Basic for Applications), you can bring a lot of automating power to your spreadsheets, whether you are creating them for yourself or others. By using a number of built-in programming tools, you can work smarter than you ever thought possible. There is no extra cost except for your willingness to become familiar with a secret window behind the Microsoft Excel application window. For a quick peek, while in Excel, hold down Alt while pressing F11. You will end up in the Visual Basic Editor (VBE) screen—Excel's programming interface.

Now that this well-guarded secret is out, let me tell you more. Apart from VBA, this book introduces you to two hot Internet technologies that can be used with Microsoft Excel. One is ASP (Active Server Pages) and the other is XML (Extensible Markup Language). You also learn a number of other supporting technologies. So, if you really want to gain some hot skills, purchase this book and waste no time beginning studying.

Learn Microsoft Excel 2002 VBA Programming with XML and ASP leads you through the process of creating VBA procedures, VBScripts, ASP pages, XML documents, and XSL stylesheets from start to finish. Along the way, there are detailed, practical "how-to" examples and plenty of illustrations. The book's approach is to learn by doing. This book begins by addressing basic VBA concepts in the early chapters and progresses to more complex topics in later chapters. Each of the 17 chapters should be worked through in order. In addition, there are four appendices that discuss working with and programming special features in Excel. Consider this book as a sort of private course that you can attend in the comfort of your office or home.

Some courses have prerequisites and so does this one. *Learn Microsoft Excel 2002 VBA Programming with XML and ASP* does not explain to the user how to use Excel features such as menus and keyboard shortcuts. The book assumes that you are comfortable working with an Excel spreadsheet and are interested in becoming more productive by learning how to communicate with Excel in its own language and learning how to integrate it with the current Internet technologies.

Chapter 1

Introduction to Spreadsheet Automation

Understanding Macros ■ Common Uses for Macros ■ Planning a Macro ■ Recording a Macro ■ Running the Macro ■ Modifying the Macro ■ Adding Comments ■ Analyzing the Macro Code ■ Cleaning Up the Macro Code ■ Testing the Modified Macro ■ Two Levels of Macro Execution ■ Improving Your Macro ■ Renaming the Macro ■ Other Methods of Running Macros ■ Saving Macros ■ Printing Macros ■ Storing Macros in the Personal Macro Workbook ■ Opening Workbooks Containing Macros ■ **The Visual Basic Editor Window** ■ Understanding the Project Explorer Window ■ Understanding the Properties Window ■ Understanding the Code Window ■ Other Windows in the Visual Basic Editor Window ■ **What's Next...**

Are you ready to build intelligence into your Microsoft Excel 2002 spreadsheets? By automating routine tasks, you can make your spreadsheets quicker and more efficient. This first chapter walks you through the process of speeding up spreadsheet tasks with macros. You learn what macros are, how and when to use them, and how to write and modify them. Getting started with macros is easy. Creating them requires nothing more than what you already have—a basic knowledge of Microsoft Excel 2002 menus and spreadsheet concepts. Are you ready to begin? Make sure you are seated at a computer and launch Microsoft Excel 2002.

Understanding Macros

Macros are programs that store a series of commands. When you create a macro, you simply combine a sequence of keystrokes into a single command that you can later "play back." Because macros can reduce the number of steps required to complete tasks, using macros can significantly decrease the time you spend creating, formatting, modifying, and printing your worksheets.

You can create macros by using Microsoft Excel's built-in recording tool, or you can write them from scratch by using the Visual Basic Editor. Microsoft Excel 2002 macros are created with the powerful programming language Visual Basic for Applications, commonly known as VBA.

Tip 1-1: The Common Language

Excel 5 was the first application on the market to feature Visual Basic for Applications. Since then, VBA has made its way into all Microsoft Office applications. This means that what you learn about VBA in this book can be used later in creating macros automating other Microsoft Office products such as Word, PowerPoint, Outlook or Access.

Common Uses for Macros

Microsoft Excel 2002 comes with dozens of built-in, timesaving features that allow you to work faster and smarter. Before you decide to automate a worksheet task with a macro, make sure there is not already a built-in feature that you can use to perform that task. Consider, however, creating a macro when you find yourself performing the same series of actions over and over again or when Excel does not provide a built-in tool to do the job.

Macros enable you to automate just about any part of your spreadsheet. For example, you can automate data entry by creating a macro that enters headings in a worksheet or replaces column titles with new labels. Macros also enable you to check for duplicate entries in a selected area of your worksheet. With a macro, you can quickly apply formatting to several worksheets, as well as combine different formats, such as fonts, colors, borders, and shading. Even though Excel has an excellent chart facility, macros are the way to go if you wish to automate the process of creating and formatting charts. Macros will save you keystrokes when it comes to setting print areas, margins, headers, and footers, and selecting special print options for printouts.

Planning a Macro

Before you create a macro, take a few minutes to consider what you want to do. Because a macro is a collection of a fairly large number of keystrokes, it is important to plan your actions in advance. The easiest way to plan your macro is to manually perform all the actions that the macro needs to do. As you enter the keystrokes, write them down on a piece of paper exactly as they occur. Don't leave anything out. Like a voice recorder, Microsoft Excel's macro recorder records every action you perform. If you do not plan your macro prior to recording, you will end up with unnecessary actions that will slow it down. Although it's easier to edit a macro than it is to erase unwanted passages from a voice recording, performing only the actions you want recorded will save you editing time and trouble later.

Suppose you want to see at a glance which areas of a worksheet are text, numbers, and formulas. Figure 1-1 shows a simple spreadsheet formatted with distinct font colors and styles to help identify the contents of the underlying cells.

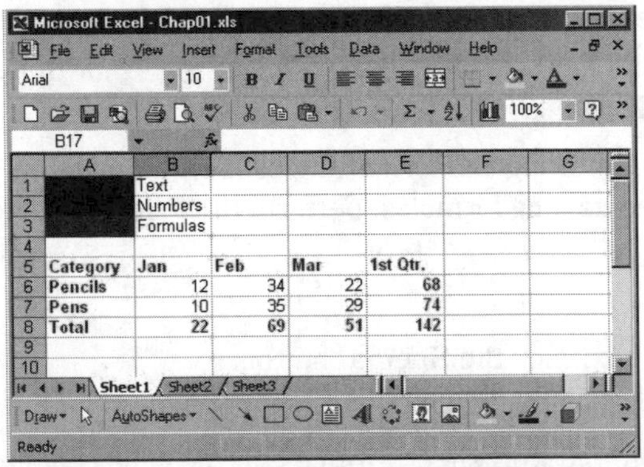

Figure 1-1:
Finding out "what's what" in a spreadsheet is easy with formatting applied by an Excel macro.

To produce the formatting results shown in Figure 1-1, open any existing spreadsheet that contains calculations or create the one shown in the figure. If you decide to use the worksheet example in the above figure, make sure you use the SUM function to calculate the monthly and quarterly totals.

Before you record the macro, manually perform the following actions:

1. Select a single cell.
2. Select **Edit | Go To**.
3. In the Go To dialog box, click the **Special** button.

4. In the Go To Special dialog box, click the **Constants** option button and then remove the check mark next to **Numbers, Logicals,** and **Errors**. Only the **Text** check box should be checked.

5. Click **OK** to return to the worksheet. Notice that the cells containing text are now selected. Be careful not to change your selection until you apply the necessary formatting in the next step.

6. With the text cells still selected, choose **Format | Cells**.

7. In the Format Cells dialog box, click the **Font** tab. Set the Font style to **Bold** and the Color to **Violet**. Then click **OK** to close the dialog box. Notice that the cells containing text now appear in a different color.

Steps 1 to 7 allowed you to locate all the cells that contain text. To select and format cells containing numbers, perform the following actions:

8. Select a single cell.

9. Select **Edit | Go To**.

10. In the Go To dialog box, click the **Special** button.

11. In the Go To Special dialog box, click the **Constants** option button and remove the check mark next to **Text, Logicals,** and **Errors**. Only the **Numbers** check box should be checked.

12. Click **OK** to return to the worksheet. Notice that the cells containing numbers are now selected. Be careful not to change your selection until you apply the necessary formatting in the following step.

13. With the number cells still selected, choose **Format | Cells**.

14. On the Font tab of the Format Cells dialog box, set the Color to **Dark blue**. Then click **OK** to close the dialog box.

Steps 8 to 14 took care of locating and formatting cells with numbers. To select and format cells containing formulas, perform the following actions:

15. Select a single cell.

16. Select **Edit | Go To**.

17. In the Go To dialog box, click the **Special** button.

18. In the Go To Special dialog box, click the **Formulas** option button.

19. Click **OK** to return to the worksheet. Notice that the cells containing numbers that are results of formulas are now selected. Be careful not to change your selection until you apply the necessary formatting in the next step.

20. With the formula cells still selected, choose **Format | Cells**.

21. On the Font tab of the Format Cells dialog box, set the Font style to **Bold** and the Color to **Red**. Then click **OK** to close the dialog box.

Steps 15 to 21 allowed you to locate and format cells containing formulas. To make it easy to understand all the formatting applied to the worksheet's cells, you will now add the color legend.

22. Select cells **A1:A3** and choose **Insert | Rows.**

23. Select cell **A1.**

24. Choose **Format | Cells,** and on the Patterns tab click the **Purple** color in the Cell shading box. Click **OK** to return to the worksheet.

25. Select cell **B1** and type **Text.**

26. Select cell **A2.**

27. Choose **Format | Cells,** and click the **Dark blue** color in the Cell shading box. Click **OK** to return to the worksheet.

28. Select cell **B2** and type **Numbers.**

29. Select cell **A3.**

30. Choose **Format | Cells,** and click the **Red** color in the Cell shading box. Click **OK** to return to the worksheet.

31. Select cell **B3** and type **Formulas.**

32. Select cell **A1.**

After completing steps 22 to 32, cells A1:A3 will display a simple color legend, as shown in Figure 1-1.

As you can see, no matter how simple your spreadsheet task appears at first, many steps may be required to get exactly what you want. Creating a macro that is capable of playing back your keystrokes can be a real time-saver, especially when you have to repeat the same process for a number of worksheets.

Recording a Macro

Now that you know what actions you need to perform, it's time to turn on the macro recorder and create your first macro.

Before you follow the recording steps outlined below, be sure to remove the formatting from the example worksheet. To do this, press Ctrl+A to select the entire worksheet. Then choose Edit | Clear | Formats. Select cells A1:A3 and choose Edit | Delete. In the Delete dialog box, select the Entire row option button. Then click OK.

To create your first macro, follow these steps:

1. Select a single cell.

   Before you record a macro, you should decide whether or not you want to record the positioning of the active cell. If you want the macro to always start in a specific location on the worksheet, turn on the macro recorder first and then select the cell you want to start in. If the location of the active cell does not matter, select a single cell first and then turn on the macro recorder.

2. Choose **Tools | Macro | Record New Macro.** The Record Macro dialog box appears.

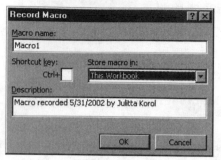

Figure 1-2:
When you record a new macro, you must name it. In the Record Macro dialog box you can also supply a shortcut key, the storage location, and a description for your macro.

3. Enter the name **WhatsInACell** for the sample macro.

Tip 1-2: Macro Names

If you forget to enter a name for the macro, Excel assigns a default name such as Macro1, Macro2, and so on. Macro names can contain letters, numbers, and the underscore character, but the first character must be a letter. For example, Report1 is a valid macro name, while 1Report is not. Spaces are not allowed. If you want a space between the words, use the underscore. For example, instead of WhatsInACell, enter Whats_In_A_Cell.

---

4. Select **This Workbook** in the Store macro in list box.

Tip 1-3: Storing Macros

Excel allows you to store macros in three locations:

- **Personal Macro Workbook** – Macros stored in this location will be available each time you work with Microsoft Excel. Personal Macro Workbook is located in the XLStart folder. If this workbook doesn't already exist, Excel creates it the first time you select this option.
- **New Workbook** – Excel will place the macro in a new workbook.
- **This Workbook** – The macro will be stored in the workbook you are currently using.

---

5. Enter the following text in the Description box: **Indicates the contents of the underlying cells: text, numbers, formulas.**

6. Choose **OK** to close the Record Macro dialog box and begin recording.

    The Stop Recording toolbar appears. The status bar at the bottom of the Excel application window displays "Ready Recording."

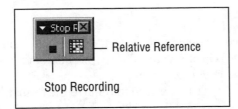

Relative Reference

Stop Recording

Figure 1-3:
The Stop Recording toolbar has buttons that allow you to stop the macro recorder or indicate how Excel should handle cell addressing when recording.

Tip 1-4: Cell Addressing in Macros: Relative or Absolute?

- **Absolute** – If you want your macro to execute the recorded action in a specific cell, no matter what cell is selected during the execution of the macro, use absolute cell addressing. Absolute cell references have the following form: $A$1, $C$5, etc. By default, the Excel macro recorder uses absolute references. Before you begin to record, make sure the Stop Recording toolbar's second button is <u>not</u> depressed. When you point the mouse to this button, its tool tip should read "Relative reference."

- **Relative** – If you want your macro to perform the action in any cell, turn on the relative references. Relative cell references have the following form: A1, C5, etc. Before you begin to record, make sure the Stop Recording toolbar's second button is depressed. Bear in mind, however, that Excel will continue recording using the relative cell references until you exit Microsoft Excel or click the Relative Reference button again.

During the process of recording your macro, you may use both methods of cell addressing. For example, you may select a specific cell (e.g., $A$4), perform an action, then choose another cell relative to the selected cell (e.g., C9, which is located five rows down and two columns to the right of the currently active cell $A$4).

Relative references automatically adjust when you copy them, and absolute references don't.

7. Perform the actions you have tried out manually in the previous section (see "Planning a Macro").

   As you record your macro, only the actions finalized by pressing Enter or clicking OK are recorded. If you press the Esc key or click Cancel before completing the entry, the macro recorder does not record that action.

8. When you have performed all the actions, click the **Stop Recording** button on the Stop Recording toolbar or choose **Tools | Macro | Stop Recording**.

Running the Macro

After you create a macro, you should run it at least once to make sure it works correctly. Later in this chapter you will learn various ways to run macros, but for now, use the menu command.

To see the results of your macro, be sure to remove the formatting from the example worksheet. To do this, press Ctrl+A to select the entire worksheet, and then choose Edit | Clear | Formats. Select cells A1:A3 and choose Edit | Delete. In the Delete dialog box, select the Entire row option button. Then click OK. Later on you can record the steps of clearing the worksheet formats in a separate macro.

1. Open any worksheet containing text, numbers, and formulas.
2. Choose **Tools | Macro | Macros** to open the Macro dialog box.
3. Click the name of the macro you want to run (see Figure 1-4).
4. Choose **Run** to execute the macro.

Quite often, you will notice that your macro does not perform as expected the first time you run it. Perhaps during the macro recording you selected the wrong font or forgot to change the cell color or maybe you just realized it would be better to include an additional step. Don't panic. Excel makes it possible to modify the macro without forcing you to go through the tedious process of recording your keystrokes again.

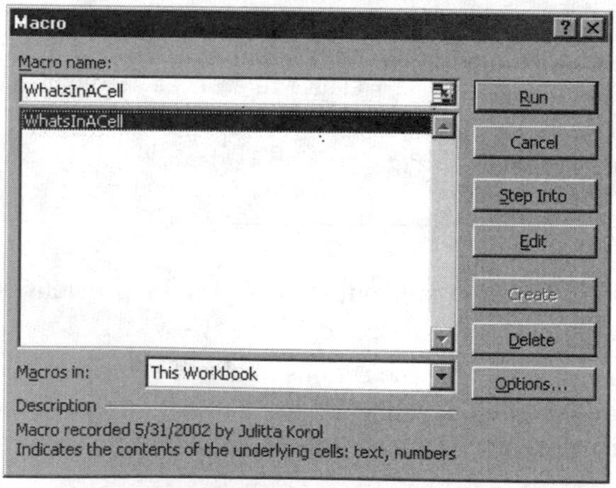

Figure 1-4:
In the Macro dialog box you can select a macro to run, edit, or delete.

Modifying the Macro

Before you can modify your macro, you must find the location where the macro recorder placed its code. As you recall, when you turned on the macro recorder, you selected This Workbook for the location. The easiest way to find your macro is by opening the Macro dialog box shown in Figure 1-4.

1. Choose **Tools | Macro**.
2. Select the name of the macro (**WhatsInACell,** in this case).
3. Click the **Edit** button.

Microsoft Excel opens a special window called Visual Basic Editor (also known as VBE), as shown in Figure 1-5. Using the keyboard shortcut Alt+F11, you can quickly move between the Microsoft Excel application window and the Visual Basic Editor window. Now take a moment and try moving between both windows. To close the Visual Basic Editor window, select Close on the VBE File menu and return to Microsoft Excel.

Don't worry if the Visual Basic Editor window seems a bit confusing at the moment. As you work with the recorded macros and start writing your own VBA procedures from scratch, you will become familiar with all the elements of this screen. For now, take a look at the menu bar and toolbar in the Visual Basic Editor window. Both of these tools differ from the ones in the Microsoft Excel window. The Visual Basic menu bar and toolbar contain tools required for programming and testing your VBA procedures. As you work through the individual chapters of this book, you will become an expert in using these tools.

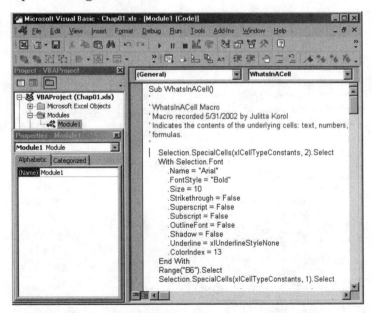

Figure 1-5: The Visual Basic Editor window is used for editing macros as well as writing new procedures in Visual Basic for Applications (VBA).

The main part of the Visual Basic Editor window is a docking surface for various windows that you will find extremely useful during the course of creating and testing your VBA procedures. Figure 1-5 displays three windows that are docked in the Visual Basic Editor window: the Project window, the Properties window, and the Code window. The Project window shows an open Module folder in which Module1 is selected. Excel records your macro actions in special worksheets called Module1, Module2, and so on. In the following chapters of this book, you will use modules to write the code of your own procedures. A module resembles a blank document in Microsoft Word. Individual modules are stored in folders called *modules*.

Tip 1-5: Macro or Procedure?

A macro is a series of commands or functions recorded with the help of a built-in macro recorder or entered manually in a Visual Basic module. Beginning with Excel 5.0, the term "macro" is often replaced with the broader term "procedure." Although the words can be used interchangeably, many programmers are in favor of procedures. While macros allow you to mimic keyboard actions, true procedures can also execute actions that cannot be performed using the mouse, keyboard, or menu options. In other words, procedures are more complex macros that incorporate language structures found in the traditional programming languages.

The Code window (see Figure 1-5) displays the following code created by the macro recorder:

```
Sub WhatsInACell()
'
' WhatsInACell Macro
' Macro recorded 5/31/2002 by Julitta Korol
' Indicates the contents of the underlying cells: text, numbers,
' formulas.
'
'
    Selection.SpecialCells(xlCellTypeConstants, 2).Select
    With Selection.Font
        .Name = "Arial"
        .FontStyle = "Bold"
        .Size = 10
        .Strikethrough = False
        .Superscript = False
        .Subscript = False
        .OutlineFont = False
        .Shadow = False
        .Underline = xlUnderlineStyleNone
        .ColorIndex = 13
    End With
    Range("B6").Select
    Selection.SpecialCells(xlCellTypeConstants, 1).Select
    With Selection.Font
        .Name = "Arial"
        .FontStyle = "Regular"
        .Size = 10
        .Strikethrough = False
```

```
            .Superscript = False
            .Subscript = False
            .OutlineFont = False
            .Shadow = False
            .Underline = xlUnderlineStyleNone
            .ColorIndex = 11
        End With
        Range("C6").Select
        Selection.SpecialCells(xlCellTypeFormulas, 23).Select
        With Selection.Font
            .Name = "Arial"
            .FontStyle = "Bold"
            .Size = 10
            .Strikethrough = False
            .Superscript = False
            .Subscript = False
            .OutlineFont = False
            .Shadow = False
            .Underline = xlUnderlineStyleNone
            .ColorIndex = 3
        End With
        Range("A1:A3").Select
        Selection.EntireRow.Insert
        Range("A1").Select
        With Selection.Interior
            .ColorIndex = 13
            .Pattern = xlSolid
            .PatternColorIndex = xlAutomatic
        End With
        Range("B1").Select
        ActiveCell.FormulaR1C1 = "Text"
        Range("A2").Select
        With Selection.Interior
            .ColorIndex = 5
            .Pattern = xlSolid
            .PatternColorIndex = xlAutomatic
        End With
        Range("B2").Select
        ActiveCell.FormulaR1C1 = "Numbers"
        Range("A3").Select
        With Selection.Interior
            .ColorIndex = 3
            .Pattern = xlSolid
            .PatternColorIndex = xlAutomatic
        End With
        Range("B3").Select
        ActiveCell.FormulaR1C1 = "Formulas"
        Range("B4").Select
    End Sub
```

For now, let's focus on finding answers to two questions: How do you read the macro code, and how can you edit macros?

Adding Comments

Take a look at the recorded macro code. Notice the lines that begin with an apostrophe. These lines indicate comments. By default, comments appear in green. When the macro code is executed, Visual Basic ignores the comment lines. Comments are often placed within the macro code for documenting the meaning of certain lines that aren't obvious. Let's now add some comments to the WhatsInACell macro.

1. Activate the Visual Basic Editor window.

2. Click in front of `Selection.SpecialCells(xlCellTypeConstants, 2).Select` and press **Enter.**

3. Move the pointer to the empty line above and add the comment shown below. Be sure to start with an apostrophe.

    `' Find and format cells containing text`

4. Click in front of `Selection.SpecialCells(xlCellTypeConstants, 1).Select` and press **Enter.**

5. Move the pointer to the empty line above and add the following comment:

    `' Find and format cells containing numbers`

6. Click in front of `Selection.SpecialCells(xlCellTypeFormulas, 23).Select` and press **Enter.**

7. Move the pointer to the empty line above and add the following comment:

    `' Find and format cells containing formulas`

8. Click in front of `Range("A1:A3").Select` and press **Enter.**

Tip 1-6: About Comments

- In the VBE Code window, every line that begins with an apostrophe is a comment. The default comment color is green. You can change the color of comments in the Options dialog box (Tools | Options | Editor Format tab).
- You can also add a comment at the end of the line of code. For example, to add a comment following the line .ColorIndex = 11, click at the end of this line, press Tab, enter the apostrophe, and then type the text of your comment. When you are done, the commented line should look as follows:

    `.ColorIndex = 11    ' Sets the font`
    `                      color to Violet`

- The comment lines don't do anything except provide information to the user about the purpose of a macro or macro action. When you write your own VBA procedures, don't forget to include comments. Comments will make your life easier if you need to return to the macro procedure several months later. They will also allow others to quickly understand various parts of your procedure.

9. Move the pointer to the empty line above and add the following comment:

```
' Create legend
```

Analyzing the Macro Code

All macro procedures begin with the keyword Sub and end with the keywords End Sub. After the Sub keyword comes the actual name of the macro, followed by a set of parentheses. Between the keywords Sub and End Sub are statements that Visual Basic executes each time you run your macro. Visual Basic reads the lines from top to bottom, ignoring the statements preceded with an apostrophe (see the previous section on comments) and stops when it reaches the keywords End Sub.

Notice that the recorded macro contains many periods. The periods appear in almost every line of code and are used to join various elements of the Visual Basic for Applications language. How do you read the instructions written in this language? They are read from the right side of the last period to the left. Here are a few statements from the WhatsInACell procedure:

```
Range("A1:A3").Select
```

Select cells A1 to A3.

```
Selection.EntireRow.Insert
```

Insert a row in the selected area. Because the previous line of code selects three cells, Visual Basic will insert three rows.

```
ActiveCell.FormulaR1C1 = "Text"
```

Let the formula of the active cell be "Text." Because the previous line of code, `Range("B1").Select`, selects cell B1, B1 is currently the active cell, and this is where Visual Basic will enter the text.

```
With Selection.Interior
    .ColorIndex = 3
    .Pattern = xlSolid
    .PatternColorIndex = xlAutomatic
End With
```

This is a special block of code that is interpreted as follows: Set the color for the interior of the currently selected cells to red (ColorIndex = 3), set the interior pattern to solid (xlSolid), and specify the default pattern for the selected cells (xlAutomatic).

The block of code that starts with the keywords With and ends with the keywords End With speeds up the execution of the macro code. Instead of repeating the following instructions each time, the macro recorder uses a shortcut.

```
Selection.Interior.ColorIndex = 3
Selection.Interior.Pattern = xlSolid
```

```
Selection.Interior.PatternColorIndex = xlAutomatic
```

It places the repeating text, Selection.Interior, to the right of the keyword
With and ends the block with the keyword End With.

Cleaning Up the Macro Code

Now, as you review and analyze your macro code line by line, you may
notice that Excel recorded a lot of information that you didn't intend to
include. For example, after selecting cells containing text, in addition to setting the font style to bold and the color to violet, Excel also recorded the
current state of options on the Font tab—font name, font size, strike-
through, superscript, subscript, shadow, and underline. Take a look at the
following code fragment:

```
With Selection.Font
    .Name = "Arial"
    .FontStyle = "Bold"
    .Size = 10
    .Strikethrough = False
    .Superscript = False
    .Subscript = False
    .OutlineFont = False
    .Shadow = False
    .Underline = xlUnderlineStyleNone
    .ColorIndex = 13
End With
```

When you use dialog boxes, Excel always records all the settings. These
additional instructions make your macro code longer and more difficult to
understand. Therefore, when you finish recording your macro, it is a good
idea to go over the recorded statements and delete the unnecessary lines.

1. In the following block of code, delete the lines that are crossed out:

```
With Selection.Font
    .Name = "Arial"
    .FontStyle = "Bold"
    .Size = 10
    .Strikethrough = False
    .Superscript = False
    .Subscript = False
    .OutlineFont = False
    .Shadow = False
    .Underline = xlUnderlineStyleNone
    .ColorIndex = 13
End With
```

After the cleanup, only two statements should be left between the
keywords With and End With. These statements are the settings that
you actually changed in the Format dialog box when you recorded this
macro:

```
With Selection.Font
    .FontStyle = "Bold"
    .ColorIndex = 13
End With
```

2. Locate the macro code that formats cells containing numbers, and make the necessary changes using the example below:

```
' Find and format cells containing numbers
    With Selection
        .SpecialCells(xlCellTypeConstants, 1).Select
        .Font.ColorIndex = 11    ' Sets the font color to Violet
    End With
    Range("C6").Select
```

3. Locate the macro code that formats cells containing formulas, and make changes following the example below:

```
' Find and format cells containing formulas
    Selection.SpecialCells(xlCellTypeFormulas, 23).Select
        With Selection.Font
            .FontStyle = "Bold"
            .ColorIndex = 3
        End With
```

4. Locate the following two lines of code:

```
Range("A1:A3").Select
Selection.EntireRow.Insert
```

5. Replace the above two lines of code with the following line:

```
Range("A1:A3").EntireRow.Insert
```

Notice that the macro recorder uses the R1C1-style notation to set the formula for the selected cell:

```
ActiveCell.FormulaR1C1 = "Text"
ActiveCell.FormulaR1C1 = "Numbers"
ActiveCell.FormulaR1C1 = "Formulas"
```

To select the active cell, the macro recorder uses the word ActiveCell once, and it applies the word Selection another time. Both of these words are called *properties*. You will learn about properties in Chapter 2. When only one cell is selected, you may use ActiveCell or Selection interchangeably.

Testing the Modified Macro

When you modify the recorded macro, it is quite possible that you may introduce errors. For example, you may delete an important line of code, or you may inadvertently remove or omit a necessary period. To make sure that your macro still works correctly after you're done editing, you must run it.

1. In the Visual Basic Editor Code window, place the cursor in any line of the WhatsInACell macro code, and choose **Run | Run Sub/UserForm**.

If you didn't introduce any problems during the modification of your macro, the macro will run smoothly and no errors will be reported. To see the result of your macro, you must switch to the Microsoft Excel window. To do this, click the button on the taskbar, or press Alt+F11.

If the Visual Basic Editor encounters an error during the execution of your macro, you will see a dialog box displaying the type of error found. Before you run macros, you must make sure that your macro can run in the worksheet that is currently selected. For example, if you try to run the WhatsInACell macro when a blank sheet is selected, you will get the "Run time error '1004'—No Cells were found" error message. Click the End button, and make sure that you select the correct worksheet before you try to run the macro again.

If the selected worksheet contains only cells with text and you try to run the WhatsInACell macro, Visual Basic will encounter a problem when attempting to select cells with numbers. The same "No cells found" message will be displayed.

If you omit the period in `With Selection.Font` on running this line of code, Visual Basic will generate the "Run time error '424'—Object required" message. Click the Debug button in the message box, and you will be placed in the Code window. At this time, Visual Basic will enter into break mode and will use the yellow highlighter to indicate the line that it had trouble executing. As soon as you correct your error, Visual Basic may announce "This action will reset your project, proceed anyway?" Click OK in response to this message. Although you can edit code in break mode, some edits prevent continuing execution. After correcting the error, run the macro again, as there may be more errors to be fixed before the macro can run smoothly. You will find more information on how to handle VBA errors in Chapters 2 and 13.

Two Levels of Macro Execution

You can run your macros from either the Microsoft Excel window or the Visual Basic Editor window. When you execute the WhatsInACell macro from the VBE screen, Visual Basic executes the macro behind the scenes. You can't see when Visual Basic selects and applies formatting to the text cells or when it inserts three empty rows for the color legend. To watch Visual Basic at work, you must run your macro from the Microsoft Excel window by choosing Tools | Macro, or arrange your screen in such a way that both Microsoft Excel and the Visual Basic windows can be viewed at the same time (see Figure 1-6).

To arrange your screen so that it matches Figure 1-6, perform the following steps:

1. Right-click the empty section of the Windows taskbar. The taskbar is the bottom area of the screen where the Start button is located.

2. From the Windows shortcut menu, select **Tile Windows Vertically**.

3. Minimize the windows that are not needed, and repeat step 1 above.

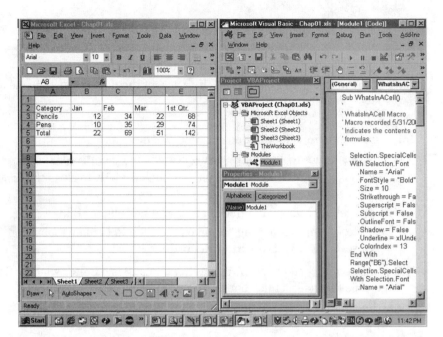

Figure 1-6: If you want to watch the execution of your macro from the level of the Visual Basic Editor, you must position the Microsoft Excel and VBE windows side by side.

4. Now that both windows are side by side, click anywhere inside the macro code, and press **F5** (or choose **Run | Run Sub/UserForm**). Now, sit back and watch. Isn't it exciting to see Visual Basic quickly perform the actions you recorded? Later, you will learn how to slow down Visual Basic so that you can watch the execution of your code step by step.

Improving Your Macro

After you record your macro, you may realize that the macro can perform some additional tasks. Adding new instructions to the macro code is not very difficult if you are already familiar with the Visual Basic language. In most situations, however, you can do this more efficiently when you delegate the extra tasks to the macro recorder. You may argue that Excel records more instructions than are necessary. One thing is for sure, however—the macro recorder does not make mistakes, and you can rely fully on it.

If you want to add additional instructions to your macro using the macro recorder, you must record a new macro, then copy the sections you want, and paste them into the correct location in your original macro.

Let's add a thick border around cells A1:B3.

1. Activate the Microsoft Excel window with the worksheet shown in Figure 1-6.

2. Choose **Tools | Macro | Record New Macro.**

3. In the Macro dialog box, click **OK** to accept the default macro name and begin recording.

4. Select cells **A1:B3.**

5. Choose **Format | Cells** and click the **Border** tab.

6. In the Presets section of the dialog box, click the **Outline** button.

7. Click the thickest line in the Style box and click **OK** to close the dialog box.

8. Click cell **A1**. Notice the thick border around cells A1:B3.

9. Click the **Stop Recording** button on the Stop Recording toolbar, or choose **Tools | Macro | Stop Recording.**

To view the recorded macro, switch to the Visual Basic Editor window. The macro code that adds a thick border around cells A1:A3 is shown here:

```
Sub Macro2()
'
' Macro2 Macro
' Macro recorded 5/31/2002 by Julitta Korol
'
'
    Range("A1:B3").Select
    Selection.Borders(xlDiagonalDown).LineStyle = xlNone
    Selection.Borders(xlDiagonalUp).LineStyle = xlNone
    With Selection.Borders(xlEdgeLeft)
        .LineStyle = xlContinuous
        .Weight = xlThick
        .ColorIndex = xlAutomatic
    End With
    With Selection.Borders(xlEdgeTop)
        .LineStyle = xlContinuous
        .Weight = xlThick
        .ColorIndex = xlAutomatic
    End With
    With Selection.Borders(xlEdgeBottom)
        .LineStyle = xlContinuous
        .Weight = xlThick
        .ColorIndex = xlAutomatic
    End With
    With Selection.Borders(xlEdgeRight)
        .LineStyle = xlContinuous
        .Weight = xlThick
        .ColorIndex = xlAutomatic
    End With
    Selection.Borders(xlInsideVertical).LineStyle = xlNone
    Selection.Borders(xlInsideHorizontal).LineStyle = xlNone
    Range("A1").Select
End Sub
```

Now let's analyze the recorded code. Do you think you can get rid of some instructions? Before you go ahead and delete the unnecessary lines of code, think of how you can use the comment feature. Before you delete any macro code, comment it out and run the macro with the commented code. If the Visual Basic Editor does not generate any errors, you can safely delete the commented lines. If you follow this guideline, you will never find yourself recording the same keystrokes more than once. And if the macro does not perform accurately, you can remove the comments from the lines that may be needed after all. For details on working with comment blocks, please see Chapter 2.

When you create macros with the macro recorder, you can quickly learn the VBA equivalents for the Excel menu options and dialog box settings. Then you can look up the meaning and the usage of these Visual Basic commands in the online help. It's quite obvious that the more instructions Visual Basic needs to read, the slower the execution of your macro. Eliminating extraneous commands will speed up your macro. However, to make your macro code easier to understand, you may want to put on your detective hat and search for a better way to perform a specific task. For example, take a look at the code the macro recorder generated for placing a border around selected cells. It appears that the macro recorder handled each line separately. It seems hard to believe that Visual Basic does not have a simple one-line command that places a border around a selection of cells. Learning the right word or expression in any language takes time. If you look long enough, you will find that Visual Basic has a BorderAround method that allows you to add a border to a range of cells and set the Color, LineStyle, and Weight for the new border.

Using Visual Basic for Applications, the quickest way to create the thick border around a selection of cells is with the following statement:

```
Range("A1:B3").BorderAround Weight:=xlThick
```

The above instruction uses the BorderAround method of the Range object. It uses the thick line to create a border around cells A1:B3. (The next chapter covers Visual Basic objects, properties, and methods.)

Now let's add the above instruction to the WhatsInACell macro:

1. Activate the Code window with the WhatsInACell macro.

2. Enter a new line after `ActiveCell.FormulaR1C1 = "Formulas"`.

3. In the blank line, enter the following instruction:

```
Range("A1:B3").BorderAround Weight:=xlThick
```

4. Place the cursor anywhere in the macro code and press **F5** to run the modified macro.

Tip 1-7: Including Additional Instructions

- To include additional instructions in the existing macro, add empty lines in the required places of the macro code by pressing Enter and type in the necessary Visual Basic statements.

- If the additional instructions are keyboard actions or menu commands, you may use the Macro recorder to generate the necessary code and then copy and paste the necessary lines into the original macro.

Let's say you would like Visual Basic to notify you when it has finished executing the last macro line. This sort of action cannot be recorded, as Excel does not have a corresponding menu option. However, using the Visual Basic language, you can add new instructions to your macro by hand.

1. In the Code window, click in front of the End Sub keywords and press **Enter.**

2. Place your cursor on the empty line and type the following statement:

    ```
    MsgBox "All actions have been performed."
    ```

3. Make sure the cursor is located anywhere in the macro code, and press **F5.**

4. When Visual Basic completes the last recorded instruction, it displays the message. Click **OK.** You now know for sure that the macro has finished running.

MsgBox is one of the frequently used VBA functions. You will learn more about its usage in Chapter 4.

Renaming the Macro

When you add additional actions to your macro, you may want to change its name to better indicate the purpose of the macro. The name of the procedure should communicate its function as closely as possible. To change the macro name, you don't need to press a specific key. In the Code window, simply delete the old macro name and enter the new name following the Sub keyword.

Other Methods of Running Macros

So far, you have learned three methods of running macros. You already know how to run a macro by choosing Tools | Macro | Macros. Unfortunately, this method of running a macro is not convenient if you need to run your macro often. You also ran the macro in the VBE Code window with the keyboard shortcut F5 or by choosing Run | Run Sub/UserForm. In addition, you can run a macro from the Visual Basic Editor window by clicking a button on the Standard toolbar (Figure 1-7) or choosing Tools | Macro.

Figure 1-7: The Visual Basic procedure can be run from the toolbar button.

Running the Macro Using a Keyboard Shortcut

A popular method to run a macro is by using an assigned keyboard shortcut. It is much faster to press Ctrl+Shift+D than it is to activate the macro from the Macro dialog box. Before you use the keyboard shortcut, you must assign it to your macro.

1. Press **Alt+F8** to quickly open the Macro dialog box.

2. In the list of macros, click the name of the **WhatsInACell** macro, and then choose the **Options** button.

3. The Macro Options dialog box appears, as shown in Figure 1-8. The cursor is located in the Shortcut key text box.

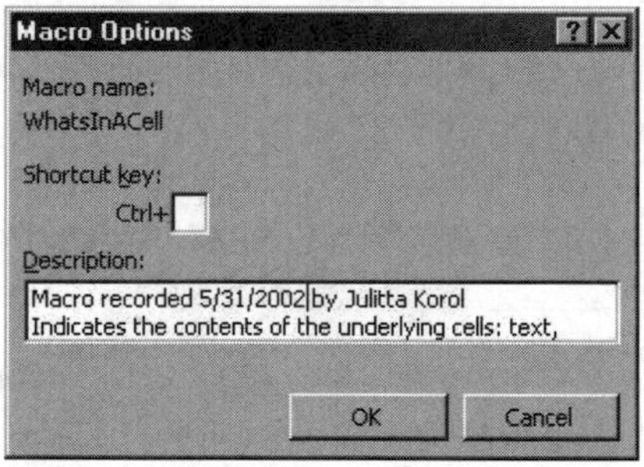

Figure 1-8:
Using the Macro Options dialog box, you can assign a keyboard shortcut for running a macro.

4. Hold down the **Shift** key and press the letter **I** on the keyboard. Excel records the keyboard combination as **Ctrl+Shift+I**.

5. Click **OK** to close the Macro Options dialog box.

6. Click **Cancel** to return to the worksheet.

Tip 1-8: Avoid Shortcut Conflicts

If you assign to your macro a keyboard shortcut that conflicts with the Microsoft Excel built-in shortcut, Excel will run your macro if the workbook containing the macro code is currently open.

To run your macro using the newly assigned keyboard shortcut, make sure the Microsoft Excel window is active and press Ctrl+Shift+I.

Running the Macro from a Menu

If you'd rather work with the menus, you can add your macro as a menu option. Using the Customize dialog box, you can quickly add your own menu command to any of Excel's built-in menus.

1. In the Microsoft Excel window, right-click the empty area of the menu bar and select **Customize** from the shortcut menu.

2. In the Customize dialog box, click the **Commands** tab.

3. In the Categories list box, select **Macros**.

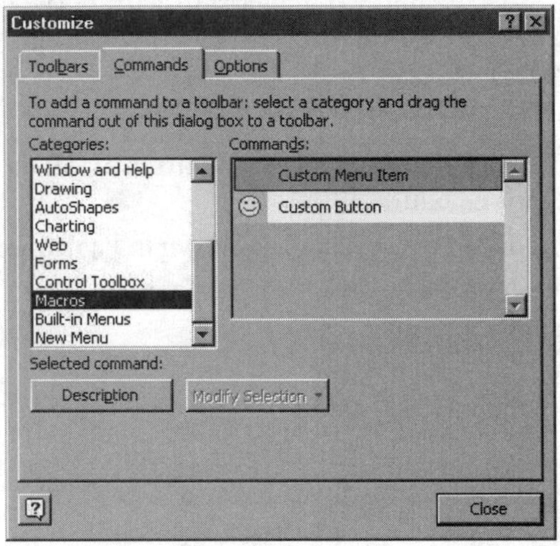

Figure 1-9:
Creating a custom menu item (Step 1)

4. Drag **Custom Menu Item** to the Tools menu. As the menu opens up, drop the button image to the position where you want to place it. Figure 1-10 shows the custom command placed as the last option on the Tools menu.

5. To change the name of the custom menu item, right-click the menu item and edit the text in the Name item on the shortcut menu (Figure 1-11). For this example, change the name to **Contents of Ce&lls**.

   The ampersand (&) character is used to indicate a keyboard shortcut. Place the ampersand immediately before the letter you want to be underlined. If you named the custom option Contents of Ce&lls, the custom menu option will be displayed as Contents of Cells. Notice that menu options can contain spaces between the words.

6. To assign a macro to the Contents of Cells menu option, select the last option—**Assign Macro**—on the shortcut menu (Figure 1-11). In the Macro dialog box, select the **WhatsInACell** macro and click **OK**. Click **Close** to close the Customize dialog box.

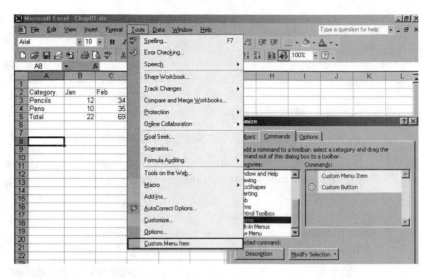

Figure 1-10: Creating a custom menu item (Step 2). You can place the custom option in any Excel menu or submenu.

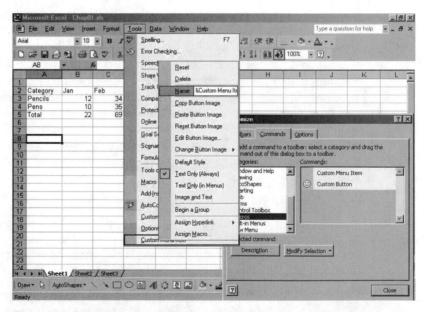

Figure 1-11: Creating a custom menu item (Step 3). Using the shortcut menu, you can rename the menu option and assign your own macro to it. To use this shortcut menu, you must first open the Customize dialog box.

Your macro can now run from your custom menu option. If you close the shortcut menu before assigning a macro to the menu option, Excel will prompt you for the macro name when you attempt to use your menu option for the first time.

7. Choose **Tools | Contents of Cells** to run your macro, or press **Alt+T** and the letter **l**.

If you removed a built-in menu or menu option while performing the above steps, open the Customize dialog box, click the Toolbars tab, and choose the Reset button. While this will bring back Microsoft Excel default options, your custom menu option will be removed.

Running the Macro from a Toolbar Button

If you like to use toolbar buttons, you can easily add a custom button to any toolbar and assign it to your own macro. Let's add the WhatsInACell macro to a toolbar.

1. Choose **Tools | Customize**.
2. In the Customize dialog box, click the **Commands** tab.
3. In the Categories list box, select **Macros**.
4. Drag the **Custom Button** image to the position on the toolbar where you want to place the button. In this example, the button is added to the Standard toolbar to the right of the Format Painter button.
5. To change the tooltip of the button, right-click the button and edit the text in the Name item on the shortcut menu. For this example, change the name of the button's tooltip to **Contents of Ce&lls**.
6. To change the image on the button, right-click the button and select the **Change Button Image** command from the shortcut menu. Forty-two predesigned images included with Excel will appear. Select the image you want. For this example, the default custom image was replaced with the pencil image.
7. To assign the macro to the button, right-click the button to open the shortcut menu and choose the **Assign Macro** command.
8. Select the **WhatsInACell** macro and choose **OK**.
9. Click the **Close** button to close the Customize dialog box.
10. Point the mouse to the custom button you just created. The Contents of Cells tooltip appears next to the button (Figure 1-12). Make sure the active sheet contains a spreadsheet with text, numbers, and formulas. Then click the custom button to run the macro.

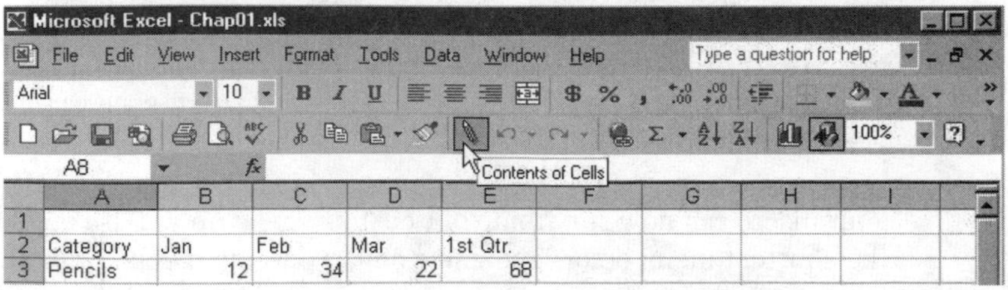

Figure 1-12: You can add a custom button to any toolbar to run your macro.

Running the Macro from a Worksheet Button

Later in this book, you will learn how buttons placed in a worksheet can help beginning Excel users with data entry. For now, let's go over the steps that will attach the WhatsInACell macro to a worksheet button.

1. Activate the example worksheet containing the data.

2. Choose **View | Toolbars** and select **Forms**. The Forms toolbar appears, as shown in Figure 1-13.

3. On the Forms toolbar, click **Button**.

4. Click anywhere in the worksheet.

5. When the Assign Macro dialog box appears, choose the name of the macro (**WhatsInACell**) and click **OK**.

6. To change the name of Button 1, make sure the button is selected, and enter the name **Contents of Cells**. When the button is selected, it looks like the one shown in Figure 1-13. If the selection handles are not displayed, right-click **Button 1** on the worksheet and choose **Edit Text** on the shortcut menu. Select the default text and enter the new name.

7. When you're done renaming the button, click anywhere in the worksheet and outside the button to exit the Edit mode.

8. To run your macro, click the button you just created.

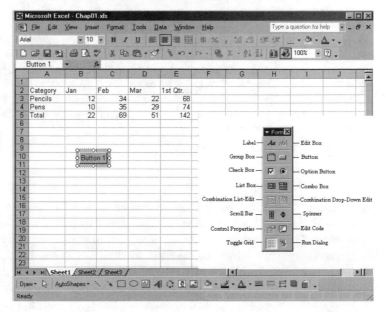

Figure 1-13: You can attach your macro to a button placed in a worksheet.

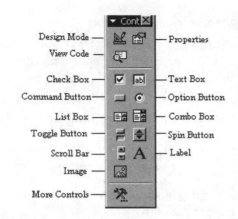

Design Mode — Properties
View Code —
Check Box — Text Box
Command Button — Option Button
List Box — Combo Box
Toggle Button — Spin Button
Scroll Bar — Label
Image —
More Controls —

Figure 1-14:
Default tools in the Control Toolbox

Tip 1-9: Adding Controls to a Worksheet

- You can add controls to a worksheet using the Forms toolbar (see Figure 1-13) or the Control Toolbox (see Figure 1-14). Both toolbars can be accessed from the View menu by selecting the Toolbars option.
- Controls accessed via the Forms toolbar are compatible with earlier versions of Excel (5.0, 7, and 97) and can be used on chart sheets, old XLM macro sheets, and worksheets when all you want to do is run a macro by clicking a control.
- The controls in the Control Toolbox are known as ActiveX controls. You can place the ActiveX controls on worksheets or your custom forms that you create by using the Visual Basic Editor. While the controls located on the Forms toolbar can only respond to the Click event, the ActiveX controls have many different actions, or events, that can occur when you use the control.
- When you use a control from the Forms toolbar, you assign a macro to it that is stored in a module of This Workbook, New Workbook, or Personal Macro Workbook. When you use an ActiveX control, write macro code that is stored with the control itself.

Saving Macros

The WhatsInACell macro you created in this chapter is located in a Microsoft Excel workbook. To save the macro on a disk, you need to save the open workbook. I suggest that you save your macro now in a workbook file named Chap01.xls. After you save the workbook, close it and then open a brand new workbook. Notice that your custom toolbar button is still available, as is the Contents of Cells option on the Tools menu. Before you try to run your macro using any of these tools, enter the text "Addition" in cell A1, the number 2 in cell A2, the number 4 in cell A3, and =Sum(A2:A3) in cell A4. When you run the macro, Excel opens the appropriate workbook file and executes the procedure assigned to your custom tool.

Printing Macros

If you want to document your macro or perhaps study the macro code when you are away from the computer, you can print your macros. You can print the entire module sheet where your macro is stored or indicate a selection of lines to print.

To print the entire module sheet that contains your macro:

1. Place the cursor anywhere in the module sheet.
2. Choose **File | Print**.
3. In the Print—VBA Project dialog box, the **Current Module** option button should be selected.
4. Click **OK** to print the module sheet.

To print selected text:

1. In the module sheet, highlight the text you want to print.
2. Choose **File | Print**.
3. In the Print—VBA Project dialog box, the **Selection** option button should be selected.
4. Click **OK** to print the highlighted text.

Storing Macros in the Personal Macro Workbook

When you record a macro, you can specify storing the macro code in the Personal Macro Workbook. When you store a macro in the Personal Macro Workbook, Excel creates a file named Personal.xls and places it in the XLStart folder, which is a subdirectory of Program Files\Microsoft Office\Office. Files that were saved to the XLStart folder are loaded automatically each time you start Excel. The Personal Macro Workbook is a convenient place to store general-purpose macros like the following one.

You will now record a general-purpose macro called FormulasOnOff. The purpose of this macro is to toggle the display of worksheet formulas on and off.

1. Choose **Tools | Macro | Record New Macro**.
2. In the Record Macro dialog box, enter **FormulasOnOff** in the Macro name box.
3. Choose **Personal Macro Workbook** from the Store macro in drop-down list.
4. Click in the Shortcut key text box, and press **Shift+F**.
5. Choose **OK** to exit the Record Macro dialog box.
6. Press **Ctrl+~** (tilde character) to turn on the display of formulas, or choose **Tools | Options** and click the **Formulas** check box on the View tab in the Windows options area. When you turn on the display of formulas, the worksheet cells show the formulas instead of the values

that the formulas produce. If you are recording this macro on a blank sheet, the only thing you'll notice is a change in the width of the worksheet columns.

7. Click the **Stop Recording** button on the Stop Recording toolbar, or choose **Tools | Macro | Stop Recording**.

8. To see the macro code, press **Alt+F11** or choose **Tools | Macro | Visual Basic Editor**.

In the Visual Basic Editor screen, the Project Explorer window now shows an additional VBA project (Personal.xls). To open the project, click the plus sign (+) to the left of the project name. The VBA project contains two folders: Microsoft Excel Objects and Modules. Click the plus sign next to the Modules folder to open it and then double-click Module1. The Code window shows the contents of the FormulasOnOff macro (Figure 1-15). Each Excel workbook contains a single project. The first time you record a macro, Excel creates a module folder and places your macro code in Module1. If you record another macro in the same workbook, Excel places it below the previously recorded macro in the same Module1 sheet. All macros recorded in the same work session are stored in the same module. If you close Excel, reopen the same workbook and record a new macro, Excel will store it in a new module.

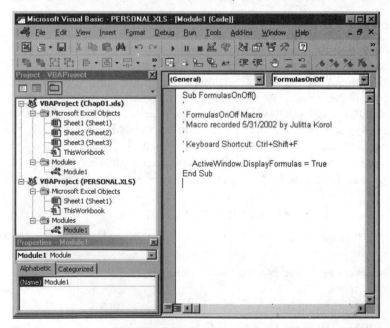

Figure 1-15: In the Project Explorer window you can select the project you want to work with.

When you recorded your macro, you turned on the display of formulas. The macro name suggests that the macro can toggle the formulas on and off. To make this macro behave exactly this way, you must edit it.

The recorded macro line sets the display of formulas in the active window to True:

```
ActiveWindow.DisplayFormulas = True
```

The False setting will turn off the display of formulas:

```
ActiveWindow.DisplayFormulas = False
```

To make a toggle in VBA, you need to connect both statements in the following way:

```
ActiveWindow.DisplayFormulas = Not ActiveWindow.DisplayFormulas
```

Replace the recorded macro line with the statement above and run the macro. No matter how many times you play this macro, it always knows what to do. You can use the same idea to create macros that toggle the display of gridlines or other Microsoft Excel features on and off.

When you close Microsoft Excel, you will be prompted to save the changes you made to the Personal Macro Workbook. Click OK to save the changes. When you restart Excel, the Personal Macro Workbook will automatically load in the background.

If you want to store other macros in the Personal Macro Workbook, you can take one of the following routes:

- Record a new macro and choose the Personal Macro Workbook for its storage location.
- Switch to the Visual Basic Editor and open the project that contains the macro you want to move to the Personal Macro Workbook. Cut the macro code from the current location and open the Personal Macro Workbook project. Paste the macro code into the existing module, or create a new module prior to pasting.
- Choose File | Import File… to bring the macro code from a text file or another Visual Basic project file (*.frm, *.bas, *.cls).

Opening Workbooks Containing Macros

Whenever you open a workbook that contains macros, Excel displays a warning message, as shown in Figure 1-16. To prevent Excel from displaying this message, you can turn off the virus protection using the Security dialog box (Figure 1-17).

When the virus message comes up, you can select:

- **Disable Macros**—Click this button if you are opening a workbook from an unfamiliar source, such as an Internet site or an e-mail, and you want to protect your computer from any macro viruses that may be in the workbook. The workbook will be opened without running any

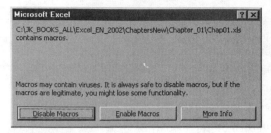

Figure 1-16:
If the virus protection is turned on, Excel displays a warning message when the workbook contains macros.

auto-macros it may contain. You will then be able to switch to the Visual Basic Editor and review the macros if they are not password protected. After checking the macros, you can close the workbook and then reopen it with macros enabled.

■ **Enable Macros**—If you know that the workbook comes from a trusted source and contains useful macros, click the Enable Macros button.

■ **More Info**—Click this button if you need more information before you decide whether to open the workbook with the macros enabled or disabled.

Microsoft Excel 2002 has a useful feature that allows you to automatically disable all macros that are not signed and sent from a trusted source. To access this feature, choose Tools | Macro | Security.

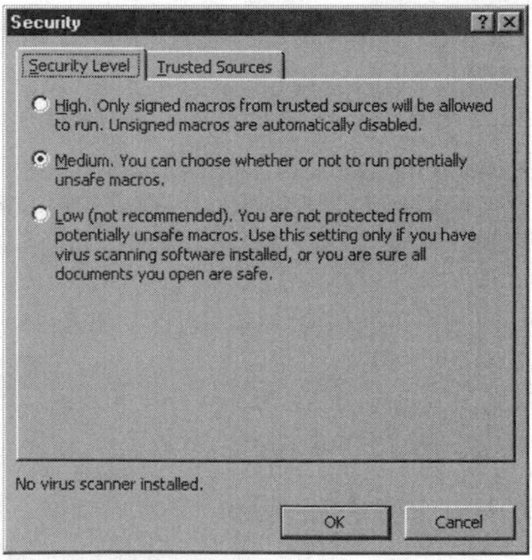

Figure 1-17:
Selecting the Medium option button will allow you to choose whether to run or not to run macros upon opening a workbook.

When you create macros that you want to distribute to others, you can use the Digital Signature feature available in the Visual Basic Editor's Tools menu to confirm that the macro does not introduce a virus.

A digital signature on a macro is similar to a handwritten signature on a printed letter. Search the Microsoft Excel online help for information on how to install and create your own digital signature. To access related topics, type "digital signature" in the Answer Wizard.

The Visual Basic Editor Window

Now that you know how to record, run, and edit macros, let's spend some time in the Visual Basic Editor window and become familiar with some of its features.

With the tools located in the Visual Basic Editor window, you can:

- Write your own VBA procedures
- Create custom forms
- View and modify object properties
- Test VBA procedures and locate errors

The Visual Basic Editor window can be accessed in two ways:

- From the Tools menu in the Microsoft Excel application window: Choose Tools | Macro | Visual Basic Editor.
- From the keyboard: Press Alt+F11.

Understanding the Project Explorer Window

The Project Explorer window displays a hierarchical list of currently open projects and its elements.

The VBA project can contain the following elements:

- Worksheets
- Charts
- This Workbook—the workbook where the project is stored
- Modules
- Classes—special modules that allow you to create your own objects
- Forms
- References to other projects

With the Project Explorer you can manage your projects and easily move between projects that are currently loaded into memory.

You can activate the Project Explorer window in one of three ways:

- From the View menu by selecting Project Explorer
- From the keyboard by pressing Ctrl+R
- From the toolbar by clicking the Project Explorer button (see Figure 1-18)

The Project Explorer window contains three buttons.

The first button from the left (View Code) displays the Code window for the selected module. The middle button (View Object) displays the selected sheet in the Microsoft Excel Object folder or a form located in the Forms folder. The first button from the right (Toggle Folders) hides and unhides the display of folders in the Project Explorer window.

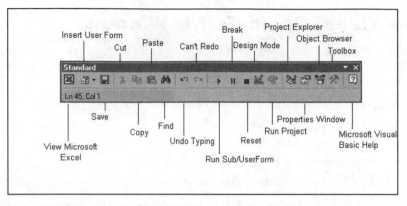

Figure 1-18: Buttons on the Standard toolbar provide a quick way to access many Visual Basic features.

Understanding the Properties Window

The Properties window allows you to review and set properties of various objects in your project. The name of the currently selected object is displayed in the Object box located just below the Properties window's title bar. Properties of the object can be viewed alphabetically or by category by clicking on the appropriate tab (Figure 1-19).

- **Alphabetic Tab**—Alphabetically lists all properties for the selected object. You can change the property setting by selecting the property name and typing or selecting the new setting.

- **Categorized Tab**—Lists all properties for the selected object by category. You can collapse the list so that you see the categories, or you can expand a category to see the properties. The plus (+) icon to the left of the category name indicates that the category list can be expanded. The minus (–) indicates that the category is currently expanded.

The Properties window can be accessed in three ways:

- From the View menu by selecting Properties Window
- From the keyboard by pressing F4
- From the toolbar by clicking the Properties Window button (see Figure 1-18)

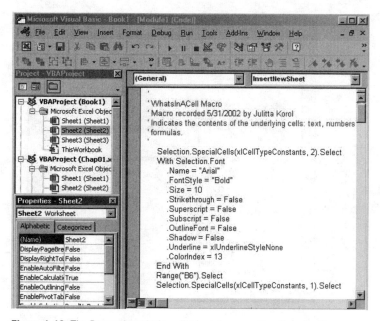

Figure 1-19: The Properties window displays the current settings for the selected object.

Understanding the Code Window

The Code window is used for Visual Basic programming as well as for viewing and modifying the code of recorded macros and existing VBA procedures. Each module can be opened in a separate code window.

There are several ways to activate the Code window:

- From the Project Explorer window, choose the appropriate UserForm or module. Then click the View Code button.
- From the menu, choose View | Code.
- From the keyboard, press F7.

At the top of the Code window, there are two drop-down list boxes (Figure 1-20) that allow you to move quickly within the Visual Basic code. In the Object box on the left side of the Code window, you can select the object whose code you want to view. The box on the right side of the Code window lets you quickly choose a particular procedure or event procedure to view. When you open this box, the names of all procedures located in a module are sorted alphabetically. If you select a procedure in the Procedures/Events box, the cursor will jump to the first line of this procedure.

By dragging the split bar (Figure 1-20) down to a selected position in the Code window, you can divide the Code window into two panes (Figure 1-21). You can then view different sections of a long procedure or a different

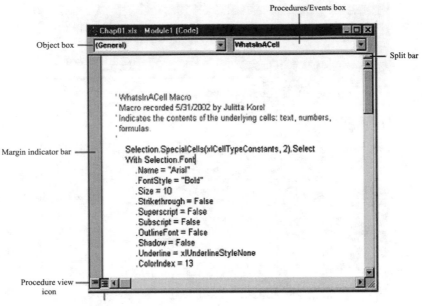

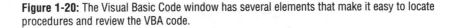

Figure 1-20: The Visual Basic Code window has several elements that make it easy to locate procedures and review the VBA code.

procedure in each pane. Setting up the Code window for the two-pane display is often used for copying or cutting and pasting sections of code between procedures of the same module. To return to the one-window display, simply drag the split line all the way to the top of the Code window.

At the bottom of the Code window, there are two icons. The Procedure View icon displays only one procedure at a time in the Code window. To select another procedure, use the Procedures/Events box. The Full Module View icon displays all the procedures in the selected module. Use the vertical scroll bar to scroll through the module's code.

The margin indicator bar is used by the Visual Basic Editor to display helpful indicators during editing and debugging. If you'd like to take a quick look at some of these indicators, skim through Chapter 13.

```
Chap01.xls - Module1 (Code)                    _ □ ×
(General)                    ▼   WhatsInACell            ▼
'
'WhatsInACell Macro
' Macro recorded 5/31/2002 by Julitta Korol
' Indicates the contents of the underlying cells: text, numbers,
' formulas.
'
    Selection.SpecialCells(xlCellTypeConstants, 2).Select
    With Selection.Font
        .Name = "Arial"
        .FontStyle = "Bold"
        .Size = 10
        .Strikethrough = False

        .ColorIndex = 11
    End With
    Range("C6").Select
    Selection.SpecialCells(xlCellTypeFormulas, 23).Select
    With Selection.Font
        .Name = "Arial"
        .FontStyle = "Bold"
        .Size = 10
        .Strikethrough = False
```

Figure 1-21:
For reviewing longer procedures, you can divide the Code window into two panes.

Other Windows in the Visual Basic Editor Window

In addition to the Code window, there are other windows that are frequently used in the Visual Basic environment:

The Form window is used for creating custom dialog boxes and user forms. You will learn how to do these sorts of things in Chapter 10.

Figure 1-22 displays the list of windows that can be docked in the Visual Basic Editor window. You will learn how to use some of these windows in Chapter 2 (Object Browser, Immediate window) and others in Chapter 13 (Locals window, Watches window).

```
Options                                          ×
  Editor │ Editor Format │ General │ Docking │
 ┌Dockable──────────────────────────────────
 │  ☑ Immediate Window
 │  ☑ Locals Window
 │  ☑ Watch Window
 │  ☑ Project Explorer
 │  ☑ Properties Window
 │  ☐ Object Browser
 │
 │
 │
 │
 │
 │
 │          OK        Cancel        Help
```

Figure 1-22:
The Docking tab in the Options dialog box allows you to choose which windows you want to be dockable.

What's Next...

By following along with some spreadsheet automating examples, you have learned not only how to record a macro but also how to view, read, and modify the Visual Basic code. In addition, you tried various methods of running macros. You ended the chapter with a quick tour of the Visual Basic Editor window. The next chapter introduces you to the fundamentals of Visual Basic for Applications. You will learn many new terms and, most importantly, you will acquire a useful VBA vocabulary that will let you delegate even more tasks to Excel.

Chapter 2

First Steps in Visual Basic for Applications

Understanding Instructions, Modules, and Procedures ■
Assigning a Name to the VBA Project ■ Renaming the Module ■
Calling a Procedure from Another Project ■ **Understanding
Objects, Properties, and Methods** ■ Learning about Objects,
Properties, and Methods ■ **Syntax Versus Grammar** ■ Breaking
Up Long VBA Statements ■ Understanding VBA Errors ■ In
Search of Help ■ On-the-fly Syntax and Programming Assistance
■ **Using the Object Browser** ■ **Using the VBA Object Library** ■
Locating Procedures with the Object Browser ■ **Using the Imme-
diate Window** ■ Obtaining Information in the Immediate Window
■ **Learning about Objects** ■ Doing Things with Spreadsheet Cells
■ Using the Range Property ■ Using the Cells Property ■ Using
the Offset Property ■ Other Methods of Selecting Cells ■
Selecting Rows and Columns ■ Obtaining Information about the
Worksheet ■ Entering Data in a Worksheet ■ Returning Informa-
tion Entered in a Worksheet ■ Finding Out about Cell Formatting
■ Moving, Copying, and Deleting Cells ■ Doing Things with
Workbooks and Worksheets ■ Doing Things with Windows ■
Managing the Excel Application ■ **What's Next...**

Language study is a long-term activity in which you pass through various stages of proficiency. The same is true about learning how to program in Visual Basic for Applications. There are no shortcuts. To become proficient in VBA, you must start at a novice level (Chapters 2-4). Only after you have a good understanding of some of the basics behind Visual Basic for Applications may you go on to the intermediate level (Chapters 5-7) and advanced level (Chapters 8-17). But, first things first. Before you can customize Microsoft Excel with VBA, you need to acquire new vocabulary and grammar. How do you say in Visual Basic, "Add a new worksheet to a workbook," "Delete the contents of cell A5," "Copy the formula from cell A1 to cell B1"? You may already know the individual words. However, do you know how to combine them correctly so that Excel can carry out these tasks? In this chapter, you will learn the terms and rules of VBA.

Understanding Instructions, Modules, and Procedures

In Chapter 1, you learned that Microsoft Excel's macro recorder creates a series of instructions that are the exact equivalents of the actions you perform. These instructions are automatically placed in a workbook sheet called a *module*. Excel stores the module in a module folder located in the current workbook, a new workbook, or in the Personal Macro Workbook. To review the recorded macro code, you must activate the Visual Basic Editor window and double-click the module folder in the Project Explorer window. When the module sheet opens up in the Code window, you are finally able to analyze your procedure's code.

A *procedure* contains all of the recorded instructions. Each line in a procedure is an *instruction*. There are various types of instructions, such as keywords, operators, or calls to other procedures. *Keywords* words carry a special meaning in Visual Basic. In Chapter 1, you learned the most popular VBA keywords—the words Sub and End Sub, which begin and end a procedure. By default, keywords appear in blue. Because keywords are reserved by Visual Basic, don't use these words for other purposes.

In addition to keywords, Visual Basic instructions can contain operators. There are four types of operators: arithmetic, string concatenation, logical, and comparison. *Operators* allow you to combine, join, and manipulate certain values. For example, the division operator (/) can be used to calculate the percentage of the total. In this book, you get many opportunities to see how operators are used in VBA procedures.

Another type of a Visual Basic instruction is a call to a procedure. Calls to procedures allow you to quickly jump to other procedures and execute other sets of instructions. Is it hard to picture this? Let's take the WhatsInACell macro you recorded in Chapter 1. Suppose you also want to include the statement you entered in the FormulasOnOff macro in this procedure.

How can you do this? You could copy the required line of code from one procedure to another. However, there is an easier and quicker way. Instead of copying instructions between procedures, you can call the procedure by specifying its name. For example, if you want to process the FormulasOnOff macro instructions before Visual Basic encounters the instruction MsgBox "All actions have been performed", you can add the following line of code:

```
FormulasOnOff
```

When Visual Basic reaches this line, it will jump right into the FormulasOn-Off procedure and execute its code. Next, it will return to the WhatsInACell macro to continue on with the remaining code, stopping when it reaches the End Sub keywords.

Before you can try out this example, you must learn how to assign names to VBA projects and modules, as well as how to call procedures from different projects.

Assigning a Name to the VBA Project

A *project* is a set of Microsoft Excel objects, modules, forms, and references. Instead of the default name, VBAProject, that precedes the name of the workbook in the Project Explorer window, each project requires a unique name.

Let's assign names to VBAProject (Chap01.xls) and VBAProject (Personal.xls):

1. Start Microsoft Excel, and open **Chap01.xls** where your WhatsInACell macro code is stored. The Personal Macro Workbook where you recorded the FormulasOnOff macro will be automatically loaded.

2. Switch to the Visual Basic Editor window.

3. In the Project Explorer window, select **VBAProject (Chap01.xls)**.

4. Double-click the **(Name)** property in the Properties window. This action selects the default project name **VBAProject**.

5. Type **FirstSteps** for the name of the VBA project, and press **Enter**. Notice that the Project Explorer window now displays FirstSteps (Chap01.xls) as the name of the VBA project.

6. In the Project Explorer window, select **VBAProject (Personal.xls)**.

7. Double-click the **(Name)** property in the Properties window.

8. Type **Personal** for the name of the VBA project, and press **Enter**.

Tip 2-1: Avoid Naming Conflicts

To avoid naming conflicts between your VBA projects, give your projects unique names. You can change the name of the project in one of the following ways:

■ In the Project Explorer window, select the name of the project, double-click the (Name) property in the Properties window, and enter a new name.

■ In the Project Explorer window, right-click the name of the project, and select ProjectName Properties, where ProjectName is the name of the highlighted project. The Project Properties dialog box appears, as shown in Figure 2-1. Type the new project name in the Project Name text box.

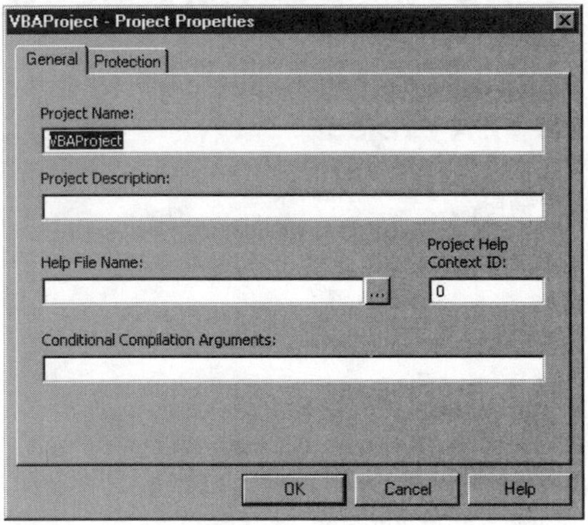

Figure 2-1:
The Project Properties window can be used for changing the name and description of the selected VBA project.

Renaming the Module

When you record a macro or create a new procedure from scratch, Visual Basic creates a module folder to store your VBA code. The first folder is called Module1, the second one Module2, and so on. When you open up a new workbook and create VBA procedures, module folders in the new VBA project are again named Module1, Module2, and so on. Having modules with the same name can be very confusing not only to you but also to Visual Basic, as it tries to execute your macros or Visual Basic procedures in an environment where several projects are open.

To avoid the module confusion, assign unique names to Module1 in the FirstSteps (Chap01.xls) project and Personal (Personal.xls) project.

1. In the Project Explorer window, select the **FirstSteps (Chap01.xls)** project and choose **Module1**.

2. Double-click the **(Name)** property in the Properties window. This action selects the default module name **Module1**.

3. Type **WorksheetFormatting** for the name of Module1, and press **Enter**. Notice that the Project Explorer window now displays WorksheetFormatting as the name of the VBA module.

4. In the Project Explorer window, select **Personal (Personal.xls)**.

5. Double-click the **(Name)** property in the Properties window.

6. Type **Switches** for the name of Module1, and press **Enter**.

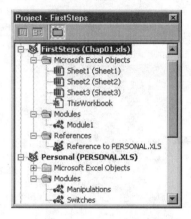

Figure 2-2:
The Project Explorer window shows unique names that were assigned to VBA projects and modules using the Name property in the Properties window.

Calling a Procedure from Another Project

You can call a procedure located in any module in the same project by specifying the procedure name.

Let's suppose that the procedure FormulasOnOff is located in another module in the same project as the WhatsInACell macro. To call the procedure FormulasOnOff from the WhatsInACell macro, all you need to do is specify the procedure name, as shown in the following example:

```
Sub WhatsInACell()
    <place recorded macro instruction here>
    FormulasOnOff
End Sub
```

However, if two or more modules contain a procedure with the same name, you must include the module name in addition to the procedure name.

Let's suppose that the FirstSteps (Chap01.xls) project has three modules. Module FormulaFormatting contains the WhatsInACell macro, while module Switches and module Formulas both contain the FormulasOnOff macro. To call FormulasOnOff (located in the Switches module) from the WhatsInACell macro, precede the procedure name with the module name, as shown in the following example:

```
Sub WhatsInACell()
    <place recorded macro instruction here>
    Switches.FormulasOnOff
End Sub
```

To call a procedure from a different project, you must set up the reference to the project. You do this in the References dialog box. Because the FormulasOnOff macro is located in the Personal (Personal.xls) project, before you can call this macro from the WhatsInACell macro, you must add the reference to the Personal project in the following way:

1. In the Project Explorer window, click **FirstSteps (Chap01.xls)**.

2. Choose **Tools | References**.

3. In the References dialog box, click the check box next to **Personal** (Figure 2-3). Then click **OK**.

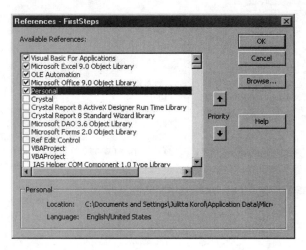

Figure 2-3:
The References dialog box lists all the references available to your project. If you want to execute a procedure located in a different project, you must establish a reference to the other project.

Now that the reference to the Personal project has been established, let's call the FormulasOnOff macro from the WhatsInACell procedure.

1. In the Project Explorer window, select **FirstSteps (Chap01.xls)** and locate the module with the WhatsInACell procedure.

2. Enter a new line before MsgBox "All actions have been performed" and type the following line of code: FormulasOnOff.

3. Return to the Microsoft Excel window and make sure that Sheet1 contains the example spreadsheet (see Figure 1-1 in Chapter 1).

4. Run the WhatsInACell macro using any of the techniques you learned in Chapter 1.

If you give the same name to two different procedures in two different projects, you must specify a project name when you call that procedure.

Let's suppose that the FormulasOnOff macro is located both in the FirstSteps (Chap01.xls) project and in the Personal (Personal.xls) project. To call the FormulasOnOff macro in the Personal (Personal.xls) project (remember that the reference to the Personal project must be established first), include the project name:

```
Sub WhatsInACell ( )
    <place recorded macro instruction here>
    Personal.Switches.FormulasOnOff
End Sub
```

Tip 2-2: How Visual Basic Locates the Called Procedure

When you call a procedure, Visual Basic first looks for it in the same module where the calling procedure (WhatsInACell) is located. If the called procedure (FormulasOnOff) is not found in the same module, Visual Basic searches other modules in the same project. If the procedure still can't be found, Visual Basic checks the references to other projects.

Tip 2-3: Project Name is Missing in the References Dialog Box

If you want to call a procedure from a project that is currently closed, when you open the References dialog to establish the reference to this project, the name of the project is not listed. Click the Browse button, and open the folder where the project is located. By default, the Add Reference dialog box lists Library Files (*.olb, .tlb, .dll). Choose Microsoft Excel Files (*.xls, *.xla) from the Files of Type drop-down list, select the file that contains the procedure you want to set the reference to, and click Open. The name of the project will be added as the last entry in the References dialog box.

Understanding Objects, Properties, and Methods

Using Visual Basic for Applications, you can create procedures that control many features of Microsoft Excel. You can also control a large number of other applications. The power of Visual Basic comes from its ability to control and manage various objects. But what is an object?

An *object* is a thing you control with VBA. A workbook, a worksheet, a range in a worksheet, a chart, or a toolbar are just a few examples of things you may want to control while working in Excel. These things are objects. Excel contains over a hundred objects that you can manipulate in different ways. All Visual Basic objects are organized in a hierarchy. Some objects may contain other objects. For example, Microsoft Excel is an Application object. The Application object contains other objects, such as workbooks or command bars. The Workbook object may contain other objects, such as worksheets or charts. In this chapter, you will learn how to control the following Excel objects: Range, Window, Worksheet, Workbook, and Application. I have listed the Range object first for a very important reason: you can't do much work in spreadsheets unless you know how to manipulate ranges of cells.

Certain objects look alike. If you open a new workbook and examine its worksheets, you won't see any differences. A group of like objects is called a *collection*. For example, a collection of worksheets includes all worksheets in a particular Workbook, and the collection of CommandBars contains all the toolbars and menu bars. Collections are also objects. In Microsoft Excel, the most frequently used collections are the Sheets collection that represents all the worksheets and charts, the Workbook collection, the Worksheets collection, and the Windows collection. When you work with collections, you can perform the same action on all the objects in the collection.

Each object has some characteristics that allow you to describe the object. In Visual Basic, the object's characteristics are called *properties*. For example, a Workbook object has a Name property, and the Range object has such properties as Column, Font, Formula, Name, Row, Style, and Value. The object properties can be set. When you set an object's property, you control its looks or its position. Object properties can only take on one specific value at any one time. For example, the active Workbook can't be called two different names at the same time. The most difficult part of Visual Basic is understanding the fact that some properties can also be objects. Consider the Range object. You can change the looks of the selected range of cells by setting the Font property. But Font can have a different name (Times New Roman, Arial, …), different size (10, 12, 14, …), and different style (Bold, Italic, Underline, …). These are Font properties. If the Font has properties, then the Font is also an object.

Properties are great. They let you change the look of the object, but how can you control the actions? Before you can make Excel carry out some tasks, you need to know another term. Objects have methods. Each action you want the object to perform is called a *method*. The most important Visual Basic method is the Add method. Using this method, you can add a new workbook or worksheet. Objects can use various methods. For example, the Range object has special methods that allow you to clear the cell contents (ClearContents method), formats (ClearFormats method), and both contents and formats (Clear method). Other methods allow the objects to be selected, copied, or moved.

Methods can have optional parameters that specify how the method is to be carried out. For example, the Workbook object has a method called Close. You can close any open workbook using this method. If there are changes to the workbook, Microsoft Excel displays a message asking whether you want to save the changes. You can use the Close method with the SaveChanges parameter set to False to close the workbook and discard any changes that have been made to it, as in the example below:

```
Workbooks("Chap01.XLS").Close SaveChanges:=False
```

Learning about Objects, Properties, and Methods

When you learn new things, theory can give you the necessary background, but how do you really know what's where? The majority of people think in pictures. To make it easy to understand the Microsoft Excel object hierarchy, the Visual Basic online help offers a diagram of the object model, as shown in the following figures.

Figure 2-4: Microsoft Excel object hierarchy (Page 1)

Notice that the Application object is positioned at the very top of the diagram. The Application object represents Microsoft Excel itself. Other Excel objects are located at lower levels.

Suppose you want to control the Range object. Before you can control an Excel object, you must create a reference to it. To get to the Range object from the top of the diagram, just follow the lines. Every time you see a line leading to a different level, make a mental note and replace the line

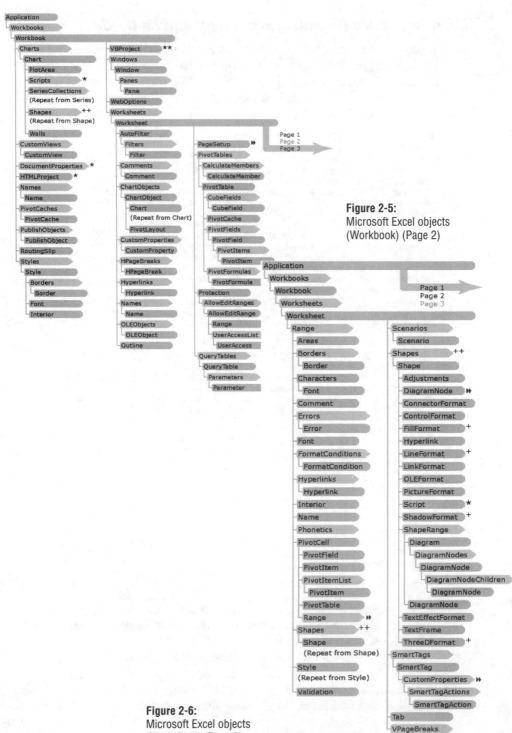

Figure 2-5:
Microsoft Excel objects
(Workbook) (Page 2)

Figure 2-6:
Microsoft Excel objects
(Worksheet) (Page 3)

with a dot operator (a simple period). This way, when you reach the Range object, you will end up with the following reference to the Range object:

```
Application.Workbook.Worksheet.Range
```

Using the Microsoft Excel object diagrams, find the paths to other objects, such as Window, Comment, AutoFilter, or ChartArea. Analyzing the object model is a great way to learn about Excel objects. The time you spend here will pay big dividends later when you start writing VBA procedures from scratch. Often, you will be required to specify the exact name of the object that is to be referenced.

Now let's make it even more practical. Suppose you want to delete the contents of cell A4. To do this manually, select cell A4 and press the Delete key on your keyboard. To perform the same operation using Visual Basic, you first need to find out how to make Excel select an appropriate cell. Cell A4, like any other worksheet cell, is represented by the Range object. Visual Basic does not have the Delete method for deleting contents of cells. Instead, use the ClearContents method, as in the following example:

```
Range("A4").ClearContents
```

Notice the dot operator between the name of the object and its method. This instruction gets rid of the contents of cell A4. However, how do you make Excel delete the contents of cell A4 located in the first sheet of the Chap02.xls workbook? Let's also assume that there are several Excel work-books open. If you don't want to end up deleting the contents of cell A4 from the wrong workbook or worksheet, you must write a detailed instruc-tion so that Visual Basic knows where to locate the necessary cell:

```
Application.Workbooks("Chap02.xls").Worksheets("Sheet1")
    .Range("A4").ClearContents
```

The above instruction should be written on one line and read from right to left as follows: Clear the contents of cell A4, which is part of a range located in a worksheet named Sheet1 contained in a workbook named Chap02.xls, which in turn is a part of the Excel application. Notice the letter "s" at the end of the collection names: Workbooks and Worksheets. All references to the names of workbooks, worksheets, or cells must be enclosed in quota-tion marks.

To locate Microsoft Excel object diagrams, choose Help | Microsoft Excel Help in the Microsoft Excel application window. On the Contents tab, click Programming Information | Microsoft Excel Visual Basic Reference | Microsoft Excel Object Model.

In addition to Microsoft Excel objects, you can use the Microsoft Office, Microsoft forms, and DAO and ADO object models. Objects that belong to these libraries can be used in Excel, as well as in other applications that are members of the Microsoft Office family of products. See Chapter 15 for examples of using DAO and ADO object models in accessing the Microsoft Access databases from Excel.

> **Tip 2-4: VBA and Prior Versions of Microsoft Excel**
>
> Microsoft Excel online help lists changes made to the Microsoft Excel object model from prior versions of Excel. Many objects, properties, and methods have been replaced with newer and improved features. To provide backward compatibility, replaced objects have been hidden.
>
> For more information, activate the online help from the Visual Basic Editor window. Hidden objects can also be located in the Object Browser. If you right-click in the Object Browser window, you can choose the option Show hidden members. You will learn how to use the Object Browser later in

Syntax Versus Grammar

Now that you know the basic elements of VBA (objects, properties, and methods), it's time to start using them. But how do you combine objects, properties, and methods into correct language structures? Every language has grammar rules that people follow in order to make themselves understood. Whether you speak English, Spanish, French, or any other language, you apply certain rules to your writing and speech. In programming, we use the term "syntax" to specify language rules. You can look up the syntax of each object, property, or method in the online help or in the Object Browser window.

Listed below are a few general Visual Basic rules you can't go without. To make Excel always understand what you mean, just stick to the following rules:

■ **Rule #1: Referring to the property of an object**

If the property does not have arguments, the syntax is as follows:

```
Object.Property
```

`Object` is a placeholder. It is where you should place the name of the actual object that you are trying to access. `Property` is also a placeholder. Here you place the name of the object's characteristics. For example, to refer to the value entered in cell A4 on your worksheet, write the following instruction:

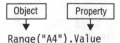

```
Range("A4").Value
```

Notice the period between the name of the object and its property. When you need to access the property of an object that is contained within several other objects, you must include the names of all objects in turn, separated by the dot operator, as shown below:

```
ActiveSheet.Shapes(2).Line.Weight
```

This example references the Weight property of the Line object and refers to the second object in the collection of Shapes located in the active worksheet.

Some properties require one or more arguments. For example, using the popular Offset property, you can select a cell relative to the active cell. The Offset property requires two arguments. The first argument indicates the row number (rowOffset), and the second one determines the column number (columnOffset).

Object	Property	Arguments

```
ActiveCell.Offset(3, 2)
```

In the example above, assuming the active cell is A1, Offset(3, 2) will reference the cell located three rows down and two columns to the right of cell A1. In other words, cell C4 is referenced.

Because the arguments placed between parentheses are often difficult to understand, it's common practice to precede the value of the argument with its name, as in the following example:

```
ActiveCell.Offset(rowOffset:=3, columnOffset:=2)
```

Notice that a colon and an equal sign always follow the named arguments (:=). When you use the named arguments, you can list them in any order. The above instruction can also be written as follows:

```
ActiveCell.Offset(columnOffset:=2, rowOffset:=3)
```

The revised instruction does not change the meaning; you are still referencing cell C4. However, if you transpose the arguments in `ActiveCell.Offset(3, 2)`, you will end up referencing D3 instead of C4.

■ **Rule #2: Changing the property of an object**

```
Object.Property = Value
```

`Value` is a new value that you want to assign to the property of the object. The value can be:

- A number

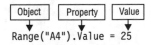

```
Range("A4").Value = 25
```

The above instruction enters the number 25 in cell A4 of the selected worksheet.

- Text entered in quotes

```
ActiveCell.Font.Name = "Times New Roman"
```

The above instruction changes the font of the active cell to Times New Roman.

- A logical value (True or False)

```
ActiveCell.Font.Bold = True
```

The above instruction applies bold formatting to the active cell.

- **Rule #3: Returning the current value of the object property**

```
Variable = Object.Property
```

`Variable` is the name of the storage location where Visual Basic is going to store the property setting. You will learn about variables in Chapter 3.

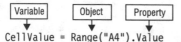

```
CellValue = Range("A4").Value
```

The above instruction saves the current value of cell A4 in the variable named `CellValue`.

- **Rule #4: Referring to the object's method**

If the method does not have arguments, the syntax is as follows:

```
Object.Method
```

`Object` is a placeholder. It is where you should place the name of the actual object that you are trying to access. `Method` is also a placeholder. Here you place the name of the action you want to perform on the object. For example, to clear the formatting in cell A4, use the following instruction:

```
Range("A4").ClearContents
```

If the method can take arguments, the syntax is as follows:

```
Object.Method (argument1, argument2, … argumentN)
```

For example, using the GoTo method, you can quickly select any range in a workbook. The syntax of the GoTo method is:

```
Object.GoTo(Reference, Scroll)
```

The `Reference` argument is the destination cell or range. The `Scroll` argument can be set to True to scroll through the window or to False to not scroll through the window.

For example, the following VBA statement selects cell P100 in Sheet1 and scrolls through the window:

```
Application.GoTo _
    Reference:=Worksheets("Sheet1").Range("P100"), _
        Scroll:=True
```

The above instruction did not fit on one line, so it was broken into sections using the special line continuation character (the underscore), as described in the next section.

Breaking Up Long VBA Statements

Although one line of VBA code can contain as many as 1,024 characters, it is a good idea to break up a long statement into two or more lines to make your procedure more readable. Visual Basic has a special line continuation character that can be used at the end of a line to indicate that the next line is a continuation of the previous one, as in the following example:

```
Selection.PasteSpecial _
    Paste:=xlValues, _
    Operation:=xlMultiply, _
    SkipBlanks: =False, _
    Transpose:=False
```

The line continuation character is the underscore (_). You must precede the underscore with a space. You can use the line continuation character in the following locations in your code:

- Before or after operators; for example: &, +, Like, NOT, AND
- Before or after a comma
- Before or after a colon and an equal sign (:=)
- Before or after an equal sign

You cannot use the line continuation character between a colon and equal sign. For example, the following use of the continuation character is not recognized by Visual Basic:

```
Selection.PasteSpecial Paste: _
    =xlValues, Operation: _
    =xlMultiply, SkipBlanks: _
    =False, Transpose: _
    =False
```

Also, you may not use the line continuation character within the text enclosed in quotes. For example, the following usage of the underscore is invalid:

```
MsgBox "To continue the long instruction, use the _
    line continuation character."
```

The above instruction should be broken up as follows:

```
MsgBox "To continue the long instruction, use the " & _
    "line continuation character."
```

Understanding VBA Errors

In the course of writing or editing VBA procedures, no matter how careful you are, you're likely to make some mistakes. For example, you may misspell a statement, misplace a comma or quote, or forget a period or ending parenthesis. These kinds of mistakes are known as syntax errors. Fortunately, Visual Basic is quite helpful in spotting this kind of error. To have Visual Basic automatically check for correct syntax after you enter a line of code, choose Tools | Options in the Visual Basic window. Make sure the Auto Syntax Check setting is checked on the Editor tab.

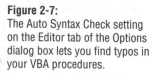

Figure 2-7:
The Auto Syntax Check setting on the Editor tab of the Options dialog box lets you find typos in your VBA procedures.

When Visual Basic finds a syntax error, it displays an error message box and changes the color of the incorrect line of code to red (Figure 2-8) or another color as indicated on the Editor Format tab in the Options dialog box.

If the explanation in the error message isn't clear, you can always click the Help button for more help. And if the Visual Basic online help cannot point you in the right direction, return to your procedure and carefully examine the offending instruction for missed letters, quotes, periods, colons, equal signs, and beginning and ending parentheses. Finding syntax errors can be aggravating and time-consuming. Certain syntax errors can be caught only during the execution of the procedure. While attempting to run your procedure, Visual Basic can find errors that were caused by using invalid arguments or omitting instructions that are used in pairs, such as If statements and looping structures.

Tip 2-5: Program Bugs

You've probably heard more than once that "computer programs are full of bugs." In programming, errors are called bugs, and debugging is the process of eliminating errors from your programs. The first step in debugging a procedure is to correct all syntax errors. Visual Basic provides a myriad of tools with which to track down and eliminate bugs. In this chapter, you will find out how you can use Visual Basic's assistance in writing code with a minimum amount of errors. In Chapter 13, you will learn how to use special debugging tools to trap errors in your VBA procedures.

In addition to syntax errors, there are two other types of errors: run-time and logic. Run-time errors occur while the procedure is running. A typical

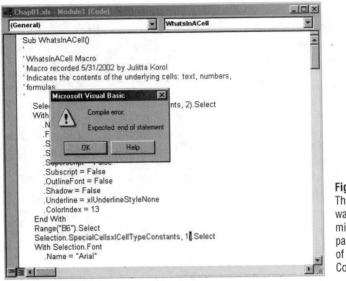

Figure 2-8:
This error message was caused by a missing beginning parenthesis in front of xlCellType-Constants.

run-time error is shown in Figure 2-9. Run-time errors are often caused by those unexpected situations that the programmer did not think of while writing the code. These occur, for example, when the program is trying to access a drive or a file that does not exist on a user's computer or copy a file to a floppy disk without first checking whether the user had inserted a floppy disk and closed the drive door.

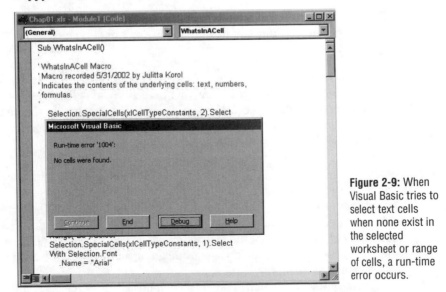

Figure 2-9: When Visual Basic tries to select text cells when none exist in the selected worksheet or range of cells, a run-time error occurs.

The third type of error, logic error, often does not generate a specific error message. The procedure may have no flaws in its syntax and may even run without errors, yet it produces incorrect results. Logic errors are usually very difficult to locate, and those that happen intermittently are so well-concealed that you can count on spending long hours, and even days, trying to locate the source of the error.

In Search of Help

When you use the macro recorder, all your actions are translated into VBA instructions and placed in a module. When studying the recorded procedure, don't forget that help is within your reach. While the meaning of some of the instructions may be pretty straightforward, you will probably find some of them less obvious. This is the time to ask for help. When you're working alone, your VBA tutor is just a click or keypress away. Using Visual Basic online help is quick and easier to use than a paper dictionary or reference manual. If you hate thumbing through the pages of a dictionary to find the needed term, you'll be amazed at how quick you can get to the necessary help page from the Visual Basic Code window.

Let's examine how, with the help of the built-in VBA tutor, you can make the first instruction in the WhatsInACell procedure a part of your VBA vocabulary:

```
Selection.SpecialCells(xlCellTypeConstants, 2).Select
```

The above instruction can be broken into three parts. What parts? Is Selection an object or a property? What is SpecialCells? What is Select? To answer these questions, perform the following:

1. Activate the Code window with a procedure you want to analyze.

2. Click anywhere within the word that you don't understand.

3. Press **F1**.

The help system opens on the correct page. If your cursor is located within the word Selection, you already know that Selection can be a property of an Application or a Window object. If you position the cursor within the next unknown term (SpecialCells) and again follow the steps above, you end up on the SpecialCells help screen (Figure 2-10).

Notice that each help screen contains lots of information. The type of instruction being looked up is shown at the top of the help window. The type of instruction allows the word to be classified. For example, SpecialCells is a method. The names of objects to which this method can apply are listed under the heading Applies To. The See Also and Example headings below the name of the instruction allow you to quickly jump to other instructions with similar usage or meaning and view a code example that uses this instruction.

The meaning of the instruction is shown below the See Also and Example headings. Next comes the syntax with the required arguments and other parameters. The Remarks section gives situations where using this particular instruction is recommended over using another instruction.

You can easily copy the code in the Example window into your own procedure. Simply highlight the lines you want to copy and press Ctrl+C, or right-click the selection and choose Copy from the shortcut menu. Switch to the Visual Basic Code window, click in the location where you want to paste the code example, and press Ctrl+V or choose Edit | Paste.

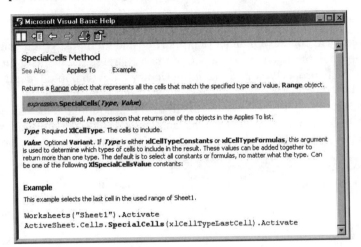

Figure 2-10:
Objects, properties, and methods of Visual Basic for Applications are explained in detail in the online help.

On-the-fly Syntax and Programming Assistance

The Edit toolbar in the Visual Basic Editor window contains several buttons that let you enter correctly formatted VBA instructions with speed and ease. If the Edit toolbar isn't currently docked in the Visual Basic Editor window, you can turn it on by choosing View | Toolbars.

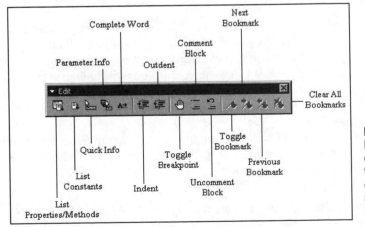

Figure 2-11:
Buttons located on the Edit toolbar make it easy to write and format VBA instructions.

Writing procedures in Visual Basic requires that you use hundreds of built-in instructions and functions. Because most people cannot learn the correct syntax of all the instructions that are available in VBA, the IntelliSense technology provides you with syntax and programming assistance on demand. While working in the Code window, you can have special windows pop up and guide you through the process of creating correct VBA code.

List Properties/Methods

Each object can contain a number of properties and methods. When you enter the name of the object and a period that separates the name of the object from its property or method in the Code window, a pop-up menu may appear. This menu lists the properties and methods available for the object that precedes the period (Figure 2-12). To turn this automated feature on, choose Tools | Options. In the Options dialog box, click the Editor tab, and make sure the Auto List Members check box is selected.

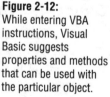

Figure 2-12:
While entering VBA instructions, Visual Basic suggests properties and methods that can be used with the particular object.

To choose an item from the pop-up menu (Figure 2-12), start typing the name of the property or method that you want to select. When Excel highlights the correct item name, press Enter to insert the item into your code and start a new line. Or, if you want to continue writing instructions on the same line, press the Tab key instead. You can also double-click the item to insert it in your code. To close the pop-up menu without inserting an item, simply press Esc.

When you press Esc to remove the pop-up menu, Visual Basic will not display it again for the same object. To display the properties/methods pop-up menu again, you can:

- Press Ctrl+J
- Use the backspace key to delete the period and type the period again
- Right-click in the Code window and select List Properties/Methods from the shortcut menu

- Choose Edit | List Properties/Methods
- Click the List Properties/Methods button 🔳 on the Edit toolbar

List Constants

Earlier in this chapter, you learned that to assign a value to a property, you need to use the following rule: Object.Property = Value. If the Options dialog box (Editor tab) has a check mark next to the Auto List Members setting, Excel displays a pop-up menu listing the constants that are valid for the property that precedes the equal sign. A *constant* is a value that indicates a specific state or result. Excel and other applications in the Microsoft Office Suite have a number of predefined, built-in constants. You will learn about constants, their types, and usage in Chapter 3.

Suppose you want your program to turn on the Page Break Preview for your worksheet. The Edit menu has two options: Normal View, which is the default view for most tasks in Excel, and Page Break Preview, which is the editing view that displays the worksheet as it prints. Both of these options are represented by a built-in constant. Microsoft Excel constant names begin with the "xl" characters. As soon as you enter in the Code window the instruction:

```
ActiveWindow.View =
```

a pop-up menu will appear with the names of valid constants for the property.

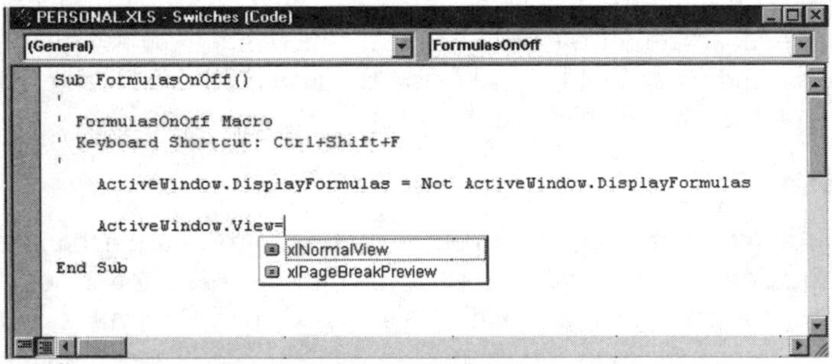

Figure 2-13: The List Constants pop-up menu displays a list of constants that are valid for the property typed.

To work with the List Constants pop-up menu, use the same techniques as the List Properties/Methods pop-up menu outlined in the previous section. The List Constants menu can be activated by pressing Ctrl+Shift+J or clicking the List Constants button 🔳 on the Edit toolbar.

Parameter Info

If you've had a chance to work with Excel functions, you already know that many functions require one or more arguments (or *parameters*). If a Visual Basic function requires an argument, you can see the names of required and optional arguments in a tip box that appears just below the cursor as soon as you type the left parenthesis (Figure 2-14). The Parameter Info feature makes it easy for you to supply correct arguments to a VBA function. In addition, it reminds you of two other things that are very important for the function to work correctly: the order of the arguments and the required data type of each argument. You will learn about data types in the next chapter.

To see how this works, enter the following in the Code window:

```
ActiveWorkbook.SaveAs(
```

As soon as you enter the beginning parenthesis, a tip window appears just below the cursor. The current argument is displayed in bold. When you supply the first argument and enter the comma, Visual Basic displays the next argument in bold. Optional arguments are surrounded by square brackets [ ].

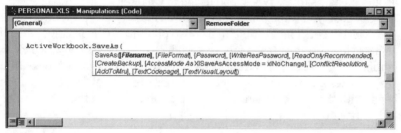

Figure 2-14: A tip window displays a list of arguments utilized by a VBA function or instruction.

To close the Parameter Info window, press Esc. To open the tip window using the keyboard, enter the instruction or function, follow it with the left parenthesis, and press Ctrl+Shift+I. You can also click the Parameter Info button 🖳 on the Edit toolbar or choose Edit | Parameter Info.

Quick Info

When you select an instruction, function, method, procedure name, or constant in the Code window and then click the Quick Info button 🖳 on the Edit toolbar (or press Ctrl+I), Visual Basic will display the syntax of the highlighted item, as well as the value of a constant. The Quick Info feature can be turned on or off using the Options dialog box. To use the feature, click the Editor tab and choose the Auto Quick Info option.

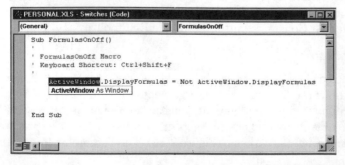

Figure 2-15:
The Quick Info feature provides a list of function paramenters, as well as constant values and VBA statement syntax.

Complete Word

Another way to increase the speed of writing VBA procedures in the Code window is with the Complete Word feature. As you enter the first few letters of a keyword and press Ctrl+Spacebar, or click the Complete Word button **A⁺** on the Edit toolbar, Visual Basic will save you time entering the remaining letters by completing the keyword entry for you.

For example, enter the first four letters of the keyword Application in the Code window and press Ctrl+Spacebar:

    Appl

Visual Basic will complete the rest of the word, and in the place of Appl, you will see the entire word Application.

If there are several VBA keywords that begin with the same letters, when you press Ctrl+Spacebar, Visual Basic will display a pop-up menu listing all the keywords. To try out this example, enter only the first three letters of the word Application, press the Complete Word button on the toolbar, and select the appropriate word from the pop-up menu.

Indent/Outdent

As you have seen, the Editor tab in the Options dialog box contains a number of settings that you can turn on to make many automated features available in the Code window. If the option Auto Indent is turned on, you can automatically indent the selected lines of code the number of characters specified in the Tab Width text box. The default entry for Auto Indent is four characters. You can easily change the Tab Width by typing a new value in the text box.

Why would you want to use indentation in your code? When you indent certain lines in your VBA procedures, you make them more readable and easier to understand. Indenting is especially recommended for entering lines of code that make decisions or repeat actions. You will learn how to create these kinds of Visual Basic instructions in Chapters 5 and 6. For now, let's practice indenting and outdenting lines of code using the WhatsInACell macro that you recorded in Chapter 1.

1. In the Project Explorer window, select the **FirstSteps (Chap01.xls)** project and activate the **WorksheetFormatting** module that contains the code of the WhatsInACell macro.

2. Select any block of code beginning with the keyword With and ending with the keywords End With.

3. Click the **Indent** button ⬚ on the Edit toolbar, or press **Tab** on the keyboard.

4. The selected block of instructions will move four spaces to the right if you are using the default setting in the Tab Width box in the Options dialog box (Editor tab).

5. Click the **Outdent** button ⯮ on the Edit toolbar, or press **Shift+Tab** to return the selected lines of code to the previous location in the Code window.

The Indent and Outdent options are also available from the Edit menu.

Comment Block/Uncomment Block

In the first chapter you learned that an apostrophe placed at the beginning of a line of code denotes a comment. Not only do comments make it easier to understand what the procedure does, but they are also very useful in testing and troubleshooting VBA procedures. For example, when you execute a procedure, it may not run as expected. Instead of deleting the lines that may be responsible for the problems, you may want to skip these lines of code for now and return to them later. By placing an apostrophe at the beginning of the line you want to avoid, you can continue checking the other parts of your procedure. While commenting one line of code by typing an apostrophe works fine for most people, when it comes to turning entire blocks of code into comments, you'll find the Comment Block and Uncomment Block buttons on the Edit toolbar very handy and easy to use. To comment a few lines of code, simply select the lines and click the Comment Block button ⯭. To turn the commented code back into VBA instructions, click the Uncomment Block button ⯭.

If you don't select text and click the Comment Block button, the apostrophe is added only to the line of code where the cursor is currently located.

Using the Object Browser

If you want to move easily through the myriad of VBA elements and features, examine the capabilities of the Object Browser. This special built-in tool is available in the Visual Basic Editor window.

To access the Object Browser, use any of the following methods:

- Press F2
- Choose View | Object Browser
- Click ⯭ on the toolbar

The Object Browser allows you to browse through the objects that are available to your VBA procedures, as well as view their properties, methods, and events. With the aid of the Object Browser, you can move quickly between procedures in your own VBA projects, as well as search for objects and methods across type libraries.

The Object Browser window is divided into three sections (see Figure 2-16). The top of the window displays the Project/Library drop-down list box with the names of all libraries and projects that are available to the currently active VBA project. A *library* is a special file that contains information about the objects in an application. New libraries can be added via the References dialog box (Tools | References). The entry for <All Libraries> lists the objects of all libraries that are installed on your computer. When you select the library called Excel, you will only see the names of the objects that are exclusive to Microsoft Excel. As opposed to the Excel library, the VBA library lists the names of objects that are exclusive to Visual Basic for Applications.

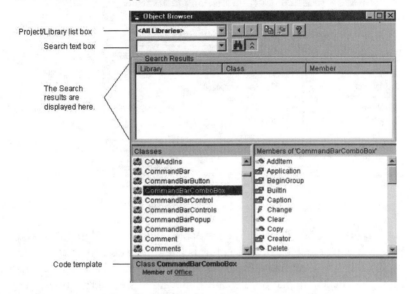

Figure 2-16: The Object Browser window allows you to browse through all the objects, properties, and methods available to the current VBA project.

Below the Project/Library drop-down list box, there is a Search text box that allows you to quickly find information in a particular library. This field remembers the last four items for which you searched. To find only whole words, right-click anywhere in the Object Browser window and choose Find Whole Word Only from the shortcut menu. The Search Results section of the Object Browser (Figures 2-16 and 2-17) displays the Library, Class, and Member element that met the criteria entered in the Search text box. When you type the search text and click the Search button ⚲, Visual Basic expands the Object Browser dialog box to show the Search Results. You can hide or show the Search Results by clicking the button located to the right of the binoculars.

Figure 2-17: Searching for answers in the Object Browser

The Classes list box displays the available object classes in the selected library. If you select a VBA project, this list shows objects in the project. In Figure 2-16 the CommandBarComboBox object class is selected. When you highlight a class, the list on the right-hand side (Members) shows the properties, methods, and events available for that class. Figure 2-16 shows some of the members of the CommandBarComboBox class. By default, members are listed alphabetically. You can, however, organize the members list by group type (properties, methods, or events) using the Group Members command from the Object Browser shortcut menu.

If you select a VBA project in the Project/Library list box, the Members list box will list all the procedures available in this project. To examine the code of a procedure, simply double-click its name. If you select a VBA library, you will see a listing of Visual Basic built-in functions and constants. If you need more information on the selected class or member, click the question mark button at the top of the Object Browser window.

The bottom of the Object Browser window displays a Code template area with the definition of the selected member. If you click the green hyperlink text in the Code template, you can quickly jump to the selected member's class or library in the Object Browser window. Text displayed in the Code template area can be copied to the Windows clipboard and then pasted to the Code window. If the Code window is visible while the Object Browser window is open, you can save time by dragging the highlighted code template and dropping it into the Code window.

You can easily adjust the size of the various sections of the Object Browser window by dragging the dividing horizontal and vertical lines.

Now that you've discovered the Object Browser, you may wonder how you can put it to use in VBA programming. Let's assume that you placed a text box in the middle of your worksheet. How can you make Excel move this text box so that it is positioned at the top left-hand corner of the sheet?

1. Open a new workbook.

2. Choose **View | Toolbars** and click **Drawing**.

3. Click **Text box** on the Drawing toolbar. Draw a box in the middle of the sheet and enter any text.

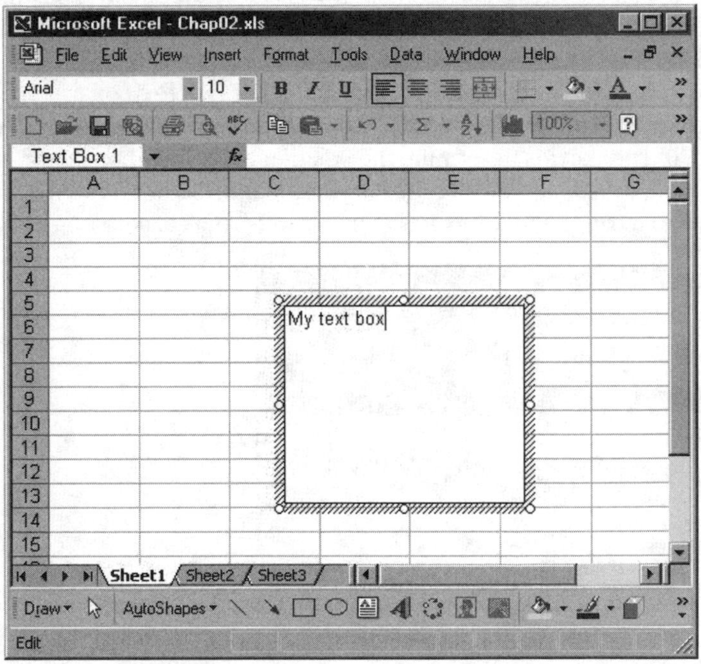

Figure 2-18: Excel displays the name of the inserted object in the Name box above the worksheet.

4. Select any cell outside the text box area.

5. Press **Alt+F11** to activate the Visual Basic Editor window, and select **Personal (Personal.xls)** in the Project Explorer window.

6. Choose **Insert | Module** to add a new module sheet to the Personal Macro Workbook.

7. In the Properties window, enter the new name for this module: **Manipulations**.

8. Choose **View | Object Browser**, or press **F2**.

9. In the Libraries/Projects list box, click the drop-down arrow and select the **Excel** type library.

10. Enter **textbox** as the search text in the Search box and click the **Search** button ▓. Make sure you don't enter a space in the search string.

Visual Basic searches the Excel library and displays the search results. It appears that the Shapes object is in control of our text box operations (Figure 2-19). Looking at the members list, you can quickly determine that the AddTextbox method is used for adding a new text box to a worksheet.

The Code template at the bottom of the Object Browser shows the correct syntax for using this method. If you select the AddTextbox method and press F1, you will see the Help window with more details on how to use this method (Figure 2-20).

When you examine the arguments of the AddTextbox method and their explanations in the Help window, you can quickly figure out that the Left and Top properties determine the position of the text box in a worksheet. All you have to do now is return to the Code window and write the procedure to move the text box to the upper left-hand corner.

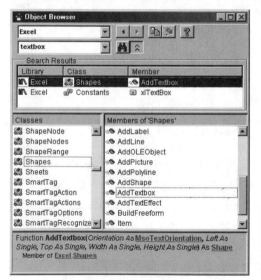

Figure 2-19:
Using the Object Browser window, you can find the appropriate VBA instructions for writing your own procedures.

11. Close the Object Browser window and the Help window (if it is still open).

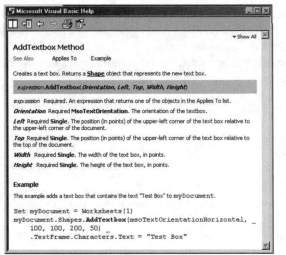

Figure 2-20: To get detailed information on any item found in the Object Browser, select the item and press F1.

12. Double-click the **Manipulations** module, and enter the procedure MoveTextBox:

```
Sub MoveTextBox()
    With ActiveSheet.Shapes("Text box 1")
        .Select
        .Left = 0
        .Top = 0
    End With
End Sub
```

13. Choose **Run | Run Sub/UserForm** to try out this procedure.

When you return to the worksheet where you placed your text box, the box will be positioned at the top left-hand corner of the worksheet.

Notice that the MoveTextBox procedure selects Text box 1 in the collection of Shapes. Text box 1 is the default name of the first object placed in the worksheet. Each time you add a new object to your worksheet, Excel assigns a new number (index) to it. Instead of using the object name, you can refer to the member of a collection by its index.

For example, instead of:

```
With ActiveSheet.Shapes("Text box 1")
```

you can enter:

```
With ActiveSheet.Shapes(1).
```

Let's manipulate another object with Visual Basic. Try this on your own. Place a small circle in the same worksheet where you originally placed the text box. Use the Ellipse tool on the Drawing toolbar to draw the circle. Insert a new procedure in the Manipulations module and write the VBA code to place the circle inside the text box. Keep in mind that Excel numbers objects consecutively. The first object is assigned a number 1, the second one a number 2, and so on. The type of object, whether it is a text box, a circle, or a rectangle, does not matter.

The MoveCircle procedure shown below demonstrates how to move a circle to the top left-hand corner of the active worksheet:

```
Sub MoveCircle()
    With ActiveSheet.Shapes(2)
        .Select
        .Left = 0
        .Top = 0
    End With
End Sub
```

Moving a circle is similar to moving a text box or any other object placed in a worksheet.

Notice that instead of referring to the circle by its name, Oval 2, the procedure uses the object's index. When you run the MoveCircle procedure, it places the circle inside the text box object.

Using the VBA Object Library

In the previous example, you used the properties of objects that are members of the Shapes collection in the Excel object library. While the Excel library contains objects specific to using Microsoft Excel, the VBA object library provides access to many built-in VBA functions grouped by categories. These functions are general in nature. They allow you to manage files, set the date and time, interact with users, convert data types, deal with text strings, or perform mathematical calculations. In the following exercise, you will see how to use one of the built-in VBA functions to create a new subfolder without leaving Excel.

1.   Return to the Manipulations module where you entered the MoveTextBox and MoveCircle procedures.

2.   Enter on a new line the name of the new procedure: **Sub NewFolder()**.

3.   Click **Enter**. Visual Basic will enter the ending keywords End Sub.

4.   Press **F2** to activate the Object Browser.

5.   Click the drop-down arrow in the Libraries/Project list box and select **VBA**.

6.   Enter **file** as the search text in the Search box, and press **Enter**.

7.   Scroll down in the Members list box and highlight the **MkDir** method (see Figure 2-21 on the following page).

8.   Click the **Copy** button in the Object Browser window to copy the selected method name to the Windows clipboard.

9. Return to the Manipulations window and paste the copied instruction inside the procedure NewFolder.

10. Enter a space, followed by **"C:\Study"**. Make sure to enter the name of the entire path in the quotes. The NewFolder procedure is:

```
Sub NewFolder()
    MkDir "C:\Study"
End Sub
```

11. Run the NewFolder procedure.

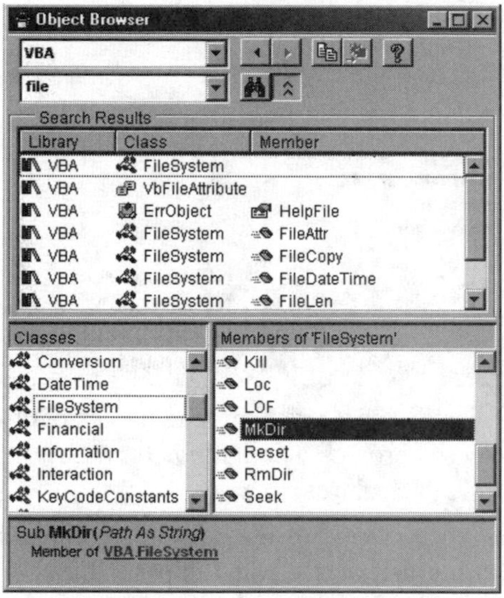

Figure 2-21:
When writing procedures from scratch, consult the Object Browser for names of the built-in VBA functions.

When you run the NewFolder procedure, Visual Basic creates a new folder on drive C. To see the folder, activate Windows Explorer. After creating a new folder, you may realize that you don't need it after all. Although you could easily delete the folder while in Windows Explorer, how about getting rid of it programmatically? The Object Browser displays many other methods that are useful for working with folders and files. The RmDir method is just as simple to use as the MkDir method. To remove the Study folder from your hard drive, simply replace the MkDir method with the RmDir method, and then rerun the NewFolder procedure. Or, create a new procedure called RemoveFolder, as shown here:

```
Sub RemoveFolder()
    RmDir "C:\Study"
End Sub
```

The RmDir method allows you to remove unwanted folders from your hard disk.

Locating Procedures with the Object Browser

In addition to locating objects, properties, and methods, the Object Browser is a handy tool for locating and accessing procedures written in various VBA projects. The following example demonstrates how you can see, at a glance, which procedures are stored in the Personal workbook.

1. Activate the Object Browser and select **Personal** from the Project/Library drop-down list.

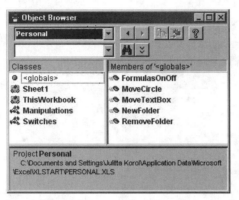

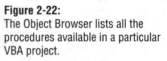

Figure 2-22:
The Object Browser lists all the procedures available in a particular VBA project.

The left side of the Object Browser displays the names of objects that are included in the selected project. The list box on the right shows the names of all the available procedures.

2. Double-click the name of the **NewFolder** procedure. Visual Basic positions the cursor in the first line of the selected procedure.

3. Close the Object Browser window.

Using the Immediate Window

Before you start creating full-fledged VBA procedures (this awaits you in the next chapter!), begin with some warm-up exercises to build up your VBA vocabulary. How can you do this quickly and painlessly? How can you try out some of the newly learned VBA statements? Here are some short, interactive language exercises: enter a simple VBA instruction, and Excel will check it out and display the result in the next line. Let's begin with setting up your exercise screen.

1. In the Visual Basic Editor window, choose **View | Immediate Window**.

    The Immediate window is used for trying out various instructions, functions, and operators present in the Visual Basic language before deciding to use them in your own VBA procedures. It is a great tool for experimenting with your new language. Instructions that you enter in this window immediately display results.

The Immediate window can be moved anywhere on the Visual Basic Editor screen, or it can be docked so that it always appears in the same area of the screen. The docking setting can be turned on and off on the Docking tab in the Options dialog box (Tools | Options).

To quickly access the Immediate window, simply press Ctrl+G while in the Visual Basic Editor screen. To close the Immediate window, click the Close button in the top right-hand corner of the window.

The Immediate window allows you to type VBA statements and test their results immediately without having to write a procedure. The Immediate window is like a scratch pad. Use it to try out your statements. If the statement produces the expected result, you can copy the statement from the Immediate pane into your procedure (or you can drag it right onto the Code window if it is visible).

2. Arrange the screen so that both the Microsoft Excel window and the Visual Basic window are placed side by side.

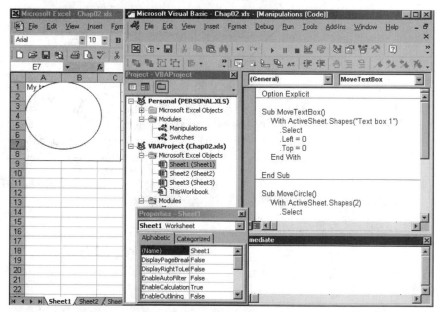

Figure 2-23: Positioning Microsoft Excel and Visual Basic windows side by side allows you to watch the execution of the instructions entered in the Immediate window.

3. In the Immediate window, type the instruction shown below, and press **Enter:**

```
Worksheets("Sheet2").Activate
```

When you press the Enter key, Visual Basic gets to work. If you entered the above VBA statement correctly, VBA activates a second sheet in the current workbook. The Sheet2 tab at the bottom of the workbook should now be highlighted.

4. In the Immediate window, type another VBA statement and make sure to press **Enter** when you're done:

   ```
   Range("A1:A4").Select
   ```

   As soon as you press Enter, Visual Basic highlights the cells A1, A2, A3, and A4 in the active worksheet.

5. Enter the following instruction in the Immediate window:

   ```
   [A1:A4].Value = 55
   ```

   When you press Enter, Visual Basic places the number 55 in every cell of the specified range, A1:A4. Although the above statement is an abbreviated way of referring to the Range object, its full syntax is more readable: `Range("A1:A4").Value = 55`.

6. Enter the following instruction in the Immediate window:

   ```
   Selection.ClearContents
   ```

   When you press Enter, VBA deletes the results of the previous statement from the selected cells. Cells A1:A4 are now empty.

7. Enter the following instruction in the Immediate window:

   ```
   ActiveCell.Select
   ```

   When you press Enter, Visual Basic makes the cell A1 active.

Figure 2-24 shows all the instructions entered in the Immediate window in the above exercise. Every time you pressed the Enter key, Excel executed the statement on the line where the cursor was located. If you want to execute the same instruction again, click anywhere in the line containing the instruction and press Enter.

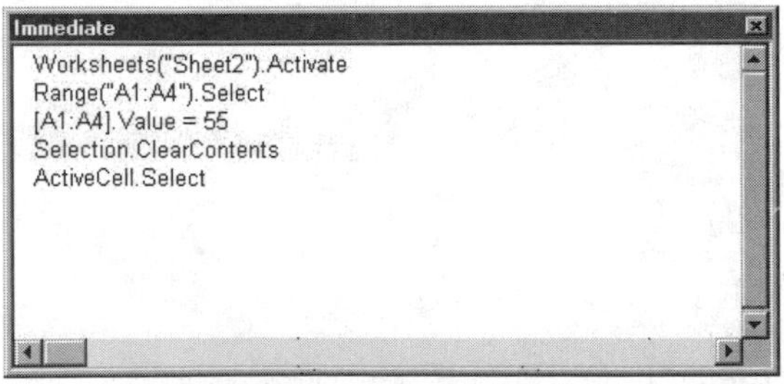

Figure 2-24:
Instructions entered in the Immediate window are executed as soon as you press the Enter key.

For more practice, rerun the statements shown in Figure 2-24. Start from the instruction displayed in the second line of the Immediate window. Execute the instructions one by one by clicking in the appropriate line and pressing the Enter key.

Obtaining Information in the Immediate Window

So far you have used the Immediate window to perform actions. These actions could have been performed manually by clicking the mouse in various areas of the worksheet and entering data. The Immediate window also allows you to ask questions. Suppose you want to find out the answers to the following: " What cells are currently selected?", "What is the value of the active cell?", "What's the name of the active sheet?", "What's the number of the current window?" When working in the Immediate window, you can easily get answers to these and other questions.

In the preceding exercise, you entered several instructions. Let's return to the Immediate window to ask some questions. Excel remembers the instructions entered in the Immediate window even after you close this window. The contents of the Immediate window are automatically deleted when you exit Microsoft Excel.

1. Click the mouse in the second line of the Immediate window where you previously entered the instruction `Range("A1:A4").Select`.

2. Press **Enter** to have Excel reselect cells A1:A4.

3. Click in the new line of the Immediate window and enter the following question:

    `?Selection.Address`

    When you press Enter, Excel will not select anything in the worksheet. Instead, it will display the result of the instruction on a separate line in the Immediate window. In this case, Excel returns the absolute address of the cells that are currently selected ($A$1:$A$4). The question mark (?) tells Excel to display the result of the instruction in the Immediate window. Instead of the question mark, you can use the Print keyword. Let's now ask for the name of the worksheet using the Print keyword.

4. In a new line in the Immediate window, enter the following question:

    `Print ActiveWorkbook.Name`

    When you press Enter, Excel enters the name of the active workbook on a new line in the Immediate window.

    How about finding the name of the application? Who's the parent of Chap02.xls?

5. In a new line in the Immediate window, enter the following question:

    `?Application.Name`

    Excel will reveal its full name: Microsoft Excel.

    The Immediate window can also be used when you require a quick calculation.

6. In a new line in the Immediate window, enter the following question:

    `?12/3`

When you press Enter, Excel shows the result of the division on the next line. But what if you want to know right away the result of 3+2 and 12*8? Instead of entering these instructions on separate lines, you can enter them on one line, as in the following example: ?3+2:?12*8.

Notice the colon separating the two blocks of instructions. When you press the Enter key, Excel displays the results 5, 96 on separate lines in the Immediate window.

Below are all the instructions you entered in the Immediate window including Excel's answers to your questions:

```
Worksheets("Sheet2").Activate
Range("A1:A4").Select
[A1:A4].Value = 55
Selection.ClearContents
ActiveCell.Select
?Selection.Address
$A$1:$A$4
Print ActiveWorkbook.Name
Chap02.xls
?Application.Name
Microsoft Excel
?12/3
 4
?3+2:?12*8
 5
 96
```

To delete the instructions from the Immediate window, highlight all the lines and press Delete.

Learning about Objects

Creating custom applications in Excel requires a working knowledge of common objects or collections of objects such as Range, Workbook (Workbooks), Worksheet (Worksheets), Window (Windows), and Application. In preceding sections, you explored several methods of learning about Visual Basic. Here's a summary of when to use a specific tool:

■ When in doubt about objects, properties, or methods in an existing VBA procedure, fire up the online help by pressing F1.

■ If you need a quick listing of properties and methods for every available object or have trouble locating a hard-to-find procedure, go with the Object Browser.

■ If you want to experiment with VBA and see the results of the VBA commands immediately, activate the Immediate window.

To help you better understand the VBA syntax, the remaining pages of this chapter contain a number of VBA language drills. You will get the most out of these drills if you take the time to work through them in the Immediate window.

Doing Things with Spreadsheet Cells

When you are ready to write your own VBA procedure to automate a particular spreadsheet task, you will most likely begin searching for instructions that allow you to manipulate spreadsheet cells. You will need to know how to select cells, how to enter data in cells, how to assign range names, how to format cells, and how to move, copy, and delete cells. Although these tasks can be easily performed with the mouse or keyboard, mastering these techniques in Visual Basic for Applications requires a little practice.

You must use the Range object to refer to a single cell, a range of cells, a row, or a column. If you take a look at the Excel object model, you will notice that the Range object is a part of another larger object—the Worksheet object. There are three properties that allow you to access the Range object: the Range property, the Cells property, and the Offset property.

Figure 2-25:
The Range object in the
Excel object model

Using the Range Property

The Range property returns a cell or a range of cells. The reference to the range must be in an A1-style and in quotation marks (for example: "A1"). The reference can include the range operator, a colon, (for example "A1:B2") or the union operator, a comma, (for example "A", "B12").

To render this into VBA:	Enter this in the Immediate window:
Select a single cell (e.g., A5).	Range("A5").Select
Select a range of cells (e.g., A6:A10).	Range("A6:A10").Select
Select several non-adjacent cells (e.g., A1, B6, C8).	Range("A1, B6, C8").Select
Select several non-adjacent cells and cell ranges (e.g., A11:D11, C12, D3).	Range("A11:D11, C12, D3").Select

Using the Cells Property

When you want to select a specific cell, the Cells property requires two arguments. The first argument indicates the row number; the second one is the column number or the column letter. Arguments are entered in parentheses. When you omit arguments, Excel selects all the cells in the active worksheet.

To render this into VBA:	Enter this in the Immediate window:
Select a singe cell (e.g., A5).	`Cells(5, 1).Select Cells(5, A).Select`
Select a range of cells (e.g., A6:A10).	`Range(Cells(6, 1), Cells(10, 1)).Select`
Select all cells in a worksheet.	`Cells.Select`

Notice how you can combine the Range property and the Cells property:

```
Range(Cells(6, 1), Cells(10, 1)).Select
```

In the above example, the first Cells property returns cell A6, while the second one returns cell A10. The cells returned by the Cells properties are then used as a reference for the Range object. As a result, Excel will select the range of cells where the top cell is specified by the result of the first Cells property and the bottom cell is defined by the result of the second Cells property.

A worksheet is a collection of cells. You can also use the Cells property with a single argument that identifies a cell's position in the collection of a worksheet's cells. Excel numbers the cells in the following way: cell A1 is the first cell in a worksheet, cell B1 is the second one, cell C1 is the third one, and so on. Cell 256 is the last cell in the first spreadsheet row. You may recall that there are 256 columns in the Microsoft Excel worksheet.

To render this into VBA:	Enter this in the Immediate window:
Select cell A1.	`Cells(1).Select` or `Cells.Item(1).Select`
Select cell C1.	`Cells(3).Select` or `Cells.Item(3).Select`
Select cell IV1.	`Cells(256).Select` or `Cells.Item(256).Select`
Select cell A2.	`Cells(257).Select` or `Cells.Item(257).Select`

Notice that the word Item is a property that returns a single member of a collection. Because Item is the default member for a collection, you can refer to a worksheet cell without explicitly using the Item property.

Now that you've discovered two ways to select cells (Range property and Cells property), you may wonder why you should bother using the more complicated Cells property. It's quite obvious that the Range property is more readable; after all, you used the Range references in Excel formulas and functions long before you decided to learn about VBA. Using the Cells property is more convenient, however, when it comes to working with cells as a collection. Use this property to access all the cells or a single cell from a collection.

Using the Offset Property

Another very flexible way to refer to a worksheet cell is with the Offset property. When automating worksheet tasks, you may not know exactly where a specific cell is located. How can you select a cell whose address you don't know? You can have Excel select a cell based on an existing selection. The Offset property calculates a new range by shifting the starting selection down or up a specified number of rows. You can also shift the selection to the right or left a specified number of columns. In calculating the position of a new range, the Offset property uses two arguments. The first argument indicates the row offset, and the second one is the column offset. Let's try out some examples.

To render this into VBA:	Enter this in the Immediate window:
Select a cell located one row down and three columns to the right of cell A1.	`Range("A1").Offset(1, 3).Select`
Select a cell located two rows above and one column to the left of cell D15.	`Range("D15").Offset(-2, -1).Select`
Select a cell located one row above the active cell.	`ActiveCell.Offset(-1, 0).Select`

In the first example above, Excel selects cell D2. As soon as you enter the second example, Excel chooses cell C13.

If cells A1 and D15 are already selected, you can rewrite the two above examples in the following way:

```
Selection.Offset(1, 3).Select
Selection.Offset(-2, -1).Select
```

Notice that the third example in the practice table above displays zero (0) in the position of the second argument. Zero entered as a first or second argument of the Offset property indicates the current row or column. The instruction `ActiveCell.Offset(-1, 0).Select` will cause an error if the active cell is located in the first row.

When working with the Offset property, you may occasionally need to change the size of a selection of cells. Suppose that the starting selection is A5:A10. How about shifting the selection two rows down and two columns to the right and then changing the size of the new selection? Let's say the new selection should highlight cells C7:C8. The Offset property can only take care of the first part of this task. The second part requires another property. Excel has a special Resize property. You can combine the Offset property with the Resize property to answer the above question. Before you combine these two properties, let's see how you can use them separately:

1. Arrange the screen so that the Microsoft Excel window and the Visual Basic window are side by side.

2. Activate the Immediate window and enter the following instructions:

```
Range("A5:A10").Select
Selection.Offset(2, 2).Select
Selection.Resize(2, 4).Select
```

The first instruction above selects the range A5:A10. Cell A5 is the active cell. The second instruction shifts the current selection to cells C7:C12. Cell C7 is located two rows below the active cell A5 and two columns to the right of A5. Now the active cell is C7. The last instruction resizes the current selection. Instead of range C7:C12, cells C7:C8 are selected. Like the Offset property, the Resize property takes two arguments. The first argument is the number of rows you intend to include in the selection, and the second argument specifies the number of columns. Hence, the instruction `Selection.Resize(2, 4).Select` resizes the current selection to two rows and four columns.

Tip 2-6: Recording a Selection of Cells

By default, the macro recorder selects cells using the Range property. If you turn on the macro recorder and select cell A2, enter any text, and select cell A5, you will see the following lines of code in the Visual Basic Editor window:

```
Range("A2").Select
ActiveCell.FormulaR1C1 = "text"
Range("A5").Select
```

You can have the macro recorder use the Offset property if you tell it to use relative references. To do this, click the Relative Reference button on the Recording toolbar prior to recording. The macro recorder produces the following lines of code:

```
ActiveCell.Offset(-3, 0).Range _
   ("A1").Select
ActiveCell.FormulaR1C1 = "text"
ActiveCell.Offset(3, 0).Range _
   ("A1").Select
```

When you record a procedure using relative references, the procedure will always select a cell relative to the active cell. Notice that the first and third line in the above instructions reference cell A1, even though nothing was said about cell A1. As you remember from Chapter 1, the macro recorder has its own way of getting things done. To make the above instructions less complex, you can delete the reference to Range("A1"):

```
ActiveCell.Offset(-3, 0).Select
ActiveCell.FormulaR1C1 = "text"
ActiveCell.Offset(3, 0).Select
```

After recording a procedure using the Relative Reference button, don't forget to click this button again if your next procedure does not require the use of relative addressing.

The last two instructions can be combined in the following way:

```
Selection.Offset(2, 2).Resize(2, 4).Select
```

In the example above, the Offset property calculates the beginning of a new range, the Resize property determines the new size of the range, and the Select method selects the specified range of cells.

Other Methods of Selecting Cells

If you often have to quickly access certain remote cells in your worksheet, you may already be familiar with the following keyboard shortcuts: End+Up Arrow, End+Down Arrow, End+Left Arrow, and End+Right Arrow. In VBA, you can use the End property to quickly move to remote cells.

To render this into VBA:	Enter this in the Immediate window:
Select the last cell in any row.	`ActiveCell.End(xlright).Select`
Select the last cell in any column.	`ActiveCell.End(xldown).Select`
Select the first cell in any row.	`ActiveCell.End(xleft).Select`
Select the first cell in any column.	`ActiveCell.End(xlup).Select`

Notice that the End property requires an argument that indicates the direction you want to move. Use the following Excel built-in constants to jump in the specified direction: xlright, xleft, xlup, xldown.

Selecting Rows and Columns

Excel uses the EntireRow and EntireColumn properties to select the entire row or column.

To render this into VBA:	Enter this in the Immediate window:
Select an entire row where the active cell is located.	`Selection.EntireRow.Select`
Select an entire column where the active cell is located.	`Selection.EntireColumn.Select`

When you select a range of cells you may want to find out how many rows or columns are included in the selection. Let's have Excel count rows and columns in Range("A1:D15").

1. Enter the following VBA statement in the Immediate window:

   ```
   Range("A1:D15").Select
   ```

   If the Microsoft Excel window is visible, when you press Enter, VBA will highlight the range A1:D15.

2. To find out how many rows are in the selected range, enter the following statement:

   ```
   ?Selection.Rows.Count
   ```

   As soon as you press Enter, VBA displays the answer on the next line. Your selection includes 15 rows.

3. To find out the number of columns in the selected range, enter the following statement:

   ```
   ?Selection.Columns.Count
   ```

Now VBA tells you that the selected `Range("A1:D15")` occupies the width of four columns.

4. Position the cursor anywhere within the word **Rows** or **Columns**, and press **F1** to find out more information about these useful properties.

Obtaining Information about the Worksheet

How big is an Excel worksheet? How many cells, columns, and rows does it contain? If you ever forget the details, use the Count property.

To render this into VBA:	Enter this in the Immediate window:
Find out the total number of cells in an Excel worksheet.	`?Cells.Count`
Find out the total number of rows in an Excel worksheet.	`?Rows.Count`
Find out the total number of columns in an Excel worksheet.	`?Columns.Count`

The Microsoft Excel 2002 worksheet has 16,777,216 cells, 65,536 rows, and 256 columns.

Entering Data in a Worksheet

The information entered in a worksheet can be text, numbers, or formulas. To enter data in a cell or range of cells, you can use any of the two properties of the Range object: the Value property or the Formula property.

Value property:

```
ActiveSheet.Range("A1:C4").Value = "=4 * 25"
```

Formula property:

```
ActiveSheet.Range("A1:C4").Formula = "=4 * 25"
```

In both examples shown above, cells A1:C4 display 100—the result of the multiplication 4 * 25.

To render this into VBA:	Enter this in the Immediate window:
Enter in cell A5 the following text: "Amount Due".	`Range("A5").Formula = "Amount Due"`
Enter the number 123 in cell D21.	`Range("D21").Formula = 123` `Range("D21").Value = 123`
Enter in cell B4 the following formula: =D21 * 3	`Range("B4").Formula = "=D21 * 3"`

Returning Information Entered in a Worksheet

In some Visual Basic procedures you will undoubtedly need to return the contents of a cell or a range of cells. Although you can use either the Value or Formula property, this time the two Range object properties are not interchangeable.

■   The Value property displays the result of a formula entered in a specified cell. If, for example, cell A1 contains the formula = 4 * 25, then the instruction ?Range("A1").Value will return the value 100.

■   If you want to display the formula instead of its result, you must use the Formula property: ?Range("A1").Formula. Excel will display the formula = 4 * 25 instead of its result (100).

Finding Out about Cell Formatting

A frequent spreadsheet task is applying formatting to a selected cell or a range. Your VBA procedure may need to find out the type of format applied to a particular worksheet cell. To retrieve the cell formatting, use the NumberFormat property:

```
?Range("A1").NumberFormat
```

Upon entering the above question in the Immediate window, Excel displays the word "General," which indicates that no special formatting was applied to the selected cell. To change the format of a cell using VBA, enter the following instruction:

```
Range("A1").NumberFormat = "$#,##0.00"
```

If you enter 125 in cell A1 after it has been formatted with the above VBA instruction, cell A1 will display $125.00. You can look up the necessary format codes in the Format Cells dialog box in the Microsoft Excel window (Format | Cells).

If the format you want to apply is not listed in the Format Cells dialog box, refer to the online help for guidelines on creating user-defined formats.

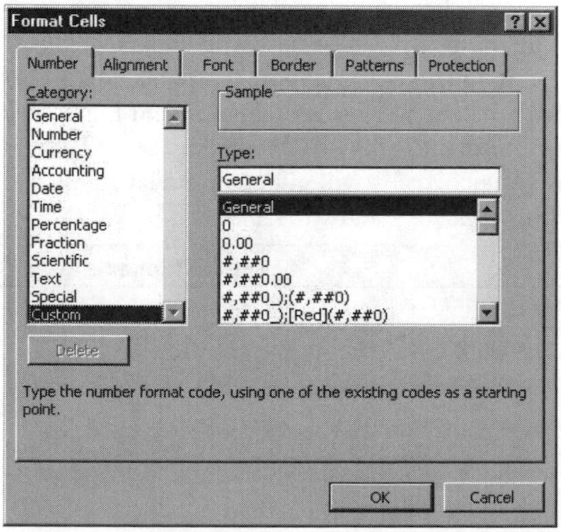

Figure 2-26:
You can apply different formatting to selected cells and ranges using the format codes displayed in the Custom category in the Format Cells dialog box.

Moving, Copying, and Deleting Cells

In the process of developing a new worksheet model, you often find yourself moving and copying cells and deleting cell contents. Visual Basic allows you to automate these worksheet editing tasks with simple-to-use methods: Cut, Copy, and Clear.

To render this into VBA:	Enter this in the Immediate window:
Move the contents of cell A5 to cell A4.	`Range("A5").Cut` `Destination:=Range("A4")`
Copy a formula from cell A3 to cells D5:F5.	`Range("A3").Copy` `Destination:=Range("D5:F5")`
Delete contents of cell A4.	`Range("A4").Clear` `Range("A4").Cut`

Notice that both the Cut and Copy methods used with the Range object require a special argument called Destination. This argument specifies the address of a cell or a range of cells where you want to place the cut or copied data. In the last example, the Cut method is used without the Destination argument to remove data from the specified cell.

The Clear method deletes everything from the specified cell or range, including any applied formats and cell comments. If you want to be specific about what you want to delete, use the following methods:

- **ClearContents**—clears only data from a cell or range of cells
- **ClearFormats**—clears only applied formats
- **ClearComments**—clears all cell comments from the specified range

Doing Things with Workbooks and Worksheets

Now that you've got your feet wet working with worksheet cells and ranges, it's time to move up one level and learn how you can control a single workbook, as well as an entire collection of workbooks. You cannot prepare a new spreadsheet if you don't know how to open a new workbook. You cannot remove a workbook from the screen if you don't know how to close a workbook. These important tasks are handled by two VBA methods: Add and Close. The next series of drills will give you the language skills necessary for dealing with workbooks and worksheets.

To render this into VBA:	Enter this in the Immediate window:
Open a new workbook.	`Workbooks.Add`
Find out the name of the first workbook.	`?Workbooks(1).Name`
Find out the number of open workbooks.	`?Workbooks.Count`
Activate the second open workbook.	`Workbooks(2).Activate`
Activate the Chap02.xls workbook.	`Workbooks("Chap02.xls").Activate`

To render this into VBA:	Enter this in the Immediate window:
Save the active workbook as "NewChap.xls."	`ActiveWorkbook.SaveAs` `Filename:="NewChap.xls"`
Close the first workbook.	`Workbooks(1).Close`
Close the active workbook without saving recent changes to it.	`ActiveWorkbook.Close` `SaveChanges:=False`
Close all open workbooks.	`Workbooks.Close`

If you worked through the last example in the practice table above, all workbooks are now closed. Before you experiment with worksheets, make sure to open a new workbook.

When you deal with individual worksheets, you must know how to add a new worksheet to a workbook, select a worksheet or a group of worksheets, name a worksheet, and copy, move, and delete worksheets. In Visual Basic, each of these tasks requires a special method or property.

To render this into VBA:	Enter this in the Immediate window:
Add a new worksheet.	`Worksheets.Add`
Find out the name of the first worksheet.	`?Worksheets(1).Name`
Select a sheet named "Sheet3."	`Worksheets(3).Select`
Select sheets 1, 3, and 4.	`Worksheets(Array(1,3,4)).Select`
Activate a sheet named "Sheet1."	`Worksheets("Sheet1").Activate`
Move "Sheet2" before "Sheet1."	`Worksheets("Sheet2").Move` `Before:=Worksheets("Sheet1")`
Rename worksheet "Sheet2" to "Expenses."	`Worksheets("Sheet2").Name =` `"Expenses"`
Find out the number of worksheets in the active workbook.	`?Worksheets.Count`
Remove the worksheet named "Expenses" from the active workbook.	`Worksheets("Expenses").Delete`

Notice the difference between the Select and Activate methods:

- The Select and Activate methods can be used interchangeably if only one worksheet is selected.
- If you select a group of worksheets, the Activate method allows you to decide which one of the selected worksheets is active. As you know, only one worksheet can be active at a time.

Tip 2-7: Sheets Other Than Worksheets

In addition to worksheets, the collection of workbooks contains chart sheets. To add a new chart sheet to your workbook, use the Add method: Charts.Add. To count the chart sheets, use: ?Charts.Count.

In Microsoft Excel prior to version 97, the Workbooks collection included two additional sheets: DialogSheets and Modules. Dialogs have been replaced with the much friendlier UserForms. Beginning with Microsoft Excel Version 97, both dialogs and modules were created in the Visual Basic Editor window.

Doing Things with Windows

When you work with several Excel workbooks and need to compare or consolidate data or when you want to see different parts of the same worksheet, you are likely to use the options available from the Microsoft Excel Window menu: New Window and Arrange.

Let's see how you can arrange your screen with Visual Basic for Applications.

To render this into VBA:	Enter this in the Immediate window:
Show the active workbook in a new window.	`ActiveWorkbook.NewWindow`
Display all open workbooks on screen.	`Windows.Arrange`
Activate the second window.	`Windows(2).Activate`
Find out the title of the active window.	`?ActiveWindow.Caption`
Change the active window's title to "My Window."	`ActiveWindow.Caption = "My Window"`

When you display windows on screen, you can decide how to arrange them. The Arrange method has many arguments. The argument that allows you to control the way the windows are positioned on your screen is called `ArrangeStyle`. If you omit the `ArrangeStyle` argument, all windows are tiled.

Constant	Value	Description
xlArrangeStyleTiled	1	Windows are tiled (the default value).
xlArrangeStyleCascade	7	Windows are cascaded.
xlArrangeStyleHorizontal	2	Windows are arranged horizontally.
xlArrangeStyleVertical	3	Windows are arranged vertically.

Instead of the names of constants, you can use the value equivalents shown above.

To cascade all windows, write the following VBA instruction:

```
Windows.Arrange ArrangeStyle:=xlArrangeStyleCascade
```

Or simply:

```
Windows.Arrange ArrangeStyle:=7
```

Managing the Excel Application

In the beginning of this chapter, you learned that objects are organized in a special structure called the object model. The topmost object in an application's object model is the application itself. By controlling the Application object, you can perform many tasks, such as saving the way your screen looks at the end of a day's work or quitting the application. As you know, Excel allows you to save the screen settings by using the Save Workspace option from the File menu. The task of saving the workspace can be easily performed with VBA:

```
Application.SaveWorkspace "Project"
```

The above instruction saves the screen settings in the workspace file named "Project." The next time you need to work with the same files and arrangement of windows, simply open the Project file and Excel will bring up the correct files and restore your screen to your liking.

To render this into VBA:	Enter this in the Immediate window:
Check the name of the active application.	`?Application.Name`
Change the title of the Excel application to "My Application."	`Application.Caption = "My Application"`
Change the title of the Excel application back to "Microsoft Excel."	`Application.Caption = "Microsoft Excel"`
Find out what operating system you are using.	`?Application.OperatingSystem`
Find out the name of the person or firm to whom the application is registered.	`?Application.OrganizationName`
Find out the name of the folder where Excel.exe resides.	`?Application.Path`
Quit working with Microsoft Excel.	`Application.Quit`

What's Next...

In this chapter you learned many basic VBA terms and built-in tools that make it easier to write and troubleshoot VBA statements. You should now have a good idea of how the most common Microsoft Excel objects are organized and controlled. I tried to keep the descriptions down to an absolute minimum and focus on teaching you how to use your new language skills to gain control over Microsoft Excel immediately without writing procedures. For this reason, I focused on the Immediate window. Visual Basic procedures usually contain more than one line of code. In fact, they can become quite complex. Before you can start creating complete VBA procedures, you still need to learn a couple of things. For example, how can you save information returned by Excel so that your procedures can use it later? While entering instructions in the Immediate window, you learned how to question Excel for vital information. You got answers to questions such as "How many worksheets are in the active workbook?" or "What's the contents of cell A4?" Excel did not mind any of your "nosy" questions. As long as you phrased your question by following the strict VBA syntax rules, Excel gave you the answer. When you start writing your own procedures, you will need to know how to save Excel answers. In the next chapter, you will learn how to save this kind of information for later by using variables. You will also explore the topic of data types and constants.

Chapter 3

Understanding Variables, Data Types, and Constants

Saving Results of VBA Statements ■ What Are Variables? ■ Data Types ■ How to Create Variables ■ How to Declare Variables ■ Specifying the Data Type of a Variable ■ Assigning Values to Variables ■ Forcing Declaration of Variables ■ Understanding the Scope of Variables ■ Procedure-Level (Local) Variables ■ Module-Level Variables ■ Project-Level Variables ■ Lifetime of Variables ■ Understanding and Using Static Variables ■ Declaring and Using Object Variables ■ Using Specific Object Variables ■ Finding a Variable Definition ■ Using Constants in VBA Procedures ■ Built-in Constants ■ What's Next...

In programming, just as in life, certain things need to be done at once while other tasks can be put off until later. When you postpone a task, you may enter it in your mental or paper "to-do" list. The individual entries on your list are often classified by their type or importance. When you delegate the task or finally get around to doing it, you cross it off the list. This chapter shows you how your VBA procedures can memorize important pieces of information for use in later statements or calculations. You will learn how a procedure can keep a "to-do" entry in a variable, how variables are declared, and how they relate to data types and constants.

Saving Results of VBA Statements

In Chapter 2, while working in the Immediate window, you tried several Visual Basic instructions that returned some information. For example, when you entered ?Cells.Count, you found out that there are 16,777,216 cells in a worksheet. However, when you write Visual Basic procedures outside of the Immediate window, you can't use the question mark. When you omit the question mark and enter Cells.Count in your procedure, Visual Basic won't stop suddenly to tell you the result of this instruction. If you want to know the result after executing a particular instruction, you must tell Visual Basic to memorize it. In programming, results returned by Visual Basic instructions can be written to variables.

What Are Variables?

A *variable* is simply a name that is used to refer to an item of data. Each time you want to remember the result of a VBA instruction, think of a name that will represent it. For example, if the number 16,777,216 has to remind you of the total number of cells in a worksheet, you can make up a name such as AllCells, NumOfCells, TotalCells, and so on.

The names of variables can contain characters, numbers, and some punctuation marks, except for the following:

, # $ % & @ !

The name of a variable cannot begin with a number or contain a space. If you want the name of the variable to include more than one word, use the underscore (_). Although the name of a variable can contain as many as 254 characters, it's best to use short and simple variable names. Using short names will save you typing time when you need to refer to the variable several times in your Visual Basic procedure. Visual Basic doesn't care whether you use uppercase or lowercase letters in variable names. However, most programmers use lowercase letters in variable names, and when the variable names are comprised of one or more words, they use the title case. That is, they capitalize each word, as in the following: NumOfCells, First_Name.

Data Types

When you create Visual Basic procedures, you have a purpose in mind. You want to manipulate data. Because your procedures will handle different kinds of information, you should understand how Visual Basic stores data. The term *data type* determines how the data is stored in the computer's memory. For example, data can be stored as a number, text, date, object, etc. If you forget to tell Visual Basic the type of your data, Visual Basic assigns the Variant data type. The Variant type has the ability to figure out on its own what kind of data is being manipulated and then take on that type. The Visual Basic data types are shown in Table 3-1. In addition to the built-in data types, you can define your own data types. (You will see an example of a user-defined data type in Chapter 8.) Because data types take up different amounts of space in the computer's memory, some of them are more expensive than others. Therefore, to conserve memory and make your procedure run faster, you should select the data type that uses the least amount of bytes and, at the same time, is capable of handling the data that your procedure has to manipulate.

Table 3-1: The VBA data types

Data Type (Name)	Size (Bytes)	Description
Boolean	2	A logical value of True or False
Byte	1	Integer from 0 to 255
Integer	2	Integer from –32,768 to 32,767
Long	4	Integer from –2,147,483,648 to 2,147,483,647
Single	4	Single precision floating-point real number: Negative numbers: –3.402823E38 to –1.401298E–45 Positive numbers: 1.401298E–45 to 3.402823E38

Data Type (Name)	Size (Bytes)	Description
Double	8	Double precision floating-point real number: Negative numbers: −1.79769313486231E308 to −4.94065645841247E−324 Positive numbers: 4.94065645841247E−324 to 1.79769313486231E308
Currency	8	(scaled integer) Used in fixed-point calculations: −922,337,203,685,477.5808 to 922,337,203,685,477.5807
Decimal	14	+/−79,228,162,514,264,337,593,543,950,335 with no decimal point; +/−7.9228162514264337593543950335 with 28 places to the right of the decimal; smallest non-zero number is +/−0.0000000000000000000000000001
Date	8	Date from January 1, 100, to December 31, 9999
String (variable-length)	10 bytes + string length	A variable-length String can contain up to approximately 2 billion characters.
String (fixed-length)	Length of string	A fixed-length String can contain up to approximately 65,400 characters.
Object	4	Object variable used to refer to any Excel object
Variant (with numbers)	16	Any numeric value up to the range of a Double
Variant (with characters)	22 bytes + string length	Same range as for a variable-length String
User-defined (using Type)	Number required by elements	The range of each element is the same as the range of its data type.

How to Create Variables

You can create a variable by declaring it with a special command or by just using it in a statement. When you declare your variable, you make Visual Basic aware of the variable's name and data type. This is called the *explicit variable declaration*.

If you don't let Visual Basic know about the variable prior to using it, you are implicitly telling VBA that you want to create this variable. Variables declared implicitly are automatically assigned the Variant data type (Table 3-1). Although implicit variable declaration is convenient (it allows you to create variables on the fly and assign values without knowing in advance the data type of the values being assigned), it can cause several problems, as outlined in Tip 3-4.

Tip 3-3: Advantages of the Explicit Variable Declaration

- Explicit variable declaration speeds up the execution of your procedure. Since Visual Basic knows the data type, it reserves only as much memory as is absolutely necessary to store the data.
- Explicit variable declaration makes your code easier to read and understand because all the variables are listed at the very beginning of the procedure.
- Explicit variable declaration helps prevent errors caused by misspelling a variable name. Visual Basic automatically corrects the variable name based on the spelling used in the variable declaration.

Tip 3-4: Disadvantages of the Implicit Variable Declaration

- If you misspell a variable name in your procedure, Visual Basic may display a run-time error or create a new variable. You are guaranteed to waste some time troubleshooting problems that could have been easily avoided had you declared your variable at the beginning of the procedure.
- Since Visual Basic does not know what type of data your variable will store, it assigns it a Variant data type. This causes your procedure to run slower because Visual Basic has to check the type of data every time it deals with your variable. Because Variant can store any type of data, Visual Basic has to reserve more memory to store your data.

How to Declare Variables

You declare a variable with the Dim keyword. Dim stands for Dimension. The Dim keyword is followed by the name of the variable and then the variable type.

Suppose you want the procedure to display the age of an employee. Before you can calculate the age, you must feed to the procedure the employee's date of birth. To do this, you declare a variable called DateOfBirth, as follows:

```
Dim DateOfBirth As Date
```

Notice that the Dim keyword is followed by the name of the variable (DateOfBirth). If you don't like this name, you are free to replace it with another word, as long as the word you are planning to use is not one of the VBA keywords. Specify the data type the variable will hold by including the As keyword followed by one of the data types from Table 3-1. The Date data type tells Visual Basic that the variable DateOfBirth will store a date.

To store the employee's age, declare the Age variable as follows:

```
Dim Age As Integer
```

The Age variable will store the number of years between today's date and the employee's date of birth. Since age is displayed as a whole number, the Age variable has been assigned the Integer data type.

You may also want your procedure to keep track of the employee's name, so you declare another variable to hold the employee's first and last name:

```
Dim FullName As String
```

Since the word "Name" is on the VBA list of reserved words, using it in your VBA procedure would guarantee an error. To hold the employee's full name, call the variable FullName, and declare it as the String data type because the data it will hold is text.

Declaring variables is regarded as good programming practice because it makes programs easier to read and helps prevent certain types of errors.

Now that you know how to declare your variables, let's take a look at a pro-

---

Tip 3-5: Implicitly Declared Variables

Variables that are not explicitly declared with Dim statements are said to be implicitly declared. These variables are automatically assigned a data type called Variant. They can hold numbers, strings, and other types of information. You can create a variable by simply assigning some value to a variable name anywhere in your VBA procedure. For example, you can implicitly declare a variable in the following way: DaysLeft = 100.

---

cedure that uses them:

```
Sub AgeCalc( )
    'variable declaration
    Dim FullName As String
    Dim DateOfBirth As Date
    Dim Age As Integer

    'assign values to variables
    FullName = "John Smith"
    DateOfBirth = #01/03/1967#

    'calculate age
    Age = Year(Now())-Year(DateOfBirth)

    'print results to the Immediate window
    Debug.Print FullName & " is " & Age & " years old."
End Sub
```

The variables are declared at the beginning of the procedure where they are going to be used. In the procedure above, the variables are declared on separate lines. If you want, you can declare several variables on the same line, separating each variable name with a comma, as shown below:

```
Dim FullName As String, DateOfBirth As Date, Age As Integer
```

Notice that the Dim keyword appears only once at the beginning of the variable declaration line.

When Visual Basic executes the variable declaration statements, it creates the variables with the specified names and reserves memory space to store their values. Then specific values are assigned to these variables. To assign a value to a variable, begin with a variable name followed by an equal sign. The value entered to the right of the equal sign is the data you want to store in the variable. The data you enter here must be of the type determined by the variable declaration. Text data should be surrounded by quotation marks and dates by the # characters.

Using the data supplied by the DateOfBirth variable, Visual Basic calculates the age of an employee and stores the result of the calculation in the variable called Age. Then the full name of the employee as well as the age are printed to the Immediate window using the instruction Debug.Print. When the Visual Basic procedure is finished, you must open the Immediate window to see the results.

Let's see what happens when you declare a variable with the incorrect data type. The purpose of the following procedure is to calculate the total number of cells in a worksheet and then display the results to the user in a dialog box.

```
Sub HowManyCells( )
    Dim NumOfCells As Integer
    NumOfCells = Cells.Count
    MsgBox "The worksheet has " & NumOfCells & " cells."
End Sub
```

A wrong data type can cause an error. In the procedure above, when Visual Basic attempts to write the result of the Cells.Count statement to the variable NumOfCells, the procedure fails and Excel displays the message "Run-time error 6—Overflow." This error results from selecting an invalid data type for that variable. The number of cells in a spreadsheet does not fit the Integer data range. To correct the problem, you should choose a data type that can accommodate a larger number. However, to quickly correct the problem you encountered in the above procedure, you can delete the variable type As Integer. When you rerun the procedure, Visual Basic will assign to your variable the Variant data type. Although Variants use up more memory than any other variable type and also slow down the speed at which your procedures run (because Visual Basic has to do the extra work to check the Variant's context), when it comes to short procedures, the cost of using Variants is barely noticeable.

Tip 3-6: What is the Variable Type?

You can quickly find out the type of a variable used in your procedure in the following way: right-click the variable name and select Quick Info from the shortcut menu.

Tip 3-7: Concatenation

You can combine two or more strings to form a new string. The joining operation is called concatenation. You have seen the example of concatenated strings in the AgeCalc and HowManyCells procedures. Concatenation is represented by an ampersand (&) character. For instance, "His name is " & FirstName will produce the following string: His name is John or His name is Michael. The name of the person is determined by the contents of the FirstName variable. Notice that there is an extra space between is and the ending quotes: "His name is ". Concatenation of strings also can be represented by a plus sign (+). However, many programmers prefer to restrict the plus sign to operations on numbers to eliminate ambiguity.

Specifying the Data Type of a Variable

If you don't specify the variable's data type in the Dim statement, you end up with the untyped variable. Untyped variables in VBA are always Variant data types. It's highly recommended that you create typed variables. When you declare a variable of a certain data type, your VBA procedure runs faster because Visual Basic does not have to stop to analyze the Variant variable to determine its type.

Visual Basic can work with many types of numeric variables. Integer variables can only hold whole numbers from –32,768 to 32,767. Other types of numeric variables are Long, Single, Double, and Currency. Long variables can hold whole numbers in the range –2,147,483,648 to 2,147,483,647. As opposed to Integer and Long variables, Single and Double variables can hold decimals. String variables are used to refer to text. When you declare a variable of String data type, you can tell Visual Basic how long the string should be. For instance:

```
Dim extension As String * 3
```

declares the fixed-length String variable named extension that is three characters long.

If you don't assign a specific length, the String variable will be dynamic. This means that Visual Basic will make enough space in computer memory to handle whatever amount of text is assigned to it.

After you declare a variable, you can only store the type of information in it that you indicated in the declaration statement. Assigning string values to numeric variables or numeric values to string variables results in the error message "Type mismatch" or causes Visual Basic to modify the value.

For example, if your variable was declared to hold whole numbers and your data uses decimals, Visual Basic will disregard the decimals and use only the whole part of the number. Try out the MyNumber procedure, as shown below, to see how Visual Basic modifies the data to fit the variable data type:

```
Sub MyNumber()
    Dim myNum As Integer

    myNum = 23.11
    MsgBox myNum
End Sub
```

If you don't declare a variable with a Dim statement, you can still designate a type for it by using a special character at the end of the variable name. To declare the FirstName variable as String, you can append the dollar sign to the variable name, as shown below:

```
Dim FirstName$
```

The above declaration is the same as Dim FirstName As String. Other type declaration characters are shown in Table 3-2.

Table 3-2: Type declaration characters

Data Type	Character
Integer	%
Long	&
Single	!
Double	#
Currency	@
String	$

Notice that the type declaration characters can only be used with six data types. To use the type declaration character, append the character to the end of the variable name.

The AgeCalc2 procedure demonstrates the use of the type declaration characters shown in Table 3-2:

```
Sub AgeCalc2()
    'variable declaration
    Dim FullName$
    DateOfBirth As Date
    Dim Age%

    'assign values to variables
    FullName$ = "John Smith"
    DateOfBirth = #01/03/1967#

    'calculate age
    Age% = Year(Now())-Year(DateOfBirth)
```

```
        'print results to the Immediate window
        Debug.Print FullName$ & " is " & Age% & " years old."
End Sub
```

Tip 3-8: Declaring Typed Variables

The variable type can be indicated by the As keyword or by attaching a type symbol. If you don't add the type symbol or the As command, the variable will be the default data type, which is the Variant type in VBA.

Assigning Values to Variables

Now that you know how to name and declare variables, it's time to start using them. Let's begin by learning how to create a variable. In Visual Basic you can create a variable anywhere within your procedure by assigning it a specific value.

1. Open a new workbook and save it as **Chap03.xls**.
2. Activate the Visual Basic Editor window.
3. In the Project Explorer window, select the new project and change the name of the project in the Properties window to **Chap03**.
4. Choose **Insert | Module** to add a new module to the Chap03 project.
5. In the Properties window, change the name of **Module1** to **Variables**.
6. In the Code window, enter the CalcCost procedure shown below. This procedure calculates the cost of purchasing a calculator using the following assumptions: the price of a calculator is 35 dollars and the sales tax equals 8.5%.

```
Sub CalcCost()
    slsPrice = 35
    slsTax = 0.085
    Range("A1").Formula = "The cost of calculator"
    Range("A4").Formula = "Price"
    Range("B4").Formula = slsPrice
    Range("A5").Formula = "Sales Tax"
    Range("A6").Formula = "Cost"
    Range("B5").Formula = slsPrice * slsTax

    Cost = slsPrice + (slsPrice * slsTax)

    With Range("B6")
        .Formula = Cost
        .NumberFormat = "0.00"
    End With

    strMsg = "The calculator total is  " & "$" & Cost & "."
    Range("A8").Formula = strMsg
```

```
End Sub
```

The CalcCost procedure uses four variables: slsPrice, slsTax, Cost, and strMsg. Because none of these variables have been explicitly declared, they all have the same data type—Variant. The variables slsPrice and slsTax were created by assigning some values to variable names at the beginning of the procedure. The Cost variable was assigned a value that is a result of a calculation: slsPrice + (slsPrice * slsTax). The cost calculation uses the values supplied by the slsPrice and slsTax variables. The strMsg variable puts together a text message to the user. This message is then entered as a complete sentence in a worksheet cell.

When you assign values to variables, place an equal sign after the name of the variable. After the equal sign, you should enter the value of the variable. This can be a number, a formula, or text surrounded by quotation marks. While the values assigned to the variables slsPrice, slsTax, and Cost are easily understood, the value stored in the strMsg variable is a little more involved. Let's examine the contents of the strMsg variable.

```
strMsg = "The calculator total is " & "$" & Cost & "."
```

- The string "The calculator total is " is surrounded by quotation marks. Notice that there is an extra space before the ending quote.
- The & character allows appending to the string another string or the contents of a variable.
- The dollar sign in quotes ("$") is used to denote the type of currency. Because the dollar symbol is a character, it is surrounded by the quotes.
- The & character must be used every time you want to append a new piece of the information to the previous string.
- The Cost variable is a placeholder. The actual cost of the calculator will be displayed here when the procedure runs.
- The & character attaches yet another string.
- The period is surrounded by quotes. When you require a period at the end of the sentence, you must attach it separately when it follows the name of the variable.

Now try out this procedure. Position the cursor anywhere within the CalcCost procedure and choose Run | Run Sub/UserForm.

Tip 3-9: Variable Initialization

When Visual Basic creates a new variable, it initializes the variable. Variables assume their default value. Numerical variables are set to zero (0), Boolean variables are initialized to False, string variables are set to the empty string (""), and Date variables are set to December 30, 1899.

Note: When you run this procedure, Visual Basic may display the following message: "Compile error: Variable not defined." If this happens, click OK to close the message box. Visual Basic will select the slsPrice variable and highlight the name of the Sub CalcCost procedure. The title bar displays "Microsoft Visual Basic – Chap03.xls [break]." The Visual Basic break mode allows you to correct the problem before you continue. Later in this book, you will learn how to fix problems in the break mode. For now, if you encounter the above-mentioned error, exit this mode by choosing Run | Reset. Next, go to the top of the Code window and delete the statement Option Explicit that appears on the first line. The Option Explicit statement means that all variables used within this module must be formally declared. You will learn about this statement in the next section. When the Option Explicit statement is removed from the Code window, rerun the procedure.

When the procedure has run, switch to Microsoft Excel. The result of the procedure should match Figure 3-1.

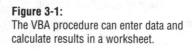

	A	B	C
1	The cost of	calculator	
2			
3			
4	Price	35	
5	Sales Tax	2.975	
6	Cost	37.97	
7			
8	The calculator total is $37.975.		

Figure 3-1:
The VBA procedure can enter data and calculate results in a worksheet.

Cell A8 displays the contents of the strMsg variable. Notice that the cost entered in cell B6 has two decimal places, while the cost in strMsg displays three decimals. To display the cost of a calculator with two decimal places in cell A8, you must apply the required format not to the cell but to the Cost variable itself.

VBA has special functions that allow you to change the format of data. To change the format of the Cost variable, you will now use the Format function. This function has the following syntax:

```
Format(expression, format)
```

Expression is a value or variable that you want to format, and format is the type of format you want to apply.

1.   Change the calculation of the Cost variable in the CalcCost procedure:

```
Cost = Format(slsPrice + (slsPrice * slsTax), "0.00")
```

2. Replace the With…End With block of instructions with the following:

```
Range("B6").Formula = Cost
```

3. Replace the statement `Range("B5").Formula = slsPrice * slsTax` with the following instruction:

```
Range("B5").Formula = Format((slsPrice * slsTax), "0.00")
```

4. Rerun the modified procedure.

After trying out the CalcCost procedure, you may wonder why you should bother declaring variables if Visual Basic can handle undeclared variables so well. The CalcCost procedure is very short, so you don't need to worry about how many bytes of memory will be consumed each time Visual Basic uses the Variant variable. In short procedures, however, it is not the memory that matters but the mistakes you are bound to make when typing variable names. What will happen if the second time you use the `Cost` variable you omit the "o" and refer to it as Cst?

```
Range("B6").Formula = Cst
```

What will you end up with if instead of `slsTax`, you use the word Tax in the formula?

```
Cost = Format(slsPrice + (slsPrice * Tax), "0.00")
```

The result of the CalcCost procedure after introducing the above mentioned mistakes is shown in Figure 3-2.

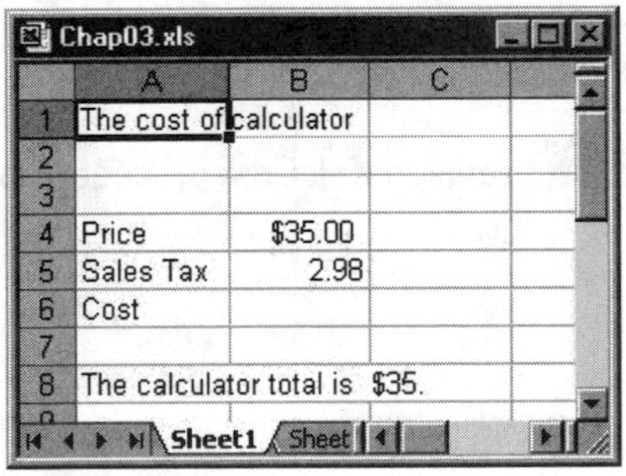

Figure 3-2:
Mistakes in the names of variables can produce wrong results.

Notice that in Figure 3-2 cell B6 does not show a value because Visual Basic does not find the assignment statement for the `Cst` variable. Because Visual Basic does not know the sales tax, it displays the price of the calculator as the total cost (see cell A8). Visual Basic does not guess. It simply does what you tell it to do. This brings us to the next section, which explains how to make sure that errors of this kind don't occur. Before you continue, make sure to replace the names of the variables Cst and Tax with Cost and slsTax.

Forcing Declaration of Variables

Visual Basic has the Option Explicit statement that automatically reminds you to formally declare all your variables. This statement has to be entered at the top of each of your modules. The Option Explicit statement will cause Visual Basic to generate an error message when you try to run a procedure that contains undeclared variables.

1. Return to the Code window where you entered the CalcCost procedure.

2. At the top of the module window (in the first line), enter **Option Explicit** and press **Enter**. Excel will display the statement in blue.

3. Run the CalcCost procedure. Visual Basic displays the error message "Compile error: Variable not defined."

4. Click **OK** to exit the message box.

    Visual Basic highlights the name of the variable slsPrice. Now you have to formally declare this variable. When you declare the slsPrice variable and rerun your procedure, Visual Basic will generate the same error as soon as it encounters another variable name that was not declared.

5. Enter the following declarations at the beginning of the CalcCost procedure:

```
'declaration of variables
    Dim slsPrice as Currency
    Dim slsTax as Single
    Dim Cost as Currency
    Dim strMsg as String
```

6. Press **F5** to run the procedure. The revised CalcCost procedure is shown below:

```
Option Explicit

Sub CalcCost()
'declaration of variables
    Dim slsPrice As Currency
    Dim slsTax As Single
    Dim Cost As Currency
    Dim strMsg As String

    slsPrice = 35
    slsTax = 0.085

    Range("A1").Formula = "The cost of calculator"
    Range("A4").Formula = "Price"
    Range("B4").Formula = slsPrice
    Range("A5").Formula = "Sales Tax"
    Range("A6").Formula = "Cost"
    Range("B5").Formula = Format((slsPrice * slsTax), "0.00")
```

```
      Cost = Format(slsPrice + (slsPrice * slsTax), "0.00")

      With Range("B6").Formula = Cost

      strMsg = "The calculator total is  " & "$" & Cost & "."
      Range("A8").Formula = strMsg
   End Sub
```

The Option Explicit statement entered at the top of the module forced you to declare variables. Because you must include the Option Explicit statement in each module for which you want to require variable declaration, you can have Visual Basic enter this statement for you each time you insert a new module.

To automatically include Option Explicit in every new module you create, follow these steps:

1. Choose **Tools | Options**.

2. Make sure the **Require Variable Declaration** check box is selected in the Options dialog box (Editor tab).

3. Choose **OK** to close the Options dialog box.

From now on, every new module will be added with the Option Explicit statement in line 1. If you want to require variables to be explicitly declared in a previously created module, you must enter the Option Explicit statement manually by editing the module yourself.

Tip 3-10: More about Option Explicit

Option Explicit forces formal (explicit) declaration of all variables in a particular module. One big advantage of using Option Explicit is that mistypings of the variable name will be detected at compile time (when Visual Basic attempts to translate the source code to executable code). The Option Explicit statement must appear in a module before any procedures.

Understanding the Scope of Variables

Variables can have different ranges of influence in a VBA procedure. The term _scope_ defines the availability of a particular variable to the same procedure, other procedures, or other VBA projects. Variables can have the following three levels of scope in Visual Basic for Applications:

■ Procedure-level scope

■ Module-level scope

■ Project-level scope

Procedure-Level (Local) Variables

From this chapter, you already know how to declare a variable by using the Dim keyword. The position of the Dim keyword in the module sheet determines the scope of a variable. Variables declared with the Dim keyword placed within a VBA procedure have a *procedure-level scope*.

Procedure-level variables are frequently referred to as *local variables*. Local variables can only be used in the procedure where they were declared. Undeclared variables always have a procedure-level scope.

A variable's name must be unique within its scope. This means that you cannot declare two variables with the same name in the same procedure. However, you can use the same variable name in different procedures. In other words, the CalcCal procedure can have the slsTax variable, and the ExpenseRep procedure in the same module can have its own variable called slsTax. Both variables are independent of each other.

Module-Level Variables

Local variables help save computer memory. As soon as the procedure ends, the variable dies, and Visual Basic returns the memory space used by the variable to the computer. In programming, however, you often want the variable to be available to other VBA procedures after the procedure in which the variable was declared has finished running. This situation requires that you change the scope of a variable. Instead of a procedure-level variable, you want to declare a module-level variable. To declare a module-level variable, you must place the Dim keyword at the top of the module sheet before any procedures (just below the Option Explicit keyword).

For instance, to make the slsTax variable available to any other procedure in the Variables module, declare the slsTax variable in the following way:

```
Option Explicit

Dim slsTax As Single
Sub CalcCost( )
    <place procedure instructions here>
End Sub
```

In the example above, the Dim keyword is located at the top of the module, just below the Option Explicit statement.

Before you can see how this works, you need another procedure that uses the slsTax variable.

1. In the Code window, cut the declaration line Dim slsTax As Single in the Variables module from the CalcCost procedure and paste it at the top of the module sheet below the Option Explicit statement.

2. Enter the code of the ExpenseRep procedure in the same module where the CalcCost procedure is located:

```
Sub ExpenseRep()
    Dim slsPrice As Currency
    Dim Cost As Currency

    slsPrice = 55.99
    Cost = slsPrice + (slsPrice * slsTax)

    MsgBox slsTax
    MsgBox Cost
End Sub
```

The ExpenseRep procedure declares two Currency type variables: slsPrice and Cost. The slsPrice variable is then assigned a value of 55.99. The slsPrice variable is independent of the slsPrice variable that is declared within the CalcCost procedure. The ExpenseRep procedure calculates the cost of a purchase. The cost includes the sales tax. Because the sales tax is the same as the one used in the CalcCost procedure, the slsTax variable has been declared at the module level. After Visual Basic executes the CalcCost procedure, the contents of the slsTax variable equals 0.085. If slsTax is a local variable, the contents of this variable would be empty upon the termination of the CalcCost procedure. The ExpenseRep procedure ends by displaying the value of the slsTax and Cost variables in two separate message boxes.

When you run the CalcCost procedure, Visual Basic erases the contents of all the variables, except for the slsTax variable, which was declared at a module level. As soon as you attempt to calculate the cost by running the ExpenseRep procedure, Visual Basic retrieves the value of the slsTax variable and uses it in the calculation.

Tip 3-11: Private Variables

When you declare variables at a module level, instead of the Dim keyword, you can use the Private keyword. For instance:

```
Private slsTax As Single
```

Private variables are available only to the procedures that are part of the module where they were declared. Private variables are always declared at the top of the module after the Option Explicit statement.

Tip 3-12: Keeping the Project-Level Variable Private

To prevent a project-level variable's contents from being referenced outside its project, you can use the Option Private Module at the top of the module sheet, just below the Option Explicit statement and before the declaration line. For example:

```
Option Explicit
Option Private Module
Public slsTax As Single

Sub CalcCost( )
    <place procedure instructions here>
End Sub
```

Project-Level Variables

Module-level variables that are declared with the Public keyword (instead of Dim) have project-level scope. This means that they can be used in any Visual Basic for Applications module. When you want to work with a variable in all the procedures in all the open VBA projects, you must declare it with the Public keyword. For instance:

```
Option Explicit

Public slsTax As Single

Sub CalcCost( )
    <place procedure instructions here>
End Sub
```

Notice that the slsTax variable declared at the top of the module with the Public keyword will now be available to any other procedure or VBA project.

Lifetime of Variables

In addition to scope, variables have a lifetime. The *lifetime* of a variable determines how long a variable retains its value. Module-level and project-level variables preserve their values as long as the project is open. Visual Basic, however, can reinitialize these variables if required by the program's logic. Local variables declared with the Dim statement lose their values when a procedure has finished. Local variables have a lifetime as long as a procedure is running, and they are reinitialized every time the program is run. Visual Basic allows you to extend the lifetime of a local variable by changing the way it is declared.

Understanding and Using Static Variables

A variable declared with the Static keyword is a special type of local variable. Static variables are declared at the procedure level. As opposed to local variables declared with the Dim keyword, static variables do not lose their contents when the program is not in their procedure. For example, when a VBA procedure with a static variable calls another procedure, after Visual Basic executes the statements of the called procedure and returns to the calling procedure, the static variable still retains the original value.

The CostOfPurchase procedure demonstrates the use of the static variable named allPurchase. This variable keeps track of the running total.

```
Sub CostOfPurchase()
    'declare variables
    Static allPurchase
```

```
Dim newPurchase As String
Dim purchCost As Single
newPurchase = InputBox("Enter the cost of a purchase:")
purchCost = CSng(newPurchase)
allPurchase = allPurchase + purchCost

'display results
MsgBox "The cost of a new purchase is: " & newPurchase
MsgBox "The running cost is: " & allPurchase
End Sub
```

The above procedure begins with declaring a static variable named allPurchase and two other local variables: newPurchase and purchCost. The InputBox function used in this procedure displays a dialog box and waits for the user to enter the value. As soon as the user inputs the value and clicks OK, Visual Basic assigns this value to the variable newPurchase. The InputBox function is discussed in detail in Chapter 4. Because the result of the InputBox function is always a string, the newPurchase variable was declared as the String data type. You can't, however, use strings in mathematical calculations. That's why the next instruction uses a type conversion function (CSng) to translate the text value into a numeric variable of the Single data type. The CSng function requires one argument—the value you want to translate. The number obtained as the result of the CSng function is then stored in the variable purchCost.

Tip 3-13: Type Conversion Functions

To find out more about the CSng function (and other type conversion functions), position the insertion point anywhere within the word CSng and press F1.

The next instruction, allPurchase = allPurchase + purchCost, adds to the current purchase value the new value supplied by the InputBox function. When you run this procedure for the first time, the content of the allPurchase variable is the same as the content of the purchCost variable. When you run the procedure the second time, the value of the static variable is increased by the new value supplied in the dialog box. You can run the CostOfPurchase procedure as many times as you want. The allPurchase variable will keep the running total for as long as the project is open.

To try out this procedure, follow these steps:

1. Position the cursor anywhere within the CostOfPurchase procedure and press **F5**.

2. When the dialog box appears, enter a number. For example, enter **100** and press **Enter**. Visual Basic displays the message "The cost of a new purchase is: 100."

3. Click **OK** in the message box. Visual Basic displays the second message "The running cost is: 100."

4. Rerun the same procedure. When the input dialog appears, enter another number. For example, enter **50** and press **Enter**. Visual Basic displays the message "The cost of a new purchase is 50."

5. Click **OK** in the message box. Visual Basic displays the second message "The running cost is: 150."

6. Run the procedure several more times to see how Visual Basic keeps track of the running total.

Declaring and Using Object Variables

The variables that you've learned so far are used to store data. Storing data is the main reason for using "normal" variables in your procedures. In addition to the normal variables that store data, there are special variables that refer to the Visual Basic objects. These variables are called *object variables*. In Chapter 2, you learned a few things about various objects. Now, you will learn how you can represent an object with the object variable.

Object variables don't store data. They tell where the data is located. For example, with the object variable you can tell Visual Basic that the data is located in cell E10 of the active worksheet. Object variables make it easy to locate data. When writing Visual Basic procedures, you often need to write long instructions, such as:

```
Worksheets("Sheet1").Range(Cells(1,1), Cells(10, 5).Select
```

Instead of using long references to the object, you can declare an object variable that will tell Visual Basic where the data is located. Object variables are declared in a similar way to the variables you already know. The only difference is that after the As keyword, you enter the word Object as the data type. For instance:

```
Dim myRange As Object
```

The statement above declares the object variable named myRange.

Well, it's not actually enough to declare the object variable. You also have to assign a specific value to the object variable before you can use this variable in your procedure. Assign a value to the object variable by using the Set keyword. The Set keyword is then followed by the equal sign and the value that the variable will refer to. For example:

```
Set myRange = Worksheets("Sheet1").Range(Cells(1,1), Cells(10, 5))
```

The above statement assigns a value to the object variable myRange. This value refers to cells A1:E10 in Sheet1. If you omit the word Set, Visual Basic will display an error message—"Run-time error 91: Object variable or With block variable not set."

Again, it's time to see a practical example. The UseObjVariable procedure shown below demonstrates the use of the object variable called
`myRange`:

```
Sub UseObjVariable()
    Dim myRange As Object

    Set myRange = Worksheets("Sheet1"). _
        Range(Cells(1, 1), Cells(10, 5))
    myRange.BorderAround Weight:=xlMedium
    With myRange.Interior
        .ColorIndex = 6
        .Pattern = xlSolid
    End With
    Set myRange = Worksheets("Sheet1"). _
        Range(Cells(12, 5), Cells(12, 10))
    myRange.Value = 54
    Debug.Print IsObject(myRange)
End Sub
```

Let's examine the code of the UseObjVariable procedure line by line. The
procedure begins with the declaration of the object variable `myRange`. The
next statement sets the object variable `myRange` to Range A1:E10 on Sheet1.
From now on, every time you want to reference this range, instead of using
the entire object's address, you'll use the shortcut—the name of the object
variable. The purpose of this procedure is to create a border around range
A1:E10. Instead of writing a long instruction:

```
Worksheets("Sheet1").Range(Cells(1, 1), _
        Cells(10, 5)).BorderAround Weight:=xlMedium
```

you can take a shortcut by using the name of the object variable:

```
myRange.BorderAround Weight:=xlMedium
```

The next series of statements changes the color of the selected range of
cells (A1:E10). Again, you don't need to write the long instruction to reference the object that you want to manipulate. Instead of the full object name,
you can use the `myRange` object variable. The next statement assigns a new
reference to the object variable `myRange`. Visual Basic forgets the old reference, and the next time you use `myRange`, it refers to another range
(E12:J12). After the number 54 is entered in the new range (E12:J12), the
procedure shows you how you can make sure a specific variable is of the
Object type. The instruction `Debug.Print IsObject(myRange)` will enter True
in the Immediate window if `myRange` is an object variable. IsObject is a VBA
function that indicates whether a specific value represents an object
variable.

> **Tip 3-14: Advantages of Using Object Variables**
>
> The advantages of object variables are as follows:
> - They can be used instead of the actual object.
> - They are shorter and easier to remember than the actual values to which they point.
> - You can change their meaning while your procedure is running.

Using Specific Object Variables

The object variable can refer to any type of object. Because Visual Basic has many types of objects, to make your programs more readable and faster, it's a good idea to create object variables that refer to a particular type of object. For instance, in the UseObjVariable procedure, instead of the generic object variable (Object), you can declare the myRange object variable as a Range object:

```
Dim myRange As Range
```

If you want to refer to a particular worksheet, you can declare the Worksheet object:

```
Dim mySheet As Worksheet
Set mySheet = Worksheets("Marketing")
```

When the object variable is no longer needed, you can assign Nothing to it. This frees up memory and system resources:

```
Set mySheet = Nothing
```

You will see additional examples of using object variables in Chapter 9.

Finding a Variable Definition

When you find an instruction in a VBA procedure that assigns a value to a variable, you can quickly locate the definition of the variable by selecting the variable name and pressing Shift+F2. Or you can choose View | Definition. Visual Basic will jump to the variable declaration line. To return your mouse pointer to its previous position, press Ctrl+Shift+F2 or choose View | Last Position. Let's try it out.

1. Locate the code of the CostOfPurchase procedure.
2. Locate the statement purchCost = CSng(newPurchase).
3. Right-click the variable name and choose **Definition** from the shortcut menu.
4. Return to the previous location by pressing **Ctrl+Shift+F2**.

5. Try finding definitions of other variables in other procedures created in this chapter. Each time use a different way to jump to the variable definition.

Tip 3-15: What Type is this Variable?

You can find out the type of a variable by using one of the Visual Basic built-in functions. See Chapter 4 for a sample usage of the VarType function.

Using Constants in VBA Procedures

The contents of a variable can change while your procedure is executing. If your procedure needs to refer to unchanged values over and over again, you should use constants. A _constant_ is like a named variable that always refers to the same value. Visual Basic requires that you declare constants before you use them. Declare constants by using the Const statement, as in the following examples:

```
Const dialogName = "Enter Data" As String
Const slsTax = 8.5
Const ColorIdx = 3
```

A constant, like a variable, has a scope. To make a constant available within a single procedure, declare it at the procedure level, just below the name of the procedure. For instance:

```
Sub WedAnniv( )
    Const Age As Integer = 25
    <place procedure instructions here>
End Sub
```

If you want to use a constant in all the procedures of a module, use the Private keyword in front of the Const statement. For instance:

```
Private Const dsk = "B:" As String
```

The Private constant has to be declared at the top of the module, just before the first Sub statement.

If you want to make a constant available to all modules in the workbook, use the Public keyword in front of the Const statement. For instance:

```
Public Const NumOfChar = 255 As Integer
```

The Public constant has to be declared at the top of the module, just before the first Sub statement.

When declaring a constant, you can use any one of the following data types: Boolean, Byte, Integer, Long, Currency, Single, Double, Date, String, or Variant.

Like variables, multiple constants can be declared on one line if separated by commas. For instance:

```
Const Age As Integer = 25, City As String = "Denver", PayCheck
    As Currency = 350
```

Using constants makes your VBA procedures more readable and easier to maintain. For example, if you refer to a certain value several times in your procedure, use a constant instead of the value. This way, if the value changes (for example, the sales tax rate goes up), you can simply change the value in the declaration of the Const statement, instead of tracking down every occurrence of that value.

Built-in Constants

Both Microsoft Excel and Visual Basic for Applications have a long list of predefined constants that do not need to be declared. These built-in constants can be looked up using the Object Browser window that was discussed in detail in Chapter 2.

Let's open the Object Browser to take a look at the list of Excel constants:

1. In the Visual Basic Editor window, choose **View | Object Browser**.

2. In the Libraries/Projects list box, click the drop-down arrow and select **Excel**.

3. Enter **Constants** as the search text in the Search box and press **Enter**, or click the **Search** button. Visual Basic shows the result of the search in the Search Results area.

4. Scroll down in the Classes list box to locate and then select **Constants**. (Figure 3-3). The right side of the Object Browser window displays a list of all built-in constants that are available in the Microsoft Excel object library. Notice that the names of all the constants begin with the prefix "xl."

Figure 3-3: Use the Object Browser to look up any built-in constant.

5. To look up VBA constants, choose **VBA** in the Libraries/Projects list box. Notice that the names of the VBA built-in constants begin with the prefix "vb."

The best way to learn about predefined constants is by using the macro recorder. Let's take a few minutes to record the process of minimizing the active window:

1. In the Microsoft Excel window, choose **Tools | Macro | Record New Macro**.

2. Type **MiniWindow** as the name of the macro. Under Store macro in, select **This Workbook**. Then click **OK**.

3. Click the **Minimize** button. Make sure you minimize the document window and not the Excel application window.

4. Click the **Stop Recording** button on the Stop Recording toolbar.

5. Maximize the minimized document window.

6. Switch to the Visual Basic Editor window and double-click the **Module** folder in the Project Explorer window. The code window displays the following procedure:

```
Sub MiniWindow( )
    ActiveWindow.WindowState = xlMinimized
End Sub
```

Sometimes you may see VBA procedures that use values instead of built-in constant names. For example, the actual value of xlMaximized is –4137. The xlMinimized constant has a value of –4140, and xlNormal has a value of –4143 (Figure 3-4).

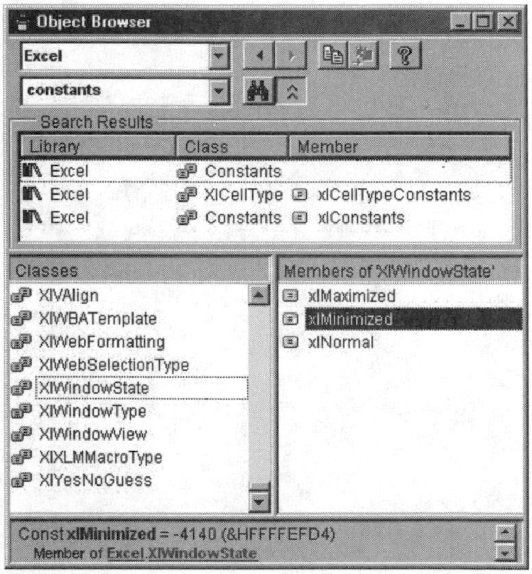

Figure 3-4: You can see the actual value of a constant by selecting its name in the Object Browser.

What's Next...

This chapter introduced several new VBA concepts, including information about data types, variables, and constants. You learned how to declare various types of variables. You also saw the difference between a variable and a constant. Now that you know what variables are and how to use them, you are capable of creating VBA procedures that can manipulate data in more meaningful ways than you saw in previous chapters. In the next chapter, you will expand your VBA knowledge by using procedures with arguments and function procedures. In addition, you will learn about functions that will allow your VBA procedure to interact with users.

Chapter 4

VBA Procedures: Subroutines and Functions

About Function Procedures ■ Creating a Function Procedure ■ Executing a Function Procedure ■ **Passing Arguments** ■ Specifying Argument Types ■ Passing Arguments by Reference and by Value ■ Using Optional Arguments ■ **Locating Built-in Functions** ■ Using the MsgBox Function ■ Using the InputBox Function ■ Using the InputBox Method ■ **Using Master Procedures and Subprocedures** ■ What's Next...

In Chapter 2 you learned that a procedure is a group of instructions that allows you to accomplish specific tasks when your program runs. VBA has three types of procedures:

- **Subroutine procedures** (*subroutines*) perform some useful tasks but don't return any values. They begin with the keyword Sub and end with the keywords End Sub. Subroutines can be recorded with the macro recorder (as you did in Chapter 1) or written from scratch in the Visual Basic Editor window (see Chapters 2 and 3). In Chapter 1, you learned various ways to execute this type of procedure.

- **Function procedures** (*functions*) perform specific tasks that return values. They begin with the keyword Function and end with the keywords End Function. In this chapter, you will create your first function procedure. Function procedures can be executed from a subroutine or accessed from a worksheet just like any Excel built-in function.

- **Property procedures** are used with custom objects. With property procedures you can set and get the value of an object's property or set a reference to an object. You will learn how to create custom objects and use property procedures in Chapter 11.

In this chapter, you will learn how to create and execute custom functions. In addition, you find out how variables (see Chapter 3) are used in passing values to subroutines and functions. Later in the chapter, you will take a thorough look at the two most useful VBA functions: MsgBox and InputBox.

About Function Procedures

With hundreds of built-in Excel functions you can perform a wide variety of calculations automatically. However, there will be times when you may require a custom calculation. With VBA programming, you can quickly fulfill this special need by creating a function procedure. You can build any functions that are not supplied with Excel.

Creating a Function Procedure

Like Excel functions, function procedures perform calculations and return values. The best way to learn about functions is to create one. So let's get started. After setting up a new VBA project, you will create a function procedure that sums up two values.

1. Open a new Excel workbook and save it as **Chap04.xls**.
2. Switch to the Visual Basic Editor window and select **VBAProject (Chap04.xls)**.
3. In the Properties window, change VBAProject to **MyFunctions**.

4. Select **MyFunctions (Chap04.xls)** in the Project Explorer window, and choose **Insert | Module**.

5. In the Properties window, change the Module1 name to **Sample1**.

6. In the Project Explorer window, click **Sample1** and choose **Insert | Procedure**. The Add Procedure dialog box appears, as shown in Figure 4-1.

7. Make the following entries in the Add Procedure dialog box:

    Name: **SumItUp**
    Type: **Function**
    Scope: **Public**

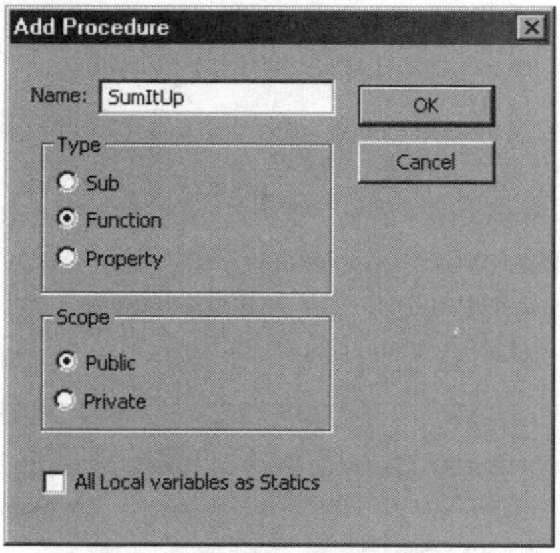

Figure 4-1:
When you use the Add Procedure dialog box, Visual Basic automatically creates the procedure type you choose.

Tip 4-1: About Function Names

Function names should suggest the role that the function performs and must conform to the rules for naming variables.

Tip 4-2: Scoping VBA Procedures

In the previous chapter you learned that the variable's scope determines which modules and procedures it can be used in. Like variables, VBA procedures have scope. A procedure scope determines whether it can be called by procedures in other modules. By default, all VBA procedures are public. This means they can be called by other procedures in any module. Since procedures are public by default, you can skip the Public keyword if you want. If you replace the Public keyword with the Private keyword, your procedure will be available only to other procedures in the same module, not to procedures in other modules.

8. Click **OK** to exit the Add Procedure dialog box. Visual Basic enters an empty function procedure that looks like this:

```
Public Function SumItUp()

End Function
```

The first statement declares the name of the function procedure. The Public keyword indicates that the function is accessible to all other procedures in all other modules. The Public keyword is optional. Notice the keyword Function followed by the name of the function (SumItUp) and a pair of empty parentheses. In the parentheses, you will list the data items that the function will use in the calculation. Every function procedure ends with the End Function statement.

9. Modify the function declaration as follows:

```
Public Function SumItUp(m,n)

End Function
```

The purpose of this function is to add up two values. Don't pass the actual values to the function. To make the function flexible, provide the function with the arguments in the form of variables. This way your custom function will be able to add up any two numbers that you supply. The variables each represent a value. You will supply the values for each of these variables when you run this function.

Tip 4-3: Some Reasons for Using Functions

Custom VBA functions can be used to:
- Analyze data and perform calculations
- Modify data and report information
- Take a specific action based on supplied or calculated data

---

10. Type the following statement between the Public Function and End Function statements:

```
SumItUp = m + n
```

This statement says to add the value stored in the n variable to the value stored in the m variable and return the result to the SumItUp function. To specify the value that you want the function to return, type the function name followed by the equal sign and the value you want it to return. In the statement above, set the name of the function equal to the total of m + n. The completed custom function procedure is shown below:

```
Public Function SumItUp(m,n)
    SumItUp = m + n
End Function
```

Congratulations! You have now created your first function. However, a function procedure is useless unless you know how to execute it. The next section shows you how to put your new function to work.

Executing a Function Procedure

In Chapter 1, you learned various ways to execute a subroutine procedure. Unlike a subroutine, a function procedure can be executed in just two ways. You can use it in a worksheet formula or you can call it from another procedure. Function procedures that you create in VBA cannot be accessed by choosing Tools | Macro | Macros in the Microsoft Excel window. And they cannot be run by pressing the F5 key when the mouse pointer is located inside the code of the function procedure. In the following sections, you will learn special techniques for executing functions.

Running a Function Procedure from a Worksheet

A custom function procedure is like built-in function. If you don't know the exact name of the function or its arguments, you can use the Insert Function dialog box to help enter the required function in a worksheet.

1. Switch to the Microsoft Excel window, and select any cell.

2. Click the **Insert Function** (*fx*) button on the formula bar. Excel displays the Insert Function dialog box. The lower portion of the dialog box displays an alphabetical listing of all the functions in the selected category.

3. In the category drop-down box, select **All** or **User Defined.** Then scroll down in the function name box to locate and select the **SumItUp** function that was created earlier in this chapter.

   When you highlight the name of the function in the function name box, the bottom part of the Insert Function dialog box displays the function's syntax: SumItUp(m,n).

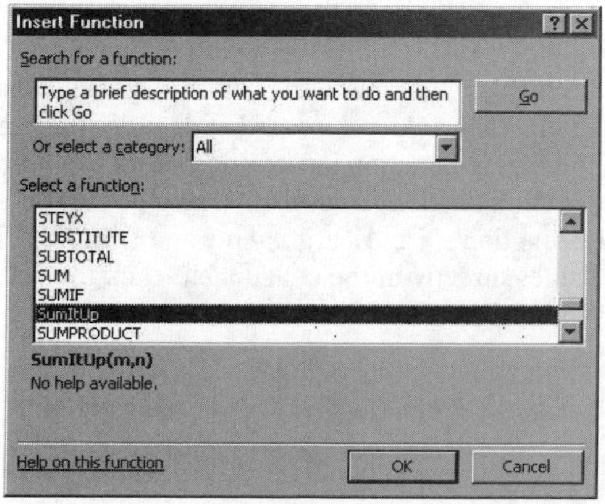

Figure 4-2:
VBA custom function procedures appear in the same list as the built-in Microsoft Excel function.

Tip 4-4: Private Functions are Not Visible to Users

Functions declared with the Private keyword do not appear in the Insert Function dialog box. Private functions cannot be used in a formula. They can only be run from another VBA procedure.

Tip 4-5: Quick Access to Custom Functions

As soon as you create your first VBA function with the Public scope, Excel adds a User Defined category in the Insert Function dialog box. By selecting this category, you can gain quick access to your custom VBA functions.

4. Click **OK** to begin writing a formula. The Function Arguments dialog box appears, as shown in Figure 4-3. This dialog displays the name of the function and each of its arguments: m and n.

5. Enter the values for the arguments as shown in Figure 4-3, or enter your own values. As you type the values in the argument text boxes, Excel displays the values you entered and the current result of the function. Because both arguments (m and n) are required, the function will return an error if you skip either of the arguments.

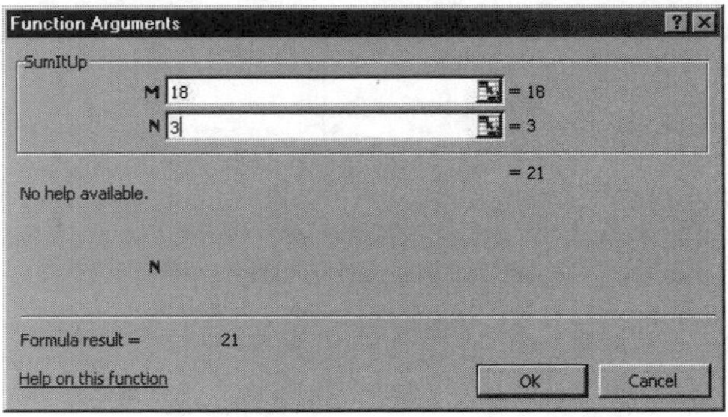

Function Arguments	? X
SumItUp	
M	18	= 18
N	3|	= 3
	= 21
No help available.	
N	
Formula result =	21
Help on this function	OK	Cancel

Figure 4-3:
The Formula Palette feature is helpful in entering any worksheet function, whether built-in or custom made with the VBA programming.

6. Click **OK** to exit the Function Arguments dialog box.

Excel enters the SumItUp function in the selected cell and displays its result. To edit the function, select the cell that displays the function's result and click the Insert Function button (*fx*). Select the function and click **OK** to access the Function Arguments dialog box. Type in different values for the function's m and n arguments and click **OK**. To edit the arguments' values directly in the cell, double-click the cell containing the function and make the necessary changes.

Tip 4-6: Ensure Availability of Your Custom Functions

Your custom VBA function is only available as long as the workbook where the function is stored is open. If you close the workbook, the function is no longer available. To make sure that your custom VBA functions are available every time you work with Microsoft Excel, you can do one of the following:

- Store your functions in the Personal Macro Workbook.
- Save the workbook with your custom VBA function in the XLStart folder.
- Set up a reference to the workbook containing your custom functions (please see Chapter 2 for information on setting up the reference to another project).

Running a Function Procedure from Another VBA Procedure

As mentioned earlier, you cannot run a function procedure from the Visual Basic Editor window by placing the mouse pointer within the code of the function procedure and pressing F5 or choosing Run | Run Sub/UserForm. To run a function, you must call the function name from another procedure. To execute a custom function, write a VBA subroutine and call the function when you need it.

The following procedure calls the SumItUp function and prints the result of the calculation to the Immediate window:

```
Sub RunSumItUp()
    Dim m As Single, n As Single
    m = 370000
    n = 3459.77

    Debug.Print SumItUp(m,n)
    MsgBox "Open the Immediate window to see the result."
End Sub
```

- The above subroutine uses the Dim statement to declare the m and n variables, which will be used to feed the data to the function.
- The next two statements assign the values to the variables.
- Next, Visual Basic calls the SumItUp function and passes the values stored in the m and n variables to it. When the function procedure statement SumItUp = m + n is executed, Visual Basic returns to the RunSumItUp subroutine and uses the Debug.Print statement to print the function's result to the Immediate window.
- The MsgBox function informs the user where to look for the result.

To try out the above procedure example, follow these steps:

1. Type the RunSumItUp procedure in the same module where you entered the code of the SumItUp function.

2. Place the mouse pointer anywhere within the RunSumItUp procedure, and press **F5**.

Tip 4-7: A Quick Test of a Function

After you write your custom function, you can quickly try it out in the Immediate window. To display the value of a function, open the Immediate window and type a question mark (?) followed by the function name. Remember to enclose the function's arguments in parentheses. For example, type:

```
? SumItUp(54, 367.24)
```

and press Enter. Your function procedure runs, using the values you passed for the m and n arguments. The result of the function appears on a line below:

```
421.24
```

Passing Arguments

So far you've created simple VBA procedures that carried out specific tasks. These procedures did not require that you provide additional data before they could be run. However, in real life, procedures (both subroutines and functions) often take arguments. *Arguments* are one or more values needed for a procedure to do something. Arguments are always entered between parentheses. Multiple arguments are separated with commas.

Having used Excel for a while, you already know that Excel's built-in functions can produce different results based on the values you supply to them. For example, if cells A4 and A5 contain numbers 5 and 10, respectively, the Sum function =SUM(A4:A5) will return 15, unless you change the values entered in the specified cells. Just like you can pass any values to Excel built-in functions, you can pass values to custom VBA procedures.

Now let's see how you can pass some values from a subroutine to the SumItUp function that you created earlier in this chapter. The purpose of this custom function is to get the sum of characters in a person's first and last name.

1. Type the following NumOfCharacters subroutine in the same module (Sample1) where you entered the SumItUp function.

    ```
    Sub NumOfCharacters()
        Dim f As Integer
        Dim l As Integer

        f = Len(InputBox("Enter first name:"))
        l = Len(InputBox("Enter last name:"))
        MsgBox SumItUp(f,l)
    End Sub
    ```

2. Place the mouse pointer within the code of the NumOfCharacters procedure and press **F5**. Visual Basic displays the input box asking for the first name. This box is generated by the following function:

```
InputBox("Enter first name:")
```

3. Enter any name, and press **Enter** or click **OK**. Visual Basic takes the text you entered and supplies it as an argument to the Len function. The Len function calculates the number of characters in the supplied text. Visual Basic places the result of the Len function in the f variable for further reference. After that, Visual Basic displays the next input box, this time asking for the last name.

4. Enter any last name, and press **Enter** or click **OK**.

   Visual Basic passes the last name to the Len function to get the number of characters. Then that number is stored in the l variable. What happens next? Visual Basic encounters the MsgBox function. This function tells Visual Basic to display the result of the SumItUp function. However, because the result is not yet ready, Visual Basic jumps quickly to the SumItUp function to perform the calculation using the values saved earlier in the f and l variables. Inside the function procedure, Visual Basic substitutes the m argument with the value of the f variable and the n argument with the value of the l variable. Once the substitution is done, Visual Basic adds up the two numbers and returns the result to the SumItUp function. There are no more tasks to perform inside the function procedure, so Visual Basic returns to the subroutine and provides the SumItUp function's result as an argument to the MsgBox function. Now the message appears on the screen displaying the total number of characters.

5. Click **OK** to exit the Message box.

   You can run the NumOfCharacters procedure as many times as you'd like, each time supplying a different first and last name.

Let's look at another example of passing arguments using variables.

1. Add a new module to the MyFunctions (Chap04.xls) project and change the module's name to **Sample2**.

2. Activate the **Sample2** module and enter the EnterText subroutine:

```
Sub EnterText()
    Dim m As String, n As String, r As String
    m = InputBox ("Enter your first name:")
    n = InputBox("Enter your last name:")
    r = JoinText(m, n)
    MsgBox r
End Sub
```

3. Enter the following function procedure:

```
Function JoinText(k,o)
    JoinText = k + " " + o
End Function
```

4. Run the EnterText procedure.

As Visual Basic executes the statements of the procedure, it collects the data from the user and stores the values of the first and last names in the variables m and n. Then these values are passed to the JoinText function. Visual Basic substitutes the variables' contents for the arguments of the JoinText function and assigns the result to the name of the function (JoinText). When Visual Basic returns to the EnterText procedure, it stores the function's value in the r variable. The MsgBox function then displays the contents of the r variable in a message box. The result is the full name of the user (first and last name separated by a space).

Tip 4-8: What Function Procedures Cannot Do

Functions cannot perform any actions. For instance, they cannot include statements for inserting, deleting, or formatting data in a worksheet, opening files, or changing the way the screen looks.

To pass a specific value from a function to a subroutine, assign the value to the name of the function. For example, the NumOfDays function shown below passes the value of 7 to the subroutine DaysInAWeek.

```
Function NumOfDays()
    NumOfDays = 7
End Function

Sub DaysInAWeek()
    MsgBox "There are " & NumOfDays & " days in a week."
End Sub
```

Specifying Argument Types

In the preceding section, you learned that functions perform some calculations based on data received through their arguments. When you declare a function procedure, you list the names of arguments inside a set of parentheses. Argument names are like variables. Each argument name refers to whatever value you provide at the time the function is called. When a subroutine calls a function procedure, it passes the required arguments as variables to it. Once the function does something, the result is assigned to the function name. Notice that the function procedure's name is used as if it were a variable.

Like variables, functions can have types. The result of your function procedure can be String, Integer, Long, etc. To specify the data type for your function's result, add the keyword As and the name of the desired data type to the end of the function declaration line. For example:

```
Function MultiplyIt(num1, num2) As Integer
```

If you don't specify the data type, Visual Basic assigns the default type (Variant data type) to your function's result. When you specify the data type for your function's result, you get the same advantages as when you specify the data type for your variables; your procedure uses memory more efficiently, and therefore it runs faster.

Let's take a look at an example of a function that returns an integer number, although the arguments passed to it are declared as Single data types in a calling subroutine.

1. Add a new module to the MyFunctions (Chap04.xls) project and change the module's name to **Sample3**.

2. Activate the **Sample3** module and enter the HowMuch subroutine, as shown below:

```
Sub HowMuch()
    Dim num1 As Single
    Dim num2 As Single
    Dim result As Single

    num1 = 45.33
    num2 = 19.24
    result = MultiplyIt(num1, num2)
    MsgBox result
End Sub
```

3. Enter the following function procedure below the HowMuch subroutine:

```
Function MultiplyIt(num1,num2) As Integer
    MultiplyIt = num1 * num2
End Function
```

Because the values stored in the variables num1 and num2 are not whole numbers, to ensure that the result of multiplication is a whole number, you may want to assign the Integer data type to the result of the function. If you don't assign the data type to the MultiplyIt function's result, the HowMuch procedure will display the result in the data type specified in the declaration line of the result variable. Instead of 872, the result of the multiplication will be 872.1492.

To make the MultiplyIt function more useful, you can pass different values each time you run the procedure by using the InputBox function, instead of hard coding the values to be used in the multiplication. Take a few minutes to modify the HowMuch procedure on your own, following the example of the EnterText subroutine that was created in the preceding section.

Passing Arguments by Reference and by Value

In some procedures, when you pass arguments as variables, Visual Basic can suddenly change the value of the variables. To ensure that the called function procedure does not alter the value of the passed arguments, you should precede the name of the argument in the function's declaration line with the keyword ByVal. Let's look at the following example.

1. Add a new module to the MyFunctions (Chap04.xls) project and change the module's name to **Sample4.**

2. Activate the **Sample4** module and type the procedures shown below:

```
Sub ThreeNumbers()
    Dim num1 As Integer, num2 As Integer, num3 As Integer
    num1 = 10
    num2 = 20
    num3 = 30

    MsgBox MyAverage(num1,num2,num3)
    MsgBox num1
    MsgBox num2
    MsgBox num3
End Sub

Function MyAverage(ByVal num1, ByVal num2, ByVal num3)
    num1 = num1 + 1
    MyAverage = (num1 + num2 + num3) / 3
End Function
```

To prevent the function from altering values of arguments, use the keyword ByVal before the arguments' names.

The ThreeNumbers subroutine assigns values to three variables and then calls the MyAverage function to calculate and return the average of the numbers stored in these variables. The function's arguments are the names of variables num1, num2, and num3. Notice that all variable names are preceded with the keyword ByVal. Also, notice that prior to the calculation of the average, the MyAverage function changes the value of the num1 variable. Inside the function procedure, the num1 variable equals 11 (10 + 1). Therefore, when the function passes the calculated average to the ThreeNumbers procedure, the MsgBox function displays the result as 20.3333333333333 and not 20, as expected. The next three functions show the contents of each of the variables. The values stored in these variables are the same as the original values assigned to them—10, 20, and 30.

What will happen if you omit the keyword ByVal in front of the num1 argument in the MyAverage function's declaration line? The function's result will still be the same, but the contents of the num1 variable displayed by MsgBox num1 is now 11. The MyAverage function has not only returned the unexpected result (20.3333333333333, instead of 20) but has also modified the original data stored in the num1 variable. To prevent Visual Basic from permanently changing the values supplied to the function, use the ByVal keyword.

Tip 4-9: Know Your Keywords: ByRef and ByVal

Because any of the variables passed to a function procedure (or a subroutine) can be changed by the receiving procedure, it is important to know how to protect the original value of a variable. Visual Basic has two keywords that give or deny permission to change the contents of a variable—ByRef and ByVal.

By default, Visual Basic passes information into a function procedure (or a subroutine) by reference (ByRef keyword), referring to the original data specified in the function's argument at the time the function is called. So, if the function alters the value of the argument, the original value is changed. You will get this result if you omit the ByVal keyword in front of the num1 argument in the MyAverage function's declaration line. If you want the function procedure to change the original value, you don't need to explicitly insert the ByRef keyword, since passed variables default to ByRef.

When you use the ByVal keyword in front of an argument name, Visual Basic passes the argument by value. It means that Visual Basic makes a copy of the original data. This copy is then passed to a function. If the function changes the value of an argument passed by value, the original data does not change—only the copy changes. That's why when the MyAverage function changed the value of the num1 argument, the original value of the num1 variable remained the same.

Using Optional Arguments

At times you may want to supply an additional value to a function. Let's say you have a function that calculates the price of a meal per person. Sometimes, however, you'd like the function to perform the same calculation for a group of two or more people. To indicate that a procedure argument is not required, precede the name of the argument with the Optional keyword. Arguments that are optional come at the end of the argument list, following the names of all the required arguments. Optional arguments must always be the Variant data type. This means that you can't specify the optional argument's type by using the As keyword.

In the preceding section, you created a function to calculate the average of three numbers. Suppose that sometimes you'd like to use this function to calculate the average of two numbers. You could define the third argument of the MyAverage function as optional. To preserve the original MyAverage function, let's create the Avg function to calculate the average for two or three numbers.

1. Add a new module to the MyFunctions (Chap04.xls) project and change the module's name to **Sample5**.

2. Activate the **Sample5** module and enter the function procedure shown
    below:

```
Function Avg(num1, num2, Optional num3)
    Dim totalNums As Integer
    totalNums = 3
    If IsMissing(num3)Then
        num3 = 0
        totalNums = totalNums -1
    End If
    Avg = (num1+num2+num3)/totalNums
End Function
```

3. Now call this function from the Immediate window:

```
?Avg(2,3)
```

As soon as you press Enter, Visual Basic displays the result: 2.5.

```
?Avg(2,3,5)
```

This time the result is: 3.3333333333333.

As you've seen, the Avg function allows you to calculate the average of two
or three numbers. You decide which values and how many values (two or
three) you want to average. When you start typing the values for the function's arguments in the Immediate window, Visual Basic displays the name
of the optional argument enclosed in square brackets.

Let's take a few minutes to analyze the Avg function. This function can
take up to three arguments. The arguments num1 and num2 are required. The
argument num3 is optional. Notice that the name of the optional argument is
preceded with the Optional keyword. The optional argument is listed at the
end of the argument list. Because the type of num1, num2, and num3 arguments
is not declared, Visual Basic treats all of these arguments as Variants.

Inside the function procedure, the totalNums variable is declared as Integer and then assigned a beginning value of 3. Because the function has to be
capable of calculating an average of two or three numbers, the handy
built-in function IsMissing checks for the number of supplied arguments. If
the third (optional) argument is not supplied, the IsMissing function puts in
its place the value of zero (0), and at the same time it deducts the value of
one from the value stored in the totalNums variable. Hence, if the optional
argument is missing, totalNums is 2. The next statement calculates the average based on the supplied data, and the result is assigned to the name of the
function.

The IsMissing function allows you to determine whether or not the
optional argument was supplied. This function returns the logical value
True if the third argument is not supplied, and it returns False when the
third argument is given. The IsMissing function is used here with a decision
making statement If...Then (see Chapter 5 for a detailed description of this
and other decision-making statements used in VBA). If the num3 argument is
missing (IsMissing), then (Then) Visual Basic supplies a zero for the value

of the third argument (num3 = 0) and reduces the value stored in the argument totalNums by one (totalNums = totalNums - 1).

How else can you run the Avg function? On your own, run this function from a worksheet. Make sure you run it with two and then with three arguments.

Tip 4-10: Testing a Function Procedure

To test whether a custom function does what it was designed to do, write a simple subroutine that will call the function and display its result. In addition, the subroutine should show the original values of arguments. This way, you'll be able to quickly determine when the values of arguments were altered. If the function procedure uses optional arguments, you'll also need to check those situations in which the optional arguments may be missing.

Locating Built-in Functions

VBA comes with many built-in functions. These functions can be looked up easily in the Visual Basic online help. To access an alphabetical listing of all VBA functions, choose Help | Microsoft Visual Basic Help in the Visual Basic Editor window. On the Contents tab, open the Visual Basic Language Reference folder. Then click Functions.

Take, for example, the MsgBox or the InputBox function. One of the features of a good program is its interaction with the user. When you work with Microsoft Excel, you interact with the application by using various dialog boxes. When you make a mistake, a dialog box comes up and displays a message informing you of the error. When you write your own procedures, you can also inform the users about an unexpected error or the result of a specific calculation. Do this with the help of the MsgBox function. So far you have seen a simple implementation of this function. In the next section, you will find out how to control the looks of your message. You will also learn how to get information from the user with the InputBox function. But before we go on to discuss these functions in detail, let's take a look at one VBA function that can be especially useful to you now that you have familiarized yourself with variables and their data types.

Visual Basic has the VarType function that returns an integer indicating the type of a variable. Figure 4-4 displays the VarType function's syntax and the values it returns.

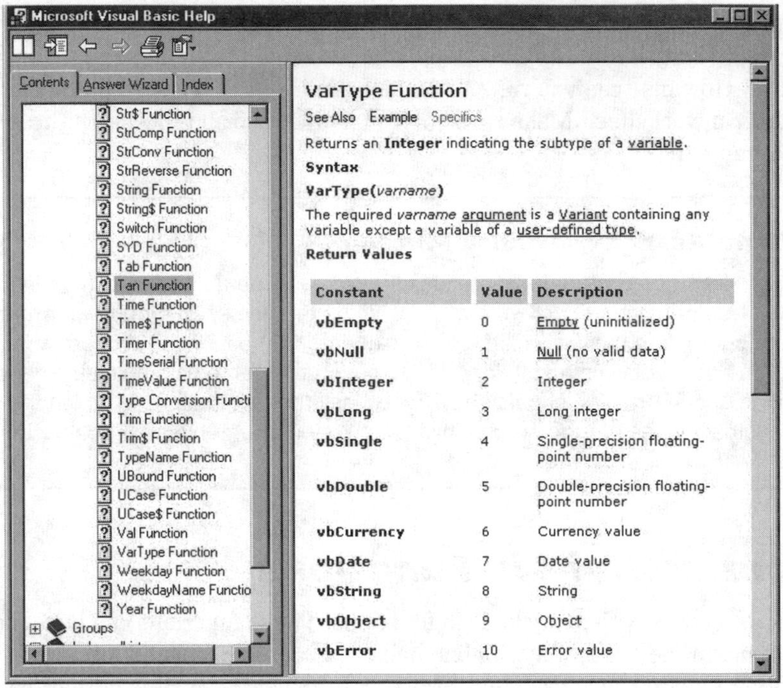

Figure 4-4: With the built-in VarType function, you can tell the data type the variable holds.

Now, let's see how you can use this function in the Immediate window.

1. Open the Immediate window.

2. Type the following statements that assign values to variables:

```
age = 18
birthdate = #1/1/1981#
firstName = "John"
```

3. Now ask Visual Basic what type of data each of the variables hold:

```
?varType(age)
```

When you press Enter, Visual Basic returns 2. As shown in Figure 4-4, the number 2 represents the Integer data type.

```
?varType(birthdate)
```

Visual Basic returns 7 for Date. If you make a mistake in the variable name (let's say you type birthday instead of birthdate), Visual Basic returns zero (0).

```
?varType(firstName)
```

Visual Basic tells you that the value stored in the variable firstName is a string (8).

Using the MsgBox Function

The MsgBox function that you have used so far was limited to displaying a message to the user in a simple, one-button dialog box. You closed the message box by clicking the OK button or pressing the Enter key. Create a simple message box by following the MsgBox function name with the text enclosed in quotation marks. In other words, to display the message "The procedure is complete," you should prepare the following statement:

```
MsgBox "The procedure is complete"
```

You can quickly try out the above instruction by entering it in the Immediate window. When you type this instruction and press Enter, Visual Basic displays the message box shown in Figure 4-5.

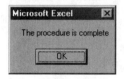

Figure 4-5:
To display a message to the user, place the text as the argument of the MsgBox function.

The MsgBox function allows you to use other arguments that make it possible to determine the number of buttons that should be available in the message box or change the title of the message box from the default, Microsoft Excel. You can also assign your own help topic. The syntax of the MsgBox is shown below.

```
MsgBox (prompt [, buttons] [, title], [, helpfile, context])
```

Notice that while the MsgBox function has five arguments, only the first one, prompt, is required. The arguments listed in square brackets are optional.

When you enter a long text string for the prompt argument, Visual Basic decides how to break the text so it fits the message box. Let's do some exercises in the Immediate window to learn various text formatting techniques.

1. Enter the following instruction in the Immediate window. Make sure to enter the entire text string on one line, and then press **Enter**.

    ```
    MsgBox "All done. Now open ""Chap04.xls"" and place an empty
    disk in the diskette drive. The following procedure will copy
    this file to the disk."
    ```

    As soon as you press Enter, Visual Basic shows the resulting dialog box.

Figure 4-6: This long message will look more appealing when you take the text formatting into your own hands.

If you get the Compile error, click OK. Then make sure that the name of the file is surrounded by double quotation marks—""Chap04.xls"".

When the text of your message is particularly long, you can break it into several lines using the VBA Chr function. The Chr function requires one argument and a number between 0 and 255, and it returns a character represented by this number. For example, Chr(13) returns a carriage return character (this is the same as pressing the Enter key), and Chr(10) returns a linefeed character (this is useful for adding spacing between the text lines).

2. Modify the instruction entered in the previous step in the following way:

```
MsgBox "All done." & Chr(13) & "Now open ""Chap04.xls"" and place"
& Chr(13) & "an empty disk in the diskette drive." & Chr(13) &
"The following procedure will copy this file to the disk."
```

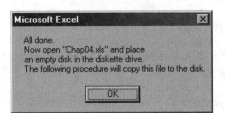

Figure 4-7:
You can break a long text into several lines by using the Chr(13) function.

You must surround each text fragment by quotation marks. Quoted text embedded in a text string requires an additional set of quotation marks, as in ""Chap04.xls"". The Chr(13) function indicates a place where you'd like to start a new line. The string concatenation character (&) is used to add a carriage return character to a concatenated string.

When you enter exceptionally long text messages on one line, it's easy to make a mistake. As you recall, Visual Basic has a special line continuation character (an underscore _) that allows you to break a long VBA statement into several lines. Unfortunately, the line continuation character cannot be used in the Immediate window.

3. Add a new module to the MyFunctions (Chap04.xls) project and change the module's name to **Sample6**.

4. Activate the **Sample6** module and enter the MyMessage subroutine shown below. Be sure to precede each line continuation character with a space.

```
Sub MyMessage()
    MsgBox "All done." & Chr(13) _
    & "Now open ""Chap04.xls"" and place" & Chr(13) _
    & "an empty disk in the diskette drive." & Chr(13) _
    & "The following procedure will copy this file to the disk."
End Sub
```

When you run the MyMessage procedure, Visual Basic displays the same message as the one shown in Figure 4-7. As you can see, the text entered on several lines is more readable, and the code is easier to maintain.

To improve the readability of your message, you may want to add more spacing between the text lines by including blank lines. To do this, use two Chr(13) or two Chr(10) functions, as shown in the following step.

5. Enter the following MyMessage2 procedure:

```
Sub MyMessage2()
    MsgBox "All done." & Chr(10) & Chr(10) _
    & "Now open ""Chap04.xls"" and place" & Chr(13) _
    & "an empty disk in the diskette drive." & Chr(13)& Chr(13)_
    & "The following procedure will copy this file to the disk."
End Sub
```

Figure 4-8 displays the message box generated by the MyMessage2 procedure.

Figure 4-8:
You can increase the readability of your message by increasing spacing between the selected text lines.

Now that you've mastered the text formatting techniques, let's take a closer look at the next argument of the MsgBox function. Although the buttons argument is optional, it's frequently used.

The buttons argument specifies how many and what types of buttons you want to appear in the message box. This argument can be a constant (see Table 4-1) or a number. If you omit this argument, the resulting message box includes only the OK button, as you've seen in the preceding examples.

Table 4-1: Settings for the MsgBox buttons argument

Constant	Value	Description
Button settings		
vbOKOnly	0	Displays only an OK button. This is the default.
vbOKCancel	1	OK and Cancel buttons
vbAbortRetryIgnore	2	Abort, Retry, and Ignore buttons
vbYesNoCancel	3	Yes, No, and Cancel buttons
vbYesNo	4	Yes and No buttons
vbRetryCancel	5	Retry and Cancel buttons
Icon settings		
vbCritical	16	Displays the Critical Message icon
vb Question	32	Displays the Question Message icon
vbExclamation	48	Displays the Warning Message icon
vbInformation	64	Displays the Information Message icon
Default button settings		
vbDefaultButton1	0	The first button is default
vbDefaultButton2	256	The second button is default
vbDefaultButton3	512	The third button is default
vbDefaultButton4	768	The fourth button is default
Message box modality		
vbApplicationModal	0	The user must respond to the message before continuing to work in the current application
vbSystemModal	4096	All applications are suspended until the user responds to the message box
Other MsgBox display settings		
vbMsgBoxHelpButton	16384	Adds Help button to the message box
vbMsgBoxSetForeground	65536	Specifies the message box window as the foreground window
vbMsgBoxRight	524288	Text is right aligned
vbMsgBoxRtlReading	1048576	Text appears as right-to-left reading on Hebrew and Arabic systems

When should you use the `buttons` argument? Suppose you want the user of your procedure to respond to a question with Yes or No. Your message box may then require two buttons. If a message box includes more than one button, one of them is considered a default button. When the user presses Enter, the default button is selected automatically.

Because you can display various types of messages (critical, warning, information), you can visually indicate the importance of the message by including in the buttons argument the graphical representation (icon) for the chosen message type.

In addition to the type of message, the buttons argument can include a setting to determine if the message box must be closed before a user switches to another application. It's quite possible that the user may want to switch to another program or perform another task before responding to the question posed in your message box. If the message box is application modal (vbApplication Modal), the user must close the message box before continuing to use your application. On the other hand, if you want to suspend all the applications until the user responds to the message box, you must include the vbSystemModal setting in the buttons argument.

The buttons argument settings are divided into five groups: button settings, icon settings, default button settings, message box modality, and other MsgBox display settings (see Table 4-1). Only one setting from each group can be included in the buttons argument.

To create a buttons argument, you can add up the values for each setting you want to include. For example, to display a message box with two buttons (Yes and No), the question mark icon, and the "No" button as the default button, look up the corresponding values in Table 4-1 and add them up. You should arrive at 292 (4+32+256). To quickly see the message box using the calculated message box argument, enter the following statement in the Immediate window:

```
MsgBox "Do you want to proceed?", 292
```

The resulting message box is shown below.

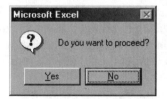

Figure 4-9:
You can specify the number of buttons to include in the message box by using the optional buttons argument.

When you derive the buttons argument by adding up the constant values, your procedure becomes less readable. There's no reference table where you can check the hidden meaning of 292. To improve the readability of your MsgBox function, it's better to use the constants instead of their values. For example, enter the following revised statement in the Immediate window:

```
MsgBox "Do you want to proceed?", vbYesNo + vbQuestion + vbDefaultButton2
```

The above statement produces the same result as shown in Figure 4-9.

The following example shows how to use the buttons argument inside the Visual Basic procedure.

1. Add a new module to the MyFunctions (Chap04.xls) project and change the module's name to **Sample7**.

2. Activate the **Sample7** module and enter the MsgYesNo subroutine shown below:

```
Sub MsgYesNo()
    Dim question As String
    Dim myButtons As Integer

    question = "Do you want to open a new workbook?"
    myButtons = vbYesNo + vbQuestion + vbDefaultButton2
    MsgBox question, myButtons
End Sub
```

In the above subroutine, the `question` variable stores the text of your message. The settings for the `buttons` argument are placed in the `myButtons` variable. Instead of using the names of constants, you can use their values, as in the following:

```
myButtons = 4 + 32 + 256
```

However, by specifying the names of the `buttons` argument's constants, you make your procedure easier to understand for yourself and others who may work with this procedure in the future.

The `question` and `myButtons` variables are used as arguments for the MsgBox function. When you run the procedure, you see the result displayed, as shown in Figure 4-9. Notice that the No button is now selected. It's the default button for this dialog box. If you press Enter, Excel removes the MsgBox from the screen. Nothing happens because your procedure does not have any more instructions following the MsgBox function. To change the default button, use the vbDefaultButton1 setting instead.

The third argument of the MsgBox function is `title`. While this is also an optional argument, it's very handy, as it allows you to create procedures that don't provide visual clues to the fact that you programmed them with Microsoft Excel. Using this argument, you can set the title bar of your message box to any text you want.

Suppose you want the MsgYesNo procedure to display in its title the text "New workbook." The following MsgYesNo2 procedure demonstrates the use of the `title` argument:

```
Sub MsgYesNo2()
    Dim question As String
    Dim myButtons As Integer
    Dim myTitle As String

    question = "Do you want to open a new workbook?"
    myButtons = vbYesNo + vbQuestion + vbDefaultButton2
    myTitle = "New workbook"

    MsgBox question, myButtons, myTitle
End Sub
```

The text for the `title` argument is stored in the variable `myTitle`. If you don't specify the value for the `title` argument, Visual Basic displays the default text "Microsoft Excel."

Notice that the arguments are listed in the order determined by the MsgBox function. If you would like to list the arguments in any order, you must precede the value of each argument with its name, as shown below:

```
MsgBox title:=myTitle, prompt:=question, buttons:=myButtons
```

The last two arguments—`helpfile` and `context`—are used by programmers who are experienced with using help files in the Windows environment. The `helpfile` argument indicates the name of a special help file that contains additional information you may want to display to your VBA procedure user. When you specify this argument, the Help button will be added to your message box. When you use the `helpfile` argument, you must also use the `context` argument. This argument indicates which help subject in the specified help file you want to display. Suppose HelpX.hlp is the help file you created, and 55 is the context topic you want to use. To include this information in your MsgBox function, you would use the following instruction:

```
MsgBox title:=mytitle, _
    prompt:=question _
    buttons:=mybuttons _
    helpFile:= "HelpX.hlp", _
    context:=55
```

The above is a single VBA statement, broken down into several lines with the line continuation character.

Returning Values from the MsgBox Function

When you display a simple message box dialog with one button, clicking the OK button or pressing the Enter key removes the message box from the screen. However, when the message box has more than one button, your procedure should detect which button was pressed. To do this, you must save the result of the message box in a variable. Table 4-2 shows values that the MsgBox function returns.

Table 4-2: Values returned by the MsgBox function

Button Selected	Constant	Value
OK	vbOK	1
Cancel	vbCancel	2
Abort	vbAbort	3
Retry	vbRetry	4
Ignore	vbIgnore	5
Yes	vbYes	6
No	vbNo	7

The MsgYesNo3 procedure is a revised version of MsgYesNo2. It shows how you determine which button the user chose.

```
Sub MsgYesNo3()
    Dim question As String
    Dim myButtons As Integer
    Dim myTitle As String
    Dim myChoice As Integer

    question = "Do you want to open a new workbook?"
    myButtons = vbYesNo + vbQuestion + vbDefaultButton2
    myTitle = "New workbook"

    myChoice = MsgBox(question, myButtons, myTitle)
    MsgBox myChoice
End Sub
```

In the above procedure, you assigned the result of the MsgBox function to the variable myChoice. Notice that the arguments of the MsgBox function are now listed in parentheses:

```
myChoice = MsgBox(question, myButtons, myTitle)
```

Tip 4-11: MsgBox Function — with or without Parentheses?

Use parentheses around the MsgBox function's argument list when you want to use the result returned by the function. By listing the function's arguments without parentheses, you tell Visual Basic that you want to ignore the function's result. Most likely, you will want to use the function's result when the MsgBox contains more than one button.

When you run the MsgYesNo3 procedure, a two-button message box is displayed. By clicking on the Yes button, the statement MsgBox myChoice displays the number 6. When you click the No button, the number 7 is displayed. In Chapter 5, you will learn how to make your procedure carry out a task depending on a button's selection.

Using the InputBox Function

The InputBox function displays a dialog box with a message that prompts the user to enter data. This dialog box has two buttons—OK and Cancel. When you click OK, the InputBox function returns the information entered in the text box. When you select Cancel, the function returns the empty string (" "). The syntax of the InputBox functon is as follows:

```
InputBox(prompt [, title] [, default] [, xpos] [, ypos] _
    [, helpfile, context])
```

The first argument, prompt, is the text message that you want to display in the dialog box. Long text strings can be entered on several lines by using the Chr(13) or Chr(10) functions (see examples of using the MsgBox function earlier in this chapter). All of the remaining InputBox arguments are optional.

The second argument, title, allows you to change the default title of the dialog box. The default value is "Microsoft Excel."

The third argument of the InputBox function, default, allows the display of a default value in the text box. If you omit this argument, the empty edit box is displayed.

The following two arguments, xpos and ypos, let you specify the exact position where the dialog box should appear on the screen. If you omit these arguments, the input box appears in the middle of the current window. The xpos argument determines the horizontal position of the dialog box from the left edge of the screen. When omitted, the dialog box is centered horizontally. The ypos argument determines the vertical position from the top of the screen. If you omit this argument, the dialog box is positioned vertically approximately one-third of the way down the screen. Both xpos and ypos are measured in special units called _twips_. One twip is an equivalent of approximately 0.0007 inches.

The last two arguments, helpfile and context, are used in the same way as the corresponding arguments of the MsgBox function discussed earlier in this chapter.

Now that you know the meaning of the InputBox arguments, let's see some examples of using this function.

1. Add a new module to the MyFunctions (Chap04.xls) project and change the module's name to **Sample8**.

2. Activate the **Sample8** module and enter the Informant subroutine shown below:

```
Sub Informant()
    InputBox prompt:="Enter your place of birth:" & Chr(13) _
        & " (e.g., Boston, Great Falls, etc.) "
End Sub
```

The above procedure displays a dialog box with two buttons. The input prompt is displayed on two lines.

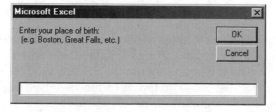

Figure 4-10:
A dialog box generated by the Informant subroutine

As with the MsgBox function, if you plan on using the data entered by the user in the dialog box, you should store the result of the InputBox function in a variable. The Informant2 procedure shown below assigns the result of the InputBox function to the variable town:

```
Sub Informant2()
    Dim myPrompt As String
    Dim town As String
    Const myTitle = "Enter data"

    myPrompt = "Enter your place of birth:" & Chr(13) _
        & "(e.g., Boston, Great Falls, etc.)"
    town = InputBox(myPrompt, myTitle)
    MsgBox "You were born in " & town & ".", , "Your response"
End Sub
```

Notice that this time, the arguments of the InputBox function are listed between parentheses. Parentheses are required if you want to use the result of the InputBox function later in your procedure. The Informant2 subroutine uses a constant to specify the text to appear in the title bar of the dialog box. Because the constant value remains the same throughout the execution of your procedure, you can declare the input box title as a constant. However, if you'd rather use a variable, you still can.

When you run a procedure using the InputBox function, the dialog box generated by this function always appears in the same area of the screen. To change the location of the dialog box, you must supply the xpos and ypos arguments, as explained earlier.

3. To display the dialog box in the top left-hand corner of the screen, modify the InputBox function in the Informant2 procedure, as follows:

```
town = InputBox(myPrompt, myTitle, , 1, 200)
```

Notice that the argument myTitle is followed by two commas. The second comma marks the position of the omitted default argument. The next two arguments determine the horizontal and vertical position of the dialog box. If you omit the second comma after the myTitle argument, Visual Basic will use the number 1 as the value of the default argument. If you precede the values of arguments by their names (for example, prompt:=myPrompt, title:=myTitle, xpos:=1, ypos:=200), you won't have to remember to place a comma in the place of each omitted argument.

What will happen if, instead of the name of a town, you enter a number? Because users often supply incorrect data in the input dialog box, your procedure must verify that the data the user entered can be used in further data manipulations. The InputBox function itself does not provide a facility for data validation. To validate user input, you must use other VBA instructions that are presented in the next chapter.

Converting Data Types

The result of the InputBox function is always a string. If the user enters a number, the string value the user entered should be converted to a numeric value before your procedure can use this number in mathematical computations. Visual Basic is capable of converting values that weren't possible in earlier versions of Excel from one data type to another.

1. Activate the **Sample8** module in MyFunctions (Chap04.xls) project and enter the following AddTwoNums procedure:

```
Sub AddTwoNums()
    Dim myPrompt As String
    Dim value1 As String
    Const myTitle = "Enter data"
    Dim mySum As Single

    myPrompt = "Enter a number:"
    value1 = InputBox(myPrompt, myTitle, 0)
    mySum = value1 + 2
    MsgBox mySum & " (" & value1 & " + 2)"
End Sub
```

The above procedure displays the dialog box shown in Figure 4-11. Notice that this dialog box has two special features that are obtained by using the InputBox function's optional `title` and `default` arguments. Instead of the default "Microsoft Excel," the dialog box displays a text string defined by the contents of the myTitle constant. The zero entered as the default value in the edit box suggests that the user enters a number instead of text.

Once the user provides the data and clicks OK, the user's input is assigned to the variable value1.

```
value1 = InputBox(myPrompt, myTitle, 0)
```

Figure 4-11:
To suggest that the user enter a specific type of data, you may want to provide a default value in the edit box.

The data type of the variable `value1` is String. You can check the data type easily if you follow the above instruction with the statement shown below:

```
MsgBox varType(value1)
```

When Visual Basic runs the above line, it will display a message box with the number 8. If you look at Figure 4-4 earlier in this chapter, you will notice that this number represents the String data type.

Tip 4-12: Define a Constant

To ensure that all the title bars in a particular VBA procedure display the same text, assign the title text to a constant. By following this tip, you will save yourself time typing the title text more than once.

Tip 4-13: Avoid the Type Mismatch Error

If you attempt to run the AddTwoNums procedure in previous versions of

Microsoft Excel (prior to version 2000), you will get the Type Mismatch error when Visual Basic tries to execute the following line of code:

```
mysum = value1 + 2
```

To avoid the Type Mismatch error, use the built-in CSng function to convert a string stored in the value1 variable to a Single type number. Write the following statement:

```
mysum = CSng(value1) + 2
```

The next line, `mySum = value1 + 2`, adds 2 to the user's input and assigns the result of the calculation to the variable `mySum`. Because the `value1` variable's data type is String, prior to using this variable's data in the computation, Visual Basic goes to work behind the scenes to perform the data type conversion. Visual Basic has the brains to understand the need for conversion. Without it, the two incompatible data types (text + number) would generate the Type Mismatch error.

The procedure ends with the MsgBox function displaying the result of the calculation and showing the user how the total was derived.

Using the InputBox Method

In addition to the InputBox function, there is the InputBox method. If you activate the Object Browser window and type "inputbox" in the Search box and then press Enter, Visual Basic will display two occurrences of InputBox—one in the Excel library and the other one in the VBA library (Figure 4-12).

The InputBox method available in the Microsoft Excel library has a slightly different syntax than the InputBox function that was covered earlier in this chapter. Its syntax is:

```
expression.InputBox(Prompt, [Title], [Default], [Left], [Top],
    [HelpFile], [HelpContextID], [Type] )
```

All bracketed arguments are optional. The `Prompt` argument is the message to be displayed in the dialog box, `Title` is the title for the dialog box, and `Default` is a value that will appear in the text box when the dialog box is initially displayed. The `Left` and `Top` arguments specify the position of the dialog box on the screen. The values for these arguments are entered in points (one point equals 1/72 inch). The arguments `HelpFile` and `HelpContextID` identify the name of the help file and specific number of the help topic to be displayed when the user clicks the Help button. The last

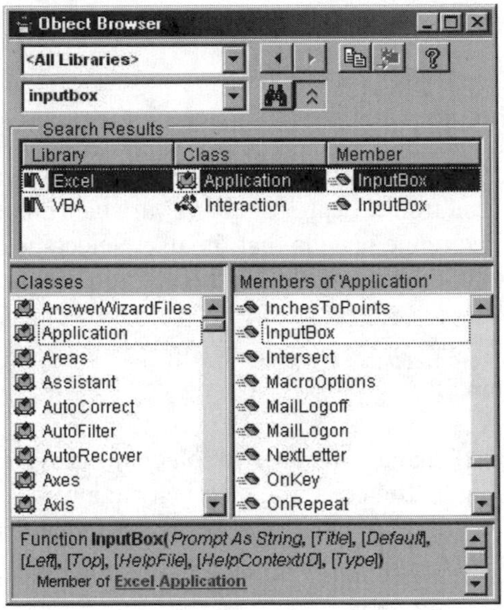

Figure 4-12:
Don't forget to use the Object Browser in researching Visual Basic functions and methods.

argument of the InputBox method, Type, specifies the return data type. If you omit this argument, the InputBox method will return text. The values of the Type argument are shown in Table 4-3.

Table 4-3: Data types returned by the InputBox method

Value	Type of Data Returned
0	A formula
1	A number
2	A string (text)
4	A logical value (True or False)
8	A cell reference, as a Range object
16	An error value; for example, #N/A
64	An array of values

You can allow the user to enter a number or text in the edit box if you use 3 for the Type argument. This value is obtained by adding up the value for a number (1) and a string (2), as shown in Table 4-3. The InputBox method is quite useful for those VBA procedures that require a user to select a range of cells in a worksheet.

1. Close the Object Browser window if you opened it before.

2. In the **Sample8** module, enter the following WhatRange procedure:

```
Sub WhatRange()
    Dim newRange As Range
    Dim tellMe As String
    tellMe = "Use the mouse to select a range:"
    Set newRange = Application.InputBox(prompt:=tellMe, _
```

```
            Title:="Range to format", _
         Type:=8)
      newRange.NumberFormat = "0.00"
      newRange.Select
   End Sub
```

The WhatRange procedure begins with a declaration of an object variable—newRange. As you recall from Chapter 3, object variables point to
the location of the data. The range of cells that the user selects is
assigned to the object variable newRange. Notice the keyword Set before
the name of the variable:

```
   Set newRange = Application.InputBox(prompt:=tellMe, _
      Title:="Range to format", _
      Type:=8)
```

The Type argument (Type:=8) enables the user to select any range of
cells. When the user highlights the cells, the next instruction:

```
   newRange.NumberFormat = "0.00"
```

changes the format of the selected cells. The last instruction selects
the range of cells that the user highlighted.

3. Run the WhatRange procedure. Visual Basic displays a dialog box
   prompting the user to select a range of cells in the worksheet.

4. Use the mouse to select any cells you want. As you drag the mouse to
   select the cells, Visual Basic enters the selected range reference in the
   edit box.

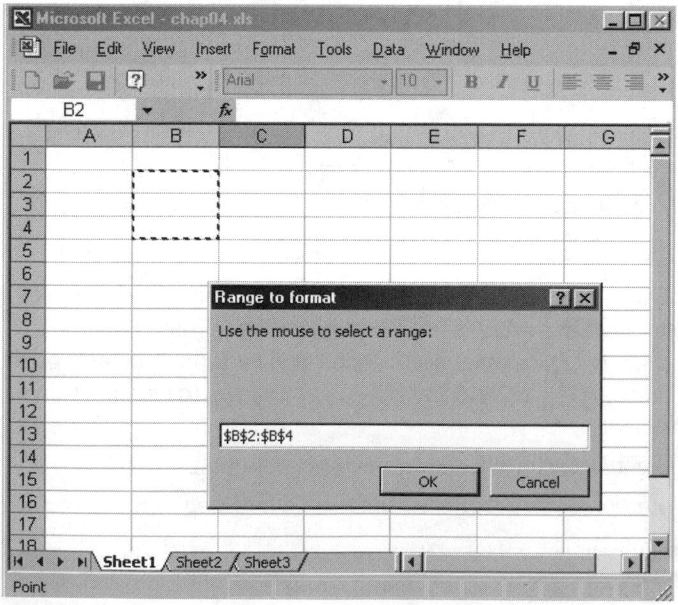

Figure 4-13:
Using Excel's InputBox method, you can get the range address from the user.

5. When you're done selecting cells, click **OK** in the dialog box. The selected range is now formatted. To check this out, enter a whole number in any of the selected cells. The number should appear formatted with two decimals.

6. Rerun the procedure, and when the dialog box appears, click **Cancel**.

The WhatRange procedure works fine if you click OK after selecting a cell or a range of cells. Unfortunately, when you click the Cancel button or press Esc, Visual Basic displays an error message—"Object Required." When you click the Debug button in the error dialog box, Visual Basic will highlight the line of code that caused the error. Because you don't want to select anything when you cancel the dialog box, you must find a way to ignore the error that Visual Basic displays. Using a special statement, On Error GoTo labelname, you can take a detour when an error occurs. This instruction has the following syntax:

```
On Error GoTo labelname
```

This instruction should be placed just below the variable declaration lines. labelname can be any word you want, except for a Visual Basic keyword. If an error occurs, Visual Basic will jump to the specified label, as shown in step 8 below.

7. Choose **Run | Reset** to cancel the procedure you were running.

8. Modify the WhatRange procedure so it looks like the WhatRange2 procedure shown below:

```
Sub WhatRange2()
    Dim newRange As Range
    Dim tellMe As String
    On Error GoTo VeryEnd
    tellMe = "Use the mouse to select a range:"

    Set newRange = Application.InputBox(prompt:=tellMe, _
        Title:="Range to format", _
        Type:=8)
    newRange.NumberFormat = "0.00"
    newRange.Select
  VeryEnd:
End Sub
```

9. Run the WhatRange2 procedure, and click **Cancel** as soon as the input box appears.

Notice that this time the procedure does not generate the error when you cancel the dialog box. When Visual Basic encounters the error, it jumps to the VeryEnd label placed at the end of the procedure. The statements placed between On Error Goto VeryEnd and the VeryEnd label are ignored. In Chapter 13 you will find other examples of trapping errors in your VBA procedures.

Tip 4-14: Subroutines and Functions: Which Should You Use?

Create a subroutine when:	Create a function when:
<ul><li>You want to perform some actions</li><li>You want to get input from the user</li><li>You want to display a message on the screen</li></ul>	<ul><li>You want to perform a simple calculation more than once</li><li>You must perform complex computations</li><li>You must call the same block of instructions more than once</li><li>You want to check if a certain expression is true or false</li></ul>

Using Master Procedures and Subprocedures

When your VBA procedure gets larger, it may be difficult to maintain its many lines of code. To make your program easier to write, understand, and change, you should use a structured approach. When you create a structured program, you simply break a large problem into small problems that can be solved one at a time. In VBA, you do this by creating a master procedure and one or more subordinate procedures. Because both master procedures and subordinate procedures are subroutines, you declare them with the Sub keyword. The master procedure can call the required subroutines and pass arguments to them. It may also call functions.

The following example shows the AboutUser procedure. The procedure requests the user's first and last name and then extracts the first and last name from the full name string. The last statement displays the user's last name followed by a comma and the first name. As you read further, this procedure will be broken down into several tasks to demonstrate the concept of using master procedures, subprocedures, and functions.

```
Sub AboutUser()
    Dim fullName As String
    Dim firstName As String
    Dim lastName As String
    Dim space As Integer

    'get input from user
    fullName = InputBox("Enter first and last name:")
    'get first and last name strings
    space = InStr(fullName, " ")
    firstName = Left(fullName, space - 1)
    lastName = Right(fullName, Len(fullName) - space)
    'display last name, first name
    MsgBox lastName & ", " & firstName
End Sub
```

The AboutUser procedure can be divided into smaller tasks. The first task is obtaining the user's full name. The next task requires that you divide the user-supplied data into two strings: last name and first name. These tasks can be delegated to separate functions (for example: GetLast and GetFirst). The last task displays a message showing the reordered full name string. Now that you know what tasks you should focus on, let's see how you can accomplish each task.

1.   Add a new module to your current VBA project and rename it **Sample9**.

2.   Enter the following AboutUserMaster procedure in the Sample9 module window.

```
Sub AboutUserMaster()
    Dim first As String, last As String, full As String
    Call GetUserName(full)
    first = GetFirst(full)
    last = GetLast(full)
    Call DisplayLastFirst(first, last)
End Sub
```

The master procedure shown above controls the general flow of your program by calling appropriate subprocedures and functions. The master procedure begins with the declaration of variables. The first statement, `Call GetUserName (full)`, calls the GetUserName subroutine (see step 3) and passes it an argument—the contents of the full variable.

Because the variable `full` is not assigned any value prior to the execution of the Call statement, it has the value of an empty string (" "). Notice that the name of the subprocedure is preceded by the Call statement. Although you are not required to use the Call keyword when calling a procedure, you must use it when the call to the procedure requires arguments. The argument list must be enclosed in parentheses.

3.   Enter the following GetUserName subroutine:

```
Sub GetUserName(fullName As String)
    fullName = InputBox("Enter first and last name:")
End Sub
```

The procedure GetUserName demonstrates two very important Visual Basic programming concepts: how to pass arguments to a subprocedure and how to pass values back from a subprocedure to a calling procedure.

In the master procedure (see step 2), you called the GetUserName procedure and passed it one argument: the variable `full`. This variable is received by a fullName parameter declared in the GetUserName subprocedure's Sub statement. Because at the time Visual Basic called the GetUserName subprocedure the variable `full` contained an empty string, the fullName parameter receives the same value—an empty string (" "). When Visual Basic displays the dialog box and gets the user's last name, this name is assigned to the fullName parameter. A value assigned to a parameter is passed back to the matching argument after the subprocedure is executed. Therefore, when Visual Basic returns to the master procedure, the full variable will contain the user's last name.

Arguments passed to a subprocedure are received by parameters. Notice that the parameter name (fullName) is followed by the declaration of the data type (As String). Although the parameter's data type must agree with the data type of the matching argument, different names may be used for an argument and its corresponding parameter.

Tip 4-15: Arguments Versus Parameters

- An argument is a variable, constant, or expression that is passed to a subprocedure.
- A parameter is simply a variable that receives a value passed to a subprocedure.

---

4. Enter the following GetFirst function procedure:

```
Function GetFirst(fullName As String)
    Dim space As Integer
    space = InStr(fullName, " ")
    GetFirst = Left(fullName, space - 1)
End Function
```

The second statement in the master procedure (see step 2), first = GetFirst(full), passes the value of the full variable to the GetFirst function. This value is received by the function's parameter—fullName. To extract the first name from the user-provided full name string, you must find the location of the space separating the first name and last name. Therefore, the function begins with a declaration of a local variable—space.

The next statement uses the VBA built-in function InStr to return the position of a space character (" ") in the fullName string. The obtained number is then assigned to the variable space. Finally, the Left function is used to extract the specified number of characters (space – 1) from the left side of the fullName string. The length of the first name is one character less than the value stored in the variable space. The result of the function (user's first name) is then assigned to the function's name. When Visual Basic returns to the master procedure, it places the result in the variable first.

5. Enter the following GetLast function procedure:

```
Function GetLast(fullName As String)
    Dim space As Integer
```

```
    space = InStr(fullName, " ")
    GetLast = Right(fullName, Len(fullName) - space)
End Function
```

The third statement in the master procedure (see step 2), `last = GetLast(full)`, passes the value of the `full` variable to the GetLast function. This function's purpose is to extract the user's last name from the user-supplied fullName string. The GetLast function uses the built-in Len function to calculate the total number of characters in the fullName string. The Right function extracts the specified number of characters (`Len(fullName) – space`) from the right side of the fullName string. The obtained string is then assigned to the function name, and upon returning to the master procedure, it is stored in the variable `last`.

6. Enter the following DisplayLastFirst subroutine:

```
Sub DisplayLastFirst(firstName As String, lastName As String)
    MsgBox lastName & ", " & firstName
End Sub
```

The fourth statement in the master procedure (see step 2), `Call DisplayLastFirst(first, last)`, calls the DisplayLastFirst subroutine and passes two arguments to it: `first` and `last`. To receive these arguments, the DisplayLastFirst subprocedure is declared with two matching parameters—firstName and lastName. Recall that different names can be used for arguments and their corresponding parameters. The DisplayLastFirst subprocedure then displays the message box showing the user's last name followed by the comma and the first name.

Tip 4-16: Advantages of Using Subprocedures

- It's easier to maintain several subprocedures than one large procedure.
- A task performed by a subprocedure can be used by several other procedures.
- Each subprocedure can be tested individually before being placed in the main program.
- Several people can work on individual subprocedures that constitute a larger procedure.

What's Next...

In this chapter you learned the difference between subroutine procedures that perform actions and function procedures that return values. While you can create subroutines by recording or typing, function procedures cannot be recorded because they can take arguments. You must write them manually. You saw examples of function procedures called from a worksheet and from another Visual Basic procedure.

You learned how to pass arguments to functions and determine the data type of a function's result. You increased your repertoire of VBA keywords with the ByVal, ByRef, and Optional keywords. You also saw how problems can be broken into simpler and smaller tasks to make your programs easier to understand. Finally, you learned how subprocedures can pass values back to the calling procedures with the help of parameters.

After working through this chapter, you should be able to create some custom functions of your own that are suited to your specific needs. You should also be able to interact easily with your procedure users by employing the MsgBox and InputBox functions. Chapter 5 introduces you to decision making. You will learn how to change the course of your VBA procedure based on the results of the conditions that you supply.

Chapter 5

Decision Making with VBA

Relational and Logical Operators ■ **If...Then Statement** ■ **Decisions Based on More Than One Condition** ■ **The If...Then...Else Statement** ■ **The If...Then... ElseIf Statement** ■ **Nested If...Then... Statements** ■ **Select Case Statement** ■ Using Is with the Case Clause ■ Specifying a Range of Values in a Case Clause ■ Specifying Multiple Expressions in a Case Clause ■ **What's Next...**

We make thousands of decisions every day. Some decisions are spontaneous. We make them automatically without having to stop and think. Other decisions require that we weigh two or more options or even plan several tasks ahead. Visual Basic for Applications, like other programming languages, offers special statements that allow you to include decision points in your own procedures. But what is decision making? Let's say someone approaches you with the question, "Do you like the color red?" After giving this question some thought, you'll answer "yes" or "no." If you're undecided or simply don't care, you might answer "maybe" or "perhaps." In programming, you must be decisive. Only "yes" or "no" answers are allowed. In programming, all decisions are based on supplied answers. If the answer is positive, the procedure executes a specified block of instructions. If the answer is negative, the procedure executes another block of instructions or simply doesn't do anything. In this chapter, you will learn how to use VBA conditional statements to alter the flow of your program. Conditional statements are often referred to as "control structures," as they give you the ability to control the flow of your VBA procedure by skipping over certain statements and "branching" to another part of the procedure.

Relational and Logical Operators

You make decisions in your VBA procedures by using conditional expressions inside the special control structures. A conditional expression is an expression that uses a relational operator (Table 5-1), a logical operator (Table 5-2), or a combination of both. When Visual Basic encounters a conditional expression in your program, it evaluates the expression to determine whether it is true or false.

Table 5-1: Relational operators in VBA

Operator	Description
=	Equal to
<>	Not equal to
>	Greater than
<	Less than
>=	Greater than or equal to
<=	Less than or equal to

Table 5-2: Logical operators in VBA

Operator	Description
AND	All conditions must be true before an action can be taken.
OR	At least one of the conditions must be true before an action can be taken.
NOT	Used for negating a condition. If a condition is true, NOT makes it false. If a condition is false, NOT makes it true.

If...Then Statement

The simplest way to get some decision-making into your VBA procedure is to use the If...Then statement. Suppose you want to choose an action depending on a condition. You can use the following structure:

```
If condition Then statement
```

For example, to delete a blank row from a worksheet, first check if the active cell is blank. If the result of the test is true, go ahead and delete the entire row that contains that cell:

```
If ActiveCell = "" Then Selection.EntireRow.Delete
```

If the active cell is not blank, Visual Basic will ignore the statement following the Then keyword.

Sometimes you may want to perform several actions when the condition is true. Although you could add other statements on the same line by separating them with colons, your code will look clearer if you use the multi-line version of the If...Then statement, as shown below:

```
If condition Then
    statement1
    statement2
    statementN
End If
```

For example, to perform some actions when the value of the active cell is greater than 50, you can write the following block of instructions:

```
If ActiveCell.Value >50 Then
    MsgBox "The exact value is " & ActiveCell.Value
    Debug.Print ActiveCell.Adress & ": " & ActiveCell.Value
End If
```

In the above example, the statements between the Then and the End If keywords are not executed if the value of the active cell is less than or equal to 50. Notice that the If...Then statement must end with the keywords End If. How does Visual Basic make a decision? It evaluates the condition it finds between the If...Then keywords.

Let's try to evaluate the following condition: `ActiveCell.Value >50`

1. Select any cell in a blank worksheet and enter **50**.
2. Switch to the Visual Basic Editor window.
3. Activate the Immediate window.
4. Enter the following statement, and press **Enter** when you're done.

```
? ActiveCell.Value >50
```

When you press Enter, Visual Basic writes the result of this test—false. When the result of the test is false, Visual Basic will not bother to read the statement following the Then keyword in your code. It will simply go on to read the next line of your procedure, if there is one. However, if there are no more lines to read, the procedure will end.

5. Now change the operator to less than or equal to, and have Visual Basic evaluate the following condition:

```
? ActiveCell.Value <= 50
```

This time, the test returns true, and Visual Basic will jump to whatever statement or statements it finds after the Then keyword.

6. Close the Immediate window.

Now that you know how Visual Basic evaluates conditions, let's try the If...Then statement in a VBA procedure.

1. Open a new workbook and save it as **Chap05.xls**.

2. Switch to the Visual Basic Editor screen and rename the VBA project **Decisions**.

3. Insert a new module in the Decisions (Chap05.xls) project and rename this module **IfThen**.

4. In the IfThen module, enter the following procedure:

```
Sub SimpleIfThen()
    Dim weeks As String
    weeks = InputBox("How many weeks are in a year:", "Quiz")
    If weeks<>52 Then MsgBox "Try Again"
End Sub
```

The SimpleIfThen procedure stores the user's answer in the variable named weeks. The variable's value is then compared with the number 52. If the result of the comparison is true (that is, if the value stored in the variable weeks is not equal to 52), Visual Basic will display the message "Try Again."

5. Run the SimpleIfThen procedure and enter a number other than 52.

6. Rerun the SimpleIfThen procedure and enter the number **52**.

When you enter the correct number of weeks, Visual Basic does nothing. The procedure simply ends. It would be nice to display a message when the user guesses right.

7. Enter the following instruction on a separate line before the End Sub keywords:

```
If weeks = 52 Then MsgBox "Congratulations!"
```

8. Run the SimpleIfThen procedure again and enter **52**.

When you enter the correct answer, Visual Basic does not execute the statement MsgBox "Try Again." When the procedure is executed, the statement to the right of the Then keyword is ignored if the result from evaluating the supplied condition is false. As you recall, a VBA procedure can call another procedure. Let's see whether it can also call itself.

Tip 5-1: Two Formats of the If...Then Statement

The If...Then statement has two formats — single line and multi-line. The short format is good for statements that fit on one line, like:

```
If secretCode <> 01W01 Then MsgBox
"Access denied"
    or
If secretCode = 01W01 Then alpha=True
: beta = False
```

Here, secretCode, alpha, and beta are the names of variables. In the first example, Visual Basic displays the message "Access denied" if the value of the secretCode variable is not equal to 01W01. In the second example, Visual Basic sets the value of the variable alpha to True and variable beta to False when the secretCode value is equal to 01W01. Notice that the second statement to be executed is separated from the first by a colon.

The multi-line If...Then statement is clearer when there are more statements to be executed when the condition is true or when the statement to be executed is extremely long, as in the following example:

```
If ActiveSheet.Name = "Sheet1" Then
    ActiveSheet.Move after:=Sheets _
            (Worksheets.Count)
End If
```

In this example, Visual Basic will examine the active sheet name. If it is "Sheet1," the condition ActiveSheet .Name = "Sheet1" will be true, and Visual Basic will proceed to execute the line following the Then keyword. As a result, the active sheet will be moved to the last position in the workbook.

9. Modify the first If statement in the SimpleIfThen procedure, as follows:

```
If weeks <> 52 Then MsgBox "Try Again" : SimpleIfThen
```

We added a colon and the name of the SimpleIfThen procedure to the end of the existing If...Then statement. If the user enters the incorrect answer, he will see a message, and as soon as he clicks the OK button in the message box, he will get another chance to supply the correct answer—the input box will appear again. The user will be able to keep on guessing for a long time. In fact, he won't be able to exit the procedure gracefully until he supplies the correct answer. If he clicks Cancel, he will have to deal with the unfriendly error message "Type mismatch." You saw in the previous chapter how to use the On Error GoTo label statement to go around the error, at least temporarily until you learn more about error handling in Chapter 13. For now, you may want to revise your SimpleIfThen procedure as follows:

```
Sub SimpleIfThen()
    Dim weeks As String
    On Error GoTo VeryEnd
        weeks = InputBox("How many weeks are in a year:", "Quiz")
        If weeks<>52 Then MsgBox "Try Again": SimpleIfThen
        If weeks=52 Then MsgBox "Congratulations!"
    VeryEnd:
End Sub
```

10. Run the SimpleIfThen procedure a few times by supplying incorrect answers. The error trap that you added to your procedure allows the user to quit guessing without having to deal with the ugly error message.

Decisions Based on More Than One Condition

The SimpleIfThen procedure that you worked with in the previous section evaluated only a single condition in the If...Then statement. This statement, however, can take more than one condition. To specify multiple conditions in an If...Then statement, use the logical operators AND and OR (see Table 5-2 at the beginning of this chapter). Here's the syntax with the AND operator:

```
If condition1 AND condition2 Then statement
```

In the above syntax, both condition1 and condition2 must be true for Visual Basic to execute the statement to the right of the Then keyword.

For example:

```
If sales = 10000 AND salary <45000 Then SlsCom = Sales * 0.07
```

In this example:

```
Condition1    sales=10000
Condition2    salary <45000
```

When AND is used in the conditional expression, both conditions must be true before Visual Basic can calculate the sales commission (SlsCom). If any of these conditions are false, or both are false, Visual Basic ignores the statement after Then.

When it's good enough to meet only one of the conditions, you should use the OR operator. Here's the syntax:

```
If condition1 OR condition2 Then statement
```

The OR operator is more flexible. Only one of the conditions has to be true before Visual Basic can execute the statement following the Then keyword. Let's look at this example:

```
If dept = "S" OR dept = "M" Then bonus = 500
```

In the above example, if at least one condition is true, Visual Basic assigns 500 to the bonus variable. If both conditions are false, Visual Basic ignores the rest of the line.

Now let's look at a complete procedure example. Suppose you can get a 10% discount if you purchase 50 units of a product, each priced at $7.00. The IfThenAnd procedure demonstrates the use of the AND operator.

1. Enter the following procedure in the IfThen module of the Decisions (Chap05.xls) project:

```
Sub IfThenAnd()
    Dim price As Single
    Dim units As Integer
    Dim rebate As Single

    Const strmsg1 = "To get a rebate you must buy an additional "
    Const strmsg2 = "Price must equal $7.00"

    units = Range("B1").Value
    price = Range("B2").Value

    If price = 7 AND units >= 50 Then
        rebate = (price * units) * 0.1
        Range("A4").Value = "The rebate is: $" & rebate
    End If
    If price = 7 AND units < 50 Then
        Range("A4").Value = strmsg1 & 50 - units & " unit(s)."
    End If
    If price <> 7 AND units >= 50 Then
        Range("A4").Value = strmsg2
    End If
    If price <> 7 AND units < 50 Then
        Range("A4").Value = "You didn't meet the criteria."
    End If
End Sub
```

The IfThenAnd procedure shown above has four If...Then statements that are used to evaluate the contents of two variables: price and units. The AND operator between the keywords If...Then allows more than one condition to be tested. With the AND operator, all conditions must be true for Visual Basic to run the statements between the Then...End If keywords.

Because the IfThenAnd procedure is based on the data entered in worksheet cells, it's more convenient to run it from the Excel window.

2. Switch to the Microsoft Excel application window, and choose **Tools | Macro | Macros**.

3. In the Macro dialog box, select the **IfThenAnd** macro and click the **Options** button.

4. Assign the shortcut key to your macro: **Ctrl+Shift+I**, and then exit the Macro Options dialog box.

5. Enter the following data in a worksheet:

	A	B
1	Units	234
2	Price	7

6. Press **Ctrl+Shift+I** to run the IfThenAnd procedure.

7. Change the values of cells B1 and B2 so that each time you run the procedure, a different If...Then statement is true.

Tip 5-2: If Block Instructions and Indenting

To make the If blocks easier to read and understand, use indentation. Compare the following:

Looking at the If...Then block statement on the right, you can easily see where the block begins and where it ends.

```
If condition Then    If condition Then
action1                  action
End If               End If
```

The If...Then...Else Statement

Now you know how to display a message or take an action when one or more conditions are true or false. What should you do, however, if your procedure needs to take one action when the condition is true and another action when the condition is false? By adding the Else clause to the simple If...Then statement, you can direct your procedure to the appropriate statement depending on the result of the test.

The If...Then...Else statement has two formats—single line and multi-line. The single line format is as follows:

```
If condition Then statement1 Else statement2
```

The statement following the Then keyword is executed if the condition is true, and the statement following the Else clause is executed if the condition is false. For example:

```
If Sales>5000 Then Bonus = Sales * 0.05 Else MsgBox "No Bonus"
```

If the value stored in the variable Sales is greater than 5000, Visual Basic will calculate the bonus using the following formula: Sales * 0.05. However, if the variable Sales is not greater than 5000, Visual Basic will display the message "No Bonus."

The If...Then...Else statement should be used to decide which of the two actions to perform.

When you need to execute more statements when the condition is true or false, it's better to use the multi-line format of the If...Then...Else statement:

```
If condition Then
      statements to be executed if condition is True
    Else
      statements to be executed if condition is False
    End If
```

Notice that the multi-line (block) If...Then...Else statement ends with the End If keywords. Use the indentation shown above to make this block structure easier to read.

In the following example, if the condition `ActiveSheet.Name = "Sheet1"` is true, Visual Basic will execute the statements between Then and Else and ignore the statement between Else and End If. If the condition is false, Visual Basic will omit the statements between Then and Else and execute the statement between Else and End If.

```
If ActiveSheet.Name = "Sheet1" Then
        ActiveSheet.Name = "My Sheet"
        MsgBox "This sheet has been renamed."
    Else
        MsgBox "This sheet name is not default."
End If
```

Let's look at the procedure example:

1. Insert a new module into the **Decisions** (Chap05.xls) project.

2. Change the module name to **IfThenElse**.

3. Enter the following WhatTypeOfDay procedure:

```
Sub WhatTypeOfDay()
    Dim response As String
    Dim question As String
    Dim strmsg1 As String, strmsg2 As String
    Dim myDate As Date

    question = "Enter any date in the format mm/dd/yyyy:" _
               & Chr(13)& " (e.g., 11/22/1999)"
        strmsg1 = "weekday"
        strmsg2 = "weekend"

        response = InputBox(question)
        myDate = Weekday(CDate(response))
        If myDate >= 2 AND myDate <= 6 Then
            MsgBox strmsg1
        Else
            MsgBox strmsg2
        End If
    End Sub
```

The above procedure asks the user to enter any date. The user-supplied string is then converted to the Date data type with the built-in CDate function. Finally, the Weekday function converts the date into an integer that indicates the day of the week (see Table 5-3). The integer is stored in the variable myDate. The conditional test is performed to check whether the value of the variable myDate is greater than or equal to two ($>=2$) and less than or equal to six ($<=6$). If the result of the test is true, the user is told that the supplied date is a weekday; otherwise, the program announces that it's a weekend.

Table 5-3: Values returned by the built-in Weekday function

Constant	Value
vbSunday	1
vbMonday	2
vbTuesday	3
vbWednesday	4
vbThursday	5
vbFriday	6
vbSaturday	7

4. Run the procedure from the Visual Basic window. Run it a few times, each time supplying a different date. Check the Visual Basic answers against your desktop or wall calendar.

Tip 5-3: What is Structured Programming?

Structured programming requires that all programs have a modular design and use only three types of logical structures: sequences, decisions, and loops. Sequences are statements that are executed one after another. Decisions allow you to execute specific statements based on a test of some condition. Loops make it possible to execute one or more statements repeatedly, as long as a specified condition is true. Loops are the subject of the next chapter. In structured programming, other logical statements, such as GoTos, are not allowed. The code of a structured program is easy to follow—it flows smoothly from top to bottom without jumping around to specified labels. Following is an example of a structured and unstructured program:

Unstructured program:
```
Sub GoToDemo()
Dim num, mystr
    num = 1
If num = 1 Then
    GoTo line1
Else
    GoTo Line2
Line1:
```
```
    mystr = "Number equals 1"
    GoTo LastLine
Line2:
    mystr = "Number equals 2"
LastLine:
    Debug.Print mystr
End sub
```

Structured program:
```
Sub Structure()
Dim num, mystr
    num = 1
    If num = 1 Then
        mystr = "Number equals 1"
        Debug.Print mystr
    Else
        mystr = "Number equals 2"
    End if
End Sub
```

When you write your VBA procedure from scratch and it needs to jump from one line of a program to another, you may be tempted to use the GoTo statement. Don't jump around. Relying on GoTo statements for changing the course of your procedure leads to confusing code referred to as spaghetti code. You can easily arrive at the required destination in your procedure by using structured programming.

Here's another practice procedure to demonstrate the use of the
If...Then...Else statement:

```
Sub EnterData()
    Dim cell As Object
    Dim strmsg As String

    On Error GoTo VeryEnd
    strmsg = "Select any cell:"
    Set cell = Application.InputBox(prompt:=strmsg, Type:=8)
    cell.Select
        If IsEmpty(ActiveCell) Then
                ActiveCell.Formula = InputBox("Enter text or number:")
            Else
                ActiveCell.Offset(1, 0).Select
        End If
    VeryEnd:
End Sub
```

The EnterData subroutine shown above prompts the user to select any cell.
The cell address is then assigned to the `cell` object variable. The
If...Then...Else structure checks if the selected cell is empty. IsEmpty is
the built-in function that is used to determine whether a variable has been
initialized. IsEmpty returns true if the variable is uninitialized. Recall that a
variable is said to be initialized when it is assigned an initial value. In this
procedure, if the active cell is empty, Visual Basic treats it as a zero-length
string (" ").

Instead of:

```
If IsEmpty(ActiveCell) Then
```

you can use the following instruction:

```
If ActiveCell.Value = "" Then
```

If the active cell is empty, the statement following Then is executed. This
statement prompts the user to enter text or number data, and once the input
is provided, the data is entered in the active cell. If the active cell is not
empty, Visual Basic will jump to the instruction following the Else clause.
This instruction will cause Visual Basic to select the next cell in the same
column.

When you run this procedure and the input box prompts you to select a
cell, click any cell in the worksheet. The selected cell address will appear in
the edit box. Click OK to exit the input box. Visual Basic will check the
contents of the selected cell and jump to the true or false section of your
procedure (the true section follows Then, and the false section follows
Else).

The If...Then...ElseIf Statement

Quite often you will need to check the results of several different conditions. To join a set of If conditions together, you can use the ElseIf clause. Using the If...Then...ElseIf statement, you can supply more conditions to evaluate than is possible with the If...Then...Else statement, which was the subject of the preceding section. Here's the syntax of the If...Then...ElseIf statement:

```
If condition1 Then
     statements to be executed if condition1 is True
ElseIf condition2 Then
     statements to be executed if condition2 is True
ElseIf condition3 Then
     statements to be executed if condition3 is True
ElseIf conditionN Then
     statements to be executed if conditionN is True
Else
     statements to be executed if all conditions are False
End If
```

The Else clause is optional; you can omit it if there are no actions to be executed when all conditions are false.

Tip 5-4: ElseIf Clause

Your procedure can include any number of ElseIf statements and conditions. The ElseIf clause always comes before the Else clause. The statements in the ElseIf clause are executed only if the condition in this clause is true.

Let's look at the following example:

```
If ActiveCell.Value = 0 Then
    ActiveCell.Offset(0, 1).Value = "zero"
    ElseIf ActiveCell.Value >0 Then
        ActiveCell.Offset(0, 1).Value = "positive"
    ElseIf ActiveCell.Value <0 Then
        ActiveCell.Offset(0, 1).Value = "negative"
End If
```

This example checks the value of the active cell and enters the appropriate label (zero, positive, negative) in the adjoining column. Notice that the Else clause is not used. If the result of the first condition (`Active.Value = 0`) is false, Visual Basic jumps to the next ElseIf statement and evaluates its condition (`ActiveCell.Value>0`). If the value is not greater than zero, Visual Basic skips to the next ElseIf and the condition `ActiveCell.Value<0` is evaluated.

Let's see how the If...Then...Else statement works in a complete procedure:

1. Insert a new module into the current project.

2. Rename the module **IfThenElseIf**.

3. Enter the following WhatValue procedure:

```
Sub WhatValue()
    Range("A1").Select
      If ActiveCell.Value = 0 Then
              ActiveCell.Offset(0, 1).Value = "zero"
          ElseIf ActiveCell.Value > 0 Then
              ActiveCell.Offset(0, 1).Value = "positive"
          ElseIf ActiveCell.Value < 0 Then
              ActiveCell.Offset(0, 1).Value = "negative"
          End If
      End If
End Sub
```

Because you need to run the WhatValue procedure several times to test each condition, let's have Visual Basic assign a temporary keyboard shortcut to this procedure.

4. Open the Immediate window and type the following statement:

```
Application.OnKey "^+y", "WhatValue"
```

When you press Enter, Visual Basic runs the OnKey method that assigns the WhatValue procedure to the key sequence Ctrl+Shift+Y. This keyboard shortcut is only temporary—it will not work when you restart Microsoft Excel. To assign the shortcut key to a procedure, use the Options button in the Macro dialog box accessed from the Tools menu in the Microsoft Excel window.

5. Now switch to the Microsoft Excel window and activate **Sheet1**.

6. Enter zero (**0**) in cell A1, and press **Ctrl+Shift+Y**. Visual Basic calls the WhatValue procedure and enters "zero" in cell B1.

7. Enter any number greater than zero in cell A1, and press **Ctrl+Shift+Y**.

   Visual Basic again calls the WhatValue procedure. Visual Basic evaluates the first condition, and because the result of this test is false, it jumps to the ElseIf statement. The second condition is true, so Visual Basic executes the statement following Then and skips over the next statements to the End If. Because there are no more statements following the End If, the procedure ends. Cell B1 now displays the word "positive."

8. Enter any number less than zero in cell A1, and press **Ctrl+Shift+Y**. This time, the first two conditions return false, so Visual Basic goes to examine the third condition. Because this test returns true, Visual Basic enters the "negative" label in cell B1.

9. Enter any text in cell A1, and press **Ctrl+Shift+Y.** Visual Basic's
    response is "positive." However, this is not a satisfactory answer. You
    may want to differentiate between positive numbers and text by dis-
    playing a "text" label. To make the WhatValue procedure smarter, you
    need to learn how to make more complex decisions by using nested
    If...Then statements.

Nested If...Then... Statements

You can make more complex decisions in your VBA procedures by placing
an If...Then or If...Then...Else statement inside another If...Then or
If...Then...Else statement. Structures in which an If statement is contained
inside another If block are referred to as nested If statements.

The following TestConditions procedure is a revised version of the
WhatValue procedure created in the previous section. The WhatValue procedure was modified to illustrate how nested If...Then statements work.

```
Sub TestConditions()
    Range("A1").Select
    If IsEmpty(ActiveCell) Then
        MsgBox "The cell is empty."
    Else
        If IsNumeric(ActiveCell.Value) Then
            If ActiveCell.Value = 0 Then
                ActiveCell.Offset(0, 1).Value = "zero"
            ElseIf ActiveCell.Value > 0 Then
                ActiveCell.Offset(0, 1).Value = "positive"
            ElseIf ActiveCell.Value < 0 Then
                ActiveCell.Offset(0, 1).Value = "negative"
            End If
        Else
            ActiveCell.Offset(0, 1).Value = "text"
        End If
    End If
End Sub
```

To make the TestConditions procedure easier to understand, each If...Then
statement is shown with different formatting. You can now clearly see that
the procedure uses three If...Then blocks.

The first If block (in bold) checks whether the active cell is empty. If
this is true, the message is displayed, and Visual Basic skips over the Else
part until it finds the matching End If. This statement is located just before
the End Sub keywords.

If the active cell is not empty, the IsEmpty (ActiveCell) condition
returns false, and Visual Basic runs the single underlined If block following
the Else formatted in bold. This (underlined) If...Then...Else statement is
said to be nested inside the first If block (in bold). This statement checks if
the value of the active cell is a number. Notice that this is done with the
help of another built-in function—IsNumeric. If the value of the active cell

is not a number, the condition is then false, so Visual Basic jumps to the statement following the underlined Else and enters "text" in cell B1.

However, if the active cell contains a number, Visual Basic runs the double-underlined If block, evaluating each condition and making the appropriate decision.

The first If block (in bold) is called the outer If statement. This outer statement contains two inner If statements (with single and double underlining).

Tip 5-5: Nesting Statements

Nesting means placing one type of control structure inside another control structure. You will see more nesting examples with the looping structures discussed in Chapter 6.

Select Case Statement

To avoid complex nested If statements that are difficult to follow, you can use the Select Case statement instead. The syntax of this statement is:

```
Select Case testexpression
Case expressionlist1
    statements if expressionlist1 matches testexpression
Case expressionlist2
    statements if expressionlist2 matches testexpression
Case expressionlistN
    statements if expressionlistN matches testexpression
Case Else
    statements to be executed if no values match testexpression
End Select
```

You can place any number of cases to test between the keywords Select Case and End Select. The Case Else clause is optional. Use it when you expect that there may be conditional expressions that return false. In the Select Case statement, Visual Basic compares each expressionlist with the value of testexpression.

Here's the logic behind the Select Case statement. When Visual Basic encounters the Select Case clause, it makes note of the value of testexpression. Then it proceeds to test the expression following the first Case clause. If the value of this expression (expressionlist1) matches the value stored in testexpression, Visual Basic executes the statements until another Case clause is encountered and then jumps to the End Select statement. If, however, the expression tested in the first Case clause does not match the testexpression, Visual Basic checks the value of each Case clause until it finds a match. If none of the Case clauses contain the expression that matches the value stored in testexpression, Visual Basic jumps to the Case Else clause and executes the statements until it encounters the End Select keywords. Notice that the Case Else clause is optional. If your procedure does not use Case Else and none of the Case clauses contain a value matching the value of the testexpression, Visual Basic jumps to the statements following End Select and continues executing your procedure.

Let's look at an example of a procedure that uses the Select Case statement. In Chapter 4, you learned about the MsgBox function that allows you to display a message with one or more buttons. You also learned that the result of the MsgBox function can be assigned to a variable. Using the Select Case statement, you can now decide which action to take based on the button the user pressed in the message box.

1. Insert a new module into the current project.

2. Rename the new module **SelectCase**.

3. Enter the following TestButtons procedure:

```
Sub TestButtons()
    Dim question As String
    Dim bts As Integer
    Dim myTitle As String
    Dim myButton As Integer

    question = "Do you want to open a new workbook?"
    bts = vbYesNoCancel + vbQuestion + vbDefaultButton1
    myTitle = "New Workbook"

    myButton = MsgBox(prompt:=question, buttons:=bts, _
                    title:=myTitle)

    Select Case myButton
        Case 6
            Workbooks.Add
        Case 7
            MsgBox "You can open a new book manually later."
        Case Else
            MsgBox "You pressed Cancel."
    End Select
End Sub
```

The first part of the TestButtons procedure displays a message with three buttons: Yes, No, and Cancel. The value of the button selected by the user is assigned to the variable myButton.

If the user clicks "Yes," the variable myButton is assigned the vbYes constant or its corresponding value—6. If the user selects "No," the variable myButton is assigned the constant vbNo or its corresponding value—7. Lastly, if Cancel is pressed, the contents of the variable myButton equals vbCancel or 2.

The Select Case statement checks the values supplied after the Case clause against the value stored in the variable myButton. When there is a match, the appropriate Case statement is executed.

The TestButtons procedure will work the same if you use the constants instead of button values:

```
Select Case myButton
    Case vbYes
        Workbooks.Add
    Case vbNo
        MsgBox "You can open a new book manually later."
    Case Else
        MsgBox "You pressed Cancel."
End Select
```

You can omit the Else clause. Simply revise the Select Case statement as follows:

```
Select Case myButton
    Case vbYes
        Workbooks.Add
    Case vbNo
        MsgBox "You can open a new book manually later."
    Case vbCancel
        MsgBox "You pressed Cancel."
End Select
```

4. Run the TestButtons procedure three times, each time selecting a different button.

Tip 5-6: Capture Errors with Case Else

Although using Case Else in the Select Case statement isn't compulsory, it's always a good idea to include one, just in case the variable you are testing has an unexpected value. The Case Else clause is a good place to put an error message.

Using Is with the Case Clause

Sometimes a decision is made based on the testexpression's condition, such as whether it is greater than, less than, equal to, or uses some other relational operator (see Table 5-1). The Is keyword lets you use a conditional expression in a Case clause. The syntax for the Select Case clause using the Is keyword is shown below:

```
Select Case testexpression
    Case Is condition1
        statements if condition1 is True
    Case Is condition2
        statements if condition2 is True
    Case Is conditionN
        statements if conditionN is True
End Select
```

For example, let's compare some numbers:

```
Select Case myNumber
    Case Is <10
        MsgBox "The number is less than 10"
    Case 11
        MsgBox "You entered eleven."
    Case Is >=100
        MsgBox "The number is greater than or equal to 100."
    Case Else
        MsgBox "The number is between 12 and 99."
End Select
```

Assuming that the variable myNumber holds 120, the third Case clause is true, and the only statement executed is the one between the Case Is >=100 and the Case Else clause.

Specifying a Range of Values in a Case Clause

In the preceding example you saw a simple Select Case statement that uses one expression in each Case clause. Many times, however, you may want to specify a range of values in a Case clause. Do this by using the To keyword between the values of expressions, as in the following example:

```
Select Case unitsSold
    Case 1 to 100
        Discount = 0.05
    Case Is <= 500
        Discount = 0.1
    Case 501 to 1000
        Discount = 0.15
    Case Is >1000
        Discount = 0.2
End Select
```

Let's analyze the above Select Case block with the assumption that the variable unitsSold currently holds the value 99. Visual Basic compares the value of the variable unitsSold with the conditional expression in the Case clauses. The first and third Case clauses illustrate how to use a range of values in a conditional expression by using the To keyword. Because unitsSold = 99, the condition in the first Case clause is true; thus, Visual Basic assigns the value 0.05 to the variable Discount.

How about the second Case clause, which is also true? Although it's obvious that 99 is less than or equal to 500, Visual Basic does not execute the associated statement Discount = 0.1. The reason for this is that once Visual Basic locates a Case clause with a true condition, it doesn't bother to look at the remaining Case clauses. It jumps over them and continues to execute the procedure with the instructions that may be following the End Select statement.

To get more practice with the Select Case statement, let's use it for a change in a function procedure. As you recall from Chapter 4, function procedures allow you to return a result to a subroutine. Suppose a subroutine has to display a discount based on the number of units sold.

You can get the number of units from the user and then run a function to figure out which discount applies.

1. Enter the following subroutine in the SelectCase module:

```
Sub DisplayDiscount()
    Dim unitsSold As Integer
    Dim myDiscount As Single
    unitsSold = InputBox("Enter the number of sold units:")
    myDiscount = GetDiscount(unitsSold)
    MsgBox myDiscount
End Sub
```

2. Enter the following function procedure:

```
Function GetDiscount(unitsSold As Integer)
    Select Case unitsSold
        Case 1 To 200
            GetDiscount = 0.05
        Case Is <=500
            GetDiscount = 0.1
        Case 501 To 1000
            GetDiscount = 0.15
        Case Is >1000
            GetDiscount = 0.2
    End Select
End Function
```

3. Place the cursor anywhere within the code of the DisplayDiscount procedure and press **F5** to run it.

   The DisplayDiscount procedure passes the value stored in the variable unitsSold to the GetDiscount function. When Visual Basic encounters the Select Case statement, it checks whether the value of the first Case clause expression matches the value stored in unitsSold. If there is a match, Visual Basic assigns a 5 percent discount (0.05) to the function name, and then jumps to the End Select keywords. Because there are no more statements to execute inside the function procedure, Visual Basic returns to the calling procedure—DisplayDiscount. Here it assigns the function's result to the variable myDiscount. The last statement displays the value of the retrieved discount in a message box.

Specifying Multiple Expressions in a Case Clause

You may specify multiple conditions within a single Case clause by separating each condition with a comma:

```
Select Case myMonth
    Case "January", "February", "March"
        Debug.Print myMonth & ": 1st Qtr."
```

```
        Case "April", "May", "June"
            Debug.Print myMonth & ": 2nd Qtr."
        Case "July", "August", "September"
            Debug.Print myMonth & ": 3rd Qtr."
        Case "October", "November", "December"
            Debug.Print myMonth & ": 4th Qtr."
    End Select
```

Tip 5-7: Multiple Conditions with Case Clause

The commas used to separate conditions within a Case clause have the same meaning as the OR operator used in the If statement. The Case clause is true if at least one of the conditions is true.

What's Next...

Conditional statements, which were introduced in this chapter, let you control the flow of your procedure. By testing the truth of a condition, you can decide which statements should be run and which ones should be skipped over. In other words, instead of running your procedure from top to bottom, line by line, you can execute only certain lines. If you are wondering what kind of conditional statement you should use, here are a few guidelines:

■ If you want to supply only one condition, the simple If...Then statement is the best choice.

■ If you need to decide which of two actions to perform, use the If...Then...Else statement.

■ If your procedure requires two or more conditions, use the If...Then...ElseIf or Select Case statements.

■ If your procedure has many conditions, use the Select Case statement. This statement is more flexible and easier to comprehend than the If...Then...ElseIf statement.

Some decisions have to be repeated. For example, you may want to repeat the same actions for each cell in a worksheet or each sheet in a workbook. The next chapter teaches you how to perform the same steps over and over again.

Chapter 6

Repeating Actions in VBA

Do Loops: Do...While and Do...Until ■ Watching a Procedure Execute ■ While...Wend Loop ■ For...Next Loop ■ For Each...Next Loop ■ Exiting Loops Early ■ Nested Loops ■ What's Next...

Now that you've learned how conditional statements can give your VBA procedures decision-making capability, it's time to get more involved. Not all decisions are easy. Sometimes you will need to perform a number of statements several times to arrive at a certain condition. On other occasions, however, after you've reached the decision, you may need to run the specified statements as long as a condition is true or until a condition becomes true. In programming, performing repetitive tasks is called *looping*. VBA has various looping structures that allow you to repeat a sequence of statements a number of times. In this chapter, you will learn how to loop through your code.

Do Loops: Do...While and Do...Until

Visual Basic has two types of Do loop statements that repeat a sequence of statements either as long as or until a certain condition is true.

The Do...While loop lets you repeat an action as long as a condition is true. This loop has the following syntax:

```
Do While condition
    statement1
    statement2
    statementN
Loop
```

When Visual Basic encounters this loop, it first checks the truth value of the condition. If the condition is false, the statements inside the loop are not executed. Visual Basic will continue to execute the program with the first statement after the Loop keyword. If the condition is true, the statements inside the loop are run one by one until the Loop statement is encountered. The Loop statement tells Visual Basic to repeat the entire process again, as long as the testing of the condition in the Do While statement is true.

Let's now see how you can put the Do...While loop to good use in Microsoft Excel. In Chapter 4, you learned how to make a decision based on the contents of a cell. Let's take it a step further and see how you can repeat the same decision for a number of cells. The decision is to apply bold formatting to any cell in a column, as long as it's not empty.

1. Open a new workbook and name it **Chap06.xls**.

2. Switch to the Visual Basic Editor screen, and change the name of the new project to **Repetition** (Chap06.xls).

3. Insert a new module into the Repetition project and rename it **DoLoops**.

4. Enter the following procedure:

```
Sub ApplyBold()
    Do While ActiveCell.Value <>""
        ActiveCell.Font.Bold = True
        ActiveCell.Offset(1, 0).Select
```

```
      Loop
   End Sub
```

5. Enter any data (text or numbers) in cells A1:A7.

6. Select cell **A1**.

7. Choose **Tools | Macro | Macros**. In the Macro dialog box, double-click the **ApplyBold** procedure (or highlight the procedure name and click **Run**).

When you run the ApplyBold procedure, Visual Basic first evaluates the condition in the Do While statement—`ActiveCell.Value <>""`. The condition says: perform the following statements as long as the value of the active cell is not an empty string (`""`). Because you have entered data in cell A1 and made this cell active (see step 6 above), the first test returns true. So Visual Basic executes the statement `ActiveCell.Font.Bold = True`, which applies bold formatting to the active cell. Next, Visual Basic selects the cell in the next row (see the Offset property in Chapter 2). Because the statement that follows is the Loop keyword, Visual Basic returns to the Do While statement and again checks the condition. If the newly selected active cell is not empty, Visual Basic repeats the statements inside the loop. This process continues until the contents of cell A8 are examined. Because this cell is empty, the condition is false, so Visual Basic skips the statements inside the loop. Because there are no more statements to execute after the Loop keyword, the procedure ends.

Let's look at another Do...While loop example. Curious to find out how to display today's date and time in Microsoft Excel's status bar? Here's how to do this for ten seconds:

```
Sub TenSeconds()
    Dim stopme
    stopme = Now + TimeValue("00:00:10")
    Do While Now < stopme
        Application.DisplayStatusBar = True
        Application.StatusBar = Now
    Loop
    Application.StatusBar = False
End Sub
```

In the above procedure, the statements inside the Do...While loop will be executed as long as the time returned by the Now function is less than the value of the variable called `stopme`. The variable `stopme` holds the current time plus ten seconds (see the online help for other examples of using the built-in TimeValue function).

The statement `Application.DisplayStatusBar` tells Visual Basic to turn on the display of the status bar. The next statement places the current date and time in the status bar. While the time is displayed (and this lasts only ten seconds), the user cannot work with the system (the mouse pointer turns into the hourglass). After the ten seconds are over (that is, when the condition Now < stopme evaluates to true), Visual Basic leaves the loop and executes the statement after the Loop keyword. This statement returns the default status bar message "Ready."

Tip 6-1: What is a Loop?

A loop is a programming structure that causes a section of a program code to execute repeatedly. VBA provides several structures to implement loops in your procedures: Do...While, Do...Until, For...Next, For...Each, and While...Wend.

The Do...While loop has an alternative syntax that lets you test the condition at the bottom of the loop in the following way:

```
Do
    statement1
    statement2
    statementN
Loop While condition
```

When you test the condition at the bottom of the loop, the statements inside the loop are executed at least once. Take a look at this example:

```
Sub SignIn()
    Dim secretCode As String
    Do
        secretCode = InputBox("Enter your secret code:")
        If secretCode = "sp1045" Then Exit Do
    Loop While secretCode <> "sp1045"
End Sub
```

Notice that by the time the condition is evaluated, Visual Basic has already executed the statements one time. In addition to placing the condition at the end of the loop, the SignIn procedure shows how to exit the loop when a condition is reached. When the Exit Do statement is encountered, the loop ends immediately.

Tip 6-2: Avoid Infinite Loops

If you don't design your loop correctly, you get an *infinite loop*—a loop that never ends. You will not be able to stop the procedure by using the Escape key. The following procedure causes the loop to execute endlessly because the user forgot to include the test condition:

```
Sub SayHello()
```

```
Do
    MsgBox "Hello."
Loop
```

To stop the execution of an infinite loop, you must press Ctrl+Break. When Visual Basic displays the message "Code execution has been interrupted," click End to end the procedure.

Another handy loop, Do...Until, allows you to repeat one or more statements until a condition becomes true. In other words, Do...Until repeats a
block of code as long as something is false. Here's the syntax:

```
Do Until condition
    statement1
    statement2
    statementN
Loop
```

Using the above syntax, you can now rewrite the previously written
ApplyBold procedure in the following way:

```
Sub ApplyBold2()
    Do Until IsEmpty(ActiveCell)
        ActiveCell.Font.Bold = True
        ActiveCell.Offset(1, 0).Select
    Loop
End Sub
```

The first line of this procedure says to perform the following statements
until the first empty cell is reached. As a result, if the active cell is not
empty, Visual Basic executes the two statements inside the loop. This process continues as long as the condition IsEmpty(ActiveCell) evaluates to
false. Because the ApplyBold2 procedure tests the condition at the beginning of the loop, the statements inside the loop will not run if the first cell is
empty. You will get the chance to try out this procedure in the next section.

Similar to the Do...While loop, the Do...Until loop has a second syntax
that lets you test the condition at the bottom of the loop:

```
Do
    statement1
    statement2
    statementN
Loop Until condition
```

If you want the statements to execute at least once, place the condition on
the line with the Loop statement no matter what the value of condition.

Let's try out the following example, which deletes each empty sheet
from a workbook.

1. Enter the DeleteBlankSheets procedure, as shown below, in the
    DoLoops module that you created earlier:

```
Sub DeleteBlankSheets()
    Dim myRange As Range
    Dim shcount As Integer
    shcount = Worksheets.Count
        Do
            Worksheets(shcount).Select
            Set myRange = ActiveSheet.UsedRange
            If myRange.Address = "$A$1" And _
                Range("A1").Value = "" Then
                    Application.DisplayAlerts = False
```

```
                    Worksheets(shcount).Delete
                    Application.DisplayAlerts = True
            End If
            shcount = shcount - 1
        Loop Until shcount = 1
    End Sub
```

2. Manually insert three worksheets into the current workbook. On one of the sheets, enter some data in cell A1. On another sheet, enter some data in cells B2 and C10. Do not enter any data on the third sheet.

3. Run the DeleteBlankSheets procedure.

When you run this procedure, Visual Basic deletes the selected sheet whenever two conditions are true—the UsedRange property address returns cell A1 and cell A1 is empty. The UsedRange property applies to the Worksheet object and contains every non-empty cell on the worksheet, as well as all the empty cells that are among them. For example, if you enter something in cells B2 and C10, the used range is $B$2:$C$10. If you later enter data in cell A1, the UsedRange will be $A$1:$C$10. The used range is bounded by the farthest upper-left and farthest lower-right non-empty cell on a worksheet.

Because the workbook must contain at least one worksheet, the code is executed until the variable shcount equals one. The statement shcount = shcount-1 makes sure that the shcount variable is reduced by one each time the statements in the loop are executed. The value of shcount is initialized at the beginning of the procedure with the following statement:

```
Worksheets.Count.
```

Notice also that when deleting sheets, Excel normally displays the confirmation dialog box. If you'd rather not be prompted to confirm the deletion, use the following statement:

```
Application.DisplayAlerts = False
```

When you are finished, turn the system messages back on with the following statement:

```
Application.DisplayAlerts = True
```

Tip 6-3: Counters

A counter is a numeric variable that keeps track of the number of items that have been processed. The Delete-BlankSheets procedure shown above declares the variable shcount to keep track of sheets that have been processed. A counter variable should be initialized (assigned a value) at the beginning of the program. This ensures you always know the exact value of the counter before you begin using it. A counter can be incremented or decremented by a specified value. See other examples of using counters with the For…Next loop later in this chapter.

Watching a Procedure Execute

When you run procedures that use looping structures, it's sometimes hard to see whether the procedure works as expected. Occasionally, you'd like to watch the procedure execute in slow motion so that you can check the logic of the program. Let's see how Visual Basic allows you to execute a procedure line by line.

1. Enter any data in cells A1:A5.

2. Select cell **A1**.

3. In the Microsoft Excel window, choose **Tools | Macro | Macros**.

4. In the Macro dialog box, select the **ApplyBold2** procedure and click the **Step Into** button. The Visual Basic Editor screen will appear with the name of the procedure highlighted in yellow (see Figure 6-1). Notice the yellow arrow at the left of the Code window.

5. Make the Visual Basic window smaller. To do this, click the **restore** button in the Visual Basic title bar and arrange the screen as shown in Figure 6-1.

6. Press **F8**. The yellow highlight in the Code window jumps to the line `DoUntil IsEmpty(ActiveCell)`.

7. Continue pressing **F8** while watching both the Code window and the worksheet window.

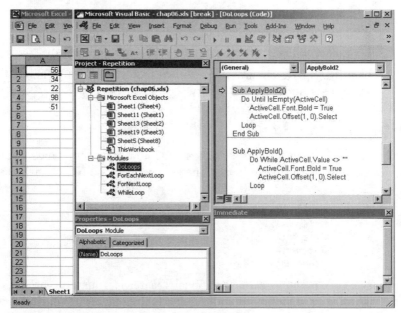

Figure 6-1: Watching the procedure code execute line by line

While...Wend Loop

The While...Wend statement is functionally equivalent to the Do...While loop. This statement is a carryover from earlier versions of Microsoft Basic and is included in VBA for backward compatibility. The loop begins with the keyword While and ends with the keyword Wend. Here is the syntax:

```
While condition
     statement1
     statement2
     statementN
Wend
```

The condition is tested at the top of the loop. The statements are executed as long as the given condition is true. Once the condition is false, Visual Basic exits the loop. Let's see an example of a procedure that uses the While...Wend looping structure.

1. Insert a new module into the current project. Rename the module **WhileLoop**.

2. Enter the following procedure in the WhileLoop module:

```
Sub ChangeRHeight()
     While ActiveCell <>""
          ActiveCell.RowHeight = 28
          ActiveCell.Offset(1, 0).Select
     Wend
End Sub
```

3. Enter some data in cells B1:B4.

4. Select cell **B1** and run the ChangeRHeight procedure.

The ChangeRHeight procedure shown above sets the row height to 28 when the active cell is not empty.

For...Next Loop

The For...Next loop is used when you know how many times you want to repeat a group of statements. The syntax of a For...Next loop looks like this:

```
For counter = start To end [Step increment]
     statement1
     statement2
     statementN
Next [counter]
```

The code in the brackets is optional. Counter is a numeric variable that stores the number of iterations. Start is the number at which you want to begin counting. End indicates how many times the loop should be executed.

For example, if you want to repeat the statements inside the loop five times, use the following For statement:

```
For counter = 1 To 5
    Your statements go here
Next
```

When Visual Basic encounters the Next keyword, it will go back to the beginning of the loop and execute the statements inside the loop again, as long as `counter` hasn't reached the `end` value. As soon as the value of `counter` is greater than the number entered after the To keyword, Visual Basic exits the loop. Because the variable `counter` automatically changes after each execution of the loop, sooner or later the value stored in `counter` exceeds the value specified in `end`.

By default, every time Visual Basic executes the statements inside the loop, the value of the variable `counter` is increased by one. You can change this default setting by using the Step clause. For example, to increase the variable `counter` by three, use the following statement:

```
For counter = 1 To 5 Step 3
    Your statements go here
Next counter
```

When Visual Basic encounters the above, it executes the statements inside the loop twice. The first time in the loop, `counter` equals 1. The second time in the loop, `counter` equals 4 (3+1). After the second time inside the loop, `counter` equals 7 (4+3). This causes Visual Basic to exit the loop.

Note that the Step increment is optional. Optional statements are always shown in square brackets (see the syntax at the beginning of this section). The Step increment isn't specified unless it's a value other than 1. You can place a negative number after Step. Visual Basic will then decrement this value from the `counter` each time it encounters the Next keyword.

The name of the variable (`counter`) after the Next keyword is also optional. However, it's good programming practice to make your Next keywords explicit by including `counter`.

How can you use the For...Next loop in a Microsoft Excel spreadsheet? Suppose in your sales report you'd like to include only products that were sold in a particular month. When you imported data from a Microsoft Access table, you also got rows with the sold amount equal to zero. How can you quickly eliminate the "zero" rows? Although there are many ways to solve this problem, let's see how you can handle it with the For...Next loop.

1. In the Visual Basic window, insert a new module into the current project and rename it **ForNextLoop**.

2. Enter the following procedure in the ForNextLoop module:

```
Sub DeleteZeroRows()
Dim totalR As Integer
Dim r As Integer
```

```
Range("A1").CurrentRegion.Select
totalR = Selection.Rows.Count
Range("B2").Select

For r = 1 To totalR-1
    If ActiveCell = 0 Then
        Selection.EntireRow.Delete
        totalR = totalR - 1
    Else
        ActiveCell.Offset(1, 0).Select
    End If
Next r
End Sub
```

3. Switch to the Microsoft Excel window and prepare the following spreadsheet:

	A	B
1	Product Name	Sales (in Pounds)
2	Apples	120
3	Pears	0
4	Bananas	100
5	Cherries	0
6	Blueberries	0
7	Strawberries	160

4. Run the DeleteZeroRows procedure.

Let's examine the DeleteZeroRows procedure line by line. The first two statements calculate the total number of rows in the current range and store this number in the variable totalR. Next, Visual Basic selects cell B2 and encounters the For keyword. Because the first row of the spreadsheet contains the column headings, decrease the total number of rows by one (totalR–1). Visual Basic will need to execute the instructions inside the loop six times.

The conditional statement (If…Then…Else) nested inside the loop tells Visual Basic to make a decision based on the value of the active cell. If the value is equal to zero, Visual Basic deletes the current row and reduces the value of totalR by one. Otherwise, the condition is false, so Visual Basic selects the next cell. Each time Visual Basic completes the loop, it jumps to the For keyword to compare the value of r with the value of totalR–1. When the procedure ends, the sales spreadsheet does not include products that were not sold.

Tip 6-4: Paired Statements

For and Next must be paired. If one is missing, Visual Basic generates the error message "For without Next."

For Each...Next Loop

When your procedure needs to loop through all of the objects of a collection or elements in an array (arrays are covered in Chapter 7), the For Each...Next loop should be used. This loop does not require a counter variable. Visual Basic can determine how many times the loop should execute.

Let's take, for example, a collection of worksheets. To remove a worksheet from a workbook, you have to first select it and then choose Edit | Delete Sheet. To leave only one worksheet in a workbook, you have to use the same command several times, depending on the total number of worksheets. Because each worksheet is an object in a collection of worksheets, you can speed up the process of deleting worksheets by using the For Each...Next loop. This loop looks like this:

```
For Each element In Group
    statement1
    statement2
    statementN
Next [element]
```

In the above syntax, element is a variable to which all the elements of an array or collection will be assigned. This variable has to be of the Variant data type for an array and an Object data type for a collection. Group is the name of a collection or an array.

Now let's use the For Each...Next loop to remove some worksheets.

1. Insert a new module into the current project and rename it **ForEachNextLoop.**

2. Type the following procedure in the ForEachNextLoop module:

```
Sub RemoveSheets()
    Dim mySheet As Worksheet
    Application.DisplayAlerts = False
    Workbooks.Add
    Worksheets("Sheet2").Select
        For Each mySheet In Worksheets
            ActiveWindow.SelectedSheets.Delete
        Next mySheet
End Sub
```

3. Run the RemoveSheets procedure.

Visual Basic will open a new workbook and delete all the sheets except for Sheet1. Notice that the variable mySheet represents an object in a collection of worksheets. Instead of declaring an object variable in a generic way as type Object, your procedure will perform better when you declare object variables according to their specific type. In this particular case, instead of Dim mySheet As Object, you can use the following declaration: Dim mySheet As Worksheet. The first instruction, Application.DisplayAlerts = False, makes sure that Excel does not display alerts and messages while the procedure is running. If you omit this statement, Excel will ask you to confirm the deletion of the selected worksheet. Next, the procedure opens a new work-book and selects Sheet2. The For Each...Next loop steps through each worksheet (starting from the selected Sheet2) and deletes it. When the procedure ends, the workbook has only one sheet—Sheet1.

Here's another example that checks whether a certain sheet is part of a workbook:

```
Sub IsSuchSheet()
Dim mySheet As Worksheet
Dim counter As Integer
counter = 0
    For Each mySheet In Worksheets
        If mySheet.name = "Sheet2" Then
            counter =counter + 1
        End If
    Next mySheet
        If counter = 1 Then
            MsgBox "This workbook contains Sheet2."
        Else
            MsgBox "Sheet2 was not found."
        End if
End Sub
```

Exiting Loops Early

Sometimes you may not want to wait until the loop ends on its own. It's possible that a user enters the wrong data, a procedure encounters an error, or perhaps the task has been completed and there's no need to do additional looping. You can leave the loop early without reaching the condition that normally terminates it. Visual Basic has two types of Exit statements:

■ The Exit For statement is used to end either a For...Next or a For Each...Next loop early.

■ The Exit Do statement immediately exits any of the VBA Do loops.

The following procedure demonstrates how to use the Exit For statement to leave the For Each...Next loop early:

1. Enter the following procedure in the current module:

```
Sub EarlyExit()
Dim myCell As Range
    For Each myCell in Range("A1:H10")
        If myCell.Value = "" Then
            myCell.Value = "empty"
        Else
            Exit For
        End If
    Next myCell
End Sub
```

The EarlyExit procedure examines the contents of each cell in the specified range—A1:H10. If the active cell is empty, Visual Basic enters the text "empty" in the active cell. When Visual Basic encounters the first non-empty cell, it exits the loop.

2. Open a new workbook and enter a value in any cell within the specified range—A1:H10.

3. Run the EarlyExit procedure.

Tip 6-5: Exiting Procedures

If you want to exit a subroutine earlier than normal, use the Exit Sub statement. If the procedure is a function, use the Exit Function statement instead.

Nested Loops

So far in this chapter you have tried out various loops. Each procedure demonstrated the use of each individual looping structure. In programming practice, however, one loop is often placed inside of another. Visual Basic allows you to "nest" various types of loops (For and Do loops) within the same procedure. When writing nested loops, you must make sure that each inner loop is completely contained inside the outer loop. Also, each loop has to have its own unique counter variable. When you use nesting loops, you can often execute the specific task more effectively.

The ColorLoop procedure shown below illustrates how one For...Next loop is nested within another For...Next loop:

```
Sub ColorLoop()
Dim myRow As Integer
Dim myCol As Integer
Dim myColor As Integer

myColor = 0
For myRow = 1 To 8
    For myCol = 1 To 7
        Cells(myRow, myCol).Select
        myColor = myColor + 1
        With Selection.Interior
            .ColorIndex = myColor
            .Pattern = xlSolid
        End With
    Next myCol
Next myRow
End Sub
```

The ColorLoop procedure shown above uses two For...Next loops to change the color of each cell located in the first eight rows and seven columns of a worksheet. While the outer loop keeps track of the row number, the inner loop does more than one thing. It determines the current column number, selects the appropriate cell based on the current row and column index, keeps track of the color index, and then applies the color to the selected cell.

The inner For…Next loop applies a different color to seven cells in the first spreadsheet row (A1, B1, C1, D1, E1, F1, and G1). When the variable myCol is greater than 7, Visual Basic jumps back to the outer loop to increment the variable myRow by one and returns to the inner loop to color the next set of cells in the second row. When the procedure ends, 56 cells (8*7) are formatted with all the colors available in the current color palette. The first cell, A1, is formatted with a black color (color index number 1). The second cell, B1, is formatted as white (color index number 2). Each time the cell address changes—Cells(myRow, myCol).Select—the contents of the variable myColor change as well—myColor = myColor + 1.

What's Next...

In this chapter you learned how to repeat certain groups of statements in procedure loops. While working with several types of loops, you saw how each loop performs repetitions in a slightly different way. As you gain experience, you'll find it easier to choose the appropriate flow control structure for your task.

In the following chapters of this book, there are many additional examples of using loops. In the next chapter, for instance, you will see how using arrays and nested loops can create a VBA procedure that picks your lottery numbers for you. In the next chapter, you will learn how to work with larger sets of data without getting lost in the sea of variables.

Chapter 7

Managing Lists and Tables of Data with VBA

Understanding Arrays ■ Declaring Arrays ■ Array Upper and Lower Bounds ■ Using Arrays in VBA Procedures ■ Arrays and Looping Statements ■ Using a Two-Dimensional Array ■ Static and Dynamic Arrays ■ **Array Functions** ■ The Array Function ■ The IsArray Function ■ The Erase Function ■ The LBound and UBound Functions ■ **Errors in Arrays** ■ **Parameter Arrays** ■ What's Next...

In previous chapters, you worked with many VBA procedures that used variables to hold specific information about an object, property, or value. For each single value that you wanted your procedure to manipulate, you declared a variable. But what if you have a series of values? If you had to write a VBA procedure to deal with larger amounts of data, you would have to create enough variables to handle all of the data. Can you imagine the nightmare of storing in your program currency exchange rates for all the countries in the world? To create a table to hold the necessary data, you'd need at least three variables for each country: country name, currency name, and exchange rate. Fortunately, Visual Basic has a way to get around this problem. By clustering the related variables together, your VBA procedures can manage a large amount of data with ease. In this chapter, you'll learn how to manipulate lists and tables of data with arrays.

Understanding Arrays

In Visual Basic an *array* is a special type of variable that represents a group of similar values that are of the same data type (String, Integer, Currency, Date, etc.). The two most common types of arrays are one-dimensional arrays (lists) and two-dimensional arrays (tables).

A one-dimensional array is sometimes referred to as a *list*. A shopping list, a list of names of the week, or an employee list are examples of one-dimensional arrays, or numbered lists. Each value in the list has an index. Below is a diagram of a list that contains six elements (items):

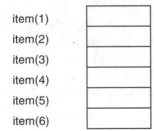

item(1)
item(2)
item(3)
item(4)
item(5)
item(6)

Notice that the column representing the one-dimensional array is currently empty. If you want to fill this array with data, instead of six individual labels, simply use one variable name followed by a number in parentheses. In the diagram above, item is a variable name and the numbers in parentheses—(1), (2), (3), (4), (5), and (6)—identify individual elements of the array.

All elements of the array must be of the same data type. In other words, one array cannot store both strings and integers. The diagrams on the following page are two examples of one-dimensional arrays: a one-dimensional array called cities is populated with text (String data type—$), and a one-dimensional array called lotto contains six lottery numbers (Integer data type—%).

One-dimensional array named cities$ (of String data type):

cities(1)	Baltimore
cities(2)	Atlanta
cities(3)	Boston
cities(4)	Washington
cities(5)	New York
cities(6)	Trenton

One-dimensional array named lotto% (of Integer data type):

lotto(1)	25
lotto(2)	4
lotto(3)	31
lotto(4)	22
lotto(5)	11
lotto(6)	5

As you can see, the contents assigned to each array element match the variable type. If you want to store values of different data types in the same array, you must declare the array as Variant.

Two-dimensional arrays are tables of data represented in rows and columns. The position of each element in a table is determined by its row and column number. Below is a diagram of an empty two-dimensional array.

rows↓	1	2	3	←columns
1	(1,1)	(1,2)	(1,3)	
2	(2,1)	(2,2)	(2,3)	
3	(3,1)	(3,2)	(3,3)	
4	(4,1)	(4,2)	(4,3)	
5	(5,1)	(5,2)	(5,3)	

Notice how items in a two-dimensional array are identified with row and column indices. In this diagram, the first element of the array is located in the first row and the first column (1, 1). The last element of the array is positioned in the fifth row and third column (5, 3). Let's now populate this array with some values. The two-dimensional array shown below stores the name of the country, its currency, and the value per U.S. dollar.

Two-dimensional array named exchange (of Variant data type):

Japan (1,1)	Japanese Yen (1,2)	128.2 (1,3)
Mexico (2,1)	Mexican Peso (2,2)	9.423 (2,3)
Canada (3,1)	Canadian Dollar (3,2)	1.567 (3,3)
Norway (4,1)	Norwegian Krone (4,2)	8.351 (4,3)
Hungary (5,1)	Hungarian Forint (5,2)	266.7 (5,3)

Although VBA arrays can have up to 60 dimensions, most people find it difficult to picture dimensions beyond 3D. A three-dimensional array is a collection of tables where each table has the same number of rows and columns. Each element of a three-dimensional array is identified by three pieces of data: row, column, and table.

Tip 7-1: What is an Array Variable?

An array is a group of variables that have a common name. While a typical variable can hold only one value, an array variable can store a large number of individual values. You refer to a specific value in the array by using the array name and an index number.

Tip 7-2: Subscripted Variables

The numbers inside the parentheses of the array variables are called subscripts, and each individual variable is called a subscripted variable or element. For example, cities(6) is the sixth subscripted variable (element) of the array cities().

Declaring Arrays

Because an array is a variable, you must declare it in a similar way that you declare other variables—by using the Dim statement. When you declare an array variable, you set aside the required memory space to hold its values.

Let's take a look at some examples of array declarations:

```
Dim cities(6) As String
Dim daysOfWeek(7) As String
Dim lotto(6) As Integer
Dim exchange(5, 3) As Variant
```

Notice that the names of variables are followed by some numbers in parentheses. One-dimensional arrays require one number between parentheses. This number specifies the maximum number of elements that can be stored in a list. The name of a two-dimensional array is always followed by two numbers—the first number is the row index, and the second number is the column index. In the example above, the exchange array can hold a maximum of 15 values (5*3=15).

The last part in the array declaration is the definition of the data type that the array will hold. An array can hold any of the following data types: Integer, Long, Single, Double, Variant, Currency, String, Boolean, Byte, or Date.

When you declare an array, Visual Basic automatically reserves enough memory space. The amount of the memory allocated depends on the array's size and data type. When you declare a one-dimensional array named lotto with six elements, Visual Basic sets aside 12 bytes—2 bytes for each element of the array (recall that the size of the Integer data type is 2 bytes, hence 2*6 = 12). The larger the array, the more memory space required to store the data. Because arrays can eat up a lot of memory and impact your computer's performance, it's recommended that you declare arrays with only as many elements as you think you'll use.

Array Upper and Lower Bounds

By default VBA assigns zero (0) to the first element of the array. Therefore, number 1 represents the second element of the array, number 2 represents the third, and so on. With numeric indexing starting at 0, the one-dimensional array cities(6) contains seven elements numbered from 0 to 6. If you'd rather start counting your array's elements at 1, you can explicitly specify a lower bound of the array by using an Option Base 1 statement. This instruction must be placed in the declaration section at the top of a VBA module before any Sub statements. If you don't specify Option Base 1 in a procedure that uses arrays, VBA assumes that the statement Option Base 0 is to be used and begins indexing your array's elements at 0.

You can have the array indexing start at a number other than 0 or 1. To do this, you must specify the bounds of an array when declaring the array variable. The bounds of an array are its lowest and highest indices. Let's take a look at the following example:

```
Dim cities(3 To 6) As Integer
```

The above statement declares a one-dimensional array with four elements. The numbers enclosed in parentheses after the array name specify the lower (3) and upper (6) bounds of the array. The first element of this array has the number 3, the second—4, the third—5, and the fourth—6. Notice the keyword To between the lower and the upper index.

Tip 7-3: The Range of the Array

The spread of the subscripts specified by the Dim statement is called the range of the array (for example: Dim mktgCodes(5 To 15)).

Using Arrays in VBA Procedures

After you declare an array, you must assign values to its elements. This is often referred to as "filling an array" or "populating an array." Let's try out a VBA procedure that uses a one-dimensional array to programmatically display a list of six American cities:

1. Open a new workbook and save it as **Chap07.xls**.
2. Switch to the Microsoft Visual Basic Editor window and rename the VBA project **Tables**.

3. Insert a new module into the Tables (Chap07.xls) project, and rename this module **StaticArrays**.

4. Enter the following FavoriteCities procedure:

```
' start indexing array elements at 1
Option Base 1

Sub FavoriteCities()

'now declare the array
Dim cities(6) As String

'assign the values to array elements
cities(1) = "Baltimore"
cities(2) = "Atlanta"
cities(3) = "Boston"
cities(4) = "Washington"
cities(5) = "New York"
cities(6) = "Trenton"

'display the list of cities

MsgBox cities(1) & Chr(13) & cities(2) & Chr(13) _
    & cities(3) & Chr(13) & cities(4) & Chr(13) _
    & cities (5) & Chr(13) & cities(6)
End Sub
```

Before the FavoriteCities procedure begins, the default indexing for an array is changed. Notice that the position of the Option Base 1 statement is at the top of the module window before the Sub statement. This statement tells Visual Basic to assign the number 1 instead of the default 0 to the first element of the array.

The array cities() is declared with six elements of String data type. Each element of the array is then assigned a value. The last statement uses the MsgBox function to display the list of cities. When you run this procedure, the city names will appear on separate lines (see Figure 7-1). You can change the order of the displayed data by switching the index values.

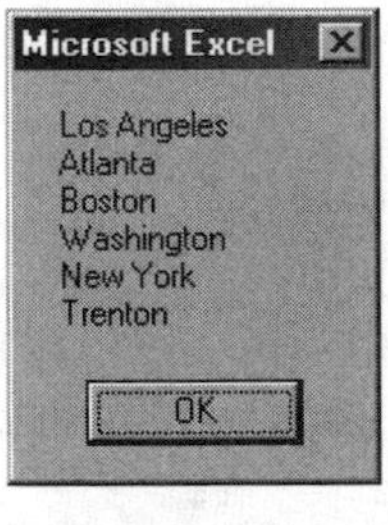

Figure 7-1:
You can display the elements of a one-dimensional array with the MsgBox function.

5. Run the FavoriteCities procedure and check the results.

6. Modify the FavoriteCities procedure so that it displays the names of the cities in the reverse order (from 6 to 1).

> **Tip 7-4: Initial Value of an Array Element**
>
> Until a value is assigned to an element of an array, the element has its default value. Numeric variables have a default value of zero (0), and string variables have the default value of the empty string ("").

Arrays and Looping Statements

Several looping statements that you learned in Chapter 6 (see the For...Next loop and For Each...Next loop) will come in handy now that you're ready to perform tasks such as populating an array or displaying the elements of an array. It's time to combine the skills you've learned so far. How can you rewrite the FavoriteCities procedure so that it shows the name of each city in a separate message box?

The FavoriteCities2 procedure shown below replaces the last statement of the original procedure with the For Each...Next loop:

```
Sub FavoriteCities2()
    'now declare the array
    Dim cities(6) As String
    Dim city As Variant

    'assign the values to array elements
    cities(1) = "Baltimore"
    cities(2) = "Atlanta"
    cities(3) = "Boston"
    cities(4) = "Washington"
    cities(5) = "New York"
    cities(6) = "Trenton"

    'display the list of cities in separate messages
    For Each city in cities
        MsgBox city
    Next
End Sub
```

Notice that the For Each...Next loop uses the variable `city` of Variant data type. As you recall from the previous chapter, For Each... Next allows you to loop through all of the objects in a collection or all of the elements of an array and perform the same action on each object or element. When you run the FavoriteCities2 procedure, the loop will execute as many times as there are elements in the array.

Let's take a look at yet another variation of the FavoriteCities procedure. In Chapter 4 you practiced passing arguments as variables to subroutines and functions. The procedure FavoriteCities3 demonstrates how you can pass elements of an array to another procedure.

1. In the current module, enter following the two procedures:

```
Sub FavoriteCities3()
    'now declare the array
    Dim cities(6) As String

    'assign the values to array elements
    cities(1) = "Baltimore"
    cities(2) = "Atlanta"
    cities(3) = "Boston"
    cities(4) = "Washington"
    cities(5) = "New York"
    cities(6) = "Trenton"

    'call another procedure and pass the array as argument
    Hallo cities()
    End Sub

Sub Hallo (cities() As String)
    Dim counter As Integer
    For counter = 1 to 6
        MsgBox "Hello " & cities(counter)
    Next
End Sub
```

The declaration of the Hallo procedure includes an array type argument —cities( ).

2. Run the FavoriteCities3 procedure. Passing array elements from a subroutine to a subroutine or function procedure allows you to reuse the same array in many procedures without unnecessary duplication of the program code.

Tip 7-5: Passing Arrays between Procedures

When an array is declared in a procedure, it is local to this procedure and unknown to other procedures. However, you can pass the local array to another procedure by using the array's name followed by an empty set of parentheses as an argument in the calling statement. For example, the statement Hallo cities() calls the procedure named Hallo and passes to it the array cities().

Here's how you can put to work your newly acquired knowledge about arrays and loops in real life. If you're an avid lotto player who is getting tired of picking your own lucky numbers, have Visual Basic do the picking. The Lotto procedure below populates an array with six numbers from 1 to 51.

```
Sub Lotto()
Const spins = 6
Const minNum = 1
Const maxNum = 51
```

```
    Dim t As Integer              'looping variable in outer loop
    Dim i As Integer              'looping variable in inner loop
    Dim myNumbers As String       'string to hold all picks
    Dim lucky(spins) As String    'array to hold generated picks

myNumbers = ""

    For t = 1 To spins
        Randomize
        lucky(t) = Int((maxNum-minNum+1) * Rnd )+ minNum)
        'see if this number was picked before
        For i = 1 To (t-1)
            If lucky(t)=lucky(i) Then
                lucky(t) = Int((maxNum-minNum+1) * Rnd)+ minNum)
                i = 0
            End If
        Next i
        MsgBox "Lucky number is " & t & lucky(t)
        myNumbers = myNumbers & " -" & lucky(t)
    Next t
    MsgBox "Lucky numbers are " & myNumbers
End Sub
```

The Randomize statement initializes the random number generator. The instruction Int((maxNum-minNum+1) * Rnd + minNum) uses the Rnd function to generate a random value between the specified minNum and maxNum. The Int function converts the resulting random number to an integer. Instead of assigning constant values for minNum and maxNum, you can use the InputBox function to get these values from the user.

The inner For...Next loop ensures that each picked number is unique—it may not be any one of the previously picked numbers. If you omit the inner loop and run this procedure multiple times, you'll likely see some occurrences of duplicate numbers pop up.

Using a Two-Dimensional Array

Now that you know how to programmatically produce a list (a one-dimensional array), it's time to take a closer look at how you can work with tables of data. The following procedure creates a two-dimensional array that will hold the country name, currency name, and exchange rate for three countries.

```
Sub Exchange()
    Dim t As String
    Dim r As String
    Dim Ex(3, 3) As Variant

        t = Chr(9)  'tab
        r = Chr(13) 'Enter

        Ex(1, 1) = "Japan"
```

```
            Ex(1, 2) = "Yen"
            Ex(1, 3) = 128.2
            Ex(2, 1) = "Mexico"
            Ex(2, 2) = "Peso"
            Ex(2, 3) = 9.423
            Ex(3, 1) = "Canada"
            Ex(3, 2) = "Dollar"
            Ex(3, 3) = 1.567
            MsgBox "Country " & t & t & "Currency" & t & "per US$" _
              & r & r _
                & Ex(1, 1) & t & t & Ex(1, 2) & t & Ex(1, 3) & r _
                & Ex(2, 1) & t & t & Ex(2, 2) & t & Ex(2, 3) & r _
                & Ex(3, 1) & t & t & Ex(3, 2) & t & Ex(3, 3), , _
                "Exchange"
        End Sub
```

When you run the Exchange procedure, you will see a message box with the information presented in three columns (Figure 7-2).

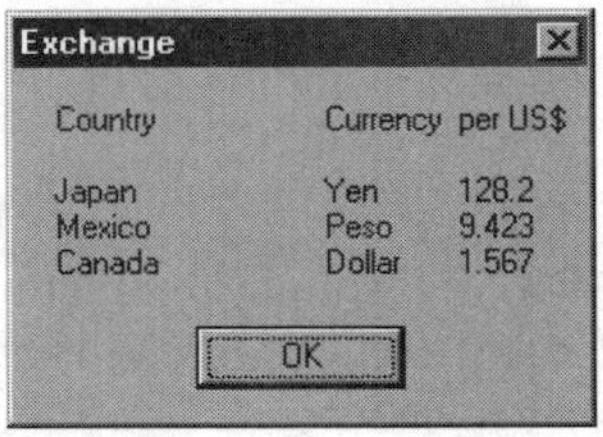

Figure 7-2:
The text displayed in a message box can be custom formatted.

Static and Dynamic Arrays

The arrays introduced so far in this chapter are static. A *static array* is an array of a specific size. Use a static array when you know in advance how big the array should be. The size of the static array is specified in the array's declaration statement. For example, the statement Dim Fruits(10) As String declares a static array called Fruits that is made up of ten elements.

But what if you're not sure how many elements your array will contain? If your procedure depends on user input, the number of user-supplied elements might vary every time the procedure is executed. How can you ensure that the array you declare is not wasting memory?

You may recall that after you declare an array, VBA sets aside enough memory to accommodate the array. If you declare an array to hold more elements than what you need, you'll end up wasting valuable computer resources. The solution to this problem is making your arrays dynamic. A *dynamic array* is an array whose size can change. You use a dynamic array when the array size is determined each time the procedure is run.

Tip 7-6: Fixed-dimension Arrays

A static array contains a fixed number of elements. The number of elements in a static array isn't going to change once it has been declared.

To declare a dynamic array, don't place a number inside the parentheses after the array name:

```
Dim Fruits( ) As String
```

A dynamic array is declared by placing empty parentheses after the array name. Before you use a dynamic array in your procedure, you must use the ReDim statement to dynamically set the lower and upper bounds of the array. The ReDim statement redimensions arrays as the code of your procedure executes. The ReDim statement informs Visual Basic about the new size of the array. This statement can be used several times in the same procedure. Now let's see how your procedure could use a dynamic array.

1. Insert a new module into the current project and rename it **DynamicArrays**.

2. Enter the following DynArray procedure:

```
Sub DynArray( )
    Dim counter As Integer
    'declare a dynamic array
    Dim myArray( ) As Integer
    'specify the initial size of the array
    Redim myArray(5)
    Workbooks.Add
    'populate myArray with values
        For counter = 1 to 5
            myArray(counter) =  counter +1
            ActiveCell.Offset(counter-1, 0).Value = myArray(counter)
        Next
    'change the size of myArray to hold 10 elements
    Redim Preserve myArray(10)
    'add new values to myArray
        For counter = 6 To 10
            myArray(counter) = counter * counter
            With ActiveCell.Offset(counter-1, 0)
                .Value = myArray(counter)
                .Font.Bold = True
            End with
    Next counter
End Sub
```

3. Set your screen so that the Microsoft Excel application window and Visual Basic Editor window are positioned side by side.

4. Run the DynArray procedure step by step. To do this, place the mouse
    pointer inside the code of this procedure and press **F8** to execute each
    statement. The result of the DynArray procedure is shown in the fol-
    lowing illustration.

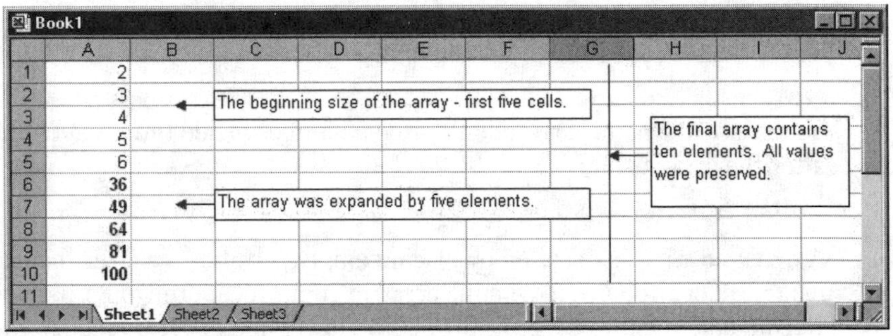

Figure 7-3: An array showing ten values

In the DynArray procedure, the statement Dim myArray() As Integer
declares a dynamic array called myArray. Although this statement declares
the array, it does not allocate any memory to the array. The first ReDim
statement specifies the initial size of myArray and reserves ten bytes of
memory for it to hold its five elements. As you know, every Integer value
requires two bytes of memory. The statement Workbooks.Add opens a new
workbook, and the For...Next loop populates myArray with data and writes
the array's elements to a worksheet. The value of the variable counter
equals 1 at the beginning of the loop. The first statement in the loop:

```
myArray(counter) =  counter + 1
```

assigns the value 2 to the first element of myArray. The second statement:

```
ActiveCell.Offset(counter-1, 0).Value = myArray(counter)
```

enters the current value of myArray's element in the active cell. The active
cell is A1. Because the variable counter equals 1, the statement above
results in the following:

```
ActiveCell.Offset(1-1, 0).Value = myArray(1)
```

or

```
ActiveCell.Offset(0,0).Value = myArray(1)
```

The above instruction enters data in cell A1. The statements inside the
loop are executed five times. Visual Basic enters data in the appropriate
worksheet cells and proceeds to the next statement:

```
ReDim Preserve myArray(10)
```

Normally, when you change the size of the array, you lose all the values that
were in that array. The ReDim statement alone reinitializes the array.

However, you can append new elements to an existing array by following the ReDim statement with the Preserve keyword. In other words, the Preserve keyword guarantees that the redimensioned array will not lose its existing data. If you omit it, the new array will be empty.

The second For…Next loop assigns values to the sixth, seventh, eighth, ninth, and tenth elements of myArray. This time, the values of the array's elements are obtained by multiplication: counter * counter. Visual Basic enters the additional array's values in the appropriate spreadsheet cells using the bold font style.

Tip 7-7: Dimensioning Arrays

Arrays must be dimensioned in a Dim or ReDim statement before they are used. This means that you can't assign a value to an array element until you have declared the array with the Dim or ReDim statement.

Array Functions

You can manipulate arrays with five built-in VBA functions: Array, IsArray, Erase, LBound, and UBound. The following sections demonstrate the use of each of these functions in VBA procedures.

The Array Function

The Array function allows you to create an array during code execution without having to dimension it first. This function always returns an array of Variants. Using the Array function, you can quickly place a series of values in a list. The CarInfo procedure shown below creates a fixed-size, one-dimensional, three-element array called auto.

1. Insert a new module into the current project and rename it **Array_Function**.

2. Enter the following CarInfo procedure:

```
Option Base 1

Sub CarInfo()
    Dim auto As Variant
    auto = Array("Ford", "Black", "1999")
  MsgBox auto(2) & " " & auto(1) & ", " & auto(3)
    auto(2) = "4-door"
    MsgBox auto(2) & " " & auto(1) & ", " & auto(3)
End Sub
```

Another example demonstrates how to use the Array function to enter column headings in a worksheet:

```
Sub ColumnHeads()
```

```
    Dim heading As Variant
    Dim cell As Range
    Dim i As Integer

    i = 1
    heading = Array("First Name", "Last Name", "Position", _
                    "Salary")
    Workbooks.Add

    For Each cell in Range("A1:D1")
        cell.Formula = heading(i)
        i = i+1
    Next

    Columns("A:D").Select
    Selection.Columns.AutoFit
    Range("A1").Select
End Sub
```

The IsArray Function

Using the IsArray function, you can test whether a variable is an array. The IsArray function returns either true, if the variable is an array, or false, if it's not an array. Here's an example:

1. Insert a new module into the current project and rename it **IsArray_Function.**

2. Enter the code of the IsThisArray procedure, as shown below:

```
Sub IsThisArray()
    'declare a dynamic array
    Dim sheetNames() As String
    Dim totalSheets As Integer
    Dim counter As Integer

    'count the sheets in the current workbook
    totalSheets = ActiveWorkbook.Sheets.Count
    'specify the size of the array
    ReDim sheetNames(1 To totalSheets)
    'enter and show the names of sheets
    For counter = 1 to totalSheets
        sheetNames(counter) = ActiveWorkbook.Sheets(counter).Name
        MsgBox sheetNames(counter)
    Next counter
    'check if this is indeed an array
    If IsArray(sheetNames) Then
        MsgBox "The sheetNames is an array."
    End If
End Sub
```

The Erase Function

When you want to remove the data from an array, you should use the Erase function. This function deletes all the data held by static or dynamic arrays. In addition, for a dynamic array, the Erase function reallocates all of the memory assigned to the array. If a procedure has to use the dynamic array again, you must use the ReDim statement to specify the size of the array. The example below shows how to erase the data from the array cities.

1.   Insert a new module into the current project and rename it **Erase_Function.**

2.   Enter the code of the FunCities procedure shown below:

```
' start indexing array elements at 1
Option Base 1

Sub FunCities()
    'declare the array
    Dim cities(1 to 5) As String

    'assign the values to array elements
    cities(1) = "Las Vegas"
    cities(2) = "Orlando"
    cities(3) = "Atlantic City"
    cities(4) = "New York"
    cities(5) = "San Francisco"

    'display the list of cities

    MsgBox cities(1) & Chr(13) & cities(2) & Chr(13)  _
        & cities(3) & Chr(13) & cities(4) & Chr(13)  _
        & cities (5)
    Erase cities
    'show all that was erased
    MsgBox cities(1) & Chr(13) & cities(2) & Chr(13)  _
        & cities(3) & Chr(13) & cities(4) & Chr(13)  _
        & cities (5)
End Sub
```

After the Erase function deletes the values from the array, the MsgBox function displays an empty message box.

The LBound and UBound Functions

The LBound and UBound functions return whole numbers that indicate the lower bound and upper bound indices of an array.

1.   Insert a new module into the current project and rename it **L_and_UBound_Function.**

2.   Enter the code of the FunCities2 procedure shown below:

```
Sub FunCities2()
    'declare the array
```

```
Dim cities(1 to 5) As String

'assign the values to array elements
cities(1) = "Las Vegas"
cities(2) = "Orlando"
cities(3) = "Atlantic City"
cities(4) = "New York"
cities(5) = "San Francisco"
'display the list of cities

MsgBox cities(1) & Chr(13) & cities(2) & Chr(13) _
    & cities(3) & Chr(13) & cities(4) & Chr(13) _
    & cities (5)

'display the array bounds
    MsgBox "The lower bound: " & LBound(cities) & Chr(13) _
        & "The upper bound: " & UBound(cities)
End Sub
```

When determining the lower- and upper-bound indices of a two-dimensional array, you must specify the dimension number: 1 for the first dimension and 2 for the second dimension.

To determine the upper and lower indices in a two-dimensional array, add the following statements at the end of the Exchange procedure that was created earlier in this chapter (add these lines of code just before the End Sub keywords):

```
MsgBox "The lower bound (first dimension) is " _
        & LBound(Ex, 1) & "."
MsgBox " The upper bound(first dimension) is " _
        & UBound(Ex, 1) & "."
MsgBox "The lower bound (second dimension) is  " _
        & LBound(Ex, 2) & "."
MsgBox " The upper bound(second dimension) is " _
        & UBound(Ex, 2) & "."
```

Errors in Arrays

When working with arrays, it's easy to make a mistake. If you try to assign more values than there are elements in the declared array, VBA will display the error message "Subscript out of range."

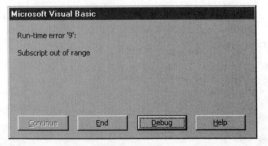

Figure 7-4:
This error was caused by an attempt to access a nonexistent array element.

Suppose you declare a one-dimensional array that consists of six elements and you are trying to assign a value to the eighth element. When you run the procedure, Visual Basic can't find the eighth element, so it displays the error message. Click the Debug button. Visual Basic will highlight the line of code that caused the error (Figure 7-5). Look at the array's declaration statement and change the index number that appears in the parentheses in the highlighted line of code.

The error "Subscript out of range" is often triggered in procedures using loops. The procedure Zoo1 shown below serves as an example of such a situation. The statements in the loop are to be executed until the user cancels out from the input box. While executing this procedure, Visual Basic will not be able to find the fourth element in a three-element array when the variable i equals 4, so the error message will appear. The modified procedure Zoo2 demonstrates how using the LBound and UBound functions introduced in the preceding section can prevent errors caused by an attempt to access a nonexistent array element.

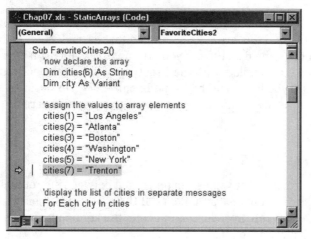

Figure 7-5:
When you click the Debug button in the error message, Visual Basic highlights the statement that triggered the error.

1. Insert a new module into the current project and rename it **Errors_In_Arrays**.

2. Enter the following procedures: Zoo1 and Zoo2:

```
Sub Zoo1()
    'this procedure triggers an error "Subscript out of range"
    Dim zoo(3) As String
    Dim i As Integer
    Dim response As String

    i = 0
    Do
        i = i +1
        response = InputBox("Enter a name of animal:")
        zoo(i) = response
```

```
          Loop until response = ""
    End Sub

    Sub Zoo2()
          'this procedure avoids the error "Subscript out of range"
          Dim zoo(3) As String
          Dim i As Integer
          Dim response As String

          i = 1
          Do While i>=LBound(zoo) And i <=UBound(zoo)
              response = InputBox("Enter a name of animal:")
              If response = "" Then Exit Sub
              zoo(i) = response
              i = i + 1
          Loop
          For i = LBound(zoo) To UBound(zoo)
              MsgBox zoo(i)
          Next
    End Sub
```

Another frequent error you may encounter while working with arrays is a
type mismatch. To avoid this error, keep in mind that each element of an
array must be of the same data type. If you attempt to assign to an element
of an array a value that conflicts with the data type of the array declared by
the Dim statement, you'll receive the "Type mismatch" error during code
execution. To hold values of different data types in an array, declare the
array as Variant.

Parameter Arrays

In Chapter 4 you learned that values can be passed between subroutines or
functions as required or optional arguments. If the passed argument is not
absolutely required for the procedure to execute, the argument's name is
preceded by the keyword Optional.

Sometimes, however, you don't know in advance how many arguments
you want to pass.

A classic example is addition. You may want to add together two numbers, or, you may use three, ten, or fifteen numbers. Using the keyword
ParamArray, you can pass an array consisting of any number of elements to
your subroutines and function procedures.

The following AddMultipleArgs function will add up as many numbers
as you require. This function begins with the declaration of an array,
myNumbers. Notice the use of the ParamArray keyword. The array must
be declared as an array of type Variant, and it must be the last argument in
the procedure definition.

1. Insert a new module into the current project and rename it
    ParameterArrays.

2. Enter the following AddMultipleArgs function procedure:

```
Function AddMultipleArgs(ParamArray myNumbers() As Variant)
     Dim mySum As Single
     Dim myValue As Variant
         For each myValue in myNumbers
             mySum=mySum+myValue
         Next
     AddMultipleArgs = mySum
End Function
```

3. To try out the above function, activate the Immediate window and type the following instruction:

```
?AddMultipleArgs(1, 23.24, 3, 24, 8, 34)
```

When you press Enter, Visual Basic returns the total of all the numbers in parentheses: 93.24. You can supply an unlimited number of arguments. To add more values, enter additional values in parentheses and press Enter. Notice that each function argument must be separated by a comma.

What's Next...

In this chapter you learned that by creating an array, you can write procedures that require a large number of variables. You worked with examples of procedures that demonstrated how to declare and use a one-dimensional array (list) and a two-dimensional array (table). You also learned the difference between a static and dynamic array. This chapter ended by introducing you to five built-in VBA functions that are frequently used with arrays, as well as the ParamArray keyword. You now know all the control structures that can make your code more intelligent: conditional statements, loops, and arrays.

Later in this book you will learn how to use collections instead of arrays to manipulate large amounts of data. By using the knowledge acquired in Chapters 1 through 7, you can now begin writing VBA procedures that can automate tasks that seemed impossible to automate before you began reading this book. The next chapter explains how to programmatically manage files and folders.

Chapter 8

Manipulating Files and Folders with VBA

Manipulating Files and Folders ■ Finding Out the Name of the Active Folder ■ Changing the Name of a File or Folder ■ Checking the Existence of a File or Folder ■ Finding Out the Date and Time the File Was Modified ■ Finding Out the Size of a File ■ Returning and Setting File Attributes ■ Changing the Default Folder or Drive ■ Creating and Deleting Folders ■ Copying Files ■ Deleting Files ■ Writing to and Reading from Files ■ **File Access Types** ■ Working with Sequential Files ■ Working with Random Access Files ■ Working with Binary Files ■ **Modern Methods of Working with Files and Folders** ■ Finding Information about Files with WSH ■ Methods and Properties of the FileSystem-Object ■ Properties of the File Object ■ Properties of the Folder Object ■ Properties of the Drive Object ■ Creating a Text File Using WSH ■ Performing Other Operations with WSH ■ **What's Next...**

In the course of your work, you've surely accessed, created, renamed, copied, and deleted hundreds of files and folders. However, you've probably never performed these tasks programmatically. So here's your chance. This chapter focuses on VBA functions and instructions that specifically deal with files and folders. By using these functions, you'll be able to:

- Find out the name of the current folder (CurDir function)
- Change the name of a file or folder (Name function)
- Check whether a file or folder exists on a disk (Dir function)
- Find out the date and time a file was last modified (FileDateTime function)
- Get the size of a file (FileLen function)
- Check and change file attributes (GetAttr and SetAttr functions)
- Change the default folder or drive (ChDir and ChDrive statements)
- Create and delete a folder (MkDir and RmDir statements)
- Copy and delete a file or folder (FileCopy and Kill statements)

In addition, this chapter gives you a working knowledge of writing to and retrieving data from three types of files: sequential, random access, and binary files. Instead of using the application's interface, you will learn how to work with files directly. At the end of this chapter, you will be introduced to the newest method of working with files and folders by utilizing the tool known as the Windows Scripting Host (WSH).

Manipulating Files and Folders

This section discusses a variety of functions for working with files and folders.

Finding Out the Name of the Active Folder (the CurDir Function)

When you work with files, you often need to find out the name of the current folder. You can get this information easily with the CurDir function:

```
CurDir([drive])
```

Drive is an optional argument. If you omit drive, VBA uses the current drive.

The CurDir function returns a file path as Variant. To return the path as String, use CurDir$ (where $ is the type declaration character for a string). To get some practice using these functions, let's perform a couple of exercises in the Immediate window:

1. Open a new workbook and switch to Microsoft Visual Basic Editor.
2. Activate the Immediate window and type the following:

```
?CurDir
```

When you press Enter, Visual Basic displays the name of the current folder. For example:

```
C:\
```

If you have a second disk drive (or a CD-ROM drive), you can find out the current folder on drive D, as follows:

```
?CurDir("D:\")
```

If you supply a letter for a drive that does not exist, Visual Basic will display the following error message: "Device unavailable."

3. To store the name of the current disk drive in a variable called myDrive, enter the following:

```
myDrive = Left(CurDir$,1)
```

When you press Enter, Visual Basic will store the letter of the current drive in the variable myDrive.

To check the contents of the variable myDrive, type the following and press **Enter**:

```
?myDrive
```

You can modify the above instruction, as follows:

```
myDrive = left(CurDir$,1) & ":"
```

Visual Basic will return the letter of the drive followed by the colon.

Changing the Name of a File or Folder (the Name Function)

To rename a file or folder, use the Name function, as follows:

```
Name old_pathname As new_pathname
```

Old_pathname is the name and path of a file or folder that you want to rename. New_pathname specifies the new name and location of the file or folder. Using the Name function, you can move a file from one folder to another; however, you can't move a folder.

Try this function out in the Immediate window (replace the example names with the actual names of your files). Here are some precautions to consider:

■ The filename in new_pathname may not refer to a file that already exists.

```
Name "C:\System.1st " As "C:\test.txt"
```

Because the file C:\test.txt already exists on drive C, Visual Basic displays the following error message: "File already exists." Similarly, the "File not found" error message will appear if the file you want to rename does not exist.

- If new_pathname already exists, and it's different from old_pathname, the Name function moves the specified file to a new folder and changes its name, if necessary.

  ```
  Name "C:\System.1st " As "D:\test.txt"
  ```

  Because the test.txt file doesn't exist in the root directory on drive D, Visual Basic moves the C:\System.1st file to the specified drive; however, it does not rename the file.

- If new_pathname and old_pathname refer to different directories and both supplied filenames are the same, the Name function moves the specified file to a new location without changing the filename.

  ```
  Name "D:\test.txt " As "C:\DOS\test.txt"
  ```

  The above instruction moves the test.txt file to the DOS folder on drive C.

Tip 8-1: You Can't Rename an Open File

You must close the file before renaming it. The name of the file cannot contain the wildcard characters * or ?.

Checking the Existence of a File or Folder (the Dir Function)

The Dir function, which returns the name of a file or folder, has the following syntax:

```
Dir[(pathname[, attributes])]
```

Both arguments of the Dir function are optional. pathname is a name of a file or folder. You can use one of the following constants or values for the attributes argument:

Table 8-1: File attributes

Constant	Value	Attribute Name
vbNormal	0	Normal
vbHidden	2	Hidden
vbSystem	4	System
vbVolume	8	Volume label
vbDirectory	16	Directory or Folder

The Dir function is often used to check whether a file or folder exists on a disk. If a file or folder does not exist, the null string ("") is returned.

Let's try out the Dir function in several exercises in the Immediate window:

1. In the Immediate window, enter the following:

```
?Dir("C:\", vbNormal)
```

As soon as you press Enter, Visual Basic returns the name of the first file in the specified folder. A normal file (vbNormal) is any file, except for one with a Hidden, Volume Label, Directory, Folder, or System file attribute.

To return the names of other files in the current directory, use the Dir function without an argument:

```
?Dir                    (and press Enter)
```

2. Enter the following instructions in the Immediate window and examine their results as you press Enter:

```
mfile = Dir("C:\", vbHidden)
?mfile
mfile = Dir
?mfile
mfile = Dir
?mfile
```

3. Enter the following instruction in the Immediate window:

```
If Dir("C:\stamp.bat") = "" Then Debug.Print "File was not found."
```

Because the stamp.bat file doesn't exist on drive C, Visual Basic writes in the Immediate window the specified text message: "File was not found."

4. To find out whether a file exists on a disk, enter the following statement on one line in the Immediate window:

```
If Dir ("C:\Autoexec.bat") <>"" Then Debug.Print "This file
    exists on your C drive."
```

The Dir function allows you to use the wild cards in the specified pathname—asterisk (*) for multiple characters and question mark (?) for a single character. For example, to find all the configuration settings files in the WINDOWS folder, you can look for all the INI files, as shown below:

```
?Dir("C:\WINNT\*.ini", vbNormal)
system.ini
?dir
WIN.INI
?dir
WINFILE.INI
?dir
control.ini
?dir
EQUIP32.INI
?dir
sxpwin32.ini
```

The procedure shown below writes the names of files in the specified directory to the Immediate window. The LCase$ function causes the names of files to appear in lowercase.

1. Open a new workbook and save it in the **Chap08.xls** file.

2. Switch to the Visual Basic Editor window and rename the VBA project **FileMan**.

3. Insert a new module into the FileMan project and rename it **DirFunction**.

4. Enter the following VBA procedure in the Code window:

```
Sub MyFiles()
Dim mfile As String
Dim mpath As String

mpath = InputBox("Enter pathname,e.g., C:\Excel")
If Right(mpath, 1) <> "\" Then mpath = mpath & "\"

mfile = Dir(mpath & "*.*")
If mfile <> "" Then Debug.Print "Files in the " & mpath _
        & "folder"
Debug.Print LCase$(mfile)
    If mfile = "" Then
        MsgBox "No files found."
    Exit Sub
    End If
    Do While mfile <> ""
        mfile = Dir
        Debug.Print LCase$(mfile)
    Loop
End Sub
```

The MyFiles procedure shown above asks the user for the pathname. If the path does not end with the backslash, the Right function appends the backslash to the end of the pathname string. Next, Visual Basic searches for all the files (*) in the specified path. If there are no files, a message is displayed. If files exist, the filenames are written to the Immediate window.

5. Enter another procedure in the same module:

```
Sub GetFiles()
Dim nfile As String
Dim nextRow As Integer      'next row index
nextRow = 1

    With Worksheets("Sheet1").Range("A1")
        nfile = Dir("C:\", vbNormal)
        .Value = nfile
            Do While nfile <> ""
                nfile = Dir
                .Offset(nextRow, 0).Value = nfile
                nextRow = nextRow + 1
```

```
                  Loop
           End With
       End Sub
```

The GetFiles procedure gets the names of files located in the root directory of drive C and writes each filename into a worksheet.

Finding Out the Date and Time the File Was Modified (the FileDateTime Function)

If your procedure must check when a file was last modified, use the FileDateTime function:

```
FileDateTime(Pathname)
```

`Pathname` is a string that specifies the file you want to work with and may include the drive and folder where the file resides. The function returns the date and time stamp for the specified file. The date and time format depends on the regional settings selected in the Windows Control Panel.

Let's practice using this function in the Immediate window:

1. Enter in the Immediate window:

    ```
    ?FileDateTime("C:\config.sys")
    ```

    When you press Enter, Visual Basic returns the date and time stamp in the following format:

    ```
    5/4/2001 10:52:00 AM
    ```

    To return date and time separately, use the FileDateTime function as an argument of the DateValue or TimeValue functions. For instance:

    ```
    ?DateValue(FileDateTime("C:\config.sys"))
    ?TimeValue(FileDateTime("C:\config.sys"))
    ```

2. Enter the following statement on one line in the Immediate window:

    ```
    If DateValue(FileDateTime("C:\config.sys"))< Date then Debug.Print
        "This file was not modified today."
    ```

    The Date function returns the current system date as it is set in the Date/Time dialog box accessed in the Windows Control Panel.

Finding Out the Size of a File (the FileLen Function)

If you want to check whether a certain file will fit on a diskette, you should use the FileLen function in the following form:

```
FileLen(Pathname)
```

`Pathname` is a string that specifies the file you want to work with and may include the drive and folder where the file resides. The FileLen function returns the size of a file in bytes. If the file is open, Visual Basic returns the size of the file when it was last saved.

Suppose that you want to find out the total size of all the files that store the configuration settings in the Windows directory.

1. Insert into the current project a new module and rename it **FileLenFunction**.

2. Enter the TotalBytesIni procedure in the Code window:

```
Sub TotalBytesIni()
    Dim iniFile As String
    Dim allBytes As Long

    iniFile = Dir("C:\WINDOWS\*.ini")
    allBytes = 0
        Do While iniFile <> ""
            allBytes = allBytes + FileLen("C:\WINDOWS\" & iniFile)
            iniFile = Dir
        Loop
    Debug.Print "Total bytes: " & allBytes
End Sub
```

Returning and Setting File Attributes (the GetAttr and SetAttr Functions)

Files and folders can have characteristics such as "read-only," "hidden," "system," and "archive."

These characteristics are called attributes. To find out the attributes of a file or folder, use the GetAttr function. The only argument of this function is the name of the file or folder that you want to work with:

```
GetAttr(Pathname)
```

The above function returns an integer that represents the sum of one or more of the constants shown below:

Table 8-2: File and folder attributes

Constant	Value	Attribute
VbNormal	0	Normal (other attributes are not set)
VbReadOnly	1	Read-only (file or folder can't be modified)
vbHidden	2	Hidden (file or folder isn't visible under normal setup)
vbSystem	4	System file
vbDirectory	16	The object is a directory
vbArchive	32	Archive (the file has been modified since it was last backed up)

To find out whether a file has any of the attributes shown above, use the AND operator to compare the result of the GetAttr function with the value of the constant. If the function returns a non-zero value, the file or folder specified in the pathname has the attribute for which you are testing.

What are the attributes of C:\MsDos.sys? You can find out quickly in the Immediate window:

```
?getattr("C:\MsDos.sys") AND vbReadOnly
 1
?getattr("C:\MsDos.sys") AND vbHidden
 2
?getattr("C:\MsDos.sys") AND vbSystem
 4
?getattr("C:\MsDos.sys") AND vbArchive
 32
```

Now let's put this information together in a procedure:

1. Insert a new module and rename it **GetAttrFunction**.

2. Enter the following GetAttributes procedure:

```
Sub GetAttributes()
Dim attr As Integer
Dim msg As String

attr = GetAttr("C:\MSDOS.SYS")
msg = ""

If attr AND vbReadOnly Then msg = msg & "Read-Only (R)"
If attr AND vbHidden Then msg = msg & Chr(10) & "Hidden (H)"
If attr AND vbSystem Then msg = msg & Chr(10) & "System (S)"
If attr AND vbArchive Then msg = msg & Chr(10) & "Archive (A)"
MsgBox msg, , "MSDOS.SYS"
End Sub
```

3. When you run the above procedure, you should see the message box shown in Figure 8-1.

Figure 8-1:
You can get the attributes of any file using the GetAttr function.

The opposite of the GetAttr function is the SetAttr function, which allows you to set the attributes for a file or a folder. Its syntax is:

```
SetAttr Pathname, Attributes
```

Pathname is a string that specifies the file or folder that you want to work with. The second argument, Attributes, is one or more constants that specify the attributes you want to set. See Table 8-1 earlier in this section for the list of constants.

Suppose you have a file called "C:\stamps.txt" and you want to set two attributes, "read-only" and "hidden." To set the file attributes, enter the following instruction in the Immediate window (replace the "C:\stamps.txt" with the name of a file that exists on your disk):

```
SetAttr "C:\stamps.txt", vbReadOnly + vbHidden
```

Tip 8-2: Invoking the SetAttr Statement

You cannot set the attributes of an open file. You must close the file before using the SetAttr function.

Changing the Default Folder or Drive (the ChDir and ChDrive Statements)

You can easily change the default folder by using the ChDir statement, as follows:

```
ChDir Path
```

In the statement above, Path is the name of the new default folder. Path may include the name of the disk drive. If Path doesn't include a drive designation, the default folder will be changed on the current drive. The current drive will not be changed.

Suppose the default folder is "C:\DOS." The statement:

```
ChDir "D:\MyFiles"
```

changes the default folder to "D:\MyFiles"; however, the current drive is still drive C.

To change the current drive, you should use the ChDrive statement in the following format:

```
ChDrive drive
```

The drive argument specifies the letter of the new default drive. For instance, to change the default drive to drive D or E, enter one of the following instructions in the Immediate window:

```
ChDrive "D"
```

or

```
ChDrive "E"
```

If you refer to a nonexistent drive, you will get the message "Device unavailable."

Creating and Deleting Folders (the MkDir and RmDir Statements)

You can create a new folder using the following syntax of the MkDir statement:

```
MkDir Path
```

Path specifies the new folder that you want to create. If you don't include the name of the drive, Visual Basic will create the new folder on the current drive. Let's run through some examples:

1. Enter the instruction in the Immediate window to create a folder called "Mail" on drive C:

   ```
   MkDir "C:\Mail"
   ```

2. Change the default folder to "C:\Mail":

   ```
   ChDir "C:\Mail"
   ```

3. Find out the name of the active folder:

   ```
   ?CurDir
   ```

   To delete a folder you no longer need, use the RmDir function. This function has the following syntax:

   ```
   RmDir Path
   ```

   Path specifies the folder you want to delete. Path may include the drive name. If you omit the name of the drive, Visual Basic will delete the folder on the current drive if a folder with the same name exists. Otherwise, Visual Basic will display the error message "Path not found."

4. Delete the C:\Mail folder that was created earlier:

   ```
   RmDir "C:\Mail"
   ```

Tip 8-3: RmDir Removes Empty Folders

You cannot delete a folder if it still contains files. You should first delete the files with the Kill statement (discussed later in this chapter).

Copying Files (the FileCopy Statement)

To copy files between folders, use the FileCopy statement shown below:

```
FileCopy source, destination
```

The first parameter of this statement, source, specifies the name of the file that you want to copy. The name may include the drive in which the file resides. The second parameter, destination, is the name of the destination file that can include the drive and folder designation. Both parameters are required.

Suppose you want to copy a file specified by a user to a folder called C:\Abort. The procedure shown below demonstrates how to do this:

```
Sub CopyToAbort()
    Dim folder As String
    Dim source As String
    Dim dest As String
    Dim msg1 As String
    Dim msg2 As String
    Dim p As Integer
    Dim s As Integer
    Dim i As Long

    On Error GoTo ErrorHandler

    folder = "C:\Abort"
    msg1 = "The selected file is already in this folder."
    msg2 = "was copied to"
    p = 1
    i = 1
    ' get the name of the file from the user
    source = Application.GetOpenFilename
    ' don't do anything if cancelled
    If source = "False" Then Exit Sub
    ' get the total number of backslash characters "\" in the source
    ' variable's contents
    Do Until p = 0
        p = InStr(i, source, "\", 1)
        If p = 0 Then Exit Do
        s = p
        i = p + 1
    Loop
    ' create the destination file name
    dest = folder & Mid(source, s, Len(source))
        ' create a new folder with this name
        MkDir folder
        ' check if the specified file already exists in the
        ' destination folder
        If Dir(dest) <> "" Then
            MsgBox msg1
        Else
        ' copy the selected file to the C:\Abort folder
            FileCopy source, dest
```

```
          MsgBox source & " " & msg2 & " " & dest
      End If
      Exit Sub
ErrorHandler:
If Err = "75" Then
    Resume Next
End If
If Err = "70" Then
    MsgBox "You can't copy an open file."
    Exit Sub
End If
End Sub
```

The procedure CopyToAbort uses the Excel application method called GetOpenFilename to get the name of the file from the user. This method causes the built-in Open dialog box to pop up. Using this dialog box, you can choose any file, in any directory, and on any disk drive. If the user cancels, Visual Basic returns the value "False" and the procedure ends. If the user selects a file and clicks Open, the selected file will be assigned to the variable source. Because for the purpose of copying you'll only need the filename (without the path), the Do...Until loop finds out the position of the last backslash ("\") in the file stored in the variable source.

Next, Visual Basic prepares a string of characters for the second argument of the FileCopy statement and assigns it to the variable dest. This variable holds the string obtained by concatenating the name of the destination folder (C:\Abort) with the user-specified filename preceded by a backslash ("\"). The MkDir function creates a new folder called C:\Abort if it doesn't yet exist on drive C. If such a folder already exists, Visual Basic will need to deal with error 75. This error will be caught by the error handler code included at the end of the procedure. Notice that the error handler is a fragment of code that begins with the label ErrorHandler followed by a colon.

When Visual Basic encounters the Resume Next statement, it will continue to execute the procedure from the instruction following the instruction that caused the error. This means that the statement MkDir folder won't be executed. After that, the procedure checks whether the selected file already exists in the destination folder. If the file already exists there, the user will get a message stored in the variable msg1. If the file does not exist in the destination folder and the file is not currently open, Visual Basic will copy the file to the specified folder and notify the user with the appropriate message. If the file is open, Visual Basic will encounter run-time error 70, and therefore it will run the corresponding instructions in the ErrorHandler section of the procedure.

1.   Enter the procedure CopyToAbort in a new module called **FileCopyStatement**.

2.   Run this procedure several times, selecting files from different folders.

3. Try to copy a file that was copied before by this procedure to the C:\Abort folder.

4. Open one file and try to copy it while it's open by using the CopyToAbort procedure.

5. Run the procedure MyFiles prepared earlier in this chapter to write to the Immediate window the contents of the folder C:\Abort.

Note: Do not delete the C:\Abort folder or the files that you have copied to it. You'll delete both the folder and the files in the next section with the VBA procedure called RemoveMe.

Deleting Files (the Kill Statement)

You already know from one of the earlier sections that you can't delete a folder if it still contains files. To delete the files from any folder, use the following Kill statement:

```
Kill Pathname
```

Pathname specifies the names of one or more files that you want to delete. Optionally, Pathname may include the drive and folder name where the file resides. To enable quick deletion of files, you can use the wildcard characters (* or ?) in the Pathname argument. You can't delete a file that is open.

If you worked through the exercises in the preceding section, your hard drive now contains the folder C:\Abort with several files. In the following exercises, you'll first delete all the files from the Abort folder and then delete the folder itself:

1. Insert a new module into the current project and rename it **KillStatement**.

2. Enter the code of the RemoveMe procedure, as shown below:

```
Sub RemoveMe()
    Dim folder As String
    Dim myFile As String

    'assign the name of folder to the folder variable
    'notice the ending backslash "\"
    folder = "C:\Abort\"
    myFile = Dir(folder, vbNormal)
    Do While myFile <> ""
        Kill folder & myFile
        myFile = Dir
    Loop
    RmDir folder
End Sub
```

3. Run the RemoveMe procedure. When the procedure ends, check Windows Explorer to see if the folder was removed.

Writing to and Reading from Files (Input/Output)

You already know from the preceding chapters how to open a spreadsheet file with VBA. For example, the instruction:

```
Application.Workbooks.Open Filename:= "C:\Excel\Report.xls"
```

opens the Report.xls workbook located in the folder C:\Excel. If, in addition to opening files within a particular application, you also want to create VBA procedures that are capable of opening other types of files and working with their contents, you should learn a few things about the process known as low-level file I/O (input/output). The following sections of this chapter on sequential, ramdom, and binary files will put you in direct contact with your data.

File Access Types

There are three types of files used by a computer:

- **Sequential access files** are files where data is retrieved in the same order as it is stored, such as files stored in the CSV format (comma-delimited text), TXT format (text separated by tabs), or PRN format (text separated by a space). Sequential file access is often used for writing text files, such as error logs, configuration settings, and reports. Sequential files have the following modes: Input, Output, and Append. The mode specifies how you can work with a file after it has been opened.

- **Random access files** are text files where data is stored in records of equal length and in fields separated by commas. Random access files have only one mode—Random.

- **Binary access files** are graphic files and other non-text files. Binary files can only be accessed in a Binary mode.

Working with Sequential Files

The hard drive of your computer contains hundreds of sequential files. Configuration files, error logs, HTML files, and all sorts of plain text files are all sequential files. These files are stored on disk as a sequence of characters. The beginning of a new text line is indicated by two special characters. One is called the *carriage return* and the other *line feed*. When you work with sequential files, you start at the beginning of the file and move forward character by character, line by line, until you encounter the end of the file. Sequential access files can be easily opened and manipulated by just about any text editor.

Tip 8-4: What is a Sequential File?

A sequential file is one in which the records must be accessed in the order they occur in the file. This means that before you can access the third record, you must first access record number 1 and then record number 2.

Tip 8-5: Opening Files with the Open Statement

When you use sequential access to open a file for input, the file must already exist.

Reading Data Stored in Sequential Files

Let's take one of the sequential files that is already present on your computer and read its contents with VBA straight from the Microsoft Excel Visual Basic Editor window. You can read the Autoexec.bat file or any other text file that you want. To read data from a file, you must first open the file with the Open statement. Here's the general syntax of this statement, followed by an explanation of each component:

```
Open pathname For mode [Access access][lock] As [#]filenumber
    [Len=reclength]
```

The Open statement has three required arguments. They are: `pathname`, `mode`, and `filenumber`. In the syntax shown above, these arguments are preceded by keywords that appear in bold.

- `Pathname` is the name of the file you want to open.
- `Pathname` may include the name of a drive and folder.
- `Mode` is a keyword that determines how the file was opened. Sequential files can be opened in one of the following modes: Input, Output, or Append. Use Input to read the file, Output to write to a file by overwriting any existing file, and Append to write to a file by appending any existing information.
- `Access` is a keyword that determines the file's read and write permissions. `Access` can be: Shared, Lock Read, Lock Write, or Lock Read Write.
- `Lock` determines which file operations are allowed for other processes. For example, if a file is open in a network environment, `lock` determines how other people can access it. The following `lock` keywords can be used: Read, Write, or Read Write.
- `Filenumber` is a number from 1 to 511. This number is used to refer to the file in subsequent operations. You can obtain a unique file number by using the Visual Basic built-in FreeFile function.
- The last element of the Open statement, `reclength`, specifies the total number of characters in the sequential files or the size of the record for random access files.

Taking the preceding into consideration, to open C:\Autoexec.bat or any other sequential file in order to read its data, you should use the following instruction:

```
Open "C:\Autoexec.bat" For Input As #1
```

If a file is opened for input, it can only be read from. After you open a sequential file, you can read its contents with the following statements: Line Input # or Input # or by using the Input function.

Reading a File Line by Line

To read the contents of the Autoexec.bat or any other sequential file line by line, use the following Line Input # statement:

Line Input #filenumber, variableName

#filenumber is the file number that was used in the process of opening the file with the Open statement. variableName is a String or Variant variable that will store the line being read.

The statement Line Input # reads a single line in an open sequential file and stores it in a variable. Bear in mind that the Line Input # statement reads the sequential file one character at a time, until it encounters a carriage return (Chr(13)) or a carriage return-linefeed sequence (Chr(13) & Chr(10)). These characters are omitted from the text retrieved in the reading process.

The ReadMe procedure that follows demonstrates how you can use the Open and Line Input# statements to read the contents of the Autoexec.bat file line by line. Try to apply the same method for reading other sequential files.

1. Insert a new module into the current project and rename it **SeqFiles**.

2. Enter the ReadMe procedure shown below:

```
Sub ReadMe()
    Dim rLine As String
    Dim i As Integer            ' line number
    i = 1

    Open "C:\Autoexec.bat" For Input As #1
    ' stay inside the loop until the end of file is reached
    Do While Not EOF(1)
        Line Input #1, rLine
        MsgBox "Line " & i & " in Autoexec.bat reads: " _
        & Chr(13) & Chr(13) & rLine
        i = i + 1
    Loop
    MsgBox i & " lines were read."
    Close #1
End Sub
```

3. Execute the procedure step by step by pressing **F8**.

The ReadMe procedure opens the Autoexec.bat file in the Input mode as file number 1 in order to read its contents. The Do...While loop tells Visual Basic to execute the statements inside the loop until the end of the file has been reached. The end of the file is determined by the result of the EOF function.

The EOF function returns a logical value of true if the next character to be read is past the end of the file. Notice that the EOF function requires one argument—the number of the open file you want to check. This is the same number that has been used previously by the Open statement. Use the EOF function to ensure that Visual Basic doesn't read past the end of the file.

The Line Input # statement stores each line's contents in the variable rLine. Next, a message is displayed that shows the line number and its contents. Then, VBA increases the line counter by one and begins reading the next line in the open file if the result of the EOF function is false (the end of the file has not been reached). Visual Basic exits the Do...While loop when the result of the EOF function is true. Before VBA ends the procedure, two more statements are executed. A message is displayed with the total number of lines that have been read. The last statement closes the open file.

Reading Characters from Sequential Files

Suppose that your procedure needs to check how many colons appear in the Autoexec.bat file. Instead of reading entire lines, you can use the Input function to return the specified number of characters. Next, the If statement can be used to compare the obtained character against the one you are looking for. Before you write a procedure that does this, let's review the syntax of the Input function:

```
Input(number, [#]filenumber)
```

Both arguments of the Input function are required. number specifies the number of characters you want to read, and filenumber is the same number that the Open statement had used to open the file. The Input function returns all the characters being read, including commas, carriage returns, end of file markers, quotes, and leading spaces.

1. In the SeqFile module, enter the Colons procedure:

```
Sub Colons()
    Dim counter As Integer
    Dim char As String
    counter = 0

    Open "C:\Autoexec.bat" For Input As #1
    Do While Not EOF(1)
        char = Input(1, #1)
        If char = ":" Then
            counter = counter + 1
        End If
    Loop
```

```
        If counter <> 0 Then
            MsgBox "Characters found: " & counter
        Else
            MsgBox "The specified character has not been found."
        End If
        Close #1
    End Sub
```

2. Execute the procedure step by step.

3. Replace the colon character with any other character you'd like to find and execute the procedure again.

The Input function allows you to return any character from the sequential file. And if you use the Visual Basic function called LOF as the first argument of the Input function, you'll be able to quickly read the contents of the sequential file without having to loop through the entire file. The LOF function returns the number of bytes in a file. Each byte corresponds to one character in a text file. The ReadAll procedure shows how to read the contents of the System.ini file to the Immediate window:

```
    Sub ReadAll()
        Dim all As String
        Open "C:\WINNT\System.ini.bat" For Input As #1
        all = Input(LOF(1), #1)
        Debug.Print all
        Close #1
    End Sub
```

Instead of printing the file contents to the Immediate window, you can read it into a text box placed in a worksheet (see Figure 8-2). The procedure that does this is shown here:

```
    Sub WriteToTextBox()
        Dim mysheet As Worksheet
        Set mysheet = ActiveWorkbook.Worksheets(1)
        On Error GoTo CloseFile
        Open "C:\WINNT\System.ini" For Input As #1
        mysheet.Shapes(1).Select
        Selection.Characters.Text = Input(LOF(1), #1)
    CloseFile:
        Close #1
    End Sub
```

Before you run the above procedure, draw a text box on Sheet1 in the Chap08.xls workbook. Notice that the statement On Error GoTo CloseFile activates error trapping. If an error occurs during the execution of a line of the procedure, the program will jump to the error-handling routine that follows the CloseFile label. The statement Close #1 will be executed, whether or not the program encounters an error.

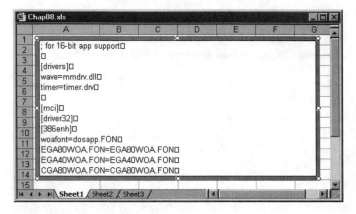

Figure 8-2:
The contents of the System.ini file are displayed in a text box placed in an Excel worksheet.

Reading Delimited Text Files

In some text files (files usually saved in CSV, TXT, or PRN format), data entered on each line of text is separated (or delimited) with a comma, tab, or space character. These types of files can be read faster with the Input # statement rather than the Line Input # statement introduced in the preceding sections. The Input # statement allows you to read data from an open file into several variables. This function looks like the following:

```
Input #filenumber, variablelist
```

filenumber is the same file number that was opened with the Open statement. variablelist is a comma-separated list of variables that you will want to use to store the data being read. You can't use arrays or object variables. You may, however, use a user-defined variable (this type of variable is explained later in this chapter).

An example of a sequential file with comma-delimited values is shown below:

```
Smith,John,15
Malloney,Joanne,28
Ikatama,Robert,15
```

To read text formatted in this way, you must specify one variable for each item of data: last name, first name, and age.

1. Open a new workbook and enter the data shown below:

	A	B	C
1	Smith	John	15
2	Malloney	Joanne	28
3	Ikatama	Robert	15

2. Save the file as **C:\Winners** in the **CSV** format (comma-delimited). Excel will display a message that the selected file type does not

support workbooks that contain multiple sheets. Click **OK** to save only the current sheet.

3. Enter the Winners procedure shown below:

```
Sub Winners()
    Dim lname As String, fname As String, age As Integer

    Open "C:\Winners.csv" For Input As #1
    Do While Not EOF(1)
        Input #1, lname, fname, age
        MsgBox lname & ", " & fname & ", " & age
    Loop
    Close #1
End Sub
```

4. Before you run the Winners procedure, make sure that the file is in the specified path or change the path in the code of this procedure to point to the actual location of the Winners.csv file on your hard drive.

The above procedure opens the Winners.csv file for input and sets up a Do...While loop that runs through the entire file until the end of the file is reached. The Input #1 statement is used to write the contents of each line of text into three variables: lname, fname, and age. Then a message box displays the contents of these variables. The procedure ends by closing the Winners.csv file.

Writing Data to Sequential Files

When you want to write data to a sequential file, you should open the file in the Append or Output mode. The differences between these modes are explained below:

- **Append** allows adding data to the end of an existing text file. For example, if you open the Readme.txt file in the Append mode and add to this file the text "Thank you for reading this document," Visual Basic won't delete or alter in any way the text that is currently in the file but will add the new text to the end of the file.

- **Output**. When you open a file in the Output mode, Visual Basic will delete the data that is currently in the file, and if the file does not exist, a brand new file will be created. For example, if you open the Readme.txt file in the Output mode and attempt to write some text to it, the previous text that was stored in this file will be removed. If you don't back up the file prior to writing the data, this mistake may be quite costly. You should open an existing file in the Output mode only if you want to replace its entire contents with new data.

Here are some examples of when to open a file in the Append or Output mode:

- To add new text to the end of C:\Readme.txt, open the file in the Append mode as follows:

```
Open "C:\Readme.txt" For Append As #1
```

- To enter some text in a brand new file called "C:\Result.txt," open the file in the Output mode as follows:

```
Open "C:\Result.txt" For Output As #1
```

- To replace the contents of an existing file C:\Winners.csv with a list of new winners, first prepare a backup copy of the original file, and then open the original file in the Output mode:

```
FileCopy "C:\Winners.csv","C:\Winners.old"
Open "C:\Winners.csv" For Output As #1
```

Tip 8-6: Can't Read and Write at the Same Time

Sequential files have to be opened separately to perform read and write operations. You cannot perform these operations simultaneously. For instance, after a file has been opened for output and data has been written to the file, the file should be closed before being opened for input.

Tip 8-7: Advantages and Disadvantages of Sequential Files

Although sequential files are easy to create and use, and don't waste any space, they have a number of disadvantages. For example, you can't easily find one specific item in the file without having to read through a large portion of the file. Also, an individual item of the file cannot be changed or deleted easily—you must rewrite the entire file. And as stated in Tip 8-6 sequential files have to be opened separately for read/write operations.

Using Write # and Print # Statements

Now that you know both methods for opening a text file with the intention of writing to it (Append or Output), it's time to learn the Write # and Print # statements that will allow you to send data to the file.

When you read data from a sequential file with the Input # statement, you usually write data to this file with the Write # statement. This statement looks like the following:

```
Write #filenumber, [outputlist]
```

filenumber, which specifies the number of the file you're working with, is the only required argument of the Write # statement. outputlist is the text you want to write to the file. outputlist can be a single text string or a list of variables that contain data that you want to write. If you specify only the file number, Visual Basic will write a single empty line to the open file.

To illustrate how the data is written to a file, let's prepare a text file with the first name, last name, birthdate, and number of siblings for three people:

1. Enter the DataEntry procedure in the current module:

```
Sub DataEntry()
    Dim lname As String
    Dim fname As String
    Dim birthdate As Date
    Dim s As Integer

    Open "C:\My Documents\Friends.txt" For Output As #1
    lname = "Smith"
    fname = "Gregory"
    birthdate = #1/2/63#
    s = 3
    Write #1, lname, fname, birthdate, s

    lname = "Conlin"
    fname = "Janice"
    birthdate = #5/12/48#
    s = 1
    Write #1, lname, fname, birthdate, s

    lname = "Kaufman"
    fname = "Steven"
    birthdate = #4/7/57#
    s = 0
    Write #1, lname, fname, birthdate, s

    Close #1
End Sub
```

The above procedure opens the C:\My Documents\Friends.txt file for output. Because this file does not yet exist on your hard disk, Visual Basic creates a brand new file and writes three records to it. The data written to the file is stored in variables. Notice that the strings are delimited with double quotes (" ") and the birthdate is surrounded by pound signs (#).

When you open the Friends.txt file using the Windows Notepad, you will see the following entries:

```
"Smith","Gregory",#1963-01-02#,3
"Conlin","Janice",#1948-05-12#,1
"Kaufman","Steven",#1957-04-07#,0
```

Notice that the Write # statement automatically inserts commas between the individual data items in each record and places the end-of-line character at the end of each line of text (Chr(13) & Chr(10)) so that each new record starts on a new line. In the above example, each line of text shows one record—each record begins with the last name and ends with the number of siblings.

If instead of separating data with commas you'd rather show the contents of a file in columns, write the data with the Print # statement. For example, if you replace the Write # statement in the DataEntry procedure above with the Print # statement, Visual Basic will write the data in the following way:

```
Smith      Gregory   1/2/63    3
Conlin     Janice    5/12/48   1
Kaufman    Steven    4/7/57    0
```

Although the Print # statement has the same syntax as the Write # statement, Print# writes data to the sequential file in a format ready for printing. The variables in the list may be separated with semicolons or spaces. To print out several spaces, you should use the Spc(n) instruction, where n is the number of spaces. Similarly, to enter a word in the fifth column, you should use the instruction Tab(5).

Let's look at some formatting examples:

- To add an empty line to a file, use the Write# statement with a comma:

  ```
  Write #1,
  ```

- To enter the text "fruits" in the fifth column:

  ```
  Write #1, Tab(5); "fruits"
  ```

- To separate the words "fruits" and "vegetables" with five spaces:

  ```
  Write #1, "fruits"; Spc(5); "vegetables"
  ```

Working with Random Access Files

When a file contains structured data, open the file in the Random mode. A file opened for random access allows you to:

- Read/write data at the same time
- Quickly access a particular record

In random access files, all records are of equal length, and each record has the same number of fixed-size fields. The length of a record or field must be determined prior to writing data to the file.

If the length of a string that is being written to a field is less than the specified size of the field, Visual Basic automatically enters spaces at the end of the string to fill in the entire size of the field. If the text being written is longer than the size of the field, the characters that don't fit will not be written.

To find out how to work with random access files, you will now create a small database for use in a foreign language study. This database will contain records made up of two fields to store an English term and its foreign language equivalent.

Tip 8-8: What is a Random Access File?

A random access file is one in which data is stored in records that can be accessed in a random order. This means that any record of a random access file can be read without having to read every record preceding it.

Creating a User-Defined Data Type

In addition to the built-in data types introduced in Chapter 3 (see Table 3-1), Visual Basic allows you to define a non-standard data type using a Type...End Type statement placed at the top of the module. This non-standard data type is often referred to as a user-defined data type. The user-defined data type can contain items of various data types (String, Integer, Date, and so on). When you work with files opened for random access, you often create a user-defined variable because such a variable provides you with easy access to the individual fields of a record.

1. Insert a new module into the current project and rename it **RandomFiles**.

2. Enter at the top of the module, just below the Option Explicit statement, the following type definition:

```
Option Explicit
' define a user-defined type
Type Dictionary
    en As String * 16    ' English word up to 16 characters
    sp As String * 20    ' Spanish word up to 20 characters
End Type
```

The user-defined type called Dictionary contains two items declared as String with the specified size. The en item can accept up to 16 characters. The size of the second item (sp) cannot exceed 20 characters. If you add up the lengths of both of these items, you will get the following record length—36 (16+20).

Do not enter the Option Explicit statement again if it already appears in your module.

3. Enter the EnglishToSpanish procedure shown below:

```
Sub EnglishToSpanish()
    Dim d As Dictionary
    Dim RecNr As Long
    Dim choice As String
    Dim totalRec As Long

    RecNr = 1
    'open the file for random access
    Open "Translate.txt" For Random As #1 Len = Len(d)
    Do
        ' get the English word
        choice = InputBox("Enter an English word", "ENGLISH")
        d.en = choice
        ' exit the loop if cancelled
        If choice = "" Then Exit Do
         choice = InputBox("Enter the Spanish equivalent for " _
            & d.en, "SPANISH EQUIVALENT  " & d.en)
        If choice = "" Then Exit Do
        d.sp = choice
```

```
            ' write to the record
            Put #1, RecNr, d
            ' increase record counter
            recNr = recNr + 1
     Loop Until choice = ""    'ask for words until Cancel
     totalRec = LOF(1) / Len(d)
     MsgBox "This file contains " & totalRec & " record(s)."
     ' close the file
     Close #1
  End Sub
```

The EnglishToSpanish procedure begins with the declaration of four variables. The variable d is declared as a user-defined type called Dictionary. This type was declared earlier with the Type statement (see step 2). After the initial value is assigned to the variable RecNr, Visual Basic opens the Translate.txt file for random access as file number 1. The Len(d) instruction tells Visual Basic that the size of each record is 36 characters. (The variable d contains two elements; sp is 20 characters, and en is 16 characters. Consequently, the total size of a record is 36.) Next Visual Basic executes the statements inside the Do…Until loop until you cancel. The first statement in the loop prompts you to enter an English word and assigns it to the variable choice. The value of this item is then passed to the first element of the user-defined variable d (d.en).

As soon as you stop entering data, Visual Basic exits the Do loop and executes the final statements in the procedure that calculates and displays the total number of records in the file. The last statement closes the file. If you enter an English word and click OK, the next dialog box will prompt you to supply a foreign language equivalent.

Of course, if you decide to quit now, Visual Basic will exit the loop and continue with the remaining statements. If everything goes fine and you enter the foreign language equivalent, Visual Basic will assign it to the variable choice and then pass it to the second element of the user-defined variable d (d.sp). Next, Visual Basic will write the entire record to the file using the following statement:

```
Put #1, recNr, d
```

After writing the first record, Visual Basic will increase the record counter by one and repeat the statements inside the loop. The EnglishToSpanish procedure allows you to enter any number of records into your dictionary. When you quit supplying the words, the procedure uses the LOF and Len functions to calculate the total number of records in the file. After displaying the message, Visual Basic closes the text file (Translate.txt).

Creating a random access file is only the beginning. Next, the VocabularyDrill procedure illustrates how to work with records in a file opened for random access. Here you will learn statements that will allow you to quickly find the appropriate data in your file.

Tip 8-9: Understanding the Type Statement

The Type command allows you to create a custom grouping of mixed variable types, called a "user-defined data type." The Type statement is generally used with random access files to store pieces of information as fields within records of a fixed size. Instead of declaring a separate variable for each field, cluster the fields used with a random access file into a user-defined variable using the Type statement. For example, define a record containing three fields in the following way:

```
Type MyRecord
    country As String * 20
```

```
    city As String * 14
    rank As Integer
End Type
```

Once the general type is defined, you must give a name to the particular variable that will be of that type:

```
Dim myInfo As MyRecord
```

Access the interior variables (country, city, rank) by using the variable name separated by a period (.) from the name of the interior variable. For example, to specify the city, enter:

```
MyInfo.city = "Warsaw"
```

---

4. Below the EnglishToSpanish procedure, enter the VocabularyDrill procedure shown below. The explanation of this code follows.

```
Sub VocabularyDrill()
    Dim d As Dictionary
    Dim totalRec As Long
    Dim recNr As Long
    Dim randomNr As Long
    Dim question As String
    Dim answer As String

    ' open a random access file
    Open "Translate.txt" For Random As #1 Len = Len(d)
    ' print the total number of bytes in this file
    Debug.Print "There are " & LOF(1) & " bytes in this file."
    ' find out and print out the total number of records
    recNr = LOF(1) / Len(d)
    Debug.Print "Total number of records: " & recNr

    Do
        ' get a random record number
        randomNr = Int(recNr * Rnd) + 1
        Debug.Print randomNr
        ' find the random record
        Seek #1, randomNr
        ' read the record
        Get #1, randomNr, d
        Debug.Print Trim(d.en); " "; Trim(d.sp)
        ' assign answer to a variable
        answer = InputBox("What's the Spanish equivalent?", d.en)
        ' finish if cancelled
```

```
        If answer = "" Then Close #1: Exit Sub
        Debug.Print answer
            ' check if the answer is correct
            If answer = Trim(d.sp) Then
                MsgBox "Congratulations!"
            Else
                MsgBox "Invalid Answer!!!"
            End If
    ' keep on asking questions, until Cancel is pressed
    Loop While answer <> ""
        ' close file
        Close #1
End Sub
```

After declaring variables, the VocabularyDrill procedure opens a file for random access and tells Visual Basic the length of each record: Len = Len(d). Next, two statements print in the Immediate window the total number of bytes and records in the open file. The number of bytes is returned by the LOF(1) statement.

The number of records is computed by dividing the entire file (LOF) by the length of one record—Len(d). Next, Visual Basic executes the statements inside the loop until Esc is pressed or Cancel is clicked. The first statement in the loop assigns the result of the Rnd function to the variable randomNr. The next statement writes this number to the Immediate window. The instruction Seek #1, randomNr moves the cursor in the open file to the record number specified by the variable randomNr.

The next instruction reads the contents of the found record. To read the data in a file opened for random access, you must use the Get statement. The instruction:

```
Get #1, randomNr, d
```

tells Visual Basic the record number (randomNr) to read and the variable (d) into which data is being read. The first record in a random access file is at position 1, the second record at position 2, and so on. Omitting a record number causes Visual Basic to read the next record.

The values of both elements of the user-defined type dictionary are then written to the Immediate window. The Trim(d.en) and Trim(d.sp) functions print the values of the record being read without the leading and trailing spaces that the user may have entered.

Next, Visual Basic displays an input box with a prompt to supply the foreign language equivalent of the shown word. The word is assigned to the variable answer. If you press Esc instead of clicking OK, Visual Basic closes the file and ends the procedure. Otherwise, Visual Basic prints your answer to the Immediate window and notifies you whether or not your answer is correct. You can press Esc or click the Cancel button in the dialog box whenever you want to quit the vocabulary drill.

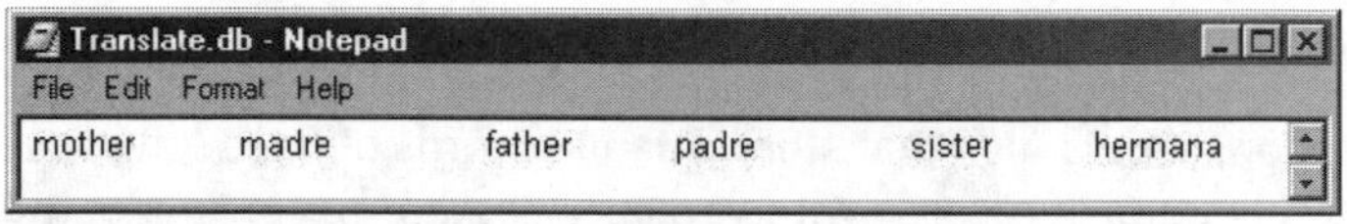

Figure 8-3: The contents of a random access file opened in Notepad

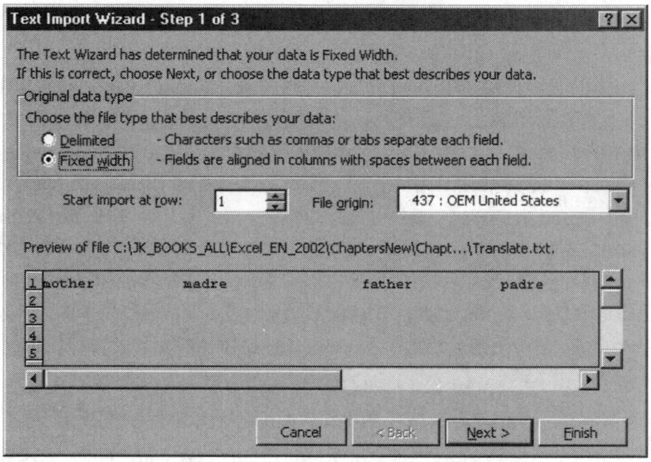

Figure 8-4: The contents of a random access file on attempt to open it with Microsoft Excel. Notice that Excel correctly recognizes the original data type—the data in a random access file is fixed width.

If you decide to continue and click OK, a new random number will be generated, and the program will retrieve the English word and ask you for the Spanish equivalent.

You can modify the VocabularyDrill procedure so that every incorrectly translated word is written to a worksheet. Also, you may want to write all the records from the Translate.txt file to a worksheet so that you always know the contents of your dictionary. You will find both of these procedures on the companion CD-ROM.

Tip 8-10: Advantages and Disadvantages of Random Access Files

Unlike sequential files, data stored in random access files can be accessed very quickly. Also, these files don't need to be closed down between placing information into them and reading from them. Random access files don't need to be read or filled in order. Random access files also have some disadvantages. For example, they often store the data inefficiently. Because they have fixed-length fields and records, the same number of bytes is used regardless of the number of characters being stored. So if some fields are left blank or contain strings shorter than the declared field size, you may waste a lot of space.

Working with Binary Files

Unlike random access files that store data in records of fixed length, binary files are a collection of records with variable lengths. For example, the first record can contain ten bytes, the second record can have only five bytes, while the third record can have 15 bytes. This method of storing data saves a lot of disk space.

Because Visual Basic doesn't need to add additional spaces to the stored string to ensure that all the fields are of the same length (as when writing data to a random access file), there is no wasted space in binary files. It's no wonder that binary files occupy less space on disk than the two types of files discussed earlier. Just like random access files, binary files can be open for simultaneous read and write operations. However, because records in binary files are of variable length, it is more difficult to manipulate these files. In order to retrieve the data correctly, you must store information about the size of each field and record.

To work with binary files, you will use the following four statements:

■ The Get statement is used to read data.

■ The Put statement allows you to enter new data to a binary file.

■ The Loc statement returns the number of the last byte that was read (in random access files the Loc statement returns the number of a record that was last read).

■ The Seek statement moves the cursor to the appropriate position inside the file.

To quickly master the usage of the above statements, open the Immediate window and enter the instructions shown in the left column below. The purpose of this exercise is to enter your first and last name in a binary file called MyData.txt and then retrieve the information you entered.

Enter in the Immediate window:	Explanation:
`Open "MyData.txt" For Binary As #1`	Open the file "MyData.txt" for binary access as file number 1.
`MsgBox "Total bytes: " & LOF(1)`	Show the number of bytes on opening the file. (The file is currently empty.)
`fname = "Julitta"`	Assign a value to the variable fname.
`ln = len(fname)`	Assign to the variable ln the length of string stored in the variable fname.
`Put #1, , ln`	Enter the value of the variable ln in the binary file in the position of the next byte.
`MsgBox "The last byte: " & LOC(1)`	Display the position of the last byte.
`Put #1, , fname`	Enter the contents of the variable fname in the next position.
`lname = "Korol"`	Assign a value to the variable lname.

Enter in the Immediate window:	Explanation:
`ln = len(lname)`	Assign to the variable ln the length of string stored in the variable lname.
`Put #1 , ,ln`	Enter the value of the variable ln in the binary file in the position of the next byte.
`Put #1,,lname`	Enter the contents of the variable lname in the next byte position.
`MsgBox "The last byte: " & LOC(1)`	Display the position of the last byte.
`Get #1,1, entry1`	Read the value stored in the position of the first byte and assign it to the variable entry1.
`MsgBox entry1`	Display the contents of the variable entry1.
`Get #1, , entry2`	Read the next value and assign it to the variable entry2.
`MsgBox entry2`	Display the contents of the variable entry2.
`Get #1, , entry3`	Read the next value and store it in the variable entry3.
`MsgBox entry3`	Display the contents of the variable entry3.
`Get #1, , entry4`	Read the next value and store it in the variable entry4.
`MsgBox entry4`	Display the contents of the variable entry4.
`Debug.Print entry1;entry2;entry3;entry4`	Print in the Immediate window all the data.
`7 Julitta 5 Korol`	The result of the previous instruction as displayed in the Immediate window.
`Close #1`	Close the file.

Note: The above instructions can be found in the EnterAndDisplay procedure on the companion CD-ROM.

When entering data to a binary file, use the following guidelines:

■ Before writing a string to a binary file, assign the length of the string to an Integer-type variable. Usually the following block of instructions can be used:

```
string_length = Len(variable_name)
Put #1, , string_length
Put #1, , variable_name
```

■ When reading data from binary files, first read the string length and then the string contents. To do this, use the Get statement and the String$ function:

```
Get #1, , string_length
variable_name=String(string_length, " ")
Get #1, , variable_name
```

Tip 8-11: Advantages and Disadvantages of Binary Access Files

In comparison with sequential and random access files, binary files are the smallest of all. Because they use variable-length records, they can conserve disk space. Like files opened for random access, you can read and write to a file opened for binary access. One big disadvantage of binary access files is that you must know precisely how the data is stored in the file to retrieve or manipulate it correctly.

Modern Methods of Working with Files and Folders

There is a hidden treasure in your computer called Windows Scripting Host (WSH), which allows you to create little programs that control the Windows operating system and its applications as well as retrieve information from the operating system. WSH is an ActiveX control found in the Wshom.ocx file. This file is automatically installed in the Windows System32 folder if you are running Windows 95, 98, NT 5.0, 2000, XP or Internet Explorer 4, 5, or 6.

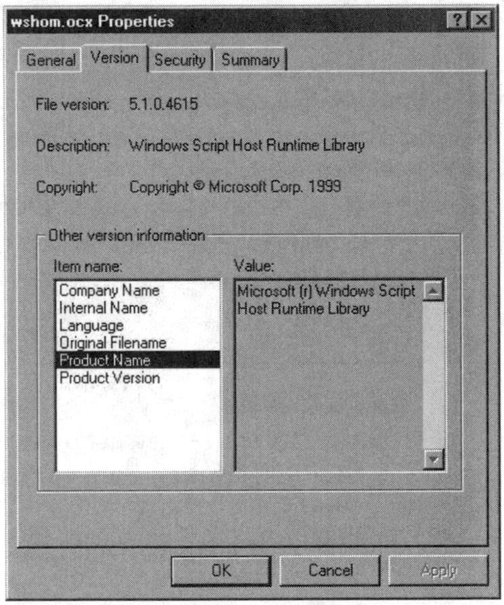

WSH is a scripting language. A *script* is a set of commands that can be run automatically. Scripts can be created and run directly from the command prompt by using the Command Scripting Host (Cscript.exe) or from Windows by using the Windows Scripting Host (Wscript.exe). In the following sections of this chapter, you will learn how the Windows Scripting Host works together with VBA.

Figure 8-5: Windows Scripting Host is an ActiveX control used to create scripts that perform simple or complex operations which previously could only be performed by writing batch files (.bat) in the MS-DOS operating system.

WSH has its own object hierarchy. Using the CreateObject function, you can refer to WSH objects from your VBA procedure. Before you start writing VBA procedures that utilize WSH objects, let's take a look at some of the objects you will be able to control.

1. In the Visual Basic Editor window, choose **Tools | References**.
2. In the References dialog box, locate and select **Microsoft Scripting Runtime**.

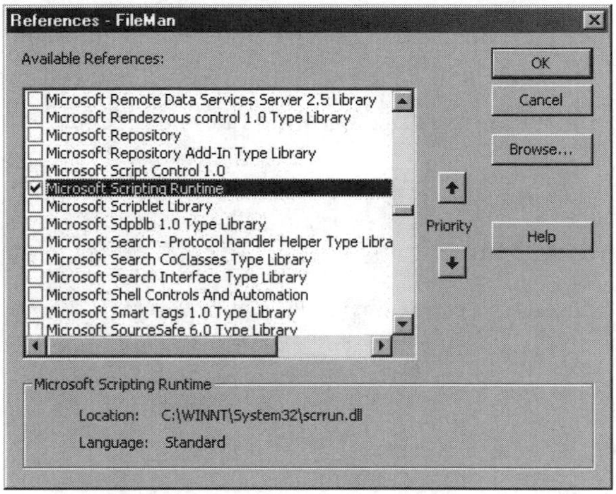

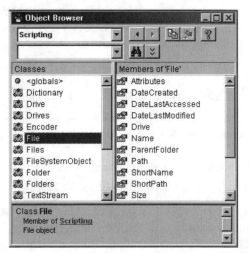

Figure 8-6:
Creating a reference to the Microsoft Scripting Runtime

3. Now press **F2** to open the Object Browser.
4. In the combo box <All libraries> choose **Scripting**. You will see a list of objects that are part of the Windows Scripting Host library.

Figure 8-7:
After establishing a reference to the Microsoft Scripting Runtime (see Figure 8-6), the Object Browser displays many objects that allow you to work with disks, folders, files, and their content.

The Windows Scripting Host allows you to quickly obtain answers to such questions as "On which disk can I locate a particular file?" (GetDrive method), "What is the extension of a filename?" (GetExtensionName method), "When was this file last modified?" (DateLastModified property), and "Does this folder or file exist on a given drive?" (FolderExists and FileExists methods).

Finding Information about Files with the WSH

The Windows Scripting Host exposes an object called FileSystemObject. This object has several methods for working with the file system.

Let's see how you can obtain some information about a specific file:

1. Insert a new module into the current VBA project and rename it **WSH**.

2. In the WSH module, enter the following FileInfo procedure:

```
Sub FileInfo()
    Dim fs As Object
    Dim objFile As Object
    Dim strMsg As String

    Set fs = CreateObject("Scripting.FileSystemObject")
    Set objFile = fs.GetFile("C:\WINNT\System.ini")
    strMsg = "File name: " & _
        objFile.Name & vbCrLf
    strMsg = strMsg & "Disk: " & _
        objFile.Drive & vbCrLf
    strMsg = strMsg & "Date Created:" & _
        objFile.DateCreated & vbCrLf
    strMsg = strMsg & "Date Modified:" & _
        objFile.DateLastModified & vbCrLf
    MsgBox strMsg, , "File Information"
End Sub
```

The FileInfo procedure shown above uses the CreateObject VBA function to create an ActiveX object (FileSystemObject) that is a part of the Windows Scripting library. This object provides access to a computer's file system.

```
Dim fs As Object
Set fs = CreateObject("Scripting.FileSystemObject")
```

The above code declares an object variable named fs. Next it uses the CreateObject function to create an ActiveX object and assigns the object to an object variable.

The second line of code in the above procedure:

```
Set objFile = fs.GetFile("C:\WINNT\System.ini"),
```

creates and returns a reference to the File object for the System.ini file in the C:\WINNT folder and assigns it to the objFile object variable. The File object has many properties that you can read. For example, the statement objFile.Name returns the full name of the file. The statement objFile.Drive returns the drive name where the file is located. The statements obj-File.DateCreated and objFile.DateLastModified return the date the file was created and last modified. This procedure can be easily modified so that it also returns the type of file, its attributes, and the name of the parent folder. Try to modify this procedure on your own by placing within its code the following instructions: objFile.Type, objFile.Attributes, objFile.ParentFolder, and objFile.Size. Check in the Object Browser for what else you can learn about the file by referencing the File object.

Methods and Properties of the FileSystemObject

The FileSystemObject is an ActiveX control that provides access to a computer's file system. This object offers a number of methods, some of which are shown in Table 8-3.

Table 8-3: Selected methods of the FileSystemObject

Method	Description
FileExists	Returns True if the specified file exists
	``Sub FileExists()
Dim fs As Object
Dim strFile As String
Set fs = CreateObject("Scripting.FileSystemObject")
strFile = InputBox("Enter the full name of the file:")
If fs.FileExists(strFile) Then
MsgBox strFile & " was found."
Else
MsgBox "File does not exist."
End If
End Sub```
GetFile	Returns a File object
GetFileName	Returns the filename with a path
GetFileVersion	Returns the file version
CopyFile	Copies a file
	``Sub CopyFile()
    Dim fs As Object
    Dim strFile As String
    Dim strNewFile As String

    strFile = "C:\Hello.doc"
    strNewFile = "C:\Program Files\Hello.doc"

    Set fs = CreateObject("Scripting.FileSystemObject")
    fs.CopyFile strFile, strNewFile
    MsgBox "A copy of the specified file was created."
    Set fs = Nothing
End Sub``` |
| MoveFile | Moves a file |
| DeleteFile | Deletes a file |
| | ```Sub DeleteFile()
    Dim fs As FileSystemObject
    Set fs = New FileSystemObject

    fs.DeleteFile "C:\Program Files\Hello.doc"
    MsgBox "The requested file was deleted."
End Sub``` |

Method	Description
DriveExists	Returns True if the specified drive exists

```
Function DriveExists(disk)
    Dim fs As Object
    Dim strMsg As String
    Set fs = CreateObject("Scripting.FileSystemObject")
    If fs.DriveExists(disk) Then
        strMsg = "Drive " & UCase(disk) & " exists."
    Else
        strMsg = UCase(disk) & " was not found."
    End If
    DriveExists = strMsg
' run this function from the worksheet
' by entering in any cell the following: =DriveExists("E:\")
End Function
```

Method	Description
GetDrive	Returns a Drive object

```
Sub DriveInfo()
    Dim fs, disk, infoStr, strDiskName
    strDiskName = InputBox("Enter the drive letter:", _
                "Drive Name", "C:\")

    Set fs = CreateObject("Scripting.FileSystemObject")
    Set disk = fs.GetDrive(fs.GetDriveName(strDiskName))
    infoStr = "Drive: " & UCase(strDiskName) & vbCrLf
    infoStr = infoStr & "Drive letter: " & _
        UCase(disk.DriveLetter) & vbCrLf
    infoStr = infoStr & "Drive Type: " & disk.DriveType & vbCrLf
    infoStr = infoStr & "Drive File System: " & _
        disk.FileSystem & vbCrLf
    infoStr = infoStr & "Drive SerialNumber: " & _
        disk.SerialNumber & vbCrLf
    infoStr = infoStr & "Total Size in Bytes: " & _
        FormatNumber(disk.TotalSize / 1024, 0) & " Kb" & vbCrLf
    infoStr = infoStr & "Free Space on Drive: " & _
        FormatNumber(disk.FreeSpace / 1024, 0) & " Kb" & vbCrLf
    MsgBox infoStr, vbInformation, "Drive Information"
End Sub
```

Method	Description
GetDriveName	Returns a string containing the name of a drive or network share

```
Function DriveName(disk)
    Dim fs As Object
    Dim strDiskName As String

    Set fs = CreateObject("Scripting.FileSystemObject")
    strDiskName = fs.GetDriveName(disk)
    DriveName = strDiskName
' run this function from the Immediate window
' by entering ?DriveName("D:\")
End Function
```

Method	Description
FolderExists	Returns True if the specified folder exists

```
Sub DoesFolderExist()
    Dim fs As Object
    Set fs = CreateObject("Scripting.FileSystemObject")
    MsgBox fs.FolderExists("C:\Program Files")
End Sub
```

GetFolder	Returns a Folder object

```
Sub FilesInFolder()
    Dim fs As Object
    Dim objFolder As Object
    Dim objFile As Object

    Set fs = CreateObject("Scripting.FileSystemObject")
    Set objFolder = fs.GetFolder("C:\")

    Workbooks.Add
    For Each objFile In objFolder.Files
        ActiveCell.Select
        Selection.Formula = objFile.Name
        ActiveCell.Offset(0, 1).Range("A1").Select
        Selection.Formula = objFile.Type
        ActiveCell.Offset(1, -1).Range("A1").Select
    Next
    Columns("A:B").Select
    Selection.Columns.AutoFit
End Sub
```

GetSpecial-Folder	Returns the path to the operating system folders: 0 – Windows folder 1 – System folder 2 – Temp folder

```
Sub SpecialFolders()
    Dim fs As Object
    Dim strWindowsFolder As String
    Dim strSystemFolder As String
    Dim strTempFolder As String

    Set fs = CreateObject("Scripting.FileSystemObject")
    strWindowsFolder = fs.GetSpecialFolder(0)
    strSystemFolder = fs.GetSpecialFolder(1)
    strTempFolder = fs.GetSpecialFolder(2)

    MsgBox strWindowsFolder & vbCrLf _
        & strSystemFolder & vbCrLf _
        & strTempFolder, vbInformation + vbOKOnly, _
            "Special Folders"
End Sub
```

Method	Description
CreateFolder	Creates a folder

```
Sub MakeNewFolder()
    Dim fs, objFolder
    Set fs = CreateObject("Scripting.FileSystemObject")
    Set objFolder = fs.CreateFolder("C:\TestFolder")
    MsgBox "A new folder named " & _
      objFolder.Name & " was created."
End Sub
```

CopyFolder	Creates a copy of a folder

```
Sub MakeFolderCopy()
    Dim fs As FileSystemObject
    Set fs = New FileSystemObject
    If fs.FolderExists("C:\TestFolder") Then
      fs.CopyFolder "C:\TestFolder", "C:\FinalFolder"
      MsgBox "The folder was copied."
    End If
End Sub
```

MoveFolder	Moves a folder
DeleteFolder	Deletes a folder

```
Sub RemoveFolder()
    Dim fs As FileSystemObject
    Set fs = New FileSystemObject

        If fs.FolderExists("C:\TestFolder") Then
            fs.DeleteFolder "C:\TestFolder"
            MsgBox "The folder was deleted."
        End If
End Sub
```

CreateTextFile	Creates a text file
OpenTextFile	Opens a text file

```
Sub ReadTextFile()
    Dim fs As Object
    Dim objFile As Object
    Dim strContent As String
    Dim strFileName As String

    strFileName = "C:\WINNT\System.ini"
    Set fs = CreateObject("Scripting.FileSystemObject")
    Set objFile = fs.OpenTextFile(strFileName)
    Do While Not objFile.AtEndOfStream
        strContent = strContent & objFile.ReadLine & vbCrLf
    Loop

    objFile.Close
    Set objFile = Nothing
    ActiveWorkbook.Sheets(3).Select
    Range("A1").Select
    Selection.Formula = strContent
End Sub
```

The FileSystemObject has only one property called Drives, which returns a reference to the collection of drives. Using this property. you can create a list of drives on a computer, as shown below:

```
Sub DrivesList()
    Dim fs As Object
    Dim colDrives As Object
    Dim strDrive As String

    Set fs = CreateObject("Scripting.FileSystemObject")
    Set colDrives = fs.Drives

        For Each Drive In colDrives
            strDrive = "Drive " & Drive.DriveLetter & ": "
            Debug.Print strDrive
        Next
End Sub
```

Properties of the File Object

The File object allows you to access all of the properties of a specified file. The following lines of code create a reference to the File object:

```
Set fs = CreateObject("Scripting.FileSystemObject")
Set objFile = fs.GetFile("C:\My Documents\myFile.doc")
```

You will find an example of using the File object in the FileInfo procedure that was created earlier in this chapter.

Table 8-4: Selected properties of the File object

Property	Description
Attributes	Returns file attributes (compare this property to the GetAttr VBA function explained at the beginning of this chapter)
DateCreated	File creation date
DateLastAccessed	File last-access date
DateLastModified	File last-modified date
Drive	Drive name followed by a colon
Name	The name of the file
ParentFolder	The parent folder of the file
Path	The full path of the file
Size	File size in bytes (compare this property to the FileLen VBA function explained at the beginning of this chapter)
Type	File type. This is the text that appears in the Type column in the Windows Explorer (e.g., Configuration settings, Application, shortcut)

Properties of the Folder Object

The Folder object provides access to all of the properties of a specified folder. The following lines of code create a reference to the Folder object:

```
Set fs = CreateObject("Scripting.FileSystemObject")
Set objFolder = fs.GetFolder("C:\My Documents")
```

Table 8-5 gives examples of VBA procedures that access the Folder object.

Table 8-5: Selected properties of the Folder object

Property	Description
Attributes	Folder attributes
DateCreated	Folder creation date
Drive	Name of the folder
Files	Collection of files in the folder

	`Sub CountFilesInFolder()`
	`    Dim fs, strFolder, objFolder, colFiles`
	
	`    strFolder = InputBox("Enter the folder name:")`
	`        If Not IsFolderEmpty(strFolder) Then`
	`            Set fs = CreateObject("Scripting.FileSystemObject")`
	`            Set objFolder = fs.GetFolder(strFolder)`
	`            Set colFiles = objFolder.Files`
	`                MsgBox "The number of files in the folder " & _`
	`                    strFolder & "=" & colFiles.Count`
	`        End If`
	`End Sub`

	The above procedure calls the IsFolderEmpty function, which is discussed with the Size property in this table.
IsRootFolder	Returns True if the folder is the root folder
Name	The name of the folder
ParentFolder	The parent folder of the specified folder
Path	The full path to the folder
Size	Folder size in bytes

	`Function IsFolderEmpty(myFolder)`
	`    Dim fs, objFolder`
	
	`    Set fs = CreateObject("Scripting.FileSystemObject")`
	`    Set objFolder = fs.GetFolder(myFolder)`
	`    IsFolderEmpty = (objFolder.Size = 0)`
	`End Function`

SubFolders	Collection of subfolders in the folder
Type	Folder type (e.g., File folder or Recycle Bin)

Properties of the Drive Object

The Drive object provides access to the properties of the specified drive on a computer or a server. The following lines of code create a reference to the Drive object:

```
Set fs = CreateObject("Scripting.FileSystemObject")
Set objDrive = fs.GetDrive("C:\")
```

You will find several procedure examples that use the Drive object in the table below.

Table 8-6: Selected properties of the Drive object

Property	Description
AvailableSpace	Available space in bytes
FreeSpace	Same as AvailableSpace
DriveLetter	The drive letter (without the colon)
DriveType	The type of drive: 0 – Unknown 1 – Removable 2 – Fixed 3 – Network 4 – CD-ROM 5 – RAM Disk ```Sub CDROM_DriveLetter()\n Const CDROM = 4\n Dim fs, colDrives\n Set fs = CreateObject("Scripting.FileSystemObject")\n Set colDrives = fs.Drives\n For Each Drive In colDrives\n If Drive.DriveType = CDROM Then\n MsgBox "The CD-ROM Drive: " & _\n Drive.DriveLetter\n End If\n Next\n End Sub```
FileSystem	File system, such as FAT, NTFS, or CDFS
IsReady	Returns True if the appropriate media (CD-ROM disk) is inserted and ready for access ```Function IsCDROMReady(strDriveLetter)\n Dim fs, objDrive\n\n Set fs = CreateObject("Scripting.FileSystemObject")\n Set objDrive = fs.GetDrive(strDriveLetter)\n\n IsCDROMReady = (objDrive.DriveType = 4) And _\n objDrive.IsReady = True\n ' run this function from the Immediate window\n ' by entering: ?IsCDROMReady("D:")\nEnd Function```

Property	Description
Path	The path of the root folder
SerialNumber	Serial number of the drive
TotalSize	Total drive size in bytes

Creating a Text File Using WSH

Windows Scripting Host (WSH) offers three methods for creating text files: CreateTextFile, OpenTextFile, and OpenAsTextStream. The syntax of each of these methods and example procedures are presented in the following table.

Table 8-7: Various methods of creating text files

Method/Syntax	Example
CreateTextFile	object.CreateTextFile(*filename*[, *overwrite*[, *unicode*]])
	Object is the name of the FileSystemObject or the Folder object.
	Filename is a string expression that specifies the file to create.
	Overwrite (optional) is a Boolean value that indicates whether you can overwrite an existing file. The value is True if the file can be overwritten and False if it can't be overwritten. If omitted, existing files are not overwritten.
	Unicode (optional) is a Boolean value that indicates whether the file is created as a Unicode or ASCII file. The value is True if the file is created as a Unicode file and False if it's created as an ASCII file. If omitted, an ASCII file is assumed.
| | ```
Sub CreateFile_Method1()
    Dim fs, objFile
    Set fs = CreateObject("Scripting.FileSystemObject")
    Set objFile = fs.CreateTextFile("C:\Phones.txt", True)
    objFile.WriteLine ("Margaret Kubiak: 212-338-8778")
    objFile.WriteBlankLines (2)
    objFile.WriteLine ("Robert Prochot: 202-988-2331")
    objFile.Close
End Sub
``` |
	The above procedure creates a text file to store the names and phone numbers of two people. Because there is a Boolean value of True in the position of the overwrite argument, the C:\Phones.txt file will be overwritten if it already exists in the specified folder.
OpenTextFile	object.OpenTextFile(filename[, iomode[, create[, format]]])
	Object is the name of the FileSystemObject.
	Filename is a string expression that identifies the file to open.
	Iomode (optional) is a Boolean value that indicates whether a new file can be created if the specified filename doesn't exist. The value is True if a new file is created and False if it isn't created. If omitted, a new file isn't created. The iomode argument can be one of the following constants:
```

Method/Syntax	Example
OpenTextFile (cont.)	ForReading (1) ForWriting (2) ForAppending (8)
	Create (optional) is a Boolean value that indicates whether a new file can be created if the specified filename doesn't exist. The value is True if a new file is created and False if it isn't created. If omitted, a new file isn't created.
	Format (optional) is one of three Tristate values used to indicate the format of the opened file. If omitted, the file is opened as ASCII.
	TristateTrue = Open the file as ASCII. TristateFalse = Open the file as Unicode. TristateUseDefault = Open the file using the system default.

	<pre>Sub CreateFile_Method2()
	    Dim fs, objFile
	    Set fs = CreateObject("Scripting.FileSystemObject")
	    Set objFile = fs.OpenTextFile("C:\Shopping.txt", _
	                                  ForWriting, True)
	    objFile.WriteLine ("Bread")
	    objFile.WriteLine ("Milk")
	    objFile.WriteLine ("Strawberries")
	    objFile.Close
	End Sub</pre>

OpenAsTextStream	`object.OpenAsTextStream([iomode, [format]])`
	Object is the name of the File object.
	Iomode (optional) indicates input/output mode. It can be one of three constants:
	ForReading (1) ForWriting (2) ForAppending (8)
	Format (optional) is one of three Tristate values used to indicate the format of the opened file. If omitted, the file is opened as ASCII.
	TristateTrue = Open the file as ASCII. TristateFalse = Open the file as Unicode. TristateUseDefault = Open the file using the system default.

	<pre>Sub CreateFile_Method3()
	    Dim fs, objFile, objText
	    Set fs = CreateObject("Scripting.FileSystemObject")
	    fs.CreateTextFile "New.txt"
	    Set objFile = fs.GetFile("New.txt")
	    Set objText = objFile.OpenAsTextStream(ForWriting, _
	                      TristateUseDefault)
	    objText.Write "Wedding Invitation"
	    objText.Close
	    Set objText = objFile.OpenAsTextStream(ForReading, _
	                      TristateUseDefault)</pre>

Method/Syntax	Example

OpenAsTextStream (cont.)	`MsgBox objText.ReadLine`
	`objText.Close`
	`End Sub`

Performing Other Operations with WSH

WSH makes it possible to manipulate any Automation object installed on your computer. In addition to accessing the file system through FileSystemObject, WSH allows you to perform such tasks as handling WSH and ActiveX objects, mapping and unmapping printers and remote drives, manipulating the registry, creating Windows and Internet shortcuts, and accessing the Windows NT Active Directory service. The WSH object model is made of the following three main objects: WScript, WshShell, and WshNetwork. This section demonstrates how you can take advantage of the WshShell object to write procedures to start other applications and create shortcuts.

Running Other Applications

In the next chapter of this book, you will learn various methods of launching external applications from Excel. You can add to these methods what you are about to find out in this section.

Suppose you want to start up Windows Notepad from your VBA procedure. The procedure that follows shows you how easy it is to run an application using the WshShell object that is a part of Windows Scripting Host. If you'd rather launch the built-in calculator, just replace the name of the Notepad application with Calc.

```
Sub RunNotepad()
    Dim WshShell As Object
    Set WshShell = CreateObject("WScript.Shell")
    WshShell.Run "Notepad"
    Set WshShell = Nothing
End Sub
```

The above procedure begins by declaring and creating a WshShell object:

```
Dim WshShell As Object
Set WshShell = CreateObject("WScript.Shell")
```

The next statement uses the Run method to run the required application:

```
WshShell.Run "Notepad"
```

Using the same concept, it is easy to run Windows utility applications such as Calculator or Explorer:

```
WshShell.Run "Calc"
WshShell.Run "Explorer"
```

The last line in the procedure destroys the WshShell object because it is no longer needed:

```
Set WshShell = Nothing
```

Instead of launching an empty application window, you can start your application with a specific document, as shown in the following procedure:

```
Sub OpenTxtFileInNotepad()
    Dim WshShell As Object
    Set WshShell = CreateObject("WScript.Shell")
    WshShell.Run "Notepad C:\Phones.txt"
    Set WshShell = Nothing
End Sub
```

To launch the MS-DOS window and print out the list of files in the current directory, try the following procedure:

```
Sub RunDOSCommand()
    Dim WshShell As Object
    Set WshShell = CreateObject("WScript.Shell")
    WshShell.Run ("Command /c Dir >lpt1:")
End Sub
```

Creating Shortcuts

When you start distributing your VBA applications, users will likely request that you automatically place a shortcut to your application on their desktop. VBA does not provide a way to create Windows shortcuts. Luckily for you, you now know how to work with WSH, and you can use its Shell object to create shortcuts to applications or web sites without any user intervention. The WshShell object exposes the CreateShortcut method, which you can use in the following way:

```
Set myShortcut = WshShell.CreateShortcut(Pathname)
```

Pathname is a string indicating the full path to the shortcut file. All shortcut files have the .lnk extension, and this extension must be included in the pathname. The CreateShortcut method returns a shortcut object that exposes a number of properties and one method, as shown in Table 8-8.

Table 8-8: Properties/methods of the CreateShortcut object

Property/Method	Description
TargetPath	The TargetPath property is the path to the shortcut's executable. `WshShell.TargetPath = ActiveWorkbook.FullName`
WindowStyle	The WindowStyle property identifies the type of window style used by a shortcut. 1 – Normal window 3 – Maximized window 7 – Minimized window `WshShell.WindowStyle = 1`

Property/Method	Description
HotKey	The HotKey property is a keyboard shortcut (for example, Alt+f, Shift+g, Ctrl+Shift+z, etc.)
	`WshShell.Hotkey = "Ctrl+Alt+w"`
IconLocation	The IconLocation property is the icon location of the shortcut. Because icon files usually contain more than one icon, you should provide the path to the icon file followed by the index of the icon number in this file. If not specified, Windows uses the default icon for the file.
	`WshShell.IconLocation = "notepad.exe, 0"`
Description	The Description property contains a string value describing a shortcut.
	`WshShell.Description = "Wordware Web Site"`
WorkingDirectory	The WorkingDirectory property identifies the working directory used by a shortcut.
	`strWorkDir = WshShell.SpecialFolders("Desktop")` `WshShell.WorkingDirectory = strWorkDir`
Save	This is the only method of the Shortcut object. After using the CreateShortcut method to create a shortcut object and set the shortcut object's properties, the Save method must be used to save the shortcut object to disk.

Creating a shortcut is a three-step process:

1. Create an instance of a WshShortcut object.

2. Initialize its properties (see Table 8-8 above).

3. Save it to disk with the Save method.

The following example creates a WshShell object and uses the CreateShortcut method to create two shortcuts: a Windows shortcut to the active Microsoft Excel workbook file and an Internet shortcut to the Wordware Publishing web site. Both shortcuts are placed on the user's desktop. The procedure uses the SpecialFolders property of the WshShell object to return the path to the Windows desktop.

```
Sub CreateShortcut()
    ' this script creates two desktop shortcuts
    Dim WshShell As Object
    Dim objShortcut As Object
    Set WshShell = CreateObject("WScript.Shell")
    ' create an internet shortcut
    Set objShortcut = WshShell.CreateShortcut(WshShell. _
      SpecialFolders("Desktop") & "\Wordware.url")
    objShortcut.TargetPath = "http://www.wordware.com"
    objShortcut.Save
    ' create a file shortcut
    Set objShortcut = WshShell.CreateShortcut(WshShell. _
      SpecialFolders("Desktop") & "\" & ActiveWorkbook.Name & ".lnk")
    With objShortcut
        .TargetPath = ActiveWorkbook.FullName
        .WindowStyle = 7
```

```
        .Save
    End With
    Set objShortcut = Nothing
    Set WshShell = Nothing
End Sub
```

Tip 8-12: Using the SpecialFolders Property

You can find out the location of a special folder on your machine using the SpecialFolders property. The following special folders are available: AllUsersDesktop, AllUsersStartMenu, AllUsersPrograms, AllUsers-Startup, Desktop, Favorites, Fonts, MyDocuments, NetHood, PrintHood, Programs, Recent, SendTo, StartMenu, Startup, and Templates. If the requested special folder is not available, the SpecialFolders property returns an empty string.

What's Next...

In the course of this chapter, you learned and tried out VBA functions and statements that allow you to work with the file system. You found out how to read and modify information pertaining to files and folders, as well as how to perform the read and write operations on files opened for sequential, random, and binary access. You also learned how to use the Windows Scripting Host (WSH) to access the FileSystemObject and perform other operations, such as launching applications and creating Windows shortcuts with the WshShell object. If you are interested in details of the discussed functions or statements, spend some time now browsing the Visual Basic online reference.

The next chapter introduces you to more automating tasks. You will learn, for example, how to use VBA to control other applications. You will learn various methods of starting applications and find out how to manipulate them directly from Microsoft Excel.

Chapter 9

Controlling Other Applications with VBA

Launching Applications ■ Moving between Applications ■ Controlling Another Application ■ Other Methods of Controlling Applications ■ Understanding Automation ■ Understanding Linking and Embedding ■ Linking and Embedding with VBA ■ COM and Automation ■ **Understanding Binding** ■ Late Binding ■ Early Binding ■ Establishing a Reference to an Object Library ■ **Creating Automation Objects** ■ Using the Create-Object Function ■ Creating a New Word Document using Automation ■ Using the GetObject Function ■ Opening an Existing Word Document ■ Using the New Keyword ■ Using Automation to Access Microsoft Outlook ■ **What's Next ...**

249

Every day, while working on your computer at work or at home, you are using various applications. To find a specific file on your hard drive or a floppy disk, you launch Windows Explorer. When you want to set the system time or change the looks of your screen, you click the appropriate icon in the Control Panel. If you have the Microsoft Office Suite installed on your computer, you use Word to create all sorts of documents and rely on Excel to perform all of your computations. Microsoft Access is great for keeping tables of your very important data, while PowerPoint helps you with sound and graphics. Finally, Microsoft Outlook makes it easy to keep your contacts, schedules, and appointments organized and easy to share with others. While working with these applications, you constantly switch between programs. You may enter data directly by using the keyboard or simply copy or move data between applications. These operations—launching applications and transferring data between them—do not need to be a manual process. These tasks can be automated with some very interesting VBA functions and instructions. In this chapter you will learn various methods of launching applications from your VBA procedures and find out how to control other applications directly from Microsoft Excel by using the technology referred to as Automation.

Launching Applications

There's more than one way to launch an application. In fact, there are at least five ways you can manually start a program: via the Start | Programs menu, a shortcut menu, the Run command, the MS-DOS window, or by double-clicking an executable file in Windows Explorer.

This section assumes that you are familiar with the manual techniques of launching applications and that you are anxious to experiment with additional techniques to start applications from inside the Microsoft Excel Visual Basic Editor window.

Let's begin with the simplest of all—the Shell function. This function allows you to start any program directly from a VBA procedure. Suppose that your procedure must open Windows Notepad. To launch Notepad, all you need is one statement between the keywords Sub and End Sub. Or better yet, you can type the following statement in the Immediate window and press Enter to see the result immediately:

```
Shell "notepad.exe", vbMaximizedFocus
```

In the above statement, "notepad.exe" is the name of the program that you want to start. This name should include the complete path (the drive and folder name) if you have any concerns that the program may not be found. Notice that the program name is in double quotes. The second argument of the Shell function can be omitted. This argument specifies the window style (that is, how the program will appear once it is launched). In the above example, Notepad will appear in a maximized window. If the window style is not specified, the program will be minimized with focus (see Table 9-1 below).

Table 9-1: Window styles used in the Shell function

Window Style Constant	Value	Window Appearance
vbHide	0	Window is hidden
vbNormalFocus	1	Normal size with focus
vbMinimizedFocus (default setting)	2	Minimized with focus (this is the default setting)
vbMaximizedFocus	3	Maximized with focus
vbNormalNoFocus	4	Normal without focus
vbMinimizedNoFocus	6	Minimized without focus

If the Shell function is capable of launching the specified executable file, it returns a number called the Task ID. This number uniquely identifies the application that has been launched. If the Shell function is unsuccessful (that is, it cannot start the specified program), Visual Basic generates an error.

If you want to work with the program launched by the Shell function, do not enter any other statements in the procedure after the Shell function. The Shell function starts the program asynchronously. That means that Visual Basic starts the program specified by the Shell function, and immediately after launching, it returns to the procedure to continue with the execution of the remaining instructions (therefore not giving you a chance of working with the application).

How would you use the Shell function to launch the Control Panel?

1. Open a new workbook and save it as **Chap09.xls**.

2. In the Visual Basic Editor window, insert a new module in the Chap09.xls VBA project.

3. Rename the project **WorkWApplets**, and change the module name to **ShellFunction**.

4. Enter the StartPanel procedure shown below:

```
Sub StartPanel()
    Shell "Control.exe", vbNormalFocus
End Sub
```

The Control Panel contains several icons. Each of these icons performs one or more tasks. As you know, behind every icon, there is a program that is activated when the user double-clicks the icon or selects the icon with the arrow keys and then presses Enter. As a rule, you can check what filename drives a particular icon by looking at the icon's properties. Unfortunately, the icons in the Control Panel have the Properties option disabled. You can, however, find out the name of the control panel icon file by creating a short-cut to the icon. For example, before you create a procedure that changes the regional settings in your computer, let's find out the name of the file that activates this icon.

1.   From the Start menu, choose **Settings**, and then **Control Panel**.

2.   In the Control Panel window, right-click the **Regional Options** icon and choose **Create Shortcut** from the shortcut menu.

3.   Click **Yes** to place the shortcut on the desktop.

4.   Close the Control Panel window.

5.   Back on the desktop, click the **Shortcut to Regional Options** icon with the right mouse button and choose **Properties**.

6.   In the Properties window, click the **Shortcut** tab and then click the **Change Icon** button.

Figure 9-1:
Each Control Panel icon has a file with the .cpl extension.

7.   Write down the name of the .cpl file (Control Panel Library) or a Dynamic Link Library file (.dll) and close all the windows that were opened in this exercise.

Table 9-2: Some of the files that activate Control Panel icons

Icon in the Control Panel	.cpl or .ddl File
Phone and Modem Options	TELEPHON.CPL or MODEM.CPL
Add/Remove Programs	APPWIZ.CPL
Network and Dial-up Connections	NETCPL.CPL or NETSHELL.DLL
32-Bit ODBC	ODBCCP32.CPL
System	SYSDM.CPL
Mail	MLCFG32.CPL
Users and Passwords	PASSWORD.CPL or NETPLWIZ.DLL
Date/Time	TIMEDATE.CPL
Regional Options	INTL.CPL
Internet Options	INETCPL.CPL

Icon in the Control Panel	.cpl or .ddl File
Sounds and Multimedia Properties	MMSYS.CPL
Display	DESK.CPL
Mouse	MAIN.CPL

The ChangeSettings procedure shown below demonstrates how to launch the Control Panel's Regional Settings icon using the Shell function. Notice that the arguments of the Shell function must appear in parentheses if you want to use the returned value later in your procedure.

1. Enter the current module of the ChangeSettings procedure, as shown below:

```
Sub ChangeSettings()
Dim nrTask
    nrTask = Shell("Control.exe intl.cpl", vbMinimizedFocus)
    Debug.Print nrTask
End Sub
```

2. Run the ChangeSettings procedure several times, each time supplying a different .CPL file according to the listing presented in Table 9-2. You may want to modify the above procedure as follows:

```
Sub ChangeSettings2()
    Dim nrTask
    Dim iconFile As String
    iconFile = InputBox("Enter the name of the CPL or DLL file:")
    nrTask = Shell("Control.exe " & iconFile, vbMinimizedFocus)
    Debug.Print nrTask
End Sub
```

If a program you want to launch is a Microsoft application, instead of the Shell function, it's more convenient to use the Visual Basic ActivateMicrosoftApp method. This method is available from the Microsoft Excel Application object. For example, to launch PowerPoint from the Immediate window, all you need to do is type the following instruction and press Enter:

```
Application.ActivateMicrosoftApp xlMicrosoftPowerPoint
```

Notice that the ActivateMicrosoftApp method requires a constant to indicate which program to start. The above statement starts Microsoft PowerPoint if it is not already running. If the program is already open, this instruction does not open a new occurrence of the program; it simply activates the already running application. You can use the following constants with the ActivateMicrosoftApp method. The name of the constant indicates the application name.

Application Name	Constant
Access	xlMicrosoftAccess
FoxPro	xlMicrosoftFoxPro
Mail	xlMicrosoftMail
PowerPoint	xlMicrosoftPowerPoint
Project	xlMicrosoftProject
Schedule	xlMicrosoftSchedulePlus
Word	xlMicrosoftWord

Moving between Applications

Because the user can work simultaneously with several applications in the Windows environment, your VBA procedure must know how to switch between the open programs. Suppose that in addition to Microsoft Excel, you have two other applications open: Microsoft Word and Windows Explorer. To activate an already open program, use the AppActivate statement using the following syntax:

```
AppActivate title [, wait]
```

Only the `title` argument is required. This is the name of the application as it appears in the title bar of the active application window or its task ID number as returned by the Shell function.

Note: The application title is compared to the title string of each running application. If there is no exact match, any application whose title string begins with title is activated.

The second argument, `wait`, is optional. This is a Boolean value (True or False) that specifies when Visual Basic activates the application. The value of False in this position immediately activates the specified application, even if the calling application does not have the focus. If you place True in the position of the `wait` argument, the calling application waits until it has the focus. Then it activates the specified application.

For example, to activate Microsoft Word, you should enter the following statement:

```
AppActivate "Microsoft Word"
```

Notice that the name of the application is surrounded by double quotation marks.

You can also use the return value of the Shell function as the argument of the AppActivate statement:

```
' run Microsoft Word
ReturnValue = Shell("C:\Microsoft Office\Office\Word.exe",1)
' activate Microsoft Word
AppActivate ReturnValue
```

The AppActivate statement is used for moving between applications and requires that the program is already running. This statement merely changes the focus. The specified application becomes the active window. The AppActivate statement will not start an application running. For an example of using this statement, see the FindCPLFiles procedure in the next section.

Let's practice some of these recently introduced VBA statements:

1. Open Windows Explorer by typing in the Immediate window the following statement:

```
Shell "Explorer"
```

After you press **Enter,** the requested application is opened. On the Windows taskbar the icon with the My Documents folder should appear.

2. Enter the following statement in the Immediate window:

```
AppActivate "My Documents"
```

After pressing **Enter,** the focus moves to the My Documents window.

Controlling Another Application

Now that you know how to use VBA statements to start a program and switch between applications, let's see how one application can communicate with another. The simplest way for an application to get control of another is by means of the SendKeys statement. This statement allows you to send a series of keystrokes to the active application window. You can send a key or a combination of keys and achieve the same result as if you worked directly in the active application window using the keyboard. The SendKeys statement looks as follows:

```
SendKeys string [, wait]
```

The required argument string is the key or key combination that you want to send to the active application. For example, to send a letter "f," use the following instruction:

```
SendKeys "f"
```

To send the key combination Alt+f, use:

```
SendKeys "%f"
```

The percent sign (%) is the string used for the Alt key.

To send a combination of keys, such as Shift+Tab, use the following statement:

```
SendKeys "+{TAB}"
```

The plus sign (+) denotes the Shift key. To send other keys and combinations of keys, see the corresponding strings listed in Table 9-3.

Tip 9-1: SendKeys versus Other Applications

You can only send keystrokes to applications that were designed for the Microsoft Windows operating system.

Tip 9-2: SendKeys and Reserved Characters

Some characters have a special meaning when used with the SendKeys statement. These keys are: plus sign (+), caret (^), tilde (~), and parentheses ( ). To send these characters to another application, you must enclose them in braces {}. To send the braces, enter {{} and {}}.

The second argument of the SendKeys statement is optional. Wait is a logical value that is true or false. If false (default), Visual Basic returns to the procedure immediately upon sending the keystrokes. If wait is true, Visual Basic returns to the procedure only after the sent keystrokes have been executed.

To send characters that aren't displayed when you press a key, use the codes in Table 9-3. Remember to enclose these codes in quotes. For example:

```
SendKeys "{BACKSPACE}"
```

Table 9-3: Keycodes used with the SendKeys statement

Key	Code	Key	Code
Backspace	{BACKSPACE}	Scroll Lock	{SCROLLLOCK}
	{BS}	Tab	{TAB}
	{BKSP}	Up Arrow	{UP}
Break	{BREAK}	F1	{F1}
Caps Lock	{CAPSLOCK}	F2	{F2}
Delete	{DELETE}	F3	{F3}
	{DEL}	F4	{F4}
Down Arrow	{DOWN}	F5	{F5}
End	{END}	F6	{F6}
Enter	{ENTER}	F7	{F7}
	~	F8	{F8}
Esc	{ESC}	F9	{F9}
Help	{HELP}	F10	{F10}
Home	{HOME}	F11	{F11}
Insert	{INSERT}	F12	{F12}
	{INS}	F13	{F13}
Left Arrow	{LEFT}	F14	{F14}
Num Lock	{NUMLOCK}	F15	{F15}
Page Down	{PGDN}	F16	{F16}
Page Up	{PGUP}	Shift	+
Print Screen	{PRTSC}	Ctrl	^
Right Arrow	{RIGHT}	Alt	%

> **Tip 9-3: SendKeys Statement is Case Sensitive**
>
> When you send keystrokes with the SendKeys statement, bear in mind that you must distinguish between the lower- and uppercase characters. Therefore, to send the key combination Ctrl+d, you must use ^d, and to send Ctrl+Shift+D, you should use the following string: ^+d.

Earlier in this chapter you learned that .cpl files launch various Control Panel icons. The purpose of the VBA procedure that you will now create is to locate on your hard drive all of the files with the .cpl extension.

1. Use the Immediate window to launch Windows Explorer with the following statement: Shell "Explorer." The "My Documents" icon should appear on the Windows taskbar at the bottom of the screen.

2. Insert a new module into the current project and rename it **SendKeysStatement.**

3. Enter the FindCPLFiles procedure, as shown below:

```
Sub FindCPLFiles()
    ' The keystrokes are for Windows 2000
    AppActivate "My Documents"
    ' activate the Search window
    SendKeys "{F3}", True
    ' move the pointer to the Search for files
    ' and folders named text box
    SendKeys "%m", True
    ' type in the search string
    SendKeys "*.cpl", True
    ' move to the Look in drop down box
    SendKeys "{Tab}{Tab}", True
    ' change to the root directory
    SendKeys "C:\", True
    ' execute the Search
    SendKeys "%s", True
End Sub
```

4. Switch to the Microsoft Excel application window and run the FindCPLFiles procedure (use Alt+F8 to open the Macro dialog, highlight the name of the procedure, and then click **Run**).

The first statement in the procedure above uses the AppActivate statement (see the preceding section) to activate the already running application. Recall that you activated the Windows Explorer with the Shell statement typed in the Immediate window. The remaining statements send necessary keystrokes to the active application. The result of this procedure is the Search Results window with a list of Control Panel files with the extension .cpl. You could use one SendKeys statement to send all of the required keystrokes (see the following example procedure). However, it's much easier to understand the procedure when keystrokes are sent in small batches.

```
Sub FindCPLFiles2()
    AppActivate "My Documents"
    SendKeys "{F3}% m*.cpl{Tab}{Tab}C:\%s", True
End Sub
```

Other Methods of Controlling Applications

Although you can pass commands to another program by using the SendKeys statement, you must resort to other methods to gain full control of another application. There are two standard ways in which applications can communicate with one another. The newest method, known as Automation, allows you to access and manipulate the objects of another application. Through Automation, you can write VBA procedures that control other applications by referencing another application's objects, properties, and methods. In the remaining sections of this chapter, you will learn how to control another application via Automation. The old data-exchange technology called DDE (Dynamic Data Exchange) is a protocol that allows you to dynamically send data between two programs by creating a special channel for sending and receiving information. DDE is quite slow and difficult to work with. DDE should be used only if you need to communicate with an older application that does not support Automation.

Understanding Automation

When you communicate with another application, you may require more functionality than activating it for sending keystrokes. For example, you may want to create and manipulate objects within that application. You can embed an entire Word document in a Microsoft Excel spreadsheet. Because both Excel and Word support Automation, you can write a VBA procedure in Excel to manipulate Word objects, such as documents or paragraphs.

The applications that support Automation are called *Automation servers* or *Automation objects*. The applications that can manipulate a server's objects are referred to as *Automation controllers*. Some applications can be only a server or a controller, and others can act in both of these roles. All Microsoft Office 2000/2002 applications can act as Automation servers and controllers. The Automation controllers can be all sorts of ActiveX objects installed on your computer. You will learn about these objects in the next chapter.

Understanding Linking and Embedding

Before you learn how to control other applications from a VBA procedure using Automation, let's take a look at how the manual method is used to link and embed an object. Object linking and embedding, known as OLE, allows you to create *compound documents*. A compound document contains objects created by other applications. For example, if you embed a Word document in a Microsoft Excel worksheet, Excel only needs to know the name of the application that was used to create this object and the method of displaying the object on the screen. Compound documents are created by either linking or embedding objects. When you use the manual method to embed an object, you first need to copy it in one application and then paste it into another. The main difference between a linked object and an embedded object is in the way the object is stored and updated. Let's try this out:

1. Activate Microsoft Word and open any document.

2. Select and copy any text.

3. In a Microsoft Excel worksheet, you can now paste the copied text using one of these four methods:

   ■ Paste as text (choose **Edit | Paste**).

   The copied text will appear in the active cell (see Figure 9-2, cell A2).

   ■ Paste as an embedded object (choose **Edit | Paste Special**, click the **Paste option** button, and select **Microsoft Word Document Object** in the As list).

   The text will be pasted into the worksheet as an embedded object (see Figure 9-2, cell A5). The embedded object becomes a part of the destination file. Because the embedded object is not connected with the original data, the information is static. When the data changes in the source file, the embedded object is not updated. To change the embedded data, you must double-click it. This will open the object for editing in the source program. Of course, the source program must be installed on the computer. When you embed objects, all of the data is stored in the destination file. This causes the file size to increase considerably. Notice that when you embed an object, the Formula bar displays:

   ```
   =EMBED("Word.Document.8","")
   ```

   ■ Paste as a linked object (choose **Edit | Paste Special**, click the **Paste Link option** button, and select **Microsoft Word Document Object** in the As list).

   Although the destination file displays all of the data, it stores only the address of the data. When you double-click the linked object (see Figure 9-2, cell A9), the source application is launched. Linking objects is a dynamic operation. This means that the linked data is updated automatically when the data in the source file changes. Because the destination document contains only information on how the object is linked with the source document, object linking doesn't increase the size of a destination file. The following formula is used to link an object in Microsoft Excel:

   ```
   =Word.Document.8|'C:\vba2002\Chap09.doc'!!OLE_LINK2'
   ```

■ Paste as a hyperlink (choose **Paste | Hyperlink**).

The pasted data appears in the worksheet as underlined, colored text (see Figure 9-2, cell A14). You can quickly activate the source file by clicking on the hyperlink.

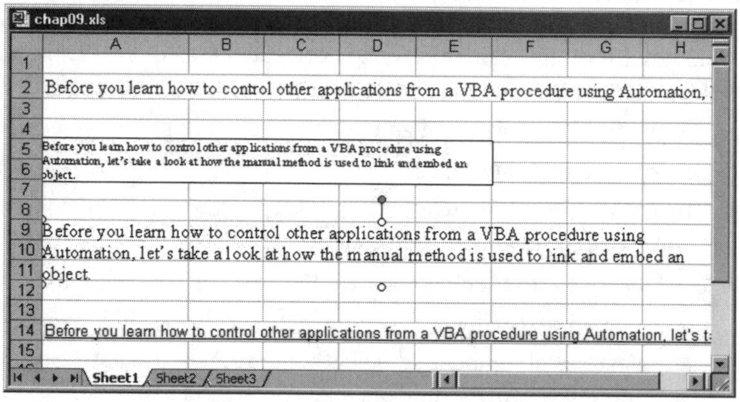

Figure 9-2: A demonstration of linking and embedding

Linking and Embedding with VBA

The InsertLetter procedure demonstrates how to programmatically embed a Word document in an Excel spreadsheet. Replace the reference to C:\Hello.doc with your own document name. The InsertLetter procedure uses the AddOleObject method. This method creates an OLE object and returns the Shape object that represents the new OLE object. To find additional arguments that the AddOLEObject method can use, look it up in the online Visual Basic documentation.

1. Insert a new module into the current project and rename it **OLE**.

2. Enter the InsertLetter procedure, as shown below:

```
Sub InsertLetter()
        Workbooks.Add
        ActiveSheet.Shapes.AddOLEObject FileName:="C:\Hello.doc"
End Sub
```

The above procedure opens a new workbook and embeds the indicated Word document in it. To link a document, you must specify an additional argument, Link, as shown below:

```
ActiveSheet.Shapes.AddOLEObject _
    FileName:="C:\Hello.doc", Link:=True
```

Tip 9-4: Objects—Linking versus Embedding

When you have to make a decision on whether to embed or link an object, use object embedding if:
- You don't mind the size of a document or you have enough disk space and memory to handle large files.

- You will never need the source file or use source text in other compound documents.
- You want to send the document to other people by e-mail or on a diskette, and you want to make sure that they can read the data without any problems.

COM and Automation

The driving force behind Automation is the Component Object Model (COM), which determines the rules for creating objects by the server application and specifies the methods that both the server and the control application must apply when using these objects. The COM standard contains a collection of functions that are made available as *Automation interfaces*.

When a server application creates an object, it automatically makes available an interface that goes along with it. This interface includes properties, methods, and events that can be recognized by the object. The controller application doesn't need to know the internal structure of the object in order to control it. It only needs to know how to manipulate the object interface that is made available by the server application.

Understanding Binding

For a controller application to communicate with the Automation object (server), you must associate the object variable that your VBA procedure uses with the actual Automation object on the server. This process is referred to as *binding*. There are two types of binding: *late binding* and *early binding*. Your choice of binding will have a great impact on how well your application performs.

Late Binding

When you declare a variable As Object or As Variant, Visual Basic uses late binding. Late binding is also known as *run-time binding*. Late binding simply means that Visual Basic doesn't associate your object variable with the Automation object at design time but waits until you actually run the procedure. Because the declaration As Object or As Variant is very general in nature, Visual Basic cannot determine at compile time that the object your variable refers to indeed has the properties and methods your VBA procedure is using.

The following declaration results in late binding of the specified object:

```
Dim mydoc As Object
```

The advantage of late binding is that all the Automation objects know how to use it.

The disadvantage is that there is no support for built-in constants. Because Visual Basic does not know at design time the type library your object is referring to, you must define constants in your code by looking up the values in the application's documentation. Also, querying an application at run time can slow down the performance of your solution.

Note: Late binding makes it possible to access objects in a type library of another application without first establishing a reference to the object library. Use late binding if you are uncertain that your users will have the referenced type libraries installed on their machines.

The following procedure demonstrates how to use late binding to print out a Word document.

```
Sub PrintWordDoc()
    Dim objWord As Object
    Set objWord = CreateObject("Word.Application")
    With objWord
        .Visible = True
        .Documents.Open "C:\Hello.doc"
        .Options.PrintBackground = False
        .ActiveDocument.PrintOut
    End With
    objWord.Documents.Close
    objWord.Quit
    Set objWord = Nothing
End Sub
```

Tip 9-5: What Kind of Binding is This?

Think of late binding whenever you declare object variables by using the generic Object or Variant data type. The main difference between late binding and early binding is how you declare your object variables.

Early Binding

When you declare object variables as specific object types, Visual Basic uses early binding. Early binding is also known as *compile-time binding*. This means that Visual Basic associates your object variable with the Automation object in the period during which the procedure source code is translated to executable code. The general syntax looks like this:

```
Dim objectVariable As Application.ObjectType
```

In the above syntax, `Application` is the name of the application as it appears in the Object Browser's Project Library drop-down list (for example, Word and Excel). `ObjectType` is the name of the object class type (for example, application, document, workbook, worksheet).

The following declarations result in early binding:

```
Dim mydoc As Word.Document
```

```
Dim mydoc As Excel.Worksheet
```

Early binding allows you to take full advantage of many of the debugging tools that are available in the Visual Basic Editor window. For example, you can look up external objects, properties, and methods with the Object Browser. Visual Basic Auto Syntax Checking, Auto List Members, and Auto Quick Info (all discussed in Chapter 2) can help you write your code faster and with less errors. In addition, early binding allows you to use built-in constants as arguments for methods and property settings. Because these constants are available in the type library at design time, you do not need to define them. The handy built-in syntax checking, IntelliSense features, and support for built-in constants aren't available with late binding. Although VBA procedures that use early binding execute faster, some very old Windows applications can only use late binding.

Note: In order to use early binding, you must first establish a reference to the object library (see the following section). Use early binding when you are certain that your users will have the referenced type libraries installed on their machines.

Establishing a Reference to an Object Library

If you decide to use early binding to connect to another application via Automation, you should start by establishing a reference to the object library whose objects you are planning to manipulate. Follow these steps to create a reference to the Microsoft Word Object Library:

1. Activate the Visual Basic Editor window.

2. Select the current project in the Project Explorer window, and choose **Tools | References**.

3. In the References dialog box, choose the name of the application in the Available References list box. For this example, click the check box next to **Microsoft Word 9.0 Object Library** or **Microsoft Word 10.0 Object Library** (Figure 9-3). Scroll down in the Available References list box to locate this object library. If the type library for an object application that is installed on your computer doesn't appear in the list of available references, click the **Browse** button.

4. Click **OK** to close the References dialog box.

The References dialog box lists the names of the references that are available to your VBA project. The references that are not used are listed alphabetically. The references that are checked are listed by priority. For example, in Excel, the Microsoft Excel 10.0 Object Library has a higher priority than Microsoft Word 10.0 or 9.0 Object Library. When a procedure references an object, Visual Basic searches each referenced object library in the order in which the libraries are displayed in the References dialog box.

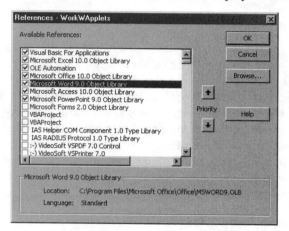

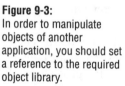

Figure 9-3:
In order to manipulate objects of another application, you should set a reference to the required object library.

After setting a reference to the required object library, you can browse the object properties and methods by using the Object Browser.

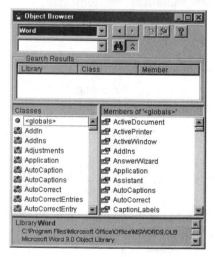

Figure 9-4:
All of the Microsoft Word objects, properties, and methods can be accessed from a Microsoft Excel VBA project after adding a reference to the Microsoft Word 9.0 Object Library (see Figure 9-3).

Creating Automation Objects

To create an Automation object in your VBA procedure, follow these steps:

- Declare an object variable using the Dim...As Object or Dim...As Application.ObjectType clause (see the topics on using late and early binding in the preceding sections).
- If you are using early binding, use the References dialog box to establish a reference to the application object type library.
- If the Automation object doesn't exist yet, use the CreateObject function. If the Automation object already exists, establish the reference to the object by using the GetObject function.
- Assign the object returned by the CreateObject or GetObject function to the object variable by using the Set keyword.

Using the CreateObject Function

To create a reference to the Automation object from a VBA procedure, use the CreateObject function with the following syntax:

```
CreateObject(class)
```

The argument `class` is the name of the application you want to reference. This name includes the object class type as discussed earlier (see the section on early binding). The Automation object must be assigned to the object variable by using the Set keyword, as shown below:

```
Set variable_name = CreateObject(class)
```

For example, to activate Word using the Automation object, include the following declaration statements in your VBA procedure:

```
'early binding
Dim wordAppl As Word.Document
Set wordAppl = CreateObject("Word.Application")
```

or

```
'late binding
Dim wordAppl As Object
Set wordAppl = CreateObject("Word.Application")
```

As a rule, the CreateObject function creates a new instance of the specified Automation object. Some applications, however, register themselves as so-called "single-instance" applications. This means that you cannot run more than one instance of the application at a time. Microsoft Word and PowerPoint are such single-instance applications. Therefore, if Word or PowerPoint are already running, the CreateObject function will simply reference a running instance instead of creating a new instance.

Creating a New Word Document Using Automation

Let's see how you can apply what you have learned in the preceding sections about binding in a real-life example. Sometimes you may be required to open a Word document programmatically and write some data to it straight from Excel. The following example uses early binding.

1. Insert a new module into the current project and rename it **Automation**.

2. In the Project Explorer window, select the project name and choose **Tools | References**.

3. If the Microsoft Word 9.0 Object Library or Microsoft Word 10.0 Object Library is not selected in the Available References list box, locate this object library and click the check box to select it. Click **OK** when done.

4. Enter the WriteLetter procedure shown below:

```
Sub WriteLetter()
Dim wordAppl As Word.Application

Application.StatusBar = "Creating Word Application Object..."
Set wordAppl = CreateObject("Word.Application")

    With wordAppl
      .Visible = True
      Application.StatusBar = "Creating a new document..."
      .Documents.Add
      .ActiveDocument.Paragraphs(1).Range.InsertBefore "Invitation"
        Application.StatusBar = "Saving document..."
      .ActiveDocument.SaveAs "C:\Invite.doc"
        Application.StatusBar = "Exiting Word..."
      .Quit
    End With
        Set wordAppl = Nothing
        Application.StatusBar = False
End Sub
```

5. Switch to the Microsoft Excel application window and choose **Tools | Macro | Macros**. Locate the WriteLetter procedure in the list of macros and click **Run**.

The WriteLetter procedure begins with the declaration of the object variable of the specific object type (Word.Application). Recall that this type of declaration (early binding) requires that you establish a reference to the Microsoft Word Object Library (this is covered in an earlier section of this chapter). The Automation object returned by the CreateObject function is assigned to the object variable called wordAppl. Because the applications launched by Automation don't appear on the screen, the statement:

```
wordAppl.Visible = True
```

makes the launched Word application visible so that you can watch VBA at work. The remaining statements of this procedure open a new document (the Add method), enter text in the first paragraph (the InsertBefore method), save the document in a disk file (the SaveAs method), and close the Word application (the Quit method). Each statement is preceded by an instruction that changes the message displayed in the status bar at the bottom of the Microsoft Excel application window. When the Word application is closed, the instruction:

```
Set wordAppl = Nothing
```

clears the object variable to reclaim the memory used by the object, and the statement:

```
Application.StatusBar = False
```

restores the default "Ready" message in the status bar.

As mentioned earlier, Microsoft Word is a _single-instance_ application. This means that you cannot run more than one instance of Word at a time. In short, the CreateObject function used in the WriteLetter procedure will launch Word if it is not already running; otherwise, it will use the currently active instance of Word.

Using the GetObject Function

If you are certain that the Automation object already exists or is already open, consider using the GetObject function. This function looks like this:

```
GetObject([pathname][, class])
```

The GetObject function has two arguments, both of which are optional. Use the first argument to specify the name of the file that you want to open. The full path should be given. If you omit this argument, you have to specify the `class` argument that indicates the type of object to work with. For example:

```
Excel.Application
Excel.Sheet
Excel.Chart
Excel.Range
Word.Application
Word.Document
PowerPoint.Application
```

To create an Excel object based on the Invite.xls spreadsheet and force the object to be an Excel 5 spreadsheet, you could use the following declaration:

```
' late binding
    Dim excelObj As Object
    Set excelObj = GetObject("C:\Invite.xls", Excel.Sheet.5")
```

To set the object variable to a specific Word document, you would use:

```
'early binding
    Dim wordObj As Word.Application
    Set wordObj = GetObject("C:\Invite.doc")
```

To access a running Office application object, leave the first argument out:

```
Dim excelObj As Object
Set excelObj = GetObject(, "Excel.Application")
```

When the GetObject function is called without the first argument, it returns a reference to an instance of the application. If the application isn't running, an error will occur.

Opening an Existing Word Document

The CenterText procedure that follows demonstrates the use of the GetObject function to access the Invite.doc file. As you recall, this file was created earlier in this chapter by the WriteLetter procedure. The Center-Text procedure will center the first paragraph in the specified Word document. The procedure uses a custom function named DocExists to check for existence of the specified document. Another custom function (IsRunning) checks whether the copy of Microsoft Word is already running. Based on the findings, the CreateObject or GetObject functions are used. If an error occurs, the error number and error description are displayed.

```
Sub CenterText()
Dim wordDoc As Word.Document
Dim wordAppl As Word.Application
Dim mydoc As String
Dim myAppl As String

On Error GoTo ErrorHandler

mydoc = "C:\Invite.doc"
myAppl = "Word.Application"

    'first find out whether the specified document exists
    If Not DocExists(mydoc) Then
        MsgBox mydoc & " does not exist." & Chr(13) & Chr(13) _
        & "Run the WriteLetter procedure to create " & mydoc & "."
        Exit Sub
    End If

    'now check if Word is running
    If Not IsRunning(myAppl) Then
        MsgBox "Word is not running - will create a new instance of _
        Word. "
        Set wordAppl = CreateObject("Word.Application")
        Set wordDoc = wordAppl.Documents.Open(mydoc)
    Else
        MsgBox "Word is running - will get the specified document. "
        'bind the wordDoc variable to a specific Word document
        Set wordDoc = GetObject(mydoc)
    End If
    'center the 1st paragraph horizontally on page
    With wordDoc.Paragraphs(1).Range
        .ParagraphFormat.Alignment = wdAlignParagraphCenter
```

```
        End With
        wordDoc.Application.Quit SaveChanges:=True
        Set wordDoc = Nothing
        Set wordAppl = Nothing
        MsgBox "The document " & mydoc & " was reformatted."
        Exit Sub
ErrorHandler:
        MsgBox Err.Description, vbCritical, "Error: " & Err.Number
End Sub

Function DocExists(ByVal mydoc As String) As Boolean
    On Error Resume Next
    If Dir(mydoc) < > "" Then
        DocExists = True
    Else
        DocExists = False
    End If
End Function

Function IsRunning(ByVal myAppl As String) As Boolean
Dim applRef As Object
On Error Resume Next

Set applRef = GetObject(, myAppl)
    If Err.Number = 429 Then
        IsRunning = False
    Else
        IsRunning = True
    End If
    'clear object variable
    Set applRef = Nothing
End Function
```

Using the New Keyword

Instead of using the CreateObject function to assign a reference to another application, you can use the New keyword. The New keyword tells Visual Basic to create a new instance of an object, return a reference to that instance, and assign the reference to the object variable being declared. For example, you can use the New keyword in the following way:

```
Dim objWord As Word.Application
Set objWord = New Word.Application

Dim objAccess As Access.Application
Set objAccess = New Access.Application
```

Object variables declared with the New keyword are always early-bound. Using the New keyword is more efficient than using the CreateObject function. Each time you use the New keyword, Visual Basic creates a new instance of the application. If the application is already running and you don't want to start another instance, you should use the GetObject function.

The New keyword can also be used to create a new instance of the object at the same time that you declare its object variable. For example:

```
Dim objWord As New Word.Application
```

Notice that when you declare the object variable with the New keyword in the Dim statement, you do not need to use the Set statement. However, this method of creating an object variable is not recommended because you lose control over when the object variable is actually created. Using the New keyword in the declaration statement causes the object variable to be created even if it isn't used. Therefore, if you want control over when the object is created, always declare your object variables using the following syntax:

```
Dim objWord As Word.Application
Set objWord = New Word.Application
```

The Set statement can be placed further in your code where you need to use the object. The following section of this chapter demonstrates how to use the New keyword to create a new instance of Microsoft Outlook and write your contact addresses to an Excel worksheet.

Using Automation to Access Microsoft Outlook

To access Outlook's object model directly from Excel, begin by establishing a reference to the Microsoft Outlook 10.0 or 9.0 Object Library. The example procedure that follows will insert your Outlook contact information into an Excel spreadsheet.

```
Sub GetContacts()
    Dim objOut As Outlook.Application
    Dim objNspc As NameSpace
    Dim objItem As ContactItem
    Dim Headings As Variant
    Dim i As Integer ' array element
    Dim r As Integer ' row index

    r = 2
    Set objOut = New Outlook.Application
    Set objNspc = objOut.GetNamespace("MAPI")

    Headings = Array("Full Name", "Street", "City", _
                            "State", "Zip Code", "E-Mail")
    Sheets(1).Activate
       For Each cell In Range("A1:F1")
          cell.FormulaR1C1 = Headings(i)
          i = i + 1
       Next
       For Each objItem In objNspc.GetDefaultFolder _
         (olFolderContacts).Items
          With ActiveSheet
             .Cells(r, 1).Value = objItem.FullName
             .Cells(r, 2).Value = objItem.BusinessAddress
```

```
                .Cells(r, 3).Value = objItem.BusinessAddressCity
                .Cells(r, 4).Value = objItem.BusinessAddressState
                .Cells(r, 5).Value = objItem.BusinessAddressPostalCode
                .Cells(r, 6).Value = objItem.EmailAddress
            End With
            r = r + 1
        Next objItem
    Set objItem = Nothing
    Set objNspc = Nothing
    Set objOut = Nothing
End Sub
```

The GetContacts procedure starts by declaring an object variable called
objOut to hold a reference to the Outlook application. This variable is
defined by a specific object type (Outlook.Application); therefore, VBA will
use early binding.

Notice that in this procedure, we use the New keyword (discussed in
the previous section) to create a new instance of an Outlook Application
object, return a reference to that instance, and assign the reference to the
objOut variable being declared.

In order to access contact items in Outlook, you also need to declare
object variables to reference the Outlook Namespace and Item objects. The
Namespace object represents the message store known as MAPI
(Messaging Application Programming Interface). The Namespace object
contains folders (Contacts, Journal, Tasks, etc.), which in turn contain
items. An item is a particular instance of Outlook data, such as an e-mail
message or a contact.

After writing column headings to the worksheet using the
For...Each...Next loop, the procedure uses another For...Each...Next loop
to iterate through the Items collection in the Contacts folder. The
GetDefaultFolder method returns an object variable for the Contact folder.
This method takes one argument, the constant representing the folder you
want to access. After all the contact items are written to an Excel spread-
sheet, the procedure releases all object variables by setting them to
Nothing.

Note: When you run the GetContacts procedure, you may get a
warning message that the program is trying to access e-mail
addresses. Click OK in the message box to allow the operation.

What's Next...

In this chapter, you learned how to launch, activate, and control other applications (Word and Outlook) from VBA procedures. You learned how to send
keystrokes to another application by using the SendKeys method. You also
learned how to manually and programmatically link and embed objects.
Finally, you used Automation to create a new Word document from Excel
and accessed this document later to change some formatting. You also

learned how to retrieve your contact addresses from Microsoft Outlook and place them in an Excel worksheet. You expanded your knowledge of VBA statements with two new functions—CreateObject and GetObject. You also learned how and when to use the New keyword. To learn how to control Microsoft Access from Excel, see Chapter 15.

In the next chapter, you will find out how to collect more data from a user with the help of custom forms.

Chapter 10

Dialog Boxes and Custom Forms

Excel Dialog Boxes ■ **File Open and File Save As Dialog Boxes** ■ **GetOpenFilename and GetSaveAsFilename Methods** ■ **Creating Forms** ■ Tools for Creating User Forms ■ Placing Controls on a Form ■ **Sample Application 1: Info Survey** ■ Adding Buttons, Check Boxes, and Other Controls to a Form ■ Changing Control Names ■ Setting Other Control Properties ■ Preparing a Worksheet to Store Custom Form Data ■ Displaying a Custom Form ■ Setting the Tab Order ■ Understanding Form and Control Events ■ Writing VBA Procedures to Respond to Form and Control Events ■ Writing a Procedure to Initialize the Form ■ Writing a Procedure to Populate the List Box Control ■ Writing a Procedure to Control Option Buttons ■ Writing Procedures to Synchronize the Text Box with the Spin Button ■ Writing a Procedure that Closes the User Form ■ Transferring Form Data to the Worksheet ■ Using the Info Survey Application ■ **Sample Application 2: Students and Exams** ■ Using MultiPage and TabStrip Controls ■ Writing VBA Procedures for the Students and Exams Custom Form ■ Using the Students and Exams Custom Form ■ **What's Next ...**

In Chapter 4 you learned how to use the built-in InputBox function to collect single items of data from the user during the execution of your VBA procedure. But what if your procedure requires more data at run time? The user may want to supply all the data at once or make appropriate selections from a list of items. If your procedure must collect data, you can:

■ Use the collection of the built-in dialog boxes

■ Create a custom form

This chapter teaches you how to display the built-in dialogs from your VBA procedures and design your own custom forms from scratch.

Excel Dialog Boxes

Before you start creating your own forms, you should spend some time learning how to take advantage of dialog boxes that are built into Excel and are therefore ready for you to use. I'm not talking about your ability to manually select appropriate options but how to call these dialog boxes from your own VBA procedures.

Microsoft Excel has a special collection of built-in dialog boxes that are represented by constants beginning with xlDialog, such as xlDialogClear, xlDialogFont, xlDialogDefineName, and xlDialogOptionsView. These built-in dialog boxes are Microsoft Excel objects that belong to the built-in Dialogs collection. Each dialog object represents a built-in dialog box.

Table 10-1: Frequently used built-in dialog boxes

Dialog Box Name	Constant
New	xlDialogNew
Open	xlDialogOpen
Save As	xlDialogSaveAs
Page Setup	xlDialogPageSetup
Print	xlDialogPrint
Font	xlDialogFont

To display a dialog box, use the Show method in the following format:

```
Application.Dialogs(constant).Show
```

For example, the following statement displays the Font dialog box:

```
Application.Dialogs(xlDialogFont).Show
```

The list of constants identifying Excel built-in dialog boxes is available in the Object Browser window after selecting the Excel library and searching for xlDialog (see Figure 10-1).

1. Open a new workbook and save it as **Chap10.xls**.
2. Switch to the Visual Basic Editor window.

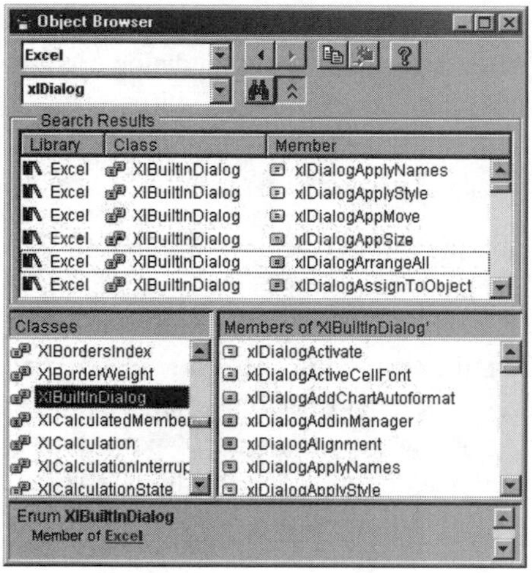

Figure 10-1:
Constants prefixed with "xlDialog" identify Excel built-in dialog boxes.

3. Open the Immediate window.

4. Enter the following statements and see the results:

```
Application.Dialogs(xlDialogClear).Show
Application.Dialogs(xlDialogFont).Show
Application.Dialogs(xlDialogFontProperties).Show
Application.Dialogs(xlDialogDefineName).Show
Application.Dialogs(xlDialogOptionsView).Show
```

The last instruction displays the Options dialog box View tab.

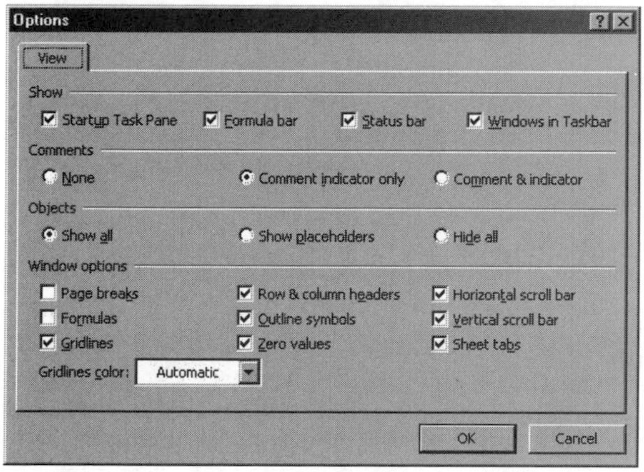

Figure 10-2:
Settings available on the Options dialog box View tab are identified by the xlDialogOptionsView constant.

After displaying a built-in dialog box, you can select an appropriate option, and Excel will format the selected cell or range, or the entire sheet. Although you can't modify the looks and behavior of a built-in dialog box, you can decide which initial setting the built-in dialog box will display when you show it from your VBA procedure. If you don't change the initial settings, VBA will display the dialog box with its default settings.

Suppose you want to display the Clear dialog box with the All option button selected. Normally, when Excel displays this dialog box, the Contents option button is selected. Enter the following statement in the Immediate window:

```
Application.DialogS(xlDialogClear).Show 1
```

You can include a list of arguments after the Show method. In the Clear dialog box, the All option button appears first in the group of four option buttons. Excel often numbers the available options. Therefore, All = 1, Formats = 2, Contents = 3, and Comments = 4. The built-in dialog box argument lists are available by searching the online help (see Figure 10-3).

To display the Font dialog box where the Arial 14-point font is already selected, try out the following instruction in the Immediate window:

```
Application.Dialogs(xlDialogFont).Show  "Arial", 14
```

To specify only the font size, enter a comma in the position of the first argument:

```
Application.Dialogs(xlDialogFont).Show  , 8
```

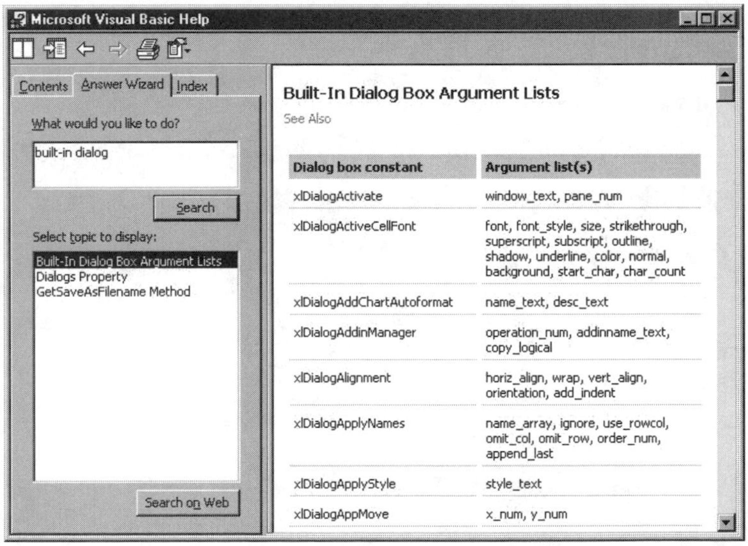

Figure 10-3: Microsoft Excel built-in dialog box argument list

The following instruction displays the Define Name dialog box, enters "John" in the Names in workbook text box, and places the reference to cell A1 in the Refers to box:

```
Application.Dialogs(xlDialogDefineName).Show "John", "=$A$1"
```

The Show method returns True if you click OK and False if you cancel.

File Open and File Save As Dialog Boxes

A new and quite powerful object in Office XP is FileDialog. This object allows you to display the File Open and File Save As dialog boxes from your VBA procedures. Because the FileDialog object is a part of the Microsoft Office 10.0 Object Library, it is available to all Office XP Applications. Programmers in all previous versions of Excel have used two special methods for displaying File Open and File Save As dialog boxes. These methods (GetOpenFilename and GetSaveAsFilename) are explained later in this section.

To display the File Open dialog box from your VBA procedure using the new FileDialog object, enter the following statement:

```
Application.FileDialog(msoFileDialogOpen).Show
```

To display the File Save As dialog box, use the following statement:

```
Application.FileDialog(msoFileDialogSaveAs).Show
```

For now, take a quick look at the File Open and File Save As dialog boxes by typing the above statements in the Immediate window.

In addition to File Open and File Save As dialog boxes, the FileDialog object is capable of displaying a Browse dialog box with a list of files and folders (Figure 10-4) or a list of folders (Figure 10-5):

```
' browse the list of files and folders
Application.FileDialog(msoFileDialogFilePicker).Show
```

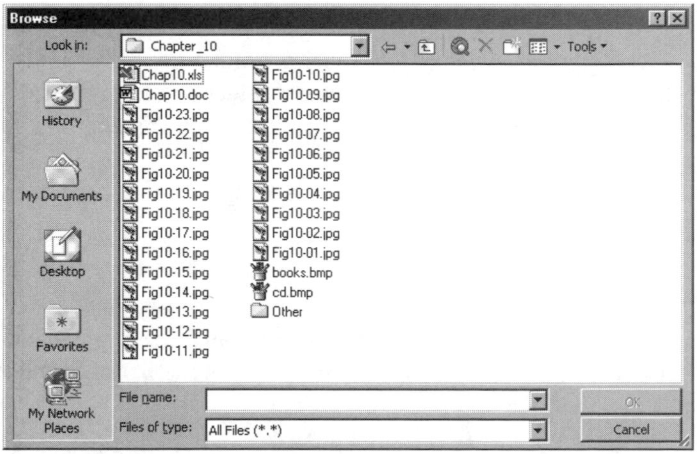

Figure 10-4: The File Picker dialog box lets users select one or more files. This dialog box displays a list of files and folders and shows Browse in the title bar.

```
' browse the list of folders
Application.FileDialog(msoFileDialogFolderPicker).Show
```

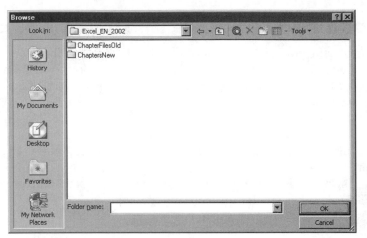

Figure 10-5:
The Folder
Picker dialog
box lets users
select a path.
This dialog box
displays a list of
directories and
shows Browse
in the title bar.

The constants that the FileDialog object uses are listed in the table below.
The "mso" prefix denotes that the constant is a part of the Microsoft Office
Object Model.

msoFileDialog Constants	Value
msoFileDialogOpen	1
msoFileDialogSaveAs	2
msoFileDialogFilePicker	3
msoFileDialogFolderPicker	4

To control the types of files that are displayed, use the FileDialog Filters
property. If you open the Files of type drop-down list box at the bottom of
the File Open dialog box, you will see quite a selection of file filters to
choose from. While there are 24 preset file filters, you can also add your
own filters to this list.

Enter the following in the Immediate window to find out the default
number of filters:

```
set f = Application.FileDialog(msoFileDialogOpen).Filters
?f.count
```

Filters are stored in the FileDialogFilters collection for the FileDialog
object. Let's create a simple procedure that returns the list of default file filters to an Excel worksheet:

1. Insert a new module into the current VBA project and rename it
    DialogBoxes.

2. In the DialogBoxes Code window, enter the ListFilters procedure, as
    shown below:

```
Sub ListFilters()
    Dim fdfs As FileDialogFilters
    Dim filt As FileDialogFilter
```

```
        Dim c As Integer

        Set fdfs = Application.FileDialog(msoFileDialogOpen).Filters
        Sheets(3).Cells(1, 1).Select
        Selection.Formula = "List of Default Filters"
        With fdfs
           c = .Count
           For Each filt In fdfs
               Selection.Offset(1, 0).Formula = filt.Description & _
                   ": " & filt.Extensions
               Selection.Offset(1, 0).Select
           Next
          MsgBox c & " filters were written to Sheet3."
          End With
    End Sub
```

This procedure declares two object variables. The fdfs variable returns a
reference to the FileDialogFilters collection of the FileDialog object, and
the filt object variable stores a reference to the FileDialogFilter object.
The Count property of the FileDialogFilters collection returns the total
number of filters. Next, the procedure iterates through the collection and
retrieves the description and extension of each defined filter.

Using the Add method of the FileDialogFilters collection, you can easily
add your own filter to the default filters. The following modified ListFilters2
procedure demonstrates how to add a filter to filter out temporary files
(*.tmp). The last statement in this procedure will open the File Open dialog
box so that you can check for yourself that the custom filter Temporary files
(*.tmp) has indeed been added to the Files of type drop-down list.

```
    Sub ListFilters2()
        Dim fdfs As FileDialogFilters
        Dim filt As FileDialogFilter
        Dim c As Integer

        Set fdfs = Application.FileDialog(msoFileDialogOpen).Filters
        Sheets(3).Cells(1, 1).Select
        Selection.Formula = "List of Default Filters"
        With fdfs
           c = .Count
           For Each filt In fdfs
               Selection.Offset(1, 0).Formula = filt.Description & _
                   ": " & filt.Extensions
               Selection.Offset(1, 0).Select
           Next
           MsgBox c & " filters were written to Sheet3."
            .Add "Temporary Files", "*.tmp", 1
            c = .Count
            MsgBox "There are now " & c & " filters." & vbCrLf _
                & "Check for yourself."
            Application.FileDialog(msoFileDialogOpen).Show
        End With
    End Sub
```

You can remove all the preset filters using the Clear method of the FileDialogFilters collection. Modify the above procedure to clear the built-in filters prior to adding the custom filter Temporary files (*.tmp).

When you select a file in the Open File dialog box, the selected file name and path is placed in the FileDialogSelectedItems collection. Use the SelectedItems property to return the FileDialogSelectedItems collection. By setting the AllowMultiSelect property of the FileDialog object to True, a user can select one or more files by holding down the Shift or Control keys while clicking filenames.

The following procedure demonstrates how to use the above-mentioned properties. The procedure opens a new workbook and inserts a list box control. The user is allowed to select more than one file. The selected files are then loaded into the list box control, and the first filename is highlighted.

```
Sub ListSelectedFiles()
    Dim fd As FileDialog
    Dim myFile As Variant
    Dim lbox As Object

    Set fd = Application.FileDialog(msoFileDialogOpen)
    With fd
        .AllowMultiSelect = True
        If .Show Then
            Workbooks.Add
            Set lbox = Worksheets(1).Shapes. _
                    AddFormControl(xlListBox, _
                    Left:=20, Top:=60, Height:=40, Width:=300)
            lbox.ControlFormat.MultiSelect = xlNone
            For Each myFile In .SelectedItems
                lbox.ControlFormat.AddItem myFile
            Next
            Range("B4").Formula = _
                "You've selected the following " & _
                lbox.ControlFormat.ListCount & " files:"
            lbox.ControlFormat.ListIndex = 1
        End If
    End With
End Sub
```

Figure 10-6:
User-selected files are loaded into a list box control placed in a worksheet by the ListSelectedFiles procedure (shown above).

Notice that the Show method does not open the files selected by the user. It merely displays the File Open dialog box. When the user clicks the Open button, the names of the files are retrieved from the SelectedItems collection via the SelectedItems property. If you'd like to immediately carry out the file open operation when the user clicks the Open button, you should use the Execute method of the FileDialog object.

The following procedure demonstrates how to open the user-selected files right away.

```
Sub OpenRightAway()
    Dim fd As FileDialog
    Dim myFile As Variant

    Set fd = Application.FileDialog(msoFileDialogOpen)
    With fd
        .AllowMultiSelect = True
        If .Show Then
            For Each myFile In .SelectedItems
                .Execute
            Next
        End If
    End With
End Sub
```

GetOpenFilename and GetSaveAsFilename Methods

For many years now, Excel has offered its programmers two handy VBA methods for displaying the File Save As and File Open dialog boxes: GetOpenFilename and GetSaveAsFilename. These methods are available only in Excel and can still be used in Excel 2002 if backward compatibility is required.

The GetOpenFilename method displays the Open dialog box, where you can select the name of a file to open. The second method (GetSaveAsFilename) shows the Save As dialog box.

1. Try out the following instructions in the Immediate window:

```
Application.GetOpenFilename
Application.GetSaveAsFilename
Application.GetSaveAsFilename ("Plan2.xls")
```

The GetOpenFilename method gets a filename from the user without actually opening the specified file. This method has four optional arguments. The most often used are the first and third arguments, as shown in the following table:

GetOpenFilename Arguments	Description
fileFilter	This argument determines what appears in the dialog box's Save as type field. For example, to display the text "Excel Files(*.xls)" in the Files of type drop-down list, you should enter the following text as fileFilter: "(Excel Files(*.xls), *.xls"). The first part of the filter (before the comma) determines the text to be displayed in the Files of type drop-down list. The second part (after the comma) specifies which files are to be displayed. Be sure to try out the example following the table.
title	This is the title of the dialog box. If omitted, the dialog box will appear with the default title "Open."

To see how these arguments are used, enter the following statement in the Immediate window (be sure to enter it on one line):

```
Application.GetOpenFilename("Excel Files(*.xls), *.xls"),,"Highlight _
    the File"
```

The GetOpenFilename method returns the name of the selected or specified file. This name can be used later by your VBA procedure to open the file. For example:

```
yourFile = Application.GetOpenFilename
?yourFile
C:\EXCEL\Mark.xls
Workbooks.Open Filename:=yourFile
```

In the example above, the filename is assigned to the variable yourFile. The two entries that follow inquire about the filename (?yourFile) and display its name (C:\EXCEL\Mark.xls). The fourth line opens the file as specified by the contents of the variable yourFile. The GetOpenFilename method returns false if you cancel the dialog box by pressing Esc or clicking Cancel.

The GetSaveAsFilename method returns a filename and path; however, it does not automatically save the specified file. To suggest the name of the file, enter the following instruction:

```
Application.GetSaveAsFilename ("Plan2.xls")
```

If you omit the filename, Excel will display the name of the active file. When using the GetSaveAsFilename method, you can specify the file filter as well as the dialog box's custom title:

```
yourFile = Application.GetSaveAsFilename("Plan2.xls", _
    "Excel Files(*.xls), *.xls",,"Name your file")
```

To display the Save As dialog box, assign the result of the GetSaveAs-Filename method to a variable, as shown above.

Creating Forms

Although ready to use and convenient, the built-in dialog boxes will not meet all of your VBA application's requirements. Apart from displaying a dialog box on the screen and specifying its initial settings, you can't control the dialog box's appearance. You can't decide which buttons to add, which ones to remove, and which ones to move around. Also, you can't change the size of the built-in dialog box. If you're looking to provide a custom interface, your only solution is to create a user form.

A user form is like a custom dialog box. You can add various controls to the form, set properties for these controls, and write VBA procedures that respond to form and control events. Forms are separate objects that you add to your VBA project by choosing Insert | UserForm from the Visual Basic Editor menu.

Forms can be shared across applications. For example, you can reuse the form you designed in Microsoft Excel in Microsoft Word or any other application that uses Visual Basic Editor.

To create a custom form, follow these steps:

- Switch to the Visual Basic Editor window
- Choose Insert | UserForm

A new folder called Forms appears in the Project Explorer window. This folder contains a blank UserForm. The work area automatically displays the form and the Toolbox with the necessary tools for adding controls.

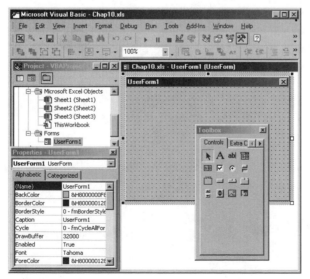

Figure 10-7:
A new form can be added to the open VBA project by selecting UserForm from the Insert menu.

The Properties window (Figure 10-8) displays a number of properties that you can set, depending on your needs. The form properties are arranged into seven categories: Appearance, Behavior, Font, Misc, Picture, Position, and Scrolling. To list form properties by category, click the Categorized tab in the Properties window. To find out information about a specific property, click the property name and press F1. The online help will be launched with the property description topic.

After adding a new form to your VBA project, you should assign a unique name to this form by setting the Name property. In addition to the name, each form should contain a title. You can set the title for your form by using the Caption property.

Tip 10-1: Sharing Forms between VBA Applications

All VBA applications that use the Visual Basic Editor share features for creating custom forms. You can share your forms by exporting and importing form files or by dragging a form object to another project. To import or export a form file, choose File | Export or File | Import. Before you export a form file, make sure to select it in the Project Explorer window. Before dragging a form to a different VBA application, arrange the VBE windows so that you can see the Project Explorer window in both applications. Drop the form on the name of another project in the Project Explorer.

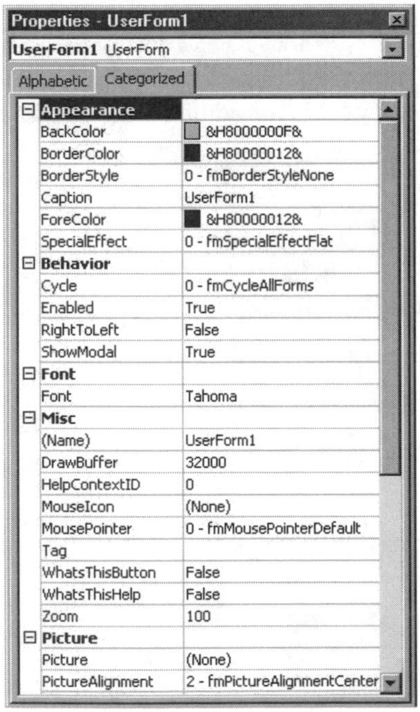

Figure 10-8:
Using the Properties window, you can easily change the appearance, behavior, and other features of your custom form.

Tools for Creating User Forms

When you design a form, you can insert appropriate controls to make it useful. The Toolbox contains standard Visual Basic buttons for all the controls that you can add to a form. It can also contain additional controls that have been installed on your computer. Controls available in the Toolbox are known as ActiveX controls. These controls can respond to specific user actions, such as clicking a control or changing its value. You will learn how to use the Toolbox controls in the remaining sections of this chapter.

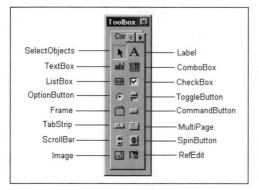

Figure 10-9:
The Toolbox displays the controls that can be added to your custom form.

The Microsoft Office Suite offers additional ActiveX controls that can be placed in the Toolbox for quick access. If you have other applications installed on your computer that contain ActiveX controls, you can also place them in the Toolbox.

To add a new ActiveX control to the Toolbox, follow these steps:

1. Right-click the **New Page** tab in the Toolbox and choose **Rename**.

2. In the Caption box, type the new name: **Extra Controls**. In the Control Tip Text box, type **Additional ActiveX Controls**. Click **OK** to return to the Toolbox.

3. Right-click anywhere within the new page area and choose **Additional Controls** from the shortcut menu. If this option is not available, make sure you are right-clicking the page area and not the Extra Controls tab itself.

4. When the Additional Controls dialog box appears, click the check box for each control you want to add. Figure 10-10 shows the Calendar Control highlighted. When you click OK, this control will appear on the Toolbox active page.

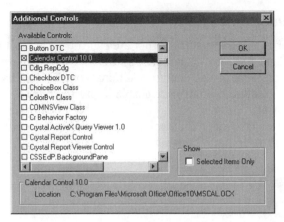

Figure 10-10:
You can add to the Toolbox additional ActiveX controls that are installed on your computer.

The standard Visual Basic controls are described in the next few sections.

Label

Labels allow you to add text to your form. The label control is often used to add captions, titles, headings, and explanations. You can use the label to assign a title to those controls that don't have the Caption property (such as text boxes, list boxes, scroll bars, and spin buttons). You can define an accelerator (shortcut) key for the label. For example, by pressing Alt and a specified letter, you can activate the control that was added to the form immediately after adding the label control and setting its Accelerator property. To add a title or a keyboard shortcut to an existing control, add a label control and type a letter in its Accelerator property in the Properties window. Next, choose View | Tab Order, and make sure that the name of the label appears before the name of the control that you want to activate with the assigned keyboard shortcut. You will learn how to use the Tab Order dialog box later in this chapter (see Figure 10-14).

Text Box

Text boxes are the most popular form controls because they can be used to display or request data from the user. You can enter text, numbers, cell references, or formulas in them. By changing the setting of the MultiLine property, you can enter more than one line of text in a text box. The text lines can automatically wrap around when you set the WordWrap property. And if you set the EnterKeyBehavior property to True when the MultiLine property is also set to True, you'll be able to start a new line in the text box by pressing Enter. Another property, EnterFieldBehavior, determines whether the text is selected when the user selects the text field. Setting this property to 0 (fmEnterFieldBehaviorSelectAll) will select the text within the field. Setting this property to 1 (fmEnterFieldBehaviorRecall-Select) will only select the text that the user selected the last time he activated this field. If you want to limit the number of characters the user

can enter inside a text box, you can do this by specifying the exact number
of characters in the MaxLength property.

Frame

Frames allow you to visually organize and logically group various controls
placed on the form. When you use the frame control around the option buttons, Visual Basic treats these buttons as mutually exclusive and allows you
to only select one of the options. Thus, if a user selects one of the available
option buttons, the other option buttons cannot be selected. Later in this
chapter, you will find an example of the Info Survey form that uses two
frames. One of them organizes the Hardware and Software option buttons
into one logical group, while the second frame groups the check boxes
related to the type of the computer (see Figure 10-11).

Option Button

The option button lets you select one of many mutually exclusive options.
Option buttons usually appear in groups of two or more buttons surrounded
by a frame control. At any given moment, only one option button can be
selected. When you select a new option button, the previously selected
option button is automatically deselected. To activate or deactivate an
option button, set its Value property to True or False. True means that the
option is activated. False means that the option is deactivated.

Check Box

Check boxes are used for turning specific options on and off. Unlike option
buttons that allow you to select only one option at a time, the user can
select concurrently one or more check boxes. If the check box is selected,
its Value property is set to True. If the check box is not selected, its Value
property is set to False.

Toggle Button

The toggle button looks like a command button and works similarly to an
option button. When you click the toggle button, the button stays pressed.
The next click on the button returns it to the normal (unpressed) state. The
pressed toggle button has its Value property set to True.

List Box

Instead of prompting the user to enter a specific value in a text box, sometimes it's better to present him with a list of available choices from which to
select. The list box reduces the possibility of data entry errors. The list box
entries can be typed in a worksheet or loaded directly from a VBA procedure using the AddItem method. The RowSource property indicates the
source of data displayed in the list box. For example, the reference $A$1:
$B$8 will display in the list box the contents of the specified range of cells.

The list box can display one or more columns when you set the Column-Count property. Another property, ColumnHeads, can be set to True to display the column titles in the list box. The user is not limited to selecting just one option. If the procedure requires that two or more list items be selected, you can set the MultiSelect property to True.

Combo Box

The combo box is a control that combines a text box and a list box. This control is often used to save space on the form. When the user clicks the down-arrow located to the right of the combo box, the box will open up to reveal a number of items to choose from. If none of the displayed choices is applicable, by setting the MatchRequired property to False, you can allow the user to enter a new value. The ListRows property determines how many items will appear when the user drops the list down. The Style property determines the type of combo box. Use 0 (fmStyleDropDownCombo) to let the user select an item from the list or enter a new item in the text box. To limit the user's selection of the items available in the combo box, set the Style property to 2 (fmStyleDropDownList).

Scroll Bar

This control allows you to place horizontal and vertical scroll bars on your form. Although normally used to navigate windows, scroll bars can be used on your form to enter values in a predefined range. The current value of the scroll bar is set or returned by the Value property. The scroll bar's Max property lets you set its maximum value. The Min property determines the minimum value. The LargeChange property determines by what value the Value property should change when the user clicks inside the scroll bar. When programming the behavior of the scroll bar, don't forget to set the SmallChange property that determines how the Value property changes when you click one of the scroll arrows.

Spin Button

The spin button works similarly to a scroll bar. You can click the spin arrow to increment or decrement a value. The spin button is often used together with a text box. The user can then type the exact value in the text box or select a value by using spin arrows. The technique of using the spin button with a text box is discussed later in this chapter.

Image

The image control lets you display a graphical image on a form. This control supports the following file formats: *.bmp, *.cur, *gif, *.ico, *.jpg, and *.wmf. Like other controls in the Toolbox, the image control has a number of properties that you can set. For example, you can control the appearance of the picture with the PictureSizeMode property. This property has three settings: 0 (fmPictureSizeModeClip crops a part of a picture that does not fit within the picture frame), 1 (fmPictureSizeModeStretch stretches the picture horizontally or vertically until it fills the entire frame area), and 3 (fmPictureSizeModeZoom enlarges the picture without distorting its proportions).

MultiPage Control

The MultiPage control displays a series of tabs at the top of the form (see Figure 10-17). Each tab acts as a separate page. Using the MultiPage control, you can design forms that contain two or more pages. You can place a different set of controls on each form page. When a form contains a lot of data, it can become less readable. It's much easier to click a form tab than move around in a long form using scroll bars. By default, each MultiPage control appears on your form with two pages. New pages can be added by using the shortcut menu or the Add method from within a VBA procedure. The second hands-on example in this chapter demonstrates how to use this control to keep track of students' exam grades.

TabStrip Control

Although the TabStrip and MultiPage controls look almost alike, each one of these controls has a different function. The TabStrip (see Figure 10-17) lets you use the same controls for displaying multiple sets of the same data. Suppose that the form shows students' exams. Each student has to pass an exam in the same subjects. Each subject can be placed on a separate page (tab). Each tab will contain the same controls to collect data showing the grade received and the date of the exam. When you activate any subject tab, you will see the same controls. Only the data in these controls will change. See the second hands-on example in this chapter to see how to use the TabStrip control.

RefEdit Control

The RefEdit control is specific to forms created in Microsoft Excel, as it allows you to select a cell or a range of cells in a worksheet and pass it to your VBA procedure. You can see how this control works by taking a look at some of the built-in dialog boxes in Excel. For example, the Consolidate dialog accessed from the Data menu has a RefEdit control labeled Reference that lets you specify the range of data that you want to consolidate. To temporarily hide the dialog box while selecting a range of cells, click the button to the right of the RefEdit control. The second hands-on example in this chapter uses the RefEdit control to populate a list box with students' names.

Placing Controls on a Form

When you create a custom form, you place various controls that are available in the Toolbox (Figure 10-9) on an empty form. The type of control you select depends on the type of data the control will have to store and the functionality of your form. The Toolbox is always visible when you work with your form. You can move it around on the screen, change its size, or close it when all controls are already on the form and all you want to do is work with their properties. The Toolbox that was temporarily removed from the screen can be redisplayed by choosing View | Toolbox.

Working with the Toolbox is easy. To add a new control to a form, first click the control image in the Toolbox and then click the form or draw a frame. Clicking on a form (without drawing a frame) will place a control in its default size. The standard settings of each control can be looked up in the Properties window. For example, the standard text box size is 18 x 72 points (see the Height and Width properties of the text box).

After placing a control on a form, the Select Object button (represented by the arrow) becomes the active control in the Toolbox. When you double-click a control in a Toolbox, you can draw as many instances of this control as you want. For example, to quickly place three text boxes on your form, double-click the text box control in the Toolbox and then click three times on the form. To deactivate the selected control, click the Select Object button in the Toolbox.

Tip 10-2: Setting Grid Options

When you drag a control on a form, Visual Basic adjusts the control so that it aligns with the form's grid. You can set the form's grid to your liking by using the Options dialog box. To access grid options, choose Tools | Options and click the General tab in the Options dialog box. The Form Grid Settings area lets you turn off the grid, adjust the grid size, and decide whether you want the controls aligned to the grid.

Sample Application 1: Info Survey

Now that you've read through the theory of creating user forms and understand the differences between various controls available in the Toolbox, you are ready for some hands-on experience. As you already know, the best way to understand a complex feature is to apply it in a real-life project. In this section, you will create a custom form for a coworker who requested that you streamline the tedious process of entering survey data into a spreadsheet.

As you work with this form (Figure 10-11), you will have the chance to experiment with many controls and their properties. Also, you will learn how to transfer data from your custom form to a worksheet (Figure 10-12).

By the end of this section, you will have the skills necessary to create a custom form to fit the unique requirements of your VBA application.

1. In the Project Explorer window, highlight the current project **VBAProject (Chap10.xls)** and change the project name in the Properties window to **CustomForms**.

2. Choose **Insert | UserForm** to add a blank form to your VBA project.

3. In the Properties window, double-click the **Name** property and type **InfoSurvey** to change the default form name (UserForm1). This is the name you will use to refer to this UserForm object in your VBA procedure.

4. Double-click the **Caption** property and type the new title for the form: **Info Survey**. This name will appear in your form's title bar.

5. Double-click the **BackColor** property, click the **Palette** tab, and select a color for the form background.

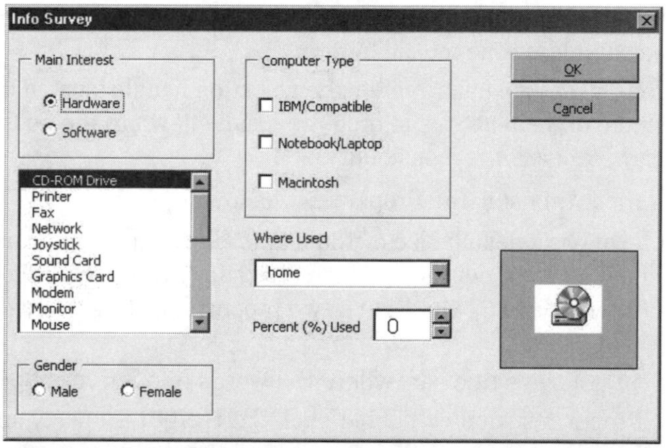

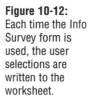

Figure 10-11:
The Info Survey custom form allows the user to quickly enter data by making appropriate selections.

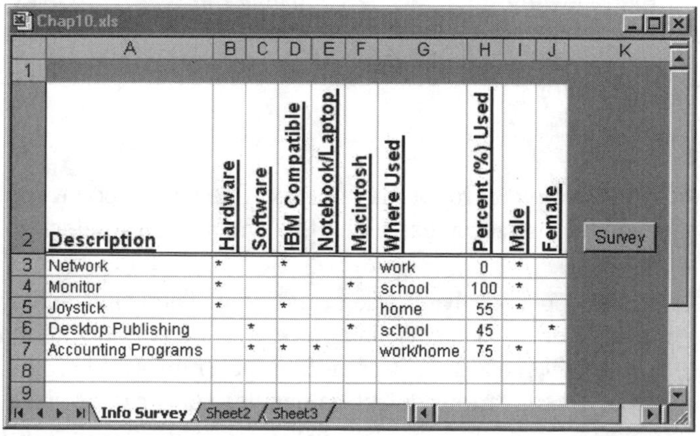

Figure 10-12:
Each time the Info Survey form is used, the user selections are written to the worksheet.

Adding Buttons, Check Boxes, and Other Controls to a Form

After setting the initial properties for a custom form (Name and Caption), proceed with placing the required controls on your form. Here are the step-by-step instructions for how to prepare the form shown in Figure 10-11.

1. **Changing the size of the form**

    When a default form inserted in your project is too small to fit all the controls required by your VBA application, you can change its size in one of the following ways:

    a. Sizing the form with the mouse:

    ■ Click on an empty part of the form. Several selection handles will appear around the form.

    ■ Position the mouse pointer over the selection handle located on the middle of the right side and drag it to the right to the position you want. Release the mouse button.

    ■ Position the mouse pointer over the selection handle located on the middle of the bottom and drag the handle down to the position you want. Release the mouse button.

    b. Sizing the form using the Properties window:

    Each new form has a default size of 180 x 240. The form's dimensions are in points. One point equals 1/72 inch. To change the size of the form, enter new values for the form's two properties: Height and Width.

    ■ Click in the form's title bar (where the words Info Survey appear).

    ■ In the Properties window, double-click the **Height** property and enter the following value: **252.75**. Change the Width property to **405.75**.

    To avoid extra work, always resize the form before adding the desired controls.

2. **Adding a frame:**

    ■ Click the **Frame** control in the Toolbox. The mouse pointer changes to a cross accompanied by the symbol of the selected control.

    ■ Point to the upper left-hand side of the form. Then click and drag the mouse to draw a small rectangle. When you release the mouse button, you will see a small rectangle titled Frame1. When the frame is selected, various selection handles appear in its sides, and the Properties window's title bar displays Properties—Frame1.

    ■ In the Properties window, double-click the **Caption** property and replace the selected default caption Frame1 with **Main Interest**.

3. **Adding option buttons:**

    ■   Click the **OptionButton** control in the Toolbox. Click the mouse pointer inside the Main Interest frame that you've just added to your form. Click and drag the mouse to the right until you see a rectangle with the default label OptionButton1.

    ■   In the Properties window, change the option button's Caption property to **Hardware**.

    ■   Using the same technique, add another option button to the Main Interest frame and change its Caption property to **Software**.

    The option buttons are used whenever the user has to select one choice from a group of mutually exclusive choices. If the user has to select more than one choice, check boxes are used.

Tip 10-3: Duplicating and Moving Controls

If you want to copy controls, select the control (a selected control will have handles at its sides), hold down the Ctrl key, position the mouse pointer inside the control, and press the left mouse button. Drag the pointer to the position you want, and then release the mouse button. Change the button's Caption property.

To select and move an entire group of controls, click the Select Objects tool in the Toolbox and start drawing a rectangle around the group of controls that you want to move together. When you release the mouse button, all the controls will be selected. (You can also select more than one control by holding down the Shift key while clicking each of the controls you want to select— don't just read it, try it now!) To move the selected group of controls to another position on the form, click within the selected area and drag the mouse to the desired position.

---

4. **Adding a list box:**

    ■   Click the ListBox control in the Toolbox. The mouse pointer will change to a cross accompanied by the symbol of the selected control. Click below the Main Interest frame, and drag the mouse down and to the right to draw a list box. When you release the mouse button, you will see a white rectangle.

    Figure 10-11 shows the list box populated with Hardware entries. In a later section of this hands-on project, you will learn how to display appropriate lists of items in a list box.

5. **Adding a frame with option buttons:**

    ■   Follow step 2 above to insert a frame below the list box that you added in step 4. Change the frame's Caption property to **Gender**. Add two option buttons inside this frame, and change the first button's Caption property to **Male** and the second one to **Female**. See Figure 10-11.

6. **Adding a frame with check boxes:**
   - Click the **Frame** control in the Toolbox and draw a rectangle to the right of the frame labeled Main Interest.
   - Change the Caption property of the new frame to **Computer Type**.
   - Click the **CheckBox** button in the Toolbox, and click inside the empty frame that you have just added. The CheckBox1 control should appear inside the frame.
   - Change the Caption property of the CheckBox1 control to **IBM/Compatible**.
   - Place two more check boxes inside the frame labeled Computer Type. Use the Caption property to assign the following new titles to these check boxes: **Notebook/Laptop** and **Macintosh**. The final result should match Figure 10-11.

Unlike option buttons that are mutually exclusive, check boxes allow the user to activate one or more options simultaneously. The check box can be checked, unchecked, or unavailable at a particular time. The unavailable check box has its label grayed out and is therefore inactive (cannot be selected). The checked box has an x in front of its caption. The check box that has the focus is indicated by a dotted line around the caption.

Tip 10-4: A Check Box or an Option Button?

Use option buttons where only one option can be selected at a given time. Use check boxes to have the user select any number of options that apply.

---

7. **Adding a label and a combo box:**
   - Click the **Label** control in the Toolbox.
   - Click the empty space below the frame labeled Computer Type. The Label1 control should appear.
   - Change the Caption property of Label1 to **Where Used**.
   - Click the **ComboBox** control in the Toolbox.
   - Click the empty space below the Where Used label and drag the mouse to draw a rectangle. Release the mouse button.

The combo box displays a list of available choices only after you click the down arrow placed at the right of this control. The combo box is sometimes referred to as a drop-down list and is used to save valuable space on the screen. Although the user can only see one element of the list at a given time, the current selection can be quickly changed by clicking on the arrow button.

8. **Adding a label, a text box, and a spin button:**
   - Click the **Label** control in the Toolbox.
   - Click on the empty place of the form just below the Where Used combo box. A label control will appear. Change the Caption property for this label to **Percent (%) Used.**
   - Click the **TextBox** control in the Toolbox.
   - Click to the right of the Percent (%) Used label control to place a default size text box.
   - Click the **SpinButton** control in the Toolbox, and then click to the right side of the text box control. A default size spin button will appear. The final result is shown in Figure 10-11.

   The spin button has two arrows that are used to increment or decrement a value in a given range. The maximum value is determined by the setting of the Max property, and the minimum value is set with the Min property. The spin button has the same properties as the scroll bar, with two differences: the spin button does not have a scroll box, and it lacks the LargeChange property. A text box is usually placed next to the spin button. This allows the user to enter a value directly into the text box or use the spin buttons to determine the value. If the spin button has to work with the text box, your VBA procedure must ensure that the value of the text box and the spin button are synchronized. In this example, you will use the spin button to indicate the percent of interest that the user has in the selected hardware or software product.

9. **Adding command buttons:**
   - Double-click the **CommandButton** control in the Toolbox. Recall that by double-clicking the control in the Toolbox, you indicate that you want to create more than one control using the selected tool.
   - Click in the top right-hand corner of the form. This will cause the CommandButton1 to appear.
   - Click below CommandButton1. CommandButton2 will appear.
   - Change the Caption property of CommandButton1 to **OK** and CommandButton2 to **Cancel.**

   Most custom forms have two command buttons, OK and Cancel, that enable the user to accept the data entered on the form or dismiss the form. In this example, the OK button will transfer the data entered on the form onto a worksheet. The user will be able to click the Cancel button whenever he is done inputting the data. To make the buttons respond to user actions, you will write appropriate VBA procedures later in this chapter.

10. **Adding an image control:**
    - Click the **Image** button in the Toolbox.

■ Click with the mouse below the Cancel button, and drag the mouse to draw a rectangle. Release the mouse button. The final result is shown in Figure 10-11. The form will display a different picture depending on whether the Hardware or Software option button is selected. The images will be loaded by a VBA procedure.

11. Checking the appearance of the form:

■ Click the title bar, or click on any empty area of the form to select it.

■ Press **F5** or choose **Run | Run Sub/UserForm** to display the form as the user will see it.

■ Visual Basic switches to the active sheet in the Microsoft Excel window and displays the custom form you designed. If you forget to select the form, the Macro dialog box will appear. Close the dialog box, and repeat the two previous steps.

■ Click the **Close** button (x) in the top right-hand corner of the form to close the form and return to the Visual Basic Editor. Recall that the OK and Cancel buttons placed on the form aren't yet functional. They require VBA procedures to make them work.

After you've added controls to the form, use the mouse or Format menu commands to adjust alignment and spacing of the controls.

Tip 10-5: Working with the UserForm Toolbar

The UserForm toolbar contains a number of useful shortcuts for working with forms, such as making controls the same size, centering a control horizontally or vertically, aligning control edges, and grouping and ungrouping controls. To display this toolbar, choose View I Toolbars I UserForm.

Changing Control Names

Before you begin to write procedures to control the form, you should assign your own names to the individual controls placed on the form. Although Visual Basic automatically assigns a default name to each control, these names are difficult to distinguish in a procedure that may reference objects of the same class that have almost identical names: OptionButton1, OptionButton2, and so on. Assigning meaningful names to the controls placed on your form makes VBA procedures referencing these controls much more readable.

To assign a new name to a control:

■ Click the appropriate control on the form.

■ Double-click the Name property in the Properties window.

Caution: Before you change the Name property, make sure that the title bar of the Properties window displays the correct type of the control. For example, to assign a new name to the frame control, click the frame control on the form. When the Properties window displays "Properties—Frame1," double-click the Name property and type the new name in place of the highlighted default name.

Do not confuse the name of the control with the control's title (caption). For example, on the Info Survey form, the default name of the frame control is Frame1, but the title of this control is Main Interest. The control title can be changed by setting a Caption property. While the control's caption allows the user to identify the purpose of the control and may suggest the type of data expected, it is the name of the control that will be used in the code of your VBA procedures to make things happen.

1. Assign names to the controls placed on the Info Survey form as shown in the following table:

Object Type	Name Property
First option button	optHard
Second option button	optSoft
List box	lboxSystems
Third option button	optMale
Fourth option button	optFemale
First check box	chkIBM
Second check box	chkNote
Third check box	chkMac
Combo box	cboxWhereUsed
Text box	txtPercent
Spin button	spPercent
First command button	butOK
Second command button	butCancel
Image	picImage

Setting Other Control Properties

The controls that you placed on the Info Survey form are objects. Each of these objects has its own properties and methods. In the previous section, you changed the Name property for all the objects that will be referenced later from within VBA procedures. The control properties can be set during the design phase of your custom form or at run time (that is, when your VBA procedure is executed).

Let's now set some control properties for selected controls. To set a property, click a control on the form, locate the desired property in the

Properties window, and type the new value in the space to the right of the property name. For example, to set the ControlTipText property of the lboxSystems control, click the list box control on the Info Survey form and locate the ControlTipText property in the Properties window. In the right-hand column of the Properties window, type the text you want to display when the user positions the mouse pointer over the list box control: Select only one item.

1. Change the object properties as shown below.

Object Name	Property	Change to
lboxSystems	ControlTipText	Select only one item
spPercent	Max	100
spPercent	Min	0
OK button	Accelerator	O
Cancel button	Accelerator	C
picImage	PictureSizeMode	0 - fmPictureSizeModeClip

The Accelerator property indicates which letter in the object name can be used to activate the control in the keyboard shortcut combination. The specified letter will appear underlined in the caption (title) of the object. For example, after displaying the form, you will be able to quickly select OK by pressing Alt+O.

The other properties of the Info Survey form objects will be set directly from VBA procedures.

Preparing a Worksheet to Store Custom Form Data

After the user selects appropriate options on the custom form and clicks OK, the selected data will be transferred to a worksheet. However, before this happens, you must prepare a worksheet to accept the data and give the user an easy interface for launching your form. Follow the steps below to get your worksheet ready:

1. Activate the Microsoft Excel window.
2. Double-click the **Sheet1** tab in the **Chap10.xls** workbook, and type the new name for this sheet: **Info Survey**.
3. Enter the column headings shown in Figure 10-13.
4. Select column **K** and row **1**, and change the background of all cells to your favorite color (use the **Fill Color** button on the Formatting toolbar).

    The easiest way to launch a custom form from a worksheet is by clicking on a button. The remaining steps walk you through the process of adding the Survey button to your Info Survey worksheet:

5. Choose **View | Toolbars**, and select **Forms**.

6. Click the **Button** control on the Forms toolbar. Click in column **K** and row **2** (cell K2) to place a button. When the Assign Macro dialog box appears, type **DoSurvey** in the Macro name box, and click **OK**. You will write this procedure later.

7. When you return to the worksheet, the button (Button1) to which you assigned the DoSurvey macro should still be selected. Type the new name for this button: **Survey**. If the button is not selected, use the right mouse button to select it. Choose **Edit Text** from the shortcut menu, and type **Survey** for the button's new name. To exit the Edit mode, click outside the button.

8. Save the changes you've made to Chap10.xls.

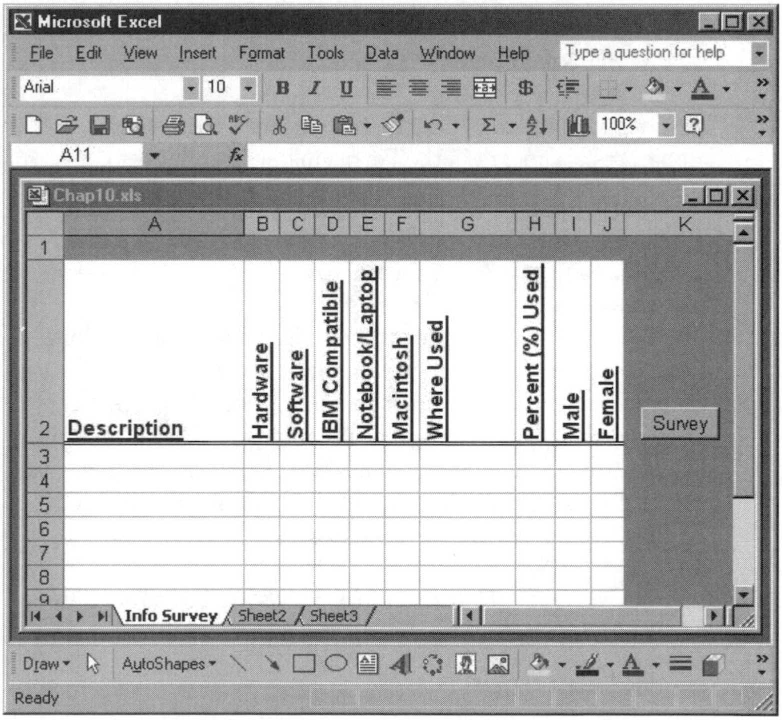

Figure 10-13: The Survey button will launch the Info Survey form. When the user clicks OK on the form, the form entries will be placed in this worksheet.

Displaying a Custom Form

Each UserForm has a Show method that allows you to display the form to the user. In the example below, you will prepare the DoSurvey procedure. Recall that in the previous section you already assigned this procedure to the Survey button placed in the Info Survey worksheet.

1. In the Visual Basic Editor window select the **CustomForms (Chap10.xls)** project in the Project Explorer window and choose **Insert | Module.**

2. In the Properties Window, change the new module's name to **ShowSurvey.**

3. Enter the following procedure to display the custom form:

```
Sub DoSurvey()
      InfoSurvey.Show
End Sub
```

Notice that the Show method is preceded by the name of the form object as it appears in the Forms folder (InfoSurvey).

4. Save the changes made to Chap10.xls.

5. Switch to the Microsoft Excel window and click the **Survey** button. The Info Survey form appears.

_____

Note: If an error message appears after you click the Survey button, you have not assigned the required macro to this button as instructed in step 6 in the previous section. To correct this problem, click OK in response to the message. Right-click the Survey button and choose Assign Macro from the shortcut menu. Click the DoSurvey macro name in the list box, and click OK. Now click the Survey button to display the form.

6. Close the Info Survey form by clicking the **Close** button (x) in the top right-hand corner of the form.

Setting the Tab Order

The user can move around a form by using a mouse or Tab key. Because many users prefer to navigate through the form using the keyboard, it is important to determine the order in which each control on the form is activated. Follow these steps to set the tab order in the Info Survey form:

1. In the Forms folder in the Project Explorer Window, double-click the **InfoSurvey** form.

2. Choose **View | Tab Order.** The Tab Order dialog box appears. This box displays the names of all the controls on the InfoSurvey form in the order that they were added. The right side of the dialog box has buttons that allow you to move the selected control up or down. To move a

control, click its name and click the Move Up or Move Down button until the control appears in the position you want.

3. Rearrange the controls of the Info Survey form as shown in Figure 10-14.

4. Close the Tab Order dialog box by clicking **OK**.

5. Return to the Microsoft Excel worksheet, and click the **Survey** button.

6. Press the **Tab** key to move forward. Press **Shift+Tab** to move backward.

7. Close the Info Survey form.

If you'd like to change the order in which the controls are activated, reopen the Tab dialog box and make the appropriate changes.

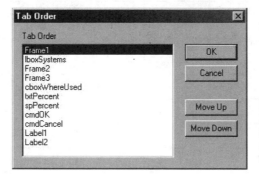

Figure 10-14:
The Tab Order dialog box lets you determine which control will be activated when you press the Tab key.

Understanding Form and Control Events

In addition to having properties and methods, each form and control has a predefined set of events. An event is some type of action, such as clicking a mouse button, pressing a key, selecting an item from a list, or changing a list of items available in a list box. Events can be triggered by the user or the system. To specify how a form or control should respond to events, write *event procedures*.

When you design a custom form, you should anticipate and program events that can occur at run time (while the form is being used). The most popular event is the Click event. Every time a command button is clicked, it triggers the appropriate event procedure to respond to the Click event for that button. A form itself can respond to more than 20 separate events, including Click, DblClick, Activate, Initialize, and Resize.

Table 10-2 lists events that are recognized by various form controls. If a control does not recognize a specific event, the table cell displays "N"; otherwise, it is blank. Take a few minutes now to familiarize yourself with the names of the events. For example, take a look at the AddControl event in the table. You can see at a glance that this event is only available for three objects: Frame, MultiPage control, and the UserForm itself.

Table 10-2: Form and control events

Event Name	UserForm	Label	TextBox	ComboBox	ListBox	CheckBox	OptionButton	ToggleButton	Frame	CommandButton	TabStrip Control	MultiPage Control	ScrollBar	SpinButton	Image	RefEdit
Activate		N	N	N	N	N	N	N	N	N	N	N	N	N	N	N
AddControl		N	N	N	N	N	N	N		N	N		N	N	N	N
AfterUpdate	N	N							N	N	N	N			N	
BeforeDragOver																
BeforeDropOrPaste																
BeforeUpdate	N	N							N	N	N	N			N	
Change	N	N							N	N					N	
Click			N										N	N		N
DblClick													N	N		
Deactivate		N		N	N	N	N	N	N	N	N	N	N	N	N	N
DropButtonClick	N	N		N	N	N	N	N	N	N	N	N	N	N	N	
Enter	N	N													N	
Error																
Initialize		N	N	N	N	N	N	N	N	N	N	N	N	N	N	N
Exit	N	N													N	
KeyDown		N													N	
KeyPress		N													N	
KeyUp		N													N	
Layout		N	N	N	N	N	N	N		N	N		N	N	N	N
MouseDown													N	N		
MouseMove													N	N		
MouseUp													N	N		
QueryClose		N	N	N	N	N	N	N	N	N	N	N	N	N	N	N
RemoveControl		N	N	N	N	N	N	N		N	N		N	N	N	N
Resize		N	N	N	N	N	N	N	N	N	N	N	N	N	N	N
Scroll		N	N	N	N	N	N			N	N			N	N	N
SpinDown	N	N	N	N	N	N	N	N	N	N	N	N		N	N	N
SpinUp	N	N	N	N	N	N	N	N	N	N	N	N			N	N
Terminate		N	N	N	N	N	N	N	N	N	N	N	N	N	N	N

Each form that you create contains a form module for storing VBA event procedures. To access the form module to write an event procedure or to find out the events recognized by a specific control, you can:

- Double-click a control
- Right-click the control, and choose View Code from the shortcut menu
- Click the View Code button in the Project Explorer window
- Double-click any unused area of the UserForm

Executing any of the above actions results in opening the code window for the form. Figure 10-15 displays the Code window activated by double-clicking a command button placed on a form. Notice the title in the Microsoft Visual Basic title bar: Chap10.xls (UserForm1(Code)). A form module contains a general section as well as individual sections for each control placed on the form. The general section is used for declaration of form variables or constants.

You can access the desired section by clicking the down arrow to the right of the combo box at the upper right-hand side. This combo box is called the Procedure box. It displays the event procedures that are recognized by the control selected in the left-hand side combo box. Events that already have procedures written for them appear in bold.

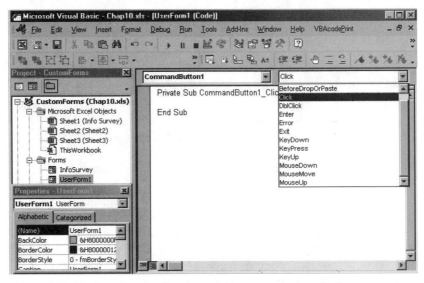

Figure 10-15: The Procedure box lists the available event procedures for the command button control.

Writing VBA Procedures to Respond to Form and Control Events

Before the user can accomplish specific tasks with a custom form, you must usually write several VBA procedures. As mentioned earlier, each form created in the Visual Basic Editor has a module for storing procedures used by that form.

Before displaying a custom form, you may want to set initial values for controls. To set the initial values, or default values, that the controls will have every time the form is displayed, write an Initialize event procedure for a UserForm.

The Initialize event occurs when the form is loaded but before it's shown on the screen. Suppose that you want the Info Survey form to appear with the following initial settings:

- The Hardware button is selected in the Main Interest frame.
- The list box below contains the items that correspond to the selected Hardware option button.
- None of the Computer Type check boxes are selected.

- The combo box below the Where Used label displays the first available item, and the user cannot add a new item to the combo box.
- The text box next to the spin button displays the initial value of zero (0).
- The image control displays a picture related to the selected Hardware or Software option button.

Writing a Procedure to Initialize the Form

1. In the Project Explorer window, double-click the **InfoSurvey** form.
2. Double-click the background of the form to open the code window for the active form.

   When you double-click the form or a control, the Code window automatically opens with the Click event for the control that you clicked and is ready for editing.

   In the procedure definition (Figure 10-15), Visual Basic automatically adds the keyword Private before the Sub keyword. Private procedures can be called only from the current form module. In other words, a procedure that is located in another module of the current project cannot call this particular (Private) procedure.

   At the top of the Code window, there are two combo boxes. The combo box on the left displays the names of all form objects. The combo box on the right shows the events recognized by the selected form object.

3. Click the down arrow in the procedure box on the right, and select the **Initialize** event. Visual Basic displays the UserForm_Initialize procedure in the Code window:

```
Private Sub UserForm_Initialize()
End Sub
```

4. Type the form's initial settings between the Private Sub and End Sub keywords. The complete UserForm_Initialize procedure is shown below:

```
Private Sub UserForm_Initialize()
    'select the Hardware option
    optHard.Value = True

    'turn off the Software option and all the check boxes
    optSoft.Value = False
    chkIBM.Value = False
    chkNote.Value = False
    chkMac.Value = False

    'display a zero in the text box
    txtPercent.Value = 0

    'call the procedure to populate the list box with
```

```
'hardware options
Call ListHardware

'populate the combo box
    With Me.cboxWhereUsed
    .AddItem "home"
    .AddItem "work"
    .AddItem "school"
    .AddItem "work/home"
    .AddItem "home/school"
    .AddItem "work/home/school"
End With

'select the first element in the combo box
Me.cboxWhereUsed.ListIndex = 0

'select the first element in the list box
Me.lboxSystems.ListIndex = 0

'load a picture file for the Hardware option
Me.picImage.Picture = LoadPicture("C:\cd.bmp")
End Sub
```

To simplify the event procedure code, you can use the Me keyword instead of the actual form name. For example, instead of using the statement:

```
InfoSurvey.cboxWhereUsed.ListIndex = 0
```

you can save time typing by using the following statement:

```
Me.cboxWhereUsed.ListIndex = 0
```

This technique is especially useful when the form name is long. Notice also that the first element of the list box has the index number zero (0). Therefore, if you'd like to select the second item in the list, you must set the ListIndex property to 1.

The procedure ends with loading a picture into the image control. Make sure that the specified graphics file can be located in the said folder. If you don't have this file, enter the complete path of a valid picture file that you want to display.

The UserForm_Initialize procedure calls the outside procedure (ListHardware) to populate its list box control with the hardware items.

5. Activate the **ShowSurvey** module and enter the code of the ListHardware procedure, as shown below:

```
Sub ListHardware
    With InfoSurvey.lboxSystems
        .AddItem "CD-ROM Drive"
        .AddItem "Printer"
        .AddItem "Fax"
        .AddItem "Network"
        .AddItem "Joystick"
        .AddItem "Sound Card"
```

```
            .AddItem "Graphics Card"
            .AddItem "Modem"
            .AddItem "Monitor"
            .AddItem "Mouse"
            .AddItem "Zip Drive"
            .AddItem "Scanner"
        End With
    End Sub
```

Now that you've prepared the UserForm_Initialize procedure and the ListHardware procedure, you can run the form to see the results.

6. Launch the form from the Survey button in the Info Survey worksheet.

After the form is displayed, the user can select appropriate options or click the Cancel button. When the user clicks the Software option button, the list box below should display different items. At the same time, the image control should load a different picture. The next section explains how you can program these events.

Writing a Procedure to Populate the List Box Control

In the preceding section, you prepared the ListHardware procedure to populate the lboxSystems list box with the Hardware items. You can use the same method to load the Software items into the list box.

1. Activate the **ShowSurvey** module and enter the code of the ListSoftware procedure, as shown below:

```
Sub ListSoftware()
    With InfoSurvey.lboxSystemy
        .AddItem "Spreadsheets"
        .AddItem "Databases"
        .AddItem "CAD Systems"
        .AddItem "Word Processing"
        .AddItem "Finance Programs"
        .AddItem "Games"
        .AddItem "Accounting Programs"
        .AddItem "Desktop Publishing"
        .AddItem "Imaging Software"
        .AddItem "Personal Information Managers"
    End With
End Sub
```

Writing a Procedure to Control Option Buttons

1. Activate the **InfoSurvey** form, and double-click the **Software** option button located in the Main Interest frame.
2. When the code window appears with the optSoft_Click procedure skeleton, highlight the code and press **Delete**.
3. Click the down arrow in the upper right-hand side combo box, and select the **Change** event procedure. Visual Basic will automatically enter the beginning and end of the optSoft_Change procedure for you.

4. Enter the code of the optSoft_Change procedure, as shown below:

```
Private Sub optSoft_Change()
    Me.lboxSystems.Clear
    Call ListSoftware
    Me.lboxSystems.ListIndex = 0
    Me.picImage.Picture = LoadPicture("C:\Books.bmp")
End Sub
```

The optSoft_Change procedure begins with the statement that uses the Clear method to remove the current list of items from the lboxSystems list box. The next statement calls the ListSoftware procedure to populate the list box with software items. In other words, when the user clicks the Software button, the procedure removes the hardware items from the list box and adds the software items. If you don't clear the list box prior to adding new items, the new items will be appended to the current list. The statement `Me.lboxSystems.ListIndex = 0` selects the first item in the list. The final statement in this procedure loads a picture file to the image control. Be sure to replace the reference to this file with the complete path to a valid picture file that is located in your computer.

Because the user may want to reselect the Hardware button after selecting the Software button, you must create a similar Change event procedure for the optHard option button.

5. Enter the following optHard_Change procedure, just below the optSoft_Change procedure:

```
Private Sub optHard_Change()
    Me.lboxSystems.Clear
    Call ListHardware
    Me.lboxSystems.ListIndex = 0
    Me.picImage.Picture = LoadPicture("C:\cd.bmp")
End Sub
```

6. Launch the form from the **Survey** button in the Info Survey worksheet and check the results. When you click the Software option button, you should see the software items in the list box below. At the same time, the image control should display the assigned picture. After clicking the Hardware option button, the list box should display the appropriate hardware items. At the same time, the image control should display a different picture.

7. Close the form by clicking the **Close** button in the form's upper right-hand corner.

Writing Procedures to Synchronize the Text Box with the Spin Button

The Info Survey form has a text box in front of the spin button control. To indicate a percent of time that the selected Hardware or Software item is used, the user can type a value in the text box or use the spin button. The initial value of the text box is set to zero (0). Suppose the user entered 10 in the text box and now wants to increase this value to 15 by using the spin button. To enable this action, the text box and the spin button have to be synchronized. Each of these objects requires a separate Change event procedure.

1. Right-click the spin button and choose **View Code** from the shortcut menu.

2. Enter the spPercent_Change procedure, as shown below:

```
Private Sub spPercent_Change()
    txtPercent.Value = spPercent.Value
End Sub
```

Using the spin buttons will cause the text box value to increase or decrease.

3. Enter the following txtPercent_Change procedure:

```
Private Sub txtPercent_Change()
    Dim entry As String

    On Error Resume Next
    entry = Me.txtPercent.Value
        If entry > 100 Then
            entry = 0
            Me.txtPercent.Value = entry
        End If
    spPercent.Value = txtPercent.Value
End Sub
```

The txtPercent_Change procedure ensures that only values between 0 and 100 can be entered into the text box. The procedure uses the On Error Resume Next statement to ignore data entry errors. If the user enters a non-numeric value into the text box (or a number greater than 100), Visual Basic will reset the text box value to zero (0). Each time a spin button is pressed, the text box value is incremented or decremented by one.

Writing a Procedure that Closes the User Form

After displaying the form, the user may want to cancel the form by pressing Esc or clicking the Cancel button. To remove the form from the screen, prepare a simple procedure that uses the Hide method.

1. Double-click the **Cancel** button and enter the following cmdCancel_Click procedure:

```
Private Sub cmdCancel_Click()
    Me.Hide
End Sub
```

The Hide method hides the object but does not remove it from memory. This way, your VBA procedure can use the form's objects and properties behind the scenes while the form isn't visible to the user.

Use the Unload method to remove the form from the screen and release memory resources:

```
Unload Me
```

When the form is unloaded, all memory associated with it is reclaimed. The user can't interact with the form, and the form's objects can't be accessed by your VBA procedure until the form is placed in the memory again by using the Load statement.

Transferring Form Data to the Worksheet

When the user clicks the OK button, the form's selections should be written to the worksheet. The user can quit using the form at any time by clicking the Cancel button.

1. Double-click the **OK** button, and enter the cmdOK_Click procedure shown below:

```
Private Sub cmdOK_Click()

    Me.Hide
    r = Application.CountA(Range("A:A"))
    Range("A1").Offset(r + 1, 0) = Me.lboxSystems.Value

    If Me.optHard.Value = True Then
        Range("A1").Offset(r + 1, 1) = "*"
    End If
    If Me.optSoft.Value = True Then
        Range("A1").Offset(r + 1, 2) = "*"
    End If
    If Me.chkIBM.Value = True Then
        Range("A1").Offset(r + 1, 3) = "*"
    End If
    If Me.chkNote.Value = True Then
        Range("A1").Offset(r + 1, 4) = "*"
    End If
    If Me.chkMac.Value = True Then
        Range("A1").Offset(r + 1, 5) = "*"
    End If
    Range("A1").Offset(r + 1, 6) = Me.cboxWhereUsed.Value
    Range("A1").Offset(r + 1, 7) = Me.txtPercent.Value
    If Me.optMale.Value = True Then
        Range("A1").Offset(r + 1, 8) = "*"
    End If
    If Me.optFemale.Value = True Then
        Range("A1").Offset(r + 1, 9) = "*"
```

```
      End If
      Unload Me
   End Sub
```

The cmdOK_Click procedure begins by hiding the user form. The statement:

```
r = Application.CountA(Range("A:A"))
```

uses the Visual Basic CountA function to count the number of cells that contain data in column A. The result of the function is assigned to the variable r. The next statement:

```
Range("A1").Offset(r + 1, 0) = Me.lboxSystems.Value
```

enters the selected list box item in a cell located one row below the last used cell in column A (r+1). Next, there are several conditional statements. The first one tells Visual Basic to place an asterisk in the appropriate cell in column B if the Hardware option button is selected. Column B is located one column to the right of column A, hence there's a "1" in the position of the second argument of the Offset method. The second If statement enters the asterisk in column C if the user selected the Software option button. Similar instructions record the actual check box values.

In column G, the procedure will enter the item selected in the Where Used combo box. Column H will show the value entered in the Percent (%) Used text box, and columns I and J will identify the gender of the person who submitted the survey.

Using the Info Survey Application

Your application is now ready for the final test.

1. Switch to the Microsoft Excel Info Survey worksheet, and click the **Survey** button.
2. When the form appears, select appropriate options and click **OK**.
3. Activate the form several times, each time selecting different options.
4. Save the changes made to Chap10.xls.

Sample Application 2: Students and Exams

In recent years, many Windows applications have been relying more and more heavily on tabbed dialog boxes for grouping sets of controls together. The Options dialog box is a good example. Using tabs, you can present a number of settings that apply to different controls in one dialog box. Tabbed dialog boxes are very easy and convenient to use. When designing custom forms for more advanced VBA applications, you can take advantage of two special tabbed controls available in the Toolbox: the MultiPage control and the TabStrip control. Sample application 2, the subject of the remaining sections of this chapter, uses these and other advanced controls (such as RefEdit and Calendar) to keep track of students and their exam grades.

Using MultiPage and TabStrip Controls

The central object of the custom form shown in Figure 10-16 is a MultiPage control that consists of two pages. The first page contains text and combo boxes to gather student data, such as Social Security number (SSN), first and last name, year of study, and major. A group of option buttons at the top of the form allows you to specify the student's status: New or Active. If the student's data has not yet been entered in a worksheet, the student's status is New. When the form is first loaded, the New option button is automatically selected. When you want to review or update data for existing students, clicking the Active option button will display the RefEdit control used to populate the list box control with students' names, as entered on the worksheet.

1. Insert a new UserForm into the current project and rename it **Students**.

2. Change the form's Caption property to **Students and Exams**.

3. Click the **MultiPage** control in the Toolbox, and then click in the upper left-hand corner of the form and drag the mouse down and to the right to draw a large frame.

4. Right-click the **Page1** tab, and choose **Rename** from the shortcut menu. Type **Students** in the Caption text box, and enter **S** in the Accelerator Key field. In the same way, rename the second page **Exams**, and enter **x** in the Accelerator Key field.

5. Click the **Students** tab. Using the controls in the Toolbox, add to the Students page all of the controls shown in Figure 10-16. Follow these guidelines:

   - The Status frame contains two option buttons. Set the Caption property of these buttons to **New** and **Active**. Next, change the Name property of the first button to **optNew** and the second one to **optActive**.

   - Text boxes are titled using label controls with their Caption property set to SSN, Last Name, and First Name. Change the Name property of the text box controls to **txtSSN**, **txtLast**, and **txtFirst**.

   - Combo boxes are titled using label controls with their Caption property set to Year and Major. Set the Name property of the combo box controls to **cboxYear** and **cboxMajor**. To allow the user to select only one of the specified items, set the following properties for each of the combo boxes: MatchRequired to **True**, MatchEntry to **1–fmMatchEntryComplete**.

- Place the Name Range label above the RefEdit control. Set the Name property of the RefEdit control to **refNames**.
- Set the Name property of the list box control to **lboxStudents**. Set the ColumnCount property to **2** to display two columns of data.
- Set the Caption property of the command buttons to **OK** and **Cancel**, and set their Name property to **cmdOK** and **cmdCancel**.

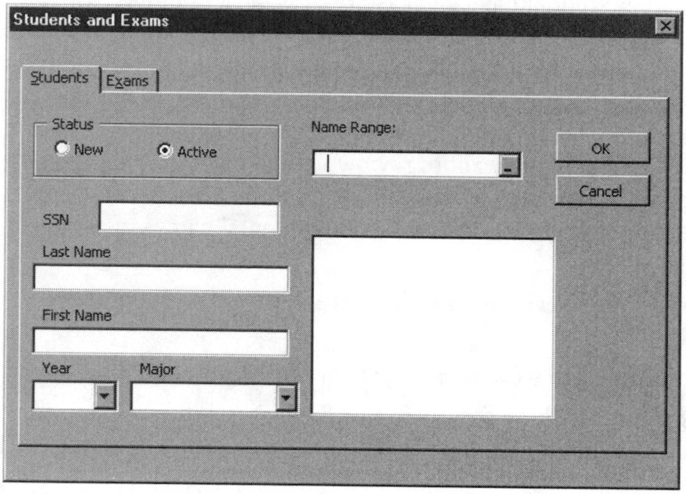

Figure 10-16: The MultiPage control can contain two or more pages. Each page shows a different set of controls.

The second page of the MultiPage control (Figure 10-17) is used to record and display information related to exams taken. This page contains two objects. The label control has a temporary title "Last, First." At run time, this label will display the student's name as selected on the previous page.

The second object on this page is the TabStrip control. It contains four tabs with the names of the exam subjects. Although this example displays the tabs at the top of the form, Visual Basic also allows you to set the orientation of the tabs to bottom, left, or right. As you navigate from tab to tab, you can see the same controls. Only the data displayed inside each control changes.

1. Click the **Exams** tab in the **MultiPage** control.

2. Click the **Label** control in the Toolbox and click in the upper left-hand corner of the Exams page. Drag a rectangle large enough to hold a person's first and last name.

3. In the Properties window, set this label's Name property to **lblWho**. Set the label's Caption property to **Last, First**. Set the Font property to **Arial, Bold, 14 point**.

4. Click the **TabStrip** control in the Toolbox. Click on the form just below the label control, and drag the mouse until the strip is the size and shape you want (see Figure 10-17). By default, the TabStrip control will display two tabs: Tab1 and Tab2. To add new tab pages, first click inside

the TabStrip control to select the TabStrip object. Click again until the hatched frame around the TabStrip object appears in bold. Right-click any tab, and choose **New Page** from the shortcut menu. Visual Basic will add Tab3. Use the same method to add Tab4. Right-click each of the tabs, and choose **Rename** from the shortcut menu. See Figure 10-17 for the names of all the tabs. Notice that each tab name has an underlined letter, which allows the user to access the tab from the keyboard. For example, pressing Alt+E will activate the English tab.

5. Click the **English** tab and begin drawing the following controls:

   ■ If the Toolbox contains only one page titled Controls, go back to the earlier section in this chapter titled "Tools for Creating User Forms" to find out how to add a Calendar control to the Toolbox. Then place the Calendar control inside the TabStrip control, as shown in Figure 10-17. Set the ShowDateSelectors property for the Calendar control to **True**.

   ■ Add the Enter/Change Grade label and a combo box control. Set the Name property for the combo box to **cboxGrade**.

   ■ Add two labels with the Caption property set to **Grade** and **Date** and the Name property set to **lblGrade** and **lblDate**. Change the SpecialEffect property for both labels to **3-fmSpecialEffect-Etched**.

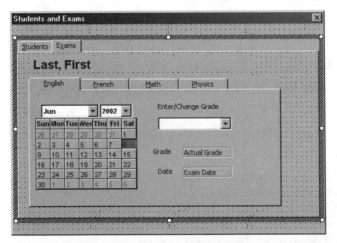

Figure 10-17: The outside frame contains the MultiPage control. The inside frame contains the TabStrip control.

Tip 10-6: Setting the TabStrip Control

The best way to set up a TabStrip control is to add it as the first control to the form and then place other controls inside it. However, if you already have controls placed on the form, you can draw the TabStrip control over these controls and use the Send to Back command to send the TabStrip to the bottom of the Z-order.

The Students and Exams custom form allows you to enter new data or display data as entered in the worksheet. Figure 10-18 shows the worksheet used by this form.

1. Prepare the worksheet displayed in Figure 10-18.

2. Add the **Display Form** button to your worksheet and assign to it the DoStudents procedure.

3. In the Visual Basic Editor screen, add a new module to the current project, and set the module's Name property to **InfoStudents**.

4. Enter the following DoStudents procedure in the InfoStudents module:

```
Sub DoStudents()
    Students.Show
End Sub
```

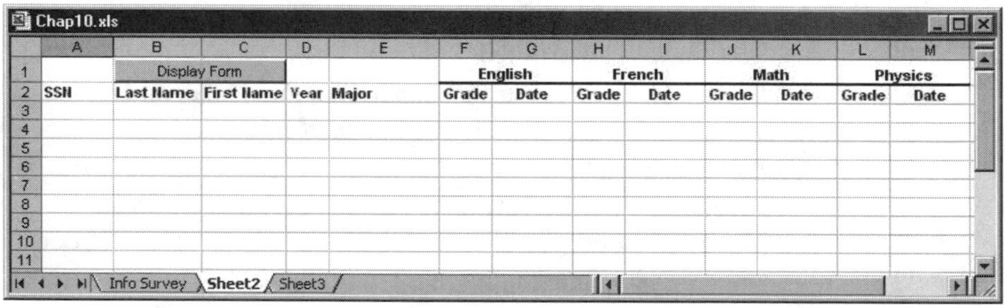

Figure 10-18: Supporting spreadsheet for Students and Exams sample application

5. Return to the worksheet, and click the **Display Form** button to test the DoStudents procedure.

6. Close the form by clicking the **Close** button in the upper right-hand corner of the form.

Writing VBA Procedures for the Students and Exams Custom Form

The custom form Students and Exams contains about a dozen VBA procedures, which are shown below. The code of these procedures has to be entered in the form module. To activate the form module, double-click the form background.

1. From the combo box at the top left-hand side of the Code window, choose **(General)**. The Procedure selection combo box on the right should display (Declarations). Type the following variable declarations:

```
'Declarations
Dim r As Integer
Dim nr As Integer
Dim indexPlus As Integer
Dim YesNo As Integer
```

2. Enter the code of the UserForm_Initialize procedure to set the form's initial settings:

```
Private Sub UserForm_Initialize()
'select first page of the MultiPage control
'page numbering begins from zero (0)

Me.MultiPage1.Value = 0

'choose the New option button
optNew.Value = True

'hide three controls on startup
lblLast.Visible = False
refNames.Visible = False
lboxStudents.Visible = False

'populate the Year combo box
    With Me.cboxYear
        .AddItem "1"
        .AddItem "2"
        .AddItem "3"
        .AddItem "4"
    End With

' populate the Major combo box
    With Me.cboxMajor
        .AddItem "English"
        .AddItem "Chemistry"
        .AddItem "Mathematics"
        .AddItem "Linguistics"
        .AddItem "Computer Science"
    End With

' populate a combo box with grades
    With Me.cboxGrade
        .AddItem "A"
        .AddItem "B"
        .AddItem "C"
        .AddItem "D"
        .AddItem "F"
    End With

    'display date in the lblDate label control
    Me.lblDate.Caption = Me.Calendar.Value

    'activate the first tab in the TabStrip control

    Me.TabStrip1.Value = 0

    'activate the SSN text box
    Me.txtSSN.SetFocus
End Sub
```

3. Enter two procedures to control the option buttons (optNew_Click and optActive_Click):

```
Private Sub optNew_Click()
    lblNames.Visible = False
    refNames.Visible = False
    lboxStudents.Visible = False
    Me.MultiPage1(1).Enabled = False
        If lboxStudents.RowSource < > "" Then
            Me.txtSSN.Text = ""
            Me.txtLast.Text = ""
            Me.txtFirst.Text = ""
            Me.cboxYear.Text = ""
            Me.cboxMajor.Text = ""
            Me.txtSSN.SetFocus
        End If
    Me.txtSSN.SetFocus
End Sub

Private Sub optActive_Click()
    lblNames.Visible = True
    refNames.Visible = True
    refNames.SetFocus
    If lboxStudents.RowSource < > "" Then
        lboxStudents.Visible = True
        Call lboxStudents_Change
    End If
End Sub
```

4. Enter the code of the lboxStudents_Change and refNames_Change procedures. These control the behavior of the RefEdit and list box control placed on the Students page:

```
Private Sub lboxStudents_Change()
indexPlus = lboxStudents.ListIndex + 3
    With ActiveWorkbook.Worksheets("Sheet2")
        Me.txtSSN.Text = Range("A" & indexPlus).Value
        Me.txtLast.Text = Range("B" & indexPlus).Value
        Me.txtFirst.Text = Range("C" & indexPlus).Value
        Me.cboxYear.Text = Range("D" & indexPlus).Value
        Me.cboxMajor.Text = Range("E" & indexPlus).Value
        Call TabStrip1_Change
        Me.MultiPage1(1).Enabled = True
    End With
End Sub

Private Sub refNames_Change()
    lboxStudents.RowSource = refNames.Value
    lboxStudents.ListIndex = 0
    lboxStudents.Visible = True
    Call lboxStudents_Change
End Sub
```

5. Enter the code to control the command buttons OK (cmdOK_Click) and Cancel (cmdCancel_Click):

```
Private Sub cmdOK_Click()
    If Me.optNew.Value = True Then
        Me.Hide
        ActiveWorkbook.Sheets("Sheet2").Select
        r = ActiveSheet.UsedRange.Rows.Count
        nr = r + 1
        Range("A" & nr).Value = Me.txtSSN.Text
        Range("B" & nr).Value = Me.txtLast.Text
        Range("C" & nr).Value = Me.txtFirst.Text
        Range("D" & nr).Value = Me.cboxYear.Text
        Range("E" & nr).Value = Me.cboxMajor.Text

        Me.txtSSN.Text = ""
        Me.txtLast.Text = ""
        Me.txtFirst.Text = ""
        Me.cboxYear.Text = ""
        Me.cboxMajor.Text = ""
        Me.txtSSN.SetFocus

    'redisplay the form
        Me.Show
    Else
        MsgBox "This control is currently unavailable."
    End If
End Sub

Private Sub cmdCancel_Click()
    Unload Me
    Set Students = Nothing
End Sub
```

6. Enter the procedure cboxGrade_Click to control the Grade combo box located on the Exams page:

```
Private Sub cboxGrade_Click()
YesNo = MsgBox("Enter the grade in the worksheet?", _
        vbYesNo, "Modify Grade")
If YesNo = 6 Then
    Me.lblGrade.Caption = cboxGrade.Value
    Select Case TabStrip1.Value
      Case 0
        Range("F" & indexPlus).Value = Me.lblGrade.Caption
      Case 1
        Range("H" & indexPlus).Value = Me.lblGrade.Caption
      Case 2
        Range("J" & indexPlus).Value = Me.lblGrade.Caption
      Case 3
        Range("L" & indexPlus).Value = Me.lblGrade.Caption
      End Select
        cboxGrade.Value = ""
    End If
End Sub
```

7. Enter the Calendar1_Click procedure, as shown below:

```
Private Sub Calendar1_Click()
```

```
    YesNo = MsgBox("Enter the date in the worksheet?", vbYesNo, _
        "Modify Date")
    If YesNo = 6 Then
        Me.lblDate.Caption = Calendar1.Value
        Select Case TabStrip1.Value
            Case 0
                Range("G" & indexPlus).Value = Me.lblDate.Caption
            Case 1
                Range("I" & indexPlus).Value = Me.lblDate.Caption
            Case 2
                Range("K" & indexPlus).Value = Me.lblDate.Caption
            Case 3
                Range("M" & indexPlus).Value = Me.lblDate.Caption
        End Select
    End If
End Sub
```

8. Enter the TabStrip1_Change and MultiPage1_Change procedures, as follows:

```
Private Sub TabStrip1_Change()
indexPlus = lboxStudents.ListIndex + 3

    With ActiveWorkbook.Worksheets("Sheet2")
        Select Case TabStrip1.Value
        Case 0  ' English
          Me.lblGrade.Caption = Range("F" & indexPlus).Value
          Me.lblDate.Caption = Range("G" & indexPlus).Value
        Case 1 'French
          Me.lblGrade.Caption = Range("H" & indexPlus).Value
          Me.lblDate.Caption = Range("I" & indexPlus).Value
        Case 2  'Math
          Me.lblGrade.Caption = Range("J" & indexPlus).Value
          Me.lblDate.Caption = Range("K" & indexPlus).Value
        Case 3 'Physics
          Me.lblGrade.Caption = Range("L" & indexPlus).Value
          Me.lblDate.Caption = Range("M" & indexPlus).Value
        End Select
    End With
End Sub

Private Sub MultiPage1_Change()
    Me.lblWho.Caption = Me.txtLast.Value & ", " _
        & Me.txtFirst.Value
    Call TabStrip1_Change
End Sub
```

Using the Students and Exams Custom Form

Now that you've prepared all of the required VBA procedures, let's see how the form responds to the user's actions:

1. Switch to Microsoft Excel window and activate **Sheet2**.
2. Click the **Display Form** button.

Clicking the Display Form button runs the DoStudents procedure. This procedure displays the Students and Exams custom form. Before the form appears on the screen, Visual Basic executes each statement entered in the UserForm_Initialize procedure. The result is the form shown in Figure 10-19.

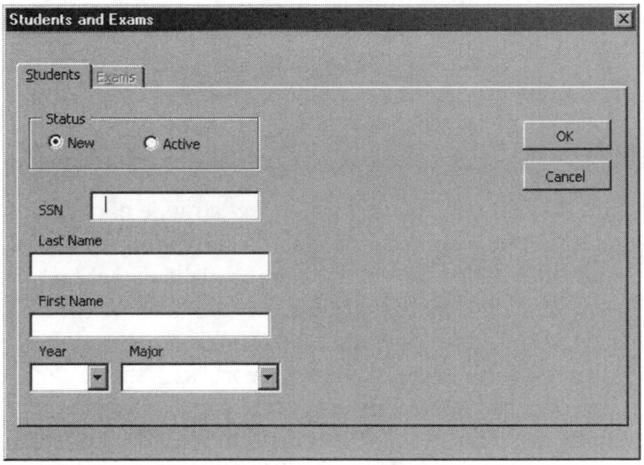

Figure 10-19: The Display Form button on the worksheet lets you quickly access the Students and Exams custom form to view or enter data. When the form is loaded, only the controls that apply to the selected option button are shown.

After the form is displayed, you can enter a new student and click OK to transfer the student's data to the worksheet. When you click the OK button, the cmdOK_Click procedure is executed. Notice that you can't enter the exams taken by the new student because the second page (Exams) of the MultiPage control is disabled at this time. Once the new student's data is written to the worksheet, the form is redisplayed. You can continue entering the data, or you can click Cancel to remove the form from the screen. When you click the Cancel button, the cmdCancel_Click procedure is run.

3. Using the Students and Exams custom form, enter data for two new students. At any time, you can click the Active option button and load the data for the existing students. When you click the Active option button, the Name Range label and the RefEdit control become visible.

4. Click the **Active** option button, and then click the minus button in the RefEdit control.

5. Select the range of names in the worksheet, as shown in Figure 10-20.

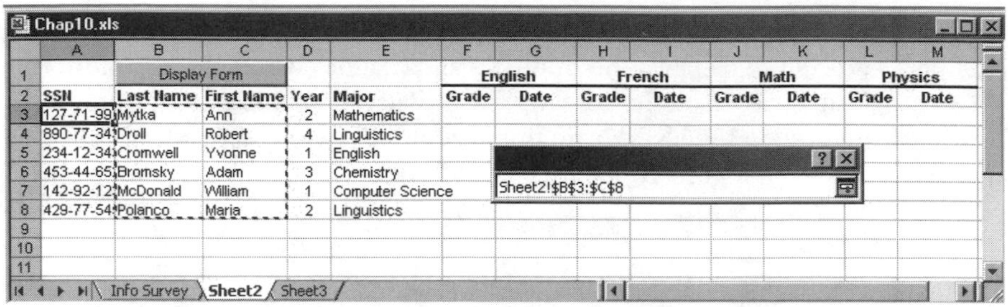

Figure 10-20: Using the RefEdit control, you can specify the range of cells containing the data that you want to work with.

Using the RefEdit control, you can select a range of cells in a worksheet. In this example, select cells containing students' last and first names. It's important that you select valid data. Start by clicking the first name below the Last Name column heading (cell B3) and drag down and to the right to include students' first names. Notice that the form is temporarily hidden while you work with the RefEdit control. The range of cells that you select appears in the RefEdit control. Click the minus button in the RefEdit control to return to the form. As you return to the form, the refNames_Change procedure is run. This procedure uses the range address to populate the list box control with the names of students.

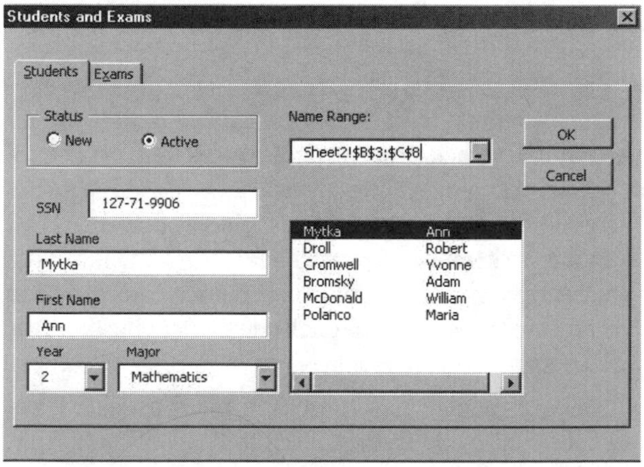

Figure 10-21:
The list box on the form is populated via the RefEdit control with the data stored in a worksheet.

The last statement of this procedure calls the lboxStudents_Change procedure to ensure that the form's text and combo boxes are synchronized with the student selection in the list box.

The list box displays the names of active students. The selected student's data is displayed in the text and combo boxes on the left (see Figure 10-21).

6. Click any name in the list box, and check the student's data.
7. Click any name in the list box, and click the **Exams** tab.

   The Exams page displays the name of the selected student (see Figure 10-22). The TabStrip control shows the exam subjects. If the selected student has taken any of the exams, the date and the exam grade are displayed when you click the appropriate subject tab.

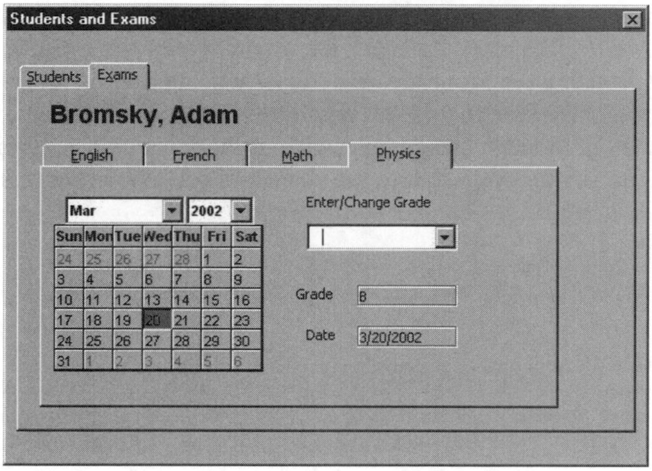

Figure 10-22: The Exams page shows the date and exam grade for the selected student and subject.

You can enter or change a student's grade and exam date by using the provided combo box and calendar control. Visual Basic asks that you confirm the modification of data (review the VBA code for the Calendar1_Click and cboxGrade_Click procedures). After responding Yes in the dialog box, the selected date or grade is written to the corresponding column in a worksheet (see Figure 10-23).

The TabStrip1_Change procedure ensures that when you click the subject tab, Visual Basic displays the exam grade and date from the appropriate spreadsheet cell. The MultiPage1_Change procedure ensures that when you click the Exams page, the lblWho label control displays the last and first name of the student who is currently selected in the list box.

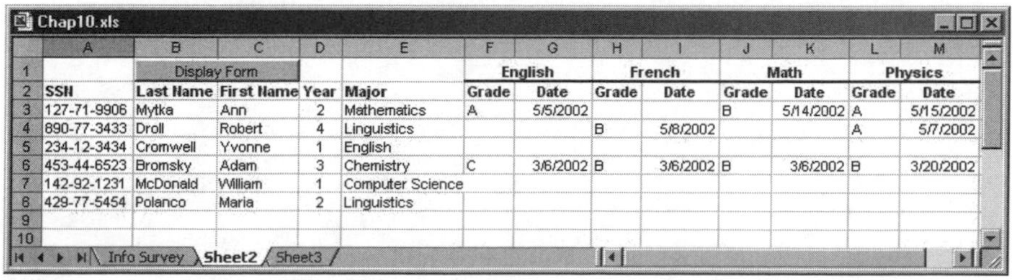

					English		French		Math		Physics	
SSN	Last Name	First Name	Year	Major	Grade	Date	Grade	Date	Grade	Date	Grade	Date
127-71-9906	Mytka	Ann	2	Mathematics	A	5/5/2002			B	5/14/2002	A	5/15/2002
890-77-3433	Droll	Robert	4	Linguistics			B	5/8/2002			A	5/7/2002
234-12-3434	Cromwell	Yvonne	1	English								
453-44-6523	Bromsky	Adam	3	Chemistry	C	3/6/2002	B	3/6/2002	B	3/6/2002	B	3/20/2002
142-92-1231	McDonald	William	1	Computer Science								
429-77-5454	Polanco	Maria	2	Linguistics								

Figure 10-23: Data in columns F-M on the spreadsheet is entered via the Exams tab on the Students and Exams user form.

What's Next...

Now that you've reached the end of this rather long chapter, you have the necessary skills for designing useful forms. Let's quickly summarize all that you've learned in this chapter. Built-in dialog boxes can be displayed from your own VBA procedures. For custom VBA applications that require user input, create a custom form. Make sure the user can move around the form in a logical order by setting the tab order. For the form to respond to user actions, write VBA procedures in a form module. Set the initial values of controls by using the Properties window or writing the UserForm_Initialize procedure. Make sure to include procedures to transfer form data to a worksheet. In the next chapter, you will get more hands-on experience with custom forms when you explore the subject of collections and custom objects.

Chapter 11

Custom Collections and Class Modules

Working with Collections ■ Declaring a Custom Collection ■ Adding Objects to a Custom Collection ■ Removing Objects from a Custom Collection ■ **Insert: Module or Class Module?** ■ Creating Custom Objects ■ **Creating a Class** ■ Variable Declarations ■ Defining the Properties for the Class ■ Creating the Property Get Procedures ■ Creating the Property Let Procedures ■ Creating the Class Methods ■ Creating an Instance of a Class ■ Event Procedures in the Class Module ■ Creating the User Interface ■ Watching the Execution of Your VBA Procedures ■ **What's Next...**

In Chapter 9, you learned how to control the objects of another application by using Automation. Recall that after setting up a reference to the Microsoft Word 10.0 Object Library, you were able to control the Word application remotely by calling upon its own objects, properties, and methods. You've also learned how to use Automation to retrieve a list of contacts from Microsoft Outlook to an Excel spreadsheet. The good news is that you are not limited to using objects built into Microsoft Excel or objects exposed by other applications. VBA allows you to create your own objects and collections of objects, complete with their own methods and properties. In this chapter, you will learn how to work with collections, including how to declare a custom Collection object. You will also learn how to use class modules to create user-defined objects.

Before diving into the theory and hands-on examples in this chapter, let's start by going over several terms that will be used throughout this chapter:

Collection—An object that contains a set of related objects.

Class—A definition of an object that includes its name, properties, methods, and events. The class acts as a sort of object template from which an instance of an object is created at run time.

Instance—A specific object that belongs to a class is referred to as an instance of the class. When you create an instance, you create a new object that has the properties and methods defined by the class.

Class Module—A module that contains the definition of a class, including its property and method definitions.

Module—A module containing Sub and Function procedures that are available to other VBA procedures and are not related to any object in particular.

Form Module—A module that contains the VBA code for all event procedures triggered by events occurring in a user form or its controls. A form module is a type of class module.

Event—An action recognized by an object, such as a mouse click or a keypress, for which you can define a response. Events can be caused by a user action or a VBA statement or can be triggered by the system.

Event Procedure—A procedure that is automatically executed in response to an event initiated by the user or program code or triggered by the system.

Working with Collections

A set of similar objects is known as a *collection*. In Microsoft Excel, for example, all open workbooks belong to the Workbooks collection, and all the sheets in a particular workbook are members of the Worksheets collection. In Microsoft Word, all open documents belong to the Documents collection, and each paragraph in a document is a member of the Paragraphs collection. Collections are objects that contain other objects.

No matter what collection you want to work with, you can do the following:

- Refer to a specific object in a collection by using an index value. For example, to refer to the second object in the Worksheets collection, use either one of the following statements:

```
Worksheets(2).Select
```
or
```
Worksheets("Sheet2").Select
```

- Determine the number of items in the collection by using the Count property. For example, when you enter in the Immediate window the statement:

```
?Worksheets.Count
```

VBA will return the total number of worksheets in the current workbook.

- Insert new items into the collection by using the Add method. For example, when you enter in the Immediate window the statement:

```
Worksheets.Add
```

VBA will insert in the current workbook a new worksheet. The Worksheets collection now contains one more item.

- Cycle through every object in the collection by using the For Each...Next loop.

Suppose that you opened a workbook containing five worksheets with the following names: "Daily wages," "Weekly wages," "Bonuses," "Yearly salary," and "Monthly wages." Use this procedure to delete the worksheets that contain the word "wages" in the name:

```
Sub DeleteSheets()
Dim ws As Worksheet
Application.DisplayAlerts = False
For Each ws In Worksheets
    If InStr(ws.Name, "wages") Then
        ws.Delete
    End If
Next
End Sub
```

While writing your own VBA procedures, you may come across a situation where there's no built-in collection to handle the task at hand. The solution is to create a custom collection. From Chapter 7, you already know how to work with multiple items of data by using dynamic or static arrays. Because collections have built-in properties and methods that allow you to add, remove, and count their elements, it's much easier to work with collections than arrays.

Declaring a Custom Collection

To create a user-defined collection, you should begin by declaring an object variable of the Collection type. This variable is declared with the New keyword in the Dim statement, as shown below:

```
Dim collection_name As New Collection
```

Adding Objects to a Custom Collection

After you've declared the Collection object, you can insert new items into the collection by using the Add method. The objects with which you populate your collection do not have to be of the same data type. The Add method looks like the following:

```
object.Add item, key, before, after
```

You are only required to specify `object` and `item`. `object` is the collection name. This is the same name that was used in the declaration of the Collection object. `item` is the object that you want to add to the collection.

Although other arguments are optional, they are quite useful. It's important to understand that the items in a collection are automatically assigned numbers from 1 on. However, they can also be assigned a unique key value. Instead of accessing a specific item with an index (1, 2, 3, and so on), you can assign a key for that object at the time an object is added to a collection. For instance, if you are creating a collection of custom sheets, you could use a sheet name as a key. To identify an individual in a collection of students or employees, you could use Social Security numbers as a key.

If you want to specify the position of the object in the collection, you should use either the `before` or `after` argument (do not use both). The `before` argument is the object before which the new object is added, and the `after` argument is the object after which the new object is added.

The GetComments procedure shown on the following page declares the custom collection object called colNotes. The procedure prompts for an author's full name and then loops through all the worksheets in the active workbook to locate this author's comments. Only comments entered by the specified author are added to the custom collection. The procedure assigns a key to the first comment and then adds the remaining comments to the collection by placing them before the comment that was added last (notice the use of the `before` argument). If the collection includes at least one comment, the procedure displays a message box with the text of the comment that was identified with the special `key` argument. Notice how the `key` argument is used in referencing an item in a collection. The procedure then prints the text of all the comments included in the collection to the Immediate window. Text functions (Mid and Len) are used to get only the text of the comment without the author's name. Next, the total number of comments in a workbook and the total number of comments in the custom collection are returned by the Count property.

Before you try out the GetComments procedure, set up the workbook file as follows:

1. Open a new workbook and save it as **Chap11.xls**.

2. Right-click any cell in Sheet1 and choose **Insert Comment** from the shortcut menu. Type any text you want. Click outside the comment frame to exit the comment edit mode. Use the same technique to enter two comments in Sheet2. Type different text for each comment. Add a new sheet (Sheet4) to the workbook, and add a comment. You should now have four comments in three worksheets.

3. Choose **Tools | Options** and click the **General** tab. The User name text box should display your name. Delete your name and enter **Joan Smith**, and click **OK**. Now, enter one comment anywhere on Sheet2 and one comment anywhere on Sheet4. These comments should be automatically stamped with Joan Smith's name. When you're done entering the comments text, return to the Options dialog box and change the entry in the User Name text box on the General tab back to your name.

4. Switch to the Visual Basic Editor, and rename the VBA project **ObjColClass**.

5. Add a new module to the current project, and rename it **MyCollection**.

6. Enter the GetComments procedure, as shown below:

```
Sub GetComments()
    Dim sht As Worksheet
    Dim colNotes As New Collection
    Dim myNote As Comment
    Dim I As Integer
    Dim t As Integer
    Dim fullName As String

    fullName = InputBox("Enter author's full name:")

    For Each sht In ThisWorkbook.Worksheets
        sht.Select
        I = ActiveSheet.Comments.Count
            For Each myNote In ActiveSheet.Comments
                If myNote.Author = fullName Then
                    MsgBox myNote.Text
                    If colNotes.Count = 0 Then
                        colNotes.Add Item:=myNote, key:="first"
                    Else
                        colNotes.Add Item:=myNote, Before:=1
                    End If
                End If
            Next
        t = t + I
```

```
        Next
        If colNotes.Count <> 0 Then MsgBox colNotes("first").Text
        MsgBox "Total comments in workbook: " & t & Chr(13) & _
                "Total comments in collection:" & colNotes.Count
        Debug.Print "Comments by " & fullName
            For Each myNote In colNotes
                Debug.Print Mid(myNote.Text, Len(myNote.Author) + 2, _
                    Len(myNote.Text))
            Next
    End Sub
```

7. Run the GetComments procedure and check its results.

Removing Objects from a Custom Collection

Removing an item from a custom collection is as easy as adding an item. To remove an object, use the Remove method in the following format:

```
object.Remove item
```

`object` is the name of the custom collection that contains the object you want to remove. `item` is the object you want to remove from the collection.

To demonstrate the process of removing an item from a collection, let's modify the GetComments procedure that you prepared in the preceding section. At the end of this procedure, we'll display the contents of the items that are currently in the colNotes collection one by one and ask the user whether the item should be removed from this collection.

1. Add the following declaration lines to the declaration section of the GetComments procedure:

```
Dim response
Dim myId As Integer
```

The first statement declares the variable called `response`. You will use this variable to store the result of the MsgBox function. The second statement declares the variable `myId` to store the index number of the collection object.

2. Locate the following statement in the GetComments procedure:

```
For Each myNote In colNotes
```

Precede the above statement with the following:

```
myId = 1
```

3. Locate the following statement in the GetComments procedure:

```
Debug.Print Mid(myNote.Text, Len(myNote.Author) + 2, _
    Len(myNote.Text))
```

Enter the following block of instructions below that statement:

```
response = MsgBox("Remove this comment?" & Chr(13) _
        & Chr(13) & myNote.Text, vbYesNo + vbQuestion)
If response = 6 Then
    colNotes.Remove Index:=myId
```

```
Else
    myId = myId + 1
End If
```

4. Enter the following statements at the end of the procedure:

```
Debug.Print "The following comments remain in the collection:"
        For Each myNote in colNotes
            Debug.Print Mid(myNote.Text, Len(myNote.Author) + 2, _
            Len(myNote.Text))
    Next
```

5. Run the GetComments procedure, and remove one of the comments displayed in the message box.

The revised GetComments procedure, GetComments2, can be found in Chap11.xls on the companion CD-ROM. This procedure removes the specified comments from the custom collection. It does not delete the comments from the worksheets.

Tip 11-1: Reindexing Collections

Collections are reindexed automatically when an object is removed. Therefore, to remove all objects from a custom collection, you can use 1 for the Index argument, as in the following example:

```
Do While myCollection.Count >0
    myCollection.Remove Index:=1
Loop
```

Insert: Module or Class Module?

There are two module commands available in the Visual Basic Editor's Insert menu: Module and Class Module. These were defined at the beginning of this chapter. So far, you've used the standard module to create Sub and Function procedures. You'll use the class module for the first time in this chapter to create a custom object and define its properties and methods.

Creating Custom Objects

Creating a new, non-standard VBA object involves inserting a class module into your project and adding code to that module. However, before you do so, you need a basic understanding of what a class is.

If you refer back to the beginning of this chapter, you will find out that a class is a sort of object template. A frequently used analogy is comparing an object class to a cookie cutter. Just as a cookie cutter defines what a particular cookie will look like, the definition of the class determines how a particular object should look and behave. Before you can actually use an object class, you must first create a new *instance* of that class. Object instances are the cookies. Each object instance has the characteristics (properties and methods) defined by its class. Just as you can cut out many cookies using the same cookie cutter, you can create multiple instances of a class. You can change the properties of each instance of a class independently of any other instance of the same class.

A class module lets you define your own custom classes, complete with custom properties and methods. Recall that a property is an attribute of an object that defines one of its characteristics, such as shape, position, color, title, and so on. A method is an action that the object can perform. You can create the properties for your custom objects by writing property procedures in a class module. The object methods are also created in a class module by writing the Sub or function procedures.

After building your object in the class module, you can use it in the same way you use other built-in objects. You can also export the object class outside the VBA project to other VBA-capable applications.

Creating a Class

The remaining sections of this chapter demonstrate the process of creating and working with a custom object called CEmployee. This object will represent an employee. The CEmployee object will have properties such as Id, FirstName, LastName, and Salary. It will also have a method for modification of the current salary.

1. Highlight **ObjColClass (Chap11.xls)** in the Project Explorer window and choose **Insert | Class Module**.

2. Highlight **Class module** in the Project Explorer window and use the Properties window to rename the class module **CEmployee**.

> **Tip 11-2: Naming a Class Module**
>
> Every time you create a new class module, give it a meaningful name. Set the name of the class module to the name you want to use in your VBA procedures using the class. The name you choose for your class should be easily understood and identify the "thing" the object class represents. As a rule, the object class name is prefaced with an uppercase "C".

Variable Declarations

After adding and renaming the class module, the next step is to declare the variables that will hold the data you want to store in the object. Each item of data you want to store in an object should be assigned a variable. Class variables are called data members and are declared with the Private keyword. This keyword ensures that the variables will be available only within the class module. Using the Private keyword instead of the familiar Dim statement hides the data members and prevents other parts of the application from referencing them. Only the procedures within the class module in which the variables were defined can modify the value of these variables.

Because the name of a variable also serves as a property name, use meaningful names for your object's data members. It's traditional to preface the variable names with m_ to indicate that they are data members of a class.

1. Type the following declaration lines at the top of the CEmployee class module:

```
Option Explicit
'declarations

Private m_LastName As String
Private m_FirstName As String
Private m_Salary As Currency
Private m_Id As String
```

Notice that the name of each data member variable begins with the prefix "m_".

Defining the Properties for the Class

Declaring the variables with the Private keyword guarantees that the variables cannot be accessed directly from outside the object. This means that the VBA procedures from outside the class module will not be able to set or read data stored in those variables. To enable other parts of your VBA application to set or retrieve the employee data, you must add special property procedures to the CEmployee class module. There are three types of property procedures:

- Property Let—This type of procedure allows other parts of the application to set the value of a property.

- Property Get—This type of procedure allows other parts of the application to get or read the value of a property.

- Property Set—This type of procedure is used instead of Property Let when setting the reference to an object.

Property procedures are executed when an object property needs to be set or retrieved. The Property Get procedure can have the same name as the Property Let procedure. You should create property procedures for each property of the object that can be accessed by another part of your VBA application.

The easiest of the three types of property statements to understand is the Property Get procedure. Let's examine the syntax of the property procedures by taking a closer look at the Property Get LastName procedure.

The property procedures contain the following parts:

■ **A procedure declaration line** that specifies the name of the property and the data type:

```
Property Get LastName ( ) As String
```

LastName is the name of the property, and As String determines the data type of the property's return value.

■ **An assignment statement** similar to the one used in a function procedure:

```
LastName = m_LastName
```

LastName is the name of the property, and m_LastName is the data member variable that holds the value of the property you want to retrieve or set. The m_LastName variable should be defined with the Private keyword at the top of the class module.

If the retrieved value is obtained as a result of a calculation, you can include the appropriate VBA statement:

```
Property Get Royalty()
    Royalty = (Sales * Percent)-Advance
End Property
```

■ **The End Property keywords** that specify the end of the property procedure

---

Tip 11-3: Immediate Exit from Property Procedures

Just like the Exit Sub and Exit Function keywords allow you to exit early from a subroutine or a function procedure, the Exit Property keywords give you a way to immediately exit from a Property procedure. Program execution will continue with the statements following the statement that called the Property Get, Property Let, or Property Set procedure.

Creating the Property Get Procedures

The CEmployee class object has four properties that need to be exposed to VBA procedures that reside in other modules in the current VBA project. When working with the CEmployee object, you would certainly like to get information about the employee ID, first and last name, and current salary.

1. Type the following Property Get procedures in the CEmployee class module, just below the declaration section:

```
Property Get Id( ) As String
    Id = m_Id
End Property

Property Get LastName( ) As String
    LastName = m_LastName
End Property
```

```
Property Get FirstName( ) As String
    FirstName = m_FirstName
End Property

Property Get Salary( ) As Currency
    Salary = m_Salary
End Property
```

Each type of the needed employee information requires a separate Property Get procedure. Each one of the above Property Get procedures returns the current value of the property. Notice how a Property Get procedure is similar to a function procedure. Like function procedures, the Property Get procedures contain an assignment statement. As you recall from Chapter 4, to return a value from a function procedure, you must assign it to the function's name.

Creating the Property Let Procedures

In addition to retrieving values stored in data members (private variables) with Property Get procedures, you must prepare corresponding Property Let procedures to allow other procedures to change the values of these variables as needed. However, you don't need to define a Property Let procedure if the value stored in a private variable is meant to be read-only. Suppose you don't want the user to change the employee ID. To make Id read-only, you simply don't write a Property Let procedure for it. Hence, the CEmployee class will only have three properties (LastName, First-Name, and Salary). Each of these properties will require a separate Property Let procedure.

1. Type the following Property Let procedures in the CEmployee class module:

```
Property Let LastName(L As String)
    m_LastName = L
End Property

Property Let FirstName(F As String)
    m_FirstName = F
End Property

Property Let Salary(ByVal dollar As Currency)
    m_Salary = dollar
End Property
```

The Property Let procedures require at least one parameter that specifies the value you want to assign to the property. This parameter can be passed by value (see the ByVal keyword in the Property Let Salary procedure shown above) or by reference (ByRef is the default). If you need a refresher on the meaning of these keywords, see "Passing Arguments by Reference and by Value" in Chapter 4. The data type of the parameter passed to the

Property Let procedure must have exactly the same data type as the value returned from the Property Get or Set procedure with the same name. Notice that the Property Let procedures have the same name as the Property Get procedures prepared in the preceding section. By skipping the Property Let procedure for the Id property, you created a read-only Id property that can be retrieved but not set.

Tip 11-4: Defining the Scope of Property Procedures

You can place the Public, Private, or Static keyword before the name of a property procedure to define its scope. For example:

To indicate that the Property Get procedure is accessible to other procedures in all modules, use the following statement format:

```
Public Property Get FirstName( ) As
    String
```

To make the Property Get procedure accessible only to other procedures in the module where it is declared, use the following statement format:

```
Private Property Get FirstName( ) As
    String
```

To preserve the Property Get procedure's local variables between procedure calls, use the following statement format:

```
Static Property Get FirstName( ) As
    String
```

If not explicitly specified using either Public or Private, property procedures are public by default. Also, if the Static keyword is not used, the values of local variables are not preserved between the procedure calls.

Creating the Class Methods

Apart from properties, objects usually have one or more methods. A *method* is an action that the object can perform. Methods allow you to manipulate the data stored in a class object. Methods are created with Sub or function procedures. To make a method available outside the class module, use the Public keyword in front of the Sub or function definition. The CEmployee object that you create in this chapter has one method that allows you to calculate the new salary. Assume that the employee salary can be increased or decreased by a specific percentage or amount.

1. Type the following CalcNewSalary function procedure in the CEmployee class module:

```
Public Function CalcNewSalary(choice As Integer, _
     curSalary As Currency, amount As Long) As Currency

   Select Case choice
     Case 1 ' by percent
        CalcNewSalary =curSalary +((curSalary + amount)/100)
     Case 2 ' by amount
        CalcNewSalary = curSalary + amount
```

```
     End Select
End Function
```

The CalcNewSalary function defined with the Public keyword in a class module serves as a method for the CEmployee class. To calculate a new salary, a VBA procedure from outside the class module must pass three arguments: choice, CurSalary, and amount. The choice argument specifies the type of the calculation. Suppose you want to increase the employee salary by 5 percent or by five dollars. Choice 1 will increase the salary by the specified percent, and choice 2 will add the specified amount to the current salary. The curSalary argument is the current salary figure for an employee, and amount determines the value by which the salary should be changed.

Tip 11-5: About Class Methods

- Only those methods that will be accessed from outside of the class should be declared as Public. All others should be Private.
- Methods perform some operation on the data contained within the class.
- If a method needs to return a value, write a function procedure. Otherwise, create a Sub procedure.

Creating an Instance of a Class

After typing all the necessary Property Get, Property Let, Sub, and function procedures for your VBA application in the class module, you are ready to create a new instance of a class, which is called an object. Before an object can be created, an object variable must be declared in a standard module to store the reference to the object. If the name of the class module is CEmployee, a new instance of this class can be created with the following statement:

```
Dim emp As New CEmployee
```

The emp variable will represent a reference to an object of the CEmployee class.

When you declare the object variable with the New keyword, VBA creates the object and allocates memory for it; however, the object isn't instanced until you refer to it in your procedure code by assigning a value to its property or running one of its methods.

You can also create an instance of the object by declaring an object variable with the data type defined to be the class of the object. For example:

```
Dim emp As CEmployee
Set emp = New CEmployee
```

If you don't use the New keyword with the Dim statement (as shown above), VBA does not allocate memory for your custom object until your procedure actually needs it.

Event Procedures in the Class Module

An *event* is basically an action recognized by an object. Custom classes recognize only two events: Initialize and Terminate. These events are triggered when an instance of the class is created and destroyed, respectively.

The Initialize event is generated when an object is created from a class (see the preceding section on creating an instance of a class). In the CEmployee class example, the Initialize event will also fire the first time that you use the emp variable in code. Because the statements included inside the Initialize event are the first ones to be executed for the object before any properties are set or any methods are executed, the Initialize event is a good place to perform initialization of the objects created from the class.

As you recall, in the CEmployee class, Id is read-only. You can use the Initialize event to assign a unique five-digit number to the m_Id variable.

1. In the CEmployee class module, enter the following Class_Initialize procedure:

```
Private Sub Class_Initialize()
    Randomize
    m_Id = Int((99999 - 10000) * Rnd + 10000)
End Sub
```

The Class_Initialize procedure initializes the CEmployee object by assigning a unique five-digit number to the variable m_Id. To generate a random integer between two given integers where ending_number = 99999 and beginning_number = 10000, the following formula is used:

```
=Int((ending_number–beginning_number)*Rnd +beginning_number)
```

The Class_Initialize procedure also uses the Randomize statement to reinitialize the random number generator. For more information on using Rnd and Integer functions, as well as the Randomize statement, search the online help.

The Terminate event occurs when all references to an object have been released. This is a good place to perform any necessary cleanup tasks. The Class_Terminate procedure uses the following syntax:

```
Private Sub Class_Terminate()
    [cleanup code goes here]
End Sub
```

To release an object variable from an object, use the following syntax:

```
Set objectVariable = Nothing
```

When you set the object variable to Nothing, the Terminate event is generated. Any code in this event is executed then.

Creating the User Interface

If you skipped the previous chapter, you may need to turn back. Implementing your custom CEmployee object requires that you design a custom form.

1. Highlight the current VBA project in the Project Explorer window and choose **Insert | UserForm**.

2. Prepare the form shown in Figure 11-1:

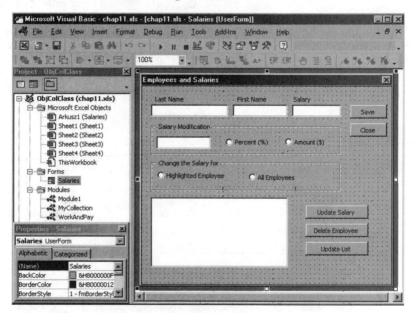

Figure 11-1: This form demonstrates the use of the CEmployee custom object.

3. Set the following properties for the form and its controls:

Object	Property	Setting
UserForm1	Name	Salaries
	Caption	Employees and Salaries
label1	Caption	Last Name
text box below the Last Name label	Name	txtLastName
label2	Caption	First Name
text box below the First Name label	Name	txtFirstName
label3	Caption	Salary
text box below the Salary label	Name	txtSalary

Object	Property	Setting
frame1	Caption	Salary Modification
text box in the frame titled "Salary Modification"	Name	txtRaise
option button 1	Name	optPercent
	Caption	Percent (%)
option button 2	Name	optAmount
	Caption	Amount ($)
frame2	Caption	Change the Salary for
option button 3	Name	optHighlighted
	Caption	Highlighted Employee
option button 4	Name	optAll
	Caption	All Employees
list box	Name	lboxPeople
	Height	91.45
	Width	180.75
command button 1	Name	cmdSave
	Caption	Save
command button 2	Name	cmdClose
	Caption	Close
command button 3	Name	cmdUpdate
	Caption	Update Salary
command button 4	Name	cmdDelete
	Caption	Delete Employee
command button 5	Name	cmdEmployeeList
	Caption	Update List

4.   Prepare a data entry worksheet, as shown in Figure 11-2:

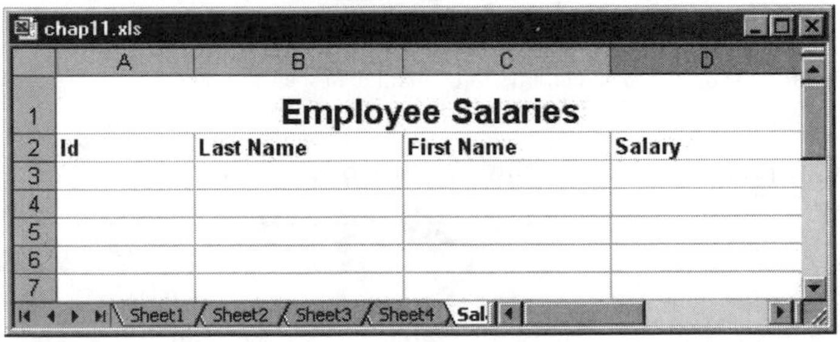

Figure 11-2: Data entered on the Employees and Salaries form will be transferred to the worksheet.

5.   Switch back to the Visual Basic Editor window, and double-click the form background to activate the form module.

6. Enter the following variable declarations at the top of the form Code window:

```
Option Explicit

Dim emp As New CEmployee
Dim CEmployees As New Collection
Dim index As Integer
Dim ws As Worksheet
Dim extract As String
Dim cell As Range
Dim lastRow As Integer
Dim empLoc As Integer
Dim startRow As Integer
Dim endRow As Integer
Dim choice As Integer
Dim amount As Long
```

The first statement declares the variable emp as a new instance of the CEmployee class. The second statement declares a custom collection. The CEmployees collection will be used to store employee data. Other variables declared here will be used by VBA procedures assigned to various controls on the form.

7. Type the following UserForm_Initialize procedure to enable or disable controls on the form:

```
Private Sub UserForm_Initialize()
    txtLastName.SetFocus
    cmdEmployeeList.Visible = False
    lboxPeople.Enabled = False
    Frame1.Enabled = False

    txtRaise.Value = ""
    optPercent.Value = False
    optAmount.Value = False

    txtRaise.Enabled = False
    optPercent.Enabled = False
    optAmount.Enabled = False

    Frame2.Enabled = False
    optHighlighted.Enabled = False
    optAll.Enabled = False

    cmdUpdate.Enabled = False
    cmdDelete.Enabled = False
End Sub
```

The statements entered inside the UserForm_Initialize procedure will enable only the desired controls when the form is loaded (Figure 11-3).

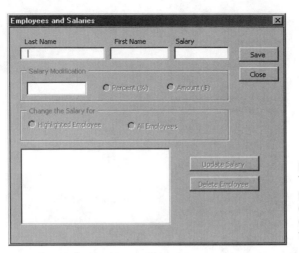

Figure 11-3:
The UserForm_Initialize
procedure disables
certain controls that
cannot be used when the
form is first loaded.

8.   Enter the following cmdSave_Click procedure to transfer the data
     entered on the form to the spreadsheet:

```
Private Sub cmdSave_Click()
    If txtLastName.Value = "" Or txtFirstName.Value = "" Or _
        txtSalary.Value = "" Then
        MsgBox "Enter Last Name, First Name and Salary."
        txtLastName.SetFocus
        Exit Sub
    End If
    If Not IsNumeric(txtSalary) Then
        MsgBox "You must enter a value for the Salary."
        txtSalary.SetFocus
        Exit Sub
    End If
    If txtSalary < 0 Then
        MsgBox "Salary cannot be a negative number."
        Exit Sub
    End If
    Worksheets("Salaries").Select
    index = ActiveSheet.UsedRange.Rows.Count + 1
    lboxPeople.Enabled = True
    'set and enter data into the CEmployees collection
    With emp
        Cells(index, 1).Formula = emp.Id
        .LastName = txtLastName
        Cells(index, 2).Formula = emp.LastName
        .FirstName = txtFirstName
        Cells(index, 3).Formula = emp.FirstName
        .Salary = CCur(txtSalary)
        If .Salary = 0 Then Exit Sub
        Cells(index, 4).Formula = emp.Salary
        CEmployees.Add emp
    End With
    'delete data from text boxes
    txtLastName = ""
```

```
        txtFirstName = ""
        txtSalary = ""
        'enable hidden controls
        cmdEmployeeList.Value = True
        cmdUpdate.Enabled = True
        cmdDelete.Enabled = True
        Frame1.Enabled = True
        txtRaise.Enabled = True
        optPercent.Enabled = True
        optAmount.Enabled = True
        Frame2.Enabled = True
        optHighlighted.Enabled = True
        optAll.Enabled = True
        txtLastName.SetFocus
End Sub
```

The cmdSave_Click procedure starts off with validating the user's input in the Last Name, First Name, and Salary text boxes. If the user entered correct data, VBA assigns to the variable Index the number of the first empty row on the active sheet for data entry purposes. The next statement enables the form's list box control.

When the program reaches the With emp... construct, a new instance of the CEmployee class is created. The LastName, FirstName, and Salary properties are set based on the data entered in the corresponding text boxes, and the Id property is set with the number generated by the statements inside the Class_Initialize event procedure. Each time VBA sees the reference to the instanced emp object, it will call upon the appropriate Property Let procedure located in the class module.

The last section of this chapter demonstrates how to walk through this procedure step by step to see exactly when the property procedures are executed. After setting the object property values, VBA transfers the employee data to the worksheet. The last statement inside the With emp... construct adds the user-defined object emp to a custom collection called CEmployees.

Next, Visual Basic removes the current entries from the form's text boxes and enables command buttons that were turned off by the UserForm_Initialize procedure. Notice the first instruction in this block: cmdEmployeeList.Value = True. This statement causes the automatic execution of the cmdEmployeeList_Click procedure attached to the Update List command button (by the way, this is the only control that the user never sees). The code for this procedure is shown below.

9. Type the cmdEmployeeList_Click procedure, as shown here:

```
Private Sub cmdEmployeeList_Click()
lboxPeople.Clear
    For Each emp In CEmployees
        lboxPeople.AddItem emp.Id & ", " & _
        emp.LastName & ", " & emp.FirstName & ", $" & _
```

```
            Format(emp.Salary, "0.00")"
    Next emp
End Sub
```

The cmdEmployeeList_Click procedure is attached to the Update List
command button. This button is controlled by the cmdSave_Click procedure and causes the new employee data to be added to the list box
control. The cmdEmployeeList_Click procedure begins with clearing
the contents of the list box and then populating it with the items stored
in the custom collection CEmployees.

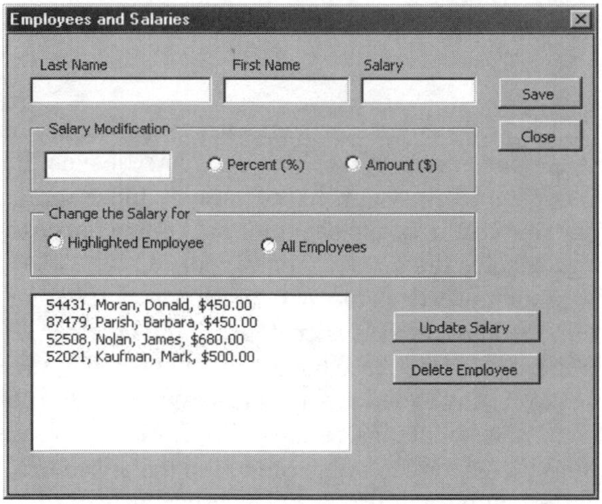

Figure 11-4:
The list box control
displays employee data
as entered in the
custom collection
CEmployees.

10. Type the following cmdClose_Click procedure:

```
Private Sub cmdClose_Click()
    Unload Me
End Sub
```

The cmdClose_Click procedure allows you to remove the user form
from the screen and finish working with the custom collection of
employees. When you run the form again, the employees you enter will
become members of a new CEmployees collection.

11. Type the following cmdDelete_Click procedure:

```
Private Sub cmdDelete_Click()
' make sure that an employee is highlighted in the
' list control

    If lboxPeople.ListIndex > -1 Then
        MsgBox "Selected item number: " & lboxPeople.ListIndex
        extract = CEmployees.Item(lboxPeople.ListIndex + 1).Id
    MsgBox extract

    Call FindId
    MsgBox empLoc
    Range("A" & empLoc).Delete (3)
```

```
    MsgBox "There are " & CEmployees.Count & _
        " items in the CEmployees collection. "
    CEmployees.Remove lboxPeople.ListIndex + 1
        MsgBox "The CEmployees collection has now " & _
    CEmployees.Count & " items."
    cmdEmployeeList.Value = True
    If CEmployees.Count = 0 Then
        Call UserForm_Initialize
    End If
    Else
        MsgBox "Click the item you want to remove."
    End If
End Sub
```

The cmdDelete_Click lets you remove an employee from the
CEmployees custom collection. To delete an employee, you must click
the appropriate item in the list box. When you click a list item, the
cmdEmployeeList_Click procedure is automatically executed. This procedure makes sure that the list box contents are refreshed. The
employee is removed both from the collection and from the list box. If
the list box contains only one employee, VBA calls the UserForm_Ini-
tialize procedure to disable certain form controls after removing the
last employee from the collection.

The cmdDelete_Click procedure contains several MsgBox statements, which allow you to examine the contents of the list box control
as you make deletions. In addition to removing the employee from the
custom collection, the cmdDelete_Click procedure must also remove
the corresponding row of employee information from the worksheet.
Locating the employee data in the worksheet is handled by the FindId
function. (The code of this procedure is in step 12 below.) This function
returns to the cmdDelete_Click procedure the row number that has to
be deleted.

12. Type the following function procedure:

```
Private Function FindId()

    Set ws = ActiveWorkbook.Sheets("Sheet5")
    startRow = ActiveSheet.UsedRange.Rows.Count + _
            1 - CEmployees.Count
    endRow = ActiveSheet.UsedRange.Rows.Count
    For Each cell In ws.Range(Cells(startRow, 1), _
            Cells(endRow, 1))
        If cell.Value = extract Then
          empLoc = cell.Row
          FindId = empLoc
            Exit Function
        End If
    Next
End Function
```

The FindId function procedure returns to the calling procedure the row number that contains the data of the employee who is currently selected in the form's list box. The search for the data in the worksheet is based on the contents of the variable extract that stores the unique employee number. The search for the employee ID is limited to the first worksheet column and begins with the row in which the first collection item was placed. This approach makes the search faster. You don't want to search the entire used area of the worksheet. Recall that if you use the form more than once, the contents of your custom collection will not include the previously entered employees.

13. Type the following cmdUpdate_Click procedure:

```
Private Sub cmdUpdate_Click()
    If optHighlighted = False And optAll = False Then
        MsgBox "Click the 'Highlighted Employee' or " _
            & " 'All Employees' option button."
        Exit Sub
    End If
    If Not IsNumeric(txtRaise) Then
        MsgBox "This field requires a number."
        txtRaise.SetFocus
        Exit Sub
    End If
    If optHighlighted = True And _
        lboxPeople.ListIndex = -1 Then
            MsgBox "Click the name of the employee."
            Exit Sub
    End If
    If lboxPeople.ListIndex <> -1 And _
        optHighlighted = True And _
        optAmount.Value = True And _
        txtRaise.Value <> "" Then
            extract = CEmployees.Item(lboxPeople.ListIndex + 1).Id
            MsgBox extract
            Call FindId
            MsgBox empLoc
            choice = 2
            amount = txtRaise
            CEmployees.Item(lboxPeople.ListIndex + 1).Salary = _
                emp.CalcNewSalary(choice, _
            CEmployees.Item(lboxPeople.ListIndex + 1).Salary, amount)
            Range("D" & empLoc).Formula = CEmployees. _
                Item(lboxPeople.ListIndex + 1).Salary
            cmdEmployeeList.Value = True
    ElseIf lboxPeople.ListIndex <> -1 And _
            optHighlighted = True And _
            optPercent.Value = True And _
            txtRaise.Value <> "" Then
            extract = CEmployees.Item(lboxPeople.ListIndex + 1).Id
            MsgBox extract
            Call FindId
            MsgBox empLoc
```

```
                        CEmployees.Item(lboxPeople.ListIndex + 1).Salary = _
                            CEmployees.Item(lboxPeople.ListIndex + 1).Salary + _
                            (CEmployees.Item(lboxPeople.ListIndex + 1).Salary * _
                            txtRaise / 100)
                        Range("D" & empLoc).Formula = CEmployees. _
                            Item(lboxPeople.ListIndex + 1).Salary
                        cmdEmployeeList.Value = True
            ElseIf optAll = True And _
                    optPercent.Value = True And _
                    txtRaise.Value <> "" Then
                        For Each emp In CEmployees
                            emp.Salary = emp.Salary + ((emp.Salary * txtRaise) _
                            / 100)
                            extract = emp.Id
                            MsgBox extract
                            Call FindId
                            MsgBox empLoc
                            Range("D" & empLoc).Formula = emp.Salary
                        Next emp
                        cmdEmployeeList.Value = True
            ElseIf optAll = True And _
                    optAmount.Value = True And _
                    txtRaise.Value <> "" Then
                        For Each emp In CEmployees
                            emp.Salary = emp.Salary + txtRaise
                            extract = emp.Id
                            MsgBox extract
                            Call FindId
                            MsgBox empLoc
                            Range("D" & empLoc).Formula = emp.Salary
                        Next emp
                        cmdEmployeeList.Value = True
        Else
            MsgBox "Enter data or select an option."
        End If
End Sub
```

With the cmdUpdate_Click procedure, you can modify the salary by the specified percentage or amount. The update can be done for the selected employee or all the employees listed in the list box control and collection. The cmdUpdate_Click procedure checks whether the user selected the appropriate option buttons and entered the increase figure in the text box. Depending on which options are specified, the Salary amount is updated for an employee or all the employees, either by the percentage or amount. The salary modification is also reflected in the worksheet. Figure 11-5 displays the salary of James Nolan, which has been increased by 10 percent. By entering a negative number in the text box, you can decrease the salary by the specified percentage or amount.

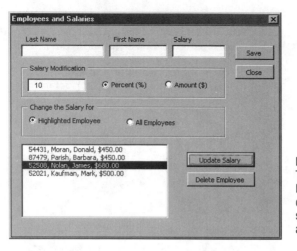

Figure 11-5:
The employee salary can be increased or decreased by the specified percentage or amount.

14. Insert a standard module into the current project by choosing **Insert | Module**. Rename this module **WorkAndPay**. Type the following procedure to display the Employees and Salaries form:

```
Sub ClassDemo( )
    Salaries.Show
End Sub
```

15. Run the ClassDemo procedure to work with the custom class.

    You can also display the Salaries form by clicking the form's background and pressing F5, or you can place a button in a worksheet and assign the ClassDemo procedure to it (see Chapter 10 for placing a button in a worksheet).

Watching the Execution of Your VBA Procedures

To help you understand what's going on when your code runs and how your custom object works, let's step through the cmdSave_Click procedure. Treat this exercise as a brief introduction to the debugging techniques that are covered in detail in Chapter 13.

1. In the Project Explorer window, select the **Salaries** form and click the **View Code** button at the top of this window.

2. When the Salaries (Code) window appears, select the **cmdSave** procedure from the combo box at the top left-hand side of the Code window.

3. Set a breakpoint by clicking in the left margin next to the following line of code:

```
If txtLastName.Value = "" Or txtFirstName.Value = "" Or _
    txtSalary.Value = "" Then
```

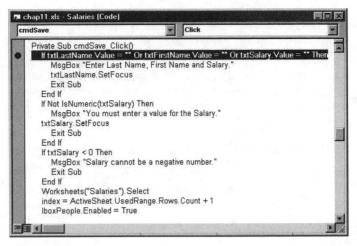

Figure 11-6: A red circle in the margin indicates a breakpoint. When VBA encounters the statement with a breakpoint, it automatically switches to the Code window and displays the text of the line as white on a red background.

4. In the Project Explorer window, highlight the **WorkAndPay** module and click the **View Code** button.

5. Place the cursor anywhere inside the ClassDemo procedure and press **F5**, or choose **Run | Run Sub/UserForm**.

6. When the form appears, enter data in the **Last Name**, **First Name**, and **Salary** text boxes, and click the form's **Save** button. Visual Basic should now switch to the Code window since it encountered the breakpoint in the first line of the cmdSave_Click procedure.

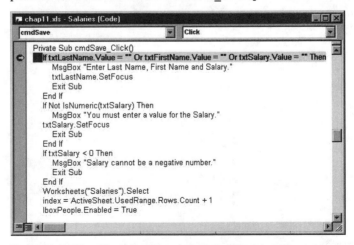

Figure 11-7: When Visual Basic encounters a breakpoint while running a procedure, it switches to the Code window and displays a yellow arrow in the margin to the left of the statement at which the procedure is suspended.

7. Step through the code one statement at a time by pressing **F8**.

Visual Basic runs the current statement and then automatically advances to the next statement and suspends execution. The current statement is indicated by a yellow arrow in the margin and a yellow background. Keep pressing F8 to execute the procedure step by step. When Visual Basic encounters the With emp statement, it will switch to the Class_Initialize procedure.

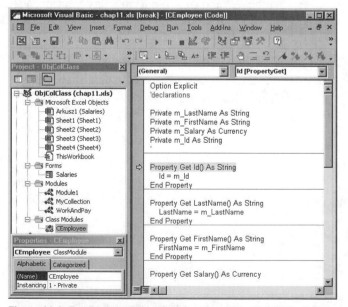

```
chap11.xls - CEmployee [Code]

Class                              Initialize

        Case 1 ' by percent
            CalcNewSalary = curSalary + ((curSalary + amount) / 100)
        Case 2 ' by amount
            CalcNewSalary = curSalary + amount
        End Select
    End Function


⇨   Private Sub Class_Initialize()
        Randomize
        m_Id = Int((99999 - 10000) * Rnd + 10000)
    End Sub
```

Figure 11-8: When Visual Basic encounters the reference to the object variable emp, it goes out to execute the Class_Initialize procedure. After executing the statements inside this procedure, VBA returns to the cmdSave_Click procedure.

When Visual Basic encounters the statement Cells(Index, 1).Formula = emp.ID, it will go out to execute the Property Get Id procedure in the CEmployee class module.

```
Microsoft Visual Basic - chap11.xls [break] - [CEmployee [Code]]

 File   Edit   View   Insert   Format   Debug   Run   Tools   Add-Ins   Window   Help

Project - ObjColClass                    (General)              Id [PropertyGet]

⊟ 🐾 ObjColClass (chap11.xls)              Option Explicit
  ⊟ 🐾 Microsoft Excel Objects             'declarations
      📗 Arkusz1 (Salaries)
      📗 Sheet1 (Sheet1)                   Private m_LastName As String
      📗 Sheet2 (Sheet2)                   Private m_FirstName As String
      📗 Sheet3 (Sheet3)                   Private m_Salary As Currency
      📗 Sheet4 (Sheet4)                   Private m_Id As String
      📗 ThisWorkbook
  ⊟ 🐾 Forms
      📋 Salaries                   ⇨      Property Get Id() As String
  ⊟ 🐾 Modules                                  Id = m_Id
      📄 Module1                            End Property
      📄 MyCollection
      📄 WorkAndPay                         Property Get LastName() As String
  ⊟ 🐾 Class Modules                             LastName = m_LastName
      📄 CEmployee                          End Property

Properties - CEmployee                    Property Get FirstName() As String
CEmployee ClassModule                          FirstName = m_FirstName
                                          End Property
Alphabetic  Categorized
(Name)       CEmployee                    Property Get Salary() As Currency
Instancing   1 - Private
```

Figure 11-9: Reading properties of your custom object is accomplished through the Property Get procedures.

8. Using the **F8** key, trace the execution of the cmdSave_Click procedure to the end.

   When VBA encounters the end of the procedure (End Sub), the yellow highlighter will be turned off. At this time, click the Microsoft Excel button on the Windows taskbar at the bottom of the screen to return to the active form. Enter data for a new employee, and click the **Save** button. When Visual Basic displays the Code window, choose **Debug | Clear All Breakpoints**. Now press **F5** to run the rest of the procedure without stepping through it.

Tip 11-6: VBA Debugging Tools

Visual Basic provides a number of debugging tools to help you analyze how your application operates, as well as locate the source of errors in your procedures. See Chapter 13 for details on working with these tools.

What's Next...

In this chapter, you learned how to create and use your own objects and collections in VBA procedures. You used a class module to create a user-defined (custom) object. You saw how to define your custom object's properties using Property Get and Property Let procedures. You also learned how to write a method for your custom object. Next, you saw how to make the class module available to the user by building a custom form. Finally, you learned how to analyze your VBA application by stepping through its code. In the next chapter, you will learn how to make your VBA procedures available to end users via custom menus and toolbars.

Chapter 12

Creating Custom Menus and Toolbars with VBA

Toolbars ■ **Using the CommandBar Object** ■ Creating a Custom Toolbar ■ Deleting a Custom Toolbar ■ Using the CommandBar Properties ■ Working with CommandBar Controls ■ **Working with Menus** ■ Menu Programming ■ Creating a Submenu ■ Modifying a Built-in Shortcut Menu ■ Creating a Shortcut Menu ■ **What's Next...**

Users have come to expect an easy way to select commands and options in any Windows application. Therefore, when you are done writing VBA procedures that provide a solution to a specific spreadsheet automation dilemma, you should spend additional time adding features that will make your application quick and easy to use. The most desired features of the user interface are custom menus and toolbars. This is especially true when your VBA application consists of a dozen or more procedures. To provide quick access to a specific command, simply create a control and place it on the built-in or custom toolbar. This chapter teaches you how to work with menus and toolbars programmatically.

Toolbars

The term *toolbars* refers both to toolbars and menu bars. Toolbars provide the user with quick and convenient access to the applications' commands. Toolbars can be easily created and modified via the Customize dialog box (Figure 12-1). One of the ways to access this dialog box is to choose Tools | Customize. You can also choose View | Toolbars | Customize or right-click any toolbar and select Customize from the shortcut menu. The toolbars can contain buttons, menus, or both. The menu bar located at the top of the application window (just below its title bar) is a special type of toolbar. In addition to commands, the menu bar can contain pictures that allow the user to quickly associate the specific command with the corresponding button on the toolbar. For example, the New and Open commands in the File menu display a picture image to the left of the command. The same images can be found on the Microsoft Excel Standard toolbar.

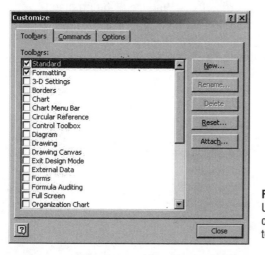

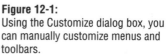

Figure 12-1:
Using the Customize dialog box, you can manually customize menus and toolbars.

The Customize dialog box consists of three tabs: Toolbars, Commands, and Options. Using the Toolbars tab, you can create a new toolbar, change the name of the existing toolbar, remove a toolbar, or reset it. The Commands tab allows you to drag new commands to the active menu or any visible toolbar. You can see the list of available commands after clicking on a particular Category. The Options tab lets you personalize your menus and toolbars by setting the size of icons, showing screen tooltips, and choosing animations. If you need a refresher on how to manipulate menus and toolbars via the Customize dialog box, see the online help. This chapter focuses on writing VBA statements and procedures to gain complete control over your application's menus and toolbars.

Using the CommandBar Object

CommandBars is a collection of objects that represents all the toolbars in the active application. Each object in this collection is called CommandBar. The term "CommandBar" is used to refer to a menu bar, a shortcut menu, or a toolbar.

Because the CommandBar object can refer to various tools (toolbar, menu bar, shortcut menu), this object comes with a special Type property that can be used to return the specific type of the toolbar as shown in Table 12-1.

Table 12-1: Types of CommandBar objects in the CommandBars collection

Type of Object	Index	Constant
Toolbar	0	msoBarTypeNormal
Menu Bar	1	msoBarTypeMenuBar
Shortcut Menu	2	msoBarTypePopup

1. Open a new workbook and save it as **Chap12.xls**.

2. Switch to the Visual Basic Editor screen.

3. Highlight the current **VBA Chap12.xls** project in the Project Explorer window and rename it **CustomTools**.

4. Add a new module to the CustomTools project.

5. Enter the MyToolBars procedure, as shown below:

```
Sub MyToolBars( )
    Dim bar As CommandBar
    Dim r As Integer
    r = 1
    ActiveSheet.Range("A1").Formula = "List of Toolbars"
    For Each bar In CommandBars
        If bar.Type = msoBarTypeNormal Then
            With Worksheets("Sheet1").Range("A1")
                .Offset(r, 0) = bar.Name
                .Offset(r, 1) = bar.Index
            End With
            r = r + 1
        End If
```

```
      Next
      Set bar = Nothing
   End Sub
```

The above procedure searches the CommandBars collection and selects only those tools with the Type Property equal to msoBarTypeNormal. If the specific element of the CommandBars collection is a toolbar, Visual Basic enters its name in the first column of the active worksheet. Column B stores the object's index.

1.   Modify the above procedure so that it writes to the spreadsheet the names of all the objects in the CommandBars collection (toolbars, menu bars, shortcut menus). Use Table 12-1 as a reference.

To refer to a specific toolbar in a CommandBars collection, you can use its name or index number.

1.   Enter the following statement in the Immediate window:

   ```
   ?CommandBars(1).Name
   ```

   When you press Enter, Visual Basic returns the name of the first element of the CommandBars collection.

2.   Enter the following statement in the Immediate window:

   ```
   ?CommandBars("Circular Reference").Type
   ```

   Visual Basic returns zero (0). This is the index number of a toolbar (see Table 12-1).

3.   To calculate the total number of tools available in the CommandBars collection, use the Count property. Try the following statement in the Immediate window:

   ```
   ?CommandBars.Count
   ```

Creating a Custom Toolbar

To create a custom toolbar, menu bar, or shortcut menu, use the Add method of the CommandBars object.

Suppose you want to create a new toolbar called "Budget Plans." The Add method that you need to invoke looks as follows:

```
CommandBars.Add(Name, Position, MenuBar, Temporary)
```

The optional argument Name is the name you want to assign to your new command bar. If you don't specify the name, Visual Basic assigns a generic name, such as "Custom1."

The Position argument determines where the new command bar will appear on the screen (see Table 12-2).

Table 12-2: Position constants for the CommandBar object

Position Constant	Index	Description
msoBarLeft	0	Command bar is docked on the left side of the application window.
msoBarRight	2	Command bar is docked on the right side of the application window.
msoBarTop	1	Command bar is docked at the top of the application window.
msoBarBottom	3	Command bar is docked at the bottom of the application window.
msoBarFloating	4	Command bar is floating (undocked).
msoBarPopup	5	Command bar is a shortcut menu.
msoBarMenuBar	6	Command bar replaces the system menu bar (Macintosh only).

The MenuBar argument is a logical value (True or False) that determines whether or not the new command bar replaces the active menu bar. Enter True if you want to replace the active menu bar; otherwise, use False.

The Temporary argument is a logical value (True or False) that determines when the command bar is deleted. Use True to have the command bar automatically deleted when the Excel application is closed. Using False will not remove the toolbar when you exit the program.

You can practice creating a toolbar in the Immediate window.

1. Enter the following statement in the Immediate window. Be sure to enter the complete statement on one line:

    ```
    set newToolbar = CommandBars.Add("Budget Plans", msoBarRight,
    False, True)
    ```

    When you press Enter, Visual Basic will add to the CommandBars collection a new toolbar with the specified name Budget Plans. To see this toolbar, switch to the Microsoft Excel application window and choose **View | Toolbars**. Excel displays a list of available toolbars, including the one you've just created (Figure 12-2).

2. Switch back to the Visual Basic Editor window, and enter the following statement in the Immediate window:

    ```
    CommandBars("Budget Plans").Visible = True
    ```

    To see the toolbar, switch to the Microsoft Excel application window. The Budget Plans toolbar is located to the right of the vertical scroll bar. Recall that when you created this toolbar, you used the msoBar-Right constant to determine its location.

3. Now close the Microsoft Excel application, and then activate it again and check whether the Budget Plans toolbar still appears on the right side of the application window. Because you have used the logical value of True in the position of the last argument of the Add method, the Budget Plans toolbar should be gone.

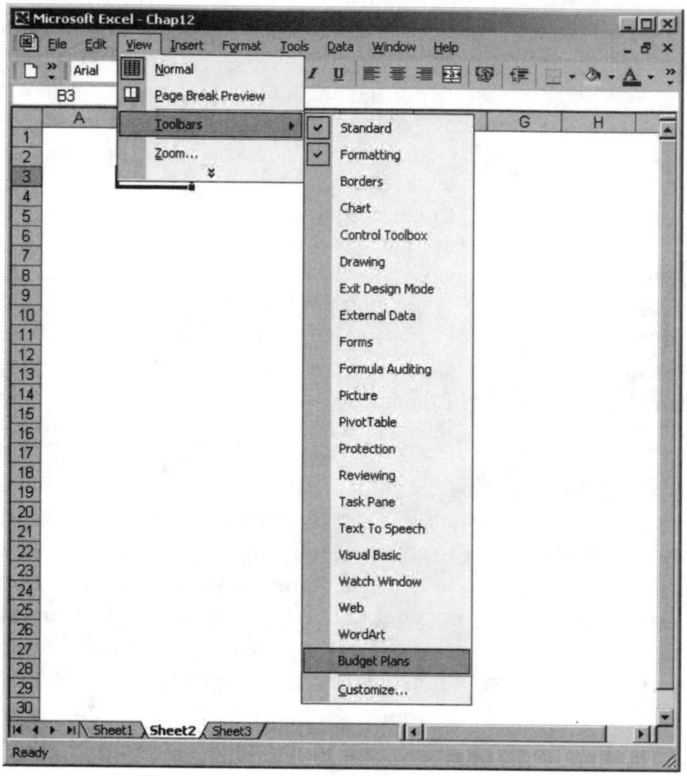

Figure 12-2: A custom toolbar is added to the list of the built-in toolbars.

Before you attempt to create a new toolbar, it's a good idea to check whether or not a toolbar with the specified name already exists in the CommandBars collection. The following procedure creates the Budget Plans toolbar, provided there is no existing command bar with such a name. Enter this procedure in the Code window of the CustomTools (Chap12.xls) project, and run it twice. The second time you execute this procedure, you should see a message notifying you that such a toolbar already exists.

```
Sub MakeToolBar()
    Dim bar As CommandBar
    Dim flagExists As Boolean

    flagExists = False
        For Each bar In CommandBars
        If bar.Name = "Budget Plans" Then
            flagExists = True
            MsgBox "The toolbar with this name already exists."
            Exit For
        End If
        Next bar
            If Not flagExists Then
                Set bar = CommandBars.Add("Budget Plans", _
```

```
                    msoBarBottom, False, True)
            CommandBars("Budget Plans").Visible = True
        End If
    Set bar = Nothing
End Sub
```

Deleting a Custom Toolbar

If you create a toolbar and decide that you don't want to keep it, you can get rid of it without closing the Excel application. Simply use the Delete method. For example, to delete the Budget Plans toolbar you can enter the following statement in the Immediate window:

```
CommandBars("Budget Plans").Delete
```

Note: You cannot delete built-in toolbars.

Using the CommandBar Properties

The CommandBar object has a number of properties. You'll work with some of them in the Immediate window.

1. Use the Immediate window to create a new toolbar named "My Reports":

    ```
    set myBar= CommandBars.Add("My Reports", msoBarBottom, False)
    ```

2. To find out whether a specific toolbar is built-in, use the statement:

    ```
    ?CommandBars("My Reports").BuiltIn
    ```

3. To determine the index number of the new toolbar in the CommandBars collection, enter the following statement:

    ```
    ?CommandBars("My Reports").Index
    ```

The toolbar is displayed on the screen when its Visible property is set to True. Set the Visible property to False to hide the command bar.

Working with CommandBar Controls

An empty toolbar does not serve any purpose. To make the toolbar useful, you need to place on it the desired controls and assign to them appropriate VBA procedures. There are three types of command bar controls, as shown in the following table.

Table 12-3: Types of controls that can be placed on toolbars

Object Name	Description
CommandBarButton	This object represents toolbar buttons and menu options. When you click a button or select a menu option, an appropriate VBA procedure is executed.

Object Name	Description
CommandBarPopup	This object represents pop-up controls that display a menu or submenu when clicked.
CommandBarComboBox	This object represents text boxes, list boxes, or combo boxes (for example, the Font and Font Size controls on the Formatting toolbar or the Zoom control on the Standard toolbar).

One of the important properties of the CommandBar object is the Controls property. This property returns the collection of all the controls on a specific toolbar.

1. Try out the following statement in the Immediate window:

```
?CommandBars(1).Controls. Count
```

When you press **Enter,** Visual Basic returns the total number of controls available in the worksheet's menu bar.

2. Enter the following statement to return the name of the first control in the worksheet's menu bar:

```
?CommandBars(1).Controls(1).Caption
```

Visual Basic returns the name of the first control: &File. The & character in front of the letter F indicates that this menu option can be executed from the keyboard by pressing Alt+F.

3. Enter this statement to execute a specific option:

```
CommandBars(1).Controls(1).Execute
```

The Execute method activates the specified control. The File menu should open up.

4. In a Code window of the current project, enter the following ControlList procedure to write to the Immediate window the names of all the controls on the active menu bar:

```
Sub ControlList()
Dim bar As CommandBar
Dim ctrl As CommandBarControl

Set bar = CommandBars(1)
    Debug.Print bar.Name & ": " & bar.Controls.Count
    For Each ctrl In bar.Controls
        Debug.Print ctrl.Caption
    Next
End Sub
```

5. Check the Immediate window after you have run the above procedure. You should see the following list:

```
Worksheet Menu Bar: 10
&File
&Edit
&View
```

```
&Insert
F&ormat
&Tools
&Data
A&ction
&Window
&Help
```

Adding Controls to a CommandBar

To run a desired VBA procedure, you can add a built-in or custom control to the built-in toolbar. If you prefer, you can add a control to a custom toolbar. Whether you add a built-in or a custom control to a built-in or custom toolbar, always use the Add method with the following syntax:

```
CommandBar.Controls.Add(Type, Id, Parameter, Before, Temporary)
```

CommandBar is the object to which you want to add a control.

Type is a constant that determines the type of custom control you want to add. You may select one of the following types:

msoControlButton	1
msoControlPopup	10
msoControlEdit	2
msoControlDropDown	3
msoControlComboBox	4

Id is an integer that specifies the number of the built-in control you want to add.

Parameter is used to send information to a Visual Basic procedure or store information about the control.

The Before argument is the index number of the control before which the new control will be added. If omitted, Visual Basic adds the control at the end of the specified command bar.

The Temporary argument is a logical value (True or False) that determines when the control will be deleted. Setting this argument to True causes the control to be automatically deleted when the application is closed.

1. Enter the AddBarAndControls procedure in the Code window, as shown below:

```
Sub AddBarAndControls( )
    With Application.CommandBars.Add("Test", , False, True)
        .Visible = True
        .Position = msoBarBottom
            With .Controls.Add(msoControlButton)
                .Caption = "List of Controls"
                .FaceId = 4
                .OnAction = "ControlList"
            End With
    End With
End Sub
```

This procedure creates a new toolbar named Test and places it at the bottom of the application window. Next, the Add method places a button on it named List of Controls identified by the printer icon. When the user clicks the button, the ControlList procedure that was prepared earlier will be executed.

Understanding and Using Control Properties

Controls placed on toolbars have many properties that you can read or set. To find out whether a control is built-in or custom, use the BuiltIn property. If the returned value is True, the control in question is built in. All user-defined controls return the value of False. If the value of the Enabled property is True, the specific control is active and can respond to a mouse click. An inactive control has its Enabled property set to False. It goes without saying that all controls have the Caption property that can be used to find out or set the control's title.

The combo type controls represented by the CommandBarComboBox object have specific properties, such as DropDownLines, DropDownWidth, List, ListCount, ListIndex, and Text. The explanation of these properties appears in Table 12-4.

Table 12-4: Selected properties of the CommandBarComboBox object

Property	Description
DropDownLines	Returns or sets the number of items that appear when the user clicks the drop-down arrow in the combo box.
DropDownWidth	Returns or sets the width of the combo box control in pixels.
List(Index)	Returns or sets the value of the list item given by Index (the index of the first item in the list equals zero (0)).
ListCount	Returns the number of items in the list.
ListIndex	Returns or sets the selected item in the list.
Text	Returns or sets the text that appears in the text box part of the combo box control.

1. Enter the MyCombo procedure in the Code window, as shown below:

```
Sub MyCombo()
    Dim cbo As CommandBarControl

    Set cbo = CommandBars(4).Controls.Add(Type:=4, Before:=1)
    With cbo
        .AddItem Text:="Row", Index:=1
        .AddItem Text:="Column", Index:=2
        .Caption = "Insert Row/Column"
        .DropDownLines = 2
        .DropDownWidth = 80
    End With
End Sub
```

The MyCombo procedure creates a combo box control (Type: =4 indicates msoControlComboBox) and places it at the very beginning of the built-in Formatting toolbar (this toolbar is the fourth CommandBar object in the CommandBars collection). Next, two items are added to the combo box control. The procedure also sets the caption and the width of the combo box control.

2. Switch to the Microsoft Excel application window and examine the first control on the Formatting toolbar.

3. Return to the Visual Basic Editor window.

4. Type the following statement in the Immediate window to remove the combo box control from the Formatting toolbar added by the MyCombo procedure:

```
CommandBars(4).Controls(1).Delete
```

When you press Enter, Visual Basic deletes the first control on the Formatting toolbar.

The buttons that appear on toolbars are easily recognized thanks to the images placed on them. If a control on a toolbar is a CommandBarButton object, the FaceId property returns or sets the ID number of the icon on the button's face. The icon ID number (FaceId), in most cases, is the same as the control's Id property. The icon image can be copied to the Windows clipboard using the CopyFace method.

	A	B	C	D
1	Image	Index	Name	Faceld
2		2520	&New	2520
3		23	Open	23
4		3	&Save	3
5		3738	&Mail Recipient	3738
6		5905	Searc&h...	5905
7		2521	Print (Lexmark Optra M412)	2521
8		109	Print Pre&view	109
9		2	&Spelling...	2
10		21	Cu&t	21
11		19	&Copy	19
12		6002	&Paste	
13		108	&Format Painter	108
14		128	&Undo	
15		129	&Redo	
16		1576	Hyperl&ink...	1576
17		226	&AutoSum	
18		210	Sort &Ascending	210
19		211	Sort Des&cending	211
20		436	&Chart Wizard	436
21		204	&Drawing	204
22		1733	&Zoom:	
23		984	Microsoft Excel &Help	984
24				

Figure 12-3: List of icons on the Standard toolbar. You can modify the Images procedure to get the complete listing of buttons and their icons on any toolbar.

The following Images procedure writes a list of buttons that appear on the Standard toolbar to a spreadsheet. In addition to the button name, the list shows its icon. Because one cannot copy the image of the icon that is currently disabled (see the Undo and Redo buttons on the Standard toolbar), when Visual Basic attempts to copy the button's face to the clipboard, it encounters an error. The Images procedure traps this error with the On Error GoTo ErrorHandler statement. This way, when Visual Basic encounters the error, it will jump to the ErrorHandler: label and execute the instructions below this label. The last statement, Resume Next, will send Visual Basic to the instruction below the one that caused the error, and the procedure will continue until all the buttons on the Standard toolbar have been checked out. You will learn more about error trapping in the next chapter.

```vba
Sub Images()
    Dim i As Integer
    Dim total As Integer
    Dim buttonId As Integer
    Dim buttonName As String
    Dim myControl As CommandBarControl
    Dim bar As CommandBar
    On Error GoTo ErrorHandler

    Workbooks.Add
    Range("A1").Select
    With ActiveCell
        .Value = "Image"
        .Offset(0, 1) = "Index"
        .Offset(0, 2) = "Name"
        .Offset(0, 3) = "FaceId"
    End With
    Set bar = CommandBars(3)
    total = bar.Controls.Count
    With bar
        For i = 1 To total
            buttonName = .Controls(i).Caption
            buttonId = .Controls(i).ID
            Set myControl = CommandBars.FindControl(ID:=buttonId)

            myControl.CopyFace  ' error could occur here
            ActiveCell.Offset(1, 0).Select
            ActiveSheet.Paste
            With ActiveCell
                .Offset(0, 1).Value = buttonId
                .Offset(0, 2).Value = buttonName
                .Offset(0, 3).Value = myControl.FaceId
            End With
        Next i
        Columns("C:C").EntireColumn.AutoFit
        Exit Sub
    ErrorHandler:
        Set myControl = CommandBars(3).Controls.Add
            With myControl
                .FaceId = buttonId
                .CopyFace
                .Delete (False)
            End With
```

```
        Resume Next
      End With
  End Sub
```

Control Methods

Controls have methods associated with them. These methods allow you to perform such tasks as moving, copying, and deleting controls. Suppose that you want to copy the Bold button from the Formatting toolbar to the Standard toolbar.

1. Enter the following three statements in the Immediate window:

```
set myBar = CommandBars(3)
set myControl = CommandBars(4).Controls(3)
myControl.Copy Bar:=myBar, Before:=1
```

2. Switch to the Microsoft Excel application window. You should see the Bold button to the left of the New button on the Standard toolbar.

3. Switch back to the Visual Basic Editor screen, and enter the following statement in the Immediate window to remove the Bold button from the Standard toolbar:

```
CommandBars(3).Controls(1).Delete
```

By replacing the Copy method with the Move method, you can move the Bold button from the Formatting toolbar to the Standard toolbar. Try this on your own. To return the toolbars to the default state, use the Reset method. When you're done practicing moving and copying buttons, type the following statements in the Immediate window:

```
CommandBars(3).Reset
CommandBars(4).Reset
```

If a control is a combo box (CommandBarComboBox), you can use the AddItem method to add a new item to the drop-down list. To remove an item from the list, use the RemoveItem method. Let's spend a few minutes and practice using these methods in the Immediate window.

1. Activate the MyCombo procedure that you prepared earlier. Run this procedure to place a custom combo box control on the Formatting toolbar.

2. Now enter the following statements in the Immediate window:

```
set myBar = CommandBars(4)
set myControl = CommandBars(4).Controls(1)
myControl.RemoveItem(1)
myControl.AddItem "Cells", 1
```

3. Switch to the Microsoft Excel application window and check the items that are available in the custom combo box control on the Formatting toolbar.

4. Return to the Visual Basic Editor window and reset the Formatting toolbar by typing in the Immediate window the following statement and pressing Enter:

```
CommandBars(4).Reset
```

Working with Menus

Just like toolbars, menus are CommandBar objects. There are two types of menus: built-in and shortcut. The built-in menu appears at the top of the application window, just below the title bar. In Microsoft Excel 2002, there are two built-in menus: Worksheet menu bar and Chart menu bar.

The Worksheet menu bar appears when a worksheet is active (Figure 12-4) and lists several main menus. Each of the main menus groups options related to specific tasks that can be performed in a worksheet or workbook. For example, the Format menu contains options allowing the application of various types of formatting to the worksheet. Some menu options have more detailed options that are grouped in a submenu (Figure 12-5).

Figure 12-4: The built-in "Worksheet Menu Bar" in Microsoft Excel

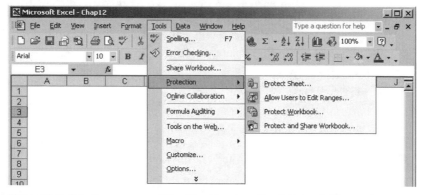

Figure 12-5: Selecting a menu option with a triangle on the right-hand side reveals a submenu with more choices.

When the user works with the chart sheet or selects a chart embedded in a worksheet, the Worksheet Menu Bar is replaced with the Chart Menu Bar (Figure 12-6). Only one menu bar can appear at a given time in the application window.

Figure 12-6: The built-in "Chart Menu Bar" in Microsoft Excel

A shortcut menu appears when you right-click on an object or press Shift+F10. Microsoft Excel 2002 has over 50 shortcut menus. A shortcut menu contains frequently used commands. For example, when you right-click any worksheet cell, the Cell shortcut menu appears (Figure 12-7). Right-clicking a worksheet tab displays the standard menu for worksheet tabs (Figure 12-8).

Figure 12-8: This shortcut menu appears when you right-click a sheet tab.

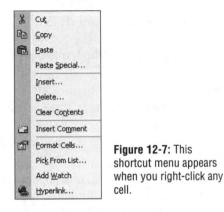

Figure 12-7: This shortcut menu appears when you right-click any cell.

Menu bars, much like toolbars, are represented by the same object—CommandBar. Use the Control object to refer to the menus, menu options, submenus, and shortcut menus. The type of the Control object is determined by an appropriate constant. Use the msoControlPopup to refer to the menu, the msoControlButton constant to refer to the menu options, and the msoBarPopup constant to refer to the shortcut menu. You will learn how to use these constants in the next section.

Menu Programming

Using Visual Basic for Applications you can perform such operations as creating a new menu bar, adding a new menu to a built-in menu bar, activating a built-in or custom menu bar, removing the user-defined (custom) menu bar, resetting the built-in menu, checking whether or not a menu bar is built-in or custom, and so on.

1. To return the name of the active menu bar, enter the following statement in the Immediate window:

    ```
    ?CommandBars.ActiveMenuBar.Name
    ```

    When you press Enter, Visual Basic returns the name of the active menu bar: Worksheet Menu Bar.

    Each menu on the menu bar has a title that can be returned or set with the Caption and Id properties.

2. To return the ID of the Format menu on the built-in Worksheet menu bar, enter the following procedure in this chapter's module:

    ```
    Sub Return_ID()
    ```

```
    Dim myControl As Object
    Set myControl = CommandBars("Worksheet menu bar"). Controls("Format")
    Debug.Print myControl.Caption & " Id is " & myControl.Id
End Sub
```

If you'd like to make the above procedure more flexible by enabling the user to return the IDs for other menus in the Worksheet menu bar, modify the Set statement as follows:

```
Set myControl = CommandBars("Worksheet menu bar").Controls
    (InputBox("Enter the menu name (Example: Format):"))
```

3. Run the Return_Id procedure, and then switch to the Immediate window to see its result.

4. To create a custom menu called Other and place it on the built-in Worksheet menu bar, enter the following statement on one line in the Immediate window:

```
CommandBars("Worksheet menu bar").Controls. Add(Type:=msoControlPopup,
    before:=10).Caption = "&Other"
```

When you press Enter and switch to the Microsoft Excel application window, the Worksheet menu bar displays your custom menu just before the Help menu. The above statement will not work if you haven't entered it on one line.

The "Other" menu is now empty. The next step demonstrates how to add menu commands.

5. To add a custom command (option) to a custom menu, enter on one line in the Immediate window the following statement:

```
CommandBars("Worksheet menu bar").Controls("Other"). Controls.Add
    (Type:=msoControlButton, before:=1).Caption = "Gridlines"
```

When you press Enter and switch to the Microsoft Excel application menu and then choose Other, you will see the Gridlines command. The above statement will not work if you haven't entered it on one line.

The next step requires that you assign to your custom menu option an appropriate VBA procedure that will be executed when the user selects this menu option.

6. Enter the following procedure that turns the gridlines on and off in the Code window of the current project:

```
Sub GridOnOff( )
    ActiveWindow.DisplayGridlines = Not ActiveWindow.DisplayGridlines
End Sub
```

7. To assign to your custom menu option the GridOnOff procedure, enter the following statement in the Immediate window on one line:

```
CommandBars("Worksheet menu bar").Controls("Other"). Controls
    ("Gridlines").OnAction = "GridOnOff"
```

When you press Enter, Visual Basic will assign the GridOnOff procedure to the Gridlines menu option. The above statement will not work if you haven't entered it on one line.

When you switch to the Microsoft Excel application window and choose **Other | Gridlines**, Visual Basic will turn the gridlines on if they are off and vice versa.

The menu option can be temporarily disabled by setting the Enabled property to False. A disabled menu option has its name grayed out, and clicking the option does nothing.

8. Disable the Gridlines command in the Other menu by entering the following statement on one line in the Immediate window:

```
CommandBars("Worksheet menu bar").Controls("Other"). Controls
  ("Gridlines").Enabled = False
```

When you press Enter, Visual Basic will disable the Gridlines menu option. The above statement will not work if you haven't entered it on one line. When you switch to the Microsoft Excel application window and choose Other, the Gridlines option is not available.

9. Enable the Gridlines command in the Other menu by replacing the logical value of False with the value of True in the Immediate window:

```
CommandBars("Worksheet menu bar").Controls("Other"). Controls
  ("Gridlines").Enabled = True
```

Notice that individual options in a built-in menu are organized in groups of similar commands separated by a horizontal line (Figure 12-9). To add such a line between menu options, use the BeginGroup method.

10. To add a horizontal line above the Hide command in the Window menu, enter the following statement on one line in the Immediate window:

```
CommandBars("Worksheet menu bar").Controls("Window").Controls
  ("Hide").BeginGroup = True
```

When you press Enter, Visual Basic will place a horizontal line just above the Hide option in the Window menu. The above statement will not work if you haven't entered it on one line. When you switch to the Microsoft Excel application window and choose Window, you'll see the Hide and Unhide commands between two horizontal lines. The upper one was added by you.

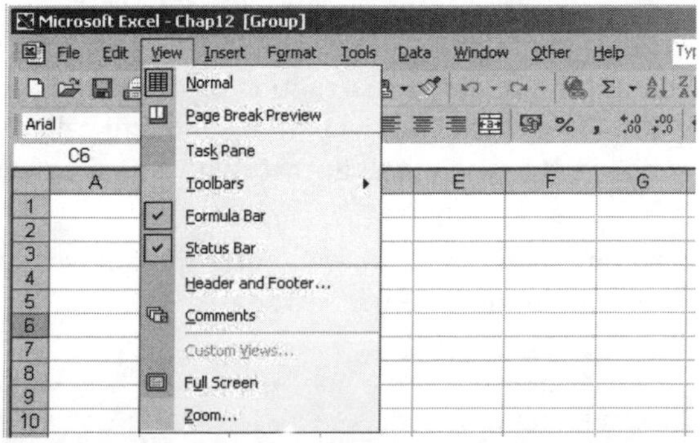

Figure 12-9: Each menu is divided into several sections by using a horizontal line.

If the menu command is selected, a check mark may appear to the left of the option name. For example, in the View menu (Figure 12-9), the check marks next to the Formula Bar and Status Bar options indicate that these options are currently in effect.

11. To indicate that your custom Gridlines option is selected in the Other menu, modify the GridOnOff procedure as follows:

```
Sub GridOnOff()
    Dim Other As Object
    Set Other = CommandBars("Worksheet menu bar").Controls("Other")
    ActiveWindow.DisplayGridlines = Not ActiveWindow.DisplayGridlines
    If ActiveWindow.DisplayGridlines = True Then
        Other.Controls("Gridlines").State = msoButtonDown
    Else
        Other.Controls("Gridlines").State = msoButtonUp
    End If
End Sub
```

Run this procedure. Then switch to the Microsoft Excel application window, and choose **Other | Gridlines**. If the gridlines in the active sheet were on, they should now be turned off. Choose **Other | Gridlines** again.

12. To remove the custom menu from the built-in Worksheet menu bar, enter the following statement in the Immediate window:

```
CommandBars("Worksheet menu bar").Controls("Other").Delete
```

When you delete a custom menu, all the commands placed in this menu are automatically deleted. Once you delete a custom menu and its commands, you can't restore them.

Creating a Submenu

Menu options containing a black triangle to the right of the menu option name display a submenu of additional commands. Suppose that you want to add a submenu to the Tools menu.

1. To add a submenu to the Tools menu, enter the following statement on one line in the Immediate window:

```
CommandBars("Worksheet menu bar").Controls("Tools").Controls.
    Add(Type:=msoControlPopup, Before:=1).Caption = "My Submenu"
```

When you press Enter, the above instruction places at the top of the Tools menu (Worksheet menu bar) a custom submenu called My Submenu. The above statement will not work if you haven't entered it on one line.

2. To add a custom command to a submenu, enter the following instruction on one line in the Immediate window:

```
CommandBars("Worksheet menu bar").Controls("Tools").
    Controls("My Submenu").Controls.Add(Type:=msoControlButton,
        Before:=1).Caption = "Option 1"
```

When you press Enter, the above instruction places the Option 1 command in the My Submenu on the Tools menu. The above statement will not work if you haven't entered it on one line. You can use the same technique to add more options to your submenu.

The following Colors procedure adds the Colors submenu to the built-in Format menu and places in it four options: red, green, blue, and black. Using these options, you can change the color of the text in a selected worksheet cell or cell ranges. The procedures that follow apply the appropriate color formatting.

```
Sub Colors()
    Dim myMenu As Object
    Dim mySubMenu As Object
    Set myMenu = CommandBars("Worksheet menu bar").Controls("Format")
    With myMenu
        .Controls.Add(Type:=msoControlPopup, Before:=2).Caption = "Colors"
    End With
    Set mySubMenu = myMenu.Controls("Colors")
    With mySubMenu
        .Controls.Add(Type:=msoControlButton).Caption = "Red"
        .Controls.Add(Type:=msoControlButton).Caption = "Green"
        .Controls.Add(Type:=msoControlButton).Caption = "Blue"
        .Controls.Add(Type:=msoControlButton).Caption = "Black"
        .Controls("Red").OnAction = "ColorRed"
        .Controls("Green").OnAction = "ColorGreen"
        .Controls("Blue").OnAction = "ColorBlue"
        .Controls("Black").OnAction = "ColorBlack"
    End With
End Sub

Sub ColorRed()
    ActiveCell.Font.Color = RGB(255, 0, 0)
End Sub

Sub ColorGreen()
    ActiveCell.Font.Color = RGB(0, 255, 0)
End Sub

Sub ColorBlue()
    ActiveCell.Font.Color = RGB(0, 0, 255)
End Sub

Sub ColorBlack()
    ActiveCell.Font.Color = RGB(0, 0, 0)
End Sub
```

Modifying a Built-in Shortcut Menu

Microsoft Excel offers 60 shortcut menus with different sets of frequently used menu options. The shortcut menu appears when you right-click on an object in the Microsoft Excel application window. Using VBA, you can return the exact number of the shortcut menus, as well as their names.

1. Enter the ShortcutMenus procedure in the current project's module, as shown below:

```
Sub ShortcutMenus()
    Dim myBar As CommandBar
    Dim counter As Integer
    For Each myBar In CommandBars
        If myBar.Type = msoBarTypePopup Then
            counter = counter + 1
            Debug.Print counter & ": " & myBar.Name
        End If
    Next
End Sub
```

Notice the use of the msoBarTypePopup constant to identify the shortcut menu in the CommandBars collection. To return the names of the built-in menus, use the msoBarTypeMenuBar constant. The msoBarTypeNormal will return the names of the toolbars. When you run the ShortcutMenus procedure, the names of all shortcut menus are returned in the Immediate window. These are listed below.

1: Query and Pivot	20: Floor and Walls	40: Shapes
2: PivotChart Menu	21: Trendline	41: Inactive Chart
3: Workbook tabs	22: Chart	42: Excel Control
4: Cell	23: Format Data Series	43: Curve
5: Column	24: Format Axis	44: Curve Node
6: Row	25: Format Legend Entry	45: Curve Segment
7: Cell	26: Formula Bar	46: Pictures Context Menu
8: Column	27: PivotTable Context Menu	47: OLE Object
9: Row	28: Query	48: ActiveX Control
10: Ply	29: Query Layout	49: WordArt Context Menu
11: XLM Cell	30: AutoCalculate	50: Rotate Mode
12: Document	31: Object/Plot	51: Connector
13: Desktop	32: Title Bar (Charting)	52: Script Anchor Popup
14: Nondefault Drag and Drop	33: Layout	53: Canvas Popup
15: AutoFill	34: Pivot Chart Popup	54: Organization Chart Popup
16: Button	35: Phonetic Information	55: Diagram
17: Dialog	36: Auto Sum	56: Add Command
18: Series	37: Paste Special Dropdown	57: Built-in Menus
19: Plot Area	38: Find Format	58: System
	39: Replace Format	59: Layout
		60: Select

Now that you know the exact names of the Excel shortcut menus, you can easily add other frequently used commands to any of these menus. Although it is easy to print a worksheet from the Print icon on the toolbar or by choosing File | Print, you may want to add the Print command to the shortcut menu that appears when the user right-clicks a worksheet tab. Let's see how you can add this option to the Ply menu that appears under these circumstances.

2.   Enter the AddToPlyMenu procedure as shown below:

```
Sub AddToPlyMenu()
    With Application.CommandBars("Ply")
        .Reset
        .Controls.Add(Type:=msoControlButton, Before:=2).Caption = _
            "Print..."
        .Controls("Print...").OnAction = "PrintSheet"
    End With
End Sub
```

The Reset method used in the above procedure prevents placing the same option in the shortcut menu when you run the procedure more than once.

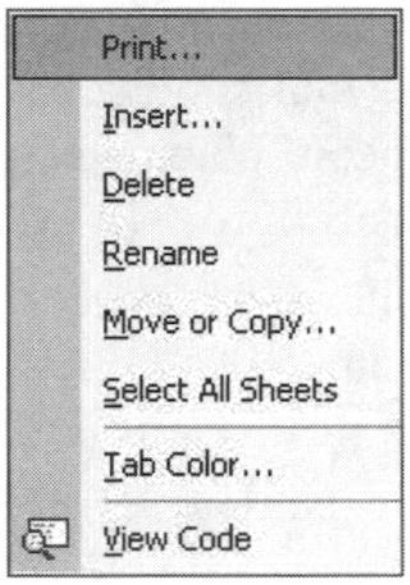

Figure 12-10: A custom option can be added to a built-in shortcut menu (see the Print option that was added by the AddToPlyMenu procedure).

3.   Run the AddToPlyMenu procedure. Then return to the Code window, and enter the code of the following procedure, which will be executed when you select the Print option from the shortcut menu:

```
Sub PrintSheet()
    Application.Dialogs(xlDialogPrint).Show
End Sub
```

4.   Switch to the Microsoft Excel application window and right-click any tab. Select the **Print** option. You should see the same dialog box that appears when you Print using other built-in tools.

Creating a Shortcut Menu

1.   Enter the Create_ShortMenu in the Code window of the current VBA project, as shown below:

```
Sub Create_ShortMenu()
Dim sm As Object
Set sm = Application.CommandBars.Add("Information", msoBarPopup)
    With sm
        .Controls.Add(Type:=msoControlButton).Caption = "Operating System"
        With .Controls("Operating System")
            .FaceId = 1954
            .OnAction = "OpSystem"
        End With
        .Controls.Add(Type:=msoControlButton).Caption = "Total Memory"
        With .Controls("Total Memory")
```

```
            .FaceId = 1977
            .OnAction = "TotalMemory"
        End With
        .Controls.Add(Type:=msoControlButton).Caption = "Used Memory"
        With .Controls("Used Memory")
            .FaceId = 2081
            .OnAction = "UsedMemory"
        End With
        .Controls.Add(Type:=msoControlButton).Caption = "Free Memory"
        With .Controls("Free Memory")
            .FaceId = 2153
            .OnAction = "FreeMemory"
        End With
    End With
End Sub
```

The above procedure creates a custom shortcut menu named Information and adds four commands to it. Notice that each command is assigned an icon. When you select a command from this shortcut menu, one of the procedures shown below in step 2 will run.

2. Enter the following procedures that are called by the Create_Short-Menu procedure:

```
Sub FreeMemory( )
    MsgBox Application.MemoryFree & " bytes", , "Free Memory"
End Sub

Sub OpSystem( )
    MsgBox Application.OperatingSystem, , "Operating System"
End Sub

Sub TotalMemory( )
    MsgBox Application.MemoryTotal, , "Total Memory"
End Sub

Sub UsedMemory( )
    MsgBox Application.MemoryUsed, , "Used Memory"
End Sub
```

To display the custom shortcut menu named Information on the screen, use the ShowPopup method, as shown in step 3.

3. Enter the following statement in the Immediate window:

```
CommandBars("Information").ShowPopup 0, 0
```

The ShowPopup method for the CommandBar object accepts two optional arguments (x, y), that determine the location of the shortcut menu on the screen. In the above example, the Information shortcut menu will appear at the top left-hand corner of the screen.

Suppose that you are designing a custom form and would like to display a shortcut menu when the user right-clicks a command button:

1. Choose **Insert | UserForm** from the Basic Editor menu.

2. Using the CommandButton control in the Toolbox, place a button anywhere on the empty user form.

3. Switch to the Code window for the form by clicking the **View Code** button in the Project Explorer window.

4. Enter the following procedure in the UserForm1 (Code) window:

```
Private Sub CommandButton1_MouseDown(ByVal Button _
                        As Integer, _
                        ByVal Shift As Integer, _
                        ByVal X As Single, _
                        ByVal Y As Single)
    If Button = 2 Then
        Call Show_ShortMenu
    Else
        MsgBox "You must right-click this button."
    End If
End Sub
```

This procedure calls the Show_ShortMenu procedure when the user right-clicks the command button placed on the form. Visual Basic has two event procedures that are executed in response to clicking a mouse button. When you click a mouse button, Visual Basic executes the MouseDown event procedure. When you release the mouse button, the MouseUp event occurs.

The MouseDown and MouseUp event procedures require the following arguments:

■ The object argument specifies the object. In this example, it's the name of the command button placed on the form.

■ The Button argument is the Integer value that specifies which mouse button was pressed.

Button Argument Value	Meaning
1	left mouse button
2	right mouse button
3	middle mouse button

■ The Shift argument determines whether the user was holding the Shift, Ctrl, or Alt keys when the event occurred.

Shift Argument Value	Meaning
1	Shift key
2	Ctrl key
3	Shift and Ctrl keys
4	Alt key
5	Alt and Shift keys
6	Alt and Ctrl keys
7	Alt, Shift, and Ctrl keys

5. Enter the code of the Show_ShortMenu procedure in the current project's module:

```
Sub Show_ShortMenu()
    Dim shortMenu As Object
    Set shortMenu = Application.CommandBars("Information")
        With shortMenu
            .ShowPopup
        End With
End Sub
```

Notice that the ShowPopup method used in this procedure does not include the optional arguments that determine the location of the short-cut menu on the screen. Therefore, the menu appears where the mouse was clicked (Figure 12-11).

6. To delete the shortcut menu named Information, enter and then run the following Delete_ShortMenu procedure in the Code window:

```
Sub Delete_ShortMenu()
    Application.CommandBars("Information").Delete
End Sub
```

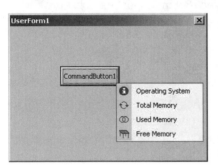

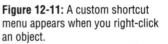

Figure 12-11: A custom shortcut menu appears when you right-click an object.

What's Next...

In this chapter, you learned how to use VBA to modify built-in menus and toolbars and how to create and display your own toolbars, menus, and short-cut menus. While working with menus and toolbars, you used various properties and methods of the CommandBar object. You learned about three types of CommandBar objects: Normal, MenuBar, and Popup. Using the Immediate window, you tried out individual statements that demonstrated how to create your own toolbars and controls on the fly.

The next chapter takes you through the process of error trapping and debugging. In other words, you will learn what to do when your procedure doesn't work correctly.

Chapter 13

Debugging VBA Procedures and Handling Errors

Testing VBA Procedures ■ Stopping a Procedure ■
Using Breakpoints ■ Using the Immediate Window in
Break Mode ■ Using the Stop Statement ■ Adding a
Watch Expression ■ Using Quick Watch ■ Using the
Locals Window and the Call Stack Dialog Box ■
Stepping through VBA Procedures ■ Stepping through
a Procedure ■ Stepping Over a Procedure ■ Setting the
Next Statement ■ Showing the Next Statement ■
Stopping and Resetting VBA Procedures ■ **Understanding and Using Conditional Compilation ■ Navigating
with Bookmarks ■ Trapping Errors ■ What's Next ...**

It does not take much for an error to creep into your VBA procedure. The truth is that no matter how careful you are, it is rare that all your VBA procedures will work correctly the first time. There's always something you have missed or haven't thought of. From Chapter 2, you already know that there are three types of errors in VBA: syntax errors, logic errors, and run-time errors. This chapter introduces you to many built-in tools that you'll find useful in the process of analyzing the code of your procedures and locating the source of errors.

Testing VBA Procedures

So far in this book you've created and executed dozens of sample procedures and functions. Because most of these procedures were quite short, finding errors wasn't very difficult. However, when writing longer and more complex procedures, locating the source of errors is more tedious and time-consuming. Fortunately, Visual Basic Editor provides a set of handy tools that can make the process of tracking down your VBA problems easier, faster, and less frustrating. Bugs are errors in computer programs and debugging is a process of locating and fixing those errors. Debugging allows you to find out the reason your procedure doesn't work the way it's supposed to work. You can do this by stepping through the code of your procedure or checking the values of variables.

When testing your VBA procedure, use the following guidelines:

- If you want to analyze your procedure, step through your code one line at a time by pressing F8, or choose Debug | Step Into.
- If you suspect that an error may occur in a specific place in your procedure, use a breakpoint.
- If you want to monitor the value of a particular variable or expression used by your procedure, add a watch expression.
- If you are tired of scrolling through a long procedure to get to sections of code that interest you, set up a bookmark to jump quickly to the desired location.

Each of these guidelines is demonstrated in this chapter in a hands-on example.

Stopping a Procedure

Do you know how to stop a Visual Basic procedure? If you are thinking of pressing the Esc key, you are correct. If you run a procedure and then suddenly press Esc, Visual Basic will halt execution of your program and display the message shown in Figure 13-1. However, in addition to the mighty and very reliable, in most circumstances, Escape key, VBA offers other methods of stopping your procedure and entering into a so-called break mode:

- Pressing Ctrl+Break
- Setting one or more breakpoints
- Inserting the Stop statement
- Adding a watch expression

A break occurs when execution of your VBA procedure is temporarily suspended. Visual Basic remembers the values of all variables and the statement from which the execution of the procedure should resume when the user decides to continue by clicking the Run Sub/UserForm on the toolbar (or the Run menu option with the same name) or by clicking the Continue button in the dialog box (Figure 13-1).

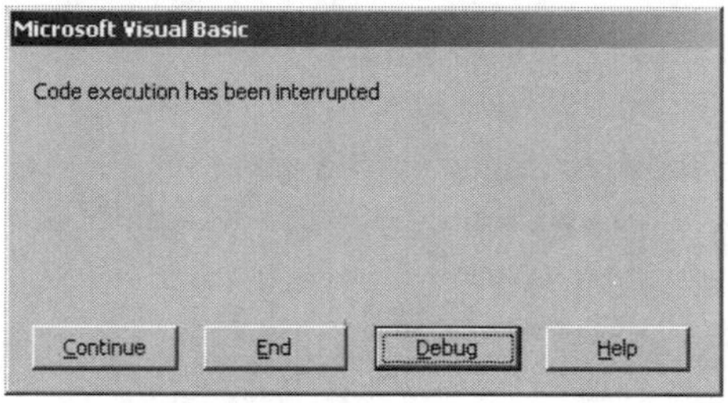

Figure 13-1:
This message appears when you press Esc or Ctrl+Break while your VBA procedure is running.

Tip 13-1: Preventing User Intervention

You can prevent the user from halting your procedure by including the following statement in the procedure code:

```
Application.EnableCancelKey = xlDisabled
```

When the user presses Esc or Ctrl+Break while the procedure is running, nothing happens. The Application object's EnableCancelKey property disables these keys.

The error dialog box shown in Figure 13-1 informs you that the procedure was halted. The following buttons are available:

Continue	Click this button to resume code execution. This button will be grayed out if an error was encountered.
End	Click this button if you do not want to troubleshoot the procedure at this time. VBA will stop code execution.
Debug	Click this button to enter break mode. The Code window will appear, and VBA will highlight the line at which the procedure execution was suspended. You can examine, debug, rest, or step through the code.
Help	Click this button to view the online help that explains the cause of this error message.

Using Breakpoints

If you know more or less where you can expect a problem in the code of your procedure, you should suspend code execution at that location (on a given line). Setting a breakpoint boils down to pressing F9 when the cursor is on the desired line of code. When VBA gets to that line while running your procedure, it will immediately display the Code window. At this point, you can step through the code of your procedure line by line by pressing F8 or choosing Debug | Step Into.

To see how this works, let's look at the following scenario. Assume that during the execution of the ChangeCode procedure the following line of code could get you in trouble:

```
ActiveCell.Formula = _
    "=VLookup(RC[1],Codes.xls!R1C1:R6C2,2)"
```

1. Prepare the spreadsheets shown in Figures 13-2 and 13-3. Save the data shown in Figure 13-2 as **Chap13.xls**. Save the data in Figure 13-3 as **Codes.xls**. Close the Codes.xls file.

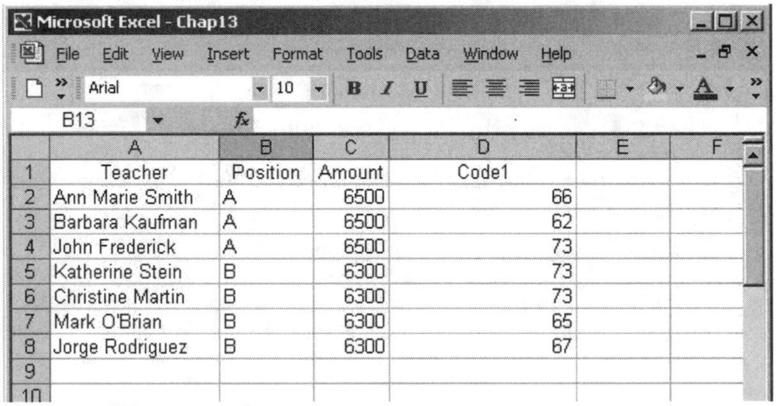

Figure 13-2: The codes entered in column D of this spreadsheet will be replaced by the ChangeCode procedure with the codes illustrated in Figure 13-3.

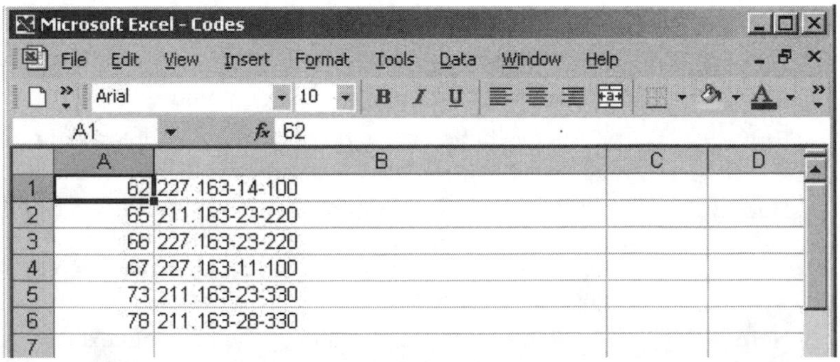

Figure 13-3: The ChangeCode procedure uses this code table for lookup purposes.

2. With Chap13.xls active, switch to the Visual Basic Editor window.

3. Use the Properties window to rename VBAProject (Chap13.xls) to **Debugging**.

4. Insert a module into the Debugging (Chap13.xls) project, and change its Name property to **Breaks**.

5. Enter the code of the ChangeCode procedure, as shown below:

```
Sub ChangeCode()
    Workbooks.Open FileName:="C:\Codes.xls"
    Windows("Chap13.xls").Activate
    Columns("D:D").Select
    Selection.Insert Shift:=xlToRight
    Range("D1").Select
    ActiveCell.Formula = "Code"
    Columns("D:D").Select
    Selection.SpecialCells(xlBlanks).Select
    ActiveCell.Formula = "=VLookup(RC[1],Codes.xls!R1C1:R6C2,2)"
    Selection.FillDown
        With Columns("D:D")
            .EntireColumn.AutoFit
            .Select
        End With
    Selection.Copy
    Selection.PasteSpecial Paste:=xlValues
    Rows("1:1").Select
        With Selection
            .HorizontalAlignment = xlCenter
            .VerticalAlignment = xlBottom
            .Orientation = xlHorizontal
        End With
    Workbooks("Codes.xls").Close
End Sub
```

6. In the ChangeCode procedure, click anywhere on the line containing the following statement:

```
ActiveCell.Formula = "=VLookup(RC[1],Codes.xls!R1C1:R6C2,2)"
```

7. Press **F9** (or choose **Debug | Toggle Breakpoint**) to set a breakpoint on the line where the cursor is located. Another way to set a breakpoint is to click in the margin indicator to the left of the line on which you want to pause the procedure. When you set the breakpoint, Visual Basic displays a red circle in the margin. At the same time, the line that has the breakpoint is indicated as white text on a red background (Figure 13-4). The color of the breakpoint can be changed on the Editor Format tab in the Options dialog box (Tools menu).

8. Run the ChangeCode procedure. When you run the procedure, Visual Basic will execute all the statements until it encounters the breakpoint. Once the breakpoint is reached, the code is suspended, and the screen displays the Code window (Figure 13-5). Visual Basic displays a yellow arrow in the margin to the left of the statement at which the procedure

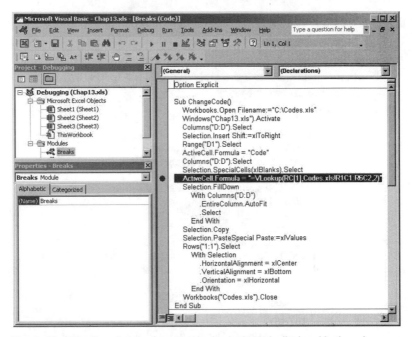

Figure 13-4: The line of code where the breakpoint is set is displayed in the color specified on the Editor Format tab in the Options dialog box.

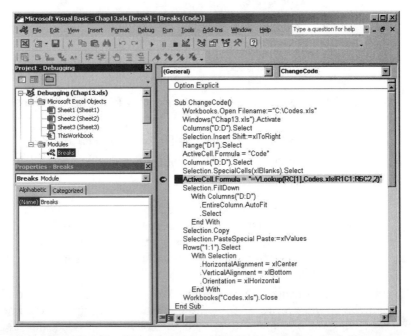

Figure 13-5: When Visual Basic encounters a breakpoint, it displays the Code window and indicates the current statement.

was suspended. At the same time, the statement appears inside a box with a yellow background. The error and the box indicate the current statement or the statement that is about to be executed. If the current statement also contains a breakpoint, the margin displays both indicators overlapping one another (the circle and the arrow).

9. Press **F8**, or choose **Debug | Step Into**.

10. Repeat the instruction in step 9 a few more times.

11. Press **F5** (or choose **Run Sub/UserForm**) to continue running the procedure without stepping through its code.

    When you finish running your procedure, Visual Basic does not automatically remove the breakpoint. Notice that the line of code with the VLookup function is still highlighted.

    In this example you have set only one breakpoint. Visual Basic allows you to set any number of breakpoints in a procedure. This way, you can suspend and continue the execution of your procedure as you please. You can analyze the code of your procedure and check the values of variables while execution is suspended. You can also perform various tests by typing statements in the Immediate window.

12. Remove the breakpoint by choosing **Debug | Clear All Breakpoints**, or press **Ctrl+Shift+F9**.

    All the breakpoints are removed. If you had set several breakpoints in a given procedure and would like to remove only one or some of them, click on the line containing the breakpoint that you want to remove and press **F9** (or choose **Debug | Clear Breakpoint**). You should clear the breakpoints when they are no longer needed. The breakpoints are automatically removed when you close the file.

Tip 13-2: When to Use a Breakpoint

Consider setting a breakpoint if you suspect that your procedure never executes a certain block of code.

Using the Immediate Window in Break Mode

Once the procedure execution is suspended, when the Code window appears, you can activate the Immediate window and type VBA instructions to find out, for instance, which cell is currently active or the name of the active sheet. You can also use the Immediate window to change the contents of variables in order to correct values that may be causing errors. By now, you should be an expert when it comes to working in the Immediate window. Figure 13-6 shows the suspended ChangeCode procedure and the Immediate window with the questions that were asked of Visual Basic while in the break mode.

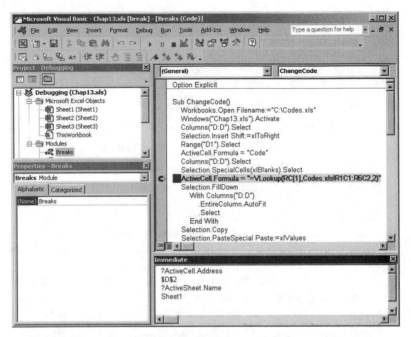

Figure 13-6: When code execution is suspended, you can find answers to many questions by entering appropriate statements in the Immediate window.

In break mode, you can quickly find out the contents of the variable at the cursor in the Code window. Simply hold the mouse pointer over any variable in a running procedure to find out the value of that variable. For example, in the VarValue procedure shown in Figure 13-7, the breakpoint has been set on the second occurrence of the Workbooks.Add statement.

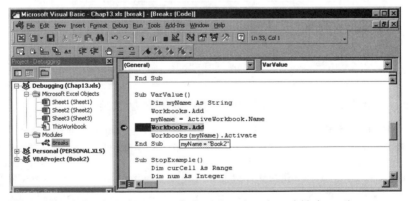

Figure 13-7: In break mode, you can find out the value of a variable by resting a mouse pointer on that variable.

When Visual Basic encounters this statement, the Code window (break mode) appears. Because Visual Basic has already executed the statement that stores the name of the active workbook in the variable myBook, you can quickly find out the value of this variable by resting the mouse pointer over its name. The name of the variable and its current value appear in a frame. To show the values of several variables used in a procedure at once, you should use the Locals window that is discussed later in this chapter.

Tip 13-3: Working within the Code Window in Break Mode

While in break mode, you can change code, add new statements, execute the procedure one line at a time, skip lines, set the next statement, use the Immediate window, and more. When Visual Basic is in break mode, all of the options on the Debug menu are available. You can enter break mode by pressing Esc, Ctrl+Break, or F8, or by setting a breakpoint.

While you work in break mode, if you change certain code, VBA will prompt you to reset the project by displaying the following error message: "This action will reset your project, proceed anyway?" You can click OK to cease the program's execution and proceed editing your code or Cancel to delete the new changes and continue running the code from the point at which it was suspended. To see this error, place your procedure in break mode, and then proceed to change the variable declaration. As you press F5 to resume code execution, VBA will prompt you to reset your project.

Using the Stop Statement

Sometimes you won't be able to test your procedure right away. If you set up your breakpoints and then close the file, Excel will remove your breakpoints, and the next time you are ready to test your procedure, you'll have to begin by setting up your breakpoints again. If you need to postpone the task of testing your procedure until later, you can take a different approach. Simply insert a Stop statement into your code wherever you want to halt a procedure. Figure 13-8 shows the Stop statement before the For...Next loop. Visual Basic will suspend the execution of the StopExample procedure when it encounters the Stop statement. The screen will display the Code window in break mode. Although the Stop statement has exactly the same effect as setting a breakpoint, it has one disadvantage, all Stop statements stay in the procedure until you remove them. When you no longer need to stop your procedure, you must locate and remove all the Stop statements.

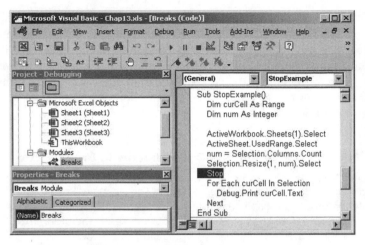

Figure 13-8:
You can insert a Stop statement anywhere in the code of your VBA procedure. The procedure will halt when it gets to the Stop statement, and the Code window will appear with the line highlighted.

Adding a Watch Expression

Many errors in procedures are caused by variables that assume unexpected values. If a procedure uses a variable whose value changes in various locations, you may want to stop the procedure and check the current value of that variable. Visual Basic offers a special Watch window, which allows you to keep an eye on variables or expressions while your procedure is running.

To add a watch expression to your procedure, perform the following:

1. In the Code window, select the variable whose value you want to monitor.

2. Choose **Debug | Add Watch.**

   The screen will display the Add Watch dialog box, as shown in Figure 13-9.

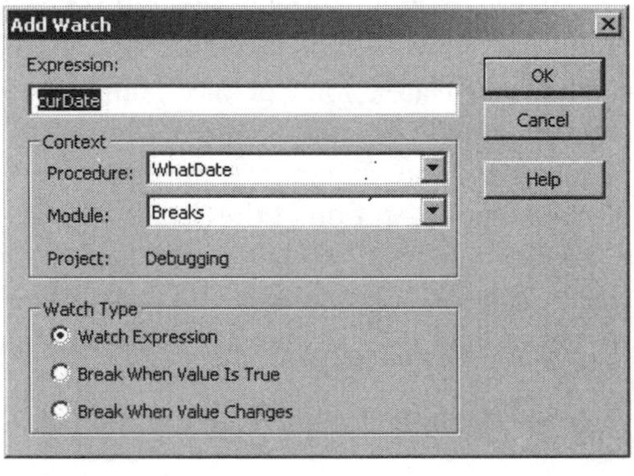

Figure 13-9:
The Add Watch dialog box allows you to define conditions that you want to monitor while a VBA procedure is running.

The Add Watch dialog box contains three sections described in the following table:

Expression	Displays the name of a variable that you have highlighted in your procedure. If you open the Add Watch dialog box without selecting a variable name, type the name of the variable you want to monitor in the Expression text box.
Context	In this section you should indicate the name of the procedure that contains the variable and the name of the module where this procedure is located.
Watch Type	Specifies how to monitor the variable. If you choose the Watch Expression option button, you will be able to read the value of the variable in the Watch window while in break mode. If you choose the Break When Value is True option button, Visual Basic will automatically stop the procedure when the variable evaluates to true (nonzero). The last option button, Break When Value Changes, stops the procedure each time the value of the variable or expression changes.

You can add a watch expression before running a procedure or after execution of your procedure has been suspended.

The difference between a breakpoint and a watch expression is that the breakpoint always stops a procedure in a specified location and the watch stops the procedure only when the specified condition (Break When Value is True or Break When Value Changes) is met. Watches are extremely useful when you are not sure where the variable is being changed. Instead of stepping through many lines of code to find out where the variable assumes the specified value, you can simply put a watch breakpoint on the variable and run your procedure as normal. Let's see how this works.

1. Prepare the procedure shown in Figure 13-10.

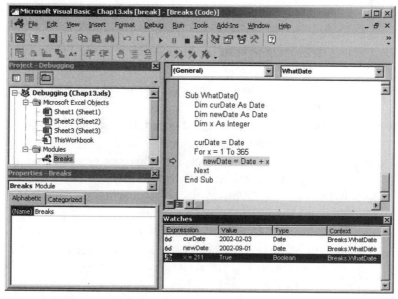

Figure 13-10: Using the Watches window

The WhatDate procedure uses the For...Next loop to calculate the date that is x days in the future. If you run this procedure, you won't get any result unless you insert the following instruction in the code of the procedure:

```
MsgBox "In " & x & " days, it will be " & NewDate
```

This time, however, you don't want to display the individual dates, day after day. Suppose that you want to stop the program when the value of the variable x reaches 211. In other words, you want to know what date will be 211 days from now. To get the answer, you could insert the following statement into your procedure:

```
If x = 211 Then MsgBox "In " & x & " days it will be " & NewDate
```

Let's say you want to get the answer without introducing any new statements into your procedure. How do you do this? If you add watch expressions to the procedure, Visual Basic will stop the For...Next loop when the specified condition is met, and you'll be able to check the values of the desired variables.

1. Choose **Debug | Add Watch**.
2. In the Expression text box, enter the following expression: **x = 211**.
3. In the Context section, choose **What Date** from the Procedure combo box, and **Breaks** from the Module combo box.
4. In the Watch Type section, select the **Break When Value is True** option button.
5. Click **OK** to close the Add Watch dialog box. You have now added your first watch expression.
6. In the Code window, position the insertion point anywhere within the name of the curDate variable.
7. Choose **Debug | Add Watch**, and click **OK** to set up the default watch type with Watch Expression.
8. In the Code window, position the insertion point anywhere within the name of the newDate variable.
9. Choose **Debug | Add Watch**, and click **OK** to set up the default watch type with Watch Expression.

    After performing the above steps, the WhatDate procedure contains the following three watches:

x = 211	Break When Value is True
curDate	Watch Expression
newDate	Watch Expression

10. Position the insertion point anywhere inside the code of the WhatDate procedure, and press **F5**. Visual Basic stops the procedure when x equals 211 (see Figure 13-10).

Notice that the value of the variable x in the Watches window is the same as the value that you specified in the Add Watch dialog. In addition, the Watches window shows the value of the variables curDate and newDate. The procedure is in break mode. You can press F5 to continue or you can ask another question: What date will be in 277 days? The next step shows how to do this.

11. Choose **Debug | Edit Watch**, and enter the following expression: **x = 27**. You can quickly display the Edit Watch dialog box by double-clicking the expression in the Watches window.

12. Click **OK** to close the Edit Watch dialog box. Notice that the Watches window now displays a new value of the expression. x is now False.

13. Press **F5**. The procedure stops again when the value of x equals 277. The value of curDate is the same. However, the newDate variable now contains a new value—a date that is 277 days from now. You can change the value of the expression again or finish the procedure.

14. Press **F5** to finish the procedure without stopping.

When your procedure is running and a watch expression has a value, the Watches window displays the value of the watch expression. If you open the Watches window after the procedure has finished, you will see < out of context> instead of the variable values. In other words, when the watch expression is out of context, it does not have a value.

Removing Watch Expressions

1. In the Watches window, click on the expression you want to remove and press **Delete**. Remove all the watch expressions you defined in the preceding exercise.

Using Quick Watch

If you want to check the value of an expression for which you have not defined a watch expression, you can use Quick Watch (Figure 13-11).

Figure 13-11:
The Quick Watch dialog box shows the value of the selected expression in a VBA procedure.

The Quick Watch dialog box can be accessed in the following way:

- While in break mode, position the insertion point anywhere inside the name of a variable or expression you wish to watch.
- Choose Debug | Quick Watch, or press Shift+F9.

The Quick Watch dialog box contains the Add button that allows you to add the expression to the Watches window.

Make sure the WhatDate procedure does not contain any watch expressions. See the preceding section on how to remove a watch expression from the Watches window. Now, let's see by example how to take advantage of the Quick Watch.

1. In the WhatDate procedure, position the insertion point on the name of the variable x.

2. Choose **Debug | Add Watch**.

3. Enter the following expression: **x = 50**.

4. Choose the **Break When Value is True** option button, and click **OK**.

5. Run the WhatDate procedure.

   Visual Basic will suspend procedure execution when x equals 50. Notice that the Watches window does not contain the newDate nor the curDate variable. To check the values of these variables, you can position the mouse pointer over the appropriate variable name in the Code window, or you can invoke the Quick Watch window.

6. In the Code window, position the mouse inside the newDate variable and press **Shift+F9**. The Quick Watch window shows the name of the expression and its current value.

7. Click **Cancel** to return to the Code window.

8. In the Code window, position the mouse inside the curDate variable and press **Shift+F9**. The Quick Watch window now shows the value of the variable curDate.

9. Click **Cancel** to return to the Code window.

10. Press **F5** to continue running the procedure.

Using the Locals Window and the Call Stack Dialog Box

If during the execution of a VBA procedure you want to keep an eye on all the declared variables and their current values, make sure to choose View | Locals Window before you run the procedure. While in break mode, Visual Basic will display a list of variables and their corresponding values in the Locals window (Figure 13-12).

The Locals window contains three columns. The Expression column displays the names of variables that are declared in the current procedure. The first row displays the name of the module preceded by the plus sign. When you click the plus sign, you can check if any variables have been declared at the module level. The class module will show here the system variable Me. In the Locals window, the global variables and variables used by other projects aren't displayed.

The second column shows the current values of variables. In this column, you can change the value of a variable by clicking it and typing the

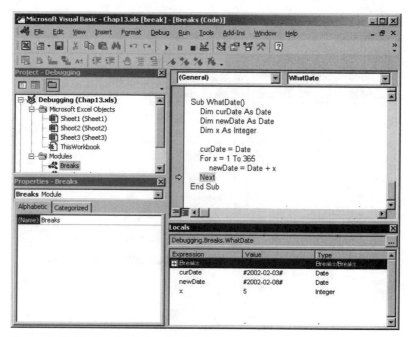

Figure 13-12: The Locals window displays the current values of all the declared variables in the current VBA procedure.

new value. After changing the value, press Enter to register the change. You can also press Tab, Shift+Tab, or the up or down arrow or click anywhere within the Locals window after you've changed the variable value. The third column displays the type of each declared variable.

To observe the values of variables in the Locals window, do the following:

1. Choose **View | Locals Window**.

2. Click anywhere inside the WhatDate procedure and press **F8**. By pressing F8, you place the procedure in break mode. The Locals window displays the name of the current module and the local variables and their beginning values.

3. Press **F8** a few more times while keeping an eye on the Locals window.

4. Press **F5** to continue running the procedure.

The Locals window also contains a button with three dots. This button opens the Call Stack dialog box (Figure 13-13), which displays a list of all active procedure calls. An active procedure call is a procedure that is started but not completed. You can also activate the Call Stack dialog box by choosing View | Call Stack. This option is only available in break mode.

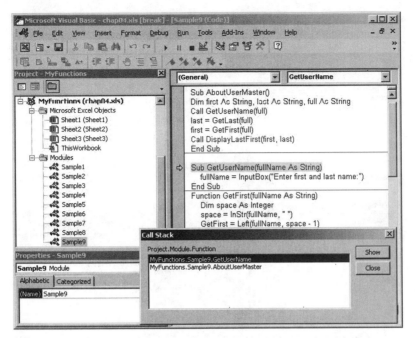

Figure 13-13: The Call Stack dialog box displays a list of the procedures that are started but not completed.

The Call Stack dialog box is especially helpful for tracing nested procedures. Recall that a nested procedure is a procedure that is being called from within another procedure. If a procedure calls another, the name of the called procedure is automatically added to the Calls list in the Call Stack dialog box. When Visual Basic has finished executing the statements of the called procedure, the procedure name is automatically removed from the Call Stack dialog box. You can use the Show button in the Call Stack dialog box to display the statement that calls the next procedure listed in the Call Stack dialog box.

Stepping through VBA Procedures

Stepping through the code means running one statement at a time. This allows you to check every line in every procedure that is encountered. To start stepping through the procedure from the beginning, place the insertion point anywhere inside the code of your procedure and choose Debug | Step Into, or press F8. The Debug menu contains several options that allow you to execute a procedure in the step mode (see Figure 13-14).

When you run a procedure one statement at a time, Visual Basic executes each statement until it encounters the End Sub keywords. If you don't want Visual Basic to step through every statement, you can press F5 at any time to run the rest of the procedure without stepping through it.

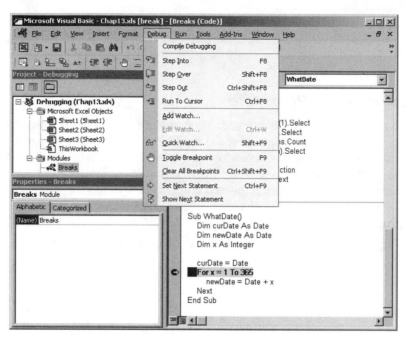

Figure 13-14: The Debug menu offers many commands for stepping through VBA procedures.

Stepping through a Procedure

1. Place the insertion point anywhere inside the code of the procedure whose execution you wish to trace.

2. Press **F8** or choose **Debug | Step Into.** Visual Basic executes the current statement and automatically advances to the next statement and suspends execution. While in break mode, you can activate the Immediate window, Watches window, or Locals window to see the effect of a particular statement on the values of variables and expressions. And, if the procedure you are stepping through calls other procedures, you can activate the Call Stack window to see which procedures are currently active.

3. Press **F8** again to execute the selected statement. After executing this statement, Visual Basic will select the next statement, and the procedure execution will be halted again.

4. Continue stepping the procedure by pressing **F8**, or press **F5** to continue the code execution without stopping. You can also choose **Run | Reset** to stop the procedure at the current statement without executing the remaining statements.

When you step over procedures (Shift+F8), Visual Basic executes each procedure as if it were a single statement. This option is particularly useful if a procedure contains calls to other procedures and you don't want to step into these procedures because they have already been tested and debugged or you want to concentrate only on the new code that has not yet been debugged.

Stepping Over a Procedure

Suppose the current statement in MyProcedure calls the SpecialMsg procedure. If you choose Debug | Step Over (Shift+F8) instead of Debug | Step Into (F8), Visual Basic will quickly execute all the statements inside the SpecialMsg procedure and select the next statement in the calling procedure MyProcedure. During the execution of the SpecialMsg procedure, Visual Basic continues to display the Code window with the current procedure.

1. Enter the following procedure in the current module:

```
Sub MyProcedure()
Dim myName As String
    Workbooks.Add
    myName = ActiveWorkbook.Name
    ' choose Step Over to avoid stepping through the
    ' lines of code in the called procedure - SpecialMsg
    SpecialMsg myName
    Workbooks(myName).Close
End Sub

Sub SpecialMsg(n As String)
    If n = "Book2" Then
        MsgBox "You must change the name."
    End If
End Sub
```

2. Add a breakpoint at the following statement:

```
SpecialMsg myName
```

3. Place the insertion point anywhere within the code of MyProcedure, and press **F5** to run it. Visual Basic halts execution when it reaches the breakpoint.

4. Press **Shift+F8**, or choose **Debug | Step Over**. Visual Basic quickly runs the SpecialMsg procedure and execution and then advances to the statement immediately after the call to the SpecialMsg procedure.

5. Press **F5** to finish running the procedure without stepping through its code.

Stepping over a procedure is particularly useful when you don't want to analyze individual statements inside the called procedure (SpecialMsg).

Another command on the Debug menu, Step Out (Ctrl+Shift+F8), is used when you step into a procedure and then decide that you don't want to step all the way through it. When you choose this option, Visual Basic will execute the remaining statements in this procedure in one step and proceed to activate the next statement in the calling procedure.

In the process of stepping through a procedure, you can switch between Step Into, Step Over, and Step Out options. The option you select depends on which code fragment you wish to analyze at a given moment.

The Debug menu Run to Cursor (Ctrl+F8) command lets you run your procedure until the line you have selected is encountered. This command is really useful if you want to stop the execution before a large loop or you intend to step over a called procedure.

Suppose you want to execute the MyProcedure procedure to the line that calls the SpecialMsg procedure.

1. Click inside the statement **SpecialMsg myName**.

2. Choose **Debug | Run to Cursor**. Visual Basic will stop the procedure when it reaches the specified line.

3. Press **Shift+F8** to step over the SpecialMsg procedure.

4. Press **F5** to execute the rest of the procedure without single stepping.

Setting the Next Statement

At times, you may want to rerun previous lines of code in the procedure or skip over a section of code that is causing trouble. In each of these situations, you can use the Set the Next Statement option on the Debug menu. When you halt execution of a procedure, you can resume the procedure from any statement you want. Visual Basic will skip execution of the statements between the selected statement and the statement where execution was suspended. Suppose that in MyProcedure (see the code of this procedure in the preceding section) you have set a breakpoint on the statement calling the SpecialMsg procedure. To skip the execution of the SpecialMsg procedure, you can place the insertion point inside the statement Workbooks(myName).Close and press Ctrl+F9 (or choose Debug | Set Next Statement). You can't use the Set Next Statement option unless you have suspended the execution of the procedure.

Tip 13-4: Skipping Lines of Code

Although skipping lines of code can be very useful in the process of debugging your VBA procedures, it should be done with care. When you use the Next Statement option, you tell Visual Basic that this is the line you want to execute next. All lines in between are ignored. This means that certain things that you may have expected to occur don't happen, which can lead to unexpected errors.

Showing the Next Statement

If you are not sure from which statement the execution of the procedure will resume, you can choose Debug | Show Next Statement, and Visual Basic will place the cursor on the line that will run next. This is particularly useful when you have been looking at other procedures and are not sure where execution will resume. The Show Next Statement option is available only in break mode.

Stopping and Resetting VBA Procedures

At any time, while stepping through the code of a procedure in the Code window, you can:

- Press F5 to execute the remaining instructions without stepping through
- Choose Run | Reset to finish the procedure without executing the remaining statements

When you reset your procedure, all the variables lose their current values. Numeric variables assume the initial value of zero, variable-length strings are initialized to a zero-length string (" "), and fixed-length strings are filled with the character represented by the ASCII character code 0 or Chr(0). Variant variables are initialized to Empty, and the value of the object variables is set to Nothing.

Understanding and Using Conditional Compilation

When you run a procedure for the first time, Visual Basic converts the VBA statements you used into the machine code understood by the computer. This process is called *compiling*. You can also perform the compilation of your entire VBA project before you run the procedure by choosing Debug | Compile (name of the current VBA project).

You can tell Visual Basic to include or ignore certain blocks of code when compiling and running by using conditional compilation. Your procedure may behave differently, depending on the condition you set. For example, conditional compilation is used to compile an application that will be run on different platforms (Windows or Macintosh, Win16 or Win32 bit). Conditional compilation is also useful in localizing an application for different languages. The program code excluded during the conditional compilation is omitted from the final file; thus, it has no effect on the size or performance of the program.

To enable conditional compilation, you should use special expressions called *directives*. First you need to declare a Boolean (True or False) constant by using the #Const directive. Next, you check this constant inside the #If...Then... #Else directive. The portion of code that you want to compile conditionally must be surrounded by these directives. Notice that the If and Else keywords are preceded by a number sign (#).

If a portion of code is to be run, the value of the conditional constant has to be set to True (–1). Otherwise, the value of this constant should be set to False (0).

Declare the conditional constant in the declaration section of the module. For example:

```
#Const User = True
```

This declares the conditional constant named User.

In the procedure that follows, data is displayed in the Polish language when the conditional constant named verPolish is True. The WhatDay procedure calls the DayOfWeek function, which returns the name of the week based on the supplied date. To compile the program in the English language, all you have to do is change the conditional constant to False and Visual Basic will jump to the block of instructions located after the #Else directive.

1. Insert a new module into the current VBA project, and rename it **Conditional.**

2. Enter the following procedure and functions:

```
' declare a conditional compiler constant
#Const verPolish = True

Sub WhatDay()
Dim dayNr As Integer
#If verPolish = True Then
    dayNr = WeekDay(InputBox("Wpisz date, np. 01/01/2000"))
    MsgBox "To bedzie " & DayOfWeek(dayNr) & "."
#Else
    WeekdayName
#End If
End Sub

Function DayOfWeek(dayNr As Integer) As String
    DayOfWeek = Choose(dayNr, "niedziela", "poniedzialek", "wtorek", _
    "sroda", "czwartek", "piatek", "sobota")
End Function

Function WeekdayName() As String
    Select Case WeekDay(InputBox("Enter date, e.g. 01/01/2000"))
        Case 1
            WeekdayName = "Sunday"
        Case 2
            WeekdayName = "Monday"
        Case 3
            WeekdayName = "Tuesday"
        Case 4
            WeekdayName = "Wednesday"
        Case 5
```

```
                WeekdayName = "Thursday"
            Case 6
                WeekdayName = "Friday"
            Case 7
                WeekdayName = "Saturday"
        End Select
        MsgBox "It will be " & WeekdayName & "."
    End Function
```

3. Run the WhatDay procedure. Because the conditional compilation constant (verPolish) is set to True at the top of the module, Visual Basic runs the Polish version of the WhatDay procedure. It asks for the user's input in Polish and displays the result in Polish. To run the English version of the code, set the verPolish constant to False, and rerun the procedure.

   Instead of declaring the conditional compiler constants at the top of a module, you can choose Tools | (Debugging) Properties (Figure 13-15). When you use the Properties window, use the following syntax in the Conditional Compilation Arguments text box to enable the English version of the WhatDay procedure:

```
verPolish = 0
```

   If there are more conditional compilation constants, each of the constants must be separated by a colon.

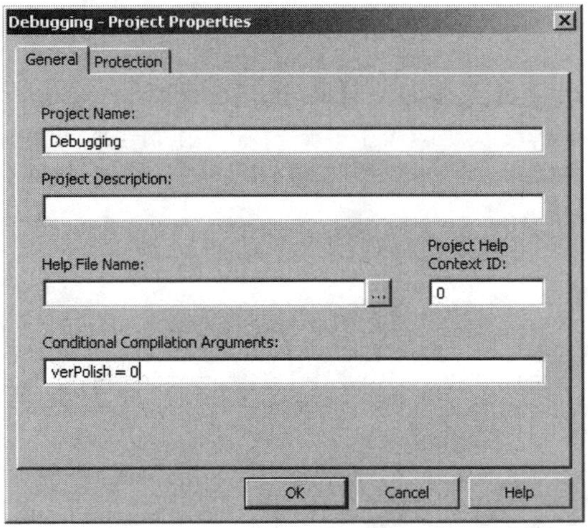

Figure 13-15:
The conditional compilation constant can be declared either at the top of the module or in the Properties window but never in both places.

4. Comment out the **#Const verPolish** directive at the top of the module and enter the conditional compilation constant in the Properties dialog box, as shown in Figure 13-15. Then run the WhatDay procedure to see how the Else branch of your program is now executed for English-speaking users.

Navigating with Bookmarks

In the process of analyzing or reviewing your VBA procedures, you will often find yourself jumping to certain code areas. Using the built-in bookmark feature, you can easily mark the spots that you want to navigate between.

To set up a bookmark:

1. Click anywhere in the statement that you want to define as a bookmark.

2. Choose **Edit | Bookmarks | Toggle Bookmark** (or click the **Toggle Bookmark** button on the Edit toolbar—see Figure 13-16). Visual Basic will place a blue, rounded rectangle in the left margin beside the statement.

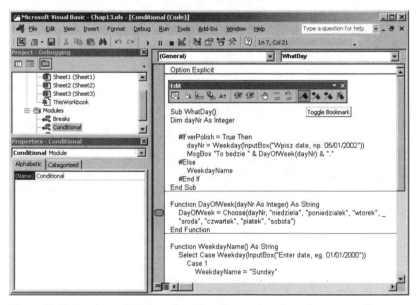

Figure 13-16: You can quickly jump between often-used sections of your procedures using bookmarks.

Once you've set up two or more bookmarks, you can jump between the marked locations of your code by choosing Edit | Bookmarks | Next Bookmark, or simply click the Next Bookmark button on the Edit toolbar. You may also right-click anywhere in the code window and select Next Bookmark from the shortcut menu. To go to the previous bookmark, select Previous Bookmark instead.

You can remove bookmarks at any time by choosing Edit | Bookmarks | Clear All, or click the Clear All Bookmarks button on the Edit toolbar. To remove a single bookmark, click anywhere in the bookmarked statement and choose Edit | Bookmarks | Toggle Bookmark, or click the Toggle Bookmark button on the Edit toolbar.

Trapping Errors

No one writes bug-free programs the first time. When you create VBA procedures, you have to determine how your program will respond to errors. Many unexpected errors happen during run time. For example, your procedure may try to give a workbook the same name as an open workbook. Run-time errors are often discovered not by a programmer but by the user who attempts to do something that the programmer has not anticipated. If an error occurs when the procedure is running, Visual Basic displays an error message and the procedure is stopped. Most often, the error message that VBA displays is quite cryptic to the user. You can prevent users from seeing many run-time errors by including error-handling code in your VBA procedures. This way, when Visual Basic encounters an error, instead of displaying a default error message, it will show a much friendlier and more comprehensive error message, perhaps advising the user how to correct the error.

How do we implement error handling in your VBA procedure? The first step is to place the On Error statement in your procedure. This statement tells VBA what to do if an error happens while your program is running. In other words, VBA uses the On Error statement to activate an error-handling procedure that will trap run-time errors. Depending on the type of procedure, you can exit the error trap by using one of the following statements: Exit Sub, Exit Function, Exit Property, End Sub, End Function, or End Property. You should write an error-handling routine for each procedure.

The On Error statement can be used in one of the following ways:

On Error GoTo *Label*	Specifies a label to jump to when an error occurs. This label marks the beginning of the error-handling routine. An error handler is a routine for trapping and responding to errors in your application. The label must appear in the same procedure as the On Error statement.
On Error Resume Next	When a run-time error occurs, Visual Basic ignores the line that caused the error and does not display an error message but continues the procedure with the next line.
On Error GoTo 0	Turns off error trapping in a procedure. When VBA runs this statement, errors are detected but not trapped within the procedure.

Tip 13-5: An Error or a Mistake?

In programming, mistakes and errors are not the same thing. A mistake, such as a misspelled or missing statement, a misplaced quote or comma, or assigning a value of one type to a variable of a different (and incompatible) type, can be removed from your program through proper testing and debugging. But even though your code may be free of mistakes, that does not mean that errors will not occur. An error is a result of an event or an operation that doesn't work as expected. For example, if your VBA procedure accesses a particular file on disk and someone deleted this file or moved it to another location, you'll get an error no matter what. An error prevents the procedure from carrying out a specific task.

The Archive procedure shown below uses the error-handling routine (see the bottom of the procedure). The procedure uses the built-in SaveCopyAs method to save the copy of the current workbook to a file without modifying the open workbook in memory.

1. Insert a new module into the current project and rename it **Traps**.

2. Enter the Archive procedure, as shown below:

```
Sub Archive()
Dim folderName As String
Dim DriveA As String
Dim BackupName As String
Dim Response As Integer

Application.DisplayAlerts = False
On Error GoTo DiskProblem
folderName = ActiveWorkbook.Path

    If folderName = "" Then
        MsgBox "You can't copy this file. " & Chr(13) _
        & "This file has not been saved.", _
        vbInformation, "File Archive"
    Else
        With ActiveWorkbook
           If Not .Saved Then .Save
             DriveA = "A:"

             MsgBox "Place a diskette in drive " & DriveA & _
             " and click OK.", , "Copying to " & DriveA
             BackupName = DriveA & .Name
             .SaveCopyAs Filename:=BackupName
             MsgBox .Name & " was copied to a disk in drive " & _
                 DriveA, , "End of Archiving"
        End With
    End If
    GoTo ProcEnd
DiskProblem:
```

```
        Response = MsgBox("There is no disk in drive A " & Chr(13) _
        & "or disk in drive " & DriveA & " is not formatted ", _
            vbRetryCancel, "Check Disk Drive")

        If Response = 4 Then
            Resume 0
        Else
            Exit Sub
        End If
ProcEnd:
        Application.DisplayAlerts = True
    End Sub
```

After the declaration of variables, the Archive procedure's `Applica-tion.DisplayAlerts = False` statement ensures that Visual Basic won't display its own alerts and messages while the procedure is running. The next statement, `On Error GoTo DiskProblem`, specifies a label to jump to when an error occurs. The path name where the active workbook was saved is stored in the variable `folderName`.

If Visual Basic can't find the workbook's path, it assumes the file was not saved and displays an appropriate message. Next, Visual Basic jumps to the statement following the End If and executes the instruction GoTo ProcEnd, which directs it to the ProcEnd label located just before the End Sub keywords. Notice that the label is followed by a colon. Visual Basic executes the statement `Application.DisplayAlerts = True`, which restores the system's built-in alerts and messages. Because there are no more statements to execute, the procedure ends.

If the active workbook's path is not an empty string, Visual Basic checks whether the recent changes in the workbook have already been saved. If they weren't, VBA uses the `If Not .Saved Then .Save` statement to save the active workbook. Saved is the VBA property of the Workbook object. Next, Visual Basic stores the name of the diskette drive "A:" in the variable `DriveA` and displays a message that prompts the user to insert a diskette into the specified drive. The name of the disk drive is then combined with the name of the active workbook and stored in the variable named BackupName.

As you know, while copying files to a diskette, all kinds of things can go wrong. For example, a diskette drive may be empty, or a diskette may be unformatted or full. When Visual Basic detects an error, it will jump to the line of code beginning with the label DiskProblem and an appropriate message will be displayed. If the user clicks the Retry button (4) in the message box, Visual Basic will execute the statement Resume 0. This statement will send Visual Basic to the statement that caused the error (`.SaveCopyAs File-Name:=BackupName`), and Visual Basic will execute it again. If the user clicks the Cancel button in the message box, VBA will execute the statement Exit Sub and the procedure will end.

If there's no problem with the diskette in drive "A:", VBA will copy the active workbook to the diskette and the message will notify the user that the copy operation was successful.

3. Run the Archive procedure several times, each time responding differently to the presented options. Make sure to test as many possibilities as you can identify. Use various debugging techniques that you have learned in this chapter.

Tip 13-6: Procedure Testing

You are responsible for the code that you produce. This means that before you give your procedure to others to test, test it yourself. After all, you will understand how it is supposed to work. Some programmers think that testing their own code is some sort of demeaning activity, especially when they work in an organization that has a team devoted to testing. Don't make this mistake. The testing process at the programmer level is as important as the code development itself. After you've tested the procedure yourself, you should give it to users to test. Users will provide you with answers to questions such as: Does the procedure produce the expected results? Is it easy and fun to use? Does it follow the standard conventions? Also, it is a good idea to give the entire application to someone who knows little about using this particular application, and ask them to play around with it and try to break it.

Let's look at another example procedure. The OpenToRead procedure shown below demonstrates the use of the Resume Next and Error statements, as well as the Err object.

```
Sub OpenToRead()
Dim myFile As String
Dim myChar As String
Dim myText As String
Dim FileExists As Boolean

FileExists = True

On Error GoTo ErrorHandler
myFile = InputBox("Enter the name of file you want to open:")
Open myFile For Input As #1
    If FileExists Then
        Do While Not EOF(1)            ' loop until the end of file
            myChar = Input(1, #1)      ' get one character
            myText = myText + myChar   ' store in the variable myText
        Loop
        Debug.Print myText       ' print to the Immediate window
        ' Close the file -commenting out this instruction will cause
        ' error 52.
        Close #1
    End If
```

```
Exit Sub
ErrorHandler:
FileExists = False
    Select Case Err.Number
        Case 71
            MsgBox "The diskette drive is empty."
        Case 53
            MsgBox "This file can't be found on the specified drive."
        Case 75
            Exit Sub
        Case Else
            MsgBox "Error " & Err.Number & " :" & Error(Err.Number)
            Exit Sub
        End Select
    Resume Next
End Sub
```

The purpose of the OpenToRead procedure is to read the contents of the user-supplied text file character by character (working with files is covered in Chapter 8). When the user enters a filename, various errors can occur. For example, the filename may be wrong, or the user may attempt to open a file from a diskette when there is no disk in the diskette drive or open a file that is already open.

To trap these errors, the error-handling routine at the end of the OpenToRead procedure uses the Name property of the Err object. The Err object contains information about run-time errors. If an error occurs while the procedure is running, the statement Err.Number will return the error number.

If errors 71, 53, or 75 occur, Visual Basic will display user-friendly messages stated inside the Select...Case block and then proceed to the Resume Next statement, which will send it to the line of code following the one that caused the error. If another (unexpected) error occurs, Visual Basic will return its error code (Err.Number) and error description (Error-(Err.Number)).

At the beginning of the procedure, the variable FileExists is set to True. This way, if the program doesn't encounter an error, all the instructions inside the If FileExists Then block will be executed. However, if VBA encounters an error, the value of the FileExists variable will be set to False (see the first statement in the error-handling routine just below the ErrorHandler label). This way, Visual Basic will not cause another error while trying to read a file that caused the error on opening. If you comment the statement Close #1, Visual Basic will encounter the error on the next attempt to open the same file.

Notice the Exit Sub statement before the ErrorHandler. Put the Exit Sub statement just above the error-handling routine. You don't want Visual Basic to carry out the error handling if there are no errors.

To test the OpenToRead procedure and better understand error trapping, let's perform the following exercise:

1. Prepare a text file named **C:\Vacation.txt** using Windows Notepad. Enter any text you want in this file.

2. Run the OpenToRead procedure four times in the step mode, each time supplying one of the following:

   - Name of the **C:\Vacation.txt** file
   - Filename that does not exist on drive C
   - Name of any file in Drive A (when the diskette slot is empty)
   - Comment the Close #1 statement and enter **C:\Vacation.txt** as the filename

---

Tip 13-7: Errors: Generating Them to Test Error Handling

You can test the ways that your program responds to run-time errors by causing them on purpose:

- Generate any built-in error by using the following syntax: Error error_number. For example, to display the error that occurs on the attempt to divide by zero, type the following in the Immediate window:

  ```
  Error 11
  ```

When you press Enter, Visual Basic will display the error message saying: _Run-time error 11. Division by zero._

- To check the meaning of the generated error, use the following syntax: Error(error_number). For example, to find out what error number 7 means, type the following in the Immediate window:

  ```
  ?Error(7)
  ```

When you press Enter, Visual Basic returns the error description: _Out of memory._

What's Next...

In this chapter you learned how to test your VBA procedures to make sure they perform as planned. You debugged your code by stepping through it using breakpoints and watches. You learned how to work with the Immediate window in break mode. You found out how the Locals window can help you monitor the values of variables and how the Call Stack dialog box can be helpful in keeping track of where you are in a complex program. You've learned to specify parts of your procedure that you want to include or exclude upon compilation. Finally, you learned how to trap errors with error-handling routines. By using the built-in debugging tools, you can quickly pinpoint the problem spots in your procedures. Try to spend more time getting acquainted with these tools. Mastering the art of debugging can save you hours of trial and error.

By completing Chapters 1 through 13, you have gained a solid, working knowledge of the Visual Basic for Applications language that you're most likely to need to get started in your own Excel spreadsheet automating projects. This chapter ends the intermediate level of your encounters with VBA in Excel 2002. VBA offers many more advanced features, which we will explore in the remaining chapters of this book.

Chapter 14

Event Programming in Microsoft Excel 2002

Introduction to Event Procedures ■ Enabling and Disabling Events ■ Event Sequences ■ Worksheet Events ■ Workbook Events ■ Chart Events ■ Embedded Chart Events ■ Events Recognized by the Application Object ■ Query Table Events ■ What's Next...

How do you disable a built-in shortcut menu when a user clicks on a worksheet cell? How do you display a custom message before a workbook is opened or closed? How can you validate data entered in a cell or range of cells? To get complete control over Microsoft Excel, you must learn how to respond to events. Learning how to program events will allow you to implement your own functionality in an Excel application. The first thing you need to learn about this subject matter is what an event is. Here's a simple definition:

    An event is something that happens.

Needless to say, events happen to objects that are part of Microsoft Excel. However, once you learn about events in Excel, you will find it easier to understand events that occur to objects in Word or any other Microsoft Office application. Events are actions recognized by an object.

Now that you know what events are, you need to know that events can be triggered by an application user (such as yourself), another program, or the system itself. So, how can you trigger an event? Suppose you right-click a worksheet cell. This particular action would display a built-in shortcut menu for a worksheet cell, allowing you to quickly access the most frequently used commands related to worksheet cells. But what if this particular built-in response isn't appropriate under certain conditions? You may want to entirely disallow right-clicking in a worksheet or perhaps ensure that a custom menu appears on a cell shortcut menu when the user right-clicks any cell. The good news is you can use VBA to write code that can react to events as they occur.

Microsoft Excel provides many events to which you can respond. The following objects can respond to events:

- Worksheet
- Chart Sheet
- Query Table
- Workbook
- Application

You can decide what should happen when a particular event occurs by writing an event procedure.

Introduction to Event Procedures

A special type of VBA procedure, an *event procedure*, is used to react to specific events. This procedure contains VBA code that handles a particular event. Some events may require a single line of code, while others can be more complex. Event procedures have names, which are created in the following way:

```
ObjectName_EventName()
```

In the parentheses after the name of the event, you can place parameters that need to be sent to the procedure. The programmer cannot change the name of the event procedure.

Before you can write an event procedure to react to an Excel event, you need to know:

■ The name of the particular object and event that you want to respond to

Objects that can respond to events display a list of events in the Procedure drop-down list in the Code window (Figure 14-1). Also, you can use the Object Browser to find out the names of the events (Figure 14-2).

■ The place where you should put the code

Some events are coded in a standard module; others are stored in a class module. While workbook, chart sheet, and worksheet events are available for any open sheet or workbook, to create event procedures for an embedded chart, query table, or Application object, you must first create a new object using the With Events keyword in the class module.

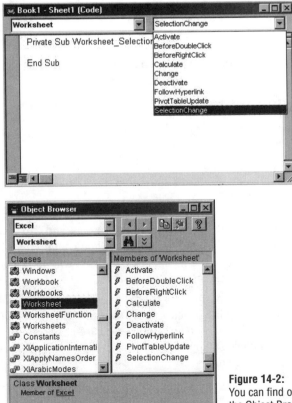

Figure 14-1:
You can find out the event names in the Code window.

Figure 14-2:
You can find out the event names in the Object Browser.

Enabling and Disabling Events

You can use the Application object's EnableEvents property to enable or disable events. If you are writing a VBA procedure and don't want a particular event to occur, set the EnableEvents property to False. For example, to avoid triggering the Workbook_BeforeClose event while running the EnterData procedure (see below), set the EnableEvents property to False before calling the Workbook object's Close method. Set EnableEvents back to True before your procedure finishes running to ensure that events are enabled.

1. Open a new workbook and save it as **DisableEvents.xls.**

2. Switch to the Visual Basic Editor screen. Double-click **ThisWorkbook** in the Project Explorer window, and enter the Workbook_BeforeSave event procedure in the Code window that appears.

```
Private Sub Workbook_BeforeSave(ByVal SaveAsUI As Boolean, _
              Cancel As Boolean)
    If MsgBox("Would you like to copy " & vbCrLf _
        & "this worksheet to " & vbCrLf _
        & "a new workbook?", vbYesNo) = vbYes Then
        Sheets(ActiveSheet.Name).Copy
    End If
End Sub
```

3. Choose **Insert | Module** to add a standard module to the active VBA project, and enter the procedure shown below:

```
Sub EnterData()
    With ActiveSheet.Range("A1:B1")
        .Font.Color = vbRed
        .Value = 15
    End With
    Application.EnableEvents = False
    ActiveWorkbook.Save
    Application.EnableEvents = True
End Sub
```

4. Switch to the Microsoft Excel application window, and choose **File | Save.** The Workbook_BeforeSave event will be triggered at this time. Click **Yes** in response to the message box. Excel will open a new workbook with the copy of the current worksheet.

5. Activate the **DisableEvents** workbook, and choose **Tools | Macro | Macros.** In the dialog box, click **EnterData** and then **Run.** Notice that when you run the EnterData procedure, you are not prompted to copy the worksheet before saving. This indicates that the Workbook_Before-Save event is not running.

Event Sequences

Events occur in response to specific actions and occur in a predefined sequence. The table below demonstrates the sequence of events while opening a new workbook, adding a new worksheet to a workbook, and closing the workbook.

Action	Object	Event Sequence
Opening a new workbook	Workbook	NewWorkbook, WindowDeactivate, WorkbookDeactivate, WorkbookActivate, WindowActivate
Inserting a new sheet into a workbook	Workbook	WorkbookNewSheet, SheetDeactivate, SheetActivate
Closing a workbook	Workbook	WorkbookBeforeClose, WindowDeactivate, WorkbookDeactivate, WorkbookActivate, WindowActivate

Worksheet Events

A Worksheet object responds to such events as activating and deactivating the worksheet, calculating a worksheet, making a change to a worksheet, and double-clicking or right-clicking a worksheet. This section discusses some of the events to which the Worksheet object can respond.

Event Name	Activate
Event Description	**Example 1**

This event occurs when the user activates a sheet.	`Dim shtName As String    'declared at the top`
	`                          ' of the module`
	
	`Private Sub Worksheet_Activate()`
	`    shtName = ActiveSheet.Name`
	`    Range("B2").Select`
	`End Sub`

The example procedure selects cell B2 each time the sheet is activated.	

- **Example 1 – Try It Out:** In the Visual Basic Editor window, activate the Project Explorer window and open the Microsoft Excel Objects folder. Double-click Sheet2 (Sheet2), and type the example procedure in the Sheet2 (Code) window. Next, switch to the Microsoft Excel application window and activate Sheet2. Notice that when Sheet2 is activated, the selection is moved to cell B2.

Event Name	Deactivate
Event Description	**Example 2**
| This event occurs when the user activates a different sheet. | ```
Private Sub Worksheet_Deactivate()
    MsgBox "You deactivated " & _
        shtName & "." & vbCrLf & _
        "You switched to " & _
        ActiveSheet.Name & "."
End Sub
``` |
| The example procedure displays a message when Sheet2 is deactivated. ||

- **Example 2 – Try It Out:** In the Visual Basic Editor window, activate the Project Explorer window and open the Microsoft Excel Objects folder. Double-click Sheet2 (Sheet2), and type the example procedure in the Sheet2 (Code) window. Next, switch to the Microsoft Excel application window and activate Sheet2. The Worksheet_Activate procedure that you created in Example 1 will run. Excel will select cell B2 and store the name of the worksheet in the shtName global variable declared at the top of the Sheet2 code module. Now click any other sheet in the active workbook and notice that Excel displays the name of the worksheet that you deactivated and the name of the worksheet to which you have switched.

Event Name	SelectionChange
Event Description	**Example 3**
| This event occurs when the user selects a worksheet cell. | ```
Private Sub Worksheet_SelectionChange(ByVal
                    Target As Excel.Range)
On Error Resume Next
Set myRange = Intersect(Range("A1:A10"), Target)
    If Not myRange Is Nothing Then
        MsgBox "Data entry or edits are not permitted."
    End If
End Sub
``` |
| The example procedure displays a message if the user selects any cell in myRange. ||

- **Example 3 – Try It Out:** In the Visual Basic Editor window, activate the Project Explorer window and open the Microsoft Excel Objects folder. Double-click Sheet3 (Sheet3), and type the example procedure in the Sheet3 (Code) window. Next, switch to the Microsoft Excel application window and activate Sheet3. Click on any cell within the specified range A1:A10. Notice that Excel displays a message whenever you click the cell in the restricted area.

Event Name	Change
Event Description	Example 4
This event occurs when the user changes a cell formula.	```Private Sub Worksheet_Change(ByVal Target _ As Excel.Range) Application.EnableEvents = False Target = UCase(Target) Columns(Target.Column).AutoFit Application.EnableEvents = True End Sub```
The example procedure changes what you type in a cell to uppercase. The column where the target cell is located is then auto-sized.	

- **Example 4 – Try It Out:** In the Visual Basic Editor window, activate the Project Explorer window and open the Microsoft Excel Objects folder. Double-click Sheet1 (Sheet1), and type the example procedure in the Sheet1 (Code) window. Next, switch to the Microsoft Excel application window and activate Sheet1. Enter any text in any cell. Notice that as soon as you press the Enter key, Excel changes the text you typed to uppercase, and the column is auto-sized.

Event Name	Calculate
Event Description	Example 5
This event occurs when the user recalculates the worksheet.	```Private Sub Worksheet_Calculate() MsgBox "The worksheet was recalculated." End Sub```
The example procedure displays a message upon recalculation of the worksheet.	

- **Example 5 – Try It Out:** Add a new sheet to the active workbook. This exercise assumes that Excel will place Sheet4 in your workbook. In cell A2 of Sheet4 enter 1, and in cell B2, enter 2. Enter the following formula in cell C2: = A2+B2. In the Visual Basic Editor window, activate the Project Explorer window and open the Microsoft Excel Objects folder. Double-click Sheet4 (Sheet4) and enter the code of the Worksheet_Calculate event procedure, as shown above. Switch to the Microsoft Excel window and activate Sheet4. Modify the entry in cell B2 by typing any number. Notice that after leaving edit mode, the Worksheet_Calculate event procedure is triggered, and you are presented with a custom message.

Event Name	BeforeDoubleClick
Event Description	Example 6
This event occurs when the user double-clicks a worksheet cell.	```Private Sub Worksheet_BeforeDoubleClick(ByVal _ Target As Range, Cancel As Boolean) If Target.Address = Range("$C$9") Then MsgBox "No double-clicking, please." Cancel = True```

Event Name	BeforeDoubleClick
| | ```
Else
    MsgBox "You may edit this cell."
End If
End Sub
``` |

The example procedure disallows in-cell editing when the user double-clicks cell C9.

- **Example 6 – Try It Out:** In the Visual Basic Editor window, activate the Project Explorer window and open the Microsoft Excel Objects folder. Double-click Sheet2 (Sheet2), and type the example procedure in the Sheet2 (Code) window. Next, switch to the Microsoft Excel application window and activate Sheet2. When you double-click cell C9, the Event procedure cancels the built-in Excel behavior, and the user is not allowed to edit the data inside the cell. However, the user can get around this restriction by clicking on the formula bar or pressing F2. When writing event procedures that restrict access to certain program features, write additional code that disallows any workaround.

Event Name	BeforeRightClick
Event Description	**Example 7**
| This event occurs when the user right-clicks a worksheet cell. | ```
Private Sub Worksheet_BeforeRightClick(ByVal _
    Target As Range, Cancel As Boolean)

    With Application.CommandBars("Cell")
        .Reset
        If Target.Rows.Count > 1 Or _
            Target.Columns.Count > 1 Then
            With .Controls.Add(Type:=msoControlButton, _
                    before:=1, temporary:=True)
                .Caption = "Print..."
                .OnAction = "PrintMe"
            End With
        End If
    End With
End Sub

Sub PrintMe()
    Application.Dialogs(xlDialogPrint).Show arg12:=1
End Sub
``` |

The example procedure adds a Print option to the cell shortcut menu when the user selects more than one cell on the worksheet.

- **Example 7 – Try It Out:** In the Visual Basic Editor window, activate the Project Explorer window and open the Microsoft Excel Objects folder. Double-click Sheet2 (Sheet2), and type the example procedure in the Sheet2 (Code) window. Insert a new module into the current project and enter the PrintMe procedure, as shown above. This procedure is called by the Worksheet_BeforeRightClick event when the user selects the Print option from the shortcut menu. Notice that the Show method of the dialog box is followed by a named argument: `arg12:=1`. This argument will display the Print dialog box with the preselected option button Selection in the Print area of the dialog box. After entering both procedures in appropriate modules, switch to the Microsoft Excel application window and activate Sheet2. Right-click on any single cell. Notice that the shortcut menu appears with the default options. Now make another selection, this time including more than one cell and right-click the selected area. You should see the Print... option as the first menu entry. Click the Print option and notice that instead of the default "Print active sheet," the Print dialog displays Print Selection.

Note: Refer to Chapter 10 for more information on working with shortcut menus programmatically. Also, see Figure 10-3 for information on how to locate Excel's built-in argument lists.

Event Name	FollowHyperlink
Event Description	Example 8

This event occurs when the user clicks a hyperlink in a Microsoft Excel worksheet.	`Private Sub Worksheet_FollowHyperlink(ByVal _`
	`        Target As Hyperlink)`
	`    Target.AddToFavorites`
	`End Sub`

The example procedure adds the hyperlink that the user clicked to the list of Favorites in Internet Explorer.	

- **Example 8 – Try It Out:** In the Visual Basic Editor window, activate the Project Explorer window and open the Microsoft Excel Objects folder. Double-click Sheet1 (Sheet1), and type the example procedure in the Sheet1 (Code) window. Switch to the Microsoft Excel application window, and enter a web address in any cell. For example, type: www.wordware.com and press Enter. Now, click the hyperlink to activate the web site. When the Internet Explorer window appears, open the Favorites menu and notice the Wordware site address has been added to the menu.

Event Name	PivotTableUpdate
Event Description	Example 9

This event occurs after a PivotTable report is updated on a worksheet.
 	
This is a new event in Excel 2002.
 	
The Target argument specifies the selected PivotTable report.
	`Private Sub pivTbl_PivotTableUpdate( _`
	`            ByVal Target As PivotTable)`
	`    MsgBox Target.Name & _`
	`        " report has been updated." & vbCrLf _`
	`    & "The PivotReport is located in cells " & _`
	`        Target.DataBodyRange.Address`
	`End Sub`

Event Name	PivotTableUpdate
pivTbl is a variable that references an object of type Worksheet declared using the WithEvents keyword in a class module.	
The example procedure displays a message stating the name of the updated PivotTable report and the range address that the report occupies on the worksheet.	

■ **Example 9 – Try It Out:** Open the PivotReport_2.xls file located on the book's companion CD-ROM. Click any cell in the PivotTable area, and click the Refresh button on the PivotTable toolbar. Figures 14-3 and 14-4 illustrate how to set up the event handler for the Pivot-TableUpdate event.

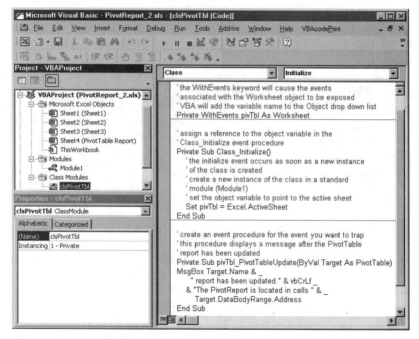

Figure 14-3: You must use a class module to trap the PivotTableUpdate event. The class module can have any valid module name. The object variable name, pivTbl, can be any valid variable name.

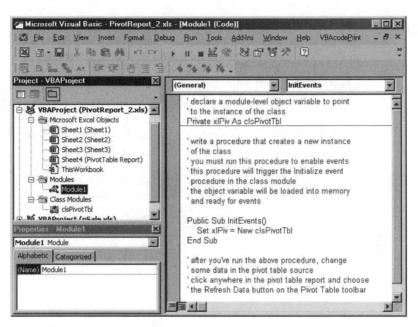

Figure 14-4: Before you can trap the PivotTableUpdate event, you must set up an instance of your class module in a standard module and assign the Worksheet object to the pivTbl property of the new object.

Workbook Events

Workbook object events occur when the user performs such tasks as opening, activating, deactivating, printing, saving, and closing a workbook. Workbook events are not created in a standard VBA module. To write code that reponds to a particular workbook event, double-click ThisWorkbook in Visual Basic Editor's Project Explorer. In the Code window that appears, open the Object drop-down list and select the Workbook object. In the Procedure drop-down list, select the event you want. The selected event procedure stub will appear in the Code window. For example:

```
Private Sub Workbook_Open()
    place your event handling code here
End Sub
```

This section describes some of the events available for Workbook objects.

Event Name	Activate
Event Description	**Example 10**

This event occurs when the user activates the workbook. This event will not occur when the user activates the workbook by switching from another application.	`Private Sub Workbook_Activate()`
	`    MsgBox "This workbook contains " & _`
	`    ThisWorkbook.Sheets.Count & "sheets."`
	`End Sub`

Event Name	Activate
The example procedure displays the total number of worksheets when the user activates the workbook containing the Workbook_Activate event procedure.	

- **Example 10 – Try It Out:** In the Visual Basic Editor window, activate the Project Explorer window and open the Microsoft Excel Objects folder. Double-click ThisWorkbook and type the example procedure in the ThisWorkbook (Code) window. Next, switch to the Microsoft Excel application window and open a new workbook. Switch to the workbook in which you entered the Workbook_Activate procedure. Excel should display the total number of sheets in this workbook.

Event Name	Deactivate
Event Description	**Example 11**
This event occurs when the user activates a different workbook within Excel. This event does not occur when the user switches to a different application.	```Private Sub Workbook_Deactivate() For Each cell In _ ActiveSheet.UsedRange If Not IsEmpty(cell) Then Debug.Print cell.Address & _ ":" & cell.Value End If Next End Sub```
The example procedure will print to the Immediate window the addresses and values of cells containing entries in the current workbook when the user activates a different workbook.	

- **Example 11 – Try It Out:** In the Visual Basic Editor window, activate the Project Explorer window and open the Microsoft Excel Objects folder. Double-click ThisWorkbook, and type the example procedure in the ThisWorkbook (Code) window. Switch to the Microsoft Excel application window and make some entries on the active sheet. Next, activate a different workbook. This action will trigger the Workbook_Deactivate event procedure. Switch to the Visual Basic Editor screen and open the Immediate window to see what cell entries got reported.

Event Name	Open
Event Description	**Example 12**
This event occurs when the user opens a workbook.	```Private Sub Workbook_Open() ActiveSheet.Range("A1").Value = Format _ (Now(), "mm/dd/yyyy") End Sub```
The example procedure places the current date in cell A1 when the workbook is opened.	

- **Example 12 – Try It Out:** Open a new workbook. In the Visual Basic Editor window, activate the Project Explorer window and open the Microsoft Excel Objects folder. Double-click ThisWorkbook, and type the example procedure in the ThisWorkbook (Code) window. Save and close your workbook. When you open the workbook again, the current date will be placed into cell A1 on the active sheet.

Event Name	BeforeSave
Event Description	Example 13

This event occurs before the workbook is saved.
 	
The SaveAsUI argument is read-only and refers to the SaveAs dialog box. If the workbook has not been saved, the value of SaveAsUI is True; otherwise, it is False.
	`Private Sub Workbook_BeforeSave(ByVal _`
	`    SaveAsUI As Boolean, Cancel As Boolean)`
	`  If SaveAsUI = True And _`
	`    ThisWorkbook.Path = vbNullString Then`
	`    MsgBox "This document has not yet " _`
	`      & "been saved." & vbCrLf _`
	`      & "The Save As dialog box will be _`
	`      displayed."`
	`  ElseIf SaveAsUI = True Then`
	`    MsgBox "You are not allowed to use " _`
	`      & "the SaveAs option. "`
	`    Cancel = True`
	`  End If`
	`End Sub`

The example procedure displays the SaveAs dialog box if the workbook hasn't been saved before. The workbook's pathname will be a NULL string (vbNullString) if the file has not been saved before. The procedure will not let the user save the workbook under a different name; the SaveAs operation will be aborted by setting the Cancel argument to True. The user will need to choose the Save option to have the workbook saved.	

- **Example 13 – Try It Out:** Open a new workbook. In the Visual Basic Editor window, activate the Project Explorer window and open the Microsoft Excel Objects folder under the newly added project. Double-click ThisWorkbook and type the example procedure in the ThisWorkbook (Code) window. Click in the Margin area next to "If SaveAsUI..." to place a breakpoint. Switch to the Microsoft Excel application window, and make an entry in any cell. Click the Save button on the toolbar. The Workbook_BeforeSave event procedure will be activated, and the statement after If SaveAsUI will be executed. Enter SaveEvent.xls as the name of your workbook in the SaveAs dialog box. After saving (and assigning a name) to this workbook, make some changes to the workbook and choose File | SaveAs. This time the ElseIf clause gets executed, and you are not allowed to save the workbook by using the SaveAs option.

Event Name	BeforePrint
Event Description	Example 14
| This event occurs before the workbook is printed and before the Print dialog appears. | ```
Private Sub Workbook_BeforePrint(Cancel _
                    As Boolean)
Dim response As Integer
response = MsgBox("Do you want to  " & vbCrLf & _
        "print the workbook's full name in the footer?", _
            vbYesNo)
    If response = vbYes Then
        ActiveSheet.PageSetup.LeftFooter = _
            ThisWorkbook.FullName
    Else
        ActiveSheet.PageSetup.LeftFooter = ""
    End If
End Sub
``` |
| The example procedure places the full workbook's name in the document footer prior to printing if the user clicks Yes in the message box. | |

- **Example 14 – Try It Out:** In the Visual Basic Editor window, activate the Project Explorer window and open the Microsoft Excel Objects folder. Double-click ThisWorkbook, and type the example procedure in the ThisWorkbook (Code) window. Next, switch to the Microsoft Excel application window and activate any sheet. Enter anything you want in any worksheet cell. When you press the Print Preview button on the toolbar, Excel will ask you if you want to place the workbook's name and path in the footer.

Event Name	BeforeClose
Event Description	Example 15
| This event occurs before the workbook is closed and before the user is asked to save changes. | ```
Private Sub Workbook_BeforeClose(Cancel _
                    As Boolean)
    If MsgBox("Do you want to change " & vbCrLf _
        & " workbook properties before closing?", _
            vbYesNo) = vbYes Then
        Application.Dialogs(xlDialogProperties).Show
    End If
End Sub
``` |
| The example procedure displays the Properties dialog box if the user responds Yes to the message box. | |

- **Example 15 – Try It Out:** In the Visual Basic Editor window, activate the Project Explorer window and open the Microsoft Excel Objects folder. Double-click ThisWorkbook and type the example procedure in the ThisWorkbook (Code) window. Next, switch to the Microsoft Excel application window, and close the workbook containing the code of the BeforeClose event procedure. Upon closing, you should see a message box asking you to view the Properties dialog box prior to closing. After viewing or modifying the workbook properties, the procedure closes the workbook. If there are any changes that you have not yet saved, you are given the chance to save the workbook, cancel the changes, or abort the closing operation altogether.

Event Name	AddInInstall
Event Description	**Example 16**

This event occurs when the user installs the workbook as an add-in.	`Private Sub Workbook_AddinInstall()`
	`    MsgBox "To create a calendar, " & vbCrLf _`
	`    & "enter CalendarMaker in the " & vbCrLf _`
	`    & "Macros dialog box."`
	`End Sub`

To trigger the Workbook_AddInInstall event procedure, please see the detailed instructions below.	

■   **Example 16 – Try It Out:**

1. Open a new workbook.

2. Switch to the Visual Basic Editor. Activate the Project Explorer window and open the **Microsoft Excel Objects** folder.

3. Double-click **ThisWorkbook** and type the Example 16 and Example 17 procedures in the ThisWorkbook (Code) window.

4. Insert a new module into the current VBA project and enter the code of the CalendarMaker procedure, shown after Example 17.

5. Switch to the Microsoft Excel application window and choose **File | Properties**. Make the following entries in the Properties dialog box:

    Title: **Calendar Maker**
    Comments: **Create a monthly calendar in an Excel spreadsheet.**

    The above information will appear in the Add-Ins dialog box when you highlight the name of your add-in.

6. Click **OK** to exit the File Properties dialog box.

7. Choose **File | SaveAs** and save the workbook as **Calendar.xls**.

8. Now choose **File | SaveAs** to save the Calendar.xls workbook as an add-in. From the Save As type drop-down list, select **Microsoft Excel Add-in**. Type the new file name (**CalendarMaker.xla**) and click **Save**.

9. Close the Calendar.xls workbook.

10. Open a new workbook.

11. Choose **Tools | AddIns**. Use the **Browse** button to add the Calendar-Maker to the list of add-ins. Select the CalendarMaker add-in in the list box by clicking the box to the left of its name. When you click **OK** in the Add-Ins dialog box, the Workbook_AddInInstall procedure will be triggered. Click **OK** in the message box.

12. To create a calendar, choose **Tools | Macro | Macros**. Type **CalendarMaker** in the Macro name text box, and click **Run**. You will be asked for the month and year. Enter the name of a month and a year (for example, October 2002) and click **OK**. A calendar page, as shown in Figure 14-5, will appear.

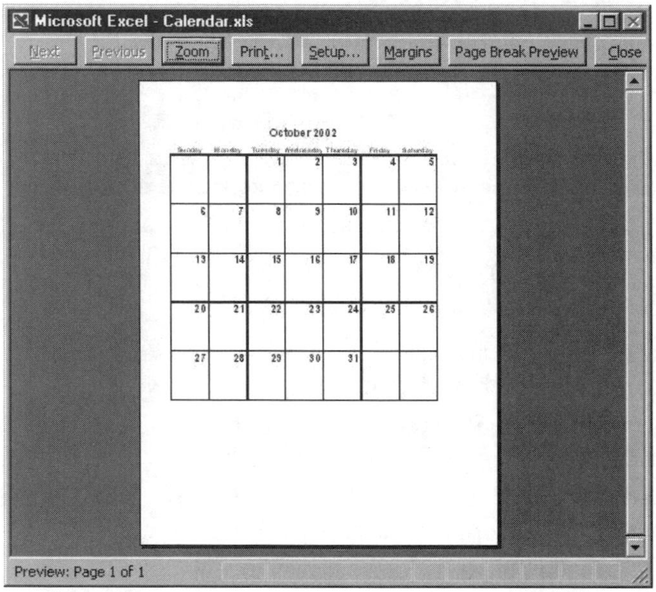

Figure 14-5: A monthly calendar as generated by the Calendar-Maker procedure

13. To trigger the AddInUninstall event procedure illustrated in Example 17, choose **Tools | AddIns** and remove the check mark next to the CalendarMaker add-in.

Event Name	AddInUninstall
Event Description	**Example 17**

This event occurs when the user uninstalls the workbook as an add-in.	`Private Sub Workbook_AddinUninstall()`
	    `MsgBox "The CalendarMaker " & vbCrLf _`
	      `& "add-in was unloaded."`
	`End Sub`

The example procedure displays a message upon uninstalling the workbook as an add-in.	

■ **Example 17 – Try It Out: See Example 16**

The following CalendarMaker procedure is available in the CodeLibrarian Add-In and is used here to demonstrate the usage of the Workbook object's AddInInstall and AddInUninstall events (see Examples 16 and 17).

```
Sub CalendarMaker()

    ' Unprotect sheet if had previous calendar to prevent error.
    ActiveSheet.Protect DrawingObjects:=False, Contents:=False, _
        Scenarios:=False
    ' Prevent screen flashing while drawing calendar.
    Application.ScreenUpdating = False
    ' Set up error trapping.
    On Error GoTo MyErrorTrap
    ' Clear area a1:g14 including any previous calendar.
    Range("a1:g14").Clear
    ' Use InputBox to get desired month and year and set variable
    ' MyInput.
    MyInput = InputBox("Type in Month and year for Calendar ")
    ' Allow user to end macro with Cancel in InputBox.
    If MyInput = "" Then Exit Sub
    ' Get the date value of the beginning of input month.
    StartDay = DateValue(MyInput)
    ' Check if valid date but not the first of the month
    ' -- if so, reset StartDay to first day of month.
    If Day(StartDay) <> 1 Then
        StartDay = DateValue(Month(StartDay) & "/1/" & _
            Year(StartDay))
    End If
    ' Prepare cell for Month and Year as fully spelled out.
    Range("a1").NumberFormat = "mmmm yyyy"
    ' Center the Month and Year label across a1:g1 with appropriate
    ' size, height and bolding.
    With Range("a1:g1")
        .HorizontalAlignment = xlCenterAcrossSelection
        .VerticalAlignment = xlCenter
        .Font.Size = 18
        .Font.Bold = True
        .RowHeight = 35
    End With
    ' Prepare a2:g2 for day of week labels with centering, size,
    ' height and bolding.
    With Range("a2:g2")
        .ColumnWidth = 11
        .VerticalAlignment = xlCenter
        .HorizontalAlignment = xlCenter
        .VerticalAlignment = xlCenter
        .Orientation = xlHorizontal
        .Font.Size = 12
        .Font.Bold = True
        .RowHeight = 20
    End With
    ' Put days of week in a2:g2.
    Range("a2") = "Sunday"
    Range("b2") = "Monday"
    Range("c2") = "Tuesday"
    Range("d2") = "Wednesday"
    Range("e2") = "Thursday"
    Range("f2") = "Friday"
```

```
Range("g2") = "Saturday"
' Prepare a3:g7 for dates with left/top alignment, size, height
' and bolding.
With Range("a3:g8")
    .HorizontalAlignment = xlLeft
    .VerticalAlignment = xlTop
    .Font.Size = 18
    .Font.Bold = True
    .RowHeight = 21
End With
' Put input month and year fully spelling out into "a1".
Range("a1").Value = Application.Text(MyInput, "mmmm yyyy")
' Set variable and get which day of the week the month starts.
DayofWeek = Weekday(StartDay)
' Set variables to identify the year and month as separate
' variables.
CurYear = Year(StartDay)
CurMonth = Month(StartDay)
' Set variable and calculate the first day of the next month.
FinalDay = DateSerial(CurYear, CurMonth + 1, 1)
' Place a "1" in cell position of the first day of the chosen
' month based on DayofWeek.
Select Case DayofWeek
    Case 1
        Range("a3").Value = 1
    Case 2
        Range("b3").Value = 1
    Case 3
        Range("c3").Value = 1
    Case 4
        Range("d3").Value = 1
    Case 5
        Range("e3").Value = 1
    Case 6
        Range("f3").Value = 1
    Case 7
        Range("g3").Value = 1
End Select
' Loop through range a3:g8 incrementing each cell after the "1"
' cell.
For Each cell In Range("a3:g8")
    RowCell = cell.Row
    ColCell = cell.Column
    ' Do if "1" is in first column.
    If cell.Column = 1 And cell.Row = 3 Then
    ' Do if current cell is not in 1st column.
    ElseIf cell.Column <> 1 Then
        If cell.Offset(0, -1).Value >= 1 Then
            cell.Value = cell.Offset(0, -1).Value + 1
            ' Stop when the last day of the month has been
            ' entered.
            If cell.Value > (FinalDay - StartDay) Then
                cell.Value = ""
                ' Exit loop when calendar has correct number of
```

```
                            ' days shown.
                            Exit For
                    End If
                End If
            ' Do only if current cell is not in Row 3 and is in Column 1.
            ElseIf cell.Row > 3 And cell.Column = 1 Then
                cell.Value = cell.Offset(-1, 6).Value + 1
                ' Stop when the last day of the month has been entered.
                If cell.Value > (FinalDay - StartDay) Then
                    cell.Value = ""
                    ' Exit loop when calendar has correct number of days
                    ' shown.
                    Exit For
                End If
            End If
    Next


    ' Create Entry cells, format them centered, wrap text, and border
    ' around days.
    For x = 0 To 5
        Range("A4").Offset(x * 2, 0).EntireRow.Insert
        With Range("A4:G4").Offset(x * 2, 0)
            .RowHeight = 65
            .HorizontalAlignment = xlCenter
            .VerticalAlignment = xlTop
            .WrapText = True
            .Font.Size = 10
            .Font.Bold = False
            ' Unlock these cells to be able to enter text later after
            ' sheet is protected.
            .Locked = False
        End With
        ' Put border around the block of dates.
        With Range("A3").Offset(x * 2, 0).Resize(2, _
                7).Borders(xlLeft)
            .Weight = xlThick
            .ColorIndex = xlAutomatic
        End With

        With Range("A3").Offset(x * 2, 0).Resize(2, _
                7).Borders(xlRight)
            .Weight = xlThick
            .ColorIndex = xlAutomatic
        End With
        Range("A3").Offset(x * 2, 0).Resize(2, 7).BorderAround _
            Weight:=xlThick, ColorIndex:=xlAutomatic
    Next
    If Range("A13").Value = "" Then Range("A13").Offset(0, 0) _
        .Resize(2, 8).EntireRow.Delete
    ' Turn off gridlines.
    ActiveWindow.DisplayGridlines = False
    ' Protect sheet to prevent overwriting the dates.
    ActiveSheet.Protect DrawingObjects:=True, Contents:=True, _
        Scenarios:=True
```

```
        ' Resize window to show all of calendar (may have to be adjusted
        ' for video configuration).
        ActiveWindow.WindowState = xlMaximized
        ActiveWindow.ScrollRow = 1

        ' Allow screen to redraw with calendar showing.
        Application.ScreenUpdating = True
        ' Prevent going to error trap unless error found by exiting Sub
        ' here.
        Exit Sub
' Error causes msgbox to indicate the problem, provides new input box,
' and resumes at the line that caused the error.
MyErrorTrap:
        MsgBox "You may not have entered your Month and Year correctly." _
            & Chr(13) & "Spell the Month correctly" _
            & " (or use 3 letter abbreviation)" _
            & Chr(13) & "and 4 digits for the Year"
        MyInput = InputBox("Type in Month and year for Calendar")
        If MyInput = "" Then Exit Sub
        Resume
    End Sub
```

Event Name	NewSheet
Event Description	**Example 18**

This event occurs after the user creates a new sheet in a workbook.	`Private Sub Workbook_NewSheet(ByVal Sh As Object)`
	`    If MsgBox("Do you want to place  " & vbCrLf _`
	`        & "the new sheet at the beginning " & vbCrLf _`
	`        & "of the workbook?", vbYesNo) = vbYes Then`
	`            Sh.Move before:=ThisWorkbook.Sheets(1)`
	`    Else`
	`        Sh.Move After:=ThisWorkbook.Sheets( _`
	`            ThisWorkbook.Sheets.Count)`
	`        MsgBox Sh.Name & _`
	`        " is now the last sheet in the workbook."`
	`    End If`
	`End Sub`

The example procedure places the new sheet at the beginning of the workbook if the user responds Yes to the message box; otherwise, the new sheet is moved to the end of the workbook.

■ **Example 18 – Try It Out:** Open a new workbook. In the Visual Basic Editor window, activate the Project Explorer window and open the Microsoft Excel Objects folder under the newly added project. Double-click ThisWorkbook, and type the example procedure in the ThisWorkbook (Code) window. Switch to the Microsoft Excel application window, and right-click any worksheet tab. Choose Insert from the shortcut menu. Select the type of sheet you want to insert, and click OK. Excel will ask where to place the new sheet.

Following is a list of other events to which Excel sheets can respond.

Event	Description
SheetActivate	This event occurs when the user activates any sheet in the workbook. The SheetActivate event also occurs at the application level when any sheet in any open workbook is activated.
SheetDeactivate	This event occurs when the user activates a different sheet in a workbook.
SheetSelectionChange	This event occurs when the user changes the selection on a worksheet. This event happens for each sheet in a workbook.
SheetChange	This event occurs when the user changes a cell formula.
SheetCalculate	This event occurs when the user recalculates a worksheet.
SheetBeforeDoubleClick	This event occurs when the user double-clicks a cell on a worksheet.
SheetBeforeRightClick	This event occurs when the user right-clicks a cell on a worksheet.

Event Name	WindowActivate
Event Description	**Example 19**

This event occurs when the user shifts the focus to any window showing the workbook.	`Private Sub Workbook_WindowActivate(ByVal _`
	`                Wn As Window)`
	`    Wn.GridlineColor = vbYellow`
	`End Sub`

The example procedure changes the color of the worksheet gridlines to yellow when the user activates the workbook containing the code of the Workbook_WindowActivate procedure.	

■ **Example 19 – Try It Out:** In the Visual Basic Editor window, activate the Project Explorer window and open the Microsoft Excel Objects folder. Double-click ThisWorkbook, and type the example procedure in the ThisWorkbook (Code) window. Next switch to the Microsoft Excel application window. Open a brand new workbook. Use the Window menu to arrange Microsoft Excel workbooks vertically on the screen. When you activate the worksheet of the workbook in which you entered the code of the Workbook_WindowActivate event procedure, the color of the gridlines should change to yellow.

Event Name	WindowDeactivate
Event Description	**Example 20**

This event occurs when the user shifts the focus away from any window showing the workbook.	`Private Sub Workbook_WindowDeactivate(ByVal _`
	`                Wn As Window)`
	`    Wn.GridlineColor = vbRed`
	`End Sub`

Event Name	WindowDeactivate
The example procedure changes the color of the worksheet gridlines to red when the user switches to another workbook from the workbook containing the code of the Workbook_WindowActivate procedure.	

- **Example 20 – Try It Out:** In the Visual Basic Editor window, activate the Project Explorer window and open the Microsoft Excel Objects folder. Double-click ThisWorkbook, and type the example procedure in the ThisWorkbook (Code) window. Next switch to the Microsoft Excel application window. Open a brand new workbook. Use the Window menu to arrange all Microsoft Excel workbooks vertically on the screen. When you deactivate the workbook containing the code of the Workbook_WindowDeactivate event and switch to the empty workbook that you just opened, the color of the gridlines in the deactivated sheet will change to red.

Event Name	WindowResize
Event Description	**Example 21**

This event occurs when the user opens, resizes, maximizes, or minimizes any window showing the workbook.	`Private Sub Workbook_WindowResize(ByVal Wn As Window)`
	`    If Wn.WindowState <> xlMaximized Then`
	`        Wn.Left = 0`
	`        Wn.Top = 0`
	`    End If`
	`End Sub`

The example procedure moves the workbook window to the top left-hand corner of the screen when the user resizes it.	

- **Example 21 – Try It Out:** In the Visual Basic Editor window, activate the Project Explorer window and open the Microsoft Excel Objects folder. Double-click ThisWorkbook, and type the example procedure in the ThisWorkbook (Code) window. Switch to the Microsoft Excel application window and click the Restore button. Change the size of the active window by dragging the window borders inside. As you complete the sizing operation, the workbook window should automatically jump to the top left-hand corner of the screen.

The following table describes the Workbook events added in Excel 2002.

Event	Description
PivotTableOpenConnection	Occurs after a PivotTable report opens the connection to its data source. This event requires that you declare an object of type Application or Workbook using the WithEvents keyword in a class module (refer to the "Chart Events" and "Events Recognized by the Application object" sections for examples of using this keyword).

Event	Description
PivotTableCloseConnection	Occurs after a PivotTable report closes the connection to its data source. This event requires that you declare an object of type Application or Workbook using the WithEvents keyword in a class module (refer to the "Chart Events" and "Events Recognized by the Application object" sections for examples of using this keyword).

SheetPivotTableUpdate
 	
It requires the following two arguments:
 	
Sh — the selected sheet
 	
Target — the selected PivotTable report
	This event occurs after the sheet of the PivotTable report has been updated. This event requires that you declare an object of type Application or Workbook using the WithEvents keyword in a class module (refer to Example 9 for information on setting up event handlers that require the WithEvents keyword). This event handler can be found in the PivotReport.xls file on the companion CD-ROM.
	
	`Private Sub App_SheetPivotTableUpdate( _`
	`    ByVal Sh As Object, ByVal Target As PivotTable)`
	`    MsgBox "Pivot Table has been updated."`
	`End Sub`

Chart Events

As you know, you can create charts in Excel that are embedded in a worksheet or located on a separate chart sheet. In this section, you will learn how to control chart events no matter where you've decided to place your chart. Before you try out selected chart events, perform the following tasks:

1. Open a new Excel workbook and save it as **ChartEvents.xls**.

2. Enter sample data, as shown in Figure 14-6.

3. Select cells **A1:D4**, and click the **Chart Wizard** button on the Standard toolbar.

4. Prepare a column chart, as shown in Figure 14-6, and embed it in a worksheet.

5. Using the same data, create a line chart on a separate chart sheet (see Figure 14-7).

6. Change the name of the chart sheet to **Sales Analysis Chart**.

The following table lists events for the Chart object. The example procedures demonstrated in this table should be tried on the chart that you've placed on a separate chart sheet (Figure 14-7). Events for a chart embedded in a worksheet require a special setup and are explained later in this chapter.

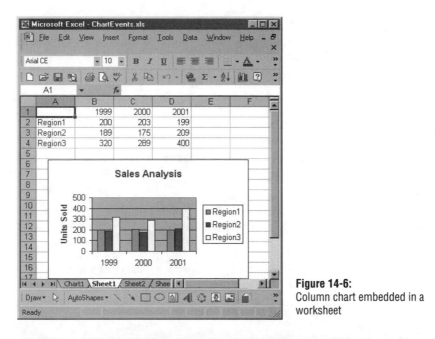

Figure 14-6:
Column chart embedded in a worksheet

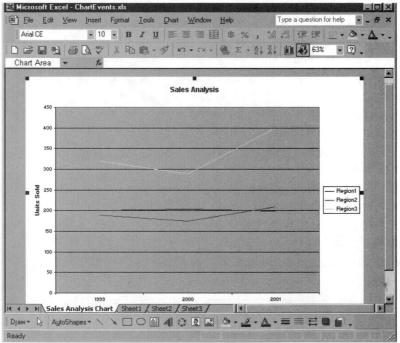

Figure 14-7: Line chart placed in a chart sheet

1. In the Visual Basic Editor window, activate the Project Explorer window and open the **Microsoft Excel Objects** folder.
2. Double-click the chart object labeled **Chart1** (Sales Analysis Chart).
3. In the Code window, enter the event procedures shown in the table below.
4. Activate the chart sheet and perform the actions that will trigger the event procedures you've written. For example, after clicking the chart title, the Chart_MouseDown and Chart_Select events should be triggered.

Event	Description

Activate	This event occurs when the user activates the chart sheet.
	
	`Private Sub Chart_Activate()`
	`    MsgBox "You've activated the chart sheet."`
	`End Sub`

Deactivate	This event occurs when the user deactivates the chart sheet.
	
	`Private Sub Chart_Deactivate()`
	`    MsgBox "It looks like you want to leave the chart sheet."`
	`End Sub`

Select	This event occurs when the user selects a chart element.
	
	`Private Sub Chart_Select(ByVal ElementID As Long, _`
	`        ByVal Arg1 As Long, ByVal Arg2 As Long)`
	`    If Arg1 <> 0 And Arg2 <> 0 Then`
	`      MsgBox ElementID & ", " & Arg1 & ", " & Arg2`
	`    End If`
	`    If ElementID = 4 Then`
	`      MsgBox "You've selected the chart title."`
	`    ElseIf ElementID = 24 Then`
	`      MsgBox "You've selected the chart legend."`
	`    ElseIf ElementID = 12 Then`
	`      MsgBox "You've selected the legend key."`
	`    ElseIf ElementID = 13 Then`
	`      MsgBox "You've selected the legend entry."`
	`    End If`
	`End Sub`

ElementId returns a constant representing the type of the selected chart element. Arguments Arg1 and Arg2 are used in relation to some chart elements. For example, the chart axis (ElementId = 21), can be specified as Main Axis (Arg1 = 0) or Secondary Axis (Arg1 = 1), while the Axis Type is specified by Arg2, which can be one of the following three values: 0 – Category Axis, 1 – Value Axis, or 3 – Series Axis.	
SeriesChange	This event occurs when the user changes the value of a chart data point. The Chart object should be declared in the class module using the WithEvents keyword.
Calculate	This event occurs when the user plots new or changed data on the chart.

Event	Description

Calculate (cont.)	`Private Sub Chart_Calculate()`
	`    MsgBox "The data in your spreadsheet has " & vbCrLf _`
	`        & "changed. Your chart has been updated."`
	`End Sub`

Resize	This event occurs when the user changes the size of the chart. The Chart object should be declared in the class module using the WithEvents keyword.
DragOver	This event occurs when the user drags data over the chart. The Chart object should be declared in the class module using the WithEvents keyword.
DragPlot	This event occurs when the user drags a range of cells over the chart. The Chart object should be declared in the class module using the WithEvents keyword.
BeforeDoubleClick	This event occurs when the user double-clicks the chart.

BeforeRightClick	This event occurs when the user right-clicks the chart.
	`Private Sub Chart_BeforeRightClick(Cancel As Boolean)`
	`    Cancel = True`
	`End Sub`

When you set the Cancel argument to True, the user will not be able to access the shortcut menu within the chart area.	

MouseDown	This event occurs when a mouse button is pressed while the pointer is over a chart.
	`Private Sub Chart_MouseDown(ByVal Button As Long, _`
	`    ByVal Shift As Long, ByVal x As Long, ByVal y As _`
	`    Long)`
	`    If Button = 1 Then`
	`        MsgBox "You pressed the left mouse button. "`
	`    ElseIf Button = 2 Then`
	`        MsgBox "You pressed the right mouse button. "`
	`    Else`
	`        MsgBox "You pressed the middle mouse button. "`
	`    End If`
	`End Sub`

The Button argument determines which mouse button was pressed (MouseDown event) or released (MouseUp event): 1 – left button, 2 – right button, and 4 – middle button. The Shift argument specifies the state of the Shift, Ctrl, and Alt keys: 1 – Shift was selected, 2 – Ctrl was selected, and 4 – Alt was selected. The x, y arguments specify the mouse pointer coordinates.	
MouseMove	This event occurs when the position of a mouse pointer changes over a chart.
MouseUp	This event occurs when a mouse button is released while the pointer is over a chart.

Embedded Chart Events

To capture events raised by the chart embedded in a worksheet, you must first create a new object in the class module using the keyword WithEvents. To see how this is done, let's follow the steps outlined below:

1. Activate the Visual Basic Editor window.

2. In the Project Explorer, select **VBAProject(ChartEvents.xls)**.

3. Choose **Insert | Class Module**.

4. In the Class Modules folder, you will see a module named Class1.

5. In the Properties window, rename Class1 to **clsChart**.

6. In the Code window of the class module, declare an object variable that will represent the events generated by the Chart object:

   ```
   Public WithEvents xlChart As Excel.Chart
   ```

   The Public keyword will make the object variable xlChart available to all modules in the current VBA project. Declaring an object variable using the WithEvents keyword exposes all of the events defined for that particular object type.

   After typing in the above declaration, the xlChart object variable is added to the drop-down Object list in the upper-left corner of the Code window, and the events associated with this object variable appear in the Procedure drop-down list box in the upper-right corner of the Code window.

7. Open the Object drop-down list box, and select the name of the xlChart variable. The Code window should now show the skeleton of the xlChart_Activate event procedure:

   ```
   Private Sub xlChart_Activate()
   End Sub
   ```

8. Add your VBA code to the event procedure. In this exercise, we will add a statement to display a message box. After adding this statement, your VBA procedure should look like the following:

   ```
   Private Sub xlChart_Activate()
       MsgBox "You've activated a chart embedded in " & _
           ActiveSheet.Name
   End Sub
   ```

   After typing in the event procedure, you still need to inform Visual Basic that you are planning on using it.

9. In the Project Explorer window, double-click the object named **ThisWorkbook**, and enter in the [ThisWorkbook (Code)] window the statement to create a new instance of the class named clsChart:

   ```
   Dim myChart As New clsChart
   ```

   The instruction shown above declares an object variable named myChart. This variable will refer to the xlChart object located in the class module clsChart. The New keyword tells Visual Basic to create a new instance of the specified object.

10. Enter the following procedure in the [ThisWorkbook (Code)] window to initialize the object variable myChart:

```
Sub InitializeChart()
    ' connect the class module and its objects with the Chart object
    Set myChart.xlChart = _
        Worksheets(1).ChartObjects(1).Chart
End Sub
```

11. Run the InitializeChart procedure. After running this procedure, the event procedures entered in the class module will be triggered in response to a particular event.

12. Activate the Microsoft Excel application window and click the embedded chart. At this time, the xlChart_Activate event procedure that you entered in step 7 should be triggered.

13. You can now enter in the class module additional event procedures for the embedded chart.

Events Recognized by the Application Object

If you want your event procedure to execute no matter which Excel workbook is currently active, you need to create the event procedure for the Application object. Event procedures for the Application object have a global scope. This means that the procedure code will be executed in response to a certain event, as long as the Microsoft Excel application remains open.

Events for the Application objects are listed in the following table. Similar to an embedded chart, event procedures for the Application objects require that you create a new object using the WithEvents keyword in the class module. The examples of the event procedures demonstrated in the table have to be entered in a class module. To do this, choose Insert | Class Module in the Visual Basic Editor window. In the Properties window change the module name to clsApplication. In the [clsApplication (Code)] window declare an object variable to represent the Application object using the WithEvents keyword as follows:

```
Public WithEvents App As Application
```

Below the declaration statement, enter the following event procedures, as shown in the table: App_NewWorkbook, App_WorkbookOpen, App_WorkbookBeforeSave, App_WorkbookBeforeClose, App_Sheet-SelectionChange, and App_WindowActivate. After you've entered the code of these procedures in the class module, insert a standard module to your current VBA project (choose Insert | Module). In the standard module, create a new instance of the clsApplication class and connect the object located in the class module clsApplication with the object variable App representing the Application object, as shown below:

```
Dim DoThis As New clsApplication

Public Sub InitializeAppEvents ()
    Set DoThis.App = Application
End Sub
```

Now place the mouse pointer within the InitializeAppEvents procedure and press F5 to run it. As a result of running the InitializeAppEvents procedure, the object App in the class module will refer to the Excel application. From now on, when a specific event occurs, the code of the event procedures you've entered in the class module will be executed. If you don't want to respond to events generated by the Application object, you can break the connection between the object and its object variable by entering in a standard module (and then running) the following procedure:

```
Public Sub CancelAppEvents()
    Set DoThis.App = Nothing
End Sub
```

When you set the object variable to Nothing, you release the memory and break the connection between the object variable and the object to which this variable refers. When you run the CancelAppEvents procedure, the code of the event procedures written in the class module will not be automatically executed when a specific event occurs.

Note: All event procedures demonstrated in this table require that you declare an object variable in a class module using the WithEvents keyword.

Event	Description

NewWorkbook	This event occurs when the user creates a new workbook.
	
	`Private Sub App_NewWorkbook(ByVal _`
	`                Wb As Workbook)`
	`    Application.DisplayAlerts = False`
	`    If Wb.Sheets.Count = 3 Then`
	`        Sheets(Array(2, 3)).Delete`
	`    End If`
	`    Application.DisplayAlerts = True`
	`End Sub`

WorkbookOpen	This event occurs when the user opens a workbook.
	
	`Private Sub App_WorkbookOpen(ByVal Wb As Workbook)`
	`    If Wb.FileFormat = xlCSV Then`
	`        If MsgBox("Do you want to save " & vbCrLf _`
	`            & " this file as an Excel workbook?", vbYesNo, _`

Event	Description

WorkbookOpen (cont.)	```
	        "Original file format: " _
	      & "Comma delimited file") = vbYes Then
	        Wb.SaveAs FileFormat:=xlWorkbookNormal
	      End If
	    End If
	End Sub
	``

WorkbookActivate	This event occurs when the user shifts the focus to an open workbook.
WorkbookDeactivate	This event occurs when the user shifts the focus away from an open workbook.
WorkbookNewSheet	This event occurs when the user add a new sheet to an open workbook.

WorkbookBeforeSave	This event occurs before an open workbook is saved.
	
	``
	Private Sub App_WorkbookBeforeSave(ByVal _
	                    Wb As Workbook, _
	                    ByVal SaveAsUI As Boolean, _
	                    Cancel As Boolean)
	
	    If Wb.Path <> vbNullString Then
	       ActiveWindow.Caption = Wb.FullName & _
	        " [Last Saved: " & Time & "]"
	    End If
	End Sub
	``

WorkbookBeforePrint	This event occurs before an open workbook is printed.
	
	``
	Private Sub App_WorkbookBeforePrint(ByVal _
	         Wb As Workbook, Cancel As Boolean)
	    Wb.PrintOut Copies:=2
	End Sub
	``

WorkbookBeforeClose	This event occurs before an open workbook is closed.
	
	``
	Private Sub App_WorkbookBeforeClose(ByVal _
	     Wb As Workbook, Cancel As Boolean)
	     Dim r As Integer
	     Sheets.Add
	     r = 1
	     For Each p In Wb.BuiltinDocumentProperties
	       On Error GoTo ErrorHandle
	         Cells(r, 1).Value = p.Name & " = " & _
	           ActiveWorkbook. _
	           BuiltinDocumentProperties _
	           .Item(p.Name).Value
	         r = r + 1
	     Next
	     Exit Sub
	ErrorHandle:
	         Cells(r, 1).Value = p.Name
	         Resume Next
	End Sub
	``

Event	Description
WorkbookAddInInstall	This event occurs when the user installs a workbook as an add-in.
WorkbookAddInUninstall	This event occurs when the user uninstalls a workbook as an add-in.
SheetActivate	This event occurs when the user activates a sheet in an open workbook.
SheetDeactivate	This event occurs when the user deactivates a sheet in an open workbook.
SheetSelectionChange	This event occurs when the user changes the selection on a sheet in an open workbook. ```\nPrivate Sub App_SheetSelectionChange(_\n ByVal Sh As Object, ByVal Target As Range)\n\n If Selection.Count > 1 Or _\n (Selection.Count < 2 And _\n IsEmpty(Target.Value)) Then\n Application.StatusBar = Target.Address\n Else\n Application.StatusBar = Target.Address & _\n "(" & Target.Value & ")"\n End If\nEnd Sub\n```
SheetChange	This event occurs when the user changes a cell formula in an open workbook.
SheetCalculate	This event occurs when the user recalculates a worksheet in an open workbook.
SheetBeforeDoubleClick	This event occurs when the user double-clicks a worksheet cell in an open workbook.
SheetBeforeRightClick	This event occurs when the user right-clicks a worksheet cell in an open workbook.
WindowActivate	This event occurs when the user shifts the focus to an open window. ```\nPrivate Sub App_WindowActivate(ByVal _\n Wb As Workbook, ByVal Wn As Window)\n\n Wn.DisplayFormulas = True\nEnd Sub\n```
WindowDeactivate	This event occurs when the user shifts the focus away from the open window.
WindowResize	This event occurs when the user resizes an open window.
WorkbookPivotTableClose-Connection (new event in Excel 2002)	This event occurs after a PivotTable report connection has been closed.

Event	Description
WorkbookPivotTableOpen-Connection (new event in Excel 2002)	This event occurs after a PivotTable report connection has been opened.

Query Table Events

A *query table* is a table in an Excel worksheet that represents data returned from an external data source, such as an SQL Server database, a Microsoft Access database, a web page, or a text file. A query table is represented by the QueryTable object. Excel provides two events for the QueryTable object: BeforeRefresh and AfterRefresh. To try out the example procedures demonstrated in the table at the end of this section, perform the tasks outlined below. This exercise assumes that you have Microsoft Access and its sample Northwind database installed on your machine.

1. In the Microsoft Excel application window, choose **Data | Import External Data** and select **New Database Query** to create a new database query.
2. In the Data Source dialog box, choose **<New Data Source>** and click **OK**.
3. In the Create New Data Source dialog box, enter **SampleDb** as the data source name.
4. Select the **Microsoft Access (*.mdb)** driver from the drop-down list next to step 2 in the Create New Data Source dialog box.
5. Click the **Connect** button.
6. In the ODBC Microsoft Access Setup dialog box, click the **Select** button.
7. In the Select Database dialog box, locate the Northwind.mdb file. This file usually can be found in the C:\Program Files\Microsoft Office\Office\Samples folder.
8. Select the file and click **OK** to close the Select Database dialog box.
9. Click **OK** again to exit the ODBC Microsoft Access Setup dialog box.
10. In the Create New Data Source dialog box's step 4, select the **Categories** table in the drop-down list box.
11. Click **OK** to close the Create New Data Source dialog box.
12. In the Choose Data Source dialog box, the SampleDb data source name should now be highlighted. Click **OK**.
13. In the Query Wizard – Choose Column dialog box, click the > button to move all the fields from the Categories table to the Columns in your query box.
14. Click the **Next** button until you see the Query Wizard – Finish dialog.

15. In the wizard's Finish dialog box, make sure the **Return Data to Microsoft Excel** option button is selected and click **Finish**.

16. In the Import Data dialog box, the current spreadsheet cell is selected. Click cell **A1** in the current worksheet to change the cell reference, and click **OK** to close the dialog box.

After completing the above steps, the data from the Category table in the Northwind database should be placed in the active worksheet. It took quite a number of steps to retrieve this data. In the next chapter, you will learn how to create a query table programmatically.

To write event procedures for a QueryTable object, you must create a class module and declare a QueryTable object by using the WithEvents keyword.

1. Insert a class module to the current VBA project and rename it **clsQryTbl**.

2. In the clsQryTbl [Code] window, type the following statement:

   ```
   Public WithEvents qrytbl As QueryTable
   ```

   After you've declared the new object (qrytbl) by using the WithEvents keyword, it appears in the Object drop-down list in the class module.

3. In the clsQryTbl [Code] window, enter the two event procedures presented in the table on the following page: QryTbl_BeforeRefresh and QryTbl_AfterRefresh. Before you can trigger these event procedures, you must connect the object that you declared in the class module (qrytbl) to the specified QueryTable object.

4. Insert a standard module into the current VBA project, and enter the following code:

   ```
   Dim sampleQry As New clsQryTbl

   Public Sub Auto_Open()
       ' connect the class module and its objects with the Query object
       Set sampleQry.qrytbl = ActiveSheet.QueryTables(1)
   End Sub
   ```

   The above procedure creates a new instance of the QueryTable class (clsQryTbl) and connects this instance with the first query table on the active worksheet. The Auto_Open procedure will run automatically when you open the workbook, so you will not need to run this procedure manually to ensure that the query events that you've entered are triggered when the data is refreshed by the user or the system.

5. Run the Auto_Open procedure that you entered in step 4. After you run this initialization procedure, the object that you declared in the class module points to the specified QueryTable object.

6. In the worksheet where you placed the Category table from Microsoft Access, change the name of one of the retrieved categories. Select any

cell in the query table and click the **Refresh** button on the External Data toolbar, or choose **Data | Refresh Data**.

At this time, the event procedure qryTbl_BeforeRefesh will be triggered, and you should see the custom message box. If you click **Yes**, the data will be refreshed with the existing data in the database and the change in the name of the category you've made will be overwritten.

Event	Description

BeforeRefresh	This event occurs before the query table is refreshed.
	
	```Private Sub qryTbl_BeforeRefresh(Cancel As Boolean)```
	``` Response = MsgBox("Are you sure you " _```
	``` & " want to refresh now?", vbYesNoCancel)```
	``` If Response = vbNo Then Cancel = True```
	```End Sub```

AfterRefresh	This event occurs after a query is completed or canceled. The Success argument is True if the query was completed successfully.
	
	```Private Sub qryTbl_AfterRefresh(ByVal Success As Boolean)```
	``` If Success Then```
	``` MsgBox "The data has been refreshed."```
	``` Else```
	``` MsgBox "The query failed."```
	``` End If```
	```End Sub```

What's Next...

In this chapter you gained hands-on experience with events and event-driven programming in Excel. These are invaluable skills, whether you are planning to create spreadsheet applications for others to use or simply automating your routine daily tasks.

Excel provides many events to which you can respond. By writing event procedures, you can change the way objects respond to events. Your event procedures can be as simple as a single line of code displaying a custom message to code including decision-making statements and other programming structures that allow you to change the flow of your program when a particular event occurs. When a certain event occurs, Visual Basic will simply run an appropriate event procedure instead of responding in the standard built-in way. You've learned that some event procedures are written in a standard module (Workbook, Worksheet, Chart Sheet), while others (Embedded Chart, Application, Query Table) require that you create a new object using the WithEvents keyword in a class module. You've also learned that you can enable or disable events using the EnableEvents property.

In the next chapter, you will learn how to work with a Microsoft Access database using the VBA procedures written in the Microsoft Excel Visual Basic environment.

Chapter 15

Using Excel with Microsoft Access

Object Libraries ■ Setting Up References to Object Libraries ■ **Connecting to Microsoft Access** ■ Using Automation to Connect to a Microsoft Access Database ■ Using DAO to Connect to a Microsoft Access Database ■ Using ADO to Connect to a Microsoft Access Database ■ **Performing Microsoft Access Tasks from Excel** ■ Creating a New Microsoft Access Database ■ Opening a Microsoft Access Form ■ Opening a Microsoft Access Report ■ Running a Microsoft Access Query ■ Calling a Microsoft Access Function ■ **Retrieving Microsoft Access Data into an Excel Spreadsheet** ■ Retrieving Data with the GetRows Method ■ Retrieving Data with the CopyFromRecordset Method ■ Retrieving Data with the Transfer-Spreadsheet Method ■ Using the OpenDatabase Method ■ Creating a Text File from Microsoft Access Data ■ Creating a Query Table from Microsoft Access Data ■ **Using Microsoft Access Data in Excel** ■ Creating an Embedded Chart from Microsoft Access Data ■ **Transferring the Excel Spreadsheet to an Access Database** ■ **Linking an Excel Spreadsheet to a Microsoft Access Database** ■ **Importing an Excel Spreadsheet to a Microsoft Access Database** ■ **Placing Excel Data in an Access Table** ■ What's Next...

In Chapter 9 you learned about controlling Microsoft Word and Outlook from Excel via Automation, which allows one application to control the objects of another application. This chapter shows you how to programmatically use Access from Excel and retrieve Access data into a spreadsheet by using the following methods: Automation, DAO (Data Access Objects), and ADO (ActiveX Data Objects). Before you learn how to use Excel VBA to perform various tasks in an Access database as well as retrieve and store data in an Access database, let's briefly introduce the data access methods that Microsoft Access uses to gain programmatic access to its objects.

Object Libraries

A Microsoft Access database consists of various types of objects stored in different object libraries to display, store, or manage data with the Visual Basic for Applications language. In this chapter you will be accessing objects, properties, and methods from several of the libraries listed below.

The Microsoft Access 10.0 Object Library provides objects that are used to display data and work with the Microsoft Access 2002 application. This library is stored in the MSACC10.OLB file and can be found in the C:\Program Files\Microsoft Office\Office folder. After setting up a reference to this library in the References dialog box (this is covered in the next section), you will be able to access this library's objects, properties, and methods in the Object Browser (see Figure 15-1).

Figure 15-1: Library Access

The Microsoft Access DAO 3.6 Object Library provides Data Access Objects (DAO) that allow you to determine the structure of your database and manipulate data using VBA. This library is stored in the DAO360.DLL file and can be found in the C:\Program Files\Common Files\Microsoft Shared\DAO folder. After setting up a reference to this library in the References dialog box (covered in the next section), you will be able to access the library's objects, properties, and methods in the Object Browser (see Figure 15-2).

Figure 15-2: Library DAO

The Microsoft ActiveX Data Objects 2.5 Library (ADO) provides ActiveX Data Objects (ADO) and allows you to access and manipulate data using the OLE DB provider. ADO objects make it possible to establish a connection with a data source and read, insert, modify, and delete data in an Access database. This library is stored in MSADO15.DLL and can be found in the C:\Program Files\Common Files\system\ado folder. After setting up a reference to this library in the References dialog, you will be able to access this library's objects, properties, and methods in the Object Browser (see Figure 15-3).

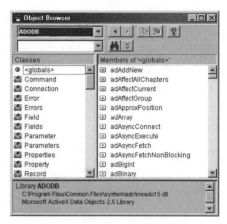

Figure 15-3: Library ADODB

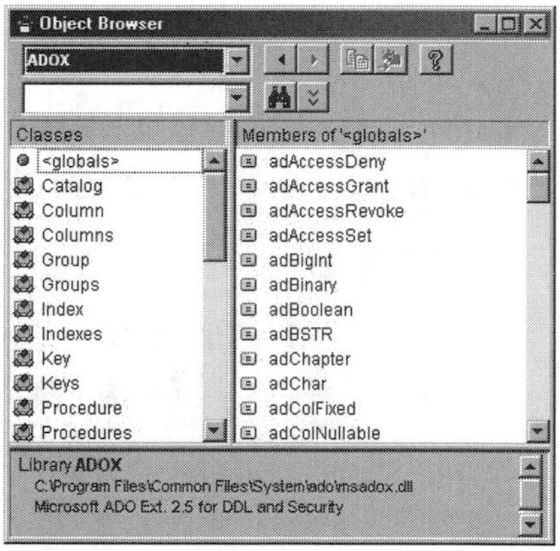

The Microsoft ADO Ext. 2.5 for DDL and Security (ADOX) stores objects that allow you to define the database structure and security. For example, you can define tables, indexes, and relationships, as well as create and modify user and group accounts.

This library is stored in MSADOX.DLL and can be found in the C:\Program Files\Common Files\System\ado folder. After setting up a reference to this library in the References dialog box, you will be able to access this library's objects, properties, and methods in the Object Browser (see Figure 15-4).

Figure 15-4: Library ADOX

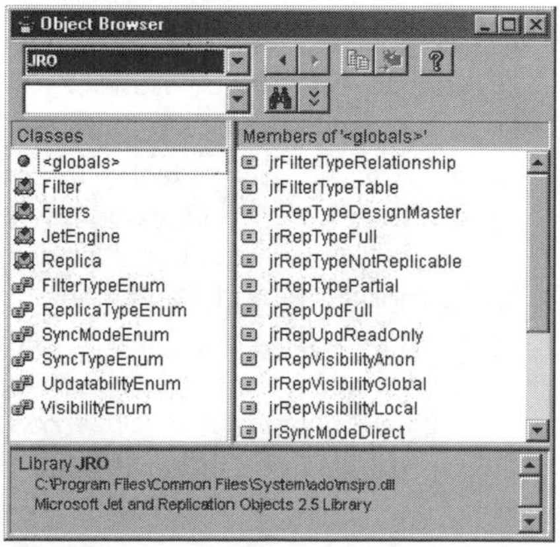

The Microsoft Jet and Replication Objects 2.6 Library (JRO) contains objects that are used in the replication of a database. This library is stored in MSJRO.DLL and can be found in the C:\Program Files\Common Files\System\ado folder. After setting up a reference to this library in the References

Figure 15-5: Library JRO

dialog box, you will be able to access this library's objects, properties, and methods in the Object Browser (see Figure 15-5).

The Visual Basic for Applications Object Library (VBA) provides many VBA objects, functions, and methods that allow you to access the file system, work with date and time functions, perform mathematical and financial computations, interact with users, convert data, and read text files. This library is stored in the VBE6.DLL file located in the C:\Program Files\Common Files\Microsoft Shared\VBA\VBA6 folder. The reference to this library is automatically set when you install Microsoft Excel 2002. This library is shared between all Office 2002 applications (see Figure 15-6).

Figure 15-6: Library VBA

Setting Up References to Object Libraries

To work with Microsoft Access 2002 objects, begin by creating a reference to the Microsoft Access 10.0 Object Library. (Choose Microsoft Access 9.00 Object Library if you are working with Microsoft Office 2000.)

1. In the Visual Basic Editor window, choose **Tools | References** to open the References dialog box. This dialog displays a list of all the type libraries that are available on your computer.

2. Locate the **Microsoft Access 10.0 Object Library** in the list of entries and select its check box.

3. Close the **References** dialog box.

Once you've created a reference to the Microsoft Access type library, you can use the Object Browser to view a list of the application's objects, properties, and methods (see Figure 15-1 in the previous section).

Use the References dialog box to set up references to other object libraries that will be accessed in the exercises of this chapter. You will find the list of libraries in the previous section. You can skip the reference to the Microsoft Jet and Replication Objects 2.6 Library (JRO), as it will not be used here. If you are interested in database replication, there are many books on Microsoft Access programming that cover this subject, including my book *Learn Microsoft Access 2000 Programming by Example* from Wordware Publishing (ISBN 1-55622-770-1).

Tip 15-1: Advantages of Creating a Reference to Microsoft Access Object Library

When you set a reference to Microsoft Access Object Library, you gain the following:

- You can look up Microsoft Access objects, properties, and methods in the Object Browser.
- You can run Microsoft Access functions directly in your VBA procedures.

- You can declare the object variable of the Application type instead of the generic Object type. Declaring the object variable as Dim objAccess As Access.Application (early binding) is faster than declaring it as Dim objAccess As Object (late binding).
- You can use Microsoft Access built-in constants in your VBA code.
- Your VBA procedure will run faster.

Connecting to Microsoft Access

The example procedures in this chapter use various methods of connecting to Microsoft Access, each of which is discussed in detail in this section. You can establish a connection to Microsoft Access by using one of the following three methods:

- Automation
- Data Access Objects (DAO)
- ActiveX Data Objects (ADO)

In order to access data in a database, you need to open it. How you open a particular database depends largely on which method you selected to establish a database connection.

Using Automation to Connect to a Microsoft Access Database

When working with Microsoft Access from Excel (or another application) using Automation, take the following steps:

1. Set a reference to the **Microsoft Access 10.0 Object Library**. (Refer to "Setting Up References to Object Libraries" earlier in this chapter).

2. Declare an object variable to represent the Microsoft Access Application object.

   ```
   Dim objAccess As Access.Application
   ```

   In this declaration line, `objAccess` is the name of the object variable, and Access.Application qualifies the object variable with the name of the Visual Basic object library that supplies the object.

3. Return the reference to the Application object and assign that reference to the object variable. Return the reference to the Application object using the CreateObject function, GetObject function, or the New keyword. Assign the reference to the object variable with the Set statement.

```
Dim objAccess As Object
Set objAccess = CreateObject("Access.Application.10")
```

Use the CreateObject function to return a reference to the Application object when there is no current instance of the object. If Microsoft Access is already running, a new instance is started and the specified object is created.

```
Dim objAccess As Object
Set objAccess = GetObject(, "Access.Application.10")
```

or

```
Set Set objAccess = GetObject("C:\Program Files\ _
    & "Microsoft Office\Office\Samples\Northwind.mdb")
```

Use the GetObject function to return a reference to the Application object to use the current instance of Microsoft Access or to start Microsoft Access and have it load a file. (For more information, see Tip 15-2.)

```
Dim objAccess As New Access.Application
```

The above statement uses the New keyword to declare an object variable, return a reference to the Application object, and assign the reference to the object variable, all in one step.

You can also declare an object variable using the two-step method, which gives more control over the object:

```
Dim objAccess As Access.Application
Set objAccess = New Access.Application
```

- When you declare the object variable with the New keyword, the Access application does not start until you begin working with the object variable in your VBA code.

- When you use the New keyword to declare the Application object variable, a new instance of Microsoft Access is created automatically and you don't need to use the CreateObject function.

- Using the New keyword to create a new instance of the Application object is faster than using the CreateObject function.

Because a computer can have more than one version of Microsoft Access installed, include the version number in the argument of the GetObject or CreateObject function. The last four versions of Microsoft Access are shown below:

Microsoft Access 2002   Access.Application.10
Microsoft Access 2000   Access.Application.9
Microsoft Access 97   Access.Application.8
Microsoft Access 95   Access.Application.7

Once you've created a new instance of the Application class by using one of the methods outlined in step 3, you can open a database or create a new database with the help of the OpenCurrentDatabase or NewCurrent-Database methods. You can close the Microsoft Access database that you opened through Automation by using the CloseCurrentDatabase method.

Tip 15-2: Arguments of the GetObject Function

The first argument of the GetObject function—Pathname—is optional. It is used when you want to work with an object in a specific file. The second argument—Class—is required and specifies which application creates the object and what type of object it is. When the first argument is optional and the second argument is required, you must place a comma in the position of the first argument, as shown below:

```
Dim objAccess As Object
Set objAccess = GetObject(, Access. _
    Application.10")
```

Because the first argument (Pathname) of the GetObject function is omitted, a reference to an existing instance of the Microsoft Access Application class is returned.

```
Dim objAccess As Object
Set objAccess = GetObject("C:\Program_
    Files\ & "Microsoft Office\Office_
    \Samples\Northwind.mdb")
```

When the first argument of the GetObject function is the name of a database file, a new instance of the Microsoft Access Application class is activated or created with the specific database.

Now that you know how to create an object variable that represents the Application object, let's take a look at an example procedure that opens an Access database straight from an Excel VBA procedure.

The AccessViaAutomation procedure shown on the next page opens the sample Northwind database that ships with Microsoft Access. This procedure will use a current instance of the Access automation server, if it is available. If Access isn't running, a run-time error will occur and the object variable will be set to Nothing. By placing the On Error Resume Next statement inside this procedure, you can trap this error. Therefore, if Access isn't running, a new instance of Access will be started. This particular example uses the New keyword to start a new instance of Access. As mentioned earlier, instead of creating a new object instance with the New keyword, you can use the CreateObject() function to start a new instance of an Automation server, as illustrated below:

```
Set objAccess = GetObject(, "Access.Application.10")
If objAccess Is Nothing Then
    Set objAccess = CreateObject("Access.Application.10")
End If
```

When you launch Microsoft Access using Automation, you will see the Microsoft Access program icon on the taskbar. The Visible property of the Access Application object is set to False. To restore the application window, set the Visible property to True.

While in use, objects consume memory and system resources. To free the resources, always close the object when you've finished working with it. The example procedure demonstrated below first closes the Northwind database by using the CloseCurrentDatabase method. Next, the Access application object is closed with the Quit method. After closing the object, you should also set the object variable to the Nothing keyword to free the memory resources used by the variable.

You can prevent an instance of Microsoft Access from closing by making an object variable a module-level variable rather than declaring it at the procedure level.

Under these circumstances, the connection to the database will remain open until you close the Automation controller (Excel) or use the Quit method in your VBA code.

```
Sub AccessViaAutomation()
    Dim objAccess As Access.Application
    Dim strPath As String

    On Error Resume Next

    Set objAccess = GetObject(, "Access.Application.9")
        If objAccess Is Nothing Then
            ' Get a reference to the Access Application object
            Set objAccess = New Access.Application
        End If

        strPath = "C:\Program Files\Microsoft Office\" _
                & "Office\Samples\northwind.mdb"
        ' Open the Northwind database
        With objAccess
            .OpenCurrentDatabase strPath
            If MsgBox("Do you want to make the Access " & vbCrLf _
                & "Application visible?", vbYesNo, _
                "Display Access") = vbYes Then
                .Visible = True
                MsgBox "Notice the Access Application icon " _
                & "now appears on the Windows taskbar."
            End If
        ' Close the database and quit Access
```

```
        .CloseCurrentDatabase
        .Quit
    End With
    Set objAccess = Nothing
End Sub
```

Run the above procedure by stepping through the code with the F8 key.

Tip 15-3: Opening a Secured Microsoft Access Database

If the Access database is secured with a password, the user will be prompted to enter the correct password. You must use Data Access Objects (DAO) or ActiveX Data Access (ADO) to programmatically open a password-protected Microsoft Access database. The following example uses the DBEngine property of the Microsoft Access object to specify the password of the database. For this procedure to work, you must set up a reference to the Microsoft DAO 3.6 Object Library, as explained in the beginning of this chapter.

```
Sub OpenSecuredDB()
  Static objAccess As _
     Access.Application
  Dim db As DAO.Database
```

```
  Dim strDb As String

  strDb = "C:\Program Files\Microsoft_
     Office\" & "Office\Samples\ _
     Northwind.mdb"

  Set objAccess = New _
     Access.Application
  Set db = objAccess.DBEngine.Open _
     Database(Name:=strDb, _
              Options:=False, _
              ReadOnly:=False, _
              Connect:=";PWD=test")
  With objAccess
     .Visible = True
     .OpenCurrentDatabase strDb
  End With
  db.Close
  Set db = Nothing
End Sub
```

Using DAO to Connect to a Microsoft Access Database

To connect to a Microsoft Access database using the Data Access Objects (DAO), you must first set up a reference to the Microsoft Data Access Objects 3.6 Library in the References dialog box (see the section titled "Setting up References to Object Libraries" earlier in this chapter). The example procedure DAOOpenJetDatabase, illustrated below, uses the OpenDatabase method of the DBEngine object to open the Northwind database and informs the user that the database has been opened. The DBEngine object allows you to initialize the standard database engine known as Microsoft Jet Engine and open a database file (.mdb). The procedure uses the Close method to close the database file.

```
Sub DAOOpenJetDatabase()
  Dim db As DAO.Database
  Set db = DBEngine.OpenDatabase _
    ("C:\Program Files\Microsoft Office\Office\Samples\Northwind.mdb")
  MsgBox "Northwind database has been opened."
  db.Close
```

```
    MsgBox "Northwind database has been closed."
End Sub
```

Using ADO to Connect to a Microsoft Access Database

The newest and most recommended method of establishing a connection with an Access database is using the ActiveX Data Objects (ADO). You must begin by setting up a reference to the Microsoft ActiveX Data Objects 2.5 Library or higher version. The example procedure ADOOpenJet-Database connects to the Northwind database using the Connection object. This object is opened via the Open method. Notice that the Open method requires a connection string argument that contains the name of the data provider (in this example, it's Microsoft.Jet.OLEDB.4.0) and the data source name (in this example, it's the full name of the database file you want to open):

```
con.Open _
    "Provider=Microsoft.Jet.OLEDB.4.0;" _
    & "Data Source=C:\Program Files\Microsoft Office\" _
    & "Office\Samples\NorthWind.mdb;"
```

After establishing a connection to the Northwind database, you can use the Recordset object to access its data. Recordset objects are used to manipulate data at the record level. The Recordset object is made up of records (rows) and fields (columns). To obtain a set of records, you need to open a Recordset by using the Open method. This method requires that you specify information such as the source of records for the Recordset:

```
rst.Open "SELECT * FROM Customers " & _
    "WHERE City = 'London'", con, _
    adOpenForwardOnly, adLockReadOnly
```

The source of records can be a name of a database table or query or the SQL statement that returns records. After specifying the source of records, you also need to indicate the connection with the database (con) and two constants, one of which defines the type of cursor (adOpenForwardOnly) and the other type of lock (adLockReadOnly). The adOpenForwardOnly constant tells VBA to create the forward-only recordset, which scrolls forward in the returned set of records. The second constant, adLockReadOnly, specifies the type of the lock placed on records during editing; the records are read-only which means that you cannot alter the data. The next part of the procedure uses the For...Each...Next loop to iterate through the Recordset and print the contents of the first record to the Immediate window:

```
For Each fld In rst.Fields
    Debug.Print fld.Name & "=" & fld.Value & vbCr
Next
```

After obtaining the data from the first record, the Close method closes the Recordset and another Close method is used to close the connection with the Access database:

```
rst.Close
con.Close
```

The ADOOpenJetDatabase procedure is given below:

```
Sub ADOOpenJetDatabase()
    Dim con As New ADODB.Connection
    Dim rst As New ADODB.Recordset
    Dim fld As ADODB.Field

        ' Connect with the database
        con.Open _
            "Provider=Microsoft.Jet.OLEDB.4.0;" _
            & "Data Source=C:\Program Files\Microsoft Office\" _
            & "Office\Samples\NorthWind.mdb;"

    ' Open Recordset based on the SQL statement
            rst.Open "SELECT * FROM Customers " & _
            "WHERE City = 'London'", con, _
            adOpenForwardOnly, adLockReadOnly

    ' Print the values for the fields in
    ' the first record in the debug window
            For Each fld In rst.Fields
                Debug.Print fld.Name & "=" & fld.Value & vbCr
            Next

    '  Close the Recordset and connection with Access
            rst.Close
            con.Close
            ' Destroy object variables to reclaim the resources
            Set rst = Nothing
            Set con = Nothing
End Sub
```

Performing Microsoft Access Tasks from Excel

After connecting to a Microsoft Access from Excel, you can perform different tasks within the Access application. This section demonstrates in particular how to use VBA code to:

- Create a new Access database
- Open an existing database form
- Create a brand new database form
- Open a database report
- Run an Access function

Creating a New Microsoft Access Database

If you want to programmatically transfer Excel data into a new Access database, you may need to create a database from scratch by using VBA code. The following example procedure demonstrates how to use the Data Access Objects (DAO) to establish a connection with Microsoft Access. The CreateDatabase method of the Workspace object is used to create a new database named ExcelDump.mdb in the root folder of the C drive. The CreateTableDef method of the Database object is then used to create a table named tblStates. Before a table can be added to a database, the fields must be created and appended to the table. The procedure creates three text fields (dbText) that can store 2, 25, and 25 characters each. As each field is created, it is appended to the Fields collection of the TableDef object using the Append method. Once the fields are created and appended to the table, the table itself is added to the database with the Append method. Because the database file named "C:\ExcelDump.mdb" may already exist in the specified location, the procedure includes the error-handling routine that will delete the file so that the database creation process can go on. Because other errors could occur, the Else clause includes a statement that will display the error and its description and allow an exit from the procedure.

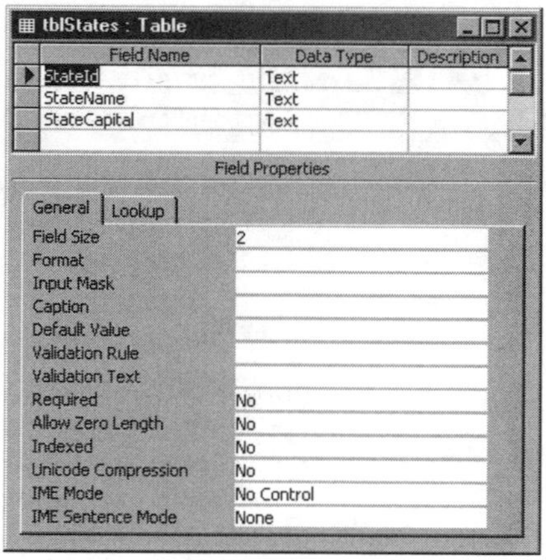

Figure 15-7: This Microsoft Access database table was created by an Excel VBA procedure.

```
Sub NewDB_DAO()
Dim db As DAO.Database
Dim tbl As DAO.TableDef
Dim strDb As String
Dim strTbl As String

On Error GoTo Error_CreateDb_DAO
strDb = "C:\ExcelDump.mdb"
strTbl = "tblStates"
' Create a new database named ExcelDump
Set db = CreateDatabase(strDb, dbLangGeneral)

' Create a new table named tblStates
Set tbl = db.CreateTableDef(strTbl)

' Create fields and append them to the Fields collection
With tbl
    .Fields.Append .CreateField("StateId", dbText, 2)
    .Fields.Append .CreateField("StateName", dbText, 25)
    .Fields.Append .CreateField("StateCapital", dbText, 25)
End With

' Append the table object to the TableDefs
db.TableDefs.Append tbl
```

```
' Close the database
db.Close
Set db = Nothing
MsgBox "There is a new database on your hard disk. " & vbCrLf _
        & "This database file contains a table " & strDb & vbCrLf _
        & "named " & strTbl & "." & vbCrLf _
        & "Before you activate this database, close the Excel _
            application."

Exit_CreateDb_DAO:
    Exit Sub
Error_CreateDb_DAO:
    If Err.Number = 3204 Then
        ' Delete the database file if it already exists
        Kill "C:\Exceldump.mdb"
        Resume
    Else
        MsgBox Err.Number & ": " & Err.Description
        Resume Exit_CreateDb_DAO
    End If
End Sub
```

Opening a Microsoft Access Form

You can open a Microsoft Access form from Microsoft Excel. You can also create a new form. The following example uses Automation to connect to Microsoft Access. Once the connection is established, the OpenCurrent-Database method is used to open the sample Northwind database. Next, the Customers form is opened with the OpenForm method of the DoCmd object. The form is opened in the normal view (acNormal). To display the form in the design view, use the acDesign constant instead. The Restore method of the DoCmd object ensures that the form is displayed on the screen in a window and not minimized. The Visible property of the Access Application object (objAccess) must be set to True for the form to become visible. Notice that the Access.Application object variable (objAccess) is declared at the top of the module. For this procedure to work correctly, you must set up a reference to the Microsoft Access Object Library. Figure 15-8 shows the Customers form after it's been opened.

```
' declare at the top of the module
Dim objAccess As Access.Application

Sub DisplayAccessForm()
    Dim strDb As String
    Dim strFrm As String
    strDb = "C:\Program Files\Microsoft Office\" _
        & "Office\Samples\Northwind.mdb"
    strFrm = "Customers"

Set objAccess = New Access.Application
    With objAccess
        .OpenCurrentDatabase(strDb)
```

```
            .DoCmd.OpenForm strFrm, acNormal
            .DoCmd.Restore
            .Visible = True
        End With
    End Sub
```

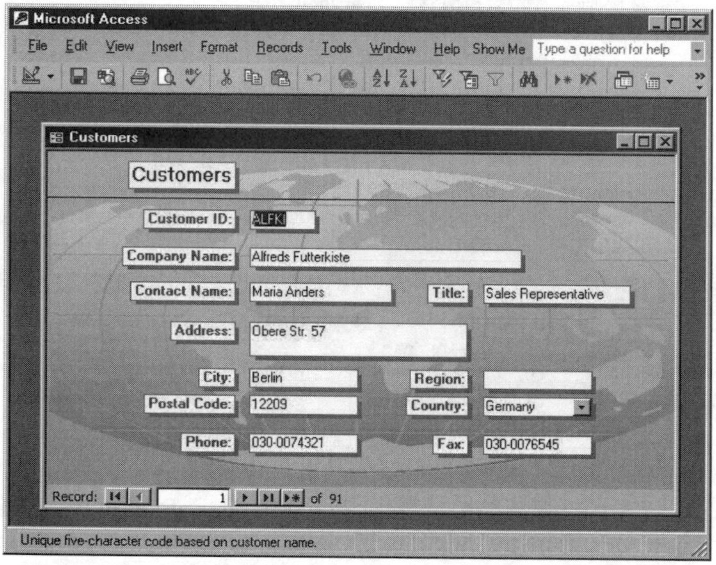

Figure 15-8: A Microsoft Access form can be opened by an Excel VBA procedure.

If you want to go a little bit further in your programming efforts, create a brand new Access form from within an Excel VBA procedure, as shown in this example:

```
' declare at the top of the module
Dim myAccess As Access.Application

Sub CreateAccessForm()
    Dim myForm As Form
    Dim myDb As String
    Dim myCtrl As Control
    Dim strFrmName As String

    On Error GoTo Error_CreateForm

    myDb = "C:\Program Files\Microsoft Office\" _
            & "Office\Samples\Northwind.mdb"
    strFrmName = "frmCustomForm"
    Set obAccess = New Access.Application
    obAccess.OpenCurrentDatabase myDb
    Set myForm = obAccess.CreateForm
    myForm.Caption = "Form created by Excel"
    myForm.RecordSource = "Employees"
    obAccess.DoCmd.Save , strFrmName
    ' Create a label and text box on the form
```

```
        Set myCtrl = CreateControl(FormName:=strFrmName, _
                                ControlType:=acLabel, _
                                Left:=1000, Top:=1000)

        myCtrl.Caption = "Last Name:"
        myCtrl.SizeToFit
        Set myCtrl = CreateControl(FormName:=strFrmName, _
                                ControlType:=acTextBox, _
                                Parent:="", _
                                ColumnName:="LastName", _
                                Left:=2200, Top:=1000)
    With obAccess
        With .DoCmd
            .Save , strFrmName
            .Close acForm, strFrmName
        End With
            .CloseCurrentDatabase
            .Quit
    End With
    Set obAccess = Nothing
    MsgBox "In the Northwind database there is now " & vbCrLf _
        & "a new form named " & strFrmName & "." & vbCrLf _
        & "Close Excel prior to opening the Northwind " & vbCrLf _
        & "database to view this form."
    ErrorHandler:
        Exit Sub
    Error_CreateForm:
        MsgBox Err & " :" & Err.Description
        Resume ErrorHandler
End Sub
```

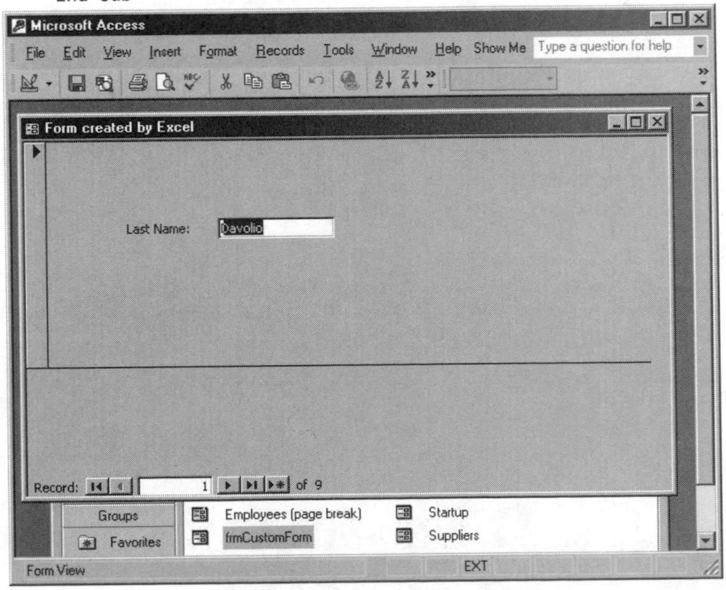

Figure 15-9: An Access form can be created by an Excel VBA procedure (see the code of the CreateAccessForm procedure shown above).

Opening a Microsoft Access Report

You can open a Microsoft Access report from Microsoft Excel. The following procedure demonstrates how you can display an existing Access report straight from Excel.

```
' declare at the top of the module
Dim objAccess As Access.Application

Sub DisplayAccessReport()
    Dim strDb As String
    Dim strRpt As String
    strDb = "C:\Program Files\Microsoft Office\" _
            & "Office\Samples\Northwind.mdb"
    strRpt = "Products by Category"

    Set objAccess = New Access.Application
        With objAccess
            .OpenCurrentDatabase (strDb)
            .DoCmd.OpenReport strRpt, acViewPreview
            .DoCmd.Maximize
            .Visible = True
        End With
End Sub
```

The example procedure below is more versatile, as it allows you to display any Access report in any Access database. Notice that this procedure takes two string arguments: the name of the Access database and the name of the report.

```
Sub DisplayAccessReport2(strDb As String, strRpt As String)

Set objAccess = New Access.Application
    With objAccess
        .OpenCurrentDatabase (strDb)
        .DoCmd.OpenReport strRpt, acViewPreview
        .DoCmd.Maximize
        .Visible = True
    End With
End Sub
```

You can run the DisplayAccessReport2 procedure from the Immediate window or from a subroutine, as shown below:

- Running the DisplayAccessReport2 procedure from the Immediate window:

```
' Enter the following statement on one line in the Immediate window
Call DisplayAccessReport2("C:\Program Files\Microsoft _
    Office\Office\Samples\Northwind.mdb", "Sales Totals by Amount")
```

- Running the DisplayAccessReport2 procedure from a subroutine:

```
' Enter the following procedure in the Code window

Sub ShowReport()
```

```
      Dim strDb As String
      Dim strRpt As String

   strDb = InputBox("Enter the name of the database (full path): ")
      strRpt = InputBox("Enter the name of the report:")
      Call DisplayAccessReport2(strDb, strRpt)
   End Sub
```

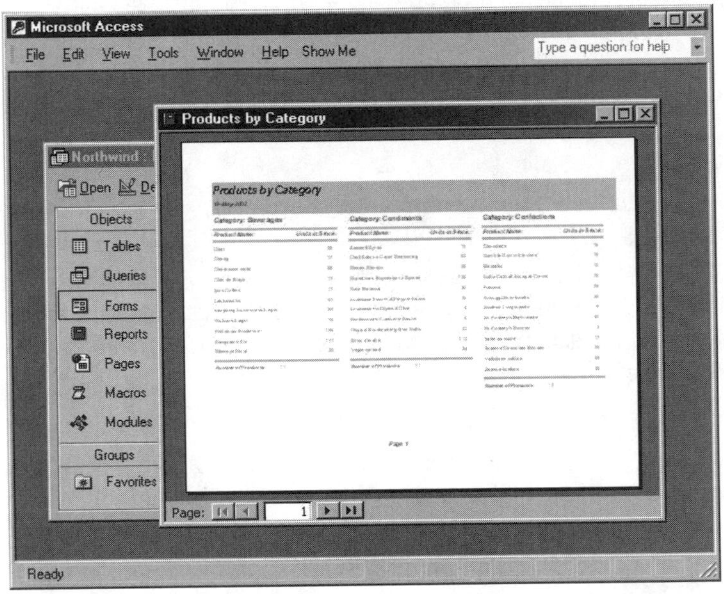

Figure 15-10: A Microsoft Access report can be opened by an Excel VBA procedure.

Running a Microsoft Access Query

The two example procedures that follow demonstrate how to run Microsoft Access queries from within an Excel VBA procedure. The most popular types of queries that are executed in the Access user interface are Select and Parameter queries. Both example procedures use the CopyFrom-Recordset method of the Range object to place the data returned by the query into an Excel worksheet. The connection with the database is established via the ADO.

The ADOX Object Library (see Figure 15-4 at the beginning of this chapter) gives you access to the database structure, security, and procedures that are stored in the database. The top object in this library is the Catalog object that represents the entire database. This object contains such database elements as tables, fields, indexes, views, and stored procedures. Using the Create method of the Catalog object, you can create a new database as follows:

```
Dim cat As ADOX.Catalog
Set cat = New ADOX.Catalog
cat.Create "Provider=Microsoft.Jet.OLEDB.4.0;" & _
    "Data Source=C:\ExcelDump2.mdb;"
```

The above example illustrates how you would create a new database using the ActiveX Data Objects. Recall that earlier in this chapter you created a new database called NewDB_DA by using the Data Access Objects.

The example procedure RunAccessQuery begins by creating an object variable cat that points to the Catalog object. Next, the ActiveConnection property of the Catalog object defines the method of establishing the connection to the database:

```
Set cat = New ADOX.Catalog
    cat.ActiveConnection = "Provider=Microsoft.Jet.OLEDB.4.0;" & _
        "Data Source=" & dbPath
```

The Command object in the ADODB Object Library (see Figure 15-3 at the beginning of this chapter) specifies the command that you want to execute in order to obtain data from the data source. Our procedure attempts to access a specific query in a database.

```
Set cmd = cat.Views(strQryName).Command
```

The Views collection, which is a part of the ADOX Object Library, contains all View objects of a specific catalog. View is a filtered set of records or a virtual table created from other tables or views. After gaining access to the required query in the database, you can run the query in the following way:

```
Set rst = cmd.Execute
```

The Execute method of the Command object allows you to activate a specific query, an SQL statement, or a stored procedure. The returned set of records is then assigned to the object variable of the type Recordset using the Set keyword. After creating the set of records, these records are placed in an Excel worksheet using the CopyFromRecordset method.

Running a Select Query

```
Sub RunAccessQuery(strQryName As String)
'   prior to running this procedure you must set up
'   references to the required object libraries

    Dim cat As ADOX.Catalog
    Dim cmd As ADODB.Command
    Dim rst As ADODB.Recordset
    Dim i As Integer
    Dim dbPath As String

    dbPath = "C:\Program Files\Microsoft Office\" _
        & "Office\Samples\Northwind.mdb"

    Set cat = New ADOX.Catalog
```

```
        cat.ActiveConnection = _
            "Provider=Microsoft.Jet.OLEDB.4.0;" & _
            "Data Source=" & dbPath
        Set cmd = cat.Views(strQryName).Command

        Set rst = cmd.Execute
        Sheets(2).Select
        For i = 0 To rst.Fields.Count - 1
            Cells(1, i + 1).Value = rst.Fields(i).Name
        Next
        With ActiveSheet
            .Range("A2").CopyFromRecordset rst
            .Range(Cells(1, 1), _
                Cells(1, rst.Fields.Count)).Font.Bold = True
            .Range("A1").Select
        End With
        Selection.CurrentRegion.Columns.AutoFit
        rst.Close
        Set cmd = Nothing
        Set cat = Nothing
End Sub
```

To run the above sub procedure, type the following statement in the Immediate window and press Enter:

```
RunAccessQuery("Current Product List")
```

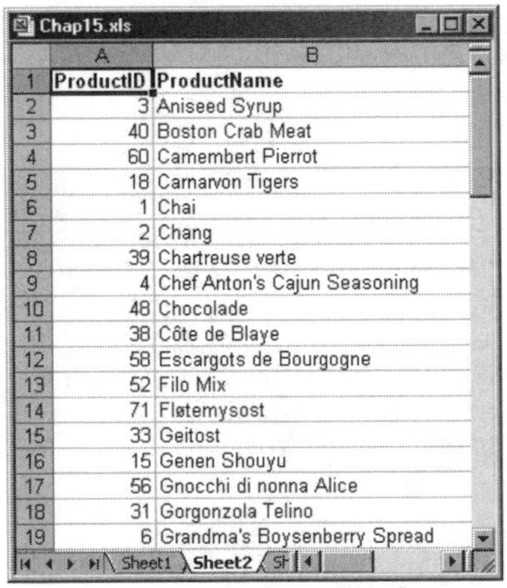

Figure 15-11: The results of running an Access query from an Excel VBA procedure are placed in a worksheet.

Running a Parameter Query

You can run a Microsoft Access parameter query and place the resulting data in a Microsoft Excel spreadsheet. For example, the RunAccessParamQuery procedure runs the Employee Sales by Country parameter query in the Microsoft Access database and retrieves the records for the period beginning 7/1/96 and ending 7/30/96. The Employee Sales by Country query requires two parameters that define the beginning and ending date.

These parameters should be defined using the Parameters collection of the Command object:

```
cmd.Parameters("[Beginning Date]") = StartDate
cmd.Parameters("[Ending Date]") = EndDate
```

After setting up the parameters, the query can be executed using the following statement:

```
Set rst = cmd.Execute
```

The set of records returned by this query is assigned to the object variable of type Recordset and then copied to a worksheet using the CopyFrom-Recordset method (see more information on using this method later in this chapter).

```
Sub RunAccessParamQuery()
'   prior to running this procedure you must set up
'   references to the required object libraries

    Dim cat As ADOX.Catalog
    Dim cmd As ADODB.Command
    Dim rst As ADODB.Recordset
    Dim i As Integer
    Dim dbPath As String
    Dim StartDate As String
    Dim EndDate As String

    dbPath = "C:\Program Files\Microsoft Office\" _
        & "Office\Samples\Northwind.mdb"
    StartDate = "7/1/96"
    EndDate = "7/31/96"

      Set cat = New ADOX.Catalog
        cat.ActiveConnection = "Provider=Microsoft.Jet.OLEDB.4.0;" & _
            "Data Source=" & dbPath

      Set cmd = cat.Procedures("Employee Sales by Country").Command
        cmd.Parameters("[Beginning Date]") = StartDate
        cmd.Parameters("[Ending Date]") = EndDate

      Set rst = cmd.Execute
        Sheets(1).Select
        For i = 0 To rst.Fields.Count - 1
            Cells(1, i + 1).Value = rst.Fields(i).Name
        Next
        With ActiveSheet
            .Range("A2").CopyFromRecordset rst
            .Range(Cells(1, 1), Cells(1, rst.Fields.Count)).Font. _
                Bold = True
            .Range("A1").Select
        End With
        Selection.CurrentRegion.Columns.AutoFit
        rst.Close
        Set cmd = Nothing
```

```
          Set cat = Nothing
      End Sub
```

Calling a Microsoft Access Function

You can run a built-in Microsoft Access function from Microsoft Excel through Automation. The example procedure below calls the EuroConvert function to convert 1000 Spanish pesetas to a Euro dollar. The EuroConvert function uses fixed conversion rates established by the European Union.

```
      Sub RunAccessFunction()
      Dim objAccess As Object
         On Error Resume Next
           Set objAccess = GetObject(, "Access.Application")
             'if no instance of Access is open, create a new one
             If objAccess Is Nothing Then
               Set objAccess = CreateObject("Access.Application")
             End If
           MsgBox "You will get " & _
              objAccess.EuroConvert(1000, "ESP", "EUR") & _
              " euro dollars. "
         Set objAccess = Nothing
      End Sub
```

Retrieving Microsoft Access Data into an Excel Worksheet

There are numerous ways to get external data into Excel. This section shows you the following different techniques of putting Microsoft Access data into an Excel worksheet:

- Using the GetRows method
- Using the CopyFromRecordset method
- Using the TransferSpreadsheet method
- Using the OpenDatabase method
- Creating a text file
- Creating a query table

Retrieving Data with the GetRows Method

To place Microsoft Access data into an Excel spreadsheet, you can use the GetRows method. This method returns a two-dimensional array where the first subscript is a number representing the field, and the second subscript is the number representing the record. Record and field numbering begins with 0.

You can programmatically return data to a Microsoft Excel worksheet by using Data Access Objects (DAO) in your VBA procedure. The following example procedure demonstrates how to run the Invoices query in the Northwind database and return records to a worksheet. For this procedure to work correctly, you must first establish a reference to the Microsoft Access 3.6 Object Library. Refer to the instructions on setting up a reference to object libraries earlier in this chapter.

After opening an Access database, the GetData_withDAO2 procedure illustrated below runs the Invoices query using the following statement:

```
Set qdf = db.QueryDefs("Invoices")
```

The QueryDefs object in the Microsoft Access 3.6 Object Library represents a Select or Action query. Select queries return data from one or more tables or queries, while Action queries allow you to modify data (you can add, modify, or delete records using Action queries).

After executing the query, the procedure places the records returned by the query in the object variable of type Recordset using the OpenRecordset method, as shown below:

```
Set rst = qdf.OpenRecordset
```

Next, the record count is retrieved using the RecordCount method and placed in the countR variable. Notice that to obtain the correct record count, the record pointer has to be moved to the last record in the recordset by using the MoveLast method.

```
rst.MoveLast
countR = rst.RecordCount
```

Next, the procedure prompts the user to enter the number of records to return to the worksheet. You can cancel at this point by clicking the Cancel button in the Input dialog box or typing the number of records to retrieve. If you enter a number that is greater than the record count, the procedure will retrieve all the records. Before retrieving records, you must move the record pointer to the first record by using the MoveFirst method. If you forget to do this, the record pointer will remain on the last record and only one record will be retrieved. The procedure then goes on to activate the Get Records worksheet and clear the current region. The records are first returned to the Variant variable containing a two-dimensional array by using the GetRows method of the Recordset object. Next, the procedure loops through both dimensions of the array to place the records in the worksheet starting at cell A2. When this is done, another loop will fill in the first worksheet row with the names of fields and autofit each column so that the data is displayed correctly.

```
Sub GetData_withDAO2()
    Dim db As DAO.Database
    Dim qdf As DAO.QueryDef
    Dim rst As DAO.Recordset
    Dim recArray As Variant
    Dim i As Integer
    Dim j As Integer
    Dim strPath As String
    Dim a As Variant
```

```
Dim countR As Long
Dim strShtName As String

strPath = "C:\Program Files\Microsoft Office\" _
          & "Office\Samples\northwind.mdb"
strShtName = "Returned records"
Set db = OpenDatabase(strPath)

Set qdf = db.QueryDefs("Invoices")
Set rst = qdf.OpenRecordset
rst.MoveLast
countR = rst.RecordCount

a = InputBox("This recordset contains " & _
    countR & " records." & vbCrLf _
    & "Enter number of records to return: ", _
    "Get Number of Records")

If a = "" Or a = 0 Then Exit Sub

If a > countR Then
    a = countR
    MsgBox "The number you entered is too large." & vbCrLf _
        & "All records will be returned."
End If

Workbooks.Add
  ActiveWorkbook.Worksheets(1).Name = strShtName
  rst.MoveFirst
    With Worksheets(strShtName).Range("A1")
        .CurrentRegion.Clear
        recArray = rst.GetRows(a)
        For i = 0 To UBound(recArray, 2)
            For j = 0 To UBound(recArray, 1)
                .Offset(i + 1, j) = recArray(j, i)
            Next j
        Next i
        For j = 0 To rst.Fields.Count - 1
            .Offset(0, j) = rst.Fields(j).Name
            .Offset(0, j).EntireColumn.AutoFit
        Next j
    End With
  db.Close
End Sub
```

Retrieving Data with the CopyFromRecordset Method

To retrieve an entire recordset into a worksheet, you can use the
CopyFromRecordset method of the Range object. This method can take up
to three arguments: Data, MaxRows, and MaxColumns. Only the first argument,
Data, is required. This argument can be the Recordset object. The optional
arguments, MaxRows and MaxColumns, allow you to specify the number of
records that should be returned (MaxRows) and the number of fields

(MaxColumns). If you omit the MaxRows argument, all the returned records will be copied to the worksheet. If you omit the MaxColumns argument, all the fields will be retrieved. The GetProducts procedure illustrated below establishes a connection with the Northwind database using the ADO objects. For this procedure to work correctly, you must create a reference to the Microsoft ActiveX Data Objects 2.6 Library (refer to the instructions on setting up a reference to object libraries earlier in this chapter).

```
Sub GetProducts()
    Dim conn As New ADODB.Connection
    Dim rst As ADODB.Recordset
    Dim strPath As String

    strPath = "C:\Program Files\Microsoft Office\" _
            & "Office\Samples\Northwind.mdb"

    conn.Open "Provider=Microsoft.Jet.OLEDB.4.0;" _
            & "Data Source=" & strPath & ";"
    conn.CursorLocation = adUseClient

    ' Create a Recordset from all the records
    ' in the Products table

    Set rst = conn.Execute(CommandText:="Products", _
                           Options:=adCmdTable)
    ' begin with the first record
    rst.MoveFirst
    ' transfer the data to Excel
    ' get the names of fields first
        With Worksheets("Sheet3").Range("A1")
            .CurrentRegion.Clear
            For j = 0 To rst.Fields.Count - 1
                .Offset(0, j) = rst.Fields(j).Name
            Next j
            .Offset(1, 0).CopyFromRecordset rst
            .CurrentRegion.Columns.AutoFit
        End With
    rst.Close
    conn.Close
End Sub
```

The above procedure copies all the records from the Products table in the Northwind database into an Excel worksheet. If you want to copy fewer records, you can use the MaxRows argument as follows:

```
.Offset(1, 0).CopyFromRecordset rst, 5
```

This statement tells Visual Basic to copy only five records. The Offset method causes the records to be entered in a spreadsheet, starting with the second spreadsheet row.

To send all the records to the worksheet using the data from only two table fields, use the following statement:

```
.Offset(1, 0).CopyFromRecordset rst, , 2
```

This statement tells Visual Basic to copy all the data from the first two columns. The comma between the rst and the number 2 is a placeholder for the omitted MaxRows argument.

Retrieving Data with the TransferSpreadsheet Method

It is possible to use the TransferSpreadsheet action to import or export data between the current Microsoft Access database (.mdb) or Access project (.adp) and a spreadsheet file. You can also link the data in a Microsoft Excel spreadsheet to the current Microsoft Access database. With a linked spreadsheet, you can view and edit the spreadsheet data with Microsoft Access while still allowing complete access to the data from your Microsoft Excel spreadsheet program.

The TransferSpreadsheet method carries out the TransferSpreadsheet action in Visual Basic and has the following syntax:

```
DoCmd.TransferSpreadsheet [transfertype][, spreadsheettype], _
    tablename, filename [, hasfieldnames][, range]
```

The transfertype argument can be one of the following constants: acImport (default setting), acExport, or acLink. These constants define whether data has to be imported, exported, or linked to the database.

The spreadsheettype argument can be one of the following constants:

0 **acSpreadsheetTypeExcel3** (default setting)
6 **acSpreadsheetTypeExcel4**
5 **acSpreadsheetTypeExcel5**
5 **acSpreadsheetTypeExcel7**
8 **acSpreadsheetTypeExcel8**
8 **acSpreadsheetTypeExcel9**
2 **acSpreadsheetTypeLotusWK1**
3 **acSpreadsheetTypeLotusWK3**
7 **acSpreadsheetTypeLotusWK4**

It is not difficult to guess that the spreadsheettype argument specifies the spreadsheet name and the version number.

The tablename argument is a string expression that specifies the name of the Microsoft Access table you want to import spreadsheet data into, export spreadsheet data from, or link spreadsheet data to. Instead of the table name, you may also specify the name of the Select query whose results you want to export to a spreadsheet.

The hasfieldnames argument is a logical value True (–1) or False (0). True indicates that the first worksheet row contains the field names. False denotes that the first row contains normal data. The default setting is False (no field names in the first row).

The range argument is a string expression that specifies the range of cells or the name of the range in the worksheet. This argument applies only to importing. If you omit the `range` argument, the entire spreadsheet will be imported. Leave this argument blank if you want to export, unless you need to specify the worksheet name.

The example procedure, ExportData, illustrated below exports data from the Shippers table in the Northwind database to the Shippers.xls spreadsheet using the TransferSpreadsheet method. Notice that this procedure uses Automation to establish a connection to Microsoft Access. After the connection has been established, the Northwind database is opened with the OpenCurrentDatabase method. After running the ExportData procedure, open the C:\Shippers.xls file to view the retrieved data.

```
' declare at the top of the module
Dim objAccess As Access.Application

Sub ExportData()
    Set objAccess = CreateObject("Access.Application")
    objAccess.OpenCurrentDatabase filepath:= _
        "C:\Program Files\Microsoft Office\Office\" _
        & "Samples\Northwind.mdb"
    objAccess.DoCmd.TransferSpreadsheet _
        TransferType:=acExport, _
        SpreadsheetType:=acSpreadsheetTypeExcel10, _
        TableName:="Shippers", _
        Filename:="C:\Shippers.xls", _
        HasFieldNames:=True, _
        Range:="Sheet1"
    objAccess.Quit
    Set objAccess = Nothing
End Sub
```

	A	B	C	D	E
1	ShipperID	CompanyName	Phone		
2	1	Speedy Express	(503) 555-9831		
3	2	United Package	(503) 555-3199		
4	3	Federal Shipping	(503) 555-9931		
5					
6					
7					
8					

Figure 15-12:
The data from a Microsoft Access table can be exported to Excel spreadsheet file using the TransferSpreadsheet method (see ExportData procedure listed above).

Using the OpenDatabase Method

Excel 2002 offers new method for working with databases. The OpenDatabase method, which applies to the Workbooks collection, is the easiest way to get the database data into a Microsoft Excel spreadsheet. This method requires that you specify the name of a database file you want to open. The following example procedure opens the Northwind database located in the C:\Program Files\Microsoft Office\Office10\Samples folder. When you run this procedure, Excel displays the dialog box listing all the tables and queries in the database (Figure 15-13). After making a selection from the list, a brand new workbook is open with the worksheet showing data from the selected table or query.

```
Sub OpenAccessDatabase()
    Workbooks.OpenDatabase _
    Filename:="C:\Program Files\Microsoft Office\" _
        & "Office10\Samples\Northwind.mdb"
End Sub
```

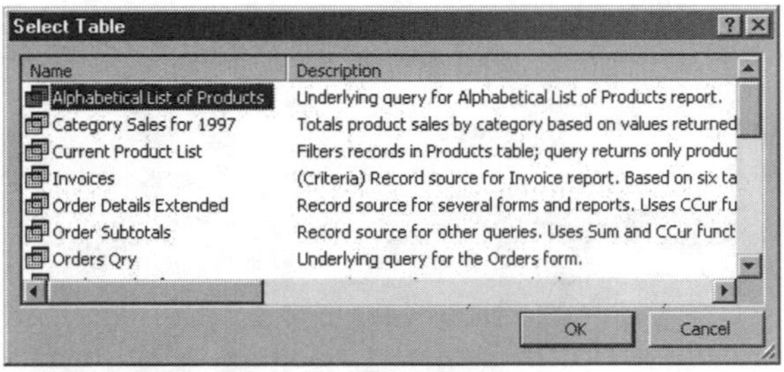

Figure 15-13:
Use the OpenDatabase method with one argument (database file name) to allow the selection of a table or query from a list box.

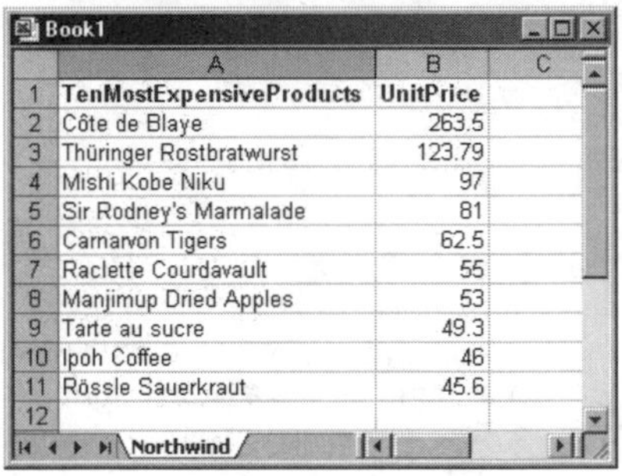

Figure 15-14:
Database data stored in a table or query can be easily retrieved into an Excel workbook using the OpenDatabase method introduced in Excel 2002.

The OpenDatabase method has four optional arguments that you can use to further qualify the data that you want to retrieve:

Optional Arguments for the OpenDatabase Method	Data Type	Description
CommandText	Variant	The SQL query string. See the following example for using this argument.
CommandType	Variant	The command type of the query. The following command types are available: Default, SQL, and Table.
BackgroundQuery	Variant	The background of the query. It can be one of the following constants: PivotCache or QueryTable.
ImportDataAs	Variant	Specifies the format of the query. Use xlQueryTable report or xlPivotTableReport to generate a Query table or PivotTable report out of the retrieved database data.

The following example procedure demonstrates how to use the OpenDatabase method with optional arguments. This procedure creates a PivotTable report out of the retrieved customer records. When you run the procedure, Excel displays a list of available fields based on the submitted query string. You can drag one or more fields to the Pivot table layout grid to create your PivotTable report. Figure 15-15 displays the CustomerId field by country.

```
Sub CountCustomersByCountry()
    Workbooks.OpenDatabase _
        Filename:="C:\Program Files\Microsoft Office\" _
            & "Office10\Samples\Northwind.mdb", _
        CommandText:="Select * from Customers", _
        BackgroundQuery:=PivotTable, _
        ImportDataAs:=xlPivotTableReport
    End Sub
```

	A	B	C	D
1				
2				
3	Count of CustomerID			
4	Country ▼	CustomerID ▼	Total	
5	Argentina	CACTU	1	
6		OCEAN	1	
7		RANCH	1	
8	Argentina Total		3	
9	Austria	ERNSH	1	
10		PICCO	1	
11	Austria Total		2	
12	Belgium	MAISD	1	
13		SUPRD	1	
14	Belgium Total		2	
15	Brazil	COMMI	1	
16		FAMIA	1	
17		GOURL	1	
18		HANAR	1	

Figure 15-15:
Using the OpenDatabase method's optional arguments, you can specify that the database data be retrieved into a specific format, such as a PivotTable report or a Query table report.

Creating a Text File from Microsoft Access Data

You can create a comma- or tab-delimited text file from Access data by using a VBA procedure in Excel. Text files are particularly useful for transferring large amounts of data to a spreadsheet. The example procedure below illustrates how you can create a tab-delimited text file from an ADO recordset. For this procedure to work correctly, you must establish a reference to the Microsoft ActiveX Data Objects 2.6 Library. Refer to Chapter 8 for details on working with text files. After running this procedure, open C:\ProductsOver50.txt in Excel.

```
Sub CreateTextFile()
    Dim strPath As String
    Dim conn As New ADODB.Connection
    Dim rst As ADODB.Recordset
    Dim strData As String
    Dim strHeader As String
    Dim strSQL As String

    strPath = "C:\Program Files\Microsoft Office\" _
            & "Office\Samples\Northwind.mdb"
    conn.Open "Provider=Microsoft.Jet.OLEDB.4.0;" _
```

```
                    & "Data Source=" & strPath & ";"
        conn.CursorLocation = adUseClient
        strSQL = "SELECT * FROM Products WHERE UnitPrice > 50"
        Set rst = conn.Execute(CommandText:=strSQL, Options:=adCmdText)
        'save the recordset as a tab-delimited file
        strData = rst.GetString(StringFormat:=adClipString, _
                            ColumnDelimeter:=vbTab, _
                            RowDelimeter:=vbCr, _
                            nullExpr:=vbNullString)
        Open "C:\ProductsOver50.txt" For Output As #1
        For Each f In rst.Fields
            strHeader = strHeader + f.Name & vbTab
        Next
        Print #1, strHeader
        Print #1, strData
        Close #1
    End Sub
```

In Chapter 8, you learned how to work with text files using the FileSystemObject. The procedure below demonstrates how to use this object to create a text file named ProductsOver100.txt:

```
Sub CreateTextFile2()
    Dim strPath As String
    Dim conn As New ADODB.Connection
    Dim rst As ADODB.Recordset
    Dim strData As String
    Dim strHeader As String
    Dim strSQL As String
    Dim fso As Object
    Dim myFile As Object

    Set fso = CreateObject("Scripting.FileSystemObject")
    Set myFile = fso.CreateTextFile("C:\ProductsOver100.txt", True)
    strPath = "C:\Program Files\Microsoft Office\" _
            & "Office\Samples\Northwind.mdb"

    conn.Open "Provider=Microsoft.Jet.OLEDB.4.0;" _
            & "Data Source=" & strPath & ";"
    conn.CursorLocation = adUseClient
    strSQL = "SELECT * FROM Products WHERE UnitPrice > 100"
    Set rst = conn.Execute(CommandText:=strSQL, Options:=adCmdText)

    'save the recordset as a tab-delimited file
    strData = rst.GetString(StringFormat:=adClipString, _
                    ColumnDelimeter:=vbTab, _
                    RowDelimeter:=vbCr, _
                    nullExpr:=vbNullString)
    For Each f In rst.Fields
        strHeader = strHeader + f.Name & vbTab
    Next
    With myFile
        .WriteLine strHeader
        .WriteLine strData
```

```
           .Close
        End With
     End Sub
```

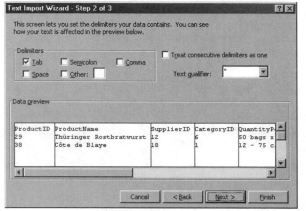

Figure 15-16:
Because text files can be easily opened in Excel, you can use them for transferring data between Microsoft Access and Microsoft Excel.

Creating a Query Table from Microsoft Access Data

If you want to work in Excel with data that comes from external data sources and you know that the data you'll be working with often undergoes changes, you may want to create a query table. A query table is a special table in an Excel worksheet that is connected to an external data source, such as a Microsoft Access database, SQL Server, web page, or text file. To retrieve the most up-to-date information, the user can easily refresh the query table. Microsoft Excel offers a special menu option for obtaining data from external data sources: simply choose Data | Import External Data and select New Database Query. By querying an external database, you can bring in data that fit your requirements exactly. For example, instead of bringing in all product information into your spreadsheet for a review, you may want to specify criteria that the data must meet prior to retrieval. Therefore, instead of bringing in all the products from an Access table, you may want to retrieve only products with a unit price greater than $20.

In VBA, you can use the QueryTable object to access external data. Each QueryTable object represents a worksheet table built from data returned from an external data source, such as an SQL server or a Microsoft Access database. To create a query programmatically, use the Add method of the QueryTables collection object. This method requires three arguments. The example procedure at the end of this section uses the following statement to create a query table on the active sheet:

```
Set myQryTable = ActiveSheet.QueryTables.Add(strConn, Dest, strSQL)
```

strConn is a variable that provides value for the first argument—Connection. This is a required argument of the Variant data type that specifies the data source for the query table.

Dest is a variable that provides value for the second argument—Destination. This is a required argument of the Range data type that specifies to the cell where the resulting query table will be placed.

strSQL is a variable that provides value for the third argument—SQL. This is a required argument of the String data type and defines the data to be returned by the query.

When you create a query using the Add method, the query isn't run until you call the Refresh method. This method accepts one argument—BackgroundQuery. This is an optional argument of the Variant data type that allows you to determine whether to return control to the procedure when a database connection has been established and the query has been submitted (True) or to return control to the procedure after the query has been run and all the data has been retrieved into the worksheet (False).

The CreateQueryTable procedure that follows only retrieves from the Northwind database's Products table those products whose UnitPrice field is greater than 20. Notice that the control is returned to the procedure only after all the relevant records have been fetched. The RefreshStyle method determines how data is inserted into the worksheet. The following constants can be used:

■ **xlOverwriteCells**—Existing cells are overwritten with the incoming data.

■ **xlInsertDeleteCells**—Cells are inserted or deleted to accommodate the incoming data.

■ **xlInsertEntireRows**—Entire rows are inserted to accommodate incoming data.

```
Sub CreateQueryTable()
    Dim myQryTable As Object
    Dim myDb As String
    Dim strConn As String
    Dim Dest As Range
    Dim strSQL As String

    myDb = "C:\Program Files\Microsoft Office\Office\" _
            & "Samples\Northwind.mdb"
    strConn = "OLEDB;Provider=Microsoft.Jet.OLEDB.4.0;" _
            & "Data Source=" & myDb & ";"
    Set Dest = Worksheets(1).Range("A1")
    strSQL = "SELECT * FROM Products WHERE UnitPrice>20"
    Set myQryTable = ActiveSheet.QueryTables.Add(strConn, _
                                        Dest, _
                                        strSQL)
    With myQryTable
        .RefreshStyle = xlInsertEntireRows
        .Refresh False
    End With
End Sub
```

	A	B	C	D	E	F	G
1	ProductID	ProductName	SupplierID	CategoryID	QuantityPerUnit	UnitPrice	UnitsInStock
2	4	Chef Anton's Cajun Seasoning	2	2	48 - 6 oz jars	22	53
3	5	Chef Anton's Gumbo Mix	2	2	36 boxes	21.35	0
4	6	Grandma's Boysenberry Spread	3	2	12 - 8 oz jars	25	120
5	7	Uncle Bob's Organic Dried Pears	3	7	12 - 1 lb pkgs.	30	15
6	8	Northwoods Cranberry Sauce	3	2	12 - 12 oz jars	40	6
7	9	Mishi Kobe Niku	4	6	18 - 500 g pkgs.	97	29
8	10	Ikura	4	8	12 - 200 ml jars	31	31
9	11	Queso Cabrales	5	4	1 kg pkg.	21	22
10	12	Queso Manchego La Pastora	5	4	10 - 500 g pkgs.	38	86
11	14	Tofu	6	7	40 - 100 g pkgs.	23.25	35
12	17	Alice Mutton	7	6	20 - 1 kg tins	39	0
13	18	Carnarvon Tigers	7	8	16 kg pkg.	62.5	42
14	20	Sir Rodney's Marmalade	8	3	30 gift boxes	81	40

Figure 15-17: Data from an external data source, such as a Microsoft Access database, can be analyzed in an Excel worksheet using the QueryTable object.

Using Microsoft Access Data in Excel

After retrieving data from a Microsoft Access database using one of the discussed methods, you can analyze the data using many of the Microsoft Excel built-in tools. Often, it is helpful to create charts based on the retrieved information.

Creating an Embedded Chart from Microsoft Access Data

Using VBA, you can easily create a chart based on the data retrieved from a Microsoft Access database. The ChartData procedure shown below uses the data fetched from the Microsoft Access Northwind database to create an embedded chart. The chart is created by using the Add method of the Charts collection. The source of the chart data is provided by the Range object. The CurrentRegion method returns all the non-blank cells surrounding cell A1. The remaining part of the procedure formats the chart by setting various properties. The chart code fragment has been recorded in a separate macro and then pasted into the VBA procedure with modifications made to the settings of some of the properties.

```
Sub ChartData()
Dim db As DAO.database
Dim qd As DAO.QueryDef
Dim rs As DAO.Recordset
Dim mySheet As Worksheet
Dim recArray As Variant
Dim i As Integer
Dim j As Integer
Dim pathDb As String
Dim qdName As String

pathDb = "C:\Program Files\Microsoft Office\" _
         & "Office\Samples\northwind.mdb"
qdName = "Category Sales for 1997"
Set db = OpenDatabase(pathDb)
```

```
Set qd = db.QueryDefs(qdName)
Set rs = qd.OpenRecordset
Set mySheet = Worksheets("Sheet2")
With mySheet.Range("A1")
      .CurrentRegion.Clear
      recArray = rs.GetRows(rs.RecordCount)
      For i = 0 To UBound(recArray, 2)
          For j = 0 To UBound(recArray, 1)
              .Offset(i + 1, j) = recArray(j, i)
          Next j
      Next i

      For j = 0 To rs.Fields.Count - 1
          .Offset(0, j) = rs.Fields(j).Name
          .Offset(0, j).EntireColumn.AutoFit
      Next j
End With

mySheet.Activate
    Charts.Add
    ActiveChart.ChartType = xl3DColumnClustered
    ActiveChart.SetSourceData _
    Source:=mySheet.Cells(1, 1).CurrentRegion, PlotBy:=xlRows
    ActiveChart.Location Where:=xlLocationAsObject, Name:=mySheet.Name
    With ActiveChart
        .HasTitle = True
        .ChartTitle.Characters.Text = qdName
        .Axes(xlCategory).HasTitle = True
        .Axes(xlCategory).AxisTitle.Characters.Text = ""
        .Axes(xlSeries).HasTitle = False
        .Axes(xlValue).HasTitle = True
        .Axes(xlValue).AxisTitle.Characters.Text = mySheet.Range("B1") _
            & "($)"
        .Axes(xlValue).AxisTitle.Orientation = xlUpward
    End With
db.Close
End Sub
```

The result of running the ChartData procedure is shown in Figure 15-18.

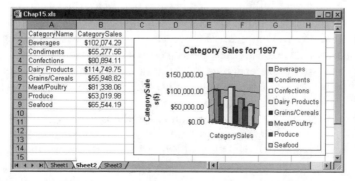

Figure 15-18:
You can create an embedded chart programmatically with VBA based on the data retrieved from a Microsoft Access table, a query, or an SQL statement.

Transferring the Excel Spreadsheet to an Access Database

Many of the world's biggest databases began as spreadsheets. When the time comes to build a database application from your spreadsheet, you can resort to a tedious manual method to transfer the data, or you can use your new VBA programming skills to automatically turn your spreadsheets into database tables. Once in a database format, your Excel data can be used in advanced company-wide reports or as a stand-alone application (needless to say, the latter requires that you possess database application design skills). The remaining sections of this chapter demonstrate how to link and import Excel spreadsheets to an Access database. Prior to moving your Excel data to Access, you should clean up the data as much as possible so the transfer operation goes smoothly. Keep in mind that each spreadsheet row you'll be transferring will become a record in a table, and each column will function as a table field. For this reason, the first row of the spreadsheet range that you are planning to transfer to Access should contain field names. There should be no gaps between the columns of data that you want to transfer. In other words, your data should be contiguous. If the data you want to transfer represents a large number of columns, you should print your data first and examine it so that there are no surprises later. If the first column of your data contains the field names, it is recommended that you use the built-in Transpose feature to reposition your data so that the data goes down rather than from left to right. The key to a smooth data import is to make your spreadsheet look as much like a database table as possible.

Linking an Excel Spreadsheet to a Microsoft Access Database

You can link an Excel spreadsheet to a Microsoft Access database by using the TransferSpreadsheet method (refer to the "Retrieving Data with the TransferSpreadsheet Method" section in this chapter for the details on working with this method). The following example procedure links the spreadsheet shown in Figure 15-19 to the Northwind database. After opening the Access database with the OpenCurrentDatabase method, the procedure uses the TransferSpreadsheet method of the Microsoft Access DoCmd object to create a linked table named ExcelSheet from the specified range of cells (A1:D7) located in the mySheet worksheet in the Chap15.xls spreadsheet file. Notice that the −1 argument in the DoCmd statement indicates that the first row of the spreadsheet contains column headings. Next, the procedure opens the linked table in Edit mode, so the user can add or modify data. If you change back to Excel after adding one or more records, you'll notice that the changes made in the linked Access table are immediately available in Excel.

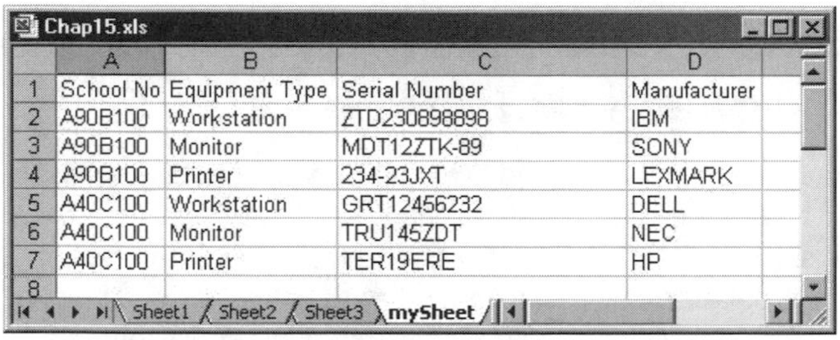

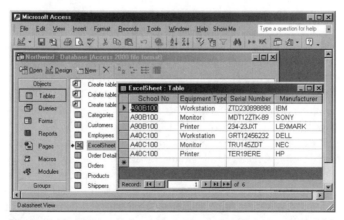

Figure 15-19: The LinkExcel_ToAccess VBA procedure links this spreadsheet to the Northwind database in Microsoft Access.

```
Sub LinkExcel_ToAccess()
    Dim objAccess As Access.Application
    Dim strName As String

    strName = "Linked_ExcelSheet"
    Set objAccess = New Access.Application
    With objAccess
        .OpenCurrentDatabase "C:\Program Files\Microsoft Office\" _
            & "Office\Samples\Northwind.mdb"
        .DoCmd.TransferSpreadsheet acLink, acSpreadsheetTypeExcel9, _
            strName, _
            "C:\Chap15.xls", _
            -1, "mySheet!A1:D7"
        .DoCmd.OpenTable strName, acViewNormal, acEdit
    End With
End Sub
```

Figure 15-20: A Microsoft Excel spreadsheet can be linked to a Microsoft Access database.

Importing an Excel Spreadsheet to a Microsoft Access Database

In the previous section, you learned how to link your Excel spreadsheet to an Access database. Importing your spreadsheet data is just as easy. You can even use the same VBA procedure you used for linking with one minor change: simply replace the acLink constant with acImport, and you are done. The following procedure imports the spreadsheet presented in Figure 15-19 (see the previous section) into the Northwind database.

```
Sub ImportExcel_ToAccess()
    Dim objAccess As Access.Application
    Dim strName As String

    strName = "Imported_ExcelSheet"
    Set objAccess = New Access.Application
    With objAccess
        .OpenCurrentDatabase "C:\Program Files\Microsoft Office\" _
            & "Office\Samples\Northwind.mdb"
        .DoCmd.TransferSpreadsheet acImport, acSpreadsheetTypeExcel9, _
            strName, _
            "C:\Chap15.xls", _
            -1, "mySheet!A1:D7"
        .DoCmd.OpenTable strName, acViewNormal, acEdit
    End With
End Sub
```

Placing Excel Data in an Access Table

What if, rather then linking or embedding your Excel spreadsheet, you wanted to create an Access table from scratch and load it with the data sitting in a worksheet? Using several programming techniques that you've already acquired in this book, you can easily achieve this task. Let's look at the VBA procedure that dynamically creates an Access table based on the Excel worksheet presented in Figure 15-19 (see the section "Linking an Excel Spreadsheet to a Microsoft Access Database"). Notice that this procedure connects to the Access database using ActiveX Data Objects (ADO) and the MicrosoftJet.OLEDB.4.0 provider. After the connection is established, the procedure creates a new Access table by using the Catalog and Table objects from the ADOX object library. Next, the fields are added to the table that correspond to the names of the spreadsheet columns. Notice that each text field specifies the maximum number of characters that it can accept. If the spreadsheet cell's length is larger than the specified field size, the error handler routine will display the Access built-in message appropriate for this error and the procedure will end.

The final task in the procedure is the data transfer operation. To perform this task, the procedure opens a Recordset object for an Access table.

Because you need to add records to the table, the procedure uses an adOpenKeyset cursor type. Now that the table is open, the procedure uses the For...Next loop to move through the Excel data rows, placing information found in each cell into the corresponding table field. Notice that a new record is added to an Access table with the AddNew method of the Recordset object. After copying data from all cells in each row, the procedure uses the Update method of the Recordset object to save the table record.

```
Sub AccessTbl_From_ExcelData()
    Dim conn As ADODB.Connection
    Dim cat As ADOX.Catalog
    Dim myTbl As ADOX.Table
    Dim rstAccess As ADODB.Recordset
    Dim rowCount As Integer
    Dim i As Integer

    On Error GoTo ErrorHandler

  ' connect to Access using ADO
    Set conn = New ADODB.Connection
    conn.Open "Provider = Microsoft.Jet.OLEDB.4.0;" & "Data Source = _
        C:\Program Files\Microsoft Office\Office\Samples\Northwind.mdb;"

  ' create an empty Access table
    Set cat = New Catalog
    cat.ActiveConnection = conn
    Set myTbl = New ADOX.Table
    myTbl.Name = "TableFromExcel"
    cat.Tables.Append myTbl

  ' add fields (columns) to the table
    With myTbl.Columns
        .Append "School No", adVarWChar, 7
        .Append "Equipment Type", adVarWChar, 15
        .Append "Serial Number", adVarWChar, 15
        .Append "Manufacturer", adVarWChar, 20
    End With
    Set cat = Nothing

    MsgBox "The table structure was created."

    ' open a recordset based on the newly created
    ' Access table

    Set rstAccess = New ADODB.Recordset
    With rstAccess
        .ActiveConnection = conn
        .CursorType = adOpenKeyset
        .LockType = adLockOptimistic
        .Open myTbl.Name
    End With
```

```
        ' now transfer data from Excel spreadsheet range

    With Worksheets("mySheet")
        rowCount = Range("A2:D7").Rows.Count

      For i = 2 To rowCount + 1
            With rstAccess
                .AddNew    ' add a new record to an Access table
                .Fields("School No") = Cells(i, 1).Text
                .Fields("Equipment Type") = Cells(i, 2).Value
                .Fields("Serial Number") = Cells(i, 3).Value
                .Fields("Manufacturer") = Cells(i, 4).Value
                .Update    ' update the table record
            End With
        Next i
    End With

      ' close the Recordset and Connection object and remove them
      ' from memory
      rstAccess.Close
      conn.Close
      Set rstAccess = Nothing
      Set conn = Nothing

AccessTbl_From_ExcelDataExit:
      Exit Sub
ErrorHandler:
      MsgBox Err.Number & ": " & Err.Description
      Resume AccessTbl_From_ExcelDataExit
End Sub
```

What's Next...

This chapter presented various examples of getting Excel data into a Microsoft Access database and retrieving data from Microsoft Access into a worksheet. You learned how to control an Access application from an Excel VBA procedure, performing such tasks as opening Access forms and reports, creating new forms, running Select and Parameter queries, and calling Access built-in functions. In addition, this chapter showed you techniques for creating text files, query tables, and charts out of the Access data. You also learned how to place Excel data in an Access database by using linked, imported, and dynamic Access tables.

In the next chapter, you will learn how to use Excel to create, view, and analyze Internet data.

Chapter 16

Excel and the Internet

Creating Hyperlinks Using VBA ■ **Creating and Publishing HTML Files Using VBA** ■ Web Server — Storing and Opening Workbooks ■ **Web Queries** ■ Creating and Running Web Queries with VBA ■ Web Queries with Parameters ■ Dynamic Web Queries ■ Refreshing Data ■ **Excel and Active Server Pages** ■ Creating an ASP Script ■ Installing Internet Information Services (IIS) or Personal Web Server ■ Creating a Virtual Directory ■ Running Your First ASP Script ■ Generating a Tab-delimited File on the Web Server ■ Creating an Excel File from User Input ■ Printing Excel Data to an Internet Browser using the GetString Method ■ Creating Charts in ASP ■ **What's Next...**

The dramatic growth of the Internet that we've been witnessing over the past several years makes it possible to gain access to enormous knowledge archives scattered all over the world. Thanks to the Internet, we now have at our fingertips databases covering various industries and fields of knowledge, dictionaries and encyclopedias, stock quotes, maps, weather forecasts, and a great deal of other types of information stored on millions of existing web servers. Often, the information retrieved from web pages becomes a subject of further analysis by computer programs. Thanks to its structure (rows and columns), Microsoft Excel 2002 is a preferred tool for working with table data found on the Internet. Using Excel, you can easily create, publish, review, and analyze data.

This chapter demonstrates the built-in tools available in Excel 2002 for retrieving data from the web and publishing Excel spreadsheets on the web. You will find many Visual Basic statements here that will allow you to obtain and publish data using custom-written Visual Basic procedures. To maximize your benefit from this chapter, you should have a connection to the Internet (a modem, telephone line, or cable, an account with an Internet service provider, and an Internet browser such as Microsoft Internet Explorer 5.0 or higher).

Creating Hyperlinks Using VBA

Excel 2002, like other applications in Microsoft Office, allows you to create hyperlinks in your spreadsheets. After clicking on a cell that contains a hyperlink, you can open a document located on a network server, an intranet, or the Internet. Hyperlinks can be created directly in the user interface with the Insert | Hyperlink option (Figure 16-1) or programmatically using VBA.

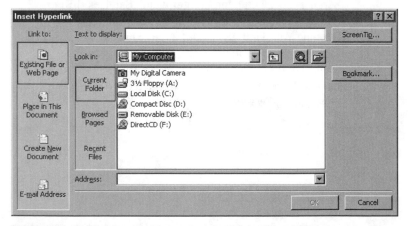

Figure 16-1: A dialog box used to insert a hyperlink in Microsoft Excel

In VBA, each hyperlink is represented by a Hyperlink object. To create a hyperlink to a web page, use the Add method of the Hyperlinks collection. This method is shown below:

```
Expression.Hyperlinks.Add(Anchor, Address, [SubAddress], [ScreenTip], _
    [TextToDisplay])
```

The arguments in square brackets are optional. Expression denotes a worksheet or range of cells where you want to place the hyperlink. Anchor is an object to be clicked. This can be either a Range or Shape object. Address points to a local network or a web page. SubAddress is the name of a range in the Excel file. ScreenTip allows the display of a screen label. TextToDisplay is a friendly name that you'd like to display in a spreadsheet cell for a specific hyperlink.

Let's see how this is done by creating a VBA procedure that places a hyperlink in a worksheet cell. This hyperlink, when clicked, should take you to the Yahoo site.

1. Open a new workbook.

2. Switch to the Visual Basic Editor screen, and insert a new module into the current VBA project.

3. In the Code window, enter the code of the FollowMe procedure shown below.

4. Activate the procedure created in step 3.

```
Sub FollowMe()
Dim myRange As Range
Set myRange = Sheets(1).Range("A1")
myRange.Hyperlinks.Add _
    Anchor:=myRange, _
    Address:="http://search.yahoo.com/bin/search", _
    ScreenTip:="Search Yahoo", _
    TextToDisplay:="Click here"
End Sub
```

When you activate the FollowMe procedure, cell A1 in the first worksheet will contain a friendly hyperlink "Click here" with the screen tip "Search Yahoo" (Figure 16-2). If you are now connected to the Internet, clicking on this hyperlink will activate your browser and load the Yahoo search engine (Figure 16-3).

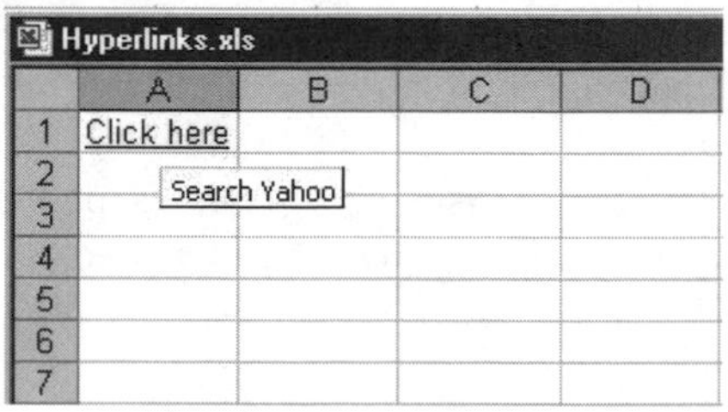

Figure 16-2:
This hyperlink was placed in a worksheet by a VBA procedure.

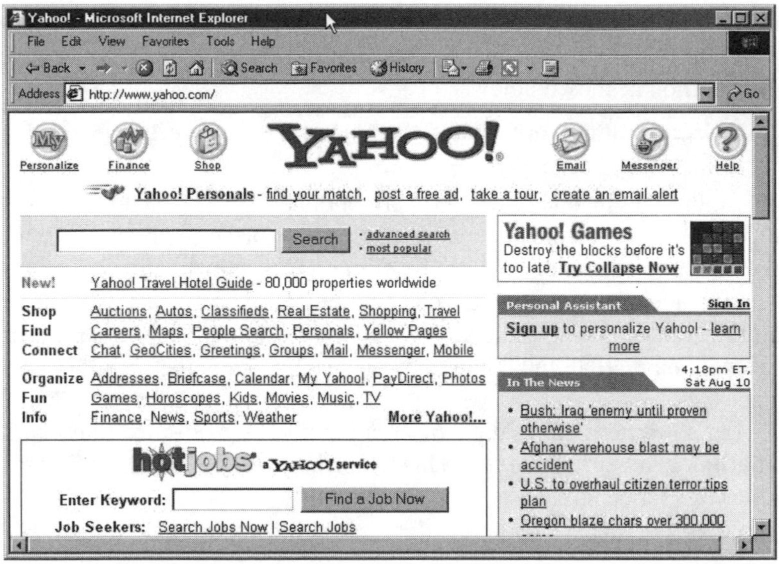

Figure 16-3: The main page of the Yahoo search engine was activated by clicking on the hyperlink placed in a worksheet cell.

If you'd rather not place hyperlinks in a worksheet but still make it possible for a user to reach the required Internet pages directly from the Excel worksheet, you can use the FollowHyperlink method. This method allows you to open the required web page without the need to place a hyperlink object in a worksheet. The format of this method looks like this:

```
Expression.FollowHyperlink(Address, [SubAddress], [NewWindow], _
     [AddHistory], [ExtraInfo], [Method], [HeaderInfo])
```

Again, the arguments in square brackets are optional. Expression returns a Workbook object. Address is the address of the web page that you want to activate. SubAddress is a fragment of the object to which the hyperlink address points. This can be a range of cells in an Excel worksheet. NewWindow indicates whether you want to display the document or page in a new window. The default setting is False. The next argument, AddHistory, is not currently used. It is reserved for future use. ExtraInfo gives additional information that allows jumping to the specific location in a document or on a web page. For example, you can specify here the text for which you want to search. Method specifies the method in which the additional information (ExtraInfo) is attached. This can be one of the following constants: msoMethodGet or msoMethodPost.

When you use msoMethodGet, ExtraInfo is a String that's appended to the URL address. When using msoMethodPost, ExtraInfo is posted as a String or byte array.

The last optional argument, HeaderInfo, is a String that specifies header information for the HTTP request. The default value is an empty string.

Let's see how to use the FollowHyperlink method in a VBA procedure. The purpose of this procedure is to find any text entered in a worksheet cell using the AltaVista search engine.

1. In the Visual Basic Editor window, activate the Project Explorer window and double-click the **Sheet2 (Sheet2)** object in the Microsoft Excel Objects folder.

2. In the Code window, enter the Worksheet_BeforeDoubleClick procedure shown below (review Chapter 14 on creating and using event procedures in Excel):

```
Private Sub Worksheet_BeforeDoubleClick(ByVal Target As Range, _
                        Cancel As Boolean)
    Dim strSearch As String

    strSearch = Sheets(2).Range("C3").Formula
        If Target = Range("C3") Then
            Cancel = True
            ActiveWorkbook.FollowHyperlink _
                Address:="http://www.altavista.com/cgi-bin/query", _
                ExtraInfo:="q=" & strSearch, _
                Method:=msoMethodGet
        End If
End Sub
```

3. Now switch to the Microsoft Excel application window and enter in cell C3 on sheet 2 any word or term you want to find information about (Figure 16-4).

4. Make sure that you are connected to Internet.

5. Double-click cell **C3**. This will cause the text entered in cell C3 to be sent to the AltaVista search engine. The screen should show the index to found topics with the specified criteria (Figure 16-5).

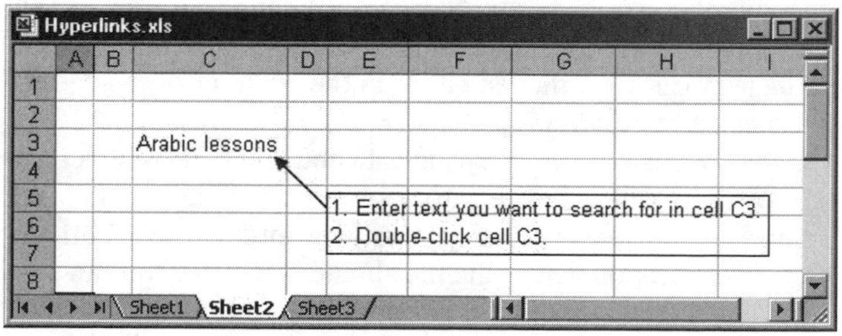

Figure 16-4: Microsoft Excel worksheets can be used to send search parameters to any search engine on the Internet (see procedure Worksheet_BeforeDoubleClick in step 2 above).

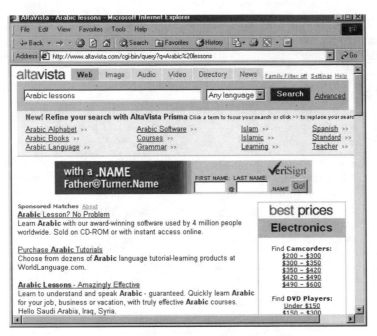

Figure 16-5: A web page opened from a Microsoft Excel worksheet lists topics that were found based on the criteria entered in a worksheet cell (see also Figure 16-4).

Creating and Publishing HTML Files Using VBA

Like previous versions, Excel 2002 allows you to save files in the HTML (Hypertext Markup Language) format. This format is recognized by Excel just like its standard .xls format. When you save an Excel file in the HTML format, you can view the spreadsheets using an Internet browser, such as Internet Explorer or Netscape Navigator. When you save a workbook or its part as HTML, Excel saves the options of the original workbook. Thanks to this, the user can view the file either in the browser or inside the Microsoft Excel application window.

Excel 2002 is capable of saving data and charts as interactive web pages. While saving an entire workbook or its part in the HTML format, you can choose between creating a static or interactive HTML document and specify a location where the file should be saved. You can save your files directly to the web server, a network server, or a local computer.

Working with nothing else but the user interface (File | Save as Web Page) you can place an entire workbook or its parts on the web page, so users can work with its information interactively or only view the data. Detailed instructions on how to place an entire workbook or any worksheet (or one of its elements — such as chart, PivotTable report) on a web page can be found in Excel online help. Because this book is about programming, we will focus only on the way these tasks are performed via VBA code.

Figure 16-6: The Save As dialog box that appears after choosing Save As Web Page from the File menu allows saving the workbook as a web page.

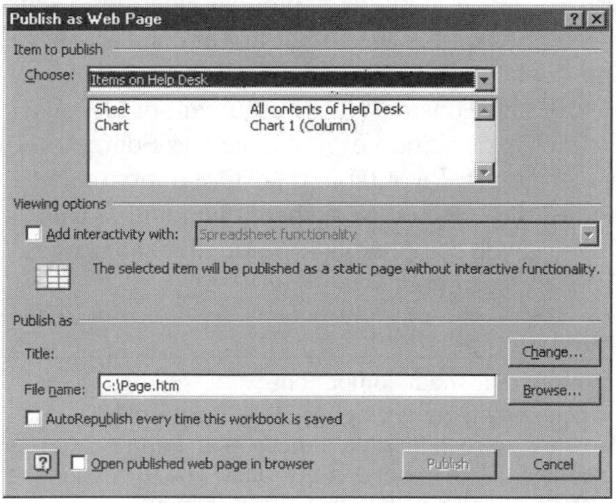

Figure 16-7: The Publish as Web Page dialog box appears after clicking the Publish button on the Save As dialog box (see Figure 16-6).

The Visual Basic for Applications (VBA) object library in Excel 2002 offers objects for publishing worksheets on web pages. To programmatically create and publish Excel files in the HTML format, you should become familiar with the PublishObject object and the PublishObjects collection.

　　PublishObject represents a worksheet element that was saved on a web page, while PublishObjects is a collection of all PublishObject objects of a specific workbook. To add a worksheet element to the PublishObjects collection, use its Add method. This method will create an object representing a specific worksheet element that was saved as a web page. The format of the Add method looks like this:

```
expression.Add(SourceType, Filename, [Sheet], [Source], [HtmlType], _
    [DivID], [Title])
```

The arguments in square brackets are optional. Expression returns an object that belongs to the PublishObjects collection. SourceType specifies the source object using one of the following constants:

Constant	Description
xlSourceAutoFilter	An AutoFilter range
xlSourceChart	A chart
xlSourcePivotTable	A PivotTable report
xlSourcePrintArea	A range of cells selected for printing
xlSourceQuery	A query table (an external data range)
xlSourceRange	A range of cells
xlSourceSheet	An entire worksheet

Filename is a string specifying the location where the source object (SourceType) was saved. This can be a URL (Unified Resource Locator) or the path to a local or network file. Sheet is the name of the worksheet that was saved as a web page. Source is a unique name that identifies a source object. This argument depends on the SourceType argument. Source is a range of cells or a name applied to a range of cells when the SourceType argument is the xlSourceRange constant. If the argument of SourceType is a constant, such as xlSourceChart, xlSourcePivotTable or xlSourceQuery, Source specifies a name of a chart, PivotTable report, or query table. HTMLType specifies whether the selected worksheet element is saved as an interactive Microsoft Office web component or static text and images. This can be one of the following constants:

Constant	Description
xlHTMLCalc	Use the Spreadsheet component. This component makes it possible to view, analyze, and calculate spreadsheet data directly in an Internet browser. This component also has options that allow you to change the formatting of fonts, cells, rows, and columns.
xlHTMLChart	Use the Chart component. This component allows you to create interactive charts in the browser.
xlHTMLList	Use the PivotTable component. This component allows you to rearrange, filter, and summarize information in a browser. This component is also able to display data from a spreadsheet or a database (for instance Microsoft Assess, SQL Server or OLAP servers).
XlHTMLStatic (default value)	Use static (non-interactive) HTML for viewing only. The data published in an HTML document does not change.

Note: The Office Web Components allow you to use Excel analytical options in an Internet browser.

DivID is a unique identifier used in the HTML DIV tag to identify the item on the web page. Title is the title of the web page.

Before we can see how to use the Add method from a VBA procedure, you also need to learn how to use the Publish method of the PublishObject. This method will allow you to publish an element or a collection of elements in a particular document on the web page. This method is quite simple and looks like this:

```
expression.Publish([Create])
```

Expression is an expression that returns a PublishObject object or PublishObjects collection. The optional argument, Create, is used only with a PublishObject. If the HTML file already exists, setting this argument to True will overwrite the file. Setting this argument to False inserts the item or items at the end of the file. If the file does not yet exist, a new HTML file is created, regardless of the value of the Create argument.

Now that you've been introduced to VBA objects and methods used for creating and publishing an Excel workbook in HTML format, you can begin programming. In the following exercises, you will create two VBA procedures. The first one will create and publish an Excel worksheet with an embedded chart as static HTML. The second procedure will demonstrate how the same worksheet can be made available as an interactive web page.

1. Create a worksheet and chart, as shown in Figure 16-8.

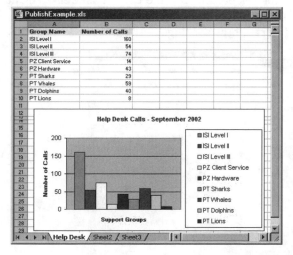

Figure 16-8:
A worksheet like this one with an embedded chart can be placed on a web page using the Save As Web Page option on the File menu or programmatically from a VBA procedure.

2. Save the workbook in a file named **PublishExample.xls**.

3. Activate the Visual Basic Editor window, and insert a new module into the current VBA project.

4. In the Code window, enter the two procedures shown below. The first one, PublishOnWeb, publishes on a web page a worksheet with an embedded chart as static HTML. The second procedure, CreateHTML-File, calls the PublishOnWeb procedure and feeds it the two required arguments: the name of the workbook that you want to publish and the name of the HTML file where the data should be saved.

```
' The procedure below will publish a worksheet
' with an embedded chart as static HTML

Sub PublishOnWeb(strSheetName As String, strFileName As String)

    Dim objPub As Excel.PublishObject
    Set objPub = ThisWorkbook.PublishObjects.Add( _
        SourceType:=xlSourceSheet, _
        Filename:=strFileName, Sheet:=strSheetName, _
        HtmlType:=xlHtmlStatic, Title:="Calls Analysis")
    objPub.Publish True
End Sub

Sub CreateHTMLFile()
    Call PublishOnWeb("Help Desk", "C:\WorksheetWithChart.htm")

End Sub
```

5. After entering both procedures, run the procedure named Create-HTMLFile. When this procedure finishes, you will see a new file called C:\WorksheetWithChart.htm. Also, there will be a folder named WorksheetWithChart_files storing supplemental files.

6. In Windows Explorer, double-click the **C:\WorksheetWithChart.htm** file created in step 5. This action will cause the published worksheet to appear in an Internet browser (Figure 16-9).

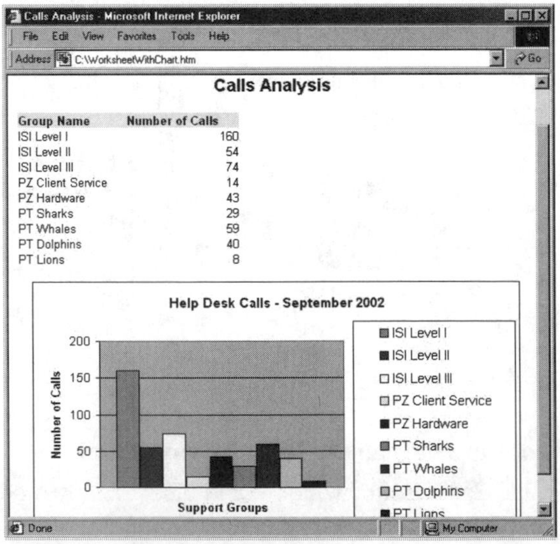

Figure 16-9:
An Excel worksheet published as a static (non-interactive) web page

To interactively publish the example worksheet with the embedded chart shown in Figure 16-8, perform the following:

1. In the Visual Basic Editor window, insert a new module into the current VBA project.

2. In the Code window, enter the InterHTML procedure, as shown below.

```
Sub InterHTML()
    Dim strSheetName As String
    strSheetName = "Help Desk"

    ' ensure that the chart is not selected
    Range("A1").Select
    ActiveWorkbook.PublishObjects _
        .Add(xlSourceChart, "C:\Inter_WorksheetWithChart.htm", _
            strSheetName, "Chart 1", xlHtmlChart).Publish (True)
End Sub
```

3. Run the procedure you've just created.

4. In Windows Explorer, double-click **C:\Inter_WorksheetWith-Chart.htm**. This will cause an Internet browser to be activated with the interactive chart (Figure 16-10). The web page also contains the interactive worksheet that supplies the chart data.

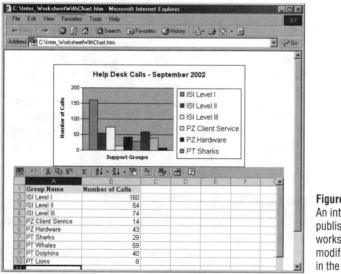

Figure 16-10: An interactively published Excel worksheet can be modified directly in the browser.

5. Change any values in column B, and see the changes on the chart.

Note: To interactively use data, you must have Microsoft Internet Explorer 4.01 or higher and Microsoft Office Web Components installed on your computer.

Web Server — Storing and Opening Workbooks

It is possible to save and open workbooks stored on a web server by using VBA statements. However, before you can store your workbooks on a web server, FrontPage Server Extensions must be running on the server.

The following statement saves a workbook to a web site:

```
ActiveWorkbook.SaveAs "http://www.yourWebSite.com/TestWkb.xls"
```

The following statement opens a workbook stored on a web site:

```
Workbooks.Open("http://www.yourWebSite.com/TestWkb.xls")
```

Web Queries

If you are planning to retrieve data from a web page to use and analyze it in Excel, you can open Excel's Data menu and select Import External Data | New Web Query. Web queries allow you to retrieve data from the web directly into Microsoft Excel. After placing data in a worksheet, you can use Excel tools for performing data analysis. Using a web query, you can retrieve into a worksheet a single table, a number of tables, or all the text that a particular web site contains.

Tip 16-1: Ready-to-Use Web Queries

Microsoft Excel 2002 comes with several built-in web queries. They are installed in the C:\Program Files\Microsoft Office\Office10\ Queries folder, and can be loaded in Excel via the Open command on the File menu. The names of these queries are:

MSN MoneyCentral Investor Currency Rates.iqy
MSN MoneyCentral Investor Major Indicies.iqy
MSN MoneyCentral Investor Stock Quotes.iqy

If your C:\Program Files\Microsoft Office\Office10\Queries folder is empty, you may need to update your current installation of Excel (use the Control Panel's Add/Remove Programs dialog box) and indicate that you want these features to be installed.

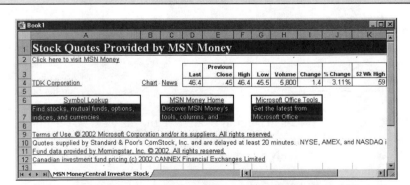

Figure 16-11: TDK corporation stock quotes were retrieved from the web using the built-in web query MSN MoneyCentral Investor Stock Quotes.iqy after typing TDK in a dialog box displayed upon activating this query.

To run web queries, you must have an active connection to the Internet.

Figure 16-12: This dialog box in the user interface allows you to create a web query without knowing anything about programming.

Web queries can be static or dynamic. Static queries always return the same data, while dynamic queries allow the user to specify different parameters to narrow down the data returned from the web page. Web queries are stored in text files with the .iqy extension. The content of the .iqy file can be viewed after opening the file in any text editor (for instance, Windows Notepad).

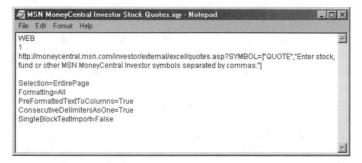

Figure 16-13: The web query file references the page from which you want to retrieve data and specifies parameters to define how data should be imported and any special instructions for the web server.

The .iqy files contain the following parts:

Section name	Description/Example
Query Type (optional section)	Set to WEB when you use the version section: `WEB`
Query Version (optional section)	Allows you to set the version number of a web query. For example: `1`

URL
(required)
	The URL of the web page where you will get your data. For example:
	`http://investor.msn.com/external/excel/quotes.asp`
	`http://www.um.lublin.pl/oswiata/sz_pdst.htm`

POST Parameters
(optional section)
	You can send parameters to the web server using the POST or GET method. This section is used for sending parameters with the POST method. These parameters need to be entered on a separate line, as in the following example:
	`http://www.xe.net/cgi-bin/ucc/convert`
	`From=USD&Amount=1&To=CAD`
	
	From, Amount, and To are the names of parameters, while the values that follow the equal (=) sign are the parameter settings. Parameters are separated from one another with the & sign.
	
	Note: When sending parameters using the GET method, the parameters are attached to the URL address using the question mark, as shown below:
	`http://uk.finance.yahoo.com/quote?symbols=met`
	
	Symbols is a parameter name, while met is a stock symbol (a parameter value), which you want to retrieve from the specified URL.

Creating and Running Web Queries with VBA

In the previous section you learned that a web query can be created by using a menu option or typing special instructions in a text editor such as Notepad. The third method of creating a web query is through VBA statements.

To programmatically create a web query, use the Add method of the QueryTables collection. This collection belongs to the Worksheet object and contains all the QueryTable objects for a specific worksheet. The Add method returns the QueryTable object that represents a new query. The format of this method is shown below:

```
expression.Add(Connection, Destination, [Sql])
```

Expression is an expression that returns the QueryTable object. Connection specifies the data source for the query table. The data source can be one of the following:

■   A string containing the address of the web page in the form "URL;<url>." For example:

```
"URL;http://www.nycenet.edu/distschweb/searchresult.asp"
```

- A string indicating the path to the existing web query file (.iqy) using the form " FINDER;<data finder file path>." For instance:

```
"FINDER;C:\Program Files\Microsoft Office\Office\Queries\ _
    MSN MoneyCentral Investor Currency Rates.iqy"
```

- A string containing an OLE DB or ODBC connection string. The ODBC connection string has the form "ODBC;<connection string>." For instance:

```
"ODBC;DSN=MyNorthwind;UID=NorthUser;PWD=UserPass;Database=Northwind"
```

- An ADO or DAO Recordset object. Microsoft Excel retains the recordset until the query table is deleted or the connection is changed. The resulting query table cannot be edited.

- A string indicating the path to a text file in the form "TEXT;<text file path and name>." For instance:

```
"TEXT;C:\myTextFile.txt"
```

Destination is the cell in the upper-left corner of the query table destination range (this is where the resulting query table will be placed). This cell must be located in the worksheet containing the QueryTable object used in the expression. The optional argument Sql is not used when a QueryTable object is used as the data source.

The example procedure shown below creates a new web query in the active workbook. The data retrieved from a web page is placed in a worksheet as static text.

1. Open a new workbook and save it as **MyWebQueries.xls**.

2. Switch to the Visual Basic Editor window, and insert a new module in the current VBA Project (MyWebQueries.xls).

3. In the Code window, enter the Manhattan_Schools procedure, which retrieves a list of NYC schools located in Manhattan from the web.

```
Sub Manhattan_Schools()
    ' create a Web query in the current worksheet, connect to the Web,
    ' retrieve data and paste it in the worksheet as static text.

    With ActiveSheet.QueryTables.Add(Connection:= _
        "URL;http://www.nycenet.edu/dist_sch/sch/" & _
            "searchresult.asp?boro=Manhattan&flag=schoolInfo2", _
        Destination:=Range("a1"))
        .BackgroundQuery = True
        .WebSelectionType = xlSpecifiedTables
        .WebTables = "Table3"
        .WebFormatting = xlWebFormattingNone
        .Refresh BackgroundQuery:=False
        .SaveData = True
    End With
End Sub
```

4. Run the Manhattan_Schools procedure. While the procedure executes, the following tasks occur: (a) a connection is established with the specified web page, (b) data from a web page is retrieved, and (c) data is placed in a worksheet.

   When you activate the above procedure, the active worksheet will display names and addresses of Manhattan schools (Figure 16-14). Notice that this worksheet does not contain any hyperlinks because we set the WebFormatting property of the QueryTable to xlWebFormattingNone in the procedure code. This property determines how much formatting from a web page, if any, is applied when you import the page into a query table. You can use one of the following constants: xlWebFormattingAll, xlWebFormattingNone (this is the default setting), or xlWebFormattingRTF. The BackgroundQuery property of the QueryTable object when set to True allows you to perform other operations in the worksheet while the data is being retrieved from the web page. The WebSelectionType property determines whether an entire web page, all tables on the web page, or only specific tables on the web page are imported into a query table. The WebSelectionType property can be one of the following constants: xlAllTables, xlEntirePage, or xlSpecifiedTables.

   The WebTables property specifies a comma-delimited list of table names or table index numbers when you import a web page into a query table.

   After retrieving data from the web page, in order to display this data in a worksheet, you must use the Refresh method of the QueryTable object. If you omit this method in your procedure code, the data retrieved from the web page will be invisible.

   By setting the SaveData property to True, the table retrieved from the web page will be saved with the workbook.

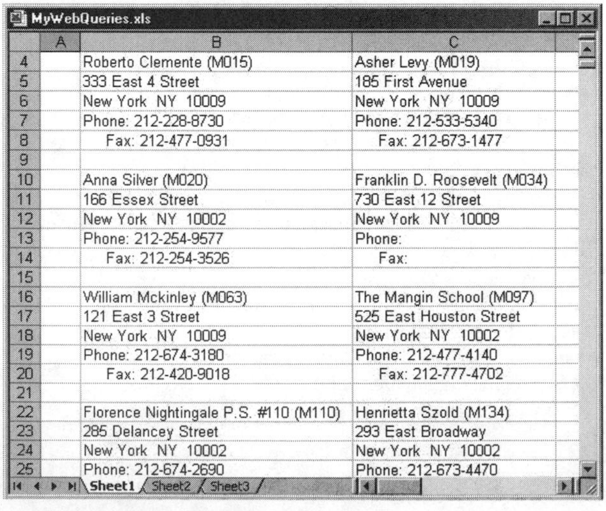
MyWebQueries.xls

	A	B	C
4		Roberto Clemente (M015)	Asher Levy (M019)
5		333 East 4 Street	185 First Avenue
6		New York NY 10009	New York NY 10009
7		Phone: 212-228-8730	Phone: 212-533-5340
8		Fax: 212-477-0931	Fax: 212-673-1477
9			
10		Anna Silver (M020)	Franklin D. Roosevelt (M034)
11		166 Essex Street	730 East 12 Street
12		New York NY 10002	New York NY 10009
13		Phone: 212-254-9577	Phone:
14		Fax: 212-254-3526	Fax:
15			
16		William Mckinley (M063)	The Mangin School (M097)
17		121 East 3 Street	525 East Houston Street
18		New York NY 10009	New York NY 10002
19		Phone: 212-674-3180	Phone: 212-477-4140
20		Fax: 212-420-9018	Fax: 212-777-4702
21			
22		Florence Nightingale P.S. #110 (M110)	Henrietta Szold (M134)
23		285 Delancey Street	293 East Broadway
24		New York NY 10002	New York NY 10002
25		Phone: 212-674-2690	Phone: 212-673-4470

Sheet1 / Sheet2 / Sheet3

Figure 16-14: This data was retrieved from a web page using the web query in a VBA procedure.

5. Right-click anywhere within the data placed by the web query in the worksheet and choose **Edit Query** from the shortcut menu. You will see the Edit Web Query dialog box. Click the **Options** button located on this dialog box's toolbar to access the Web Query Options dialog box, as shown in Figure 16-15. Notice that in the Formatting area the option button None is selected. This option button represents the setting of xlWebFormattingNone of the WebFormatting property in the procedure code.

Figure 16-15: The Web Query Options dialog box

Web Queries with Parameters

Often, in order to retrieve data from a web page, you need to specify parameters. To send parameters to the web server in your web query, use the POST or GET method after checking which of these methods the particular web server uses. You can find out this information in the following way:

1. Activate your browser and enter the address of a web page from which you want to retrieve information. For example, enter:

```
http://www.xe.net/ucc/
```

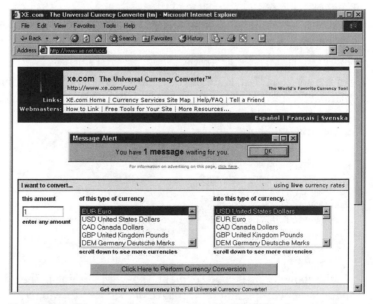

Figure 16-16: This web page allows you to convert one type of currency into another type.

2. Choose **Source** from your browser's View menu. The underlying code for this web page appears in Notepad (Figure 16-17).

3. In Notepad, choose **Find** from the Edit menu and type **POST** as the text to search for. If the parameters are being sent to the web server using the POST method, the word POST should appear highlighted, as shown below. Next to the POST method, there is a URL of the web server that supplies the data.

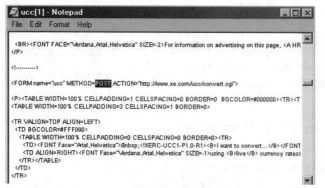

Figure 16-17:
You can view the source of the underlying data for a particular web page by selecting View | Source from your browser's menu. The underlying code will appear in Notepad.

Now that you know which method is used to send the parameters, you need to find out how the parameters are called.

4. In Notepad, choose **Find** from the Edit menu and type the word **name** as the search string. Next to the word "name" you should see text in quotes. This text is the name of the first parameter. After the word "value=", you should see the current value of a parameter. For example:

```
<INPUT TYPE="text" NAME="Amount" VALUE="1" SIZE=10><BR>
```

In the above HTML statement, the word "Amount" is the name of a parameter and "1" is the current value of this parameter. A value of the parameter can also be one of the options located in the HTML <option> tag. For example:

```
<SELECT NAME="From" SIZE=5 onChange="CheckMore()">
    <OPTION VALUE="EUR" SELECTED>EUR Euro</OPTION>
    <OPTION VALUE="USD">USD United States Dollars</OPTION>
    <OPTION VALUE="CAD">CAD Canada Dollars</OPTION>
    <OPTION VALUE="GBP">GBP United Kingdom Pounds</OPTION>
    <OPTION VALUE="DEM">DEM Germany Deutsche Marks</OPTION>
    ...
    ...
</SELECT><BR>
```

In the above HTML code segment, the word "From" is the name of a parameter. This parameter can have one of the following values: USD, CAD, GBP, DEM.

If a web server receives parameters using the GET method, you can see the parameter names and their values in your browser's address bar:

```
http://www.nycenet.edu/dist_sch/sch/searchresult/asp?boro=Manhattan _
&flag= schoolInfo2
```

Notice that the first parameter is preceded by a question mark. Parameters are separated from one another using the & sign.

Static and Dynamic Parameters

Web query parameters can be static or dynamic. When you use static parameters, you do not need to enter any values when running a web query (see the code of the Portfolio procedure below). A static web query always returns the same data.

If you use dynamic parameters, you can specify one or more values as criteria for your data retrieval while executing your web query (see the Portfolio2 procedure in the next section). A dynamic web query returns data based on the supplied parameters.

In the following example you will see how you can create a static web query programmatically. This web query will send parameters to the web server using the GET method. These parameters are static because you are not prompted to supply their values when the web query is run. The values of the parameters, which the server expects to receive, are coded inside the VBA procedure.

1. In the Visual Basic Editor window, insert a new module into the current VBA project—**VBAProject (MyWebQueries.xls)**.

2. In the Code window, enter the code of the Portfolio procedure:

```
Sub Portfolio()
    Dim sht As Worksheet
    Dim qryTbl As QueryTable

  ' insert a new worksheet in the current workbook
    Set sht = ThisWorkbook.Worksheets.Add
    ' create a new Web query in a worksheet
    Set qryTbl = sht.QueryTables.Add(Connection:= _
      "URL;http://uk.finance.yahoo.com/quote?symbols=met&symbols=aol", _
      Destination:=sht.Range("a1"))
    ' retrieve data from Web page and specify formatting
    ' paste data in a worksheet
    With qryTbl
        .BackgroundQuery = True
        .WebSelectionType = xlSpecifiedTables
        .WebTables = "17"
        .WebFormatting = xlWebFormattingAll
        .Refresh BackgroundQuery:=False
        .SaveData = True
    End With
End Sub
```

3. Run the Portfolio procedure. The result of this procedure is shown in Figure 16-18.

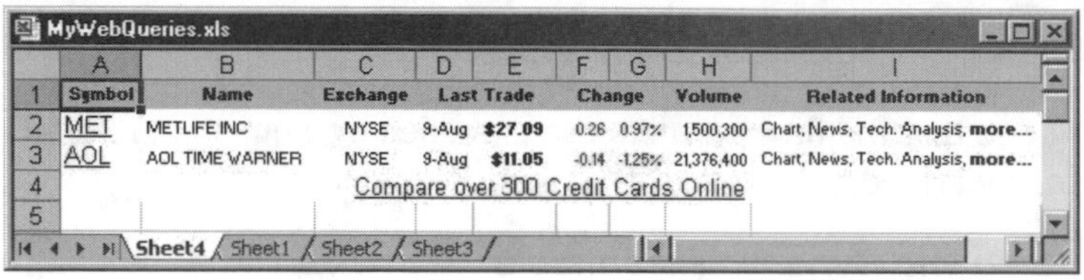

Figure 16-18: A web query can retrieve data from a specific table on a web page.

Notice that the Portfolio procedure imports data contained in the 17th table of the specified web site (see the WebTables property setting). To retrieve data from two or more tables, separate their indices or names with commas. The table names or indices must appear in quotes. To view the explanations of other properties used in this procedure, see the Manhattan_Schools procedure earlier in this chapter.

When sending several values using the same parameter name, instead of repeating the parameter name (as shown in the Portfolio procedure), you can separate parameter values with the plus (+) sign, like this:

```
http://uk.finance.yahoo.com/quote?symbols=met+aol+ibm
```

Tip 16-2: Which Table Should I Import?

Web pages may contain many tables. Tables allow you to organize the content of the page. When viewing the HTML source code in Notepad, you can easily recognize tables by the following tags: <TABLE> (beginning of table) and </TABLE> (end of table). The <TD> tag indicates table data. This data will be placed in a worksheet cell when retrieved by Excel. Every new table row begins with the <TR> tag and ends with the </TR> tag. Many times, one table is placed inside another table (referred to as table nesting). Because tables are usually numbered in the HTML code, finding the correct table number containing the data you want to place in the worksheet usually requires experimentation. The Excel 2002 New Web Query dialog box provides a visual clue to which tables a particular page contains (see Figure 16-12 earlier in this chapter). By clicking on the arrow pointing to the table, you can mark a particular table for selection. You can then click the Save Query button to save the query to a file. When you open the prepared .iqy file in Notepad, you will see the number assigned to the selected table (as shown below). You can now use this number in your VBA procedure.

```
WEB
1
http://uk.finance.yahoo.com/quote? _
symbols=met+aol+ibm

Selection=17
Formatting=None
PreFormattedTextToColumns=True
ConsecutiveDelimitersAsOne=True
SingleBlockTextImport=False
DisableDateRecognition=False
DisableRedirections=False
```

Dynamic Web Queries

Instead of hard coding the parameter values in the code of your VBA procedures, you can create a dynamic query that will prompt the user for the parameter setting when the query is run.

The Portfolio2 procedure shown below uses the GET method for sending dynamic parameters. This procedure displays a dialog box prompting the user to enter stock symbols separated by spaces. Notice that the message is placed within square brackets and surrounded by double quotes, like this:

```
symbols=[""Enter symbols separated by spaces""]
```

When the web query is activated, a dialog box appears, as shown in Figure 16-19. Here the user may specify any stock symbols in which he or she is interested.

```
Sub Portfolio2()
    Dim sht As Worksheet
    Dim qryTbl As QueryTable

    ' insert a new worksheet in the current workbook
    Set sht = ThisWorkbook.Worksheets.Add
    ' create a new Web query in a worksheet
    Set qryTbl = sht.QueryTables.Add(Connection:= _
        "URL;http://uk.finance.yahoo.com/quote?symbols=[""Enter " & _
        "symbols separated by spaces""]", _
      Destination:=sht.Range("a1"))
    ' retrieve data from Web page and specify formatting
    ' paste data in a worksheet
    With qryTbl
        .BackgroundQuery = True
        .WebSelectionType = xlSpecifiedTables
        .WebTables = "17"
        .WebFormatting = xlWebFormattingAll
        .Refresh BackgroundQuery:=False
        .SaveData = True
    End With
End Sub
```

Figure 16-19:
A dynamic web query requests parameter values from the user.

The next example demonstrates a web query that uses the POST method with dynamic parameters:

1. In the Code window, enter the Currency_Exchange_POST procedure, as shown below.

```
Sub Currency_Exchange_POST()
  With ActiveSheet.QueryTables.Add(Connection:= _
        "URL;http://www.xe.net/cgi-bin/ucc/convert", _
        Destination:=Range("D1"))
    .PostText = "From=[""Enter the currency symbol from which " & _
    "you want to convert""]&Amount=[""'Enter amount you wish " & _
    "to convert""]&To=[""Enter the currency symbol you want to obtain""]"
    .BackgroundQuery = True
    .WebSelectionType = xlSpecifiedTables
    .WebTables = "8"
    .WebFormatting = xlWebFormattingAll
    .RefreshStyle = xlOverwriteCells
    .AdjustColumnWidth = True
    .Refresh BackgroundQuery:=False
    .SaveData = True
  End With
End Sub
```

2. Run the above procedure. Notice that the Currency_Exchange_POST procedure uses the PostText property of the QueryTable object for sending dynamic parameters to the web server. A web query can use a combination of static and dynamic parameters, as shown in the following code fragment:

```
"From=[""Enter the currency symbol from which " & _
"you want to convert ""]&Amount="1"& To=[""Enter the currency symbol " & _
" you want to obtain""]"
```

Because Amount is a static parameter, the user will only be prompted for the From and To currency symbols.

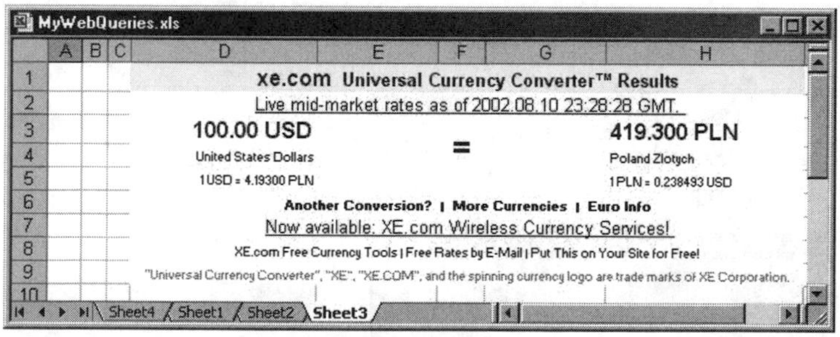

Figure 16-20: This worksheet has been generated by the Currency_Exchange_POST procedure.

Note: Web pages undergo frequent modifications. It's not uncommon to find out that a web query you prepared a while ago suddenly stops working because the web page address or parameters required to process the data have changed. If you plan on using web queries in your applications, you must watch for any changes introduced on the web sites that supply you with vital information. Particularly watch for table references. "Table 13" from a while ago could now be a totally different number, causing your query to retrieve data that you don't care about (or no data at all).

Refreshing Data

You can refresh data retrieved from a web page by using the Refresh data option on a shortcut menu. To get this menu, right-click any cell in the range where the data is located. Try this out using the data placed in a worksheet by the Currency_Exchange_POST procedure in the previous section. When the dialog box appears, prompting you for currency symbols and amount, specify USD as the From currency and CAD as the To currency. Enter any amount you want to convert.

The Refresh data option is also available from the Data menu and the External Data toolbar. Data can be refreshed in the background while per-forming other tasks in the worksheet when the file is being opened or at the specified time intervals. You can specify when the data should be refreshed in the External Data Range Properties dialog box; right-click anywhere in the data range and choose Data Range Properties from the shortcut menu (see Figure 16-21).

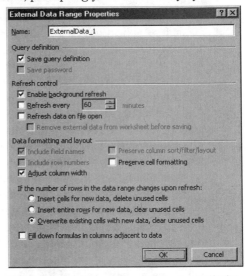

Figure 16-21: After retrieving data from a particular web page using the web query, you can use the External Data Range Properties dialog to control when data is refreshed and how it is formatted.

Excel and Active Server Pages

In Chapter 15 you learned various methods of retrieving data from a Micro-soft Access database and placing this data in an Excel worksheet. This section explores another technology, known as ASP, that you can use for accessing and displaying data stored in databases.

Active Server Pages (ASP) is a technology developed a few years ago by Microsoft. Using this technology, you can design powerful and dynamic web applications that change every time they are viewed. ASP is platform independent. This means that you can view ASP pages in any browser. The current version of ASP is 3.0 and is available with Microsoft Internet Information Server (IIS 5.0 and above). While HTML (Hypertext Markup Language), which is used for creating web pages, contains text and formatting tags, ASP pages are a collection of HTML standard formatting elements, text, and embedded scripting statements. You can easily recognize an ASP page in a browser by its .asp extension in the URL address:

```
http://www.nycenet.edu/dist_sch/sch/searchresult.asp
```

Simply put, ASP pages are text files with the .asp extension. ASP code is processed entirely by the web server and sent to the user browser as pure HTML code. Users cannot view the script commands that created the page that they are viewing. All they can see is the HTML source code for the page. However, if you have access to the original ASP file and open this file in any text editor, you will be able to view the ASP code.

Creating ASP pages is quite easy for those who already know Visual Basic for Applications. VBScript, a subset of Visual Basic and VBA, is one of the built-in scripting languages in ASP (another built-in language is JScript). To create an ASP file, you need a simple text editor, such as Notepad. But if you are planning to create professional Internet applications using ASP, it's worthwhile to purchase Microsoft Visual InterDev 6.0, which offers many tools for creating and debugging ASP scripts and viewing HTML. It is also a good idea to acquire some working knowledge of HTML. Needless to say, a good place to start is the Internet. For easy, step-by-step tutorials and lessons, check out the following web site addresses: http://www.html-goodies.com or http://www.bfree.on.ca/HTML.

The ASP has its own object model consisting of merely five objects (Request, Response, Application, Server, and Session). The ASP objects have methods, properties, and events that can be called to manipulate various features. For example, the CreateObject method of the Server object enables you to create a link between a web page and your Access database, while the Write method of the Response object allows you to write text to the client browser. You will use these methods while creating an example ASP script later in this chapter.

Let's see how you can use ASP to retrieve some data from the Shippers table in the sample Microsoft Access Northwind database and how to display this data as an HTML table in an Excel worksheet inside your Internet browser.

To create your first ASP script, you will use the following tags:

<% and %>	Beginning and end of the ASP script fragment. The script code between the <% and %> tags will be executed on the server before the page is delivered to the user browser.
<HTML> and </HTML>	You should place the <HTML> tag at the beginning of each web page. To indicate the end of a web page, use the closing tag: </HTML>.

<BODY> and **</BODY>**	The text you want to display on the web page should be placed between these tags.
<TABLE> and **</TABLE>**	Beginning and end of a table
<TABLE Border = "1">	The Border parameter specifies the width of the table border.
<TH> and **</TH>**	Place table headings between these tags.
<TR> and **</TR>**	The <TR> tag begins a new row in a table. Each table row ends with the </TR> tag.
<TD> and **</TD>**	Use these tags to specify table cells. Each table data cell starts with the <TD> tag and ends with the </TD> tag. Table cells can contain any content, including another table.

Creating an ASP Script

1.   Open Notepad and enter the following ASP script:

```
<%
' declare variables
Dim accessDB
Dim conn
Dim rst
Dim sql

Response.ContentType = "Application/vnd.ms-excel"

' name of the database
accessDB="Northwind"

' establish connection to the database
conn="DRIVER={Microsoft Access Driver (*.mdb)};"
conn=conn & "DBQ=" & Server.Mappath(accessdb)

' Create a Recordset
Set rst = Server.CreateObject("ADODB.Recordset")

' select all records from Shippers table
sql = "SELECT * FROM Shippers"

' Open Recordset (and execute SQL statement above)
rst.Open sql, conn

%>

<HTML>
<BODY>
<TABLE Border="1">

<%
      For Each fld in rst.Fields
%>
         <TH>
```

```
        <% Response.Write fld.Name %>
      </TH>
 <%

    Next
    rst.MoveFirst
    Do While Not rst.EOF
    %>
      <TR>
  <%
      For Each fld in rst.Fields
    %>
      <TD>
        <% Response.Write fld.Value %>
      </TD>
    <% Next %>
      </TR>
    <% rst.MoveNext
    Loop
    %>
  </TABLE>
  </BODY>
  </HTML>
  <%
  rst.Close
  Set rst=Nothing
  %>
```

2. Save the file as **C:\AccessTbl.asp**.

3. Close Notepad.

Notice that the above ASP script begins by declaring variables. In ASP scripts, all variables are of the Variant type. Therefore, you don't need to use the As keyword to specify the type of variable:

```
Dim accessDB
Dim conn
Dim rst
Dim sql
```

You can also declare all your variables on one line, like this:

```
Dim accessDB, conn, rst, sql
```

To tell the browser that the code that follows should be formatted for display in Excel, use the following directive:

```
Response.ContentType = "Application/vnd.ms-excel"
```

The ContentType property of the Response object specifies which format should be used for displaying data obtained from a web server. If you don't set this property, the data will default to text/HTML format.

To connect with the Access database, the ASP script shown above uses the following connection that accesses the Microsoft Access driver directly:

```
conn="DRIVER={Microsoft Access Driver (*.mdb)};"
```

```
conn=conn & "DBQ=" & Server.Mappath(accessDB)
```

Conn is an object variable that stores the string specifying how to connect to the database. The DRIVER parameter specifies the name of the driver that you are planning to use for this connection (Microsoft Access Driver (*.mdb")). The DBQ parameter indicates the database path. The exact path will be supplied by the Mappath method of the Server object:

```
Server.Mappath(accessDB)
```

You can also connect to your Access database by using the OLE DB data provider as follows:

```
Set conn = Server.CreateObject("OLEDB.Connection")
conn.Open "Provider=Microsoft .Jet.OLEDB.4.0; Data Source=" _
     & Server.MapPath(accessDB)
```

To connect to an SQL server database, use the following format:

```
Set conn = Server.CreateObject("OLEDB.Connection")
conn.Open "Provider="SQLOLEDB;" & _
     "Data Source=YourServerName;" & _
     "Initial Catalog=accessDB;" & _
     "UID=yourId; Password=yourPassword;"
```

To gain access to database records, the ASP script creates the Recordset object using the CreateObject method of the Server object:

```
Set rst = Server.CreateObject("ADODB.Recordset")
```

After creating the Recordset, open it using the Open method, like this:

```
rst.Open sql, conn
```

The above statement opens a set of records. The sql variable indicates that you want to select all the records from the Shippers table (sql = "SELECT * FROM Shippers"). The conn variable indicates how you will connect with the database.

The next part of the ASP script contains HTML formatting tags that prepare a table. The table headings are read from the Fields collection of the Recordset object using the For...Each...Next loop. Notice that all instructions that need to be executed on the Server are enclosed by the <% and %> tags. To enter the data returned by the Server in the appropriate worksheet cells, use the Write method of the Response object:

```
Response.Write fld.Name
```

The above statement will return the name of a table field. Because this instruction appears between the <TH> and </TD> formatting tags, the names of the table fields will be written in the first worksheet row in bold type.

After reading the headings, the next loop reads the values of the fields in each record:

```
Response.Write fld.Value
```

Because this statement is located between the <TD> and </TD> formatting tags, the values retrieved from each field in a particular record will be written to table cells. The ASP script ends by closing the recordset and relasing the memory used by it:

```
rst.Close
set rst = Nothing
```

To try out this ASP script on your own computer, you must first:

1. Install Microsoft Information Services (IIS) 5.0 or a newer version (for Windows NT/ 2000 Professional or Windows XP) or Personal Web Server 4.0 (if you are working on Windows 95/98 or NT Workstation 4.0). The installation instructions are presented below.

2. Create a virtual folder (see the section following installation instructions).

Installing Internet Information Services (IIS) or Personal Web Server

Windows 2000 Installing Internet Information Services 5.0	Windows 98 Installing Personal Web Server
Insert the Windows 2000 Professional CD-ROM into a drive.	Insert the Windows 98 CD-ROM into a drive.
Click **Start**, select **Settings**, and click **Control Panel**.	When the Windows 98 CD-ROM window appears, double-click **Browse This CD**.
Double-click **Add/Remove Programs**.	Double-click **Add-ons**.
Click the **Add/Remove Windows Components** button in the left-hand side panel.	Double-click **pws**.
	Double-click **Setup.exe**.
Click the box beside **Internet Information Services (IIS)**.	When the Microsoft Personal Web Server Setup dialog box appears, click **Typical** to indicate the type of installation that you want to perform.
Click **Next** to start the installation.	
When the installation is complete, click **Finish** to close the wizard.	The screen indicating the location of the Personal Web Server home directory will appear. Press **Next** to continue the installation.
Restart your computer.	
	When the installation is complete, click **Finish**.
	A message will appear, asking you to restart your computer. Click **Yes** to restart.

After completing the installation steps above, you should see the Inetpub folder on your computer (Figure 16-22).

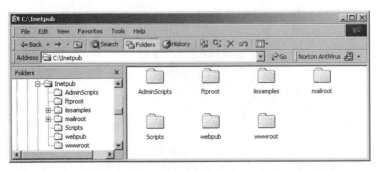

Figure 16-22: The C:\Inetpub\wwwroot folder is automatically set as the home directory for IIS 5.0 or higher and Personal Web Server.

Creating a Virtual Directory

The default home directory for the WWW service is C:\InetPub\wwwroot. Files located in the home directory and its subdirectories are automatically available to visitors to your web site. You can create virtual directories to make web pages that are not stored in the home directory or its subdirectories available for viewing. A virtual directory appears to client browsers as if it were physically contained in the home directory. For the purposes of this chapter, in order to try out the example script you've just prepared, you should create a directory called C:\ExcelWithASP on your computer and set it up as a virtual directory.

1. Open Windows Explorer and create a new folder on your C drive named **C:\ExcelWithASP**.

2. Right-click the **ExcelWithASP** folder and select **Properties**. The ExcelWithASP Properties box appears (see Figure 16-23).

3. Click the **Web Sharing** tab. A dialog box appears where you can set up an alias that users will use to access pages in that directory.

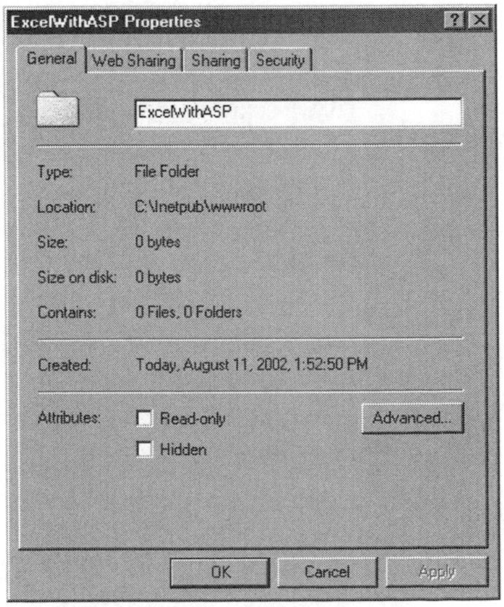

Figure 16-23: Creating a virtual directory— folder properties

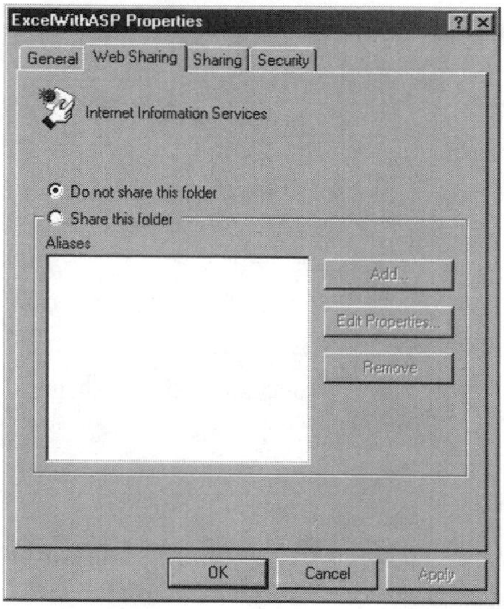

Figure 16-24:
Creating a virtual directory—
sharing web folder

4. Click the **Share this folder** option. The Edit Alias dialog box will appear. A virtual directory has an alias, a name that client browsers use to access that directory. An alias is often used to shorten a long directory name. In addition, an alias provides increased security. Because users do not know where your files are physically located on the server, they cannot modify them.

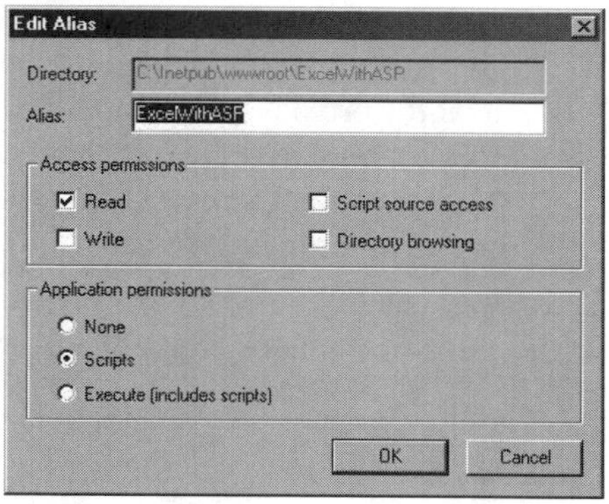

5. Enter **accessDB** in the Alias box, as shown in Figure 16-26. In the Access permissions area, make sure that the **Read** and **Write** permissions are selected. In the Application permissions area, make sure that the **Scripts** option button is selected. Click **OK**.

    When you set up a virtual directory, it is important to specify the access permissions for that directory. The Read

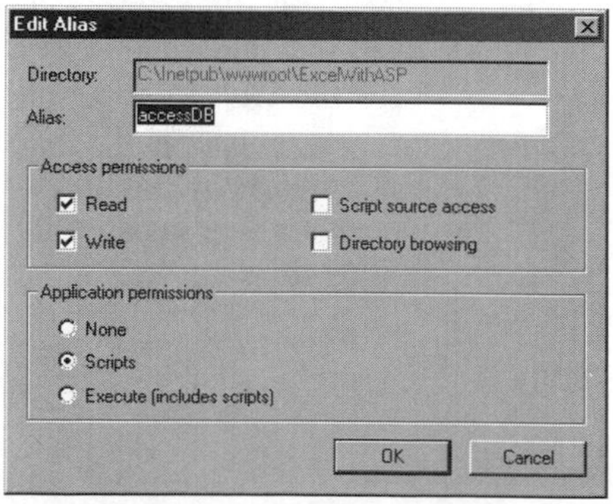

Figure 16-25: Creating a virtual directory—Edit Alias dialog box

Figure 16-26: Creating a virtual directory—changing the alias and setting permissions

permission allows users to access web pages. This option must be turned on so that the directory content can be viewed. The Read permission is turned on by default. The Write permission will make it possible to perform an update or some other action that alters the information in the database or creates files on the server. In addition, the Scripts permission should be turned on for virtual directories that will contain ASP pages. For the exercises in this chapter, make your Edit Alias dialog box look like Figure 16-26.

6. When you click **OK** in the Edit Alias dialog, a Warning dialog box will appear. Click **Yes** in response to the message. You should now see the alias named accessDB listed in the Aliases box (Figure 16-27).

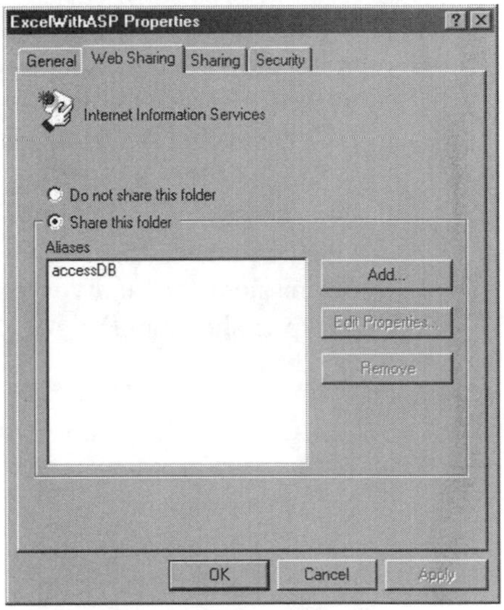

7. Click the **Security** tab and set permissions for the Everyone group, as shown in Figure 16-28.

8. Click **OK** to close the ExcelWithASP Properties dialog box.

9. To ensure that all of the components that you need can be quickly accessed, copy the sample **Northwind.mdb** database file from the C:\Windows\ Program Files\Microsoft Office\Office10\Samples folder to your **C:\ExcelWithASP** folder.

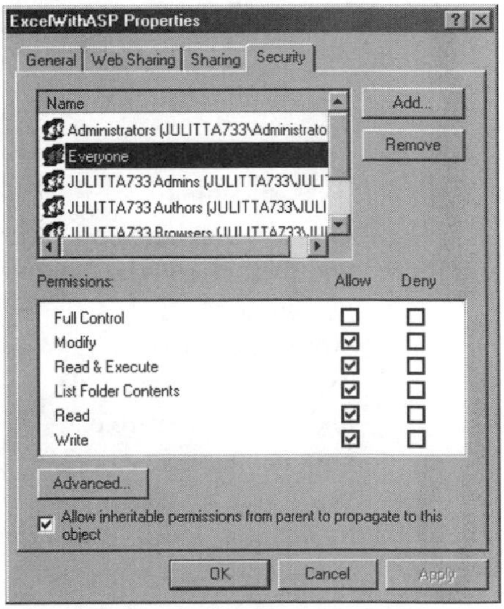

Figure 16-27: The physical folder named ExcelWithASP will be shared over the web as accessDB.

Figure 16-28: Give the Internet Guest account (IUSR_MACHINE), which is by default part of the "Everyone" group, Write permissions on the directory containing the .mdb file.

10. Copy the **AccessTbl.asp** file that you created earlier to the **C:\ExcelWithASP** folder.

11. Right-click the **Northwind.mdb** file that you placed in the C:\ExcelWithASP folder, and choose **Properties**. When the Properties dialog box appears, click the **Security** tab and set up permissions for the Everyone group as shown in Figure 16-29.

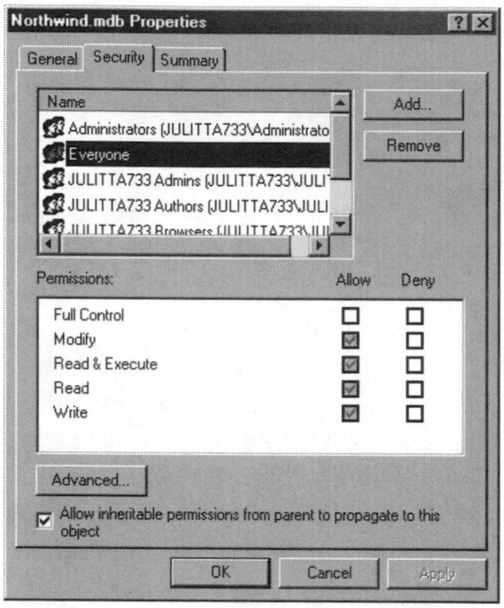

Figure 16-29: Give the Internet Guest account (IUSR_MACHINE), which is by default part of the "Everyone" group, Write permissions to the database file.

Running Your First ASP Script

Now that you've prepared the ASP file and set up the virtual directory, including the necessary permissions, it's time to see the result of your efforts.

1. Open your Internet browser.

2. Enter the following address: **http://localhost/accessDb/ AccessTbl.asp**.

   Localhost is the name of the web server installed on your computer, and accessDb is the name of the virtual folder where the ASP script file named AccessTbl.asp is stored. Type the address exactly as shown above and press **Enter** to execute the .asp file.

3. When the File Download dialog box appears, choose **Open this file from its current location** and click **OK**.

Figure 16-30: Opening the ASP script in an Internet browser

When you click OK after choosing the first option in the File Download window, the data from the Microsoft Access Northwind database Shippers table appears in a Microsoft Excel workbook opened in the browser (Figure 16-31). Choosing Save this file to disk in the File Download dialog box will allow you to download the file to your computer so that you can work with it later.

Notice the main menu in the browser. This is a Microsoft Excel menu bar merged with your browser's menu. You can use the Excel menu options to apply formatting to your data, add calculations, or use available analysis tools. Inside the browser, you can see a worksheet with a table containing data retrieved from Access. Now try to write another ASP script on your own to retrieve data from another Access table.

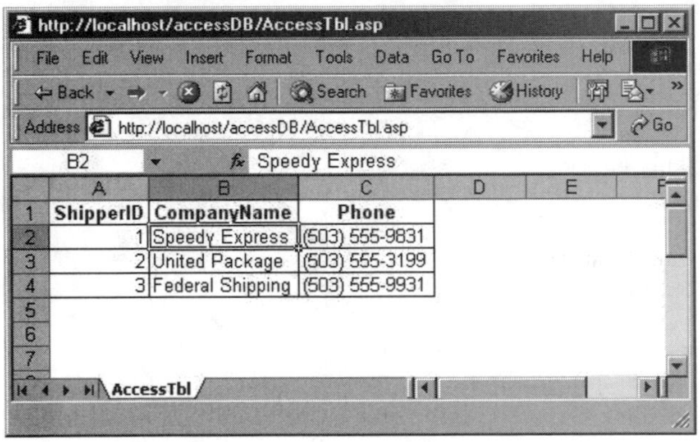

Figure 16-31:
The Excel application opened in an Internet browser displays a table of data retrieved from an Access database.

Generating a Tab-delimited File on the Web Server

In your first ASP script (see the code in the AccessTbl.asp file earlier in this chapter), you found out that to retrieve data from a table in a Microsoft Access database and display it in an Internet browser as an Excel spreadsheet, you must use the following directive in your ASP script:

```
<% Response.ContentType = "Application/vnd.ms-excel" %>
```

If you comment out the above statement in the AccessTbl.asp file, you will see a static table of data upon requesting this .asp page.

The next example ASP script demonstrates another way to generate an Excel file on the server. This script creates a tab-delimited file on the web server with an .xls extension. The user can open the generated Excel file in the browser or download it. After the session ends, the file is automatically deleted by the server. This example uses two files. The first one is named AccessTbl_2.asp and contains the code to generate the Excel file on the server. The second one is the Global.asa file that changes the session timeout when the session starts and deletes the file when the session ends.

Step 1: Creating the Active Server Page That Generates an Excel File on the Server

1. Open Notepad and type the ASP code shown below.

2. Save the file in your virtual folder as **C:\Inetpub\wwwroot\Excel-WithASP\AccessTbl_2.asp**.

3. Close Notepad when you are finished.

AccessTbl_2.asp code

```
<%@ Language=VBScript %>
<%

' declare variables
Dim accessDB
Dim conn
Dim rst
Dim sql
Dim strFileN
Dim fso
Dim excelFile
Dim strLine

' name of the database
accessDB="Northwind"

' connection string to the database
conn="DRIVER={Microsoft Access Driver (*.mdb)};"
conn=conn & "DBQ=" & Server.Mappath(accessDB)

' create a Recordset
Set rst = Server.CreateObject("ADODB.Recordset")

' select some records from Products table
sql = "SELECT * FROM Products WHERE CategoryId = 2"

' Open Recordset (and execute SQL statement above)
' using the connection to the database
rst.Open sql, conn

' use the Session ID as the name for the Excel file
' get the complete path to the file (needed for the hyperlink)
strFileN=Server.MapPath("./") & "\" & Session.SessionID & ".xls"

' create a text file
Set fso = Server.CreateObject("Scripting.FileSystemObject")
Set excelFile=fso.CreateTextFile(strFileN, True)

'read and write table headings
For Each fld in rst.Fields
   strLine = strLine & fld.Name & vbTab
Next
   excelFile.WriteLine strLine
```

```
'read and write records
Do While Not rst.EOF
  strLine = ""
  For Each fld in rst.Fields
    strLine = strLine & fld.Value & vbTab
  Next
  excelFile.WriteLine strLine
  rst.MoveNext
Loop

' store the filename in the Session object for cleanup by the server
Session("strExcelFile") = strFileN

' close and release the variables
rst.Close
Set rst = Nothing
Set fso = Nothing
set excelFile = Nothing

' write file information and link to the browser
Response.Write "Excel file from Products table was generated as " & _
    Session.SessionID & ".xls<BR>"
Response.Write "<A href=" & strFileN & ">Click here to open " & _
    "this file in Excel</A>"

%>
```

The above ASP script shows how to generate an Excel file from scratch.
The script connects to the Access database on the server and retrieves data
from the Products table. This time, however, we are not retrieving all table
data but only a subset of data that belongs to the product category 2. Instead
of creating a table using HTML tags, the ASP script stores retrieved data to
the strLine variable. This variable is then used as a parameter to the
WriteLine method that actually writes the data to a file (see the "Modern
Methods of Working with Files and Folders" section in Chapter 8). Notice
that the vbTab constant is used to separate columns. In this ASP script
example, the file name is generated using the SessionID property of the
Session object:

```
strFileN = Server.MapPath("./") & "/" & Session.SessionID & ".xls"
```

The above statement guarantees that each time the ASP page is requested,
a unique file name is created. The SessionID property returns the session
identifier, a unique identifier that is generated by the server when the session is created. The session ID is returned as a Long data type.

Note: You can also generate a unique file name by using the GetTempName method of the FileSystemObject.

```
Dim fso, strFileN
Set fso = Server.CreateObject("Scripting.FileSystemObject")
strFileN = fso.GetBaseName(fso.GetTempName()) & ".xls"
```

The GetBaseName method of the FileSystemObject will remove the .tmp file extension from the file name returned by the GetTempName method.

Next, the code stores the filename in the Session object for cleanup by the server:

```
Session("strExcelFile") = strFileN
```

The above statement stores the variable `strFileN` in the Session object named strExcelFile. You can use the Session object to store information needed for a particular user session. Variables stored in the Session object persist for the entire user session. The server destroys the Session object when the session expires or is abandoned.

After retrieving and writing all data to the text file, you will want to close and release the variables, notify the user that the file was generated, and provide a hyperlink to download or display the file:

```
Response.Write "Your Excel file was generated as " & strFileN & "<BR>"
Response.Write "<A href=" & strFileN & ">Click here to open " & _
    "this file in Excel</A>"
```

In the above statements, the Response.Write statement writes the text to the browser. The <BR> tag indicates a line break. This way, two statements that you write to the browser will appear on separate lines. The second line includes a link that the user can click to download the file or open it in the browser. The link begins with the <A href=" & strFileN & "> tag and ends with the </A> tag. Between these tags, you should enter the text for the user to click on.

Step 2: Creating a Global.asa File

To ensure that the server is not burdened with many files created by users requesting your ASP script, you need to somehow remove these files when they are no longer needed. The technique commonly used is to perform the cleanup in the Global.asa file when the user session ends. The Global.asa file is an optional file that contains Application events, Session events, object declarations, and type library declarations. An application can only have one Global.asa file. Before you can try out your AccessTbl_2.asp script, use these steps to create the Global.asa file:

1. Open Notepad and type the Global.asa code shown on the following page.
2. Save the file in your virtual folder as **C:\ExcelWithASP\Global.asa**.

3. Close Notepad when you are finished.

Global.asa code

```
<SCRIPT LANGUAGE=VBScript RUNAT="Server">

Sub Session_OnStart
' make the session expire after 1 minute
' (for demonstration purpose only)
  Session.Timeout = 1
End Sub

Sub Session_OnEnd
  ' delete the file created during the session
  set Session("fso") = CreateObject("Scripting.FileSystemObject")
  Session("fso").DeleteFile Session("strExcelFile"), True
End Sub

</SCRIPT>
```

Notice that the Global.asa file presented above has two event procedures. The Session_On start procedure will run when the user requests a page from your ASP application. A session automatically ends if a user has not requested or refreshed a page in an application for a specified period of time. This value is 20 minutes by default. Because we don't want to wait that long to see if the Excel file actually gets deleted by the server, we will change the default by setting the Session Timeout property of the Session object to 1 minute:

```
Session.Timeout = 1
```

When the session ends, the Session_OnEnd event will fire. Here we will use the DeleteFile method of the FileSystemObject to remove the file created during the session from the server directory:

```
set Session("fso") = CreateObject("Scripting.FileSystemObject")
Session("fso").DeleteFile Session("strExcelFile"), True
```

Notice that the name of the file to be deleted is stored in the Session object named strExcelFile. Recall that you created this object in your ASP script. The second, optional argument of the DeleteFile method with the value of True indicates that the files with the read-only attribute set should be deleted.

Step 3: Running the ASP Script—AccessTbl_2.asp

Now that your ASP script file (AccessTbl_2.asp) and the Global.asa file are ready, it's time to try out our script.

1. Open your Internet browser.

2. Enter the following address: **http://localhost/accessDB/Access-Tbl_2.asp.**

You should see the page shown in Figure 16-32.

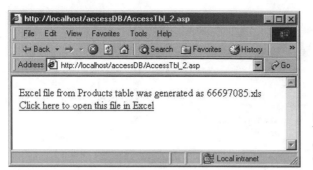

Figure 16-32:
The ASP script can generate an Excel file on the server

3. Click on the provided hyperlink. You should see the File Download dialog box, as shown earlier in Figure 16-30. Notice that with the provided options, you can either open the file in the browser or download it to your computer.

4. Activate Windows Explorer and navigate to your virtual directory named C:/ExcelWithASP. If you stay inactive for a minute or so, you will notice that the .xls file disappears after the set timeout interval. You may need to press F5 to refresh the window. If you switch back to your browser after the file has been removed from the virtual directory and click the provided link, you will get the "Page cannot be displayed" screen.

Creating an Excel File from User Input

An ASP script can contain a form that is used for collecting user input. Assume that you need to gather information about patients visiting an urgent care center in your town. It's been requested that your data entry/display screen has a web interface. Normally when you collect data on a web page, the information is saved into some sort of a database, like SQL Server or Access. However, your client particularly requested that the data from the input fields be saved directly to an Excel file. Let's see how you can provide this interface.

Even though Excel is primarily a spreadsheet application, because of its layout (rows and columns), it can easily act as a database. It's not recommended to store a lot of records in a spreadsheet, but if the spreadsheet is currently the only container you have for storing the data, why not use it to your advantage? The following example will demonstrate how to use Excel as a database. You will learn here how to query your Excel spreadsheet in order to display data from it on a web page. In addition, you will learn how to take the information entered on a web page and save it to your Excel file. As an additional feature, your application will allow the clearing of existing data in your Excel database.

Step 1: Creating an Excel Spreadsheet File to Act as a Database

1. Open the Excel application and create a new workbook.

2. In cell A1, enter **Patient**. In cell B1, enter **Phone**. These labels will serve as headings for your two-field Excel database.

3. Select columns **A:B**. With columns A and B highlighted, choose **Insert | Name | Create.** When the Create Names dialog box appears with the Top Row check box selected, click **OK.** The performed tasks will result in creating two named ranges in your workbook: Patient and Phone. If you open the Define Name dialog box (choose Insert | Name | Define Name), you will see that Patient refers to cells =Sheet1!$A$2:$A$65536, and the Phone range name references cells =Sheet1!$B$2:$B$65536.

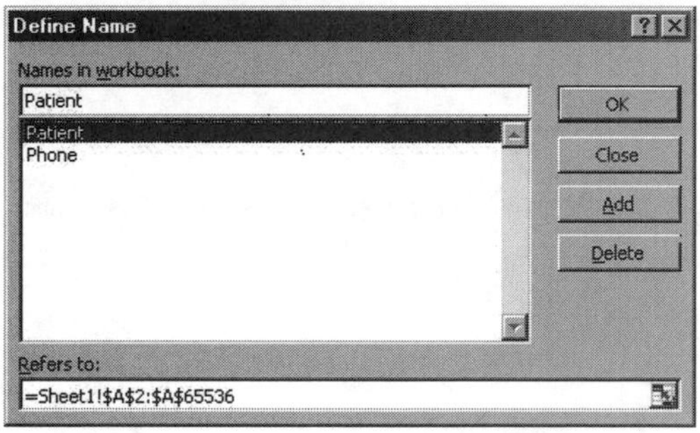

Figure 16-33:
Defining named ranges in a workbook

This is all you need for your Excel database.

4. Save your Excel workbook file as **C:\ExcelWithASP\WriteTo-Excel.xls**. Notice that we are using the same virtual directory as in previous examples.

5. Close the Excel application.

Step 2: Creating an ASP Script to Provide User Interface (Form Input) and Excel Database Operations

1. Open Notepad.

2. Enter the ASP script shown below.

3. Save the ASP file as **C:\ExcelWithASP\ExcelEntry.asp**.

4. Close Notepad.

ExcelEntry.asp code

```
<%@ Language=VBScript %>
<%
' Variable Declarations
Dim con        ' The ADODB connection object
Dim rst        ' The ADODB recordset object
Dim strCon     ' Variable to hold connection string to Excel database
Dim strSQL     ' Variable to hold SQL query string to perform the insert
Dim name       ' Variable to hold patient's name
Dim phone      ' Variable to hold patient's phone
```

```
Dim key            ' Iterator (dummy variable) in the For Each loop
Dim GoAhead        ' The flag to indicate whether we can proceed
Dim myStr          ' Variable to hold the message to display in the
                   ' right-hand side table

' ADODB Constants
'---- CursorTypeEnum Value ----
Const adOpenKeyset = 1

'---- LockTypeEnum Value ----
Const adLockPessimistic = 2

On Error Resume Next
name=Request("txtPatientName")
phone=Request("txtPhone")

  For Each key In Request.Form
    If Request.Form(key)= "" Then
      If key = "txtPatientName" Then
      Response.Write "<FONT Color = 'Blue'>Please enter the Patient name.</Font>"
      Else
      Response.Write "<FONT Color = 'Red'>Please enter the Phone number.</Font>"
      End If
        goAhead = False
        Exit For
    End If
  GoAhead=True
 Next

If goAhead = True Then
name=Replace(Request("txtPatientName"),"'","''")
  If Len(name)<> 0 Or _
    Len(phone)<>0 Then
       Set con = Server.CreateObject("ADODB.Connection")
       strCon="Provider=Microsoft.Jet.OLEDB.4.0;Data Source="
       strCon=strCon & server.MapPath("WriteToExcel.xls") & ";"
       strCon=strCon & "Extended Properties=Excel 8.0"
       If Request("cmdSubmit")="Enter Data in Excel" Then
         strSQL = "INSERT INTO [Sheet1$] (Patient, Phone)"
         strSQL = strSQL & " VALUES ('" & name & "'"
         strSQL = strSQL & ",'" & Phone & "')"
       End If
       With con
          .Open strCon
          If Request("cmdDelete")<>"Delete Data" Then
            .Execute(strSQL)
          Else
            set rst = Server.CreateObject("ADODB.Recordset")
            rst.Open "Select * from [Sheet1$] Where Patient='" & name & "'" & _
                 " AND phone ='"& phone &"'", con, adOpenKeyset, _
                 adLockPessimistic
            rst.fields(0).value = ""
            rst.fields(1).value = ""
            rst.Update
```

```
                    rst.Close
                End If
            End With
            If err.Number =3021 Then
                Response.Write "The information you entered cannot be deleted." _
                    & "<BR>"
                Response.Write "Either name or phone number is incorrect. " & "<P>"
            Else
                name = ""
                phone = ""
                set rst = Server.CreateObject("ADODB.Recordset")
                rst.Open "Select * from [Sheet1$]", con
                Response.Write "<TABLE Border=""1"">"
                For Each fld in rst.Fields
                    %>
                        <TH>
                    <% Response.Write fld.Name %>
                        </TH>
                    <%
                Next
                rst.MoveFirst
                Do While Not rst.EOF
                    %>
                        <TR>
                    <% For Each fld in rst.Fields %>
                        <TD>
                    <% Response.Write fld.Value %>
                        </TD>
                    <% Next %>
                        </TR>
                <% rst.MoveNext
                Loop
                %>
                    </TABLE>
                <%
                rst.Close
                Set rst=Nothing
                con.Close
                Set con=Nothing
            End If
        End If
    End If
%>

<HR>
<HTML>
<HEAD>
    <TITLE>Patient Data Entry Screen</TITLE>
</HEAD>
<BODY>
    <FORM Action="ExcelEntry.asp" Method = "POST" Name="form1">
    <P>
    <TABLE BORDER="1" CELLPADDING="2" CELLSPACING="4">
        <TR>
```

```
<TD>
  <TABLE BORDER="1" CELLPADDING="2" CELLSPACING="3">
  <TR>
    <TD>Patient Name: </TD>
    <TD>
      <INPUT Type="text1" Name="txtPatientName" Value="<%=name%>" Size= "30">
    </TD>
  </TR>
  <TR>
    <TD>Phone: </TD>
    <TD>
        <INPUT Type="text2" Name="txtPhone" Value="<%=phone %>">
    </TD>
  </TR>
  <INPUT Type="Submit" Name="cmdSubmit" Value="Enter Data in Excel">
  <INPUT Type="Submit" Name="cmdDelete" Value="Delete Data">
  </TABLE>
  </TD>
<TD>
<%
  If err.number = 0 Then
    If (Request("cmdSubmit")="Enter Data in Excel" or _
    Request("cmdDelete") = "Delete Data") and Request.Form(key) <>"" Then
    myStr = "The following data has been successfully "
      If Request("cmdSubmit")="Enter Data in Excel" Then
        Response.Write "<I><FONT Color = 'Green'>" & _
      myStr & "added:</I></FONT><HR>"
      ElseIf Request("cmdDelete") = "Delete Data" Then
        Response.Write "<I><FONT Color = 'Green'>" & _
      myStr & "deleted:</I></FONT><HR>"
      End If
    End If
    If Request("txtPatientName") <>"" or Request("txtPhone") <>"" Then
      Response.Write "Patient Name: <B>" & Request("txtPatientName") & "</B></P>"
      Response.Write "Phone Number: <B>" & Request("txtPhone") & "</B>"
    End If
  End If
%>
  </TD>
</TR>
</TABLE>
</FORM>
</BODY>
</HTML>
```

Because forms are used to gather information from users, you will often want to place the information from the form's fields into variables. Instead of constantly calling the Request.Form (variablename) to get the content of each variable, you can use an iterator (dummy variable) in a For…Each loop. The ExcelEntry.asp script shown above uses the following code to display an appropriate message when a form's input field has been left empty:

```
For Each key In Request.Form
  If Request.Form(key)= "" Then
```

```
       If key = "txtPatientName" Then
         Response.Write "<FONT Color = 'Blue'>Please enter the Patient _
             name.</Font>"
       Else
          Response.Write "<FONT Color = 'Red'>Please enter the Phone _
             number.</Font>"
       End If
       goAhead = False
       Exit For
     End If
    GoAhead=True
  Next
```

The above code fragment checks for any blanks in the form.

Next, if the user has filled in the two text boxes, the code uses the Microsoft Jet database engine to access data in other database file formats, such as Excel workbooks. Notice that to connect to a Microsoft Excel file (WriteToExcel.xls) that serves as our database, you need to specify the database type in the extended properties for the connection. You should use the Excel 8.0 source database type for Microsoft Excel 8.0 and higher. Therefore, the connection string looks like this:

```
strCon="Provider=Microsoft.Jet.OLEDB.4.0;Data Source="
      strCon=strCon & server.MapPath("WriteToExcel.xls") & ";"
      strCon=strCon & "Extended Properties=Excel 8.0"
```

Note: When you use Excel as a database, the first row is considered the header, unless you specify HDR=No in the extended properties in your connection string.

Depending on which button the user has clicked, an SQL INSERT INTO statement or the Recordset's Update method are executed. When inserting data into an Excel spreadsheet, we use the sheet name followed by a dollar sign (Sheet1$):

```
If Request("cmdSubmit")="Enter Data in Excel" Then
    strSQL = "INSERT INTO [Sheet1$] (Patient, Phone)"
    strSQL = strSQL & " VALUES ('" & name & "'"
    strSQL = strSQL & ",'" & Phone & "')"
End If
```

It is also possible to reference data in a range with a defined name or a specific address. For example, if your spreadsheet contains the Patient list in cells A1:B15, you can use the following statement to select data based on what the user has entered in the web form's text boxes:

```
rst.Open "Select * from [Sheet1$A1:B15] Where Patient='" & name & "'" & _
         " AND phone ='"& phone &"'", con, adOpenKeyset, adLockPessimistic
```

Or, if you assigned the name PatientList to cells A1:B15, you can refer to the named range as follows:

```
rst.Open "Select * from PatientList Where Patient='" & name & "'" & _
        " AND phone ='"& phone &"'", con, adOpenKeyset, adLockPessimistic
```

To insert data into the Excel spreadsheet, the code uses the Execute method of the ADO connection:

```
If Request("cmdDelete")<>"Delete Data" Then
   .Execute(strSQL)
Else
   set rst = Server.CreateObject("ADODB.Recordset")
   rst.Open "Select * from [Sheet1$] Where Patient='" & name & "'" & _
   " AND phone ='"& phone &"'", con, adOpenKeyset, adLockPessimistic
   rst.fields(0).value = ""
   rst.fields(1).value = ""
   rst.Update
   rst.Close
End If
```

The Else clause in the code fragment above locates the data in an Excel file based on the user's input. Once found, the data is cleared from the spreadsheet cells using the Recordset's Value method, and the change is saved with the Recordset's Update method. Note that when using ADO from the ASP, you are not allowed to delete entire rows in a spreadsheet. The SQL statement DELETE FROM will not work. To get rid of the existing data in a spreadsheet, you can only blank it out. This of course will cause empty lines within your data range. To get rid of the empty lines, you can write some code in the Open event for the workbook.

If the data the user wants to remove from the Excel file cannot be located, error 3021 will occur; therefore, we display the user-friendly message:

```
Response.Write "The information you entered cannot be deleted." & "<BR>"
Response.Write "Either name or phone number is incorrect. " & "<P>"
```

Every time the user clicks any of the provided buttons, we want to keep him posted about the data currently contained in the Excel database by building a table on the fly:

```
set rst = Server.CreateObject("ADODB.Recordset")
rst.Open "Select * from [Sheet1$]", con
Response.Write "<TABLE Border=""1"">"
For Each fld in rst.Fields
   %>
     <TH>
   <% Response.Write fld.Name %>
     </TH>
   <%
Next
rst.MoveFirst
Do While Not rst.EOF
   %>
   <TR>
   <% For Each fld in rst.Fields %>
```

```
<TD>
    <% Response.Write fld.Value %>
</TD>
    <% Next %>
</TR>
 <% rst.MoveNext
Loop
%>
 </TABLE>
<%
rst.Close
Set rst=Nothing
con.Close
Set con=Nothing
```

The above code fragment writes the data contained in an Excel spreadsheet to a table. Notice that the first For…Each loop iterates through the Fields collection to write out the names of column headings, while the second For…Each loop places the actual data in table cells.

Finally, the remaining part of the ASP script creates an HTML table within another HTML table to provide a user interface. The table on the right-hand side will serve to advise the user whether the requested operation (insert or delete) was successfully completed.

Step 3: Running the ASP Script—ExcelEntry.asp

To try out the above script, you may want to perform the following steps:

1. Open your Internet browser.
2. Enter the following address: **http://localhost/accessDB/Excel-Entry.asp**. You should see the following form:

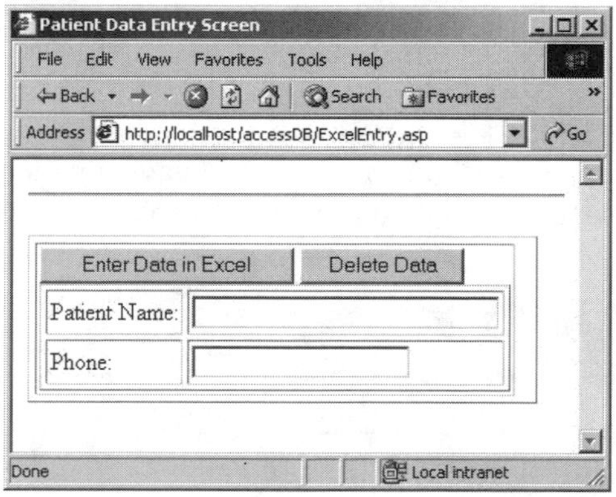

Figure 16-34:
An ASP form can be used for collecting data from a user.

3. Enter any name and phone number in the provided text boxes and press the **Enter Data in Excel** button. After entering data, my screen looked like Figure 16-35.

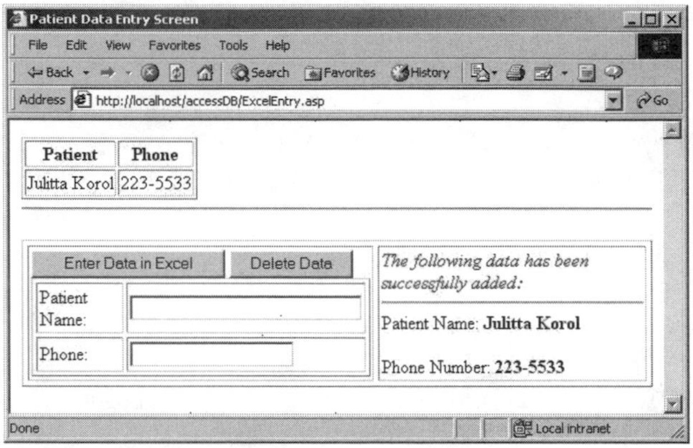

Figure 16-35:
Entering data into
Excel via a user
form

4. Add data for another patient.

5. Remove the data for the patient that you entered in step 3 by typing it
    in the text boxes and pressing the **Delete Data** button. You should see
    a screen similar to the one in Figure 16-36.

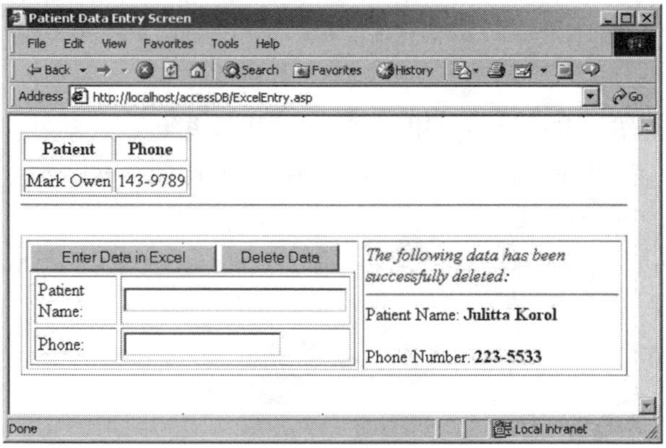

Figure 16-36:
Deleting data from
an Excel database via
an ASP form

6. Try to delete the data entered in step 4 by supplying only the patient
    name. The screen should prompt you to enter the phone number.

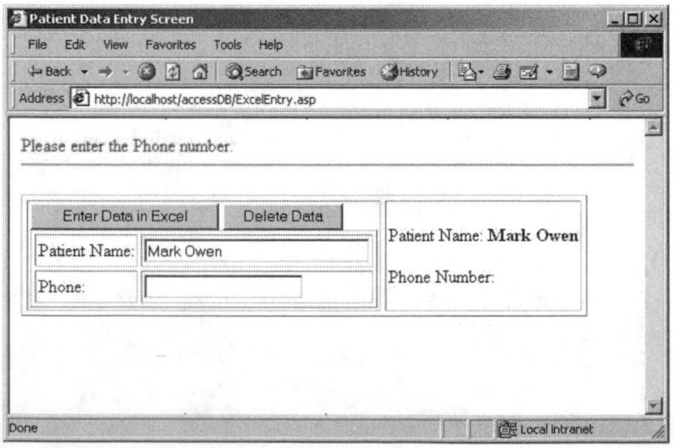

Figure 16-37:
ASP form with data
validation during the
data entry

7. Try to delete the data that does not exist. The result is shown in Figure 16-38.

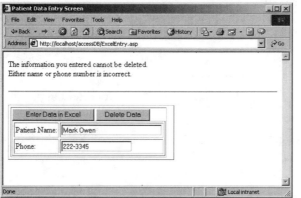

Figure 16-38:
ASP form with data validation during the delete operation

8. Open the spreadsheet file **C:\ExcelWithASP\WriteToExcel.xls** and view the results.

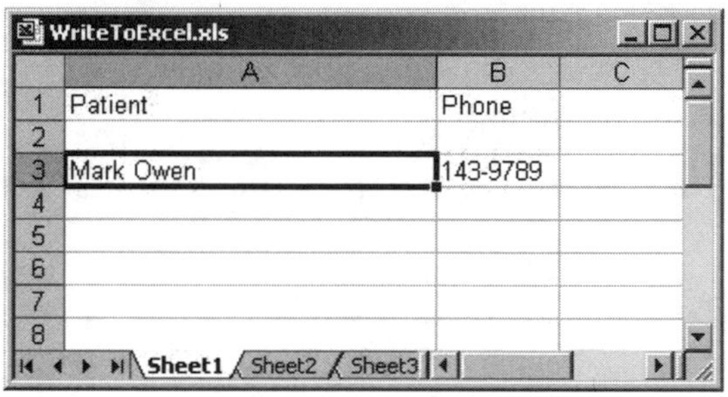

Figure 16-39:
Excel spreadsheet after removing the first entry (in row 2)

Printing Excel Data to an Internet Browser using the GetString Method

You can use the Recordset object's GetString method to print the data contained in an Excel spreadsheet in an Internet browser. This method returns a set of records into a string and is faster than looping through the recordset. The GetString method has the following syntax:

```
variant = recordset.GetString(StringFormat, NumRows, _
                    ColumnDelimiter, RowDelimiter, NullExpr)
```

The first argument (`StringFormat`) determines the format for representing the recordset as a string. The second argument (`NumRows`) specifies the number of recordset rows to return. If blank, GetString will return all the rows. The third argument (`ColumnDelimiter`) specifies the delimiter for the columns within the row (the default is a tab). The fourth argument (`RowDelimiter`) specifies a row delimiter (the default is a carriage return).

The fifth argument (`NullExpr`) specifies an expression to represent NULL values (the default is an empty string).

Now let's see how you can use the GetString method to retrieve the data from the Excel file created in an earlier example (or simply substitute the file name with any Excel spreadsheet name you want to read).

1. Open Notepad.
2. Enter the ASP script shown below.
3. Save the ASP file as **C:\ExcelWithASP\GetExcel.asp**.
4. Close Notepad.

GetExcel.asp code

```
<% @Language=VBSCRIPT %>
<%
dim myConn
dim myExcel
dim strCon
dim mySQL

' Create the connection object
 set myConn = Server.CreateObject("ADODB.Connection")

' Specify the connection string
 strCon="Provider=Microsoft.Jet.OLEDB.4.0;Data Source="
     strCon=strCon & server.MapPath("WriteToExcel.xls") & ";"
     strCon=strCon & "Extended Properties=Excel 8.0"

' Open the connection
 myConn.Open strCon

' Create the Recordset
 set myExcel=Server.CreateObject("ADODB.Recordset")
 mySQL="Select * from [Sheet1$]"

' Open the Recordset
 myExcel.Open mySQL, myConn

' Show data in a table
 Response.Write "<TABLE BORDER=1><TR><TD>"

' Get the column names
  For each fld in myExcel.Fields
   Response.Write fld.Name & "<TD>"
  Next
 Response.Write "</TR><TR><TD>"

' Get the actual data
 Response.Write myExcel.GetString(, -1, "</TR><TD>", _
     "</TD></TR><TR><TD>", NBSPACE)

' Close the Recordset and release the object
 myExcel.Close
```

```
      set myExcel = Nothing

' Close the connection
  myConn.Close
  set myConn = Nothing
%>
</TABLE>
```

The above ASP script connects to the specified Excel file and retrieves the data located in Sheet1. After reading the column names from the Fields collection, the code uses the above-mentioned GetString method to pull the data:

```
Response.Write myExcel.GetString(, -1, "</TR><TD>", _
    "</TD></TR><TR><TD>", NBSPACE)
```

Notice that –1 indicates that all rows should be read. The </TR><TD> tags are used for delimiting columns while </TD></TR> <TR><TD> specify the row delimiter. If the cell does not contain any data, a non-breaking space will be entered (NBSPACE) so that there are no gaps in the table structure.

Creating Charts in ASP

When you present dynamic data in web pages, you can enhance the comprehension of the data by the user by providing a nice chart. Although there are many ways to generate charts in ASP, in this section we will focus on using a tool that you are already familiar with. Simply put, you will use the Microsoft Excel Chart Wizard to create a chart. A word of caution: Using Chart Wizard requires that you have a copy of Microsoft Office installed on your web server. Also, keep in mind that with this technique, Excel needs to be loaded into memory; therefore, using this approach for a high-volume web site is not recommended.

The example below demonstrates how to create a chart based on data pulled dynamically from the Microsoft Access sample Northwind database.

Step 1: Creating the ASP Script to Obtain the Data and Generate the Chart

1. Open Notepad.
2. Enter the ASP script shown below.
3. Save the ASP file as **C:\ExcelWithASP\MakeChart.asp**.
4. Close Notepad.

    MakeChart.asp code

```
<% @Language=VBSCRIPT %>
<%
' Constant declaration
 Const adOpenStatic = 3
 Const adLockReadOnly = 1
```

```
Const xlColumnClustered = 51
Const xlRows = 1
Const xlLocationAsObject = 2
Const xlCategory = 1
Const xlPrimary = 1
Const xlValue = 2
Const xlHtml = 44

' Variable declaration
dim myExcel        ' Object variable representing Excel Application.
dim fso            ' Object variable representing the FileSystemObject.
dim filename       ' String variable to hold the name of the chart file.
dim conn           ' Object variable representing the Connection object.
dim rst            ' Object variable representing the Recordset object.
Dim wkb            ' Object variable representing the Workbook object.
Dim rng            ' Object variable representing the Range object.
Dim fld            ' Dummy variable for enumerating fields.
Dim rowNum         ' Row counter.
Dim colNum         ' Column counter.
Dim varData        ' Variant to hold returned Recordset.

Set myExcel= Server.Createobject("Excel.Application")
Set fso = Server.Createobject("Scripting.FileSystemObject")

' If exists, delete the previously prepared chart
filename = "c:\xlsChart.htm"
If fso.FileExists(filename) Then
    fso.DeleteFile filename, True
End If

' Release the FileSystemObject
Set fso = Nothing

' Create a new workbook
set wkb = myExcel.Workbooks.Add

' Get data to chart from Microsoft Access database
' Create and establish connection to the database
Set conn = Server.CreateObject("ADODB.Connection")

' Open the Northwind database
conn.Open "Driver={Microsoft Access Driver (*.mdb)};" & _
        "DBQ=" & Server.MapPath("Northwind.mdb")

' Create recordset and retrieve values using the open connection
Set rst = Server.CreateObject("ADODB.Recordset")

' Open the Recordset with a static cursor (3) in read-only mode (1)
    rst.Open "SELECT CategoryName As [Product Category], " & _
        "SUM(Quantity) AS [Total Quantity Sold] " & _
        "FROM Categories " & _
          "INNER JOIN (Products INNER JOIN [Order Details] ON " & _
        "Products.ProductID = [Order Details].ProductID) ON " & _
        "Categories.CategoryID = Products.CategoryID " & _
```

```
            "GROUP BY Categories.CategoryName " & _
            "ORDER BY Categories.CategoryName", _
               conn, adOpenStatic, adLockReadOnly


' Add field names as column headers.
 For fld = 0 to rst.Fields.Count - 1
    colNum = colNum + 1
    wkb.ActiveSheet.Cells(1, colNum).Value = _
        rst.Fields(fld).Name
 Next


' Store the records in a variable
 varData = rst.GetRows()


'Place data from the database in a worksheet.
 For rowNum = 1 To rst.RecordCount
   For colNum = 0 To UBound(varData)
     wkb.ActiveSheet.Cells(rowNum + 1, colNum + 1).Value = _
        varData(colNum, rowNum - 1)
   Next
 Next


' Close the Recordset and release the object
 rst.Close
 set rst = Nothing


' Close the Connection to the database
 conn.Close
 Set conn = Nothing


' Autofit the used range
 wkb.ActiveSheet.UsedRange.Columns.Autofit


' Set the range of the chart
 set rng = wkb.Sheets("Sheet1").Range("A1").CurrentRegion


' Create a chart based on pulled data
 wkb.Charts.Add


' Format the chart
 wkb.ActiveChart.ChartType = xlColumnClustered


' Specify the data source of the chart
 wkb.ActiveChart.SetSourceData rng, xlRows


' Place the chart on the second sheet
 wkb.ActiveChart.Location xlLocationAsObject, "Sheet2"


' Add chart and value axis titles
 With wkb.ActiveChart
   .HasTitle = True
   .ChartTitle.Characters.Text = "Quantity Sales by Category"
   .Axes(xlValue, xlPrimary).HasTitle = True
   .Axes(xlValue, xlPrimary).AxisTitle.Characters.Text = "Quantity"
```

```
End With

' Save the workbook file as a Web Page (in HTML format)
wkb.SaveAs filename, xlHtml

' Close the workbook
myExcel.ActiveWorkbook.Close

' Shut down Excel application and release the object
myExcel.Quit
Set myExcel = Nothing

' Display the generated Web Page in the browser
Response.Redirect filename
%>
```

The ASP script shown above is well commented, so you should not have
any trouble understanding the entire process. In short, we will start by
defining constants and variables. Constant declaration will allow you to use
the intrinsic constants instead of their values and make the code easier to
understand. Before creating a new workbook, the script uses the
FileSystemObject to delete the previously prepared HTML file if it exists.
The remaining part of the ASP script can be broken into the following main
sections:

- Creating a new workbook
- Connecting to the Access database and obtaining the data
- Writing out column headings and the data to a web page (notice how
  the GetRows method is used to store the data in a two-dimensional
  array)
- Closing the Recordset and connection to the Access database
- Creating and formatting the chart. Some of the code for this section can
  be recorded using the macro recorder if you are not very familiar with
  Chart objects, methods, and properties.
- Saving the workbook as a web page. When you save a workbook file as
  a web page, the document is saved as an HTML file. In addition, a
  folder containing all the supporting files that are referenced by the
  HTML file is created on your hard drive. This folder is named
  name_files, where name is the document name. Therefore, when your
  ASP code saves the workbook in HTML format using the following
  statement:

```
wkb.Save As filename, xlhtml
```

you should see on your computer a folder of supporting files named
xlsChart_files.

If you'd rather keep the supporting files in the same folder as the
HTML file, you can indicate your preference in the Options dialog box.
Simply click the General tab and press the Web options button. Next,

click the Files tab, and clear the Organize supporting files in a folder check box.

■ Closing the open file and quitting Excel

■ Displaying the generated web page in a browser. Response.Redirect tells the browser to request a different page (in this case, the newly created xlsChart.htm file).

Step 2: Running the ASP Script—MakeChart.asp

To try out your ASP script, perform the following:

1. Open your Internet browser.

2. Enter the following address: **http://localhost/accessDB/Make-Chart.asp**. You should see the xlsChart.htm file in the browser with Sheet1 displaying the data pulled from the Access database.

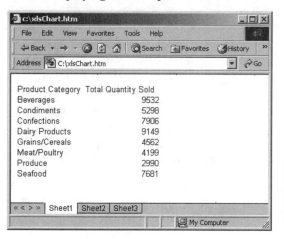

Figure 16-40:
Data used for charting can be obtained dynamically from the Microsoft Access database.

3. Click the **Sheet2** tab to view the chart.

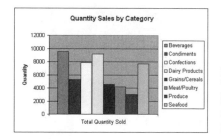

Figure 16-41:
You can use the Microsoft Excel Chart Wizard to generate a chart in an ASP page.

Note: To see other examples of charting using Excel, see Appendices A and D.

What's Next...

In this chapter, you were introduced to using Excel with the Internet. Let's quickly summarize the information that we've covered here:

■ Hyperlinks allow you to activate a specified web page from a worksheet cell.

■ Excel files can be easily viewed in an Internet browser.

■ HTML files can be created and published from Excel using menu options or VBA procedures.

■ Web queries allow you to retrieve "live" data from a web page into a worksheet. These queries can be created using built-in menu options or programmatically with VBA. Web queries let you retrieve an entire web page or specific tables that a particular web page contains. The retrieved data can be refreshed as often as required. There are two types of web queries: static and dynamic.

■ Active Server Pages (ASP) is a technology from Microsoft enabled by the Internet Information Services (IIS) or Personal Web Server. ASP allows you to create dynamic web pages. Using ASP, you can retrieve information stored in external data sources (such as a Microsoft Access database or SQL Server database) into an Excel spreadsheet.

■ Using several hands-on examples, you've learned how to write and run ASP scripts, generate a tab-delimited file on the web server, create an Excel file from user input, and use the Excel Chart Wizard to create charts in ASP.

In the next chapter, you will explore another Internet technology known as XML and find out how it is integrated with Excel.

Chapter 17

XML and Excel 2002

What is XML? ■ XML Support in Excel 2002 ■ Creating XML Spreadsheet Files with VBA ■ Viewing the XML Source File in Notepad ■ Well-Formed XML Documents ■ Viewing the XML Source File in Internet Explorer ■ Building XML Files Outside of Microsoft Excel 2002 ■ The XML Flattener ■ Formatting XML Data with Stylesheets ■ Linking an XML Document to a Stylesheet ■ Viewing XML Documents Formatted with Stylesheets ■ Using an XSLT Template ■ XML Data Islands ■ Using VBScript to Transform the Contents of XML Data Islands ■ Saving a Range of Cells as an XML Document ■ The XML Document Object Model ■ Transforming XML into HTML with an XSL Stylesheet Programmatically ■ Using VBScript and XML DOM to Transform XML Documents ■ Working with XML Document Nodes ■ Retrieving Information from Element Nodes ■ XML via ADO ■ Saving an ADO Recordset as XML to Disk ■ Two Types of XML Files ■ Applying an XSL Stylesheet ■ Transforming Attribute-Based XML Data into an HTML Table ■ Loading an ADO Recordset ■ Saving the ADO Recordset to XML in Memory ■ Saving the ADO Recordset into the XML DOMDocument Object ■ XML and ASP ■ Posting Excel XML Data to a Web Server ■ What's Next...

In the previous chapter you mastered several techniques of using Excel with the Internet. You've used HTML, ASP, and VBScript to put Excel worksheets on the web and retrieved web data via web queries for further manipulation in Excel. This chapter expands your knowledge of Internet technologies by introducing you to new XML functionality that has been added to Excel 2002.

What is XML?

XML, which stands for *Extensible Markup Language,* is an exciting new technology that provides a mechanism for designing your own custom markup language and using that language for describing the data in your own documents. Although XML was designed specifically for delivering information over the World Wide Web, it is being utilized in other areas, such as storing, sharing, and exchanging data.

Like HTML, XML is a markup language. However, HTML and XML serve different functions: HTML describes web page layout by using a set of fixed non-customizable tags, while XML lets you describe data content using custom tags.

The main goal of XML is the separation of content from presentation. Because XML documents are text files, XML is independent of an operating system platform, a software vendor, and a natural or programming language. XML makes it easy to describe any data structure (structured or unstructured) and send it anywhere across the web using common protocols, such as HTTP or FTP. As long as any two organizations can agree on the XML tag set to be used to represent the data being exchanged, it doesn't matter what back-end systems these organizations run or databases they use.

Although anyone can describe the data by creating a set of custom tags, the representatives of many industry groups have defined and published XML schemas that dictate how XML documents are formatted to represent data for their industry. A good example is the Microsoft XML-SS schema, which finally allows you to describe spreadsheet data (more details on it later in this chapter), or Chemical Markup Language (CML), which defines how to use XML to describe data for the chemical industry.

You can find information on XML-related specifications and proposals and domain-specific XML vocabularies at http://www.w3.org or http://www.wdvl.com/Authoring/Languages/XML/Specifications.html or by searching for "XML Vocabularies" in your browser.

XML Support in Excel 2002

Microsoft Excel 2002 offers extensive XML support. To begin with, instead of saving your workbook file as a standard *.xls file, you can just as easily save it as an XML spreadsheet. To do this, no programming skills are required. In the Microsoft Excel application window, simply choose File | Save As and select XML Spreadsheet in the Save as type drop-down box of the Save As dialog box (Figure 17-1). You can also open the XML spreadsheet back into Excel and use it as if it were a standard Excel file (Figure 17-2).

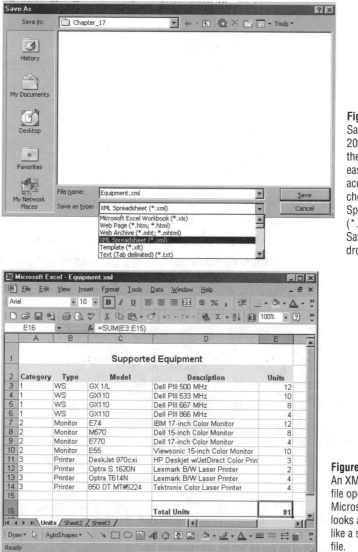

Figure 17-1:
Saving the Excel 2002 workbook in the XML format is easily accomplished by choosing XML Spreadsheet (*.xml) in the Save as type drop-down box.

Figure 17-2:
An XML spreadsheet file opened in Microsoft Excel looks and behaves like a standard .xls file.

The following sections in this chapter demonstrate how XML files are created programmatically with VBA and how XML data can be formatted for display in a web page by using XSL (Extensible Stylesheet Language) and data binding. You also learn how to use ActiveX Data Objects (ADO) to save data retrieved from the Microsoft Access sample database as XML to disk or to XML in memory. The chapter ends with a more complex hands-on project demonstrating how to post timesheet data to a web server directly from a Microsoft Excel spreadsheet.

Creating XML Spreadsheet Files with VBA

Now that you know how to save and open the XML file using the manual method (see Figure 17-1), let's see how you can save and open XML files in Excel 2002 programmatically with VBA.

The following exercise demonstrates how to use VBA to save and open spreadsheet files in XML format.

1. Create the worksheet file shown in Figure 17-2 or load the Equipment.xls file from the book's companion CD-ROM. If you are creating the file from scratch, save it as **Equipment.xls**.

2. With the Equipment.xls workbook open, activate the Visual Basic Editor window (**Alt+F11**) and press **Ctrl+G** to open the Immediate window.

3. To save the Equipment.xls file in the XML spreadsheet format, enter the following instruction in the Immediate window:

```
ActiveWorkbook.Worksheets("Units").SaveAs "Units.xml", xlXMLSpreadsheet
```

When you press Enter, Visual Basic displays the message shown in Figure 17-3 below. Click **Yes** to continue. The above instruction saves the workbook file in the current directory in the XML spreadsheet format by using the xlXMLSpreadsheet file format parameter.

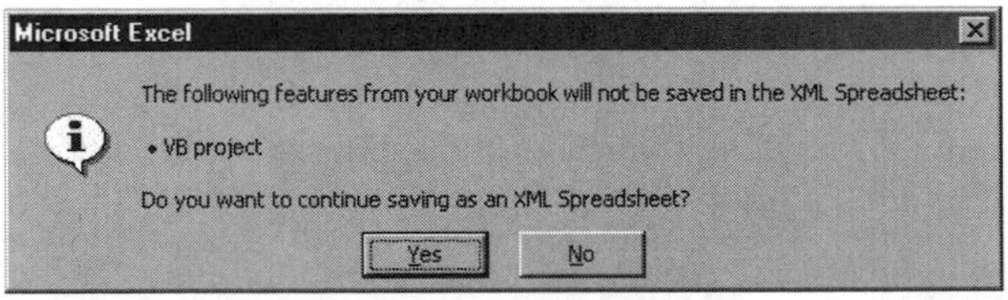

Figure 17-3: When a workbook feature cannot be saved in the XML spreadsheet format, Excel displays a message.

Tip 17-1: Saving Excel Workbooks in XML Format

When you save an Excel workbook in XML format, all the information about the workbook and its data is saved, except for charts, images, OLE and drawing objects, groups/outlines, and VBA projects.

---

4. To find out where the file was saved, type the following in the Immediate window:

```
?ActiveWorkbook.Path
```

When you press Enter, the file path appears in the Immediate window. You can save the file directly to a specific directory on a web server by specifying the path as follows:

```
ActiveWorkbook.Worksheets("Units").SaveAs _
    "http://localhost/myfolder/Units.xml", xlXMLSpreadsheet
```

The above statement must be entered on one line when used in the Immediate window. This statement saves the XML file to a virtual directory, myfolder, on the web server named localhost (see Chapter 16 for how to create a virtual directory).

5. Now go back to the Immediate window and close the Units.xml file by entering the following instruction:

```
ActiveWorkbook.Close
```

The Units.xml file is now closed. However, the Excel application is still running and you should be in the Visual Basic Editor window.

6. Reopen the Units.xml file by typing the following statement in the Immediate window:

```
Workbooks.Open "Units.xml"
```

Excel opens the Units.xml file. This file looks like the Equipment.xml file shown in Figure 17-2. You can use the XML file as a standard XLS file. You can also open an XML file in Microsoft Excel by using the OpenXML method, as shown below:

```
Workbooks.OpenXML "Units.xml"
```

The OpenXML method requires a string indicating the name of the file to open. It can also take a second, optional argument—a value or an array of values specifying which XSLT stylesheet processing instructions to apply. You will learn about stylesheets later in this chapter.

Tip 17-2: What's the Difference between XML and XLS Files?

XLS files in proprietary binary format are recognized by Excel. XML files created in Excel 2002 either manually or with VBA are text files. XML files can be opened or written from scratch in any ASCII text editor.

Viewing the XML Source File in Notepad

You have now created programmatically your first XML spreadsheet document. You've also opened it and saw no difference in the way the XML document appears in the Microsoft Excel user interface. This is because the XML document created from within Excel 2002 preserves the Microsoft Excel spreadsheet format, structure, and data. But let's open the Units.xlm file in Windows Notepad and view the underlying XML code. As mentioned earlier, XML is a markup language that uses custom tags. In order to understand XML files, you must become familiar with the way XML files are tagged. We will continue working in the Immediate window to get some programming practice while learning the new XML concepts.

The following exercise demonstrates how to use Notepad to view the content of XML files.

1. In the Immediate window type the following instruction to open the XML file in Notepad:

```
Shell "Notepad.exe Units.xml"
```

Visual Basic launches Notepad and loads the Units.xml file. Switch to Notepad by clicking the appropriate icon in the Windows taskbar. Notepad displays the XML file, as shown in Figure 17-4.

Figure 17-4:
The XML file created with Excel VBA can be displayed in Notepad.

An XML document contains a tree of elements. Each element has an element type name (often called the tag name) and a set of attributes. Notice that the XML tags are the labels within < >. Each attribute consists of a name followed by an equals sign and an attribute value. For instance, ss:ID="Default", ss:Name="Sheet1", ss:StyleId="s22", ss:Type="

Number", ss:Size="12", and ss:Formula="=SUM(R[-13]C:R[-1]C)" are just a few examples of attributes that you will find in the Units.xml source code.

The topmost element of an XML spreadsheet document is <Workbook>. This is also the root tag of the spreadsheet document. Under the root you will find other tags that represent child elements. These elements precisely define the spreadsheet document. As you scroll down in the Notepad window, you will find the <Styles> tag that contains the style definitions for the workbook and the <Worksheet> tag that defines a worksheet within the current workbook. At least one instance of this element is required within a valid XML spreadsheet document. Below the Worksheet tag, you should find the <Table> tag that defines a table of cells in the current worksheet with some optional attributes, such as ss:ExpandedColumnCount or ss:ExpandedRowCount that specify the total number of columns and rows in the table. The child element of a table is <Row>. Each Row element may contain one or more <Cell> elements, which in turn contain <Data> elements specifying the value of a cell. If you apply more formatting to your orginal spreadsheet and resave the file in the XML spreadsheet format, you will find other tags describing your spreadsheet document. For example, named and/or autofilter ranges within the worksheet will be indicated with the <Names>, <NamedRange>, and <AutoFilter> tags.

Tip 17-3: The XML Spreadsheet Tag Hierarchy

The details on each XML spreadsheet element and the required and optional attributes can be found at http://msdn.microsoft.com/library/default.asp?url=/library/en-us/dnexcl2k2/html/odc_xlsmlinss.asp.

As you can see, the structure of the XML spreadsheet document is very logical and therefore easy to follow. Tags are nested inside other tags. Each element must have both a start tag and an end tag. Unlike HTML, XML is less forgiving; it does not allow you to omit the end tag. The name of the start tag must match the name in the corresponding end tag exactly. For example, a start tag of <Row> must have an end tag of </Row>.

The first line in the XML file is a processing instruction:

```
<?xml version="1.0"?>
```

This instruction identifies the file as an XML file. If you remove this processing instruction and attempt to open the XML file in Excel, the file won't be recognized as XML and Excel will open it as a text file. Note that the processing instruction begins and ends with a question mark (?) and contains the name of the application (in this example "xml") to which the instruction is directed, as well as additional information that needs to be passed to the XML processor, such as the version number, character set to be applied, name of a file to use, etc.

The second instruction:

```
<Workbook xmlns="urn:schemas-microsoft-com:office:spreadsheet"
xmlns:o="urn:schemas-microsoft-com:office:office"
xmlns:x="urn:schemas-microsoft-com:office:excel"
xmlns:ss="urn:schemas-microsoft-com:office:spreadsheet"
xmlns:html="http://www.w3.org/TR/REC-html40">
```

lists namespaces referenced in the Excel XML spreadsheet document (see Tip 17-4).

Tip 17-4: What is a Namespace?

A namespace is a collection of names in which all names are unique. Because XML allows you to invent your own tag names, how can you ensure that your tags will not conflict with someone else's tags when two or more XML documents are combined? The <TABLE> tag will certainly have a different meaning and content in an Excel XML spreadsheet document than the <TABLE> element used to describe different types of tables listed in a catalog for a furniture store chain. There must be some way to differentiate elements and attributes that have the same name. The XML Namespaces specification ensures that element names do not conflict with one another and are unique within a particular set of names (a namespace). The attribute "xmlns" is an XML keyword for a namespace declaration. The namespace is identified by a Uniform Resource Identifier (URI) — either a Uniform Resource Locator (URL) or a Uniform Resource Name (URN).

Usually the namespace declaration is placed within the start tag of the element where you want to use the namespace, as in the following:

```
<Workbook xmlns="urn:schemas-
  microsoft-com:office:spreadsheet"
  xmlns:o="urn:schemas-microsoft-com:
  office:office"
```

```
...
...
xmlns:html="http://www.w3.org/TR/
  REC-html40">
```

In this example, the first declaration indicates that the urn:schemas-microsoft-com:office:spreadsheet namespace is the default XML namespace. A namespace without a prefix is referred to as a "default namespace." All elements and attributes within the Workbook element are by default from that namespace.

The second declaration associates the "o" prefix with the urn:schemas-microsoft-com:office:office namespace. The last declaration declares the html namespace. This is a special namespace that always points to the following URL: http://www.w3.org/TR/REC-html40.

There is no requirement that the specified URI is valid or that it conforms to any sort of specification. Most namespaces use URIs for the namespace names because URIs are guaranteed to be unique. What you should remember from this tip is that namespaces don't really exist. They are arbitrary names that allow you to distinguish between tags with the same names that need to be processed differently. Namespaces prevent naming conflicts that might arise in XML documents.

Well-Formed XML Documents

When you create or modify an XML document, you must make sure that your XML file is well-formed. See Tip 17-5 for what makes a document well-formed. The well-formedness of an XML document is similar to syntax checking in VBA. When you try to open an XLM file in Excel that is not well-formed, you will receive an error message similar to the one in Figure 17-5. I have forced this error by removing the end tag </CELL> from the Units.xml file while it was opened in Notepad. I then resaved the file in Notepad and closed it. When I attempted to open the file again in Excel, I received the error message in Figure 17-5. As you can see, the error dialog box specifies the type of error that was found and indicates that the error log XMLErr.log file can be found in the Temp folder. Figure 17-6 displays the contents of the error log file. You must fix all the errors to successfully open the file in Excel.

Tip 17-5: What is a Well-Formed XML Document?

An XML document must have one root element. While in HTML the root element is always <HTML>, in the XML document you can name your root element anything you want. Element names must begin with a letter or underscore character.

The root element must enclose all other elements. Elements must be properly nested. The XML data must be hierarchical; the beginning and ending tags cannot overlap.

```
<Employee>
   <Employee Id>090909</Employee Id>
</Employee>
```

All element tags must be closed. A begin tag must be followed by an end tag:

```
<Sessions>5</Sessions>
```

You can use shortcuts, such as a single slash (/), to end the tag so you don't have to type the full tag name. For example, if the current Sessions

element is empty (does not have value), you could use the following tag: <Sessions />.

Tag names are case-sensitive: The tags <Title> and </Title> aren't equivalent to <TITLE> and </TITLE>. For example, the following:

```
<Title>Beginning VBA Programming
   </Title>
```

is not the same as:

```
<TITLE>Beginning VBA Programming
   </TITLE>
```

All attributes must be in quotation marks:

```
<Course Id="VBAEX1"/>
```

You cannot have more than one attribute with the same name within the same element. If the <Course> element has two Id attributes, they must be written separately, as shown below:

```
<Course Id="VBAEX1"/>
<Course Id="VBAEX2"/>
```

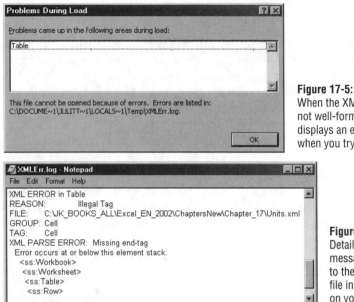

Figure 17-5:
When the XML document is not well-formed, Excel displays an error message when you try to open the file.

Figure 17-6:
Details of the error messages are written to the XMLErr.log text file in the Temp folder on your computer.

Viewing the XML Source File in Internet Explorer

To become more familiar with the structure of the XML document, let's open it now in the browser.

The following exercise demonstrates how to use Internet Explorer to view the content of XML files.

1. Open the Units.xml file in Internet Explorer by typing the following instruction in the Immediate window:

```
Shell "Explorer.exe Units.xml"
```

Explorer opens with the specified file (Figure 17-7).

When you open an XML file in Internet Explorer, you can see the hierarchical layout of an XML document very clearly. IE automatically places a

---

Tip 17-6: What is a Parser?

If you want to read, update, create, or manipulate any XML document, you will need an XML parser. A parser is a software engine, usually a dynamic-link library (DLL), that can read and extract data from XML. Microsoft Internet Explorer 5 or higher has a built-in XML parser (MSXML.DLL, MSXML2.DLL, MSXML3.DLL) that can read and detect all non well-formed documents. MSXML has its own object model, known as DOM (Document Object Model), that you can use from VBA to quickly and easily extract information from an XML document.

Figure 17-7:
Raw (unformatted)
XML file opened in
Internet Explorer

plus/minus (+ / –) sign, so it is possible to expand and collapse your XML data in the browser. Earlier in this chapter, you learned that XML documents must be well-formed. To verify that the document is well-formed, it's a good idea to open it in the browser. Figure 17-8 shows how the browser displays the document with the same error that was presented earlier (see Figure 17-5).

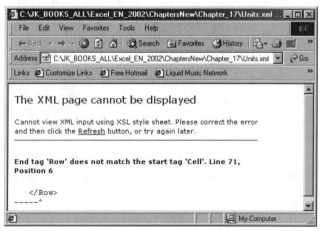

Figure 17-8:
A quick way to check
whether an XML
document is
well-formed is by
opening it in a
browser, such as
Internet Explorer.

Tip 17-7: Two Types of Validation

In XML there are two types of validation. One is checking whether the document is well-formed (see Tip 17-5). The other type of validation requires that you create a Document Type Definition (DTD) or a set of rules (known as schema) to determine the type of elements and attributes an XML document should contain, how these elements and attributes should be named, and the relationship between the elements. The DTD or schema for an XML document is optional. You create either one only if you are planning to validate data. In XML, data validation is accomplished by comparing the document with the DTD or schema. When you open the XML document in a parser, the parser compares the DTD to the data and raises an error if the data is invalid. This book does not explore the creation and use of DTDs or schemas. What you should remember from this tip is that a valid XML document is not the same as a well-formed XML document. A valid XML document conforms to a structure outlined in the Document Type Definition (DTD) or schema, while well-formed documents follow the basic formatting rules mentioned in Tip 17-5.

Building XML Files Outside of Microsoft Excel 2002

When you save a Microsoft Excel 2002 workbook in the XML spreadsheet file format, the program uses the XML Spreadsheet Schema (XML-SS) to encode the data and formatting of the spreadsheet. Based on what you've already learned in this chapter about XML spreadsheet elements and attributes, it is quite easy to create an XML spreadsheet file outside of Microsoft Excel. Assume that you are working on a computer where Excel is not installed and need to prepare a spreadsheet containing quarterly sales figures for the East region. For the following exercise, you can use Notepad as your editor.

The following exercise demonstrates how to use Notepad to create an Excel spreadsheet in XML format.

1. Enter the XML code shown in Figure 17-9.

2. Save the file as **EastRegion.xml**.

3. Assume you've just received an e-mail with the EastRegion.xml file attachment. Open the EastRegion.xml document in Microsoft Excel 2000. The XML output is shown in Figure 17-10.

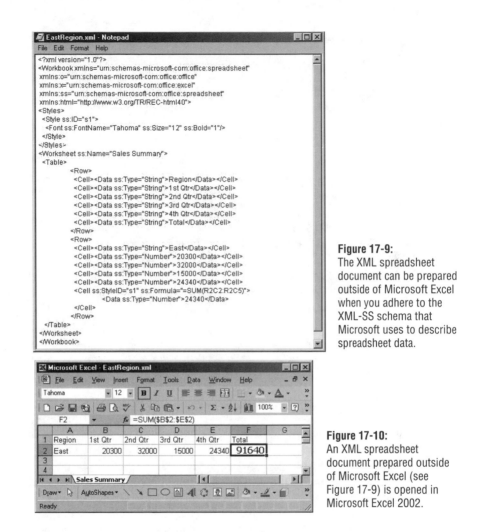

Figure 17-9:
The XML spreadsheet document can be prepared outside of Microsoft Excel when you adhere to the XML-SS schema that Microsoft uses to describe spreadsheet data.

Figure 17-10:
An XML spreadsheet document prepared outside of Microsoft Excel (see Figure 17-9) is opened in Microsoft Excel 2002.

The XML Flattener

It's quite interesting to see how Excel 2002 deals with XML files that have been created outside of Excel but do not use the XML-SS that Microsoft uses to describe spreadsheet data. Let's again assume that you've just received an e-mail with an XML file attachment listing the VBA course schedule for the coming year. The Courses.xml file is shown in Figure 17-11. You don't care how this file was generated. It could have been typed directly in a text editor or outputted from a database using a programming language. Now that you've got the data, you want to view it in Excel. Figure 17-12 displays the Courses.xml file opened in Excel.

With Excel being a spreadsheet application, it looks at your XML file and tries to display it in a familiar spreadsheet format using its built-in

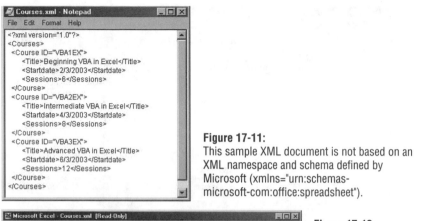

Figure 17-11:
This sample XML document is not based on an XML namespace and schema defined by Microsoft (xmlns="urn:schemas-microsoft-com:office:spreadsheet").

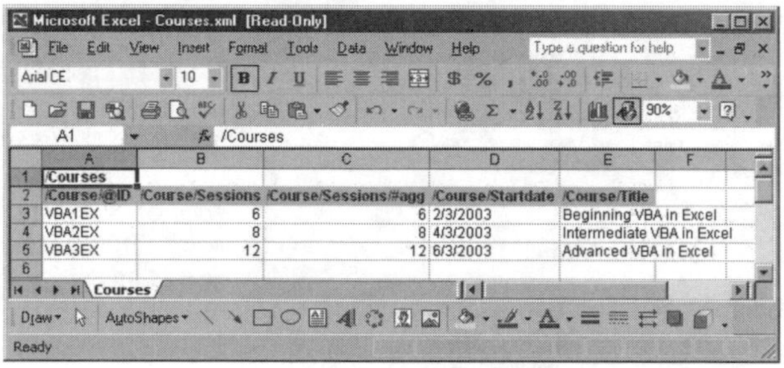

Figure 17-12:
Microsoft Excel 2002 transforms an XML document that is not in XML spreadsheet format (see Figure 17-11) into rows and columns using a built-in mechanism known as the XML Flattener.

mechanism known as the XML Flattener. Because your XML file is not in a spreadsheet format, the XML Flattener must convert the hierarchical structure that is present in the XML document into a flat spreadsheet format. To do this, it must reshape the XML tree structure so that the data can be presented in spreadsheet rows and columns. Notice that in the original Courses.xml file (see Figure 17-11), the root element <Courses> has three child elements (also called nodes) positioned at the same level. The flattener reshapes the tree structure by collapsing the <Course> elements into a single node that contains all the children elements of the course elements that were collapsed. Notice also that in the original XML file, each of the <Course> elements has an attribute. Each attribute of the <Course> node will be appended to the node as a child node. The XML Flattener adds the @symbol to the beginning of the attribute name to avoid redundant naming and opens the file as read-only to prevent you from accidentally saving the original source file in the XML spreadsheet format (XML-SS). The XML Flattener performs the necessary trasformations behind the scenes. If you wanted to do manually what the XML Flattener does automatically, you would end up with the XML tree similar to the example shown below. Notice, however, that you could not add the @ symbol in front of the ID attribute because XML does not allow this character in names.

```
<?xml version="1.0"?>
<Courses>
    <Course>
```

```
<ID>VBA1EX
    <Title>Beginning VBA in Excel</Title>
    <startdate>2/3/2003</startdate>
    <Sessions>6</Sessions>
</ID>
<ID>VBA2EX
    <Title>Intermediate VBA in Excel</Title>
    <startdate>4/3/2003</startdate>
    <Sessions>8</Sessions>
</ID>
<ID>VBA3EX
    <Title>Advanced VBA in Excel</Title>
    <startdate>6/3/2003</startdate>
    <Sessions>12</Sessions>
</ID>
    </Course>
</Courses>
```

The following exercise demonstrates how to open an XML file in Excel.

1. Enter the above example code using Notepad and save it as **Courses2.xml**.

2. Open this file in Excel 2002 and compare the output with Figure 17-12.

If you take a look at Figure 17-12, you will notice that the XML Flattener places the root element <Courses> in cell A1 and treats it as a title for the data presented below. The column headings are not displayed in the same order as in the original file (see Figure 17-11) but are sorted alphabetically. Depending on the structure of the XML file, the XML Flattener may have to add a column named #Id when a node is collapsed to prevent the loss of information. To avoid calculation errors, an extra column with #agg is added (see the column labeled /Course/Sessions/#agg). Because Microsoft Excel does not know whether a value should exist individually in every column or if it should be an aggregate (a single value obtained from a calculation), it places an extra column with the #agg designation if the XML source file contains numeric values.

Formatting XML Data with Stylesheets

Although it is easy to view the XML file in the browser, nowadays users expect to see documents nicely formatted. Your raw XML data can be formatted with the Extensible Stylesheet (XSL) to meet users' expectations. Because the XML document does not contain any formatting instructions, you should prepare a stylesheet that can be applied to your document to make it visually more appealing to the user. You are not limited to one stylesheet. By creating more than one stylesheet, you can present the same XML document to various users formatted differently. The XSL document is just another XML document that contains HTML formatting instructions as to how to format the elements in your XML document.

In the following exercise, you will learn how to create a stylesheet for the Courses.xml file that we created earlier in this chapter. When you have completed this exercise, you will have an XSL stylesheet that transforms an XML document into HTML. Like any XML document, the XSL stylesheet can be created using a text editor such as Notepad.

The following exercise demonstrates how to create an XSL stylesheet to render XML documents into HTML.

1. Open Notepad and type the following line:

```
<?xml version="1.0"?>
```

Because the XLS document is just another XML application, it must contain the XML declaration, which states that this is an XML document and specifies the version number of the latest XML specification. Note that the declaration line must be entered in lowercase.

2. Type the following declaration line:

```
<HTML xmlns:xsl="http://www.w3.org/TR/WD-xsl">
```

This line of the XSL code specifies the namespace used by the stylesheet.

3. Now enter HTML tags to change the browser's title bar:

```
<HEAD>
      <TITLE>VBA Course Schedule</TITLE>
</HEAD>
```

This will cause the text "VBA Course Schedule" to appear in your browser's title bar when you open the formatted XML document.

4. Let's make the browser background more colorful:

```
<BODY bgcolor="yellow">
```

5. It's a good idea to place the same title in the browser's title bar on the web page. Let's make it stand out, centered on the page:

```
<CENTER>
<STRONG>VBA Course Schedule</STRONG><P/>
```

The <P/> tag will put a blank line between the page title and the table that you will write next.

6. Start writing out the table that you want to display. The table will obviously need headings, so we will begin with the following code:

```
<TABLE border="1" cellPadding="4" cellSpacing="2">
<TR>
      <TH>Course Id</TH>
      <TH>Course Title</TH>
      <TH>Start Date</TH>
      <TH>No of Sessions</TH>
</TR>
```

This HTML code segment will place a table on the web page when it's finished. Notice there is no closing </TABLE> tag, as we are not yet finished.

7. Now the tricky part begins, as we will need to refer to the XSL namespace to use one of its formatting commands: for-each. Write the following instruction:

```
<xsl:for-each select="Courses/Course">
```

The above line tells the XML processor to apply the same formatting to every <Course> element within the <Courses> element. Having said this, we will proceed to write out the remaining part of our table and place the actual data in it.

8. Type the following lines of code to complete the table:

```
<TR>
    <TD><xsl:value-of select="@ID"/></TD>
    <TD><xsl:value-of select="Title"/></TD>
    <TD><xsl:value-of select="Startdate"/></TD>
    <TD><xsl:value-of select="Sessions"/></TD>
</TR>
</xsl:for-each>
</TABLE>
```

The above code segment uses the HTML <TD> tag to place the actual data in a table row for each element, as specified in the <xsl:for-each select="Courses/Course"> statement (see step 7). The formatting element <xsl:value-of> returns the actual value of the specified element. The select attribute uses the XML Path Language (XPath) expression to locate the child elements to be processed. The tag <xsl:value-of select="Title"/> tells the XSL processor to find the Title element (here, "Title" is the XPath expression) and replace it with its value. If an expression refers to an attribute rather than an element, you need to prefix the attribute name with the @ character in order to read its value, as in the following:

```
<TD><xsl:value-of select="@ID"/></TD>
```

The tag <xsl:value-of> returns the content of the specified tag. It gets replaced with the actual data when the document is presented in the browser. After reading all the data elements, you must not forget about the ending tag to close the loop:

```
</xsl:for-each>
```

and the ending tag to close the table:

```
</TABLE>
```

Tip 17-8: What is XPath?

XML Path Language (XPath) is a query language used to create expressions for finding data in the XML. These expressions can manipulate strings, numbers, and Boolean values. They can also be used to navigate an XML tree structure and process its elements with XSLT instructions. XPath is designed to be used by XSL Transformations (XSLT) (see Tip 17-9). With XPath expressions, you can easily identify and extract from the XML document specific elements (nodes) based on their type, name, values, or the relationship of a node to other nodes. When preparing stylesheets for transforming your XML documents into HTML, you will often use various XPath expressions in the Select attribute. For example, to tell the XSLT processor to display the value of the current <Sessions> element, you will use the following tag:

```
<xsl:value-of select="Sessions"/>
```

To gather nodes of the same type so that you can iterate through them in your stylesheet, you might use the following tag:

```
<xsl:for-each select="Courses/Course"/>
```

The above directive tells the XSLT processor to go through all the course elements in the root node (Courses) and retrieve the value from the node's contents.

---

9.   At this point, you can write the closing tags </CENTER>, </BODY>, and </HTML> to complete your stylesheet document, or you can proceed to add additional information that you want to display for users to see once the formatted XML document is viewed in the browser. Let's add the information about the author and the name of the stylesheet used. Because we don't want this information centered, we will start off by closing the <CENTER> tag:

```
</CENTER>
<H6 align="left">
<HR/>
<FONT face="Tahoma">
Using Sample XSL stylesheet 'Courses.xsl' prepared by 'put your name here'
</FONT></H6>
</BODY>
</HTML>
```

Notice that before displaying the text, we placed a horizontal line using the <HR/> tag. While in a plain vanilla HTML document you can use the <HR> tag to place a horizontal line, the XSL stylesheet is an XML document and requires that all tags be closed. Hence, you need to write it as <HR/> or you'll get an error.

10. Save your document as **Courses.xsl**. Make sure to use the .xsl extension. Pay attention to this extension, as it is easy to get carried away and mix it up with the Excel .xls file extension. The completed XSL stylesheet is illustrated in Figure 17-13.

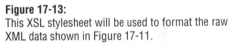

Figure 17-13:
This XSL stylesheet will be used to format the raw XML data shown in Figure 17-11.

The XSL document contains many HTML formatting instructions. (Take a look at Figure 17-13 and notice the following tags: <HEAD>, <TITLE>, <BODY>, <CENTER>, <STRONG>, <TABLE>, <TR>, <TD>, <H6>, <HR>, and <FONT>.) The example stylesheet also uses two special XSL formatting instructions. The first one:

```
<xsl:for-each select="Courses/Course"/>
```

tells the XSL processor to loop through all the <Course> elements within the <Courses> root element. The first part of this tag, xsl:for-each, tells the XSL processor to do something every time it finds a pattern, while the second part of the tag, select="Courses/Course", specifies the pattern for which to look. Notice that you must close each loop with a closing loop tag:

```
</xsl:for-each>
```

The stylesheet can also sort the information by using the order-by attribute on the xsl:for-each element, as shown below:

```
<xsl:for-each select="Courses/Course" order-by="Title"/>
```

The second type of special formatting instructions uses the <xsl:value-of> tags to tell the XSL processor to look inside the <Course> element and retrieve the value of the tag specified in the select attribute:

```
<TD><xsl:value-of select="@ID"/></TD>
<TD><xsl:value-of select="Title"/></TD>
<TD><xsl:value-of select="Startdate"/></TD>
<TD><xsl:value-of select="Sessions"/></TD>
```

Because the above block of code is located below the <xsl:for-each> tag, the XSL processor will retrieve the specified values for each <Course> element.

The Courses.xsl stylesheet contains formatting instructions that generate an HTML table and use the values of selected XML elements to fill the table with information. You can create as many stylesheets for your XML document as desired. Later in this chapter you will see other examples of XLS stylesheets and enhance your understanding of this subject.

Linking an XML Document to a Stylesheet

To establish a link between the XML and XSL files, you must include in your XML file a reference to the XSL file.

The following exercise demonstrates how to add a reference to a stylesheet in your XML document.

1. Open the Courses.xml document in Notepad.

2. Enter the following instruction below the XML declaration line:

    ```
    <?xml-stylesheet type="text/xsl"
    href="Courses.xsl"?>
    ```

    The modified XML document is shown in Figure 17-14.

3. Save your modified Courses.xml file.

4. Close Notepad.

Figure 17-14: Linking an XML document to an XSL stylesheet

Viewing XML Documents Formatted with Stylesheets

An XML document formatted with an XSL stylesheet can be viewed in a browser or in Microsoft Excel 2002.

The following exercise demonstrates how to view XML documents formatted with stylesheets.

1. In Windows Explorer, double-click the **Courses.xml** file. The file should open in the browser. Because this file is now linked to a stylesheet, instead of raw XML data you should see a nicely formatted table.

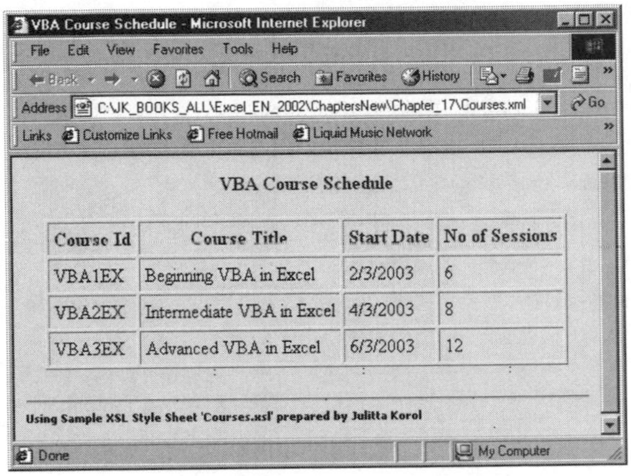

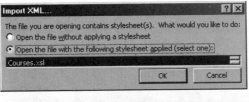

Figure 17-15:
An XML document formatted with an XSL stylesheet opened in the browser

2. Now let's open the Courses.xml file in Excel 2002. When you open an XML document in Excel that is linked to a stylesheet, Excel displays the Import XML dialog box (Figure 17-16) in which you can specify to either open the file without applying a stylesheet or apply a specific stylesheet. If you open the file without applying a stylesheet, the file will be opened, as described earlier in the section titled "XML Flattener."

Figure 17-16:
Excel allows you to open an XML file with or without a stylesheet if the XML file is linked to a stylesheet.

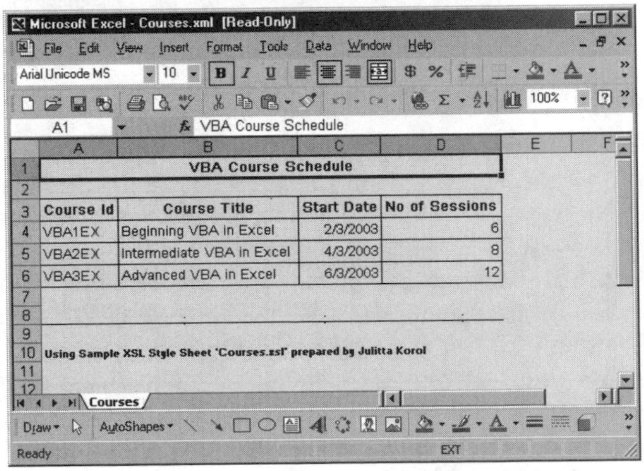

Figure 17-17:
An XML document formatted with an XSL stylesheet opened in Microsoft Excel 2002

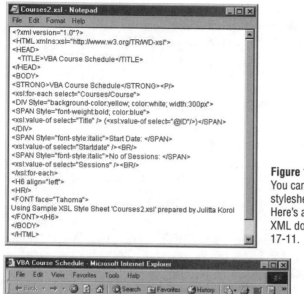

Figure 17-18:
You can apply more than one stylesheet to an XML document. Here's another stylesheet for the XML document shown in Figure 17-11.

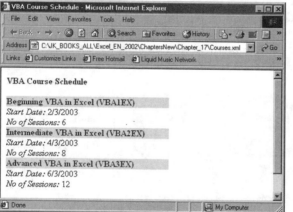

Figure 17-19:
This XML document was formatted with the XSL stylesheet shown in Figure 17-18.

Tip 17-9: What's the Difference between XSL and XSLT?

XSL (Extensible Stylesheet Language) is a style language for XML. This language consists of two parts:

- An XML vocabulary for specifying how an XML document should be formatted for display. XSL is often referred to as XSL-FO (Extensible Stylesheet Language Formatting Objects).

- A language for transforming XML documents to HTML or other XML documents: XSLT (XSL Transformations). XSLT is designed to be used independently of XSL. Tranformations also allow you to change the order of elements and selectively process elements.

To find out the details about the XSLT recommendation, visit the following web site: http://www.w3.org/TR/xslt. To read the XSL specification details, visit http://www.w3.org/TR/xsl.

Tip 17-10: XSLT Formatting Elements

The <xsl:for-each> and <xsl:value-of> elements used in the example stylesheet (Courses.xsl) in Figure 17-13 are only two of a number of XSLT formatting elements that are available for transforming raw XML data into HTML that the browser can display. Other XSLT elements allow you to define and apply templates for the output of elements (<xsl:template>, <xsl:apply-templates>, <xsl:call-template>), create additional elements and attributes in the output file (<xsl:element>, <xsl:attribute>), and declare parameters and variables (<xsl:param>, <xsl:variable>), as well as provide you with several ways to perform conditional processing (<xsl:if>, <xsl:choose>). To find out more about XSLT elements, visit the following web site: http://www.w3.org/TR/xslt.

Using an XSLT Template

Earlier in this chapter, you prepared an XSL stylesheet using the <xsl:for-each> formatting instruction. In addition to for-each processing of XML elements, you can use templates to perform tranformations of XML documents. The XSL stylesheet can contain one or more XSLT templates. You can think of templates as special blocks of code that apply to one or more XML tags. Templates contain rules for displaying a particular branch of elments in the XML document. The use of templates is made possible via special formatting tags. In this section, you will learn how to use two of these tags, <xsl:template> and <xsl:apply-templates>, while creating a stylesheet named CoursesMatch.xsl that is based on a single template.

The following exercise demonstrates how to create a stylesheet that uses a template.

1. Open Notepad and enter the code shown below.

2. Save the file as **CoursesMatch.xsl**.

```
<?xml version="1.0"?>
<xsl:stylesheet xmlns:xsl="http://www.w3.org/TR/WD-xsl">

<xsl:template match="/">

<STRONG>VBA Course Schedule</STRONG><P/>
<TABLE border="1" cellPadding="4" cellSpacing="2">
<TR>
     <TH>Course Id</TH>
     <TH>Course Title</TH>
     <TH>Start Date</TH>
     <TH>No of Sessions</TH>
</TR>
<xsl:apply-templates select="//Course"/>
</TABLE>
</xsl:template>
```

```
<xsl:template match="Course">
<TR>
      <TD><xsl:value-of select="@ID"/></TD>
      <TD><xsl:value-of select="Title"/></TD>
      <TD><xsl:value-of select="Startdate"/></TD>
      <TD><xsl:value-of select="Sessions"/></TD>
</TR>
</xsl:template>
</xsl:stylesheet>
```

The first line of the stylesheet code declares that this is an XML document that follows the XML 1.0 standard (version). As mentioned earlier, an XSL document is a type of XML document. While XML documents store data, XSL documents specify how the data should be displayed. The next line declares the namespace to be used to identify the tags in the xsl:stylesheet document (see Tip 17-4 for more information about namespaces). The third line of the code is where the template definition begins. The instruction:

```
<xsl:template match="/">
```

defines a template for the entire document. Notice that the <xsl:template> element has a match attribute. The value of the match attribute indicates the nodes (elements) for which this template is appropriate. For example, the special pattern "/" in the match attribute tells the XSL processor that this is the template for the document root. If you wanted to indicate that the template is appropriate only for <Title> elements, you would place "Title" as the value of the match attribute.

Following the definition of the template, the example code uses standard HTML tags to format the document title and table headings. The next instruction:

```
<xsl:apply-templates select="//Course"/>
```

directs the XSLT processor to find an appropriate <xsl:template> to apply. The select attribute of the <xsl:apply-templates> element selects the "Course" elements below the document root and asks the processor to find and apply an appropriate template. The text "//Course" is an XPath expression (see Tip 17-8) that tells the XSLT processor to get all the <Course> nodes. The first backslash represents the XML document's root node.

The apply-templates instruction is similar to the for-each instruction that was introduced in an earlier section. The major difference is that with apply-templates you can implement different processing by invoking many templates, depending on the rules that you've defined for each template. The for-each instruction, although easier to read and faster to process, allows only the code between the for-each open and close tags to be applied.

Now that you've defined the template to be used and asked the XSL processor to apply it, you need to write the closing tags </TABLE> and </xsl:template> and proceed to write a template that is appropriate for the "Course" elements.

The instruction:

```
<xsl:template match="Course">
```

tells the XSL processor that what follows are template rules to be used for all "Course" elements. The <xsl:template> element defines a template to be used to generate the desired output for the specified nodes. The match attribute identifies the source node or nodes to which the template rule applies. The next code fragment:

```
<TR>
    <TD><xsl:value-of select="@ID"/></TD>
    <TD><xsl:value-of select="Title"/></TD>
    <TD><xsl:value-of select="Startdate"/></TD>
    <TD><xsl:value-of select="Sessions"/></TD>
</TR>
```

uses the <xsl:value-of> element that was discussed earlier in this chapter. Recall that this element's select attribute tells the XSL processor to retrieve the value of the specified element or attribute. Each node selected by the <xsl:apply-templates> element will be associated with a template and become the current node for the template.

The above lines are applied to each "Course" node found under the root element and will create a row of table data for each element matching the "Course" pattern.

To finish off your stylesheet, you need to write two closing tags:

```
</xsl:template>
</xsl:stylesheet>
```

Now that the stylesheet is ready, you can link it to the Courses.xml document, as described in an earlier section titled "Linking an XML Document to a Stylesheet." When you open the Courses.xml document in your browser or inside Microsoft Excel 2002, you should see the data formatted in a table similar to Figure 17-21 (in the next section).

XML Data Islands

If you are looking for a hassle-free way to display your XML data in the browser in the HTML format (without using stylesheets), you should familiarize yourself with the concept of an XML data island. With XML data islands (introduced in Internet Explorer 5.0), you can easily bind HTML tags to data fields in your XML document. A *data island* is a segment of XML code within an HTML document. You can embed data in XML format directly into an HTML page by using the xml element. To see how this is done, take a look at Figure 17-20. In this example, the XML data island is the code fragment between the following comment lines: <!-- BEGINNING OF XML Data Island --> and <!-- END OF XML Data Island -->.

An HTML document can contain one or more data islands (groups of XML). Notice that the xml element contains an attribute named ID that specifies a reference to the data island. This reference is used later in the code to refer to the source data for the HTML table (see the datasrc attribute within the <TABLE> tag in the HTML Formatting Instructions section in Figure 17-20).

Tip 17-11: Comments in XML Documents

To make your XML documents legible and clear, you should use comments. the XML processor ignores all commented text. A comment begins with the <! -- characters and ends with the -- > characters. Within your comment, you can use any characters, except for a double-hyphen (--). A comment can be placed anywhere within an XML document provided that it's outside (not within) other markup tags.

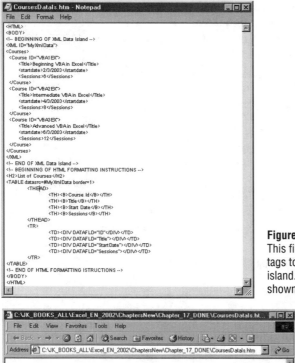

Figure 17-20:
This file shows how to bind HTML tags to data fields in an XML data island. The result of this code is shown in Figure 17-21.

Figure 17-21:
This table was generated by binding HTML tags to data fields in an XML data island (see Figure 17-20).

Data islands can also be used to refer to an external XML document by specifying the src attribute in association with the xml element. This way, instead of embedding the XML data within an HTML document, you can create a reference to the existing XML document, as shown in the code below.

The following exercise demonstrates how to create XML data islands in an HTML document.

1. Open Notepad and enter the code shown below.

2. Save this code as **CoursesDataIs2.htm**.

3. Open the file in your browser. The result should match Figure 17-21.

```
<HTML>
<BODY>
<! -- BEGINNING OF XML Data Island -->
<XML ID="MyXmlData" src="Courses.xml">
</XML>
<! -- END OF XML Data Island -->

<! -- BEGINNING OF HTML FORMATTING INSTRUCTIONS -->
<H2>List of Courses</H2>
<TABLE datasrc=#MyXmlData border=1>
    <THEAD>
        <TH><B>Course Id</B></TH>
        <TH><B>Title</B></TH>
        <TH><B>Start Date</B></TH>
        <TH><B>Sessions</B></TH>
    </THEAD>
    <TR>
        <TD><DIV DATAFLD="ID"</DIV></TD>
        <TD><DIV DATAFLD="Title"></DIV></TD>
        <TD><DIV DATAFLD="StartDate"></DIV></TD>
        <TD><DIV DATAFLD="Sessions"></DIV></TD>
    </TR>
</TABLE>
<! -- END OF HTML FORMATTING ISTRUCTIONS -->
</BODY>
</HTML>
```

The code above demonstrates how to create an XML data island that references an external XML document.

Using VBScript to Transform the Contents of XML Data Islands

When you have an XML document and XSL stylesheet in external files, you can place a reference to them in separate data islands and use simple VBScript code to perform the tranformation to HTML. The following exercise demonstrates this technique using the Courses.xml and Courses.xsl files that you created earlier in this chapter.

The following exercise demonstrates how to use VBScript to transform XML data islands into HTML.

1. Open Notepad, and enter the code presented below.

2. Save the file as **DataIslandTransformation.htm**.

```
<HTML>
  <BODY>
  <! -- Data Island #1 contains raw XML data in External file -->
    <XML id="source" src="Courses.xml"></XML>
  <! -- Data Island #2 contains the XSL stylesheet in External file -->
    <XML id="style" src="Courses.xsl"></XML>
  <! -- Insert the Transform result into a DIV element -->
    <DIV id="displayOutput"></DIV>

  <SCRIPT language=vbscript>
    displayOutput.innerHTML = source.transformNode(style.XMLDocument)
  </SCRIPT>
  </BODY>
</HTML>
```

3. Open the newly created HTML file in your browser. The code above begins with the definition of two data islands named source and style and a blank HTML <DIV> tag named displayOutput. The source data island contains a reference to the raw XML document. The style data island points to the XSLT stylesheet containing the formatting instructions. In order to apply XSLT formatting instructions to the XML data, you need to write client-side VBScript code with the following statement:

```
displayOutput.innerHTML = source.transformNode(style.XMLDocument)
```

This line uses the tranformNode method of the XMLDocument object to apply the stylesheet to the Raw XML document named source. The result of the transformation is then assigned to the innerHTML property of the DIV tag named displayOutput for displaying in a web page. The result of the preceding code is illustrated in Figure 17-22.

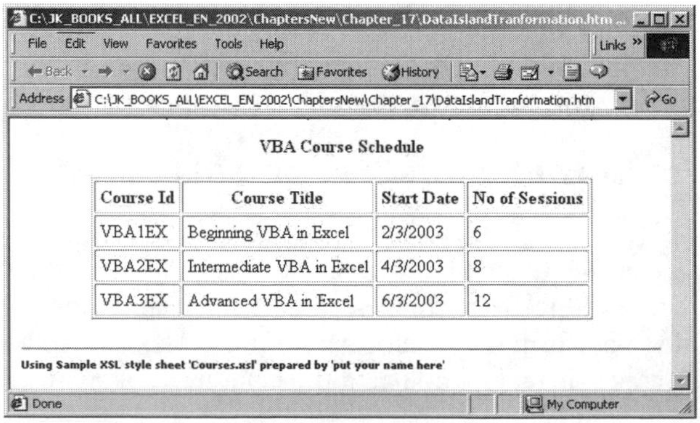

Figure 17-22:
By using client-side VBScript with Dynamic HTML and XSLT stylesheet, you can transform the contents of XML data islands to render them on the web page.

Saving a Range of Cells as an XML Document

In the beginning of this chapter you learned how to save an Excel spreadsheet in the XML-SS spreadsheet format, both by using File | Save As and programmatically via the Save As method of the Workbook object and the special parameter xlXMLSpreadsheet. At times, however, it may be desirable to save only a specific range of cells in the XML format. While the user interface does not offer such an option, Excel 2002 now offers a Value property of the Range object with the xlRangeValueXMLSpreadsheet parameter to let you programmatically retrieve or set a range as an XML spreadsheet. Let's look at how you can persist an Excel range in an XML document. We will use the Equipment.xls file shown in Figure 17-2 earlier and demonstrate how to use VBA to save cell ranges in XML format.

1. Open the Equipment.xls file illustrated in Figure 17-2.
2. Switch to the Visual Basic Editor window and insert a new module.
3. Type the following procedure in a module:

```
Sub SaveRangeAsXML_Spreadsheet()
    Dim objFSO As Object
    Dim objTextFile As Object
    Dim myRange As Range
    Dim strGetThisRange As String
    Dim strFile As String

    strFile = "C:\myRange.xml"

    Set objFSO = CreateObject("Scripting.FileSystemObject")
    Set objTextFile = objFSO.CreateTextFile(strFile, True)

    Set myRange = Worksheets("Units").Range("A2:E6")
    ' retrieve the range as XML spreadsheet
    strGetThisRange = myRange.Value(xlRangeValueXMLSpreadsheet)

    ' write the string to the Immediate window
    Debug.Print strGetThisRange
    ' Write the string to a file
    objTextFile.Write strGetThisRange
    objTextFile.Close
    'open the newly prepared XML document in Excel
    Workbooks.Open strFile
End Sub
```

The procedure shown above retrieves the specified range of cells ("A2:E6") as an XML spreadsheet by passing the xlRangeValueXMLSpreadsheet parameter to the Value property of the Range object. The XML representation of a selected range of cells in the spreadsheet is printed to the Immediate window and saved to a file using the CreateTextFile method of the FileSystemObject (see Chapter 8 for details on creating and working with text files). The source code of the XML document (MyRange.xml) created by the SaveRangeAsXML_Spreadsheet procedure is presented below:

```xml
<?xml version="1.0"?>
<Workbook xmlns="urn:schemas-microsoft-com:office:spreadsheet"
 xmlns:o="urn:schemas-microsoft-com:office:office"
 xmlns:x="urn:schemas-microsoft-com:office:excel"
 xmlns:ss="urn:schemas-microsoft-com:office:spreadsheet"
 xmlns:html="http://www.w3.org/TR/REC-html40">
 <Styles>
   <Style ss:ID="Default" ss:Name="Normal">
     <Alignment ss:Vertical="Bottom"/>
     <Borders/>
     <Font/>
     <Interior/>
     <NumberFormat/>
     <Protection/>
   </Style>
   <Style ss:ID="s21">
     <Alignment ss:Horizontal="Left" ss:Vertical="Bottom"/>
   </Style>
   <Style ss:ID="s22">
     <Alignment ss:Horizontal="Center" ss:Vertical="Bottom"/>
     <Font x:Family="Swiss" ss:Bold="1"/>
     <Interior ss:Color="#CCFFCC" ss:Pattern="Solid"/>
   </Style>
 </Styles>
 <Worksheet ss:Name="Units">
  <Table ss:ExpandedColumnCount="5" ss:ExpandedRowCount="5">
   <Column ss:Index="3" ss:AutoFitWidth="0" ss:Width="89.25"/>
   <Column ss:Width="149.25"/>
   <Row ss:AutoFitHeight="0" ss:Height="24">
    <Cell ss:StyleID="s22"><Data ss:Type="String">Category</Data></Cell>
    <Cell ss:StyleID="s22"><Data ss:Type="String">Type</Data></Cell>
    <Cell ss:StyleID="s22"><Data ss:Type="String">Model</Data></Cell>
    <Cell ss:StyleID="s22"><Data ss:Type="String">Description</Data></Cell>
    <Cell ss:StyleID="s22"><Data ss:Type="String">Units</Data></Cell>
   </Row>
   <Row>
    <Cell ss:StyleID="s21"><Data ss:Type="Number">1</Data></Cell>
    <Cell ss:StyleID="s21"><Data ss:Type="String">WS</Data></Cell>
    <Cell ss:StyleID="s21"><Data ss:Type="String">GX 1/L</Data></Cell>
    <Cell ss:StyleID="s21"><Data ss:Type="String">Dell PIII 500 MHz</Data></Cell>
    <Cell><Data ss:Type="Number">12</Data></Cell>
   </Row>
   <Row>
    <Cell ss:StyleID="s21"><Data ss:Type="Number">1</Data></Cell>
    <Cell ss:StyleID="s21"><Data ss:Type="String">WS</Data></Cell>
    <Cell ss:StyleID="s21"><Data ss:Type="String">GX110</Data></Cell>
    <Cell ss:StyleID="s21"><Data ss:Type="String">Dell PIII 533 MHz</Data></Cell>
    <Cell><Data ss:Type="Number">10</Data></Cell>
   </Row>
   <Row>
    <Cell ss:StyleID="s21"><Data ss:Type="Number">1</Data></Cell>
```

```
   <Cell ss:StyleID="s21"><Data ss:Type="String">WS</Data></Cell>
   <Cell ss:StyleID="s21"><Data ss:Type="String">GX110</Data></Cell>
   <Cell ss:StyleID="s21"><Data ss:Type="String">Dell PIII 667 MHz</Data></Cell>
   <Cell><Data ss:Type="Number">8</Data></Cell>
  </Row>
  <Row>
   <Cell ss:StyleID="s21"><Data ss:Type="Number">1</Data></Cell>
   <Cell ss:StyleID="s21"><Data ss:Type="String">WS</Data></Cell>
   <Cell ss:StyleID="s21"><Data ss:Type="String">GX110</Data></Cell>
   <Cell ss:StyleID="s21"><Data ss:Type="String">Dell PIII 866 MHz</Data></Cell>
   <Cell><Data ss:Type="Number">4</Data></Cell>
  </Row>
 </Table>
</Worksheet>
</Workbook>
```

The XML Document Object Model

You can create, access, and manipulate XML documents programmatically via the XML DOM (Document Object Model). The DOM has properties, methods, and constants for interacting with XML documents. The XML DOM is supplied with Internet Explorer. To use the XML DOM from your VBA procedures, you need to set up a reference to the MSXML object library. To do this, switch to the Visual Basic Editor window and choose Tools | References. In the References dialog box, locate and select Microsoft XML, v3.0 (see Figure 17-23). If you are using Microsoft Internet Explorer 4.0, you'll need to choose the version 2.0 type library (or upgrade your browser to the higher version). Now that you have the reference set, you can open the Object Browser and examine XML DOM's objects, methods, and properties (see Figure 17-24).

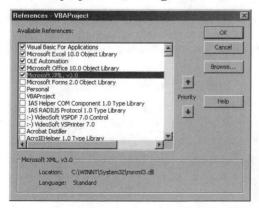

Figure 17-23:
To work with XML documents programmatically, you need to establish a reference to the Microsoft XML type library.

The DOMDocument object is the top level of the XML DOM hierarchy. This object represents a tree structure composed of nodes. You can navigate through this tree structure and manipulate the data contained in the nodes by using various methods and properties. The DOMDocument object is the parent for all other elements in the DOM hierarchy. Because every XML object is created and accessed from the document, the DOMDocument object must be created first.

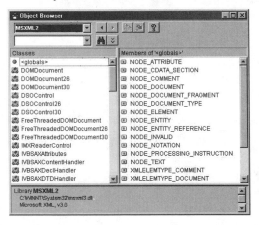

Figure 17-24:
To see objects, properties, and methods exposed by the DOM (Document Object Model), open the Object Browser after setting up a reference to the Microsoft XML type library (see Figure 17-23).

To work with an XML document, you need to create an instance of the DOMDocument object, as in the following example:

```
Dim myXMLDoc as MSXM2.DOMDocument30
Set myXMLDoc = New MSXML2.DOMDocument30
```

To make the instantiated DOMDocument object useful, you should load it with some data. The following VBA procedure demonstrates how to get started with the XML DOM. You will perform the following tasks:

- Create an instance of the DOMDocument
- Load XML information from a file using the Load method
- Use the DOMDocument object's XML property to retrieve the raw data
- Use the DOMDocument object's Text property to retrieve the text stored in nodes

The following exercise demonstrates how to read XLM documents programmatically.

1. Enter the following Load_ReadXMLDoc procedure in a new module. Change the path to point to the Courses.xml file on your hard disk.

2. Run the procedure and examine the results in the Immediate window and in an Excel spreadsheet.

```
Sub Load_ReadXMLDoc()
    ' Create an instance of the DOMDocument
    Dim xmldoc As MSXML2.DOMDocument30
    Set xmldoc = New MSXML2.DOMDocument30
    ' Disable asynchronous loading
    xmldoc.async = False
    ' Load XML information from a file
```

```
        If xmldoc.Load("C:\JK_BOOKS_ALL\Excel_EN_2002\" _
            & "ChaptersNew\Chapter_17\Courses.xml") Then
                ' Use the DOMDocument object's XML property to
                ' retrieve the raw data
                Debug.Print xmldoc.XML
                ' Use the DOMDocument object's Text poperty to
                ' retrieve the actual text stored in nodes
                Sheets(2).Range("A1").Value = xmldoc.Text
        End If
    End Sub
```

The XML DOM has two methods for loading XML information: Load and LoadXML. Use the Load method to load XML information from a text file. Use the LoadXML method when loading from a string in memory (we will discuss the Stream object later in this chapter). MSXML uses an asynchronous loading mechanism by default for working with documents. Asynchronous loading allows you to perform other tasks during long database operations, such as providing feedback to the user as MSXML parses the XML file or giving the user the chance to cancel the operation. Before calling the Load method, however, it's a good idea to set the Asynch property of the DOMDocument object to False to ensure that when the load returns, the entire document has finished loading. The Load method returns True if it successfully loaded the data and False otherwise. Having loaded the data into a DOMDocument object, you can use the XML property to retrieve the raw data or use the Text property to obtain the text stored in document nodes.

Transform XML into HTML with an XSL Stylesheet Programmatically

Earlier in this chapter, we created an XSL stylesheet for the Courses.xml document. Now that you are familiar with the XML DOM object model, you can use the TransformNode method of the DOMDocument object to apply this XSL to your XML file. The procedure you need to write will have two DOMDocument objects, one with the XML file (Courses.xml) and one with the XSL file (Courses.xsl). To see the results of XML to HTML transformation, save the generated HTML to a string variable and print it to the Immediate window. Next, write the variable's content to a text file (refer to Chapter 8 for details on creating text files). Finally, open the newly created HTML file in Excel 2002.

The following exercise demonstrates how to transform XML into HTML programmatically.

1.   Open the Courses.xml file in Notepad.

2.   Locate the line that links the XML file to a stylesheet and comment it out as follows:

```
<!-- <?xml-stylesheet type="text/xsl" href="Courses2.xsl"?> -->
```

Because the example TransformXML procedure will apply a stylesheet programmatically to this XML document, you can get rid of this line or simply comment it out as shown.

3. Save and close the Courses.xml file.

4. In the Visual Basic Editor window, enter the Transform XML procedure shown below. Be sure to modify the file paths to point to a valid location of the required documents on your hard disk.

```
Sub TransformXML()
        Dim xmldoc As MSXML2.DOMDocument30
        Dim xsldoc As MSXML2.DOMDocument30
        Dim fs As Object
        Dim myFile As Object
        Dim strHTML As String
        Dim strFile As String

        ' Load XML document
        Set xmldoc = New MSXML2.DOMDocument30
        xmldoc.Load "C:\JK_BOOKS_ALL\Excel_EN_2002\" _
         & "ChaptersNew\Chapter_17\Courses.xml"

        ' Load XSL stylesheet
        Set xsldoc = New MSXML2.DOMDocument30
        xsldoc.Load "C:\JK_BOOKS_ALL\Excel_EN_2002\" _
         & "ChaptersNew\Chapter_17\MyCourses.xsl"

        ' apply the stylesheet to transform XML to HTML
        ' and write out the HTML to a string
        strHTML = xmldoc.transformNode(xsldoc)
        Debug.Print strHTML

        ' save the string to HTML file
        strFile = "C:\NewCourses.htm"
        Set fs = CreateObject("Scripting.FileSystemObject")
        Set myFile = fs.CreateTextFile(strFile, True)
        myFile.Write strHTML
        myFile.Close

        ' Open the file in Excel
        Workbooks.Open strFile
    End Sub
```

After you run the TransformXML procedure shown above, both the Immediate window and the C:\NewCourses.htm file contain the following HTML code:

```
<HTML xmlns:xsl="http://www.w3.org/TR/WD-xsl">
<HEAD>
<TITLE>VBA Course Schedule</TITLE>
</HEAD>
<BODY bgcolor="yellow">
<CENTER>
<STRONG>VBA Course Schedule</STRONG><P />
```

```
            <TABLE border="1" cellPadding="4" cellSpacing="2">
            <TR>
            <TH>Course Id</TH>
            <TH>Course Title</TH>
            <TH>Start Date</TH>
            <TH>No of Sessions</TH>
            </TR>
            <TR>
            <TD>VBA3EX</TD>
            <TD>Advanced VBA in Excel</TD>
            <TD>6/3/2003</TD>
            <TD>12</TD>
            </TR>
            <TR>
            <TD>VBA1EX</TD>
            <TD>Beginning VBA in Excel</TD>
            <TD>2/3/2003</TD>
            <TD>6</TD>
            </TR>
            <TR>
            <TD>VBA2EX</TD>
            <TD>Intermediate VBA in Excel</TD>
            <TD>4/3/2003</TD>
            <TD>8</TD>
            </TR>
            </TABLE>
            </CENTER>
            <H6 align="left">
            <HR />
            <FONT face="Tahoma">
            Using Sample XSL stylesheet 'Courses.xsl' prepared by 'put _
                  your name here'
            </FONT></H6>
            </BODY>
        </HTML>
```

Tip 17-12: Avoid Mixing DOM Objects from Different Versions of the MSXML Parser

If you take a look at Figure 17-24 (presented earlier in this chapter), you will notice three occurrences of the DOMDocument object: DOMDocument, DOMDocument26, and DOMDocument30. To avoid ugly errors, do not mix the DOMDocument objects from different versions of MSXML parser. Notice how the TransformXML procedure shown above declares two instances of DOMDocument object—both of which use the DOM objects from the same version of MSXML parser (3.0). If you attempt to load one document into an instance of MSXML DOMDocument 2.6 and another one into an instance of MSXML DOMDocument 3.0, you are asking for trouble.

Using VBScript and XML DOM to Transform XML Documents

In the previous section you wrote a VBA procedure to transform the XML document into HTML. In this section you will learn how to process the formatting of an XML document on the client machine by creating an HTML file with some code written in VBScript.

The following exercise demonstrates how to use VBScript to transform an XML document into HTML.

1. Create a folder named **TestXML** under C:\Inetpub\wwwroot.

2. Right-click the folder name and choose **Web Sharing** from the shortcut menu.

3. When the TestXML Properties dialog box appears, activate the Web Sharing tab and click the **Share This Folder** option button.

4. In the Edit Alias dialog box, enter **TestX** in the Alias text box and click **OK**.

5. The Alias name (TestX) should appear in the Aliases list box. Click **OK** to exit the TestXML Properties dialog.

6. Copy the Courses.xml and MyCourses.xsl files to the TestXML folder.

7. Open Notepad and add the following code. When you are done, save the file as **ClientTransform.htm** in the TestXML folder.

```
<HTML>
<HEAD>

<SCRIPT LANGUAGE="VBScript">
Dim xslDoc
Dim xmlDoc

Sub LoadAndCombine()
  Set xslDoc = CreateObject("Microsoft.XMLDOM")
  Set xmlDoc = CreateObject("Microsoft.XMLDOM")
  xslDoc.Async = False
  xmlDoc.Async = False
  xslDoc.Load "MyCourses.xsl"
  xmlDoc.Load "Courses.xml"
  Placeholder.innerHTML = xmlDoc.transformNode(xslDoc)
End Sub
</SCRIPT>

</HEAD>
<BODY ONLOAD="LoadAndCombine">
<DIV ID="Placeholder"></DIV>
</BODY>
</HTML>
```

Notice that the example code above contains a VBScript code fragment placed in the Head section of the HTML document. First, two global object variables are declared—one will hold the reference to the XML document and the other will point to the XSL stylesheet. Next, within the subprocedure named LoadAndCombine, two references to the XML DOM are set via the CreateObject(Microsoft.XMLDOM) method. The next two lines tell the parser to load both the XML and the XSL document synchronously. Therefore, the browser will wait until both documents are loaded before proceeding with the transformation. The next two lines use the Load method to load the XML document (Courses.xml) and the XSL stylesheet document (MyCourses.xsl) into the client's memory. The last line of the procedure uses the transform-Node method to apply the stylesheet (xslDoc) to the XML document (xmlDoc) and uses the innerHTML property to fill a <DIV> tag (identified by the ID="Placeholder") with the result of the transform (the result of the transformation is XML text).

Following the VBScript code fragment is HTML code. Inside the <BODY> tag, you should specify the name of the procedure to be executed when the OnLoad event occurs. Finally, the line <DIV ID="Placeholder"></DIV> tells the browser to replace the information between the DIV tags with the obtained XML text.

8. Open the HTML file that you created in step 7. When you open the file in the browser, the OnLoad event fires and the browser displays a nicely formatted document.

Working with XML Document Nodes

As you already know, the XML DOM represents a tree-based hierarchy of nodes. An XML document can contain nodes of different types. For example, an XML document can include a document node that provides access to the entire XML document or one or more element nodes representing individual elements. Some nodes represent comments and processing instructions in the XML document, and others hold the text content of a tag. To determine the type of node, use the nodeType property of the IXMLDOMNode object. Node types are identified either by a text string or a constant. For example, the node representing an element can be referred to as NODE_ELEMENT or 1, while the node representing the comment is named NODE_COMMENT or 8. See the MSXML2 Library in the Object Browser (Figure 17-24 earlier in this chapter) for the names of other node types.

In addition to node types, nodes can have parent, child, and sibling nodes. The hasChildNodes method lets you determine if a DOMDocument object has child nodes. There's also a childNodes property with which it's quite simple to retrieve a collection of child nodes. Before you start looping through the collection of child nodes, it's a good idea to use the length property of the IXMLDOMNode to determine how many elements the collection contains.

The LearnAboutNodes procedure shown below will get you working with nodes programmatically in no time. The result of the procedure, as printed in the Immediate window, is shown following the procedure code.

The following exercise demonstrates how to experiment with XML document nodes.

1. Enter the following procedure in a module. Remember to add References to the MSXML type library and change the path of the XML document to point to the file location on your disk.

2. Run the LearnAboutNodes procedure in a step mode by pressing **F8**.

```
Sub LearnAboutNodes()
  ' Create an instance of the DOMDocument
    Dim xmldoc As MSXML2.DOMDocument30
    Dim xmlNode As MSXML2.IXMLDOMNode

    Set xmldoc = New MSXML2.DOMDocument30
    xmldoc.async = False
    ' Load XML information from a file
    ' Be sure to change the file path to point to the location
    ' of the Courses.xml file on your computer
    xmldoc.Load ("C:\ExcelVBA2002\Chap17\Courses.xml")
    ' find out the number of child nodes in the document
    If xmldoc.hasChildNodes Then
        Debug.Print "Number of Child Nodes: " & xmldoc.childNodes.Length
        ' iterate through the child nodes to gather information
        For Each xmlNode In xmldoc.childNodes
            Debug.Print "Node Name: " & xmlNode.nodeName
            Debug.Print vbTab & "Type: " & xmlNode.nodeTypeString _
                                    & "(" & xmlNode.nodeType & ")"
            Debug.Print vbTab & "Text: " & xmlNode.Text
        Next xmlNode
    End If
End Sub
```

The LearnAboutNodes procedure prints to the Immediate window the information about child nodes found in the Courses.xml document. Notice that the text property of a node returns all the text from all the node's children in one string (see the text for the Courses node below):

```
Number of Child Nodes: 3
Node Name: xml
      Type: processinginstruction(7)
      Text: version="1.0"
Node Name: #comment
      Type: comment(8)
      Text:  <?xml-stylesheet type="text/xsl" href="Courses2.xsl"?>
Node Name: Courses
      Type: element(1)
      Text: Beginning VBA in Excel 2/3/2003 6 Intermediate
            VBA in Excel 4/3/2003 8 Advanced VBA in Excel 6/3/2003 12
```

Retrieving Information from Element Nodes

Let's assume that you want to read the information only from the text
element nodes and place it in an Excel spreadsheet. Use the getElements-
ByTagName method of the DOMDocument object to retrieve an
IXMLDOMNodeList object containing all the element nodes. The getElementsByTagName method takes one argument specifying the tag name for
which to search. To search for all the element nodes, use the "*" as the tag
to search for (as illustrated in the procedure below).

The following exercise demonstrates how to obtain data from XML
document element nodes.

1. Enter the following procedure in a module. Remember to add Refer-
    ences to the MSXML type library and change the path of the XML
    document to point to the file location on your disk.

2. Run the procedure in a step mode by pressing **F8**.

```
Sub IterateThruElements()
    Dim xmldoc As MSXML2.DOMDocument30
    Dim xmlNodeList As MSXML2.IXMLDOMNodeList
    Dim xmlNode As MSXML2.IXMLDOMNode
    Dim myNode As MSXML2.IXMLDOMNode

    ' Create an instance of the DOMDocument
    Set xmldoc = New MSXML2.DOMDocument30
    xmldoc.async = False
    ' Load XML information from a file
    xmldoc.Load ("C:\ExcelVBA2002\Chap17\Courses.xml")
    ' find out the number of child nodes in the document
    Set xmlNodeList = xmldoc.getElementsByTagName("*")
    Workbooks.Add
    Range("A1:B1").Formula = Array("Element Name", "Text")
    For Each xmlNode In xmlNodeList
        For Each myNode In xmlNode.childNodes
          If myNode.nodeType = NODE_TEXT Then
              ActiveCell.Offset(0, 0).Formula = xmlNode.nodeName
              ActiveCell.Offset(0, 1).Formula = xmlNode.Text
          End If
        Next myNode
        ActiveCell.Offset(1, 0).Select
    Next xmlNode
End Sub
```

The IterateThruElements procedure fills in two spreadsheet columns
with the XML element name and the corresponding text for all the text
elements in the Courses.xml document (see the procedure result in
Figure 17-25). Notice that this procedure uses two For...Each... Next
loops. The first one (outer For...Each...Next loop) iterates through
the entire collection of element nodes. The second one (inner
For...Each...Next loop) uses the nodeType property to find only those
element nodes that contain a single text node.

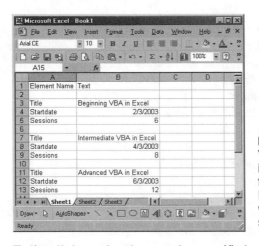

Figure 17-25:
You can programmatically retrieve information about element nodes from the XML document. The IterateThruElements procedure was used to create this spreadsheet.

To list all the nodes that match a specified criterion, use the selectNodes method. The following procedure (SelectNodes_Specify-Criterion) returns to the Immediate window the text for all Title nodes in the Courses.xml file. The "//Title" criterion of the SelectNodes method looks for the element named "Title" at any level within the tree structure of the nodes.

3. Enter the following procedure in a module. Remember to change the path of the XML document to point to the file location on your disk.

4. Run the procedure in a step mode by pressing **F8**.

```
Sub SelectNodes_SpecifyCriterion()
    Dim xmldoc As MSXML2.DOMDocument30
    Dim xmlNodeList As MSXML2.IXMLDOMNodeList

    ' Create an instance of the DOMDocument
    Set xmldoc = New MSXML2.DOMDocument30
    xmldoc.async = False
    ' Load XML information from a file
    xmldoc.Load ("C:\ExcelVBA2002\Chap17\Courses.xml")
    ' Retrieve all the nodes that match the specified criterion
    Set xmlNodeList = xmldoc.selectNodes("//Title")
    If Not (xmlNodeList Is Nothing) Then
        For Each myNode In xmlNodeList
            Debug.Print myNode.Text
        Next myNode
    End If
End Sub
```

The criterion in the selectNodes method can be more complex. Let's assume that you are only interested in the title for the Course element with the ID of "VBA2EX." To retrieve this information, use the following statement:

```
Set xmlNodeList = xmldoc.selectNodes("//Course[@ID='VBA2EX']//Title")
```

The above statement tells the XML processor to start searching for an element named Course at any level within the tree structure of nodes and find only the course element whose ID attribute contains the value of "VBA2EX," and return the Title element.

If all you want to do is retrieve the first node that meets the specified criterion, use the selectSingleNode method of the XML document. As the argument of this method, specify the string representing the node that you'd like to find. For example, the following procedure finds the first node that matches the criterion "//Title" in the Courses.xml document. The result of this procedure is the text "Beginning VBA in Excel" written to the Immediate window.

5. Enter the following procedure in a module. Remember to change the path of the XML document to point to the file location on your disk.

6. Run the procedure in a step mode by pressing **F8**.

```
Sub Select_SingleNode()
    Dim xmldoc As MSXML2.DOMDocument30
    Dim xmlSingleN As MSXML2.IXMLDOMNode

    ' Create an instance of the DOMDocument

    Set xmldoc = New MSXML2.DOMDocument30
    xmldoc.async = False
    ' Load XML information from a file
    xmldoc.Load ("C:\ExcelVBA2002\Chap17\Courses.xml")
    ' Retrieve the reference to a particular node
    Set xmlSingleN = xmldoc.selectSingleNode("//Title")
    Debug.Print xmlSingleN.Text
End Sub
```

The following statements will retrieve the first Course node with the ID attribute:

```
Set xmlSingleN = xmldoc.selectSingleNode("//Course//@ID")
Debug.Print xmlSingleN.Text
```

If you replace the last two lines in the Select_SingleNode procedure with the above statements and run the procedure again, you should see the text "VBA1EX" in the Immediate window.

Once you find the correct node to work with, you can easily modify its value. For example, to change the text of the first Course element with the ID attribute, use the following lines of code:

```
Set xmlSingleN = xmldoc.selectSingleNode("//Course//@ID")
xmlSingleN.Text = "VBA1EX2002"
xmldoc.Save "C:\ExcelVBA2002\Chap17\Courses.xml"
```

Notice that to make a permanent change in the XML document, you must resave it using the Save method.

When using the selectSingleNode method, you should use the Is Nothing conditional expression to determine whether a matching element was found in the loaded XML document. The modified Select_SingleNode_2 procedure shown below will display the user-friendly message if the criterion specified as the argument of the selectSingleNode method is invalid. To try out this example, replace the XPath expression "//Course//@ID" with "//Cours//@ID" and run the procedure. You should see the text "No nodes selected" in the Immediate window.

7. Enter the following procedure in a module. Remember to change the path of the XML document to point to the file location on your disk.

8. Run the procedure in a step mode by pressing **F8**.

```
Sub Select_SingleNode_2()
    Dim xmldoc As MSXML2.DOMDocument30
    Dim xmlSingleN As MSXML2.IXMLDOMNode

    ' Create an instance of the DOMDocument
    Set xmldoc = New MSXML2.DOMDocument30
    xmldoc.async = False
    ' Load XML information from a file
    xmldoc.Load ("C:\ExcelVBA2002\Chap17\Courses.xml")
    ' Retrieve the reference to a particular node
    'Set xmlSingleN = xmldoc.selectSingleNode("//Title")
    Set xmlSingleN = xmldoc.selectSingleNode("//Course//@ID")
    If xmlSingleN Is Nothing Then
        Debug.Print "No nodes selected."
    Else
        Debug.Print xmlSingleN.Text
        xmlSingleN.Text = "VBA1EX2002"
        Debug.Print xmlSingleN.Text
        xmldoc.Save "C:\JK_BOOKS_ALL\Excel_EN_2002\" _
           & "ChaptersNew\Chapter_17\Courses.xml"
    End If
End Sub
```

XML DOM provides a number of other methods that make it possible to programmatically add or delete elements. Covering all of the details of the XML DOM object model is beyond the scope of this chapter. When you are ready for more information on this subject, visit the following web links: http://www.w3.org/DOM/ and http://www.w3.org/XML/.

XML via ADO

In Chapter 15 you learned how to perform database operations using the
ActiveX Data Objects (ADO). This section will show you what you can do
with XML and ADO. Since ADO version 2.5 (released in 2000), you can
save all types of recordsets as XML to disk. You can also save any type of
ADO recordset to XML in memory, using the ADO Stream object.

> **Tip 17-13: ADO is Part of Microsoft Data Access Components (MDAC)**
>
> You can download the latest version of MDAC from the Microsoft
> web site.

Saving an ADO Recordset as XML to Disk

To save an ADO recordset as XML to a disk file, use the Save method of the
Recordset object with the adPersistXML constant. The procedure illustrated below establishes a connection to the sample Northwind database
using the ADO Connection object. Next it executes an SQL SELECT statement against the database to retrieve all of the records from the Products
table. Once the records are placed in a recordset, the Save method is called
to store the recordset to a disk file. If the disk file already exists, the procedure deletes the existing file using the VBA Kill statement. The On Error
Resume Next statement allows bypassing the Kill statement if the file that
you are going to create does not yet exist.

The following exercise demonstrates how to create XML files from
ADO recordsets.

1. Open a new workbook and activate the Visual Basic Editor window.
2. Insert a new module and type the SaveRst_ADO procedure, as shown
   below.
3. Save the spreadsheet file as **XMLviaADO.xls**.
4. Run the SaveRst_ADO procedure.
5. Open the C:\Products.xml file created by the SaveRst_ADO procedure
   and examine its content.

```
Sub SaveRst_ADO()
    Dim rst As ADODB.Recordset
    Dim conn As New ADODB.Connection

    Const strConn = "Provider=Microsoft.Jet.OLEDB.4.0;" _
        & "Data Source=C:\Program Files\Microsoft Office\" _
        & "Office\Samples\Northwind.mdb"

    ' open a connection to the database
```

```
        conn.Open strConn

        ' execute a select SQL statement against the database
        Set rst = conn.Execute("SELECT * FROM Products")

        ' delete the file if it exists
        On Error Resume Next
        Kill "C:\Products.xml"

        ' save the recordset as an XML file
        rst.Save "C:\Products.xml", adPersistXML
    End Sub
```

Two Types of XML Files

Once you've saved the recordset to a disk file, you can send it to someone via e-mail, or you can work with it yourself. If you open the XML file created by the SaveRst_ADO in your web browser, you will see the raw XML.

Figure 17-26:
Saving a recordset to an XML file with ADO 2.5 produces an attribute-based XML file.

XML files can be element-based or attribute-based. The XML files produced by ADO 2.5 or higher are all attribute-based. XML files generated by ADO are self-describing objects that contain data and metadata (information about the data). If you take a look at the XML file generated by the example procedure (see Figure 17-26), you will notice that below the XML document's root tag there are two children nodes: <s:Schema> and <rs:data>. The schema node describes the structure of the recordset, while the data node holds the actual data. Inside the <s:Schema id="RowsetSchema"> and </s:Schema> tags, ADO places information about each column: field name, position, data type and length, nullability, and whether the column is writable. Each field is represented by the <s:AttributeType> element. Notice that the value of the name attribute is the field name. The <s:AttributeType> element also has a child element <s:datatype>, which holds information about its data type (integer, number, string, etc.) and the maximum field length. Below the schema definition, you can find the actual data. The ADO schema represents each record using the <z:row > tag. The fields in a record are expressed as attributes of the <z:row> element. Every XML attribute is assigned a value that is enclosed in a pair of single or double quotation marks; however, if the value of a field in a record is NULL, the attribute on the z:row is not created. Notice that each record is written out in the following format:

```
<z:row ProductID='1' ProductName='Chai' SupplierID='1' CategoryID='1'
QuantityPerUnit='10 boxes x 20 bags' UnitPrice='18'  UnitsInStock='39'
UnitsOnOrder='0' ReorderLevel='10' Discontinued='False'/>
```

The above code fragment is an attribute-based XML document. However, you may want to have each record written out as follows:

```
<Product>
  <ProductID>1</ProductID>
  <ProductName>Chai</ProductName>
  <SupplierID>1</SupplierID>
  <CategoryID>1</CategoryID>
  <QuantityPerUnit>10 boxes x 20 bags</QuantityPerUnit>
  <UnitPrice>18</UnitPrice>
  <UnitsInStock>39</UnitsInStock>
  <UnitsOnOrder>0</UnitsOnOrder>
  <ReorderLevel>10</ReorderLevel>
  <Discontinued>False</Discontinued>
  </Product>
```

The above code fragment represents an element-based XML. Each record is wrapped in a <Product> tag, and each field is an element under the <Product> tag.

Changing the Type of an XML File

Because it is much easier to work with element-based XML files, you can write an XSL stylesheet to transform your attribute-based XML file to an element-based file. Figure 17-27 shows an example of such a stylesheet.

The following exercise demonstrates how to write a stylesheet to convert an XML document from attribute-based to element-based.

1. Open Notepad and type the code shown in Figure 17-27.

2. Save the stylesheet file as **AttribToElem.xsl**. We will use this stylesheet for the transformation in the next example procedure.

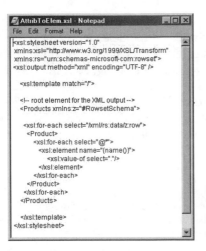

Figure 17-27:
This XSL stylesheet will convert an attribute-based XML document prepared by ADO to an element-based XML document.

Notice that in the above stylesheet example, the @* wild card matches all attribute nodes. Each time the <z:row> tag is encountered, an element named <Product> will be created. And for each attribute, the attribute name will be converted to the element name using the built-in XPath Name( ) function. Expressions in curly braces are evaluated and converted to strings. The select="." returns the current value of the attribute being read.

Tip 17-14: Character Encoding in XML

When you type an XML document into Notepad and save it, you can choose from one of several supported character encodings, including ANSI, Unicode (UTF-16), Unicode (Big Endian), or UTF-8. The encoding declaration in the XML document identifies which encoding is used to represent the characters in the document. UTF-8 encoding allows the use of non-ASCII characters, regardless of the language of the user's operating system and browser or the language version of Office. When you use UTF-8 or UTF-16 character encoding, an encoding declaration is optional. XML parsers can determine automatically if a document uses UTF-8 or UTF-16 Unicode encoding.

Applying an XSL Stylesheet

Now that you've created the stylesheet to transform an attribute-based XML file into an element-based file, you can use the transformNodeTo-Object method of the DOMDocument object to apply the stylesheet. The procedure that follows demonstrates how to do this programmatically.

1. Enter the code of the ApplyStyleSheet procedure, as shown below, in the same module where you've entered the code of the SaveRst_ADO procedure (XMLviaADO.xls).

2. Run the ApplyStyleSheet procedure to reformat the original XML file.

3. Open the C:\Products_Converted.xml file generated by the ApplyStyleSheet procedure (see Figure 17-28 following the procedure code).

```vba
Sub ApplyStyleSheet()
    Dim myXMLDoc As New MSXML2.DOMDocument30
    Dim myXSLDoc As New MSXML2.DOMDocument30
    Dim newXMLDoc As New MSXML2.DOMDocument30
    Dim strXML As String

    myXMLDoc.async = False
    If myXMLDoc.Load("C:\Products.xml") Then
        myXSLDoc.Load "C:\AttribToElem.xsl"

    ' apply the transformation
        If Not myXSLDoc Is Nothing Then
            Set newXML = New DOMDocument30
            myXMLDoc.transformNodeToObject myXSLDoc, newXMLDoc

    ' Save the output
            newXMLDoc.Save "C:\Products_Converted.xml"
        End If
    End If

    ' Cleanup
        Set myXMLDoc = Nothing
        Set myXSLDoc = Nothing
        Set newXMLDoc = Nothing
End Sub
```

Figure 17-28:
This element-based XML file is a result of applying a stylesheet to the attribute-based ADO recordset saved to an XML file. The original file is shown in Figure 17-26, and the stylesheet used in the transformation can be found in Figure 17-27.

Transforming Attribute-Based XML Data into an HTML Table

As you've seen in earlier examples, after creating an XML file from the ADO Recordset, the generated output is quite far from what you'd like to present to users. How about converting this output directly to an HTML table? You can create a generic XSL stylesheet that draws out a simple table for the users when they open the file in their browser. Before we get started, open the Products.xml file in your browser and print it out. Keep the copy handy as we analyze the code of the stylesheet.

The following exercise demonstrates how to create a stylesheet to transform an attribute-based XML document into HTML.

1. Open Notepad and type the following code for the stylesheet.

2. Save the file as **AttribToHTML.xsl**.

3. Close Notepad.

4. Open the AttribToHTML.xsl file in the browser to test whether it is well-formed.

5. Close the browser.

```
<?xml version="1.0"?>
<xsl:stylesheet xmlns:xsl="http://www.w3.org/TR/WD-xsl"
  xmlns:html="http://www.w3.org/TR/REC-html40" >

<xsl:template match="/">
 <html>
<head>
<title>Using Stylesheet to convert attribute based XML to HTML</title>
<style type="text/css">
 .myHSet { font-Family:verdana; font-Size: 9px; color:blue; }
 .myBSet { font-Family:Garamond; font-Size; 8px; }
</style>
</head>

<body>
  <table width="100%" border="1">

   <xsl:for-each select="xml/s:Schema/s:ElementType/s:AttributeType">
     <th class="myHSet">
         <xsl:value-of select="@name" />
     </th>
   </xsl:for-each>

   <xsl:for-each select="xml/rs:data/z:row">
   <tr>
     <xsl:for-each select="@*">
         <td class="myBSet" valign="top"><xsl:value-of match="@*"/></td>
     </xsl:for-each>
   </tr>
     </xsl:for-each>
  </table>
```

```
  </body>
  </html>
  </xsl:template>
  </xsl:stylesheet>
```

The above stylesheet uses the feature known as cascading stylesheets (CSS) to format the HTML table. A style comprises different properties—bold, italic, font size, font weight, color, etc.—that you want to apply to a particular text (titles, headers, body, etc.) and assigns to these properties a common name. Thus, in the above stylesheet, two styles are defined. A style named myHSet is applied to the table headings, and the style named myBSet is used for formatting the text in the body of the table. Using styles is very convenient. If you don't like the formatting, you can simply change the style definition and get a new look in no time. Notice that to define a style, you type a period and a class name. Using letters and numbers, you can define any name for your style class. After the class name, type the definition for the class between curly brackets { }. The definition of the class includes the name of the property followed by a colon and the property value. Properties are separated by a semicolon. A semicolon is also placed before the ending } bracket. A style class can be applied to any HTML tag. The following code fragment defines the style:

```
<style type="text/css">
  .myHSet { font-Family:verdana; font-Size: 9px; color:blue; }
  .myBSet { font-Family:Garamond; font-Size; 8px; }
</style>
```

The example stylesheet AttribToHML.xsl uses a template-based processing. We begin by matching on the root document:

```
<xsl:template match="/">
```

The code between the initial and the closing tags will be processed for all tags whose names match the value of the attribute match. In other words, you want the pattern matching that follows to be applied to the entire document.

Next, a loop is used to write out the column headings. To do this, you must move through all the AttributeType elements of the root element outputting the value of the name attribute:

```
<xsl:for-each select="xml/s:Schema/s:ElementType/s:AttributeType">
  <th class="myHSet">
      <xsl:value-of select="@name" />
  </th>
</xsl:for-each>
```

An attribute's name is always preceded by @. Next, another loop runs through all the <z:row> elements representing actual records:

```
<xsl:for-each select="xml/rs:data/z:row">
```

All the attributes of any <z:row> element are enumerated:

```
<xsl:for-each select="@*">
     <td class="myBSet" valign="top"><xsl:value-of match="@*"/></td>
</xsl:for-each>
```

The string @* denotes any attribute. For each attribute found under the <z:row> element, you need to match the attribute name with its corresponding value.

Now that you are finished with the stylesheet, you need to establish a link between the XML and XSL files. Recall that you've already learned how to do this in the exercise on how to add a reference to a stylesheet in your XML document. Continue with the following steps to finish off this exercise:

6. Save the Products.xml file as **ProductsTable.xml** (do not use the original file, as it will be used in other examples).
7. Open the ProductsTable.xml file with Notepad.
8. Type the following definition in the first line of this file:

```
<?xml-stylesheet type="text/xsl" href="AttribToHTML.xsl"?>
```

9. Save the changes made to the file and close Notepad.
10. Open the ProductsTable.xml file in your browser. You should see the data formatted in a table.

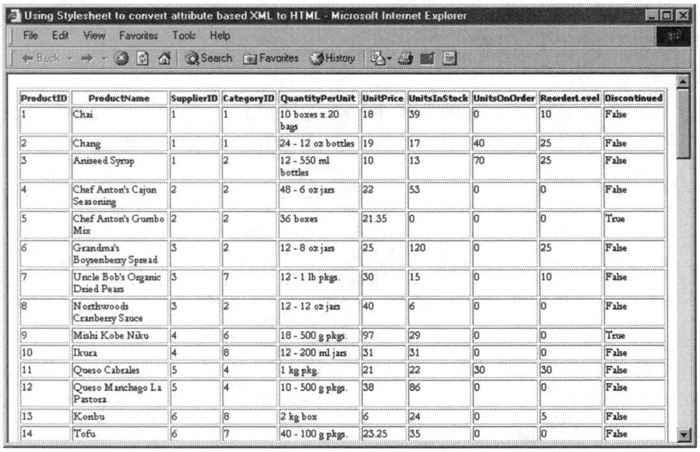

ProductID	ProductName	SupplierID	CategoryID	QuantityPerUnit	UnitPrice	UnitsInStock	UnitsOnOrder	ReorderLevel	Discontinued
1	Chai	1	1	10 boxes x 20 bags	18	39	0	10	False
2	Chang	1	1	24 - 12 oz bottles	19	17	40	25	False
3	Aniseed Syrup	1	2	12 - 550 ml bottles	10	13	70	25	False
4	Chef Anton's Cajun Seasoning	2	2	48 - 6 oz jars	22	53	0	0	False
5	Chef Anton's Gumbo Mix	2	2	36 boxes	21.35	0	0	0	True
6	Grandma's Boysenberry Spread	3	2	12 - 8 oz jars	25	120	0	25	False
7	Uncle Bob's Organic Dried Pears	3	7	12 - 1 lb pkgs.	30	15	0	10	False
8	Northwoods Cranberry Sauce	3	2	12 - 12 oz jars	40	6	0	0	False
9	Mishi Kobe Niku	4	6	18 - 500 g pkgs.	97	29	0	0	True
10	Ikura	4	8	12 - 200 ml jars	31	31	0	0	False
11	Queso Cabrales	5	4	1 kg pkg.	21	22	30	30	False
12	Queso Manchego La Pastora	5	4	10 - 500 g pkgs.	38	86	0	0	False
13	Konbu	6	8	2 kg box	6	24	0	5	False
14	Tofu	6	7	40 - 100 g pkgs.	23.25	35	0	0	False

Figure 17-29: You can apply a generic stylesheet to an XML document generated by the ADO to display the data in a simple HTML table.

Loading an ADO Recordset

After saving an ADO recordset to an XML file on disk, you can load it back and read it as if it were a database. To gain access to the records saved in the XML file, use the Open method of the Recordset object and specify the filename including its path and the persisted recordset service provider as "Provider=MSPersist." Let's look at an example.

The following exercise demonstrates how to open a persisted recordset.

1. In the same module where you entered previous procedures, enter the procedure OpenAdoFile, as shown below.

2. Run the OpenAdoFile procedure.

3. Open the C:\Products.xls file created by running this procedure.

```
Sub OpenAdoFile()
    Dim rst As ADODB.Recordset
    Dim StartRange As Range

    Set rst = New ADODB.Recordset
    ' open your XML file and load it
    rst.Open "C:\Products.xml", "Provider=MSPersist"
    ' display the number of records
    MsgBox rst.RecordCount

    ' open a new workbook
    Workbooks.Add
    ' copy field names as headings to the first row of the worksheet
        For h = 1 To rst.Fields.Count
            ActiveSheet.Cells(1, h).Value = rst.Fields(h - 1).Name
        Next

    ' specify the cell range to receive the data (A2)
    Set StartRange = ActiveSheet.Cells(2, 1)

    'copy the records from the recordset beginning in cell A2
    StartRange.CopyFromRecordset rst

    'autofit the columns to make the data fit
    Range("A1").CurrentRegion.Select
    Columns.AutoFit

    ' close the workbook and save the file
    ActiveWorkbook.Close SaveChanges:=True, _
        Filename:="C:\Products.xls"
End Sub
```

The example procedure shown above creates a Recordset object and places in it the XML file created by an earlier procedure. After displaying the number of records in the file, the procedure opens a new workbook and fills the first worksheet row with field names. Next, the CopyFromRecordset method is used to retrieve the records into the worksheet. After adjusting the size of the columns to fit the data, the workbook is saved using the standard Excel file format (XLS).

Saving the ADO Recordset to XML in Memory

If you are working with ADO 2.5 or higher, you can take advantage of the Stream object to save your ADO recordset in XML format directly to memory, instead of a disk file. You can then process your recordset as needed. The contents of the Stream object can be printed out using the Stream object's ReadText method. Saving the recordset to memory is much faster and more scalable than saving to a disk file, especially when all you need to do is manipulate the recordset and you don't need a physical XML file to send to someone.

The example procedure that follows demonstrates how to use the Stream object. The procedure retrieves the records from the Shippers table; however, instead of creating an XML disk file, it saves the recordset to memory. Once the data is in the Stream object, you can close the recordset and work with the data as needed; for instance, remove one or more document nodes from the final output presented to the user. You can also save the contents of the Stream object to a local file with the Stream object's SaveToFile method. This method takes two parameters—a String value with the fully-qualified name of the file to which the contents of the Stream should be saved and a constant that specifies whether a file should be created (adSaveCreateNotExist) or overwritten (adSaveCreateOver-Write) when saving from a Stream object.

The following exercise demonstrates how to create in memory XML files with the ADO Stream object.

1. In a new module, enter the code of the SaveToStream procedure shown below.

2. Run the procedure in a step mode by pressing **F8**. Make sure the Immediate window is open so you can see at once the results of various Debug.Print statements that the example procedure contains.

```
Sub SaveToStream()
    Dim conn As ADODB.Connection
    Dim rst As ADODB.Recordset
    Dim myStream As ADODB.Stream
    Dim xmlDoc As MSXML2.DOMDocument30
    Dim xslDoc As MSXML2.DOMDocument30
    Dim myNode As MSXML2.IXMLDOMNode
    Dim parentNode As MSXML2.IXMLDOMNode
    Dim objFSO As Object
    Dim objTextFile As Object
    Dim strContents As String
    Dim strFileN As String

    On Error GoTo ErrorHandler

    ' declare constant used as database connection string
    Const strConn = "Provider=Microsoft.Jet.OLEDB.4.0;" _
        & "Data Source=C:\Program Files\Microsoft Office\" _
        & "Office\Samples\Northwind.mdb"

    ' open a connection to the database
    Set conn = New ADODB.Connection
    conn.Open strConn

    ' open the Products table
```

```vb
    Set rst = New ADODB.Recordset
    rst.Open "Shippers", conn, adOpenStatic, adLockOptimistic

    ' create a Stream object
    Set myStream = New ADODB.Stream

    ' save the recordset to XML in memory
    rst.Save myStream, adPersistXML

    ' close the recordset
    rst.Close
    Set rst = Nothing

    ' save the contents of the Stream object to a variable
    strContents = myStream.ReadText
    Debug.Print strContents

    ' use SaveToFile method to copy the contents
    ' of a Stream object to a local file
    strFileN = "C:\xmlFromStream.xml"
    myStream.SaveToFile strFileN, adSaveCreateNotExist

    ' Load the XML content to the DOM object
    Set xmlDoc = New MSXML2.DOMDocument30
    xmlDoc.loadXML strContents
    Debug.Print xmlDoc.XML

    ' manipulate the contents of the Stream object here
    ' for example, the following code removes a node from final output
    Set myNode = xmlDoc.selectSingleNode( _
        "//z:row[@CompanyName='United Package']")
    Set parentNode = xmlDoc.selectSingleNode("//rs:data")
    parentNode.removeChild myNode
    Debug.Print xmlDoc.XML

    ' load the XSL stylesheet from disk
    Set xslDoc = New MSXML2.DOMDocument30
    xslDoc.async = False
    xslDoc.Load "C:\AttribToHTML.xsl"

    ' transform XML
    strHTML = xmlDoc.transformNode(xslDoc)
    Debug.Print strHTML

    ' save the strHTML to a File
    strFileN = "C:\XmlFromStream_Transformed.htm"
    Set objFSO = CreateObject("Scripting.FileSystemObject")
    Set objTextFile = objFSO.CreateTextFile(strFileN, True)
    objTextFile.Write strHTML
    objTextFile.Close

ExitHere:
    ' Cleanup
    Set xmlDoc = Nothing
```

```
        Set xslDoc = Nothing
        Set myStream = Nothing
        Set conn = Nothing
        Exit Sub
ErrorHandler:
    If Err.Number = 3004 Then
        myStream.SaveToFile strFileN, adSaveCreateOverWrite
        Resume Next
    Else
        MsgBox Err.Number & ": " & Err.Description
        GoTo ExitHere
    End If
End Sub
```

Saving the ADO Recordset into the XML DOMDocument Object

Instead of saving the recordset into a stream (see the previous section) and then loading the stream into the XML DOMDocument for further manipulation, you can save the recordset directly into the XML DOMDocument object using the following code:

```
Set xmlDoc = New MSXML2.DOMDocument30
rst.Save xmlDoc, adPersistXML
```

The following exercise demonstrates how you can use DOM to modify XML generated by the ADO Save method. After saving the recordset into the XML DOMDocument object, the procedure locates a node matching a specified search string by using the selectSingleNode method. Notice that the XPath expression used as an argument of this method searches for the Phone attribute in the z:row element nodes that have a CompanyName attribute set to "Speedy Express":

```
Set myNode = xmlDoc.selectSingleNode( _
        "//z:row[@CompanyName='Speedy Express']/@Phone")
```

Once the required phone number is located, the procedure modifies the area code, as follows:

```
strCurValue = myNode.Text
myNode.Text = "(508)" & Right(strCurValue, 9)
```

If you'd rather remove the Phone entry completely, you could use the following code:

```
Set myNode = xmlDoc.selectSingleNode( _
        "//z:row[@CompanyName='Speedy Express']")
myNode.Attributes.removeNamedItem "Phone"
```

The removeNamedItem method removes an attribute from the attributes of a given node. This method requires one parameter—a String specifying the name of the attribute to remove from the collection.

The following exercise demonstrates how to save an ADO recordset into the XML DOMDocument object.

1. In a module, enter the code of the SaveToDOM procedure, as shown below.

2. Run the procedure in a step mode by pressing **F8**. Make sure the Immediate window is open so you can see at once the results of various Debug.Print statements that the example procedure contains.

```
Sub SaveToDOM()
    Dim conn As ADODB.Connection
    Dim rst As ADODB.Recordset
    Dim xmlDoc As MSXML2.DOMDocument30
    Dim xslDoc As MSXML2.DOMDocument30
    Dim myNode As IXMLDOMNode
    Dim objFSO As Object
    Dim objTextFile As Object
    Dim strFileN As String
    Dim strCurValue As String

    ' declare constant used as database connection string
    Const strConn = "Provider=Microsoft.Jet.OLEDB.4.0;" _
        & "Data Source=C:\Program Files\Microsoft Office\" _
        & "Office\Samples\Northwind.mdb"

    ' open a connection to the database
    Set conn = New ADODB.Connection
    conn.Open strConn

    ' open the Products table
    Set rst = New ADODB.Recordset
    rst.Open "Shippers", conn, adOpenStatic, adLockOptimistic

    ' create a new XML DOMDocument object
    Set xmlDoc = New MSXML2.DOMDocument30

    ' save the recordset directly into the XML DOMDocument object
    rst.Save xmlDoc, adPersistXML
    Debug.Print xmlDoc.XML

    ' modify shipper's phone
    Set myNode = xmlDoc.selectSingleNode( _
    "//z:row[@CompanyName='Speedy Express']/@Phone")
    strCurValue = myNode.Text
    myNode.Text = "(508)" & Right(strCurValue, 9)

    ' load the XSL stylesheet from disk
    Set xslDoc = New MSXML2.DOMDocument30
    xslDoc.async = False
    xslDoc.Load "C:\AttribToHTML.xsl"

    ' transform XML
    strHTML = xmlDoc.transformNode(xslDoc)
```

```
      Debug.Print strHTML

      ' save the strHTML to a File
      strFileN = "C:\XmlFromDom_Transformed.htm"
      Set objFSO = CreateObject("Scripting.FileSystemObject")
      Set objTextFile = objFSO.CreateTextFile(strFileN, True)
      objTextFile.Write strHTML
      objTextFile.Close

   ' Cleanup
      Set xmlDoc = Nothing
      Set xslDoc = Nothing
      Set conn = Nothing
      Set myNode = Nothing
      Set objTextFile = Nothing
      Set objFSO = Nothing
   End Sub
```

XML and ASP

In the previous chapter you got a quick introduction to using Active Server Pages (ASP). This section will add to your knowledge by demonstrating how you can use ASP to transform an existing XML document to HTML on the server. You will also learn here how to dynamically generate XML from ADO recordsets on the server and send it as pure HTML to the browser.

Before you can work with an XML document in a web page, you must load the XML document. Start by creating an instance of the XML DOM object as follows:

```
Set xmlDoc = Server.CreateObject("Microsoft.xmldom")
xmlDoc.async = False
xmlDoc.Load("Products.xml")
```

To create the DOM object on the server, the server should have IE 5 or higher installed. Remember to set the async property of the document object to False to load the XML document synchronously. This causes the browser to wait until the entire XML document is loaded before processing further instructions.

After creating a DOM object, you can load an existing XML document or create one from scratch. As mentioned earlier in this chapter, an XML document can be loaded from a string or from a file. Let's do some processing on the server.

The following exercise demonstrates how to transform XML into HTML on the server.

1. Create a new folder under C:\Inetpub\wwwroot and name it **XML_ASP.**

2. Right-click the **XML_ASP** folder name, select **Sharing** from the shortcut menu, and click the **Web Sharing** tab. Click the **Share this folder** option button and type **myXML** in the Alias text box. Click **OK** twice to exit.

3. Open Notepad and type the ASP code shown below.

4. Save the ASP file as **C:\Inetpub\wwwroot\XML_ASP\Server-Transform.asp**.

5. Open the browser and type the following in the address bar: **http://localhost/myXML/ServerTransform.asp.** The resulting page should list products from the Northwind database Products table (compare it with Figure 17-29 earlier in this chapter).

```
<% @Language="VBScript" %>
<%
Option Explicit

Dim xmlDoc
Dim xslDoc
Dim strXMLDoc
Dim strXSLDoc
Dim strResult

On Error Resume Next

' instantiate the XMDOM object to hold the XML file
set xmlDoc = Server.CreateObject("Microsoft.xmldom")

' get the XML file name
strXMLDoc = Server.MapPath("Products.xml")

' get the XSL file name
strXSLDoc = Server.MapPath("AttribToHTML.xsl")

If err.number = 0 then
 ' parse the XML Document
 ' turn off asynchronous loading
 xmlDoc.async = False
 ' load the XML file
 xmlDoc.Load (strXMLDoc)
 If xmlDoc.parseError.errorCode = 0 then
  ' instantiate the XMDOM object to hold the XSL file
  set xslDoc = Server.CreateObject("Microsoft.xmldom")
  ' turn off asynchronous loading
  xslDoc.async=False
  ' load the XSL stylesheet
  xslDoc.Load (strXSLDoc)
   If xslDoc.parseError.errorCode = 0 then
    ' transform the XML into HTML using the stylesheet
    strResult = xmlDoc.TransformNode(xslDoc)
   else
    strResult = "Error processing XSL stylesheet: <BR>" & _
     "Code: " & xslDoc.parseError.errorCode & "<BR>" & _
     "Description: " & xslDoc.parseError.reason
   End if
 Else
   strResult = "Error processing XML document: <BR>" & _
```

```
      "Code: " & xmlDoc.parseError.errorCode &  "<BR>" & _
      "Description: " & xmlDoc.parseError.reason
   End if
 Else
      strResult = Err.number & ":" & Err.Description
 End if

 ' output result to the client
 Response.Write strResult

 ' cleanup
 set xmlDoc = Nothing
 set xslDoc = Nothing
 %>
```

This ASP code loads an XML document and a stylesheet from files previously saved on disk. The Server.MapPath method converts the virtual file path into a physical file path. Once the XML and XSL documents are successfully parsed, the Document object's TransformNode method is called to apply the stylesheet to the XML document. The result of the transformation is then written to the client using the Response.Write method.

Notice that the ASP script above also includes error-handling code. The On Error Resume Next statement at the top of the ASP script will force the script to continue when an error occurs. By using the ParseError property of the XML DOMDocument object, you can find out if any errors occurred parsing either document. The errorCode property will return the error code, and the reason property will display the error description. Because other errors besides parsing errors might occur while running the script, you can use the Visual Basic Err object to trap these errors.

Instead of using an existing XML document, you can write ASP code to dynamically generate XML from a database, as shown in the following exercise. By dynamically generating the XML document, you can rest assured that the XML document will be updated as the database changes. By taking this route, your XML document will always stay in sync with the database.

The following exercise demonstrates how to dynamically generate XML from a database.

1. Open Notepad and type the ASP code on the following page.

2. Save the ASP file as **C:\Inetpub\wwwroot\XML_ASP\Display-Products.asp**. See the previous exercise on creating a virtual directory.

3. Open the browser and type the following in the address bar: **http://localhost/myXML/DisplayProducts.asp**.

   Figure 17-30 presents the resulting page listing products and unit prices from the Northwind database Products table in descending order.

```
<% @Language="VBScript" %>
<%
Option Explicit
' declare variables
Dim strSQL
Dim strConnect
Dim rst

' declare constants
const adUseClient =3
const adOpenStatic=3
const adLockOptimistic=3
const adPersistXML=1

' assign values to variables
strSQL="Select ProductName, UnitPrice from Products Order By UnitPrice DESC"
strConnect="Provider=Microsoft.Jet.OLEDB.4.0; Data Source="& _
  Server.MapPath("Northwind.mdb")

' create and open the Recordset
set rst = Server.CreateObject("ADODB.Recordset")
rst.CursorLocation = adUseClient
rst.Open strSQL, strConnect, adOpenStatic, adLockOptimistic

' output as XML and apply stylesheet
Response.ContentType="text/xml"
Response.Write "<?xml:stylesheet type=""text/xsl"" href=" _
    "AttribToHTML.xsl"" ?>" & vbCrLf

' Save the Recordset to the Response object
rst.Save response, adPersistXML

' Close the Recordset
rst.Close
set rst=Nothing
%>
```

The ASP code above uses the Microsoft.Jet.OLEDB.4.0 provider to establish a connection to the Northwind database. If the database is on the SQL Server, you can use the following connection format (substitute relevant data with your own):

```
"Provider=SQLOLEDB;Data Source=11.2.19.215;" _
    & "Initial Catalog=Northwind;UserId=tester;Password=password;"
```

Once the database connection is open, the code creates and opens a recordset based on the specified SQL statement. Notice that the recordset is saved directly into the ASP Response object using the following code:

```
rst.Save response, adPersistXML
```

Notice also that prior to sending the response to the client machine, the code specifies the type of the file content and the name of a stylesheet file to be applied:

```
Response.ContentType="text/xml"
Response.Write "<?xml:stylesheet type=""text/xsl"" _
     href=""AttribToHTML.xsl"" ?>" & vbCrLf
```

When the ASP page is requested in the browser, the XML is formatted using the appropriate stylesheet. The user sees a table with a simple product price list in descending order.

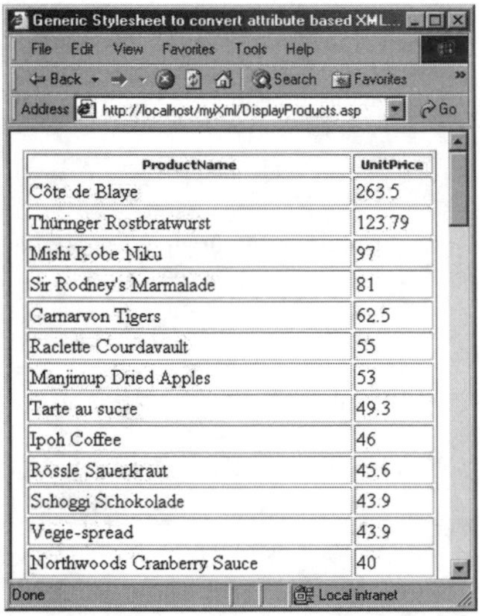

Generic Stylesheet to convert attribute based XML...
File Edit View Favorites Tools Help
Back Search Favorites
Address http://localhost/myXml/DisplayProducts.asp Go
ProductName UnitPrice
Côte de Blaye 263.5
Thüringer Rostbratwurst 123.79
Mishi Kobe Niku 97
Sir Rodney's Marmalade 81
Carnarvon Tigers 62.5
Raclette Courdavault 55
Manjimup Dried Apples 53
Tarte au sucre 49.3
Ipoh Coffee 46
Rössle Sauerkraut 45.6
Schoggi Schokolade 43.9
Vegie-spread 43.9
Northwoods Cranberry Sauce 40
Done
Local intranet

Figure 17-30:
This page was generated dynamically by the ASP page.

Tip 17-15: Important Facts about ADO Recordsets

An ADO recordset can be saved directly to an XML file.

```
Dim rst As ADODB.Recordset
Set rst = New ADODB.Recordset
...
...
rst.Save "C:\myfile.xml", adPersistXML
```

An ADO recordset can be saved directly to the Stream object so XML does not have to be saved in a physical file before you can work with it.

```
Dim rst As ADODB.Recordset
Dim myStream As ADODB.Stream
Set rst = New ADODB.Recordset
Set myStream = New ADODB.Stream
...
...
rst.Save myStream, adPersistXML
```

An ADO recordset can be saved directly into the XML DOMDocument object so you don't need to first save to a stream and then load that stream into the DOM. This method is faster and more scalable.

```
Dim rst As ADODB.Recordset
Dim myDom As MSXML2.DOMDocument30
Set rst = New ADODB.Recordset
Set myDom = New MSXML2.DOMDocument30
...
...
rst.Save myDom, adPersistXML
```

An ADO recordset can be saved directly into the ASP Response object.

```
<%
Dim rst As ADODB.Recordset
Set rst = New ADODB.Recordset
...
...
Rst.Save response, adPersistXML
%>
```

Posting Excel XML Data to a Web Server

Armed with your newly acquired XML skills, you can now write a useful business application that will handle the required processing on the server without human intervention. Take, for example, a common problem related to collecting employee timesheets. Each week, an employee fills in a timesheet that reports regular hours worked and overtime. The timesheets are collected by a designated person, often an administrative assistant, who must then summarize the data and perhaps rekey each timesheet into a database system. Using your Excel, XML, and ASP skills, you can now eliminate the timesheet task from the administrator's weekly routine. Each employee can be given an Excel spreadsheet with a custom-designed timesheet. When he is done reporting his time, the information can be processed automatically with the press of a button.

The following exercise demonstrates how to go about extracting data from an Excel range in the XML format (this was discussed earlier in this chapter) and posting the extracted data to a web application for further processing. The example web application is an ASP page that receives the posted Excel range, transforms that range into a custom XML using a stylesheet, and enters data into two Microsoft Access tables. When the processing is complete, the application automatically sends the status of the processing back to the client machine so that the employee does not have to wonder whether the data was successfully received or not. To make this application even more useful, you will allow the employee to query our Access tables for their timesheet data. This project will take several steps to complete, as outlined below.

Step 1: Creating a virtual directory
Step 2: Creating an Access database
Step 3: Creating a timesheet spreadsheet
Step 4: Writing VBA procedures for the command buttons
Step 5: Protecting the timesheet
Step 6: Writing a stylesheet
Step 7: Creating an ASP page
Step 8: Using the timesheet application

Step 1: Creating a Virtual Directory

We will store all of the files required by our web timesheet application in a virtual directory under C:\Inetpub\wwwroot. Follow these steps to set up a virtual folder on your computer:

1. Create a new folder under C:\Inetpub\wwwroot and name it **TimeTrack**.

2. Right-click the **TimeTrack** folder name, select **Sharing** from the shortcut menu, and click the **Web Sharing** tab.

3. Click the **Share this folder** option button and type **Time** in the Alias text box.

4. In the Access Permission area, click the check box next to the **Write** label.

5. The Application permissions area should have the **Scripts** option button selected.

6. Click **OK** to exit the Alias box. Click **OK** to the message.

7. In the TimeTrack Properties dialog box, click the **Security** tab.

8. Give the Everyone group **Read** and **Write** access to this folder (see Figure 17-31). If the Everyone group is not listed, you can add the group by clicking **Add**.

9. Click **OK** to exit the TimeTrack Properties dialog box.

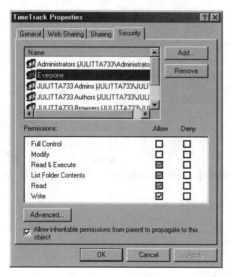

Figure 17-31:
Setting the Security permissions for the Everyone group

Step 2: Creating an Access Database

The first file to place in the TimeTrack folder is the Microsoft Access database. This database will contain two tables for storing and retrieving employee timesheet data.

1. Launch Microsoft Access (version 2000 or 2002) and create a new database named **C:\Inetpub\wwwroot\TimeTrack\TimeTrack.mdb**.

2. Create two tables, as shown in Figures 17-32 and 17-33.

3. Set up primary keys in both tables. In the tblTimeSheets table the PrimaryKey is TSheetId. In tblTimeSheetDetails the PrimaryKey is based on two fields: TSheetId and DayOfWeek. Because the tblTimeSheet details will be searched by EmployeeName, it is a good idea to define the index on the EmployeeName field as well.

4. Close the Access database and exit Microsoft Access.

5. Locate the newly created TimeTrack.mdb file in the C:\Inetpub\wwwroot\TimeTrack folder, and right-click the filename. Choose **Properties** from the shortcut menu. In the TimeTrack.mdb Properties dialog box click the **Security** tab, and assign the **Read & Execute**, **Read**, and **Write** permissions to the Everyone group. Click **OK** to exit the dialog box.

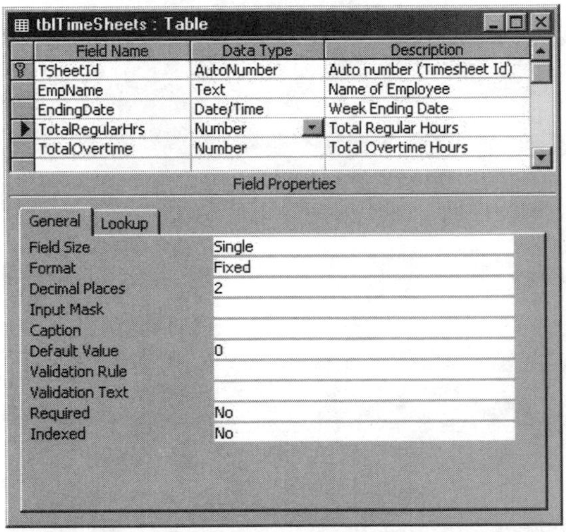

Figure 17-32:
Table tblTimeSheets holds the Summary data from the employee timesheet.

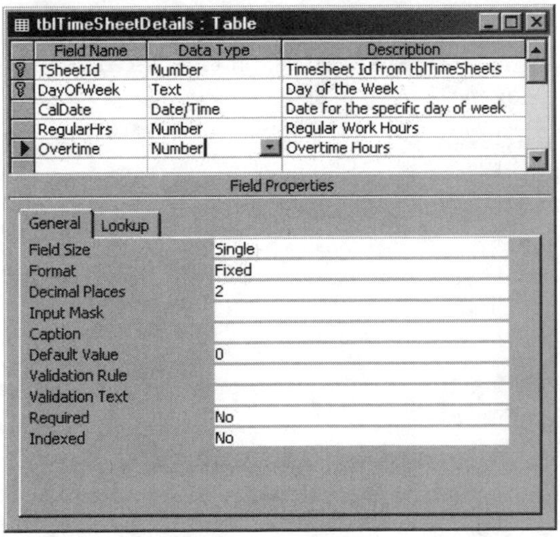

Figure 17-33:
Table tblTimeSheetDetails holds the timesheet details.

Step 3: Creating a Timesheet Spreadsheet

Now is the time to set up the user interface for your web application (Figure 17-34). Because most users are familiar with the spreadsheet format, they will welcome the idea of keeping track of their time in a worksheet, especially if you make it quick and easy for them to use.

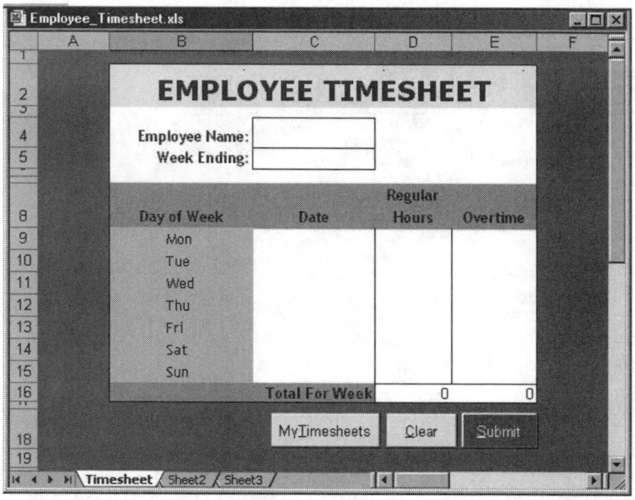

Figure 17-34:
This custom Timesheet worksheet will allow users to report their time to the central server for further processing.

1. Create a worksheet, as shown in Figure 17-34 above. Use the following guidelines to place formulas:

   - Each day of the week has a corresponding date that is calculated, as shown below:

Mon	=IF(C5<>"",$C$5-6,"")
Tue	=IF($C$5<>"",C9+1,"")
Wed	=IF($C$5<>"",C10+1,"")
Thu	=IF($C$5<>"",C11+1,"")
Fri	=IF($C$5<>"",C12+1,"")
Sat	=IF($C$5<>"",C13+1,"")
Sun	=IF($C$5<>"",C14+1,"")

   - Use the SUM function to calculate totals in the Regular Hours and Overtime columns:

     Total For Week =SUM(D9:D15) =SUM(E9:E15)

   - Place the formulas that calculate week-ending dates, as shown in Figure 17-35. Notice that these formulas are out of view when the spreadsheet is first presented to the user. The formulas assume that Sunday is the last day of the week.

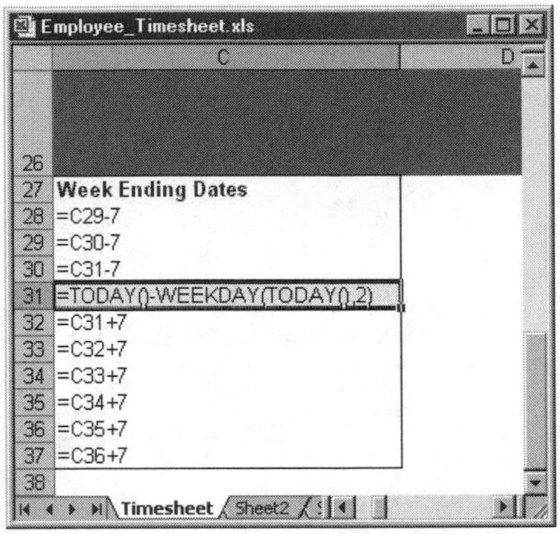

Figure 17-35:
Week-ending dates are based on simple formulas.

2. Link cell C5 to Week Ending Dates in cells C28:C37 as follows: Select cell **C5**. Choose **Validation** from the Data menu. The Data Validation dialog box will appear. Fill in the Data Validation dialog, as shown in Figure 17-36.

   In the Data Validation dialog box, click the **Input Message** tab and type the following input message: **Select Week Ending Date**. Make sure to mark the **Show input message when cell is selected** check box. In the Data Validation dialog box, click the **Error Alert** tab and fill it out as shown in Figure 17-37.

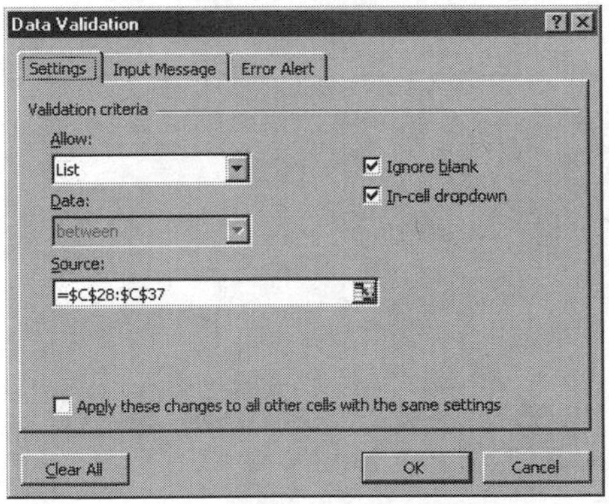

Figure 17-36: The list setting in the Data Validation dialog box allows you to create a dropdown list that gets its choices from cells elsewhere on the worksheet.

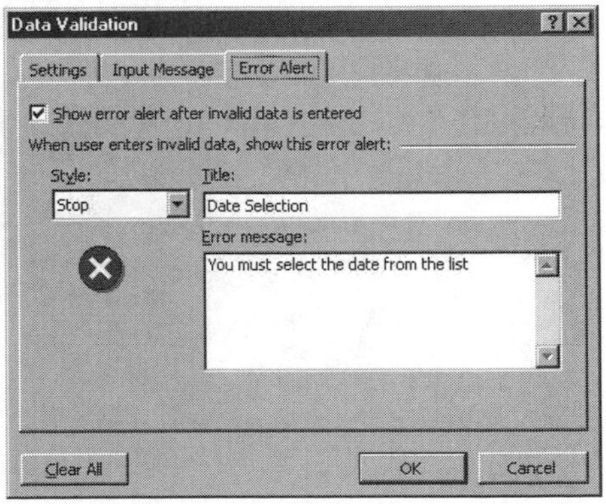

Figure 17-37: Use the Error Alert tab in the Data Validation dialog box to create a message that appears when incorrect data has been entered.

   Click **OK** to exit the Data Validation dialog box.

3. Use the Define Name dialog box (Figure 17-38) to assign the following names to spreadsheet cells:

Name	Refers to
CalDate	=Timesheet!$C$9:$C$15
DayOfWeek	=Timesheet!$B$9:$B$15
EmployeeName	=Timesheet!$C$4
EMPLOYEETIMESHEET	=Timesheet!$B$2:$E$16
EndingDate	=Timesheet!$C$5
Overtime	=Timesheet!$E$9:$E$15
RegularHrs	=Timesheet!$D$9:$D$15
TotalOvertime	=Timesheet!$E$16
TotalRegularHrs	=Timesheet!$D$16

Figure 17-38:
Use this dialog box to define names in the Timesheet spreadsheet.

4. Place three command buttons on the worksheet using the Control Toolbox: Choose **View | Toolbars | Control Toolbox** to display the Control Toolbox.

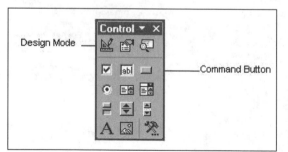

Figure 17-39:
Use the Control Toolbox to add interactive features to your worksheet.

Click the **Command Button** tool in the Control Toolbox and click in cell **E18** to place a command button on the worksheet. Right-click the button and choose **Properties** from the shortcut menu. Fill in the properties for the Submit button, as shown in Figure 17-40.

Using the same method, place the other two buttons (Clear and MyTimesheets) on the worksheet. Assign **cmdClear** and **cmdMy-Time** to the Name properties of these buttons.

Right-click each button and choose **View Code** from the shortcut menu. You will get skeletons for your VBA procedures in the Sheet1 (Timesheet) Code window:

```
Private Sub cmdClear_Click()

End Sub

Private Sub cmdClear_Click()

End Sub

Private Sub cmdClear_Click()

End Sub
```

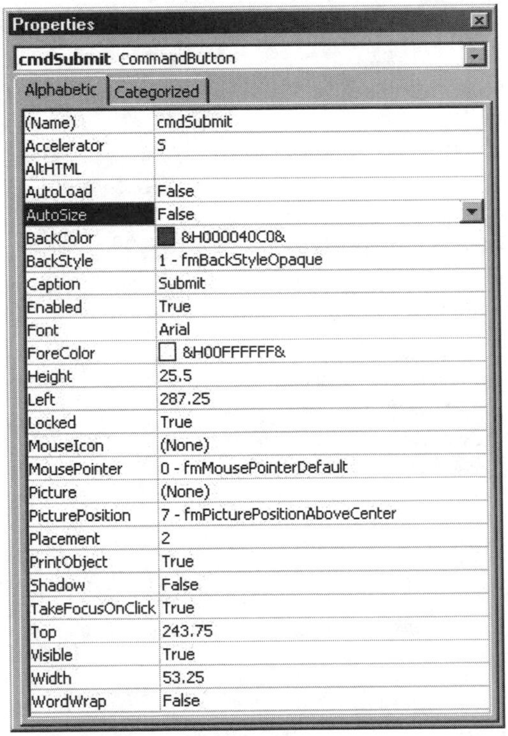

Figure 17-40:
The Properties sheet lists all properties that apply to the selected control.

Step 4: Writing VBA Procedures for the Command Buttons

1. Start by writing a simple VBA procedure that will clear the timesheet when the user clicks the Clear button. This procedure should clear unprotected cells in the spreadsheet, except for the Employee name stored in cell C4. Note that when you are done writing VBA procedures, you should protect your timesheet so users can enter data only in the designated cells and cell ranges. The procedure assigned to the

Clear button will also be automatically called after the timesheet data has been successfully submitted. The cmdClear_Click procedure is shown below.

```
Private Sub cmdClear_Click()
    ActiveSheet.Unprotect
        Range("C5").ClearContents
        Range("RegularHrs").ClearContents
        Range("Overtime").ClearContents
    ActiveSheet.Protect
End Sub
```

2. Write the code for the cmdMyTime_Click procedure that is assigned to the My Timesheets button on the spreadsheet. This procedure will retrieve data from the TimeTrack database for the indicated employee when the user clicks the My Timesheets button.

```
Private Sub cmdMyTime_Click()
    Dim conn As ADODB.Connection
    Dim rst As ADODB.Recordset
    Dim strEmpName As String
    Dim strDB As String
    Dim strSQL As String
    Dim fldCount As Integer
    Dim recCount As Long
    Dim c As Integer            ' column index
    Dim r As Integer            ' row index
    Dim TShId As String

    On Error GoTo ErrorHandler

    If IsEmpty(Range("C4")) Then
        MsgBox "Please enter Employee Name.", _
            vbInformation, "Missing Employee Name"
        Exit Sub
    End If
    strEmpName = Range("C4").Value

    ' Set the path of your TimeTrack database
    strDB = "c:\inetpub\wwwroot\TimeTrack\timeTrack.mdb"

    ' Open connection to the database
    Set conn = New ADODB.Connection
    conn.Open "Provider=Microsoft.Jet.OLEDB.4.0;" & _
        "Data Source=" & strDB & ";"

    ' Open recordset based on tblTimeSheets table
    Set rst = New ADODB.Recordset
    strSQL = "SELECT * From tblTimeSheets"
    strSQL = strSQL & " WHERE EmpName ='" & strEmpName & "'"
    rst.Open strSQL, conn

    If rst.EOF Then
        MsgBox "Database does not have any records for " & _
```

```
                    strEmpName & "."
        GoTo ExitHere
    End If

    Sheets(2).Select
    ActiveSheet.Cells.Clear

    ' Copy field names to the first row of the worksheet
    fldCount = rst.Fields.Count
    For c = 1 To fldCount
        ActiveSheet.Cells(1, c).Value = rst.Fields(c - 1).Name
    Next

    ' Copy the recordset to the worksheet, starting in cell A2
    ActiveSheet.Cells(2, 1).CopyFromRecordset rst

    ' store all timesheet IDs in a variable
    ActiveSheet.Cells(2, 1).Select
    Do Until IsEmpty(ActiveCell)
        TShId = TShId & ActiveCell.Value & ","
        ActiveCell.Offset(1, 0).Select
    Loop

    ' Open a new recordset based on the tblTimesheetDetails table
    Set rst = New ADODB.Recordset
    strSQL = "SELECT * FROM tblTimesheetDetails"
    strSQL = strSQL & " WHERE TSheetId in (" & TShId & ")"
    strSQL = strSQL & " ORDER BY TSheetId, Weekday(CalDate, 2)"
    rst.Open strSQL, conn

    ' Copy field names to the first row of the worksheet
    ' beginning in Column G
    fldCount = rst.Fields.Count
    For c = 1 To fldCount
        ActiveSheet.Cells(1, c + 6).Value = rst.Fields(c - 1).Name
    Next
    ActiveSheet.Range("G2").CopyFromRecordset rst
    ActiveSheet.Cells(1, 1).Select

ErrorHandler:
    If Err.Number <> 0 Then
        MsgBox Err.Description
        GoTo ExitHere
    End If
ExitHere:
    rst.Close
    Set rst = Nothing
    conn.Close
    Set conn = Nothing
End Sub
```

3. Write the code for the cmdSubmit_Click procedure that is assigned to the Submit button on the spreadsheet. This procedure posts data from the spreadsheet range to the ASP page (Timesheet.asp). Notice that

the procedure begins with a call to the ValidateData function. See this function's code following the code of the cmdSubmit_Click procedure.

You can post data to Active Server Pages by using the XMLHTTP object of the XML DOM object model. When you use the XMLHTTP object, the XML data is passed over the Internet using the standard HTTP protocol. Sending data begins by opening a "POST" connection to your web server. To create the XMLHTTP object and set it up, the procedure uses the following code:

```
' Submit the XMLSS to the ASP page for processing
Set myHTTP = New MSXML2.XMLHTTP30
myHTTP.Open "Post", sFolder & "TimeSheet.asp", False
```

In the above code fragment the sFolder is a constant pointing to the "http://localhost/Time/" folder where the ASP page (which you will create later) is located. The False, in the place of the third parameter of the Open method, indicates that communication between client and server will be handled synchronously. This means that the client machine will wait until the response is returned from the server.

Once the connection to the web server is open, use the Send method of the XMLHTTP object to send the XML data to the receiving ASP page:

```
myHTTP.send resultXML
```

In the above statement, resultXML is the XML document that you obtained after transforming the XML spreadsheet data from the Excel range into the custom format using the Timesheet.xls stylesheet (the code of the stylesheet is shown later in this chapter).

It is always useful during procedure testing to see what was actually sent to the web server, so use these two debugging statements to find out:

```
Debug.Print resultXML.XML
Debug.Print resultXML.Text
```

The ASP page that receives the data will contain code to process the data and write the response to the client. You can retrieve the processing result from the XMLHTTP object's responseText property:

```
' Get response from ASP page
Set myResponse = New MSXML2.DOMDocument30
myResponse.Load myHTTP.responseXML
Debug.Print myHTTP.responseText
```

Here's the complete code for the cmdSubmit_Click procedure:

```
Private Sub cmdSubmit_Click()
    ' Declarations
    Dim timeRangeXML As MSXML2.DOMDocument30
    Dim timeXSL As MSXML2.DOMDocument30
    Dim resultXML As MSXML2.DOMDocument30
    Dim myHTTP As MSXML2.XMLHTTP30
    Dim myResponse As MSXML2.DOMDocument30
```

```vba
        Dim strStatus As String

        On Error GoTo ErrorHandler
        Const sFolder = "http://localhost/Time/"

        ' call the ValidateData function
        If ValidateData = False Then Exit Sub

        ' Load a new DOMDocument using range B4:E16
        Set timeRangeXML = New MSXML2.DOMDocument30
        timeRangeXML.LoadXML Range("B4:E16").Value(xlRangeValueXMLSpreadsheet)

        ' Transform the XMLSS spreadsheet to custom XML
        Set timeXSL = New MSXML2.DOMDocument30
        timeXSL.Load ThisWorkbook.Path & "\Timesheet.xsl"

        Set resultXML = New MSXML2.DOMDocument30
        timeRangeXML.transformNodeToObject timeXSL, resultXML

        ' Submit the XMLSS to the ASP page for processing
        Set myHTTP = New MSXML2.XMLHTTP30
        myHTTP.Open "Post", sFolder & "TimeSheet.asp", False
        myHTTP.send resultXML

        ' See what was sent
        Debug.Print resultXML.XML
        Debug.Print resultXML.Text

        ' Get response from ASP page
        Set myResponse = New MSXML2.DOMDocument30
        myResponse.Load myHTTP.responseXML

        Debug.Print myHTTP.responseText
        strStatus = myResponse.selectSingleNode("//Status").Text

        If strStatus = "Success" Then
            MsgBox "You have successfully submitted  " & vbCrLf _
                & "the timesheet for the week ending " & _
                Range("EndingDate").Value & ".", _
                vbInformation, "Congratulations!"
        Else
            MsgBox strStatus
        End If
        cmdClear_Click
        Exit Sub
ErrorHandler:
        MsgBox Err.Number & ": " & Err.Description
    End Sub
```

Prior to posting data to the server, it is always a good idea to validate it on the client. The ValidateData function is called by the cmdSubmit_Click procedure. This function ensures that users enter complete and valid data.

4. Enter the following ValidateData function below the code of the
    cmdSubmit_Click procedure.

```
Function ValidateData()
    Dim strMsg As String
    Dim strReg As String
    Dim strOvt As String
    Dim response As Integer
    Dim cell As Variant
    Dim blnNotNumber As Boolean

    ValidateData = True
    strMsg = ""

    If Range("C4").Value = "" Then
        strMsg = strMsg & " * Employee name" & vbCrLf
    End If
    If Range("C5").Value = "" Then
        strMsg = strMsg & " * Week-ending date" & vbCrLf
    End If

    For Each cell In Range("D9:D15")
        If IsEmpty(cell) Or Not IsNumeric(cell) Then
            strReg = strReg & cell.Offset(0, -2).Value & " "
        End If
    Next
    If strReg <> "" Then
        strMsg = strMsg & " * Regular hrs for: " & strReg & vbCrLf
    End If

    For Each cell In Range("E9:E15")
        If IsEmpty(cell) Or Not IsNumeric(cell) Then
            strOvt = strOvt & cell.Offset(0, -3).Value & " "
            If Not IsNumeric(cell) Then
                blnNotNumber = True
            End If
        End If
    Next

    If strOvt <> "" Then
        strMsg = strMsg & " * Overtime hrs for: " & strOvt
        strMsg = strMsg & vbCrLf & vbCrLf
        If blnNotNumber = False Then
            strMsg = strMsg & "Do you want to enter zeros for overtime?"
        End If
    End If

    If strMsg <> "" Then
        strMsg = "The following data is missing: " & vbCrLf & vbCrLf & strMsg
    Else
        Exit Function
    End If

    If strOvt <> "" And blnNotNumber = False Then
```

```
            response = MsgBox(strMsg, vbYesNo + vbExclamation, _
                "Incomplete Data")
            If response = vbYes And blnNotNumber = False Then
                Range("E9:E15").Select
                ActiveSheet.Unprotect
                Selection.SpecialCells(xlCellTypeBlanks).Select
                Selection.FormulaR1C1 = "0"
                ActiveSheet.Protect
            End If
        Else
            MsgBox strMsg, vbExclamation, "Incomplete Data"
        End If
        ValidateData = False
    End Function
```

Step 5: Protecting the Timesheet

Now that you are done writing VBA procedures that clear the cells and request, validate, and submit the data, you should take the time to protect your work.

1. Unlock the following cells and cell ranges by choosing **Format | Cells** (**Protection** tab) and clearing the check box next to the **Locked** label:

    ■ C4:C5: User must be able to enter his/her name in the EmployeeName cell (C4) and make a selection from the drop-down list in cell C5. These cells must be unlocked.

    ■ D9:E15: Cells to which you assigned the names RegularHrs and Overtime should be unlocked.

    ■ C28:C37: Cells calculating the Week Ending Date should be both locked and hidden from the user.

2. Use **Tools | Options** (**View** tab) to adjust window options so users don't scroll around in the worksheet sheet or view row and column headings and gridlines. Clear the check box next to the following labels: **Gridlines, Row & column headers, Horizontal scroll bars, Vertical scroll bars**.

3. Protect the timesheet by choosing **Tools | Protection | Protect Sheet**. When the Protect Sheet dialog box appears, make sure the check box next to **Select unlocked cells** is selected. All other check boxes in the section "Allow all users of this worksheet to" should be cleared. The top of the dialog box should indicate that you want to protect the worksheet and the contents of the locked cells. Ensure that this box is checked and click **OK** to exit the dialog box.

Note: You can protect the timesheet with a password to not allow users to unprotect the sheet and make any changes to the underlying data (unless they happen to know the password, they won't be able to make any design changes).

After applying the sheet protection, the user won't be able to click on any locked cell. Also, because you have removed the scroll bars, they won't be able to move past the initial screen.

4. With the sheet protection in place, save your work in the **Employee_Timesheet.xls** file. Place this file in the **C:\Inetpub\ wwwroot\timetrack** folder that you created at the very beginning of this project. This way, all the files related to the timesheet project are kept in one place.

Step 6: Writing a Stylesheet

The following stylesheet is used to format XML data requested from an Excel range in the cmdSubmit_Click procedure assigned to the Submit button.

1. Open Notepad and type the code of the stylesheet presented below.

2. Save the stylesheet as **C:\Inetpub\wwwroot\timetrack\Time- sheet.xsl**.

3. Close Notepad.

4. Open the stylesheet in the browser by double-clicking the filename. Recall that by opening the XML file in the browser, you can quickly check whether the file is well-formed.

Timesheet.xsl – The XSL Stylesheet

```
<?xml version="1.0" encoding="UTF-16"?>
<xsl:stylesheet version="1.0" xmlns:xsl ="http://www.w3.org/1999/XSL/ _
    Transform"
xmlns:xl="urn:schemas-microsoft-com:office:spreadsheet"
xmlns:ss="urn:schemas-microsoft-com:office:spreadsheet"
exclude-result-prefixes="xl ss">
  <xsl:template match="/xl:Workbook/xl:Worksheet/xl:Table">
  <Timesheet>
    <GeneralInfo>
      <EmployeeName>
        <xsl:value-of select="xl:Row/xl:Cell[xl:NamedCell[@ss:Name= _
            'EmployeeName']] / xl:Data "/>
      </EmployeeName>
      <EndingDate>
       <xsl:value-of select="substring(xl:Row/xl:Cell[xl:NamedCell _
           [@ss:Name='EndingDate']] /xl:Data,1,10) "/>
      </EndingDate>
      <TotalRegularHrs>
        <xsl:value-of select="xl:Row/xl:Cell[xl:NamedCell[@ss:Name='Total _
            RegularHrs']] /xl:Data "/>
      </TotalRegularHrs>
      <TotalOvertime>
        <xsl:value-of select="xl:Row/xl:Cell[xl:NamedCell[@ss:Name='Total _
            Overtime']] /xl:Data "/>
      </TotalOvertime>
    </GeneralInfo>
```

```
    <Days>
     <xsl:for-each select="xl:Row/xl:Cell[xl:NamedCell _
           [@ss:Name='DayOfWeek']]">
     <Day>
     <DayOfWeek>
       <xsl:value-of select="../xl:Cell[xl:NamedCell _
           [@ss:Name='DayOfWeek']] /xl:Data "/>
     </DayOfWeek>
     <CalDate>
       <xsl:value-of select="substring(../xl:Cell[xl:NamedCell _
           [@ss:Name='CalDate']] /xl:Data,1,10) "/>
     </CalDate>
     <RegularHrs>
       <xsl:value-of select="../xl:Cell[xl:NamedCell _
           [@ss:Name='RegularHrs']] /xl:Data "/>
     </RegularHrs>
     <Overtime>
       <xsl:value-of select="../xl:Cell[xl:NamedCell _
           [@ss:Name='Overtime']] /xl:Data "/>
     </Overtime>
     </Day>
     </xsl:for-each>
    </Days>
   </Timesheet>
  </xsl:template>
 </xsl:stylesheet>
```

When you get data out of a Microsoft Excel spreadsheet using the Value property of the Range object (as you did in the cmdSubmit_Click procedure), the data is formatted using the XML-SS schema. The XML Spreadsheet Schema (SS) outputs the data in a tree structure like this:

XML-SS schema	Example row in the XML-SS schema format

`<Worksheet>`
  `<Table>`
   `<Row>`
    `<Cell>`
     `<Data></Data>`
    `</Cell>`
   `</Row>`
  `</Table>`
`</Worksheet>`
	`<Row ss:AutoFitHeight="0" ss:Height="20.25">`
	  `<Cell ss:StyleID="s31">`
	   `<Data ss:Type="String">Employee Name:</Data>`
	  `</Cell>`
	  `<Cell ss:StyleID="s42">`
	   `<Data ss:Type="String">Margaret Hanson</Data>`
	   `<NamedCell ss:Name="EmployeeName"/>`
	  `</Cell>`
	  `<Cell ss:StyleID="s32"/>`
	  `<Cell ss:StyleID="s27"/>`
	`</Row>`

The Timesheet.xsl stylesheet that we are applying to the XML data obtained from an Excel range will transform this XML-SS tree structure into an easy-to-read element-based XML document that looks like this:

```
<?xml version="1.0" encoding="UTF-16" ?>
- <Timesheet>
 - <GeneralInfo>
    <EmployeeName>Mark Brown</EmployeeName>
```

```
          <EndingDate>2002-07-21</EndingDate>
          <TotalRegularHrs>37</TotalRegularHrs>
          <TotalOvertime>0</TotalOvertime>
        </GeneralInfo>
    -   <Days>
    -   <Day>
          <DayOfWeek>Mon</DayOfWeek>
          <CalDate>2002-07-15</CalDate>
          <RegularHrs>7</RegularHrs>
          <Overtime>0</Overtime>
    -   </Day>
    -   <Day>
          <DayOfWeek>Tue</DayOfWeek>
          <CalDate>2002-07-16</CalDate>
          <RegularHrs>7</RegularHrs>
          <Overtime>0</Overtime>
        </Day>
    -   <Day>
          <DayOfWeek>Wed</DayOfWeek>
          <CalDate>2002-07-17</CalDate>
          <RegularHrs>7</RegularHrs>
          <Overtime>0</Overtime>
        </Day>
    -   <Day>
          <DayOfWeek>Thu</DayOfWeek>
          <CalDate>2002-07-18</CalDate>
          <RegularHrs>7</RegularHrs>
          <Overtime>0</Overtime>
        </Day>
    -   <Day>
          <DayOfWeek>Fri</DayOfWeek>
          <CalDate>2002-07-19</CalDate>
          <RegularHrs>7</RegularHrs>
          <Overtime>0</Overtime>
        </Day>
    -   <Day>
          <DayOfWeek>Sat</DayOfWeek>
          <CalDate>2002-07-20</CalDate>
          <RegularHrs>2</RegularHrs>
          <Overtime>0</Overtime>
        </Day>
    -   <Day>
          <DayOfWeek>Sun</DayOfWeek>
          <CalDate>2002-07-21</CalDate>
          <RegularHrs>0</RegularHrs>
          <Overtime>0</Overtime>
        </Day>
        </Days>
        </Timesheet>
```

Tip 17-16: Examining XML-SS Data Prior to Applying a Stylesheet

To see the XML output prior to applying the stylesheet, activate the Visual Basic Editor window and place a breakpoint on the following statement in the cmdSubmit_Click procedure:

```
timeRangeXML.LoadXML Range("B4:E16")
.Value(xlRangeValueXMLSpreadsheet)
```

Next fill in the timesheet data and click the Submit button. When the code

window appears, press F8 to run the above statement. Activate the Immediate window and enter the following statement:

```
?timeRangeXML.xml
```

When you press Enter, you will be able to examine the XML that is stored in this object variable.

Notice that the Timesheet.xsl stylesheet uses a single template to reshuffle the original data. The statement:

```
<xsl:template match="/xl:Workbook/xl:Worksheet/xl:Table">
```

tells the XSL processor to find a Table branch, which is a child of a worksheet and a grandchild of a workbook, and process the data found within this branch according to the instructions that follow. The first tag inside the template, <Timesheet>, is the name of the document element, also known as a root element. This top-level element will contain all other elements in the transformed XML document. Within the root, we are dividing the data into two subtrees: General Info and Days. The General Info comprises information from the Employee Name, Ending Date, Total Regular Hrs, and Overtime cells. To get relevant information, we need to locate the cell with the appropriate range name and return its Data element. Therefore, to get the Employee Name, the stylesheet uses the following expression:

```
<xsl:value-of select="xl:Row/xl:Cell[xl:NamedCell[@ss:Name=
  'EmployeeName']] / xl:Data "/>
```

Reading the Ending Date value is a bit more complicated, as the date is reported in the XML-SS schema format like this:

```
<Row ss:AutoFitHeight="0" ss:Height="14.25">
    <Cell ss:StyleID="s31">
      <Data ss:Type="String">Week Ending:</Data>
    </Cell>
    <Cell ss:StyleID="s44">
      <Data ss:Type="DateTime">2002-07-28T00:00:00.000</Data>
      <NamedCell ss:Name="EndingDate"/>
    </Cell>
    <Cell ss:StyleID="s33"/>
    <Cell ss:StyleID="s27"/>
</Row>
```

Because you only need to obtain the date portion of the XML data node's value (2002-07-28T00:00:00.000), the stylesheet uses an XPath substring function. This function has the same syntax as the VBA Mid function, allowing you to extract a specified number of characters from a string starting at a specific position. The format of the substring function is shown below:

```
Substring(string, startpos, length)
```

startpos is the position of the first character to extract, and length represents the number of characters to be returned from string. Therefore, the expression:

```
<xsl:value-of select="substring(xl:Row/xl:Cell[xl: NamedCell _
    [@ss:Name='EndingDate']] /xl:Data,1,10) "/>
```

tells the XSL processor to retrieve only the first ten characters from the value found in the EndingDate cell.

Reading the other two elements (TotalRegularHrs and TotalOvertime) for the GeneralInfo subtree follows the same rules. Following GeneralInfo, the stylesheet creates a Days subtree with elements showing Day of Week, Calendar Date (CalDate), Regular Hrs, and Overtime. To retrieve the individual days of the week, you need to start a loop with the following expression:

```
<xsl:for-each select="xl:Row/xl:Cell[xl:
    NamedCell[@ss:Name='DayOfWeek']]">
```

For each day of the week, you need to get the corresponding value of CalDate, RegularHrs, and Overtime using the following example expression:

```
<xsl:value-of select="../xl:Cell[xl:
    NamedCell[@ss:Name='RegularHrs']] /xl:Data "/>
```

Notice that the two dots in front of /xl:Cell refer to the row that is the parent of the cell. When you are done looping through the day cells, you must end the loop with the ending tag, like this:

```
</xsl:for-each>
```

and make sure to close all the other tags that were started:

```
    </Days>
        </Timesheet>
    </xsl:template>
</xsl:stylesheet>
```

This completes the analysis of the stylesheet and brings us one step closer to the completion of our timesheet application.

Step 7: Creating an ASP Page

Now that the design of the user interface and the XML transformation are out of the way, you need to design the Active Server Page that will receive the XML data from the client and perform the required processing.

1. Open Notepad and type the ASP script shown on the following page.

2. Save the file as **Timesheet.asp** in the C:\Inetpub\wwwroot\timetrack folder.

TimeSheet.asp – Active Server Page

```
<%@ Language="vbscript"%>
<%
    Dim clientXML    ' XML Data received from the client
    Dim Conn         ' ADO Connection to the database
    Dim strConn      ' Database connection string
    Dim rst          ' ADO Recordset for the table - tblTimesheets
    Dim rstDetails   ' ADO Recordset for the table - tblTimesheetDetails
    Dim myDays       ' Collection of Day nodes
    Dim myDay        ' Single day node in the collection of myDays
    Dim strStatus    ' Timesheet processing status
    Dim blnProceed   ' Boolean value to indicate whether to continue
                     ' processing
    Dim strTSheetId  ' Id of the newly entered record in the
                     ' tblTimesheets
    Dim strReceipt   ' XML string to send as receipt to the client

    On Error Resume Next

    'Load the XML data passed by client
    Set clientXML = CreateObject("Microsoft.XMLDOM")
    clientXML.Load(Request)

    'save XML on the server (for practice only)
    clientXML.save(Server.MapPath("LastSubmit.xml"))
    blnProceed = True

    'Open a connection to the TimeTrack.mdb Access database
    If blnProceed Then
        Set Conn = CreateObject("ADODB.Connection")
        strConn = "Provider=Microsoft.Jet.OLEDB.4.0;Data Source=" _
            & Server.MapPath("TimeTrack.mdb")
        Conn.Open strConn
        If err.Number <> 0 Then
            strStatus = err.Description & " " & err.number
            blnProceed = False
        End If
    End If

    'Open the tblTimesheets table to add new records
    If blnProceed Then
      If err.number = 0 Then
            Set rst = CreateObject("ADODB.Recordset")
            rst.Open "SELECT * FROM tblTimesheets", Conn, 2, 3
            rst.AddNew
            rst("EmpName").Value = _
                clientXML.selectSingleNode("//EmployeeName").Text
            rst("EndingDate").Value = _
                clientXML.selectSingleNode("//EndingDate").Text
            rst("TotalRegularHrs").value = _
                clientXML.selectSingleNode("//TotalRegularHrs").Text
```

```
            rst("TotalOvertime").value = _
                clientXML.selectSingleNode("//TotalOvertime").Text
            rst.Update
            strTSheetId = rst("TSheetId").Value
    End If
      If err.number = 0 Then
          'Open the tblTimesheetDetails table to add new records
          Set rstDetails = CreateObject("ADODB.Recordset")
          rstDetails.Open _
                "SELECT * FROM tblTimesheetDetails", Conn, 2, 3
          ' set up loop to read and write individual days
          Set myDays = clientXML.SelectNodes("Timesheet/Days/Day")
          For Each myDay In myDays
              rstDetails.AddNew
              rstDetails("TSheetId").Value = strTSheetId
              rstDetails("DayOfWeek").Value = myDay.childnodes(0).Text
              rstDetails("CalDate").Value = myDay.childnodes(1).Text
              rstDetails("RegularHrs").Value = myDay.childnodes(2).Text
              rstDetails("Overtime").Value = myDay.childnodes(3).text
              rstDetails.Update
          Next
      End If
      If err.Number <> 0 Then
          strStatus = err.Description
      Else
          strStatus = "Success"
      End If

      'Close the recordsets and connection
      rstDetails.Close
      Set rstDetails = Nothing
      rst.Close
      Set rst = Nothing
      Conn.Close
      Set Conn = Nothing
    End If

    'Return to the client the Timesheet status in the XML format
    strReceipt = "<?xml version=""1.0""?>"
    strReceipt = strReceipt & "<TimeSheetSubmitted>"
    strReceipt = strReceipt & "<Status>" & strStatus & "</Status>"
    strReceipt = strReceipt & "<TSheetId>" & strTSheetId & "</TSheetId>"
    strReceipt = strReceipt & "</TimeSheetSubmitted>"
    Response.ContentType = "text/xml"
    Response.Write strReceipt
    Response.End
%>
```

The ASP page shown above begins with retrieving the XML data passed by the client. The ASP does not care who the client is (that is, which application has posted the data). All the ASP page on the server side needs to know is how to retrieve the passed data. This task is accomplished through the ASP Request object. Notice that to obtain data, the Request object is loaded into an instance of the XMLDOM, like this:

```
Set clientXML = CreateObject("Microsoft.XMLDOM")
clientXML.Load(Request)
```

After the XML data has been retrieved, the ASP page can do with the data whatever is required before sending the report back to the client. In this particular scenario, you first save the posted data to a disk file using the following statement:

```
clientXML.save(Server.MapPath("LastSubmit.xml"))
```

Note that saving the XML to a disk file is not required. It is presented here for demonstration purposes only. Next, open the connection to your custom Microsoft Access database that you prepared in the second step of this project. If the connection is successful (there are no errors—err.number <>0), open the recordset based on the tblTimeSheets table and add a new record using the AddNew method of the Recordset object. Then retrieve values of the appropriate XML elements using the Text property of the selectSingleNode method. When you've written values for each field, use the Update method of the Recordset object. After you've successfully added the new record with the employee timesheet, retrieve the ID of this record (TSheetId) and store it in the strTSheetId variable. If everything goes well (there are no errors), open the second recordset on the tblTimeSheet-Details table and proceed to add detail records.

You must loop through individual days of the week and make a record for each day. The easiest way to accomplish this is via the For Each...Next loop. Notice that each day record contains five fields named TSheetId, DayOfWeek, CalDate, RegularHrs, and Overtime. Except for the first field whose value you obtained from tblTimeSheets, you need to retrieve values for the remaining fields by using the Text property of the childnodes collection. For example, to write the name of the day of the week to the DayOfWeek field, use the following statement:

```
rstDetails("DayOfWeek").Value = myDay.childnodes(0).Text
```

Because collections are zero-based, the first element in the collection has an index value of 0.

Once you've added a detailed record for each day of the week, close both recordsets and break the connection to the database. When the processing is done by the ASP page, send some sort of notification to the client. The last fragment of the ASP script does that by first building a reply in the XML format and placing it in the strReceipt variable. Next, the content of the variable is written to the page using the statement:

```
Response.Write strReceipt
```

Then it is sent to the client using Response.End.

Step 8: Using the Timesheet Application

Now that you are finished writing the last part of the timesheet application, you should spend some time testing and debugging it. I suggest that you set up several breakpoints in your VBA code and step through the procedures while querying the contents of objects in the Immediate window. You may also expand this application by adding additional features.

Here are some illustrations of running the application from the user interface.

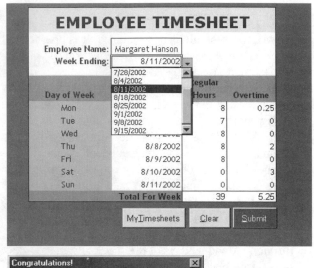

Figure 17-41: Entering employee timesheet data for a specific week-ending date

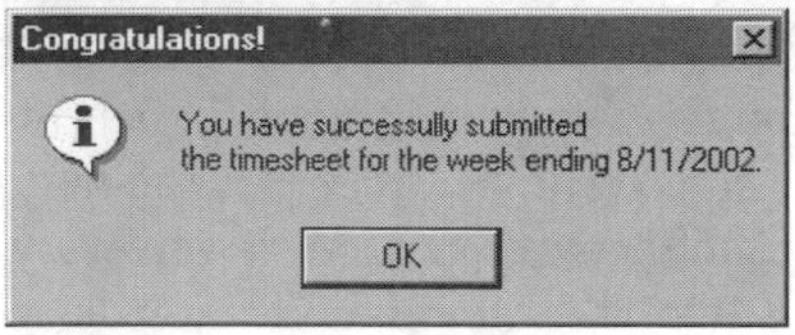

Figure 17-42: When the timesheet data is successfully submitted, the employee receives the confirmation message.

Employee_Timesheet.xls

	A	B	C	D	E	F	G	H	I	J	K
1	TSheetId	EmpName	EndingDate	TotalRegularHrs	TotalOvertime		TSheetId	DayOfWeek	CalDate	RegularHr:	Overtime
2	6	Margaret Hans	8/4/2002	33	0		6	Mon	7/29/2002	7	0
3	7	Margaret Hans	7/28/2002	40	3		6	Tue	7/30/2002	5	0
4	8	Margaret Hans	8/11/2002	39	5.25		6	Wed	7/31/2002	7	0
5							6	Thu	8/1/2002	7	0
6							6	Fri	8/2/2002	7	0
7							6	Sat	8/3/2002	0	0
8							6	Sun	8/4/2002	0	0
9							7	Mon	7/22/2002	8	0
10							7	Tue	7/23/2002	8	0
11							7	Wed	7/24/2002	8	0
12							7	Thu	7/25/2002	8	3
13							7	Fri	7/26/2002	8	0
14							7	Sat	7/27/2002	0	0
15							7	Sun	7/28/2002	0	0
16							8	Mon	8/5/2002	8	0.25
17							8	Tue	8/6/2002	7	0
18							8	Wed	8/7/2002	8	0
19							8	Thu	8/8/2002	8	2
20							8	Fri	8/9/2002	8	0
21							8	Sat	8/10/2002	0	3
22							8	Sun	8/11/2002	0	0
23											

Timesheet | Sheet2 | Sheet3

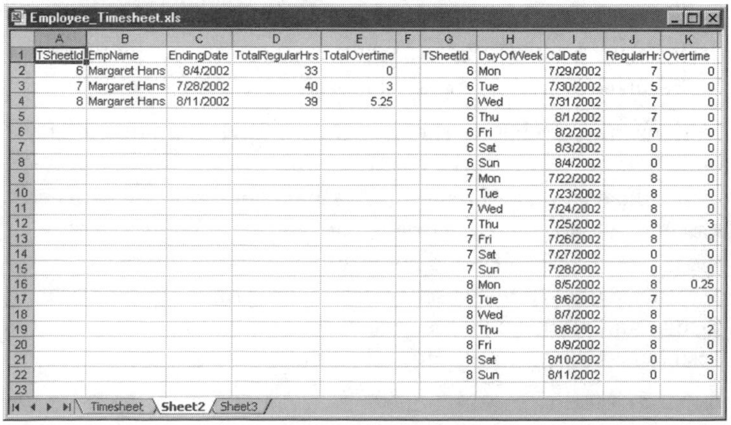

Figure 17-43: Upon pressing the My Timesheets button, the user is switched to Sheet2 to view the information on his or her existing timesheets in the database. You can view information for any employee by changing the name that appears next to the Employee Name

What's Next...

It's hard to stop when you really get going. New ideas will start to flow, and you will be anxious to test (and most likely implement) them right away. This chapter has only scratched the surface of what's possible with the technology known as XML. You learned here what XML is and how it is structured. While HTML consists of markup tags that define how the information should be formatted for display in a web browser, XML allows you to invent your own tags in order to define and describe data stored in a wide range of documents. XML will supply you with numerous ways to accomplish a specific task. Because XML is stored in plain text files, it can be read by many types of applications, independent of the operating system or hardware. This chapter has shown you how to perform many tasks with XML and Excel together. You've learned how to transform data from XML to HTML and from one XML format to another. You explored the ADO recordset methods suitable for working with XML programmatically and saw how to send data to the web server from an Excel worksheet. You were introduced to XML data islands and XSL stylesheets. All of these new methods and techniques that you've studied here will need time to sink in. XML is not like VBA. It is not very independent. It needs many supporting technologies to assist it in its work. So do not despair if you don't understand something right away. Learning XML requires learning many other new concepts (like XSLT, XPath, schemas, etc.) at the same time. Take XML step by step by experimenting with it. The time that you invest studying this new technology will not be in vain. XML is here to stay, and future versions of Excel are bound to offer even better integration with XML than the current 2002 version. Here are three main reasons why you should really consider XML:

- XML separates content from presentation. This means that if you are planning to design any web pages, you no longer need to make changes to your HTML files when the data changes. Because the data is kept in separate files, it's easy to make modifications.

- XML is perfect for sharing and exchanging data. This means that you no longer have to worry if your data needs to be processed by a system that's not compatible with yours. Because all systems can work with text files (and XML documents are simply text files), you can share and exchange your data without a headache.

- XML can be used as a database. This means that you no longer need a database system to have a database. What a great value!

The appendixes describe how to work with and program Excel special features.

Appendix A

Programming PivotTables and PivotCharts

Introduced in Excel 5, the PivotTable Wizard continues to serve millions of Microsoft Office application users as a powerful tool for organizing and presenting information from various sources. If you are not familiar with this feature, now is the time to get your feet wet. Using PivotTables, you can analyze your data from multiple perspectives. PivotTables make it possible to drag headings around a table to rearrange them so that your data is displayed dynamically any way you (or your users) want it. If you need to focus on understanding your data, rather than on organizing it, you need to get to know PivotTables.

Creating a PivotTable Report

Before you can create a PivotTable, you need to prepare the data. You can get the data from one of the following sources:

- A range on an Excel worksheet (type in your data or paste from other sources)
- External data source (such as a Microsoft Access or SQL Server database)
- Multiple consolidation ranges
- Another PivotTable or PivotChart report

Figure A-1 displays the data that was dumped into a Microsoft Excel worksheet from an SQL Server database. The workbook file named WarrantyCounts.xls is located in the Appendix A folder on the companion CD-ROM. This file contains approximately 1,5000 rows of data that would be difficult to summarize if it weren't for the built-in Excel PivotTable feature.

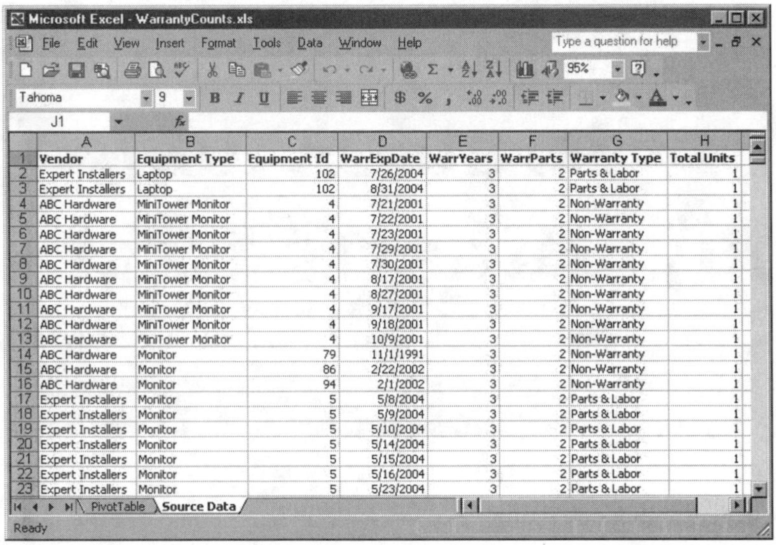

	A	B	C	D	E	F	G	H
1	Vendor	Equipment Type	Equipment Id	WarrExpDate	WarrYears	WarrParts	Warranty Type	Total Units
2	Expert Installers	Laptop	102	7/26/2004	3	2	Parts & Labor	1
3	Expert Installers	Laptop	102	8/31/2004	3	2	Parts & Labor	1
4	ABC Hardware	MiniTower Monitor	4	7/21/2001	3	2	Non-Warranty	1
5	ABC Hardware	MiniTower Monitor	4	7/22/2001	3	2	Non-Warranty	1
6	ABC Hardware	MiniTower Monitor	4	7/23/2001	3	2	Non-Warranty	1
7	ABC Hardware	MiniTower Monitor	4	7/29/2001	3	2	Non-Warranty	1
8	ABC Hardware	MiniTower Monitor	4	7/30/2001	3	2	Non-Warranty	1
9	ABC Hardware	MiniTower Monitor	4	8/17/2001	3	2	Non-Warranty	1
10	ABC Hardware	MiniTower Monitor	4	8/27/2001	3	2	Non-Warranty	1
11	ABC Hardware	MiniTower Monitor	4	9/17/2001	3	2	Non-Warranty	1
12	ABC Hardware	MiniTower Monitor	4	9/18/2001	3	2	Non-Warranty	1
13	ABC Hardware	MiniTower Monitor	4	10/9/2001	3	2	Non-Warranty	1
14	ABC Hardware	Monitor	79	11/1/1991	3	2	Non-Warranty	1
15	ABC Hardware	Monitor	86	2/22/2002	3	2	Non-Warranty	1
16	ABC Hardware	Monitor	94	2/1/2002	3	2	Non-Warranty	1
17	Expert Installers	Monitor	5	5/8/2004	3	2	Parts & Labor	1
18	Expert Installers	Monitor	5	5/9/2004	3	2	Parts & Labor	1
19	Expert Installers	Monitor	5	5/10/2004	3	2	Parts & Labor	1
20	Expert Installers	Monitor	5	5/14/2004	3	2	Parts & Labor	1
21	Expert Installers	Monitor	5	5/15/2004	3	2	Parts & Labor	1
22	Expert Installers	Monitor	5	5/16/2004	3	2	Parts & Labor	1
23	Expert Installers	Monitor	5	5/23/2004	3	2	Parts & Labor	1

Figure A-1: Source data for the PivotTable

Once you have the data, it's time to create your first PivotTable report. The easiest way to create this report is with the PivotTable Wizard (accessed from the Data menu). Before starting the wizard, select any cell anywhere in the data range. This will cause the data range to be automatically selected by Excel. When you choose Data | PivotTable and PivotChart Report, the Pivot Table Wizard – Step 1 of 3 dialog box appears. Choose the source of your data (Microsoft Excel List or Database) on this screen and click the Next button. The PivotTable Wizard – Step 2 of 3 dialog box appears. Ensure that the range displayed in the Range field incorporates all the data on which you want to report. The range will appear automatically if the active cell is within the data range. If the currently selected cell is outside of the data range, you will need to make your own selection.

When you click the Next button, the Step 3 of 3 dialog box appears. Here you can indicate where you would like to place your PivotTable report (select New Worksheet for this exercise). If you press the Finish button at this time, you will see a new worksheet with an empty PivotTable and a list of fields (columns in your source data), which you can drag to the indicated PivotReport layout. If, however, you press the Layout button in the Step 3 of 3 dialog box, you will see a PivotTable layout, as shown in Figure A-2, that explains how to place required fields in the pivot diagram.

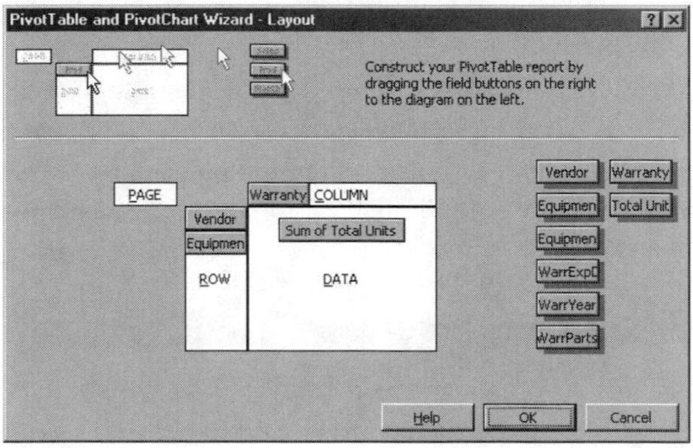

Figure A-2:
PivotTable Layout

A PivotTable report has four areas where you place fields:

- **The Row area** should contain the fields that you want to display your data "by." For example, if you want to produce the report by Vendor, place the Vendor field in the Row area. The Row area can contain more than one field. In our example report (see Figure A-3), we also want to see the report by Equipment Type, so the Equipment Type field is placed in the Row area as well. If you position the Equipment Type field to the right of the Vendor field, the data will be grouped first by Vendor and then by Equipment Type within those vendors.

- **The Column area** should contain fields that answer the question "what." For example, what type of information do you want to display for each of the fields in the Row area? Our example PivotTable reports on the Warranty type. Because we want to see all types of warranties for each vendor and equipment type, we placed the Warranty Type field in the Column area.

However, if you want to view your data from a different perspective, you can place the fields from the Row area in the Column area and vice versa. It is up to you.

- **The Data area** displays the data that you want to analyze. In our example, we want to find out the total number of units (Equipment Type) covered by each of the Warranty types. The Data area must contain a field that has numeric data. Once we place the field containing numeric data in the Data area, we can choose what calculation (sum, count, average, and so on) we want to perform on the data.

- **The Page area** is optional. Page fields add a third dimension to your data analysis. For example, if you want to look at the total units under each warranty type for a particular Equipment Id, you would place EquipmentId in the Page area. This would allow you to drill down your

PivotTable by the Equipment Id or show the data for all the equipment. Later in this appendix, when you generate a PivotTable programmatically, you will add a field to the Page area and be able to experiment with the data.

Note that you do not have to place all the fields in the PivotTable. Place only those fields that you need; you can easily add other fields at any time via PivotTable toolbar buttons or a shortcut menu. If you position the fields as shown in Figure A-2 and press the Finish button in the PivotTable Step 3 of 3 dialog box, you should see a PivotTable report, that resembles Figure A-3.

Sum of Total Units	Warranty Type				
Vendor / Equipment Type	Full Warranty	Non-Warranty	Parts & Labor	Parts Only	Grand Total
Expert Installers — Laptop			344		344
Monitor	1398		23	15	1436
Scanner	42				42
Server	19		20	15	54
Server Monitor	9		76		85
WS	3901		2460	10405	16766
Expert Installers Total	5369		2923	10435	18727
ABC Hardware — Laptop		6933			6933
MiniTower Monitor		41			41
Monitor		10251			10251
Scanner		110			110
Server Monitor		61			61
WS		24780			24780
ABC Hardware Total		42176			42176
Experts R Us — Monitor				5888	5888
Server				15	15
Server Monitor			2	13	15
WS			100	5784	5884
Experts R Us Total			102	11700	11802
Grand Total	5369	42176	3025	22135	72705

Figure A-3: PivotTable report

PivotTables are for data analysis and presentation only. This means that you are not permitted to enter data directly into a PivotTable. To make any changes or additions to the data, you must do this in the underlying source data and then use the Refresh button on the PivotTable toolbar or the Refresh Data option on the Data menu to bring the PivotTable up to date.

To see new versions of the same information, drag PivotTable headings to new positions. Figure A-4 presents a different view of the same data.

You can examine the contributing data by double-clicking a cell containing a total. For example, if you double-click cell C8 (Figure A-3), Excel will add a new worksheet to the active workbook showing all the records that contributed to the selected total value (Figure A-5).

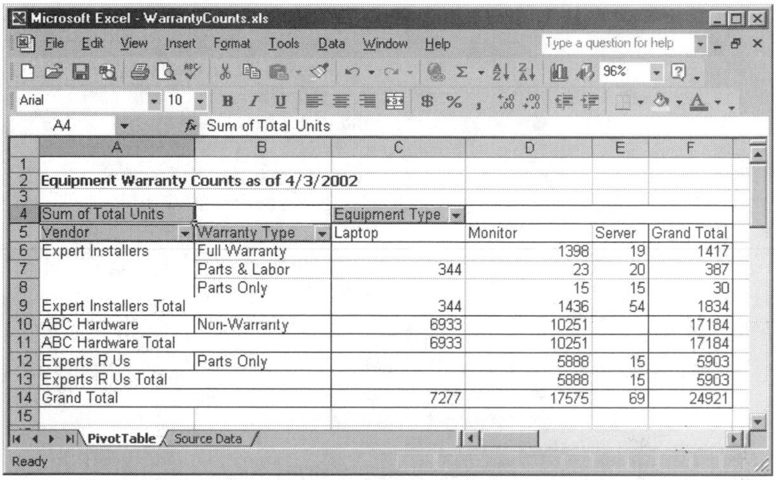

Equipment Warranty Counts as of 4/3/2002

Sum of Total Units		Equipment Type			
Vendor	Warranty Type	Laptop	Monitor	Server	Grand Total
Expert Installers	Full Warranty		1398	19	1417
	Parts & Labor	344	23	20	387
	Parts Only		15	15	30
Expert Installers Total		344	1436	54	1834
ABC Hardware	Non-Warranty	6933	10251		17184
ABC Hardware Total		6933	10251		17184
Experts R Us	Parts Only		5888	15	5903
Experts R Us Total			5888	15	5903
Grand Total		7277	17575	69	24921

Figure A-4: Another PivotTable view of the source data

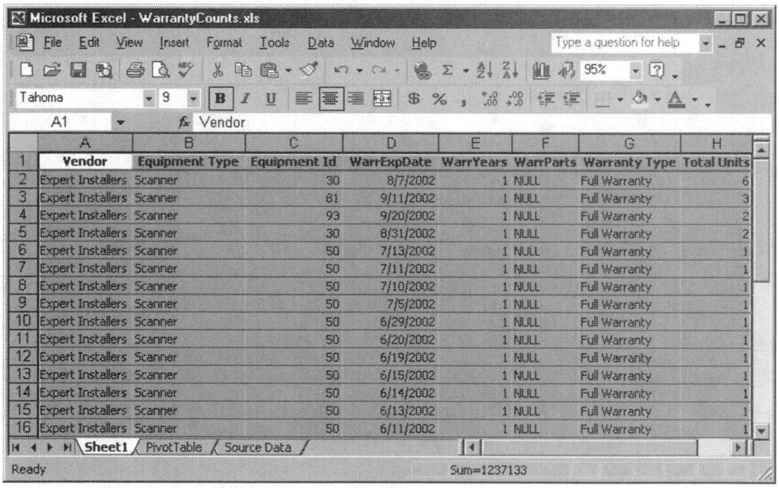

Vendor	Equipment Type	Equipment Id	WarrExpDate	WarrYears	WarrParts	Warranty Type	Total Units
Expert Installers	Scanner	30	8/7/2002	1	NULL	Full Warranty	6
Expert Installers	Scanner	81	9/11/2002	1	NULL	Full Warranty	3
Expert Installers	Scanner	93	9/20/2002	1	NULL	Full Warranty	2
Expert Installers	Scanner	30	8/31/2002	1	NULL	Full Warranty	2
Expert Installers	Scanner	50	7/13/2002	1	NULL	Full Warranty	1
Expert Installers	Scanner	50	7/11/2002	1	NULL	Full Warranty	1
Expert Installers	Scanner	50	7/10/2002	1	NULL	Full Warranty	1
Expert Installers	Scanner	50	7/5/2002	1	NULL	Full Warranty	1
Expert Installers	Scanner	50	6/29/2002	1	NULL	Full Warranty	1
Expert Installers	Scanner	50	6/20/2002	1	NULL	Full Warranty	1
Expert Installers	Scanner	50	6/19/2002	1	NULL	Full Warranty	1
Expert Installers	Scanner	50	6/15/2002	1	NULL	Full Warranty	1
Expert Installers	Scanner	50	6/14/2002	1	NULL	Full Warranty	1
Expert Installers	Scanner	50	6/13/2002	1	NULL	Full Warranty	1
Expert Installers	Scanner	50	6/11/2002	1	NULL	Full Warranty	1

Figure A-5: You can obtain details of any summary figure by double-clicking on a data field in the PivotTable.

Drilling down on the data is a nice feature, except for the fact that if you do a lot of double-clicking, you will end up with many additional and most likely unwanted worksheets in your workbook. You may want to delete the drill-down worksheet after examining the detail data. You can do this manually, or you can perform the cleanup programmatically by writing VBA procedures for the Workbook_SheetBeforeDoubleClick and Workbook_SheetActivate events. To try this out, switch to the Visual Basic Editor screen and double-click the ThisWorkbook object in the Project Explorer window. In the Code window WarrantyCounts.xls – ThisWorkbook (Code) window, enter the global variable declaration and event procedures shown on the following page.

```
' Global variables
Dim flag As Boolean         ' Boolean variable to indicate whether
                            ' to delete a drill-down worksheet
Dim pivSheet As String      ' String to hold the name of the sheet
                            ' containing the PivotTable
Dim drillSheet As String    ' String to hold the name of the drill-down sheet
Dim pivSource As String     ' String to hold the name of the worksheet with
                            ' the PivotTable source data

Private Sub Workbook_SheetActivate(ByVal Sh As Object)
    If pivSheet = "" Then Exit Sub
    If Sh.Name <> pivSheet Then
      If InStr(1, pivSource, Sh.Name) = 0 Then
        If MsgBox("Do you want to Delete " & Sh.Name & _
           " from the workbook" & vbCrLf _
           & "upon returning to PivotTable?", _
            vbYesNo + vbQuestion, _
            "Sheet: Delete or Keep") = vbYes Then
             flag = True
             drillSheet = Sh.Name
      Else
         flag = False
         Exit Sub
      End If
    End If
  End If
  If ActiveSheet.Name = pivSheet And flag = True Then
      Application.DisplayAlerts = False
      Worksheets(drillSheet).Delete
      Application.DisplayAlerts = True
      flag = False
  End If
End Sub
```

The Workbook_SheetActivate event procedure shown above will ask the user whether the drill-down worksheet should be deleted when the user returns to the worksheet containing the PivotTable. If the user answers "Yes" in the message box, the Boolean variable flag will be set to True. Because Excel by default displays a confirmation message whenever the worksheet is about to be deleted, the procedure code turns off the application messages so that deletion can be performed without further user intervention. After the deletion, don't forget to turn the alerts back on.

```
Private Sub Workbook_SheetBeforeDoubleClick(ByVal Sh As Object, _
                        ByVal Target As Range, Cancel As Boolean)
    With ActiveSheet
      If .PivotTables.Count > 0 Then
         pivSource = ActiveSheet.PivotTables(1).SourceData
         If ActiveCell.PivotField.Name <> "" And IsEmpty(Target) Then
            MsgBox "There is no data in the selected cell - cannot drill down"
            Cancel = True
            Exit Sub
         End If
```

```
            flag = True
            pivSheet = ActiveSheet.Name
        End If
    End With
End Sub
```

The Workbook_SheetBeforeDoubleClick procedure shown above will disable the drill-down if the user clicks on a PivotTable cell that is empty; otherwise, it will set the Boolean variable flag to True to indicate that a drill-down was requested. At the same time, the name of the worksheet containing the PivotTable will be written to a global variable. Also, because we do not want to delete the worksheet containing the PivotTable source data, we will use the SourceData property of the PivotTables collection to store the name of the source data worksheet and the underlying data range in a variable. To find out exactly how these two event procedures work together, use some of the skills that you acquired in Chapter 13.

Creating a PivotTable Report Programmatically

Although the PivotWizard utility has undergone many improvements to make it easy to use, some users still find the process of creating PivotTable reports confusing. For those users, you may want to generate PivotTables via VBA code. Also with VBA, you can make many formatting changes to the existing PivotTables. This section demonstrates how you can work with PivotTables programmatically. We will start by creating the PiviotTable report shown earlier in Figure A-3 using the data source presented in Figure A-1. Here's the code that generates that PivotTable:

```
Sub CreateNewPivot()
    Dim wksData As Worksheet
    Dim rngData As Range
    Dim wksDest As Worksheet
    Dim pvtTable As PivotTable

    ' Set up object variables
    Set wksData = ThisWorkbook.Worksheets("Source Data")
    Set rngData = wksData.UsedRange
    Set wksDest = ThisWorkbook.Worksheets("Sheet1")

    ' Create a skeleton of a PivotTable
    Set pvtTable = wksData.PivotTableWizard(SourceType:=xlDatabase, _
        SourceData:=rngData, TableDestination:=wksDest.Range("B5"))

    ' Close the Pivot Table Field list that appears automatically
    ActiveWorkbook.ShowPivotTableFieldList = False

    ' Add fields to the PivotTable
    With pvtTable
        .PivotFields("Vendor").Orientation = xlRowField
```

```
          .PivotFields("Equipment Type").Orientation = xlRowField
          .PivotFields("Warranty Type").Orientation = xlColumnField
          With .PivotFields("Total Units")
              .Orientation = xlDataField
              .Function = xlSum
          End With
          .PivotFields("Equipment Id").Orientation = xlPageField
      End With

      ' Autofit columns so all headings are visible
      wksDest.UsedRange.Columns.AutoFit
  End Sub
```

The procedure shown above creates a new PivotTable report using the PivotTableWizard method of a Worksheet object. Notice that this method takes a few arguments that allow you to specify the type of the data source, its location, and the location where the PivotTable reports should be placed. All these arguments of the PivotTableWizard method are optional. However, it is a good idea to specify these arguments, as we did in our example code. Because you can create a PivotTable from various sources of data, by using the xlDatabase constant, our code specifically says that our data comes from an Excel range. If you want to create a PivotTable report from another PivotTable, use xlPivotTable for the `SourceType` argument. And if your data is to be pulled from an external database (as shown in a later example), specify xlExternal as the `SourceType`.

The `SourceData` argument in the example procedure is a reference to the used range on the worksheet containing the source data. The `Table-Destination` argument has a reference to cell B5 on Sheet1 in the current worksheet. This is where the upper left-hand corner of the PivotReport will be placed. This code assumes that Sheet1 exists in the workbook. If you don't have Sheet1, it's easy enough to add one via the VBA code prior to setting the reference.

It is important to understand that when you call the PivotTableWizard method, you create a blank PivotTable report. All the fields from the data source are hidden. To make the fields visible, you need to add them to appropriate areas of the PivotTable report. As you recall, there are four such areas. PivotTable Wizard automatically displays the list of fields that you can add. However, because you are creating a PivotTable programmatically, there is no need to display that list on the screen. By setting the ShowPivotTableFieldList property to False, the list will go off the screen and you can concentrate on specifying the position of the fields in the PivotTable report areas. For each field that you want to display in the PivotTable report, set the Orientation property of the PivotField object. Use the following constants for the Orientation property: xlRowField, xlColumnField, xlDataField, and xlPageField. Note that for the Total Units field placed in the Data area, the procedure sets the Function property of the PivotField object to Sum.

When you are creating a PivotTable report via code, you may need to check whether a PivotTable already exists in the destination worksheet. You can place the following code just below the code that sets variables (see the CreateNewPivot procedure above):

```
' Check if PivotTable already exists
If wksDest.PivotTables.Count > 0 Then
    MsgBox "Worksheet " & wksDest.Name & " already contains a pivot _
            table."
    Exit Sub
End If
```

When you run the CreateNewPivot procedure, you should see a PivotTable report resembling the one in Figure A-3.

Creating a PivotTable Report from an External Data Source

You can use the same PivotTableWizard method of the Worksheet object (demonstrated in the previous example procedure) to create a PivotTable report from an external data source. We will look at two examples that pull data for the PivotTable from a Microsoft Access database. The first one will use a Microsoft Access driver to connect to a Microsoft Access database and then use the PivotTableWizard method to create an empty PivotTable. The second example will employ a newer technology known as ADO (ActiveX Data Objects) to obtain the data and will then use the PivotCaches collection to create a new PivotCache; it will use the CreatePivotTable method of the PivotCache object to create an empty PivotTable. In both examples we will also set the Orientation property of the retrieved fields to populate the PivotTable report with the data.

Creating a PivotTable Report Using the PivotTableWizard Method

1. Add a new module to a VBA project and enter the PivotTable_External1 procedure shown below. This procedure is also available on the companion CD-ROM in the ProgramPivots.xls file.

2. Run the procedure to generate the PivotTable.

```
Sub PivotTable_External1()
    Dim strConn As String
    Dim strQuery_1 As String
    Dim strQuery_2 As String
    Dim myArray As Variant
    Dim destRange As Range
    Dim strPivot As String

    strConn = "Driver={Microsoft Access Driver (*.mdb)};" & _
            "DBQ=" & "C:\Program Files\Microsoft Office\Office\" & _
```

```
                    "Samples\Northwind.mdb;"

    strQuery_1 = "SELECT Customers.CustomerID, Customers.CompanyName, " & _
                "Orders.OrderDate, Products.ProductName, Sum([Order " & _
                "Details].[UnitPrice]*[QUantity]*(1-[Discount])) AS Total " & _
                "FROM Products INNER JOIN ((Customers INNER JOIN Orders " & _
                "ON Customers.CustomerID = "

    strQuery_2 = "Orders.CustomerID) INNER JOIN [Order Details] " & _
                "ON Orders.OrderID = [Order Details].OrderID) ON " & _
                "Products.ProductID = [Order Details].ProductID " & _
                "GROUP BY Customers.CustomerID, Customers.CompanyName, " & _
                "Orders.OrderDate, Products.ProductName;"

    myArray = Array(strConn, strQuery_1, strQuery_2)
    Worksheets.Add

    Set destRange = ActiveSheet.Range("B5")
    strPivot = "PivotFromAccess"

    ActiveSheet.PivotTableWizard _
            SourceType:=xlExternal, _
            SourceData:=myArray, _
            TableDestination:=destRange, _
            TableName:=strPivot, _
            SaveData:=False, _
            BackgroundQuery:=False

        ' Close the Pivot Table Field list that appears automatically
        ActiveWorkbook.ShowPivotTableFieldList = False

        ' Add fields to the PivotTable
        With ActiveSheet.PivotTables(strPivot)
            .PivotFields("ProductName").Orientation = xlRowField
            .PivotFields("CompanyName").Orientation = xlRowField
            With .PivotFields("Total")
                .Orientation = xlDataField
                .Function = xlSum
                .NumberFormat = "$#,##0.00"
            End With
            .PivotFields("CustomerID").Orientation = xlPageField
            .PivotFields("OrderDate").Orientation = xlPageField
        End With

        ' Autofit columns so all headings are visible
        ActiveSheet.UsedRange.Columns.AutoFit
    End Sub
```

When you use the PivotTableWizard method of the Worksheet object to create a PivotTable report from an external data source, you need to specify (at a minimum) the following arguments:

SourceType	Use the xlExternal constant to indicate that the data for the PivotTable comes from an external data source.

SourceData	Specify an array containing two or more elements. The first element of the array must be a connection string to the database; the second argument is the SQL statement for querying an external database. If the SQL statement is longer than 255 characters, break it up into several strings and pass each string as a separate element of the array. In the PivotTable_External1 procedure, the SQL statement necessary for obtaining the required data from an external database is longer than 255 characters; therefore, the SQL string is broken into two strings: strQuery_1 and strQuery_2. Next, the connection string and the SQL statement are placed in an array like this: `myArray = Array(strConn, strQuery_1, strQuery_2)` myArray is then used as the SourceData argument of the PivotTableWizard method.
TableDestination	Specify a worksheet range where the PivotTable should be placed.
TableName	Specify the name of the PivotTable that you want to create.

In addition to the above arguments, the example procedure uses the SaveData and BackgroundQuery arguments. The SaveData argument tells Visual Basic whether to save the PivotTable when the workbook file is saved. By setting this argument to False, the PivotTable will not be saved. This setting allows you to save space on disk. Setting the BackgroundQuery argument to False tells Visual Basic to refrain from executing other operations in Excel in the background until the query is complete.

After creating a PivotTable, the procedure specifies where the fields returned by the SQL statement should be placed in the PivotTable layout. The resulting PivotTable report is illustrated in Figure A-6.

Figure A-6:
A PivotTable report can be created programmatically from an external data source, such as the Microsoft Access database.

ProductName	CompanyName	Total
Alice Mutton	Antonio Moreno Taquería	$702.00
	Berglunds snabbköp	$312.00
	Blondel père et fils	$936.00
	Bólido Comidas preparadas	$1,170.00
	Bon app'	$592.80
	Bottom-Dollar Markets	$1,404.00
	Du monde entier	$585.00
	Ernst Handel	$3,730.35
	Godos Cocina Típica	$748.80
	Hanari Carnes	$585.00
	Hungry Coyote Import Store	$62.40
	La corne d'abondance	$234.00
	Lehmanns Marktstand	$351.00
	Mère Paillarde	$2,074.80
	Old World Delicatessen	$624.00
	Piccolo und mehr	$2,496.00
	Rattlesnake Canyon Grocery	$2,305.68
	Reggiani Caseifici	$741.00
	Ricardo Adocicados	$468.00
	Save-a-lot Markets	$7,392.45
	Seven Seas Imports	$877.50
	Suprêmes délices	$1,248.00
	Tortuga Restaurante	$639.60

OrderDate (All), CustomerID (All), Sum of Total

Creating a PivotTable Report Using the CreatePivotTable Method of the PivotCache Object

When you use the macro recorder to generate the code for creating a PivotTable programmatically, Excel uses the Add method of the PivotCaches collection to create a new PivotCache. A PivotCache object represents the data behind a PivotTable. It is an area in memory where data is stored and accessed as required from a data source.

The example procedure connects to the Microsoft Access Northwind database using the Microsoft.Jet.OLEDB.4.0 provider. To use this type of connection, you must set up a reference to the Microsoft ActiveX Data Objects (ADO) in the References dialog box (available in the Microsoft Excel Visual Basic Editor screen).

After establishing a connection with a database and executing the SQL statement to obtain the data, the procedure creates a PivotCache using the following line of code:

```
Set objPivotCache = ActiveWorkbook.PivotCaches.Add( _
        SourceType:=xlExternal)
```

The code then places the data from the external data source in the PivotCache by assigning a Recordset object to the PivotCache object, like this:

```
Set objPivotCache.Recordset = rst
```

Next, the code uses the CreatePivotTable method of the PivotCache object to create an empty PivotTable:

```
With objPivotCache
        .CreatePivotTable TableDestination:=Range("B6"), _
            TableName:="Invoices"
End With
```

Once the skeleton of the PivotTable is created, the code adds appropriate fields to the PivotTable.

You should use the PivotCache when you need to generate multiple PivotTables from the same data source. By using a PivotCache, you can gain a high level of control over your external data source. The PivotCache object can also be used to change and refresh data stored in the cache. The last several lines of the example procedure demonstrate how to find out information about the PivotCache.

To force the PivotCache to refresh automatically when the workbook file containing the PivotTable is opened, set the RefreshOnFileOpen property to True. Add the following statement at the end of the procedure shown below:

```
ActiveSheet.PivotTables("Invoices").PivotCache.RefreshOnFileOpen = True
```

1.   Add a new module to the current workbook and enter the following procedure code.

2.   Run the procedure to generate the PivotTable.

```
Sub Pivot_External2()
    Dim objPivotCache As PivotCache
    Dim cmd As New ADODB.Command
    Dim rst As New ADODB.Recordset
    Dim dbPath As String

    dbPath = "C:\Program Files\Microsoft Office\Office\" & _
        "Samples\Northwind.mdb"
    With cmd
        .ActiveConnection = "Provider=Microsoft.Jet.OLEDB.4.0;" & _
            "Data Source =" & dbPath
        .CommandText = "Select Country, ProductName, " & _
            "ExtendedPrice from Invoices"
    End With
    Set rst = cmd.Execute

    ' Create a PivotTable cache and report
    Set objPivotCache = ActiveWorkbook.PivotCaches.Add( _
        SourceType:=xlExternal)
    Set objPivotCache.Recordset = rst

    Worksheets.Add
    With objPivotCache
        .CreatePivotTable TableDestination:=Range("B6"), _
            TableName:="Invoices"
    End With

    ' Add fields to the PivotTable
    With ActiveSheet.PivotTables("Invoices")
        .SmallGrid = False
        With .PivotFields("Country")
            .Orientation = xlRowField
            .Position = 1
        End With
        With .PivotFields("ProductName")
            .Orientation = xlRowField
            .Position = 2
            .Name = "Product Name"
        End With
        With .PivotFields("ExtendedPrice")
            .Orientation = xlDataField
            .Position = 1
            .NumberFormat = "$#,##0.00"
        End With
    End With

        ' Autofit columns so all headings are visible
    ActiveSheet.UsedRange.Columns.AutoFit

    ' Clean up
    Set cmd = Nothing
    Set rst = Nothing
```

```
' Obtain information about PivotCache
With ActiveSheet.PivotTables("Invoices").PivotCache
    Debug.Print "Information about the PivotCache:"
    Debug.Print "Number of Records: " & .RecordCount
    Debug.Print "Data was last refreshed on: " & .RefreshDate
    Debug.Print "Data was last refreshed by: " & .RefreshName
    Debug.Print "Memory used by PivotCache: " & .MemoryUsed & _
        " (bytes)"
End With
End Sub
```

Formatting, Grouping, and Sorting a PivotTable Report

You can modify the display and format of a PivotTable programmatically by using a number of different properties of the PivotTable object. For example, you may want to reposition the fields within the PivotTable layout, sort the data by a specific field, or group your data by years, quarters, months, and so on. The example procedure below reformats the PivotTable report generated earlier in this appendix (see Figure A-6).

1. Add a new module to the current workbook and enter the procedure code, as shown below.

2. Activate the worksheet containing the PivotTable, as presented in Figure A-6.

3. Run the procedure to reformat the PivotTable shown in Figure A-6.

```
Sub FormatPivotTable()
    Dim pvtTable As PivotTable
    Dim strPiv As String

    If ActiveSheet.PivotTables.Count > 0 Then
        strPiv = ActiveSheet.PivotTables(1).Name
        Set pvtTable = ActiveSheet.PivotTables(strPiv)
    Else
        Exit Sub
    End If

    With pvtTable
        .PivotFields("OrderDate").Orientation = xlRows
        .PivotFields("CompanyName").Orientation = xlHidden

        ' use this statement to group OrderDate by year
        .PivotFields("OrderDate").DataRange.Cells(1).Group _
            Start:=True, End:=True, _
            periods:=Array(False, False, False, False, False, False, True)

        ' use this statement to group OrderDate both by quarter and year;
        ' if you use this statement, comment the preceding line of code
        ' .PivotFields("OrderDate").DataRange.Cells(1).Group _
            Start:=True, End:=True, _
```

```
                periods:=Array(False, False, False, False, False, True, True)

            .PivotFields("OrderDate").Orientation = xlColumns
            .TableRange1.AutoFormat Format:=xlRangeAutoFormatColor2
            .PivotFields("ProductName").DataRange.Select

            ' sort the Product Name field in descending order based on the Sum
            ' of Total
            .PivotFields("ProductName").AutoSort xlDescending, "Sum of Total"
        Selection.IndentLevel = 2
        With Selection.Font
            .Name = "Times New Roman"
            .FontStyle = "Bold"
            .Size = 10
        End With
        With Selection.Borders(xlInsideHorizontal)
            .LineStyle = xlContinuous
            .Weight = xlThin
            .ColorIndex = xlAutomatic
        End With
    End With
End Sub
```

By studying the code presented above, you can easily conclude that:

- To change the layout of a PivotTable, you should set the Orientation property of the required field to a different constant. The example code above moves the OrderDate field from the Page area to the Row area of the PivotTable layout.

- To display a PivotTable without a particular field, you need to set the Orientation property of the required field to xlHidden.

- To group the OrderDate field by year, you should use the Group method of the Range object. For example, the code uses the following statement to group the data in the OrderDate field by year:

```
.PivotFields("OrderDate").DataRange.Cells(1).Group _
    Start:=True, End:=True, _
    periods:=Array(False, False, False, False, False, False, True)
```

- The Start and End arguments specify the start and end date to be included in the grouping. By setting these arguments to True, all dates are included. The Periods argument is an array of Boolean values that specifies the period for the group, as shown in the following table:

Array Element	Period
1	Seconds
2	Minutes
3	Hours
4	Days
5	Months
6	Quarters
7	Years

Note: The following statement will ungroup the dates:

```
ActiveSheet.PivotTables(1).PivotFields("OrderDate").LabelRange.Ungroup
```

■   You can apply automatic formatting to the entire PivotTable report by using the AutoFormat property of the Range object. The TableRange1 property returns a Range object that represents the range containing the entire PivotTable report without the page fields:

```
.TableRange1.AutoFormat Format:=xlRangeAutoFormatColor2
```

■   You can select the data items in a particular field by using the DataRange property and the Select method, like this:

```
.PivotFields("ProductName").DataRange.Select
```

■   You can sort a particular field in descending or ascending order. The example procedure uses the following statement to sort the ProductName field in descending order based on the Sum of Total:

```
.PivotFields("ProductName").AutoSort xlDescending, "Sum of Total"
```

■   You can change the text indentation, and the font name, size, and style, as well as the borders of the selected range, as demonstrated in the last statements of the example procedure.

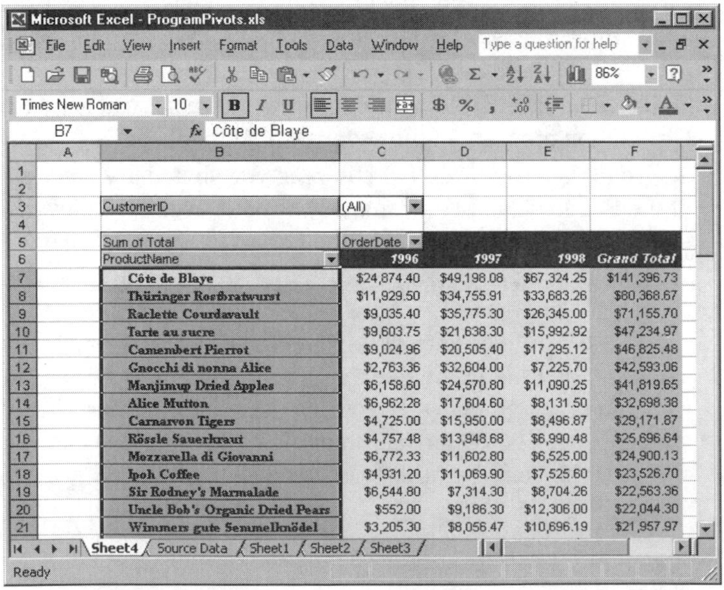

Figure A-7: A PivotTable report can be reformatted to view data from a different perspective.

Hiding Items in a PivotTable

In the previous example procedure, you grouped the data in the
PivotReport by year based on the OrderDate field. To hide some of the
grouped data, you can set the Visible property of the PivotItem object to
False. For instance, the following procedure will hide the 1996 column of
data in the PivotTable report presented in Figure A-7.

```
Sub Hide1996Data()
    Dim myPivot As PivotTable
    Dim myItem As PivotItem
    Dim strFieldLabel As String

    strTitle = "1996"

    Set myPivot = ActiveSheet.PivotTables(1)
    For Each myItem In myPivot.PivotFields("OrderDate").PivotItems
        If myItem.Name <> strTitle Then
            myItem.Visible = True
        Else
            myItem.Visible = False
        End If
    Next
End Sub
```

Adding Calculated Fields and Items to a PivotTable

You can customize a PivotTable report by defining calculated fields and
items. Using the contents of other numeric fields in a PivotTable, you can
create a calculated field that performs the required calculation. For example,
the procedure demonstrated below creates two calculated fields named
Change: 2001/2000 and Change: 2000/1999 to calculate the difference in
number of products sold from year to year. Figure A-8 shows the source
data and the PivotTable generated by the procedure listed below.

```
Sub PivotWithCalcFields()
    ActiveWorkbook.PivotCaches.Add( _
        SourceType:=xlDatabase, _
        SourceData:="Sheet1!R1C1:R4C4").CreatePivotTable _
        TableDestination:="'[PivotFields.xls]Sheet1'!R4C7", _
        TableName:="Piv1", _
        DefaultVersion:=xlPivotTableVersion10
    With ActiveSheet.PivotTables("Piv1").PivotFields("Product")
        .Orientation = xlRowField
        .Position = 1
    End With
    ActiveSheet.PivotTables("Piv1").AddDataField _
            ActiveSheet.PivotTables("Piv1").PivotFields("2001"), _
            "Sum of 2001", xlSum
    ActiveSheet.PivotTables("Piv1").AddDataField _
```

```
                ActiveSheet.PivotTables("Piv1").PivotFields("2000"), _
                "Sum of 2000", xlSum
        ActiveSheet.PivotTables("Piv1").AddDataField _
                ActiveSheet.PivotTables("Piv1").PivotFields("1999"), _
                "Sum of 1999", xlSum
        ActiveSheet.PivotTables("Piv1").CalculatedFields.Add _
                "Change: 2001/2000", "='2001' -'2000'", True
        ActiveSheet.PivotTables("Piv1").CalculatedFields.Add _
                "Change: 2000/1999", "='2000' -'1999'", True
        ActiveSheet.PivotTables("Piv1"). _
                PivotFields("Change: 2001/2000"). _
                Orientation = xlDataField
        ActiveSheet.PivotTables("Piv1"). _
                PivotFields("Change: 2000/1999"). _
                Orientation = xlDataField
    End Sub
```

Notice that calculated fields are defined by using the Add method of the CalculatedFields object and supplying two arguments: the name for the new field and a formula.

```
    ActiveSheet.PivotTables("Piv1").CalculatedFields.Add _
                "Change: 2001/2000", "='2001' -'2000'", True
    ActiveSheet.PivotTables("Piv1").CalculatedFields.Add _
                "Change: 2000/1999", "='2000' -'1999'", True
```

The third (optional) argument set to True indicates that the strings in field names will be interpreted as having been formatted in standard U.S. English instead of using local settings. The default setting is False.

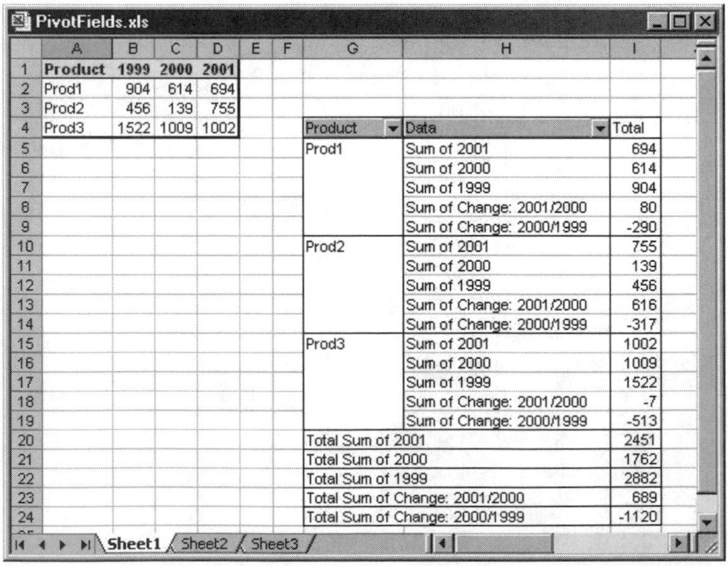

	A	B	C	D	E	F	G	H	I
1	Product	1999	2000	2001					
2	Prod1	904	614	694					
3	Prod2	456	139	755					
4	Prod3	1522	1009	1002			Product	Data	Total
5							Prod1	Sum of 2001	694
6								Sum of 2000	614
7								Sum of 1999	904
8								Sum of Change: 2001/2000	80
9								Sum of Change: 2000/1999	-290
10							Prod2	Sum of 2001	755
11								Sum of 2000	139
12								Sum of 1999	456
13								Sum of Change: 2001/2000	616
14								Sum of Change: 2000/1999	-317
15							Prod3	Sum of 2001	1002
16								Sum of 2000	1009
17								Sum of 1999	1522
18								Sum of Change: 2001/2000	-7
19								Sum of Change: 2000/1999	-513
20							Total Sum of 2001		2451
21							Total Sum of 2000		1762
22							Total Sum of 1999		2882
23							Total Sum of Change: 2001/2000		689
24							Total Sum of Change: 2000/1999		-1120

Figure A-8: You can add additional calculations to a PivotTable by defining additional fields, such as Change: 2001/2000 and Change: 2000/1999 depicted here.

A *calculated field* uses a formula that refers to other Pivot fields that contain numeric data. This can be a simple formula, such as addition (+), subtraction (−), multiplication (*), and division (/), or an Excel function. In the PivotWithCalcFields procedure example, we created two calculated fields:

Calculated Field Name	Formula
Change: 2001/2000	='2001' −'2000'
Change: 2000/1999	='2000' −'1999'

"2001," "2000," and "1999" are the names of the fields placed in the Data area of the PivotTable. When you use multiple Pivot fields in the Data area, Excel creates a new Pivot field named Data (Figure A-8). The labels for the multiple Pivot fields in the Data area can be displayed going down the rows (as shown in Figure A-8) or across columns. You can specify the orientation of the labels by setting the Orientation property of the Data field to xlRowField or xlColumnField. The following statement:

```
ActiveSheet.PivotTables("Piv1"). _
            PivotFields("Data").Orientation = xlColumnField
```

will modify the PivotTable in Figure A-8 to look like this:

Once you define a calculated field, the field is added to the PivotTable field

	Data ▾				
Product ▾	Sum of 2001	Sum of 2000	Sum of 1999	Sum of Change: 2001/2000	Sum of Change: 2000/1999
Prod1	694	614	904	80	-290
Prod2	755	139	456	616	-317
Prod3	1002	1009	1522	-7	-513
Grand Total	2451	1762	2882	689	-1120

list and maintained in the PivotTable cache.

Note: You can add a calculated field manually by using the PivotTable toolbar. Click PivotTable, point to Formulas, and click Calculated Field.

You must not confuse a calculated item with a calculated field. A calculated item is a custom item you define in a PivotTable field to perform calculations using the contents of other fields and items in the PivotTable. Let's say you have created a report showing the total product sales for each of your salespeople by country. Then you want to look at the data differently and show the sales made by each salesperson on three continents. You will need three new (calculated) items under the Country field. These items will be named North America, South America, and Europe. After you create these items, you can change the name of the Country field to Continent (see Figure A-9) to make your data easier to read. The following procedure retrieves the data for this demonstration example from the Microsoft Access sample Northwind database. The code of this procedure was generated by a macro recorder. You may need to change it to point to a valid location of the example database on your computer.

```vba
Sub PivotWithCalcItems()
    Dim strConn As String
    Dim strSQL As String
    Dim myArray As Variant
    Dim destRng As Range
    Dim strPivot As String

    strConn = "Driver={Microsoft Access Driver (*.mdb)};" & _
                "DBQ=" & "C:\Program Files\Microsoft Office\Office10\" & _
                "Samples\Northwind.mdb;"

    strSQL = "SELECT Invoices.Customers.CompanyName, " & _
                "Invoices.Country, Invoices.Salesperson, " & _
                "Invoices.ProductName, Invoices.ExtendedPrice " & _
                "FROM Invoices ORDER BY Invoices.Country"

    myArray = Array(strConn, strSQL)
    Worksheets.Add

    Set destRange = ActiveSheet.Range("B5")
    strPivot = "PivotTable1"

    ActiveSheet.PivotTableWizard _
            SourceType:=xlExternal, _
            SourceData:=myArray, _
            TableDestination:=destRange, _
            TableName:=strPivot, _
            SaveData:=False, _
            BackgroundQuery:=False

    With ActiveSheet.PivotTables(strPivot).PivotFields("CompanyName")
        .Orientation = xlPageField
        .Position = 1
    End With
    With ActiveSheet.PivotTables(strPivot).PivotFields("Country")
        .Orientation = xlRowField
        .Position = 1
    End With
    ActiveSheet.PivotTables(strPivot).AddDataField _
        ActiveSheet.PivotTables(strPivot).PivotFields("ExtendedPrice"), _
        "Sum of ExtendedPrice", xlSum
    With ActiveSheet.PivotTables(strPivot).PivotFields("Salesperson")
        .Orientation = xlRowField
        .Position = 1
    End With
    Range("A6").Select
    With ActiveSheet.PivotTables(strPivot).PivotFields("Salesperson")
        .Orientation = xlPageField
        .Position = 1
    End With
    Range("A3").Select
    With ActiveSheet.PivotTables(strPivot).PivotFields("Salesperson")
        .Orientation = xlColumnField
        .Position = 1
```

```
      End With
      Range("A6").Select
      ActiveSheet.PivotTables(strPivot).PivotFields("Country").CalculatedItems. _
          Add "North America", "=USA+Canada", True
      ActiveSheet.PivotTables(strPivot).PivotFields("Country").CalculatedItems. _
          Add "South America", "=Argentina+Brazil+Venezuela", True
      ActiveSheet.PivotTables(strPivot).PivotFields("Country").CalculatedItems( _
          "North America").StandardFormula = "=USA+Canada+Mexico"
      ActiveSheet.PivotTables(strPivot).PivotFields("Country").CalculatedItems. _
          Add "Europe", _
          "=Austria+Belgium+Denmark+Finland+France+Germany+Ireland+Italy" & _
          "+Norway+Poland+Portugal+Spain+Sweden+Switzerland+UK", True

      With ActiveSheet.PivotTables(strPivot).PivotFields("Country")
          .PivotItems("Argentina").Visible = False
          .PivotItems("Austria").Visible = False
          .PivotItems("Belgium").Visible = False
          .PivotItems("Brazil").Visible = False
          .PivotItems("Canada").Visible = False
          .PivotItems("Denmark").Visible = False
          .PivotItems("Finland").Visible = False
          .PivotItems("France").Visible = False
          .PivotItems("Germany").Visible = False
          .PivotItems("Ireland").Visible = False
          .PivotItems("Italy").Visible = False
          .PivotItems("Mexico").Visible = False
          .PivotItems("Norway").Visible = False
          .PivotItems("Poland").Visible = False
          .PivotItems("Portugal").Visible = False
          .PivotItems("Spain").Visible = False
          .PivotItems("Sweden").Visible = False
          .PivotItems("Switzerland").Visible = False
          .PivotItems("UK").Visible = False
          .PivotItems("USA").Visible = False
          .PivotItems("Venezuela").Visible = False
      End With
      Range("A6").Select
      ActiveSheet.PivotTables(strPivot).PivotFields("Country").Caption = _
          "Continent"
      Range("A5").Select
      With ActiveSheet.PivotTables(strPivot). _
        PivotFields("Sum of ExtendedPrice").NumberFormat = "$#,##0.00"
      End With
      With ActiveSheet.PivotTables(strPivot).PivotFields("ProductName")
          .Orientation = xlRowField
          .Position = 2
      End With
      Range("B6").Select
      ActiveSheet.PivotTables(strPivot). _
        PivotFields("ProductName").Orientation = xlHidden
End Sub
```

A *calculated item* uses a formula that refers to other items in the specified PivotTable field. For example, a PivotTable that contains a Country field listing a number of different country items (Austria, UK, Brazil, Argentina, etc.) could have a calculated item named "South America" defined as the sum of countries located on the South American continent:

Calculated Item	Formula
South America	=Argentina+Brazil+Venezuela

All the calculated items in the specified PivotTable are members of the CalculatedItems collection. Calculated items are defined by using the Add method of the CalculatedItems object and supplying two arguments: the name for the new item and a formula:

```
ActiveSheet.PivotTables(strPivot).PivotFields("Country").CalculatedItems. _
    Add "South America", "=Argentina+Brazil+Venezuela", True
```

The third (optional) argument set to True indicates that the strings in field names will be interpreted as having been formatted in standard U.S. English instead of using local settings. The default setting is False.

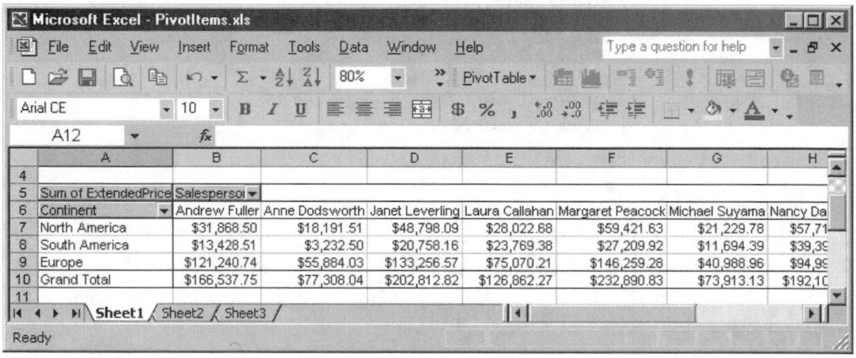

Figure A-9: By defining new items in a PivotTable report, you can present information summaries according to specific needs. Here the Continent field has been renamed from the Country field to present information summarized by continent. North America, South America, and Europe are calculated items in this PivotTable report.

You can modify the PivotWithCalcItems procedure by defining new calculated items in the Salesperson PivotTable field. The following report displays the sales by continent for the Female and Male teams:

Sum of ExtendedPrice	Salesperson		
Continent	Female	Male	Grand Total
North America	$212,144.09	$107,312.50	$319,456.59
South America	$114,368.41	$59,350.50	$173,718.91
Europe	$505,469.02	$267,148.35	$772,617.37
Grand Total	$831,981.52	$433,811.35	$1,265,792.87

You can find out if the PivotField or PivotItem is calculated by using the IsCalculated property of the PivotField or PivotItem object. The procedure shown below prints a list of fields and items in the PivotTable to the Immediate window, indicating whether the field or item is calculated. In addition, this procedure prints the names of all calculated items and their formulas to an Excel worksheet.

```
Sub ListCalcFieldsItems()
    Dim fld As PivotField      ' field enummerator
    Dim itm As PivotItem       ' item enummerator
    Dim r As Integer           ' row number

    Set pivTable = Worksheets(1).PivotTables(1)

    On Error Resume Next

    ' print to the Immediate window the names of fields
    ' and calculated items
    For Each fld In pivTable.PivotFields
        If fld.IsCalculated Then
            Debug.Print fld.Name & ":" & _
                    fld.Name & vbTab & "-->Calculated field"
        Else
            Debug.Print fld.Name
        End If
        For Each itm In pivTable. _
            PivotFields(fld.Name).CalculatedItems
                Debug.Print fld.Name & ":" & _
                    itm.Name & vbTab & "-->Calculated item"
                ' enter information about Calculated items
                ' in a worksheet
                r = r + 1
                With Worksheets(2)
                    .Cells(r, 1).Value = itm.Name
                    .Cells(r, 2).Value = Chr(39) & itm.Formula
                End With
        Next
    Next
End Sub
```

Creating a PivotChart Report Using VBA

A PivotChart represents the data in a PivotTable report. Using VBA code, you can create a PivotChart based on an existing PivotTable report, and you can change the layout and data displayed in a PivotChart just as easily as you can reformat a PivotTable report. Similar to PivotTable reports, PivotCharts are interactive and allow you to view data in different ways by changing the position or detail of the PivotChart fields. Excel creates a PivotChart report on a separate chart sheet. You may, however, copy the resulting chart to a worksheet to produce an embedded chart that can be viewed or printed on the same page with the PivotTable report. A PivotChart report is linked to a PivotTable report. This means that when you rearrange the data in a PivotTable report, the PivotChart report displays the same view of the data, and vice versa. The default chart type for a PivotTable chart report is a stacked column chart. This type of chart is useful for comparing the contribution of each value to a total across categories. You can generate any type of a PivotChart report, except xy (scatter), stock, or bubble.

Creating a PivotChart report programmatically boils down to using the SetDataSource method of the PivotChart object and specifying a reference to the PivotTable range. The PivotTable object has the following two properties that return ranges representing part or all of the PivotTable report:

- TableRange1—Returns a range representing the PivotTable report without page fields
- TableRange2—Returns a range representing the entire PivotTable report

The following procedure creates a PivotChart report based on the PivotTable report depicted in Figure A-10.

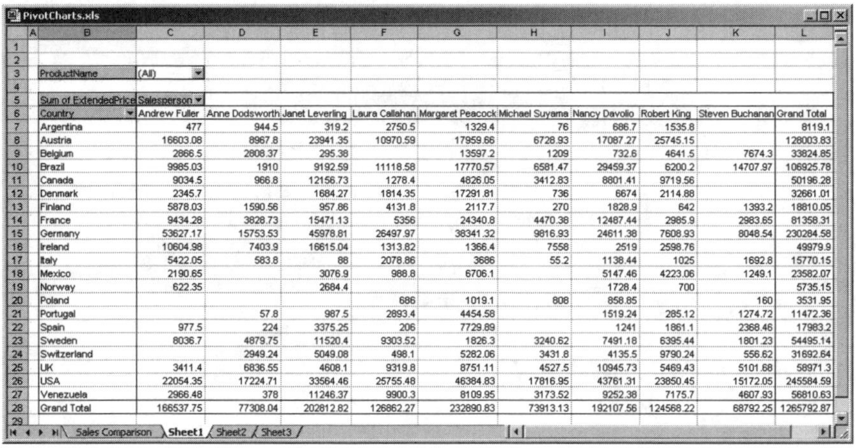

PivotCharts.xls

ProductName (All)

Sum of ExtendedPrice	Salesperson									
Country	Andrew Fuller	Anne Dodsworth	Janet Leverling	Laura Callahan	Margaret Peacock	Michael Suyama	Nancy Davolio	Robert King	Steven Buchanan	Grand Total
Argentina	477	944.5	319.2	2750.5	1329.4	76	686.7	1535.8		8119.1
Austria	16603.08	8967.8	23941.35	10970.59	17959.66	6728.93	17087.27	25745.15		128003.83
Belgium	2866.5	2808.37	295.38		13597.2	1209	732.6	4641.5	7674.3	33824.85
Brazil	9985.03	1910	9192.59	11118.58	17770.57	6581.47	29459.37	6200.2	14707.97	106925.78
Canada	9034.5	966.8	12156.73	1278.4	4826.05	3412.83	8801.41	9719.56		50196.28
Denmark	2345.7		1684.27	1814.35	17291.81	736	6674	2114.88		32661.01
Finland	5878.03	1590.56	957.86	4131.8	2117.7	270	1828.9	642	1393.2	18810.05
France	9434.28	3828.73	15471.13	5356	24340.8	4470.38	12487.44	2985.9	2983.65	81358.31
Germany	53627.17	15753.53	45978.81	26497.97	38341.32	9816.93	24611.38	7608.93	8048.54	230284.58
Ireland	10604.98	7403.9	16615.04	1313.82	1366.4	7558	2519	2598.76		49979.9
Italy	5422.05	583.8	88	2078.86	3686	55.2	1138.44	1025	1692.8	15770.15
Mexico	2190.65		3076.9	988.8	6706.1		5147.46	4223.06	1249.1	23582.07
Norway	622.35		2684.4				1728.4	700		5735.15
Poland				686	1019.1	808	858.85		160	3531.95
Portugal		57.8	987.5	2893.4	4454.58		1519.24	285.12	1274.72	11472.36
Spain	977.5	224	3375.25	206	7729.89		1241	1861.1	2368.46	17983.2
Sweden	8036.7	4879.75	11520.4	9303.52	1826.3	3240.62	7491.18	6395.44	1801.23	54495.14
Switzerland		2949.24	5049.08	498.1	5282.06	3431.8	4135.5	9790.24	556.62	31692.64
UK	3411.4	6836.55	4608.1	9319.8	8751.11	4527.5	10945.73	5469.43	5101.68	58971.3
USA	22054.35	17224.71	33564.46	25755.48	46384.83	17816.95	43761.31	23850.45	15172.05	245584.59
Venezuela	2966.48	378	11246.37	9900.3	8109.95	3173.52	9252.38	7175.7	4607.93	56810.63
Grand Total	166537.75	77308.04	202812.82	126862.27	232890.83	73913.13	192107.56	124568.22	68792.25	1265792.87

Sales Comparison | Sheet1 | Sheet2 | Sheet3

Figure A-10: This PivotTable report is used to graph data in the PivotChart report.

```
Sub CreatePivotChart()
    Dim myChart As Chart
    Dim strChartName As String
    Dim rngSource As Range
    Dim pvtTable As PivotTable

    Set pvtTable = Worksheets("Sheet1").PivotTables(1)
    Set rngSource = pvtTable.TableRange2
    strChartName = "Sales Comparison"
    Set myChart = ActiveWorkbook.Charts.Add
    With myChart
        .Name = strChartName
        .SetSourceData Source:=rngSource
        .ChartType = xlColumnClustered
```

```
End With

' set the current page for the PivotTable report to the
' page named "Tofu"
pvtTable.PivotFields("ProductName").CurrentPage = "Tofu"

End Sub
```

After creating a PivotChart report based on the PivotTable report in Sheet1 (Figure A-10), the procedure changes the current page for the PivotTable report to display information about the product named Tofu. The resulting PivotChart report is shown in Figure A-11. Notice that the fields in a PivotChart report are shown as drop-down lists to allow you to play with the data on the chart.

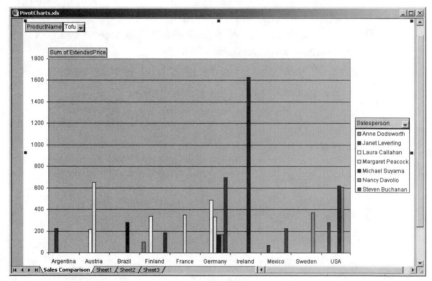

Figure A-11: The PivotChart report is generated from the PivotTable report data on a separate chart sheet.

The following procedure lists the names of the PivotChart report fields to a worksheet:

```
Sub GetChartInfo()
    ' list of all the PivotTable field names used
    ' in the first PivotChart report

    Dim sht As Worksheet
    Dim r As Integer
    Dim fld As PivotField

    Set sht = Worksheets.Add
    sht.Activate
    r = 1
    For Each fld In _
        Charts("Sales Comparison").PivotLayout.PivotFields
```

```
            sht.Cells(r, 1).Value = fld.Caption
            r = r + 1
        Next fld
    End Sub
```

Saving PivotTable Report and PivotChart Report as a Web Page

Check out Appendix D on using Microsoft Office web components. By publishing a PivotTable report or PivotTable chart as a web page, you can work with your PivotTable or PivotChart interactively inside Microsoft Internet Explorer. When you select the PivotTable report, Excel uses the Microsoft PivotTable web component to publish your data. When you save your PivotChart report as a web page, the publishing job is handled by the Microsoft Chart web component. To manually save your PivotTable report and PivotChart report as a web page, perform the following tasks (for programming examples, see Appendix D):

1. Select the sheet containing the PivotTable report (see Figure A-10).

2. Choose **File | Save As**.

3. In the Save As dialog box, choose **Web Page (*.htm; *.html)** from the Save as file type drop-down list. Make sure the **Selection: Sheet** option button is selected. Click the **Add interactivity** check box. At this point, the name of the file changes to PivotCharts.htm.

4. Click the **Publish** button.

5. In the Publish as Web Page dialog box, select **PivotTable** from items on Sheet1 (see Figure A-12).

6. Click **Publish**.

The page should now open in your browser (see Figure A-13).

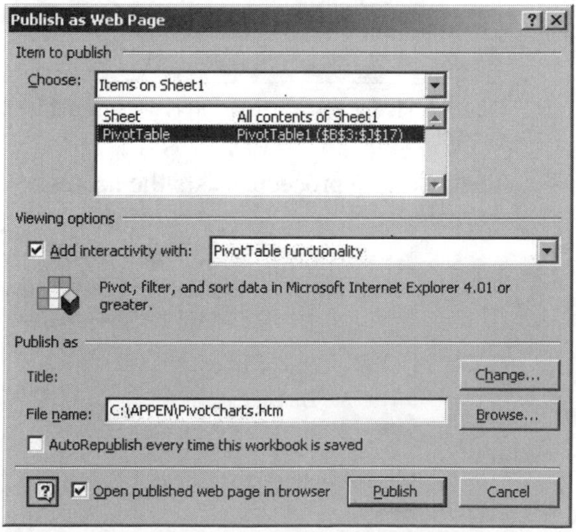

Figure A-12: Publishing a PivotTable report as a web page

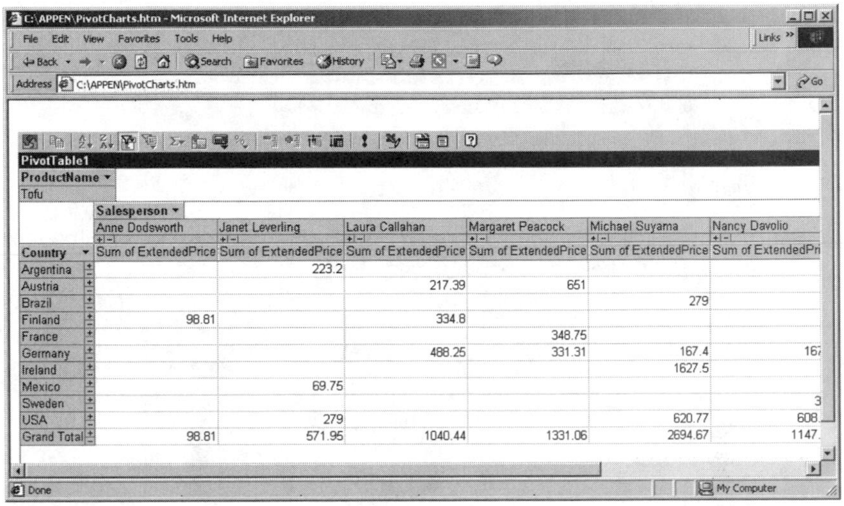

Figure A-13: A PivotTable report published from Excel as a web page is displayed in Internet Explorer using the PivotTable Office web component. Office web components are covered in Appendix D.

A PivotTable report and a PivotChart report can be published together by saving the chart sheet as a web page.

1. Select the Sales Comparison chart sheet containing the PivotChart report (see Figure A-11).

2. Choose **File | Save As**.

3. In the Save As dialog box, choose **Web Page (*.htm; *.html)** from the Save as file type drop-down list. Make sure the **Selection: Chart** option button is selected. Click the **Add interactivity** check box. At this point, the name of the file changes to PivotCharts.htm. Change the filename to **PivotCharts2.htm**.

4. Click the **Publish** button.

5. In the Publish as Web Page dialog box, the Chart item is automatically selected (see Figure A-14).

6. Click **Publish**.

7. The web page should now open in your browser (see Figure A-15).

Note: To browse a web page interactively with the Office web components, you must have a Microsoft Office 2000/XP license.

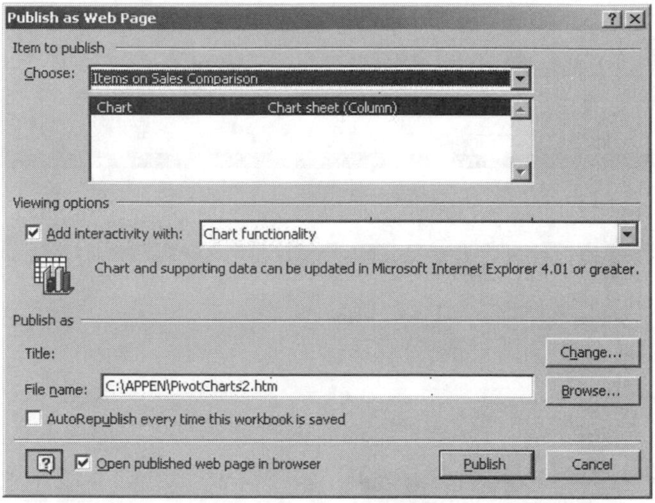

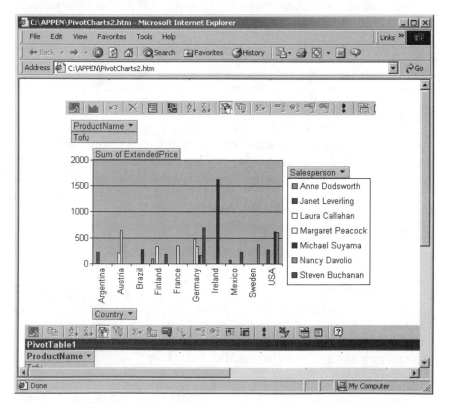

Figure A-14: You can publish a PivotChart report as a web page.

Figure A-15: When you publish a PivotChart report from Excel as a web page, the browser uses the Microsoft Office web chart component to graph the data and allow you to interact with the chart. Also, presented on the same page (inside the Microsoft Office PivotReport component) is the source data for the ChartReport.

Appendix B

Programming Special Features

The Excel 2002 Object Model contains hundreds of objects that allow you to control various aspects of the Excel application. In addition to native objects, you can call upon objects exposed by the Office XP Object Model when programming Excel. For this appendix, I have selected a number of objects from these two libraries to give you a feel of what can be accomplished by calling upon the many available objects.

Selected Objects in the Excel 2002 Object Model

The Excel 2002 objects presented here will show you how to make worksheets more attention grabbing with special formatting (see the following objects: Tab, CellFormat, Characters, PageSetup, Format-Condition, Graphic, and Diagram). Other objects, such as Speech, SpellingOptions, and AutoCorrect, can help you make sure that the worksheets your users distribute are void of as many errors as possible. Objects such as Reference, VBProject, and VBComponent will give you a taste of what it is like programming the Visual Basic Editor (VBE).

Tab Object

Sheet tabs at the bottom of an Excel chart sheet or worksheet are represented by the Tab object. Excel 2002 has a new feature that allows you to change the color of sheet tabs by using the Color or ColorIndex properties of the Tab object. The Color property requires that you use the RGB function to create a color value. For example, to set the Sheet1 tab color to purple, use the following statement:

```
' color - purple
ActiveWorkbook.Worksheets(1).Tab.Color = RGB(128, 0, 255)

Sub ColorTabs()
    Dim wks As Worksheet
    Dim i As Integer

    i = 5
    For Each wks In ThisWorkbook.Worksheets
        If wks.Tab.ColorIndex = xlColorIndexNone Then
            wks.Tab.ColorIndex = i
            i = i + 1
        End If
    Next
End Sub
```

Speech Object

Office XP comes with a speech recognition feature that makes it possible to read text on demand. The text can be read automatically on data entry by clicking the Speak on Enter button on the Text to Speech toolbar (choose Tools | Speech). You can also control the speech feature via the Speech object from a VBA procedure. This object has the Speak method that causes the text to be spoken by Excel. To cause the active cell to be spoken on entry or when it is finished being edited, set the SpeakCellOnEnter property of the Speech object to True:

```
Application.Speech.SpeakCellOnEnter = True
```

Notice that the Speech object is accessed via the Application object.

Name	Scores
Ann Matluck	133
John Brick	248
Adam Bryan	187
Micky Mack	345
Tonya Walsh	149

```
Sub ReadNamesWithHighScores()
Dim v As Integer

v = InputBox("Enter the minimum expected score:", "Approved Minimum")

    For Each cell In ActiveSheet.Columns("B").Cells
        If IsNumeric(cell.Value) And cell.Value >= v Then
```

```
          Application.Speech.Speak "Congratulations" & _
              cell.Offset(0, -1).Text
          Application.Speech.Speak "your score is " & cell.Text
       End If
   Next
End Sub
```

SpellingOptions Object

This object represents the various spell-checking options for a worksheet. Spelling options can also be set manually on the Spelling tab in the Options dialog box. The following procedure sets some spelling options and adds a new dictionary named Special.dic, where you can add correct words found during the spell check. Use the following spreadsheet for the test run.

Citricidal	Liquid	10 onz
Vitamin B12	Tablets	50
Licorice Root	Tablets	100
Ginger Root	Tablets	150

```
Sub SpellCheck()
    ' set spelling options
    With Application.SpellingOptions
        .SuggestMainOnly = True
        .IgnoreCaps = True
        .IgnoreMixedDigits = True
        .SuggestMainOnly = False
        .IgnoreFileNames = True
        .UserDict = "Special.dic"
    End With

    ' run a spell check
    Cells.CheckSpelling
End Sub
```

CellFormat Object

Two new properties of the Application object (FindFormat and Replace-Format) return the CellFormat object that represents the search criteria for the cell format.

- FindFormat property—Sets or returns the search criteria for the type of cell formats to find

- ReplaceFormat property—Sets the replacement criteria to use in replacing cell formats

Name	Scores
Ann Matluck	133
John Brick	248
Adam Bryan	187
Micky Mack	345
Tonya Walsh	149

```
Sub Reformat()
    ' Set search criteria
    With Application.FindFormat.Font
        .Name = "Arial"
        .FontStyle = "Regular"
        .Size = 10
    End With

    ' Set replacement criteria
    With Application.ReplaceFormat.Font
        .Name = "Tahoma"
        .FontStyle = "Bold"
        .Size = 11
    End With

    With Application.ReplaceFormat.Borders(xlEdgeBottom)
        .LineStyle = xlContinuous
        .Weight = xlThick
    End With

    ' Perform the replace
    Sheets(1).UsedRange.Replace What:="", Replacement:="", _
        SearchFormat:=True, _
        ReplaceFormat:=True

    ' Reset the Find and Replace formats
    Application.FindFormat.Clear
    Application.ReplaceFormat.Clear
End Sub
```

Characters Object

The Characters object allows you to modify individual characters in a text string. Use Characters (start, length), where start is the start character number and length is the number of characters, to return a Characters object. The following procedure changes the font color of the first letter of every word found in the UsedRange. The result of this procedure is shown below.

Student Name	Scores
Ann Matluck	133
John Brick	248
Adam Bryan	187
Micky Mack	345
Tonya Walsh	149

```
Sub Format1stLetters()
    Dim myChr As Characters
    Dim i As Integer

    For Each cell In Sheets(1).UsedRange
        If Not IsNumeric(cell) Then
```

```
                  Set myChr = cell.Characters(1, 1)
                  myChr.Font.Color = RGB(128, 0, 255)
                  For i = 1 To Len(cell.Text)
                    If Asc(Mid(cell, i, 1)) = 32 Then
                      Set myChr = cell.Characters(i + 1, 1)
                      myChr.Font.Color = RGB(255, 0, 0)
                    End If
                  Next
              End If
        Next
    End Sub
```

AutoCorrect Object

The AutoCorrect object has properties and methods that allow you to work with Excel's AutoCorrect features. The following two procedures will get you started working with AutoCorrect programmatically. The first procedure uses the ReplacementList method to retrieve common misspelled words and their automatic replacements into an array. The procedure then reads the values of this array and enters them into a worksheet so that you can print them out easily. If you need to update your AutoCorrect list with a number of new entries, you may want to enter them in a worksheet instead of working with the provided dialog box. The first column would hold the misspelled words, and the next column would contain the corrected word. You could then use the second VBA procedure shown below to update the AutoCorrect list with your new entries quickly and easily.

```
' this procedure generates a list of AutoCorrect entries
Sub Auto_Correct()
    Dim myList As Variant
    Dim i As Integer

    myList = Application.AutoCorrect.ReplacementList
    ActiveSheet.Cells(1, 1).Select
        For i = LBound(myList) To UBound(myList)
            With ActiveCell
                .Offset(0, 0).Value = myList(i, 1)
                .Offset(0, 1).Value = myList(i, 2)
                .Offset(1, 0).Select
            End With
        Next
    ActiveSheet.Columns("A:B").AutoFit
    Cells(1, 1).Select
End Sub
```

To add a number of entries to the AutoCorrect list, type your entries in any two columns of a worksheet (as shown below) and run the procedure that follows.

adventage	advantage
knowlge	knowledge

```
Sub Auto_Correct_Batch_Add()
    Dim myRange As Range
    Dim myList As Variant
    Dim strReplaceWhat As String
    Dim strReplaceWith As String

    ' prompt user to select data for processing
    ' the Type argument ensures that the return value is
    ' a valid cell reference (a Range object).
    Set myRange = Application.InputBox( _
        Prompt:="Highlight the range containing your list", _
        Title:="List Selection", _
        Type:=8)

    If myRange.Columns.Count <> 2 Then Exit Sub

    ' save all the values in the selected range to an array
    myList = myRange.Value

    ' retrieve the values from the array and
    ' add them to the AutoCorrect replacements
    For i = LBound(myList) To UBound(myList)
        strReplaceWhat = myList(i, 1)
        strReplaceWith = myList(i, 2)
        If strReplaceWhat <> "" And strReplaceWith <> "" Then
          Application.AutoCorrect.AddReplacement _
            strReplaceWhat, strReplaceWith
        End If
    Next
End Sub
```

PageSetup Object

If you need to programmatically read or set various options available in the PageSetup dialog box (such as paper size, orientation, margins, print area, and so on), use the PageSetup property to return a PageSetup object. The following example procedure prints several settings from the Page Setup dialog to the Immediate window and asks whether to set the orientation to portrait mode.

```
Sub ReadPageSetup()
    Dim objPageS As PageSetup

    Set objPageS = ActiveSheet.PageSetup
    With objPageS
        Debug.Print "Orientation:"; .Orientation
        Debug.Print "Paper Size:"; .PaperSize
        Debug.Print "Print Area: "; .PrintArea
        Debug.Print "Left Margin: "; .LeftMargin
        Debug.Print "Top Margin: "; .TopMargin
        Debug.Print "Print Gridlines: "; .PrintGridlines
        .Orientation = xlLandscape
        If .Orientation <> xlPortrait Then
```

```
                    If MsgBox("Do you want to set the orientation " & _
                    "mode to Portrait?", vbYesNo + vbQuestion) = vbYes Then
                        .Orientation = xlPortrait
                    End If
                End If
            End With
        End Sub
```

FormatCondition Object

You can add conditional formatting to your spreadsheet by using the For-matCondition object. Conditional formatting is associated with a particular range of cells. The FormatCondition object is a member of the Format-Conditions collection. This collection can contain up to three FormatCondition objects for a given range. Use the Count method of the FormatConditions collection to return the number of objects in the collec-tion. Use the Add method of the FormatConditions collection to create a new conditional format. This method requires that you specify the type con-stant (xlCellValue, xlExpression) to indicate whether the conditional format is based on a cell value or an expression. The Add method also has three optional arguments (Operator, Formula1, and Formula2) that allow you to spec-ify the condition. Use the Modify method to modify the formatting condition. Use the Delete method to delete a formatting condition. The example procedure below creates a conditional format to be applied to all non-numeric cells in the active sheet when the cell value is greater than or equal to 150. Notice how the cell with a value of 150 is formatted with white font color and colored background.

Citricidal	Liquid	10 onz
Vitamin B12	Tablets	50
Licorice Root	Tablets	100
Ginger Root	Tablets	150

```
Sub ApplyConditionalFormat()
    Dim objFormatCon As FormatCondition
    Dim objFormatColl As FormatConditions
    Dim myRange As Range

    ' select range containing numeric cells only
    Set myRange = ActiveSheet.UsedRange. _
        SpecialCells(xlCellTypeConstants, 1)
    Set objFormatColl = myRange.FormatConditions

    ' find out if any conditional formatting already exists
    If objFormatColl.Count > 0 Then
        MsgBox "There are " & objFormatColl.Count & " conditions " & _
            "defined for the used range."
    End If

    ' remove existing conditions if they exist
```

```
    For Each objFormatCon In objFormatColl
        objFormatCon.Delete
    Next

        ' add first condition
        Set objFormatCon = objFormatColl.Add(Type:=xlCellValue, _
            Operator:=xlGreaterEqual, _
            Formula1:="150")
        With objFormatCon
            .Font.Bold = True
            .Font.ColorIndex = 2  ' white
            .Interior.Pattern = xlSolid
            .Interior.Color = RGB(0, 0, 255)  ' blue
        End With
    End Sub
```

Graphic Object

Use the Graphic object to place a picture in the header or footer area of an Excel worksheet. There are six properties of the PageSetup object (Center-FooterPicture, CenterHeaderPicture, LeftFooterPicture, LeftHeader-Picture, RightFooterPicture, and RightHeaderPicture) that can return the Graphic object. The following procedure displays the File Picker dialog box where the user can select a picture file. Next, the file is inserted in the left header of the active sheet. Notice that to make the picture visible, you must set the LeftHeader property to the following string: "&G." To make this procedure more user friendly, modify it so that it asks the user in which of the six areas to display the picture.

```
Sub AddWatermarkImage()
    Dim strFilename As String
    With Application.FileDialog(msoFileDialogFilePicker)
        .Title = "Custom image selection"
        .AllowMultiSelect = False
        .Filters.Add "Pictures", "*.gif; *.jpg; *.jpeg; *.bmp", 1
        .InitialView = msoFileDialogViewThumbnail
        If .Show = -1 Then
            strFilename = .SelectedItems(1)
            With ActiveSheet.PageSetup
                With .LeftHeaderPicture
                    .Filename = strFilename
                    .Brightness = 0.85
                    .ColorType = msoPictureWatermark
                    .Contrast = 0.15
                    .Height = 72
                    .Width = 72
                End With
                .TopMargin = Application.InchesToPoints(1.25)
                .LeftHeader = "&G"
            End With
        End If
    End With
End Sub
```

Diagram Object

You can illustrate various concepts using diagramming tools in Excel 2002. A diagram is a collection of shapes. Diagram types include Cycle, Target, Radial, Venn, and Pyramid.

Each diagram contains nodes. A node represents an individual shape object in a diagram. To add a Diagram object programmatically to a worksheet, use the AddDiagram method of the Shapes collection. To add shapes to the diagram, use the DiagramNode object within the Shape object. The following procedure creates a diagram with four nodes. A problem in Microsoft Excel 2002 makes it impossible to programmatically set the text in a diagram node. Microsoft has posted a workaround to this problem, where you can use Microsoft Word or PowerPoint to create a diagram and then copy it to Excel (see article Q317293 in the Microsoft Knowledge Base for an example VBA procedure).

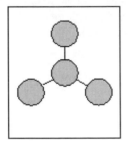

```
Sub AddADiagram()
    Dim dgnNode As DiagramNode
    Dim shpDiagram As Shape
    Dim intNodes As Integer

    Worksheets.Add
    ' Add diagram and first child node
    Set shpDiagram = ActiveSheet.Shapes.AddDiagram _
        (Type:=msoDiagramCycle, Left:=10, Top:=15, _
        Width:=400, Height:=475)
    Set dgnNode = shpDiagram.DiagramNode.Children.AddNode

    ' Add three additional child nodes
    For intNodes = 1 To 3
        dgnNode.AddNode
    Next intNodes

    ' Automatically format the diagram
    dgnNode.Diagram.AutoFormat = msoTrue

    ' Change the diagram type
    dgnNode.Diagram.Convert Type:=msoDiagramRadial

    ' Display the number of nodes in the diagram
```

```
        MsgBox dgnNode.Diagram.Nodes.Count

        ' Select all nodes
        ActiveSheet.Shapes(1).Diagram.Nodes.SelectAll
    End Sub
```

CustomProperty Object

When you write VBA procedures, you often need to store specific information regarding a worksheet. Excel offers many ways to preserve information for later use. For example, you can store information in worksheet-level range names or hidden worksheets, or you can write it directly to the registry. The fourth, and newest, method is storing information using custom properties. A CustomProperty object can store information with a worksheet or SmartTag. Use the Add method of the CustomProperties collection to add custom property information and return a CustomProperty object. You must specify the name and value of the custom property. The following example procedure demonstrates how to store student names and scores shown below as custom properties.

Student Name	Scores
Ann Matluck	133
John Brick	248
Adam Bryan	187
Micky Mack	345
Tonya Walsh	149

```
    Sub StoreScores()
        Dim mySheet As Worksheet
        Dim custPrp As CustomProperty
        Dim i As Integer
        Dim rng As Range
        Dim totalCount As Integer

        Set mySheet = Application.Workbooks("Special.xls"). _
            Worksheets("Speech")

        ' find out if custom properties exist
        If mySheet.CustomProperties.Count > 0 Then
            ' Display custom properties
            totalCount = mySheet.CustomProperties.Count
            For i = 1 To totalCount
                With mySheet.CustomProperties(1)
                    Debug.Print .Name & vbTab; .Value
                    Set rng = mySheet.Range("A:A").Find(what:=.Name)
                    ' Delete the custom property
                    If Not rng Is Nothing Then .Delete
                End With
            Next
        End If
```

```
mySheet.Activate
Cells(2, 1).Select
Do While ActiveCell <> ""
    If Not IsEmpty(ActiveCell) Then
        Set custPrp = mySheet.CustomProperties.Add( _
          Name:=ActiveCell.Text, _
          Value:=ActiveCell.Offset(0, 1).Text)
        Debug.Print custPrp.Name & vbTab & custPrp.Value
        ActiveCell.Offset(1, 0).Select
    End If
Loop

If mySheet.CustomProperties.Count > 0 Then
' Display custom properties
    For i = 1 To mySheet.CustomProperties.Count
        With mySheet.CustomProperties(i)
            Debug.Print .Name & vbTab; .Value
        End With
    Next
End If
End Sub
```

VBProject Object, VBComponent Object, and Reference Object

To program and manipulate Visual Basic Editor (VBE) in code, you need to access objects contained in the Microsoft Visual Basic for Applications Extensibility 5.3 Library (VBIDE). Before you can use the objects from the VBIDE library, you must do two things:

1. Enable access to VBProjects.

   In the Microsoft Excel application window, choose **Tools | Macro | Security**. Click the **Trusted Sources** tab, select the **Trust Access to Visual Basic Project** check box, and click **OK**.

   Note: If access to VBProjects is not enabled, an attempt to run a VBA procedure that accesses objects from the VBIDE Library results in the following error message: "Programmatic access to Visual Basic Project is not trusted."

2. Create a reference to the VBIDE Library.

   In the Visual Basic Editor window, choose **Tools | References**, check **Microsoft Visual Basic for Applications Extensibility 5.3 Library**, and click **OK**.

The top-level object in the VBA Extensibility Library object model is the VBE object, which represents the Visual Basic Editor itself. The VBE object contains the collection of projects. A VBA project that is open in the Visual Basic Editor is represented by the VBProject object. Each VBA project can reference one or more type libraries or projects. Use the Reference object to find out what references are currently selected in the References dialog box for the specific VBA Project.

A VBProject object has a collection of VBComponents consisting of VBComponent objects. A VBComponent object represents a component in the project, such as a standard module, class module, or user form. Each VBComponent has a CodeModule property, which you can use to access the underlying CodeModule object. A CodeModule object represents each component's code module.

The following procedure creates a new standard module in a workbook and prints to the Immediate window the names of all VBA projects, the names and full paths of selected references for each VBA project, and the names of each project's components. The procedure also demonstrates how you can programmatically export the contents of a module to a file.

```
Sub VB_Project()
    Dim objVBPrj As VBIDE.VBProject
    Dim objVBCom As VBIDE.VBComponent
    Dim vbrRef As VBIDE.Reference

    ' Create new workbook
    Application.Workbooks.Add
    ' Create a new module in a workbook
    Application.VBE.ActiveVBProject. _
        VBComponents.Add (vbext_ct_StdModule)

    ' List VBA projects as well as references and
    ' component names they contain
    For Each objVBPrj In Application.VBE.VBProjects
        Debug.Print objVBPrj.Name
        For Each vbrRef In objVBPrj.References
            With vbrRef
                Debug.Print .Name & "---" & .FullPath
            End With
        Next
        For Each objVBCom In objVBPrj.VBComponents
            Debug.Print vbTab & objVBCom.Name
        Next
    Next

    ' Export the entire Module1 in the activeVB project to disk
    With ThisWorkbook.VBProject. _
        VBComponents("Module1")
        If MsgBox("Module1 contains " & _
            .CodeModule.CountOfLines & _
            " lines." & vbCrLf & _
            "Do you want to export it to a file?", _
            vbYesNo) = vbYes Then
                .Export "C:\myCode1.bas"
        End If
    End With
End Sub
```

Selected Objects in the Office XP Object Model

The Office XP objects presented here will enhance your knowledge about files and folders (see the following objects: FileSearch, SearchScope, ScopeFolder, and NewFile). Objects such as HTMLProject and HTMLProjectItem will enable you to work with the HTML code in an Office document. The last topic in this appendix will also introduce you to a powerful built-in development tool that you can use for this purpose.

FileSearch Object

Use the FileSearch object to search for any file type based on various criteria. You can search for an exact filename, files of a specific type, or files containing a specific text located in a specific folder including or not including subfolders. The following function allows searching for a specific file or group of files. To search a specific folder, including subfolders, change the SearchSubFolders property to True. Any time you perform the new search, remember to reset the search settings using the NewSearch method. Note, however, that this method does not reset the LookIn property.

You can call the function shown below from a separate subroutine or by typing the following statement in the Immediate window:

```
FindFile("*.*")

Function FindFile(strFileName As String)
    Dim objFS As FileSearch
    Dim strFiles As String
    Dim varFile As Variant

    Set objFS = Application.FileSearch
     With objFS
        .NewSearch
        .LookIn = "C:\"
        .Filename = strFileName
        .SearchSubFolders = False
        If .Execute() > 0 Then
            For Each varFile In .FoundFiles
                strFiles = strFiles & varFile & vbCrLf
            Next varFile
        End If
     End With
     MsgBox strFiles
End Function
```

Because the FileSearch object belongs to the Microsoft Office XP Object Model, it can be called from any Office XP application.

SearchScope Object and ScopeFolder Object

A SearchScope object denotes a type of folder that can be searched by using the FileSearch object. Each local or network drive, and even a Microsoft Outlook folder on your computer, represents a single search scope. Search scope types are represented by the following constants: *msoSearchInMyComputer, msoSearchInMyNetworkPlaces, msoSearchInOutlook,* and *msoSearchInCustom.* Within each SearchScope object, there is a single ScopeFolder object that corresponds to the root folder of the search scope. A ScopeFolder represents a searchable folder and is part of a SearchFolders collection. Use the SearchFolders collection to define the folders to search when using the FileSearch object. The following procedure lists all searchable folders on your computer:

```
Sub SearchableFolders()
    Dim objSScope As SearchScope
    Dim objSFolder As ScopeFolder
    Dim strPaths As String

    With Application.FileSearch
        For Each objSScope In .SearchScopes
            Select Case objSScope.Type
                Case msoSearchInMyComputer
                    For Each objSFolder In objSScope. _
                    ScopeFolder.ScopeFolders
                        strPaths = strPaths & objSFolder.Path & vbCrLf
                    Next
                Case Else
            End Select
        Next objSScope
    End With
    MsgBox "The following paths are searchable:" & vbCrLf & strPaths
    Debug.Print strPaths
End Sub
```

NewFile Object

Microsoft Office XP applications contain a new feature known as a task pane. A *task pane* is a dialog box docked within the host application (see Figure B-1). This dialog box can contain one or more pages broken into sections. For example, the New Workbook page in Excel 2002 contains the following five sections: Open a workbook, New, New from existing workbook, New from template, and an unnamed section at the bottom of the task pane. The NewFile object represents a new document that can be listed in the task pane. To access the NewFile object in Excel, use the NewWorkbook property. The following procedures demonstrate how to add and remove a workbook from the New from existing workbook section of the task pane:

```
Sub AddToTaskPane()
    Application.NewWorkbook.Add _
```

```
            Filename:="C:\BlueGrid.xls", _
            Section:=msoNewfromExistingFile, _
            DisplayName:="New Blue Grid", _
            Action:=msoCreateNewFile
        CommandBars("Task Pane").Visible = False
        CommandBars("Task Pane").Visible = True
    End Sub

    Sub RemoveFromTaskPane()
        Application.NewWorkbook.Remove _
            Filename:="C:\BlueGrid.xls", _
            Section:=msoNewfromExistingFile, _
            DisplayName:="New Blue Grid"
        CommandBars("Task Pane").Visible = False
        CommandBars("Task Pane").Visible = True
    End Sub
```

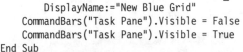

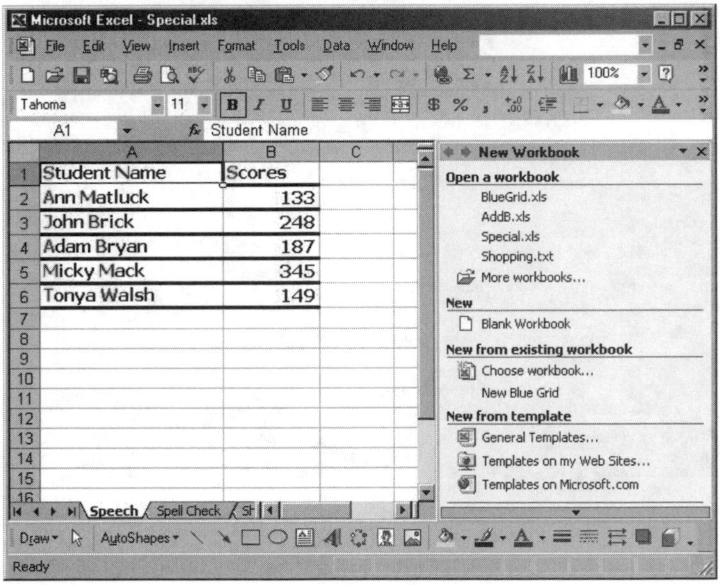

Figure B-1: You can programmatically add files to the New Workbook page of the task pane.

HTMLProject Object and HTMLProjectItem Object

Both Office 2000 and Office XP contain a special development tool called Microsoft Script Editor (MSE) that allows you to work with documents as web pages. To access this tool in Excel 2002, open the Tools menu, point to Macro, and choose Microsoft Script Editor. The MSE can also be accessed by pressing Alt+Shift+F11 or programmatically by using the HTML-Project object. Try the latter by opening any workbook you want in Microsoft Excel, switch to the Visual Basic Editor screen, activate the Immediate window, and type the following statement:

```
ActiveWorkbook.HTMLProject.Open
```

When you press Enter, the above statement will open the Active workbook in the Microsoft Script Editor (Figure B-2). Notice that the MSE user interface is similar to the VBE (Visual Basic Editor) interface. It contains a Project Explorer, a Properties window, a Toolbox, and a Code window. In addition to that, you can access the Object Browser and Document Outline windows by choosing Other Windows from the MSE View menu.

When you open an Excel workbook in the MSE, the Project Explorer displays a Sheet object for each sheet in the workbook. To see the HTML code for any sheet, double-click the sheet name in the Project Explorer. Note that the Code window displays both the HTML and XML code.

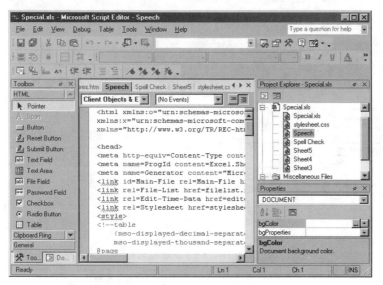

Figure B-2: The Microsoft Script Editor (MSE)

Using the Microsoft Script Editor is beyond the scope of this book. You can learn all you want about this subject by using the built-in help. Simply choose Microsoft Script Editor Help from MSE's Help menu to gain access to various topics (Figure B-3).

Using the HTMLProject object and HTMLProjectItem object from the Microsoft Office XP object model, you can access and manipulate the HTML objects of an Excel workbook or another Office document.

The HTMLProject object represents the HTML code in an Office document. The HTMLProject object contains a collection of HTMLProjectItem objects. Each HTMLProjectItem represents an individual project item, as displayed in the Project Explorer in the Microsoft Script Editor. You can use the Name property to return and display the name of the project item. Use the Count property of the HTMLProjectItems collection to return the number of project items in the HTML project for the specified workbook. The

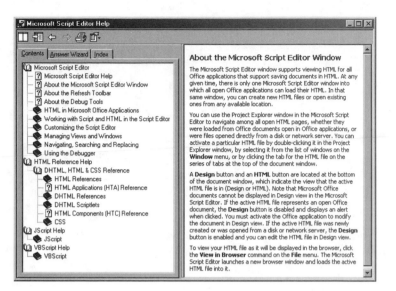

Figure B-3: Study the Microsoft Script Editor Help to learn about scripting.

following procedure will get you started working with these objects and their properties and methods programmatically. Notice that after retrieving the number of project items in the current HTML project of the Active-Workbook, the procedure loops through these items and prints their names to the Immediate window. If the found project item's name is "Speech," the procedure will store the HTML text of the project item in a text file.

```vba
Sub HTML_Project()
    Dim objHTMLPrj As HTMLProject
    Dim itm As Variant

    Set objHTMLPrj = ActiveWorkbook.HTMLProject

    With objHTMLPrj
        Debug.Print "The HTML Project contains " & _
            .HTMLProjectItems.Count & " items as follows:"
        For Each itm In .HTMLProjectItems
            Debug.Print itm.Name
            If itm.Name = "Speech" Then
                .HTMLProjectItems(itm).SaveCopyAs "C:\Scores.txt"
            End If
        Next
        If .State = msoHTMLProjectStateDocumentProjectUnlocked Then
                .Open
        End If
    End With
End Sub
```

Appendix C

Introduction to Using and Programming Smart Tags

When you enter certain text into a Microsoft Excel 2002 spreadsheet cell, you may notice a small purple triangle that appears in the lower-right corner of that cell. This feature is a result of a new technology called *smart tags* that was introduced in Office XP. When you move your mouse pointer over the text that has been tagged, you will see a button representing a circle with a lowercase "i" inside it. When clicked, this Smart Tag button displays a list of available actions that are relevant to the marked text (Figure C-1).

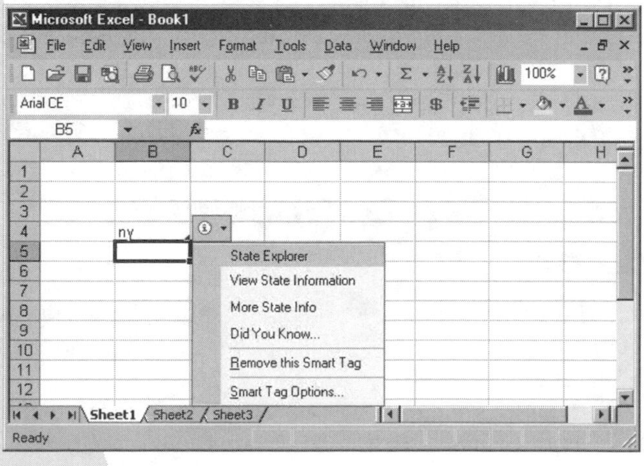

Figure C-1:
A custom smart tag implemented in the Microsoft Excel 2002 worksheet

The purpose of smart tags is to recognize frequently accessed data, such as stock symbols, zip codes, customer names, part numbers, dates, and so on, and make it easy for users to perform actions on those pieces of data regardless of what application they are currently using. For example, a smart tag could check warranty information on a specific part number entered in a spreadsheet or check prices on specific products. Or, it could retrieve flight information when an airline and flight number are recognized.

With the implementation of smart tag technology, your spreadsheet applications can become more intelligent and user friendly. Users will no longer need to manually launch other applications, as smart tags can return data from any data source or open a browser and navigate to a web site—all automatically. In summary, smart tags allow you to eliminate extra steps that you would normally have to take to perform a certain action.

At this point, you are probably anxious to get started. So, how can you create your own smart tags? There are two ways to develop smart tags. If you studied Chapter 17 of this book, you already have the necessary skills to develop some simple smart tags. This approach requires that you are familiar with the Extensible Markup Language (XML). With XML, you can define a set of terms that smart tags will recognize and create a list of actions to display whenever a term from the list is encountered in a worksheet or another Microsoft Office XP document. This approach is very limited, as it allows you to only use web-based actions (more about this later). If you require more dynamic and powerful smart tags, you must develop ActiveX DLLs (dynamic-link libraries) using development environment tools provided within Microsoft Visual Basic 6.0 or Microsoft Visual C++.

Smart tags are currently available for Microsoft Excel 2002, Microsoft Word 2002, Microsoft Outlook 2002 (when Word 2002 is used as an e-mail editor), and Internet Explorer. This appendix expands your knowledge of XML by showing you how to get started creating smart tag lists. If you are interested in learning more about developing your own smart tags (using either the XML or DLL approach), download a free Smart Tags software development kit (SDK) provided by Microsoft (http://msdn.microsoft.com).

Checking Smart Tag Options in an Excel Workbook

Let's start by checking whether your workbook is set to recognize smart tags. To do this, choose Tools | AutoCorrectOptions and click the Smart Tags tab (Figure C-2).

Notice that both built-in and custom smart tags are listed as a group in the Recognizers section. Microsoft Excel 2002 comes with the MSN MoneyCentral smart tag that allows you to check the latest stock prices. So if you enter a financial symbol, such as "MSFT," in a spreadsheet cell and the smart tag lists are selected as shown in Figure C-2, you will be presented with a list of actions allowing you to insert a refreshable stock price, obtain a stock quote on MSN MoneyCentral, look at the company report on MSN MoneyCentral, or read recent news on MSN MoneyCentral. The smart tag options allow you to turn off the display of smart tags, label data with smart tags, configure how you want to display a smart tag on a per-workbook basis, save the

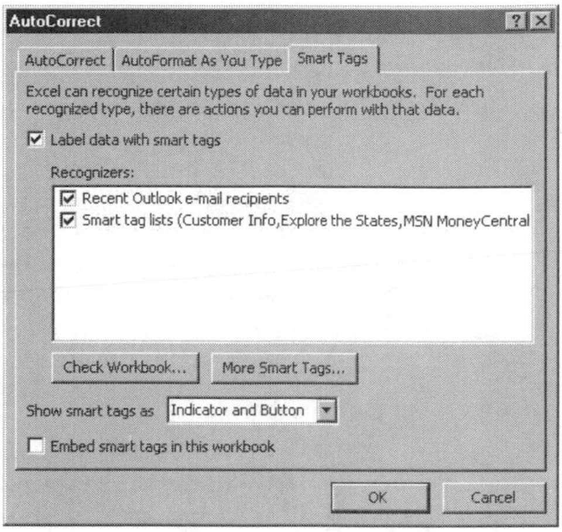

Figure C-2: Configuring smart tags

smart tags with the workbook, and search for more smart tags on the web. Two other smart tags listed in Figure C-2 (Customer Info, Explore the States) are custom-made. You will learn how to create and use these smart tags in the next sections.

Creating Your First Simple Smart Tag

Smart tags are based on *actions* and *recognizers*. Recognizers check whether the term entered by the user belongs to the list of stored terms. When the user has entered a term that has been recognized, the action associated with the term is executed. Each term can have one or more actions associated with it. Actions are also called *verbs*. Your first tag will recognize certain state abbreviations as smart-tag actionable. For example, when you enter "ny," "ca," or another state abbreviation included in your list of terms in a spreadsheet cell, you will be presented with smart tag actions as depicted in Figure C-1. We will call this smart tag State Explorer. By default, smart tags are case-sensitive, therefore entering "NY," "CA," or other abbreviations included in your list of terms in uppercase will not be recognized as a smart tag.

Now let's proceed to write some XML code to define the list of terms and the actions for our State Explorer smart tag.

1. Open Notepad.

2. Type in the following XML document in Notepad. When you are done, save the file as **State.xml** anywhere on your hard drive. Later on, you will copy this file to the appropriate location to put your smart tags to work.

C:\State.xml

```
<FL:smarttaglist xmlns:FL="urn:schemas-microsoft-com:smarttags:list">
    <FL:name>Explore the States</FL:name>
    <FL:description>Shows detailed state info</FL:description>
    <FL:updateable>false</FL:updateable>
    <FL:updatefrequency>10080</FL:updatefrequency>
    <FL:autoupdate>true</FL:autoupdate>
    <FL:smarttag type="urn:schemas-microsoft-com:office:smarttags#States">
        <FL:caption>State Explorer</FL:caption>
        <FL:terms>
            <FL:termlist>"mt", "sd", "ny", "ca", "oh", "ne", "ar", "md", _
            "fl", "ga"</FL:termlist>
        </FL:terms>
        <FL:actions>
            <FL:action id="StateLookup">
              <FL:caption>View State Information</FL:caption>
              <FL:url>http://www.americaslibrary.gov/cgi-bin/page.cgi/ _
                  es?subject={TEXT}</FL:url>
        </FL:action>
            <FL:action id="MoreInfo">
              <FL:caption>More State Info</FL:caption>
              <FL:url>http://www.ipl.org/div/kidspace/stateknow/ _
                  {TEXT}1.html</FL:url>
        </FL:action>
         <FL:action id="Facts">
              <FL:caption>Did You Know...</FL:caption>
              <FL:url>http://www.ipl.org/div/kidspace/stateknow/ _
                  {TEXT}2.html</FL:url>
         </FL:action>
         </FL:actions>
    </FL:smarttag>
</FL:smarttaglist>
```

The XML code that you have just entered describes your smart tag using a specific syntax defined by Microsoft. As mentioned in Chapter 17, the XML document begins by specifying a root element and declaring a namespace. The namespace is stated in the form of the Uniform Resource Indicator (URI) to uniquely identify a group of XML tags belonging to a logical category. For smart tags, the "urn:schemas-microsoft-com:smarttags:list" URI is used. Notice that this name is preceded by an alias "FL"—a short name for this namespace. The root element is named smarttaglist. This element is contained within the FL namespace. Therefore, each smart tag list that you develop using XML should begin with:

```
<FL:smarttaglist xmlns:FL="urn:schemas-microsoft-com:smarttags:list">
```

and end with a closing tag:

```
</FL:smarttaglist>
```

Once you've declared a smart tag, you need to specify certain properties, such as a friendly name for the smart tag recognizer:

```
<FL:name>Explore the States</FL:name>
```

The name element is required. The optional description element is a longer string describing the smart tag:

```
<FL:description>Shows detailed state info</FL:description>
```

The optional elements, such as updateable, updatefrequency, and autoupdate, as well as lastcheckpoint, lastupdate, and updateurl (not specified here), tell if the smart tag list can be updated, and if so, how often the update should occur, when the last update occurred, and which URL to check for updates to the smart tag list. The default value of updatefrequency is 10,080 minutes (seven days). The State Explorer smart tag uses some of these elements for demonstration only. Our term list will not be updatable as coded here. To recognize more states, you will have to manually add new state abbreviations to the term list, save the modified XML file, and relaunch Excel before your changes can take effect. To find out how you can replace one smart tag list with another on a scheduled basis, check this topic in the Smart Tag software development kit (Smart Tag SDK).

A smart tag type is defined by a unique namespace in the form of a URI and a tag name, as in the following line of code:

```
<FL:smarttag type="urn:schemas-microsoft-com:office:smarttags#States">
```

The smart tag element is absolutely required. In the above line, "urn:schemas-microsoft-com:office:smarttags" is the name of the namespace and "States" is the tag name. The tag name is always preceded with the "#" symbol. The tag name can be any unique string.

After the definition of the smart tag type, you need to define the caption and terms for the tag type. For example:

```
<FL:caption>State Explorer</FL:caption>
    <FL:terms>
        <FL:termlist>"mt", "sd", "ny", "ca", "oh", "ne", "ar", "md", _
            "fl", "ga"</FL:termlist>
    </FL:terms>
```

The caption is what will appear at the top of the Smart Tag Actions menu when the user clicks the Smart Tag button. The terms element can be one of the following: a termlist or a termfile. A _termlist_ is a comma-delimited list of terms. Double quotes denote that the terms are case-sensitive. The specified state abbreviations will be recognized only when typed in lowercase. A _termfile_ is a special binary file (.bin) containing your terms. Microsoft offers two utilities (MakeTrie and TestTrie) that can be used to prepare such a file. You may download these advanced tools from the Microsoft web site.

Once you have defined the terms, you need to specify the actions that will take place when the user clicks on the Smart Tag button. In this example, we have defined three actions:

```
<FL:actions>
    <FL:action id="StateLookup">
        <FL:caption>View State Information</FL:caption>
        <FL:url>http://www.americaslibrary.gov/cgi-bin/page.cgi/ _
                es?subject={TEXT}</FL:url>
    </FL:action>
    <FL:action id="MoreInfo">
        <FL:caption>More State Info</FL:caption>
        <FL:url>http://www.ipl.org/div/kidspace/stateknow/ _
                {TEXT}1.html</FL:url>
    </FL:action>
    <FL:action id="Facts">
        <FL:caption>Did You Know...</FL:caption>
        <FL:url>http://www.ipl.org/div/kidspace/stateknow/ _
                {TEXT}2.html</FL:url>
    </FL:action>
</FL:actions>
```

Notice that each action has an action ID, a caption, and the URL that should be activated when the user selects a smart tag menu item. The first action will open the browser, navigate to the americaslibrary.gov web site, and invoke the cgi application named page.cgi located in the cgi-bin folder. Once there, it will run the script named "es," passing to it the name of the term as the subject argument. Note that {TEXT} will be substituted with the term that caused the smart tag to be invoked. The other two actions in this example will navigate to another web address and run appropriate HTML files. Notice that in both examples the name of the HTML file includes the name of the term. Before you define your smart tag actions, you need to investigate which arguments are required to get the information you need from a specific web site.

Storing Smart Tag List Definition Files

Before you or your users can take advantage of the State Explorer tag you've just defined, you must save your smart tag list definition code in an XML file in a proper location on your computer.

1. Move or copy the State.xml file that you prepared in the previous section into the following folder:

    `\Program Files\Common Files\Microsoft Shared\Smart Tag\Lists`

Smart tag lists placed in the above directory will be available to all users.

Note: If the smart tag has been designed for a specific user, you should place it in the following folder:

`\Documents and Settings\username\Application Data\Microsoft\Smart Tag Lists`

Placing the smart tag list in the above directory will ensure that the list roams with the user.

Smart tag lists created with XML use the MOFL.DLL file included with Microsoft Office XP. This file is installed in the C:\Program Files\Common Files\Microsoft Shared\Smart tag folder.

Using Custom Smart Tags

Before you distribute your smart tag solutions to other users, be sure to test the solution on your computer to ensure that it performs as desired. After moving or copying your smart tag definition file (.xml) into the \Program Files\Common Files\Microsoft Shared\Smart Tag\Lists folder on your computer, launch Excel and open a blank worksheet. Next, click in any cell and type one of the terms that you defined in the terms file, using upper- or lowercase letters as required. Recall that the State Explorer smart tag will recognize only the state abbreviations written in lowercase letters. If you find that your smart tag does not perform as planned, you should quit Excel and edit your XML file. Resave the file with the newly made changes and relaunch Excel. You must restart Excel each time you make changes in the smart tag list definition files because the workbooks are scanned for smart tag recognizers only once (when the Excel application starts).

Information Lookups via ASP Pages

Earlier in this appendix you learned how to create smart tag actions that navigate to a specific web site when a user enters a term that is stored in the XML term list. Instead of sending users to public or commercial web sites, you may want to program actions that link to your own ASP pages and return appropriate data from your database. The XML smart tag list description file can call the ASP script and pass to it the required term to look up, as well as other arguments that you may find necessary for your script. To illustrate how you can provide information lookups via ASP pages, let's create a new XML smart tag list description file that will display information related to some customers in the Northwind database. We will call this new smart tag Customer Information. Figure C-3 displays smart tag actions that we will implement for this smart tag.

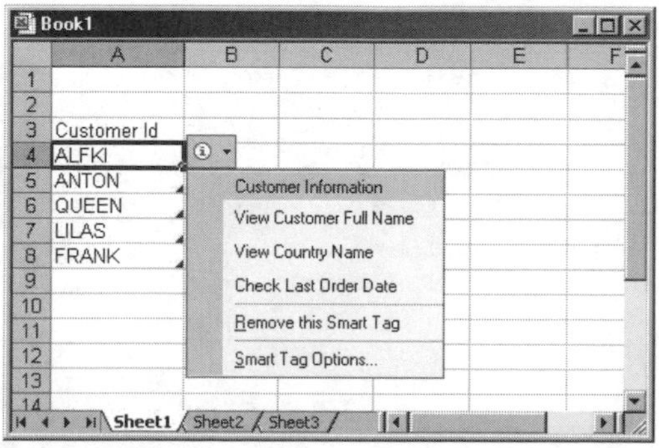

Figure C-3:
This custom smart tag will access data from the Northwind database.

1. Open Notepad and prepare the XML document shown in Figure C-4.
    When you are done, save the file as **Customer.xml** in the C:\Program
    Files\Common Files\Microsoft Shared\Smart Tag\Lists folder.

Note: The next few steps will walk you through setting up a
virtual directory on your computer. You will use this directory to
store your ASP script, which you will prepare later. For more
information on creating virtual directories and Active Server
Pages (ASP), refer to Chapter 16 of this book.

2. Create a new folder on your computer named **C:\Inetpub\www-
    root\SmartTags**.

3. Right-click the **C:\Inetpub\wwwroot\SmartTags** folder name and
    choose **Properties**.

4. In the Properties dialog box, click the **Web Sharing** tab.

5. Click the **Share This Folder** option button and click the **Add** button.

6. In the Alias text box, enter **Tags** as the name of your virtual directory.
    The Edit Alias dialog box should have the Read Access permission and
    Scripts Application permission selected. Click **OK** to exit the Edit Alias
    dialog box.

7. Locate the Northwind.mdb file on your computer and copy it to the
    C:\Inetpub\wwwroot\SmartTags folder.

```
Customer.xml - Notepad
File  Edit  Format  Help
<FL:smarttaglist xmlns:FL="urn:schemas-microsoft-com:smarttags:list">
 <FL:name>Customer Info</FL:name>
 <FL:lcid>1033,0</FL:lcid>
 <FL:description>Displays Information about Customers</FL:description>
 <FL:updateable>false</FL:updateable>
 <FL:updatefrequency>10080</FL:updatefrequency>
 <FL:autoupdate>true</FL:autoupdate>
 <FL:smarttag type="urn:schemas-internal-office:northwind#Customers">
  <FL:caption>Customer Information</FL:caption>
   <FL:terms>
    <FL:termlist>ALFKI, ANTON, FRANK, LILAS, QUEEN</FL:termlist>
   </FL:terms>
   <FL:actions>
    <FL:action id="NameLookup">
     <FL:caption>View Customer Full Name</FL:caption>
     <FL:url>http://localhost/tags/getInfo.asp?Term={TEXT}&amp;ActionId=NameLookup</FL:url>
    </FL:action>
    <FL:action id="CountryLookup">
     <FL:caption>View Country Name</FL:caption>
     <FL:url>http://localhost/tags/getInfo.asp?Term={TEXT}&amp;ActionId=CountryLookup</FL:url>
    </FL:action>
    <FL:action id="LastOrderDateLookup">
     <FL:caption>Check Last Order Date</FL:caption>
     <FL:url>http://localhost/tags/getInfo.asp?Term={TEXT}&amp;ActionId=LastOrderDateLookup</FL:url>
    </FL:action>
   </FL:actions>
 </FL:smarttag>
</FL:smarttaglist>
```

Figure C-4: The XML smart tag list definition file can link to ASP script.

The XML code shown above uses the same elements as the State Explorer smart tag that you prepared in an earlier example. This time, however, the termlist contains the customer IDs that you would like to look up in a database on your server. Because the customer IDs are not enclosed in double quotes, they will be recognized whether they are typed in upper- or lowercase letters. Let's take a closer look at the defined actions because they differ a bit from what you've seen in the State Explorer smart tag. To query a database, you need to reference your ASP script in the URL element, as follows:

```
<FL:action id="NameLookup">
  <FL:caption>View Customer Full Name</FL:caption>
  <FL:url>http://localhost/tags/getInfo.asp?Term= _
      {TEXT}&amp;ActionId=NameLookup</FL:url>
</FL:action>
```

The above code will execute the getInfo.asp script (which is located in the virtual directory named tags on the local server) upon selection of the View Customer Full Name option from the Smart Actions menu. The code of the getInfo.asp script is shown below. Notice that this script file expects two parameters that are provided at the end of a URL following the "?" character. The first parameter will pass the customer ID, and the second one will pass the action ID. The action ID will allow the script to decide which SQL statement should be run to return the data. This way, you can have one Active Server Page handle all of your smart actions. Recall that when you pass parameters to ASP pages, they are separated by the ampersand (&). In your XML code, however, to ensure proper parsing and interpretation, the parameters must be separated by "&" like this:

```
<FL:url>http://localhost/tags/getInfo.asp?Term={TEXT} _
    &amp;ActionId=NameLookup</FL:url>
```

When you call the ASP page, the URL will be parsed as follows:

```
http://localhost/tags/getInfo.asp?Term=ALFKI&ActionId=NameLookup
```

8. Open Notepad and prepare the ASP script file shown below. When you are done, save the file as **getInfo.asp** in the C:\Inetpub\wwwroot\ SmartTags folder.

C:\Inetpub\wwwroot\SmartTags\GetInfo.asp

```
<%@ Language=VBScript %>
<%

Dim conn
Dim strSearch
Dim strstrSQL

strSearch = Request.QueryString("Term")
strAction = Request.QueryString("ActionId")
```

```
' establish connection to the database
 conn="Provider=Microsoft.Jet.OleDB.4.0; Data Source=" & _
   Server.Mappath("Northwind.mdb")

' build SQL statement
Select Case strAction
 Case "NameLookup", "CountryLookup"
  strSQL = strSQL & "SELECT * FROM Customers"
  strSQL = strSQL & " WHERE Customers.CustomerId = "
  strSQL = strSQL & "'" & strSearch & "'"
 Case "LastOrderDateLookup"
  strSQL = strSQL & "SELECT Customers.CustomerID,"
  strSQL = strSQL & " Max(Orders.OrderDate) AS LastDate"
  strSQL = strSQL & " FROM Customers INNER JOIN Orders"
  strSQL = strSQL & " ON Customers.CustomerID = Orders.CustomerID"
  strSQL = strSQL & " GROUP BY Customers.CustomerID"
  strSQL = strSQL & " HAVING (((Customers.CustomerID)="
  strSQL = strSQL & "'" & strSearch & "'))"
End Select

' Create a Recordset
 Set rst = CreateObject("ADODB.Recordset")

' Open a static (3) Recordset (and execute the SQL
' statement above) using the open connection
 rst.Open strSQL, conn, 3

' Display information if found
If not rst.EOF then
 Response.Write strSearch & ": "

 Select Case strAction
  Case "NameLookup"
   Response.Write "<B>" & rst("CompanyName").value & "</B>"
  Case "CountryLookup"
   Response.Write "<B>" & rst("Country").value & "</B>"
  Case "LastOrderDateLookup"
   Response.Write "<B>" & rst("LastDate").value & "</B>"
 End Select
Else
 Response.Write "No match for the specified ID: "
 Response.Write strSearch
End if

rst.close
set rst = Nothing
Set conn = Nothing
%>
```

The ASP script that you've just created begins by retrieving the required
parameters. Notice that this is done through the QueryString collection of
the Request object:

```
strSearch = Request.QueryString("Term")
```

```
strAction = Request.QueryString("ActionId")
```

Next, a connection to the Northwind database is established using the Microsoft Jet OLEDB.4.0 provider. For this connection to work properly, you need to place the Northwind.mdb file in the virtual directory that you created earlier, or change the connection string to point to a different location where this file is located. To look up a customer ID and return a different type of information from the database depending on a selected Smart Tag action, you need to build appropriate SQL statements. The first two actions will use the same SQL statement, as the information that you want to return is located in the same table. This SQL statement simply says to select all fields from the Customers table where CustomerId is the ID (term) that the user had typed:

```
strSQL = strSQL & "SELECT * FROM Customers"
  strSQL = strSQL & " WHERE Customers.CustomerId = "
  strSQL = strSQL & "'" & strSearch & "'"
```

In the above statement, the strSearch variable holds the value of the customer ID that was typed by the user in a worksheet cell.

The date lookup will require a different, more complex SQL statement. This statement says to select the CustomerId field and a calculated field named LastDate obtained by applying the Max function to the OrderDate field in the Orders table. The two tables (Customers, Orders) necessary to obtain this information are to be joined on the CustomerId field. All information will be grouped by CustomerId. The Having clause will limit the returned records to the one record meeting our criteria—the CustomerId (term) provided by the user in a worksheet:

```
strSQL = strSQL & "SELECT Customers.CustomerID,"
  strSQL = strSQL & " Max(Orders.OrderDate) AS LastDate"
  strSQL = strSQL & " FROM Customers INNER JOIN Orders"
  strSQL = strSQL & " ON Customers.CustomerID = Orders.CustomerID"
  strSQL = strSQL & " GROUP BY Customers.CustomerID"
  strSQL = strSQL & " HAVING (((Customers.CustomerID)="
  strSQL = strSQL & "'" & strSearch & "'))"
```

The Select Case statement will allow you to build an SQL statement based on the action ID.

The next statements in the code create and open the recordset based on the SQL statement using the open connection to the database. The remaining code deals with the display of data. If the returned recordset is not empty, we will read the value of the CompanyName, Country, or LastDate field, depending on the type of action that the user has selected. Otherwise, we will display a message that the data for the specified ID was not found. This ASP script is pretty straightforward. For more practice with scripting, check out Chapter 16.

9. Now that you have both the XML smart tag description file (Customer.xml) and the ASP script file (getInfo.asp) ready and placed in the

appropriate directories, launch Microsoft Excel. Activate any cell in any workbook and type one of the terms defined in the Customer.xml file. When the Smart Tag options button appears, select one of the options. You should see the requested information appear in your browser (see Figure C-5).

Note: If you are looking for the ability to feed information that you have looked up back into Microsoft Excel, you will need to take the DLL approach to creating smart tags. You can find examples on how to do this in the Smart Tags SDK.

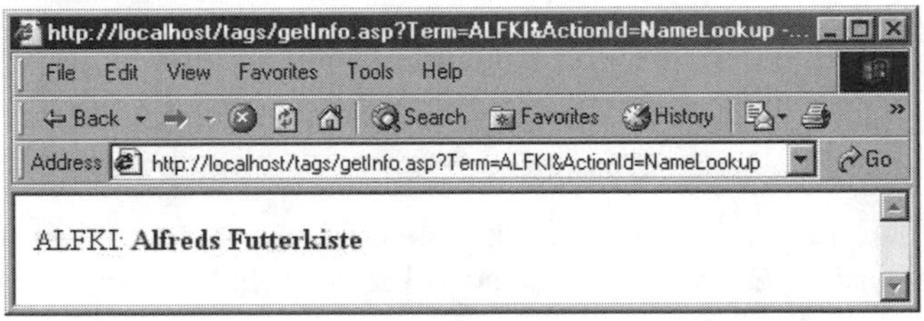

Figure C-5:
A simple smart tag can pull the requested information from a database and display it in a browser.

Manipulating Smart Tags with VBA

To support new smart tag functionality, new objects have been added to the Microsoft Excel 2002 object model. You can use VBA to control the display of smart tags, add a smart tag to a worksheet cell, and execute any of the smart tag actions. The following sections introduce you to smart tag objects and get you started manipulating them with VBA.

SmartTag Object

A SmartTag object represents an identifier assigned to a worksheet cell. Each SmartTag object belongs to a SmartTag collection. To return a SmartTag object, use the Add method of the SmartTags collection. Once the SmartTag object is returned, you can access its properties and methods as shown below.

Figure C-6:
Properties and methods of the SmartTag object

SmartTagAction Object

Use the SmartTagAction object to access actions that can be performed with smart tags. Each SmartTagAction object is a member of a SmartTag-Actions collection. Use the Item property of the SmartTagActions collection to return the SmartTagAction object. This object has four properties and one method, as illustrated in Figure C-7. Use the Execute method to invoke a smart tag action.

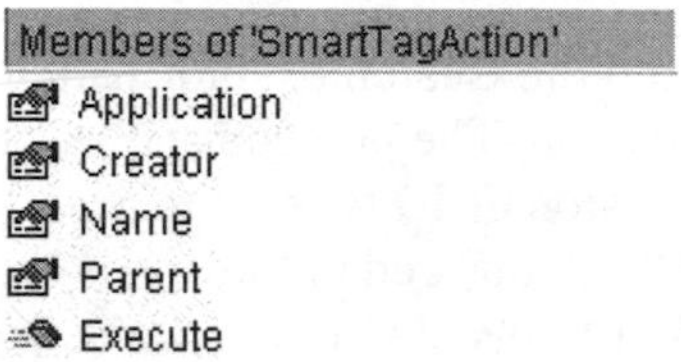

Members of 'SmartTagAction'
🔊 Application
🔊 Creator
🔊 Name
🔊 Parent
▪◈ Execute

Figure C-7:
Properties and methods of the
SmartTagAction object

SmartTagOptions Object

You can control options that can be performed with smart tags with the SmartTagOptions object. Use the SmartTagOptions property of the Workbook object to return a SmartTagOptions object. Use the EmbedSmartTags property of the SmartTagOptions object to turn on or off the embedding of smart tags in a workbook. Use the DisplaySmartTags property of the SmartTagOptions object to control the display features of the smart tags.

SmartTagRecognizer Object

When you type certain data in Microsoft Excel, data that is recognized by the installed recognition engine is tagged. Use the SmartTagRecognizer object to determine if tag recognizers are enabled for the entire application. The SmartTagRecognizer is a member of the SmartTagRecognizers collection. You can return a single SmartTagRecognizer via the Item property of the SmartTagRecognizers collection.

Now let's spend a few minutes working with the above-mentioned objects.

1. Enter **MSFT** in cell **B5** in any worksheet.

2. Switch to a Visual Basic Editor window.

3. Press **Ctrl+G** to activate the Immediate window.

4. In the Immediate window, enter the following statements and review the results:

```
?Range("B5").SmartTags(1).Name
urn:schemas-microsoft-com:office:smarttags#stockticker

?Range("B5").SmartTags(1).SmartTagActions(1).Name
Insert refreshable stock price...
```

```
?Range("B5").SmartTags(1).SmartTagActions(2).Name
LatestQuoteData

?Range("B5").SmartTags(1).SmartTagActions(2).Parent
urn:schemas-microsoft-com:office:smarttags#stockticker

Range("B5").SmartTags(1).SmartTagActions(2).Execute

?Range("B5").SmartTags(1).XML
<xml xmlns:fa1="urn:schemas-microsoft-com:office:smarttags"> _
        <fa1:stockticker>MSFT</fa1:stockticker></xml>
```

The following example procedure relates to the Customer Information
smart tag that was created in an earlier section. The procedure illustrates
how, by using VBA, you can recognize a customer ID typed into a worksheet cell, even though that particular ID is not stored in the smart tag list
description file that was created using the Extensible Markup Language
(XML). Recall that the Customer.xml file contains just a few customer IDs.
This procedure prompts you for a customer ID and then executes the first
smart action, which returns the customer's full name.

```
Sub AddNExecute_SmartTag()
    Dim strValue
    Dim strLink

    strLink = "urn:schemas-internal-office:northwind#Customers"

    ' get Customer Id from the user
     strValue = InputBox("Enter an ID of a Northwind customer " _
    & "that is not in the Customer.xml " _
    & "Smart Tag list description file:", "Enter: Customer Id")

    ' exit if user clicked Cancel
    If strValue = "" Then Exit Sub

     ' set Smart Tag options to embed and recognize smart tags
    ActiveWorkbook.SmartTagOptions.EmbedSmartTags = True
    Application.SmartTagRecognizers.Recognize = True

    With Range("B5")
        .Formula = strValue
        .SmartTags.Add(strLink).SmartTagActions(1).Execute
    End With
End Sub
```

Appendix D

Microsoft Office XP Web Components

Some of the powerful functionality of Microsoft Excel 2002 can be made available outside of Microsoft Excel via a collection of ActiveX controls known as Microsoft XP web components. This collection is composed of four components: a spreadsheet, chart, pivot table, and data source. Web components can be used not only in web pages (as the name implies) but also in other applications and environments, such as Microsoft Access, Visual Basic, and C++.

Let's say you need to display information on a web site or an Access form in an Excel-like interface. By incorporating the Spreadsheet component into your application, you can provide your users with features that Microsoft Excel handles extremely well: recalculation, filtering, and sorting. Or, if you want to perform these operations just in the background, you can use the Spreadsheet component as an invisible calculation engine. The Chart component will allow you to create flexible solutions that require graphing, while the PivotTable component will provide your users with data manipulation options for viewing data from different perspectives, similar to those found in the built-in Excel PivotTable feature. The fourth component, Data Source, does not have a graphical user interface. It is invisible to the user and used for managing connections to a database and binding to other web components.

> **Tip:** **Licensing Required.** To personally use Microsoft Office XP web components, you must have the Microsoft Office XP web components installed and an appropriate Office XP license. If your applications utilize Office XP web components, your users do not need to have Office XP installed on their computers, but they do need to have a license for it. You can get an Office XP site license that permits intranet distribution and configure the components to allow the users to download them from your corporate intranet.

Each Office web component is identified with a ClassId, as shown below:

Component Name	ClassId
Spreadsheet	classid="CLSID:0002E510-0000-0000-C000-000000000046"
Chart	classid="CLSID:0002E500-0000-0000-C000-000000000046"
PivotTable	classid="CLSID:0002E520-0000-0000-C000-000000000046"
Data Source	classid="CLSID:0002E530-0000-0000-C000-000000000046"

If used on web pages, web components require Internet Explorer 4.01 or later. For best functionality, use Internet Explorer 5 or later. To use web components in other applications, make a reference to the Microsoft Office XP Web Components Library (OWC10). This library is stored in C:\Program Files\Common Files\Microsoft Shared\Web Components\10\OWC-10.DLL. After setting up a reference to the OWC10 Library, you can open the Object Browser and take a look at numerous properties, methods, and events that you can use to manipulate various web components.

Figure D-1:
Use the Object Browser to look up properties, methods, and events of the Spreadsheet, Chart, PivotTable, and Data Source web components.

You can find a lot of useful information on the OWC10 object model and many code samples in the online help files located in the folder C:\Program Files\Common Files\Microsoft Shared\Web Components\10\1033. Consider this appendix as a quick, hands-on introduction to scripting web components from a web page.

The Spreadsheet Web Component

Because you already know how to use a Microsoft Excel Workbook object, you will find it extremely easy to work with the Spreadsheet component. This component is very useful for displaying formatted data, performing calculations, or simply providing your users with a quick way to enter, calculate, and store data. The current XP version of the Spreadsheet component supports multiple worksheets containing 262,144 rows and 18,278 columns (ZZZ) each. Creating business solutions that utilize the Spreadsheet component is not complicated because the component uses Excel properties, methods, and events that you are already familiar with. The best way to learn about the Spreadsheet and the other three Office web components is, of course, by example. Our example for the Spreadsheet component is very simple. You will create an HTML form with the embedded Spreadsheet component. This form will have three buttons (see Figure D-2) for performing different operations, such as renaming the active worksheet, populating the worksheet with data, and saving the data to an Excel file. Let's get started.

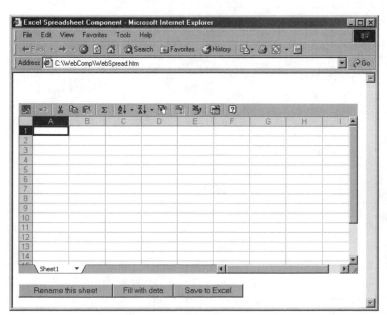

Figure D-2:
The Spreadsheet web component on a web page. Notice the familiar spreadsheet tools at the top of this ActiveX control. Use the Commands and Options buttons to the left of the Help tool to access additional formatting options. Many options are available via a shortcut menu by right-clicking on any cell.

1. Create a new folder named **C:\WebComp**.
2. Open Notepad and enter the script shown below.
3. Save the file as **C:\WebComp\WebSpread.htm**.

```
<html>
<Title>Excel Spreadsheet Component</Title>
<body>
<br/>
<br/>
<object classid="clsid:0002E551-0000-0000-C000-000000000046"
    id="Spread1" width=600 height=300>
</object>
<br/>
<br/>
<button id="btnRename">Rename this sheet</button>
<button id="btnFill">Fill with data</button>
<button id="btnSave">Save to Excel</button>

<SCRIPT LANGUAGE="VBScript">

Dim num      ' global variable (Integer)

Sub btnRename_OnClick()
Dim curSh  ' ActiveSheet

set curSh = Spread1.ActiveSheet

Alert "Spreadsheet Web Component contains: " & vbCrLf _
     & curSh.rows.count & " rows" & vbCrLf _
     & curSh.columns.count & " columns "

  If curSh.UsedRange.Address = "$A$1" and _
     curSh.Cells(1,1).value = "" then
         Alert "No data in this sheet."
  Else
   num = num + 1
   curSh.name = "My Data" & num
  End if
End Sub

Sub btnFill_OnClick()
Dim conn
Dim rst
Dim strSQL
Dim count
Dim r
Dim c
Dim myData

  ' establish connection to the database
   conn="Provider=Microsoft.Jet.OleDB.4.0; Data Source=" & _
     "C:\Program Files\Microsoft Office\Office\" & _
     "Samples\Northwind.mdb"
```

```
' Create a Recordset
Set rst = CreateObject("ADODB.Recordset")
' select all records from Order Details table
strSql = "SELECT * FROM [Order Details]"

' Open a static (3) Recordset (and execute the SQL
' statement above) using the open connection
rst.Open strSql, conn, 3

' enter field names as column headings
For count = 0 to rst.fields.count - 1
     r = r + 1
     With Spread1.ActiveSheet.Cells(1, r)
        .Value = rst.Fields(count).Name
        .Font.Bold = True
     End with
Next

' store data in the Recordset into the variable
' data is stored as a two-dimensional array
myData = rst.GetRows()
returnedRows = UBound(mydata, 2) + 1

' enter data into worksheet cells
For r = 1 to returnedRows
 For c = 1 to rst.Fields.Count
    Spread1.ActiveSheet.Cells(r+1, c).value = myData(c-1, r-1)
 Next
Next
 ' close the Recordset
 rst.close
 set rst = Nothing
End Sub

Sub btnSave_OnClick()
 Dim strFileName
 Dim fso
 Dim txtStream
 Dim strData

 strFileName="C:\myDataBook.xls"
 set fso = CreateObject("Scripting.FileSystemObject")
 set txtStream = fso.CreateTextFile(strFileName)
 Spread1.DataType="HTMLData"
 strData = Spread1.HTMLData
 txtStream.WriteLine strData
 txtStream.Close
 set txtStream = Nothing
 Set fso = Nothing
 MsgBox "Your spreadsheet data was saved in " & _
              strFileName & " file."
End Sub
</SCRIPT>
```

```
</body>
</html>
```

Use the HTML <OBJECT> tag to add an Office web component to a web page. The component type is specified by the control's class identifier. For example, the following code places a Spreadsheet web component on a web page:

```
<object classid="clsid:0002E551-0000-0000-C000-000000000046"
    id="Spread1" width=600 height=300>
</object>
```

You can assign a name to the component by using the Id attribute. Also, you can specify the size and width of the ActiveX control via the width and height attributes. Notice that after you add the web component to a web page, you need to write some script to react to user actions. Each of the three buttons placed on the web page has an OnClick procedure attached to it. In your script, you reference the Spreadsheet web component by using the value of its Id attribute (in this case, Spread1). Figure D-3 illustrates the Spreadsheet web component after it has been filled with data from the Northwind database.

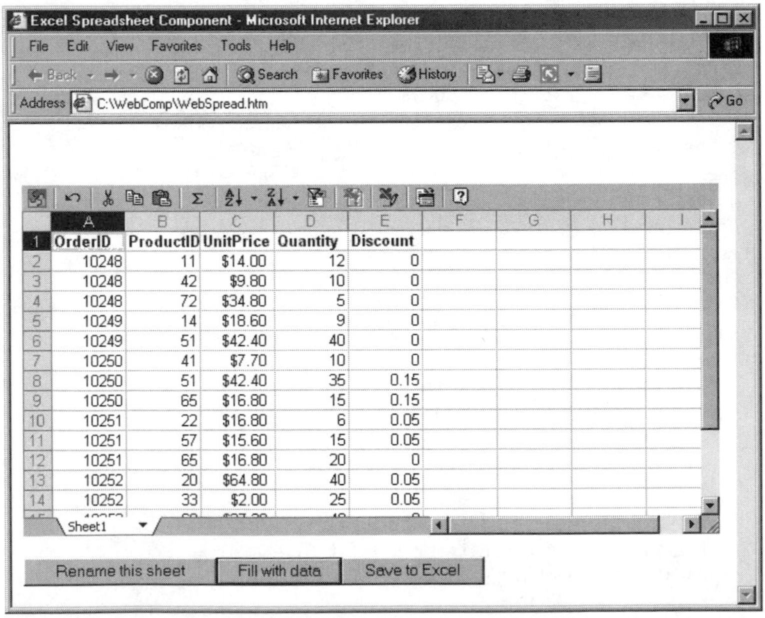

Figure D-3: The Spreadsheet web component populated with the data from a database

The btnFill_OnClick procedure (attached to the second button) demonstrates how to connect with the Access database using the Microsoft Jet OleDB provider and the GetRows method of the Recordset object to retrieve the data. If the worksheet already contains data, the existing data will be replaced.

The Spreadsheet web component can be populated with data using several methods not presented here. For example, the user can enter the data manually, copy it from another file, or import data by using special properties of the LoadText method of the Range object (the CSVURL property will allow you to load data from the tab-delimited text file, CSV file, or an ASP script; HTMLURL will load data from the HTML file specified in URL; CSVData loads data using comma-separated values; HTMLData loads data using the HTMLData property; and XMLData loads data using the XMLData property).

Saving the spreadsheet data into an Excel file is accomplished via the third button placed on the web form. The btnSave_OnClick procedure that is attached to this button creates a file using the CreateTextFile method of the FileSystemObject (see details on working with text files in Chapter 8). The data is saved in the HTML format on the client's computer, using the following code:

```
Spread1.DataType="HTMLData"
strData = Spread1.HTMLData
txtStream.WriteLine strData
```

In the above code, the DataType property specifies the spreadsheet's data source and its format. It can be one of the following values: HTMLURL, HTMLData, CSVURL, or CSVData. The HTMLData value used in the example procedure indicates that the data source is the string specified by the HTMLData property. The HTMLData property returns a string that represents the spreadsheet data as a properly formatted HTML string.

Once you have the HTML string, you can write this string to a file by using the WriteLine method of the TextStream object. Recall that the TextStream object was returned by the CreateTextFile method of the FileSystemObject:

```
set fso = CreateObject("Scripting.FileSystemObject")
set txtStream = fso.CreateTextFile(strFileName)
```

Note: If you get a message saying the the CreateObject method of the Scripting.FileSystem object failed, ensure that the Internet Explorer security setting for Initialize and script ActiveX controls not marked as safe (see the Security tab (Custom Level) in the Internet Options dialog box) is set to either Prompt or Enable.

The Chart Web Component

The Office XP Chart component can display data from various sources, such as other web components (Spreadsheet, PivotTable, and Data Source controls), arrays, tab-delimited strings, and ADO recordsets. When the Chart component is bound to other web components, changes that are made to the data placed in those controls are immediately displayed on the chart. To create complex charts, you need to know numerous properties and methods that the chart object exposes. You can learn a lot about the Chart component object model from the OWCDCH10.CHM file located in the folder C:\Program Files\Common Files\Microsoft Shared\Web Components\10\1033.

This section will get you started creating simple charts on a web page. The first chart that you create will be bound to the spreadsheet component that was discussed in an earlier section. The second example will demonstrate how you can create multiple charts within the Web Chart component. Both examples use the client-side scripting code (VBScript) to create an HTML file, and they both chart data obtained dynamically from the Microsoft Access sample database (Northwind.mdb).

Charts are created within a chart workspace. The chart workspace can contain more than one chart (currently you can place as many as 16 charts in a chart workspace). Each chart in a workspace is represented by a chChart object. When the chart workspace is first created, it is empty. To insert a Chart web component on a web page, add an <OBJECT> tag and specify its class ID. The following statement will create a chart workspace named chrtSpace on an HTML page:

```
<object classid="clsid:0002E500-0000-0000-C000-000000000046" id= _
    "chrtSpace"></object>
```

Use the Clear method to clear the chart workspace of any existing charts. The chart workspace will then be completely empty.

To add a chart to the chart workspace, use the Add method of the chChart object, as follows:

```
chrtSpace.Charts.Add
```

The above statement creates a new chart. At this time, the chart is blank. To place data into the chart, use the SetData method. This method has three arguments, as described in the following table.

Argument Name	Description
Dimension	Specifies which part of the chart you want to populate with data. The following constants refer to the portion of the chart and are passed to the SetData method with the indicated enumerated constant:

Argument Name	Description	
Dimension (cont.)	SeriesNames	chDimSeriesNames
	Categories	chDimCategories
	Values	chDimValues
	Yvalues	chDimYValues
	Xvalues	chDimXValues
	OpenValues	chDimOpenValues
	CloseValues	chDimCloseValues
	HighValues	chDimHighValues
	LowValues	chDimLowValues
	BubbleValues	chDimBubbleValues
	Rvalues	chDimRValues
	ThetaValues	chThetaValues
DataSourceIndex	Specifies the source of data. This can be done via one of the following enumerated constants: chDataBound, chData-Linked, chDataLiteral, and chDataNone. The two code examples in this section demonstrate how to use the chDataBound and chDataLiteral constants.	
DataReference	Used to send the actual data for the chart. If the chart is bound to the Spreadsheet web component, you can specify an Excel range (for example, A2:A11). If the chart is bound to the ADO recordset, place the field name here (for example, rst.Fields(1)). If the data for the chart comes from an array or a tab-delimited string, place the name of the variable representing the array or string here.	

The following code fragment illustrates the use of the SetData method for a chart bound to the Spreadsheet component. Notice that the data is added here to the Series object.

```
With objChart.SeriesCollection(0)
    .SetData cons.chDimSeriesNames, chDataBound,"B1"
    .SetData cons.chDimCategories, chDataBound,"A2:A9"
    .SetData cons.chDimValues, chDataBound,"B2:B9"
End With
```

In the above code fragment, chDimSeriesNames, chDimCategories, and chDimValues are passed as the first argument of the SetData method. Notice that the names of these arguments are prefaced by the "cons" object. This object has been defined earlier in the VBScript code, like this:

```
set cons = chrtSpace.Constants
```

Because VBScript does not support the use of named constants, you must create a reference by using the Constants property, as shown above, and preface the constants with this object.

The chDataBound constant in the code snippet above serves as the DataSourceIndex argument of the SetData method. When the chart is bound to the first data source, you can use the data source index of 0 as the second argument of the SetData method, like this:

```
With objChart.SeriesCollection(0)
```

```
      .SetData cons.chDimSeriesNames, 0,"B1"
      .SetData cons.chDimCategories, 0,"A2:A9"
      .SetData cons.chDimValues, 0,"B2:B9"
End With
```

The index of 0 specifies the first data source in the WCDataSources collection. If your chart is based on multiple data sources, you can set data from the second data source by using index 1, and so on.

The third argument of the SetData method in the code fragment above uses an Excel Range reference to indicate that the data for the indicated chart portion is located in the specified worksheet range. Hence, "B1" above tells VBScript that the name of the series should be taken from cell B1. If you change the contents of cell B1, the name that appears in the legend will also be changed. It is not required, however, to bind the series name to the spreadsheet. You can use the SeriesCollection (0) Caption property to specify an independent name for the series. The "A2:A9" reference in the code above tells where the names of the categories are, and "B2:B9" indicates the location of data to be graphed. If the chart is bound to a recordset, you will place the required recordset field name instead of range references, like this:

```
With myChart
    .SetData cons.chDimCategories, 0, rst.Fields(0).Name
    .SetData cons.chDimValues, 0, rst.Fields(1).Name
End With
```

If you need to give your users the capability of saving the chart as a graphics file, use the ExportPicture method of the Chart component to generate a GIF, JPG, or PNG image of that chart, like this:

```
myChart.ExportPicture Server.MapPath(chartfilename), "gif", _
    width:=400, height:=200
```

Figure D-4 displays the result of opening the HTML file in a web browser created by the code that follows. Notice that the Spreadsheet component is presented here without its toolbar. Also, the control is sized exactly to the data, and its viewable range is limited to the data. The user is not allowed to scroll to other areas of the spreadsheet. Change the data in the spreadsheet, and notice that the chart is updated accordingly.

To prepare the web page shown in Figure D-4, open Notepad and enter the following HTML and VBScript code. Ensure that the path points to the Northwind database on your server. Save the file as WebChart.htm. You can find this file on the companion CD-ROM.

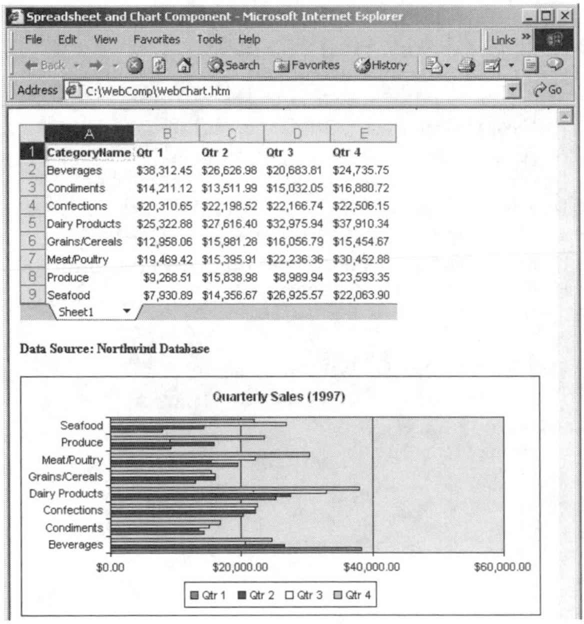

Figure D-4:
A web Chart component is bound to the Spreadsheet component that retrieves data from a database.

WebChart.htm

```
<html>
<Title>Spreadsheet and Chart Component</Title>
<body>
<object classid="clsid:0002E551-0000-0000-C000-000000000046" id="Spread1" >
</object>
<br/>
<h5>Data Source: Northwind Database </h5><p>
<object classid="clsid:0002E500-0000-0000-C000-000000000046" id="chrtSpace"
width=500 height=230></object>
<br/>

<SCRIPT LANGUAGE="VBScript">

Sub Window_OnLoad()

' Declare variables
Dim strConnection, rst, strSQL, count, r, c, myData, cons, objChart

' the connection string
strConnection="Provider=Microsoft.Jet.OleDB.4.0; data source=" & _
    "C:\Program Files\Microsoft Office\Office\Samples\Northwind.mdb"

' Create a Recordset
Set rst = CreateObject("ADODB.Recordset")

' define the SQL query to supply the data for charting
strSql = "TRANSFORM Sum([Order Details].[Quantity]*(" _
            & "[Order Details].[UnitPrice]-" _
```

```
                 & "([Order Details].[Discount]/100)*"
                 & "[Order Details].[UnitPrice])) AS Sales  " _
                 & "SELECT [Categories].[CategoryName]  " _
                 & "FROM (Categories INNER JOIN Products " _
                 & "ON [Categories].[CategoryID]=[Products].[CategoryID])" _
                 & "INNER JOIN (Orders INNER JOIN [Order Details] " _
                 & "ON [Orders].[OrderID]=[Order Details].[OrderID]) " _
                 & "ON [Products].[ProductID]=[Order Details].[ProductID]  " _
                 & "WHERE (((DatePart('yyyy',[OrderDate]))=1997))  " _
                 & "GROUP BY [Categories].[CategoryName]  " _
                 & "ORDER BY [Categories].[CategoryName]  " _
                 & "PIVOT 'Qtr ' & DatePart('q',[OrderDate])  "

' Open Recordset (and execute the SQL statement above)
' use the connection string with a client-side cursor (3)
' and static dataset (3)
rst.Open strSql, strConnection, 3, 3

' Enter field names as column headings in Spreadsheet control
For count = 0 to rst.fields.count - 1
    r = r + 1
    With Spread1.ActiveSheet.Cells(1, r)
      .Value = rst.Fields(count).Name
      .Font.Bold = True
      .Font.Color = "blue"
    End with
Next

' retrieve rows from the Recordset
' and fill an array with the resulting data
myData = rst.GetRows()

' determine how many rows were actually returned
returnedRows = UBound(mydata, 2) + 1

' read the array and copy data to the Spreadsheet control
For r = 1 to returnedRows
   For c = 1 to rst.Fields.Count
      Spread1.ActiveSheet.Cells(r+1, c).value = myData(c-1, r-1)
   Next
Next

' cleanup
rst.close
set rst = Nothing

'format the Spreadsheet control including the data
With Spread1
  .DisplayGridlines = False
  .DisplayToolbar = False
  .ViewableRange = Spread1.ActiveSheet.UsedRange.Address
  .AutoFit = True
  With .ActiveSheet.UsedRange
   .Font.Size = 8
```

```
        .Columns.AutoFit
      End With
End With


'-------------------------------------------------------------
' Create a column chart with four series showing the category
' sales by quarter in 1997
'-------------------------------------------------------------
' Clear the contents of the chrtspace object
' and format the title
With chrtSpace
  .Clear
  .HasChartSpaceTitle = True
    With  .ChartSpaceTitle
      .Caption = "Quarterly Sales (1997)"
      .Font.Size = 9
      .Font.Bold = True
    End With
End With


' Bind the Spreadsheet component to the chart
chrtSpace.DataSource = Spread1

' Get constants for the Chart component
set cons = chrtSpace.Constants

' Add a new chart to chrtSpace
set objChart = chrtSpace.Charts.Add

' Specify that the chart is a column chart
objChart.Type = cons.chChartTypeBarClustered

' Add four series to the chart
objChart.SeriesCollection.Add
objChart.SeriesCollection.Add
objChart.SeriesCollection.Add
objChart.SeriesCollection.Add

' Series one contains Qtr 1 sales
With objChart.SeriesCollection(0)
    .SetData cons.chDimSeriesNames, chDataBound,"B1"
    .SetData cons.chDimCategories, chDataBound,"A2:A9"
    .SetData cons.chDimValues, chDataBound,"B2:B9"
End With

' Series two contains Qtr 2 sales
With objChart.SeriesCollection(1)
    .SetData cons.chDimSeriesNames, chDataBound,"C1"
    .SetData cons.chDimCategories, chDataBound,"A2:A9"
    .SetData cons.chDimValues, chDataBound,"C2:C9"
End With

' Series three contains Qtr 3 sales
With objChart.SeriesCollection(2)
```

```
        .SetData cons.chDimSeriesNames, chDataBound,"D1"
        .SetData cons.chDimCategories, chDataBound,"A2:A9"
        .SetData cons.chDimValues, chDataBound,"D2:D9"
End With

' Series four contains Qtr 4 sales
With objChart.SeriesCollection(3)
        .SetData cons.chDimSeriesNames, chDataBound,"E1"
        .SetData cons.chDimCategories, chDataBound,"A2:A9"
        .SetData cons.chDimValues, chDataBound,"E2:E9"
End With

'Specify position for the chart legend
With objChart
        .HasLegend = True
        .Legend.Position = cons.chLegendPositionBottom
End With

End Sub

</SCRIPT>
</body>
</html>
```

Programmatically, you can add as many as 16 charts to the chart workspace. Multiple charts can be displayed in rows or columns. You can control the chart layout with the ChartLayout property of the ChartSpace object. The following statement will position the charts side by side:

```
chrtSpace.ChartLayout = cons.chChartLayoutHorizontal
```

The following layout values are available:

0	chChartLayoutAutomatic
1	chChartLayoutHorizontal
2	chChartLayoutVertical

You can control the number of charts on a row or column by setting the ChartWrapCount property to the required number of charts. For example, to place four charts in a row or column, use the following statement:

```
chrtSpace.ChartWrapCount = 4
```

Figure D-5 presents a web page with a Chart component containing a bar chart and a doughnut chart placed in two rows. The data for both charts is supplied dynamically from the Northwind database when the web page is opened. The data is bound to arrays obtained from the ADO recordset and passed to the SetData method via the chDataLiteral constant, like this:

```
' Bind the charts to arrays
With chrtSpace.Charts(0)
        .SeriesCollection.Add
        .SeriesCollection(0).SetData cons.chDimSeriesNames, _
            cons.chDataLiteral, "Unit Price"
```

```
            .SeriesCollection(0).SetData cons.chDimCategories, _
                cons.chDataLiteral, categ
            .SeriesCollection(0).SetData cons.chDimValues, _
                cons.chDataLiteral, values1
            .HasLegend = True
            .Type = cons.chChartTypeBarClustered
            .Axes(cons.chAxisPositionBottom).NumberFormat = "$##"
    End With
```

The categ and values1 in the code fragment above are the names of Variants that hold arrays with the list of categories and values to be charted. See the code below on how these arrays are filled from the ADO recordset.

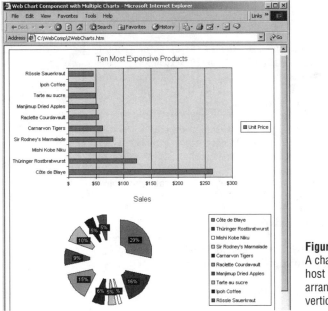

Figure D-5:
A chart workspace can host multiple charts arranged horizontally or vertically.

To prepare the web page shown in Figure D-5, open Notepad and enter the HTML and VBScript code, as shown below. Ensure that the path points to the Northwind database on your server. Save the file as 2WebCharts.htm. You can find this file on the companion CD-ROM.

2WebCharts.htm

```
<html>
<Title>Web Chart Component with Multiple Charts</Title>
<body>
<object classid="clsid:0002E500-0000-0000-C000-000000000046" id="chrtSpace"
width=600 height=600></Object
<br/>
<H4>Data Source: Northwind Database </H4>

<SCRIPT LANGUAGE="VBScript">
```

```
Sub Window_OnLoad()

' Declare variables
Dim strConnection, rst, strSQL
Dim i, myData, cons
Dim categ(10)
Dim values1(10)
Dim values2(10)

  ' specify the connection string
strConnection="Provider=Microsoft.Jet.OleDB.4.0; data source=" & _
  "C:\Program Files\Microsoft Office\Office\Samples\Northwind.mdb"

' Create a Recordset
Set rst = CreateObject("ADODB.Recordset")

' define the SQL query to supply the data for charting
strSql = "SELECT DISTINCTROW TOP 10 [Products].[ProductName] " _
 & "AS TenMostExpensiveProducts, [Products].[UnitPrice], " _
 & "Sum(CCur(([Order Details].[UnitPrice]*[Quantity])*" _
 & "(1-[Discount])/100)*100)" _
 & " AS [Sales Total] FROM Products INNER JOIN [Order Details] " _
 & " ON [Products].[ProductID]=[Order Details].[ProductID]" _
 & "GROUP BY [Products].[ProductName], [Products].[UnitPrice]" _
 & "ORDER BY [Products].[UnitPrice] DESC;"

' Open Recordset (and execute the SQL statement above)
' use the connection string with a client-side cursor (3)
' and static dataset (3)
rst.Open strSql, strConnection, 3, 3

' get categories and values for the chart
' from the Recordset and fill the arrays

        rst.MoveFirst
        Do Until rst.EOF
        i = i + 1
           categ(i) = rst.Fields(0)
        values1(i) = rst.Fields(1)
        values2(i) = rst.Fields(2)
           rst.MoveNext
        Loop

'Cleanup
rst.close
set rst = Nothing

' Clear the chrtspace object
With chrtSpace
  .Clear
  .HasChartSpaceTitle = True
  .ChartSpaceTitle.Caption = "Ten Most Expensive Products"
End With
```

```
' Get constants for the Chart component
set cons = chrtSpace.Constants

' Add two charts to the chartspace
chrtSpace.Charts.Add 0
chrtSpace.Charts.Add 1

' Bind the charts to arrays
With chrtSpace.Charts(0)
    .SeriesCollection.Add
    .SeriesCollection(0).SetData _
      cons.chDimSeriesNames, cons.chDataLiteral, "Unit Price"
    .SeriesCollection(0).SetData _
            cons.chDimCategories, cons.chDataLiteral, categ
    .SeriesCollection(0).SetData _
            cons.chDimValues, cons.chDataLiteral, values1
    .HasLegend = True
    .Type = cons.chChartTypeBarClustered
        .Axes(cons.chAxisPositionBottom).NumberFormat = "$##"
End With

With chrtSpace.Charts(1)
    .SeriesCollection.Add
    .SeriesCollection(0).SetData _
      cons.chDimSeriesNames, cons.chDataLiteral, "Sales"
    .SeriesCollection(0).SetData _
            cons.chDimCategories, cons.chDataLiteral, categ
    .SeriesCollection(0).SetData _
            cons.chDimValues, cons.chDataLiteral, values2
    .HasLegend = True
    .HasTitle = True
    .Type = cons.chChartTypeDoughnutExploded
    .holeSize = 20
        .SeriesCollection(0).Explosion = 15
        'Include data labels on the slices as percentages
        With .SeriesCollection(0).DataLabelsCollection.Add
          .HasValue = False
          .HasPercentage = True
          .Font.Size = 8
          .Font.Color = RGB(255, 255, 255) ' white
          .Interior.Color = RGB(0, 0, 0)    ' black
        End With
    End With
End With
End Sub

</SCRIPT>
</body>
</html>
```

You can make very complex charts with custom layout and drawings, as well as apply special formatting to different sections of your chart by using numerous properties, methods, and events organized neatly for easy lookup in the OWCDCH10.CHM help file located in the folder C:\Program Files\Common Files\Microsoft Shared\Web Components\10\1033.

The Data Source Web Component

Unlike the other Office XP web components (Spreadsheet, Chart, and PivotTable), the Data Source web component is an ActiveX control without a user interface. Its main purpose is managing connections to the underlying data source and fetching records for display by other controls on a web page. This section demonstrates how to set up the Data Source control for providing data to a chart control. The next section in this appendix shows how to bind the Data Source control to a PivotTable.

You can use the Data Source control to connect to such databases as the SQL Server, Oracle, or Microsoft Access. To insert a Data Source web component on a web page, add an <OBJECT> tag and specify its class ID. The following statement places a Data Source control named dsc1 on an HTML page:

```
<object id=dsc1 classid=CLSID:0002E530-0000-0000-C000-000000000046></object>
```

Remember that the Data Source control has no visible interface at run time. To take advantage of this control, you must use the programming code to initialize it. After placing the <OBJECT> tag on a web page, specify the source for the data in the Data Source control. This is done by setting the control's ConnectionString property, as follows:

```
strConnection="Provider=Microsoft.Jet.OleDB.4.0; data source=" & _
 "C:\Program Files\Microsoft Office\Office\Samples\Northwind.mdb"
 dsc1.ConnectionString = strConnection
```

Next, build the SQL query string to define the data that you want to retrieve from the database. This can be a simple query string like "SELECT * from Customers" or a more complex one like the one presented in the code section later in this section. To execute the query, add a recordset definition to the data source control by using the AddNew method of the RecordsetDefs collection:

```
Set rstdef = dsc1.RecordsetDefs.AddNew(strSQL, dsc1.Constants.dscCommandText)
```

The above statement says that you want to use the string specified by the first argument of the AddNew method (strSQL) for the new schema row source of type dscCommandText. Because VBScript does not understand enumerated constants, you need to precede the name of the second (optional) argument with the constant definition, like this: dsc1.Constants.dscCommandText. The Data Source control can use table names, views, stored procedures, SQL statements, or XML files as the record row source. Each row source type is represented by a different enumerated constant (dscTable (1), dscView (2), dscCommandText (3), dscProcedure (4), and dscCommandFile (5)). You can add multiple recordset definitions to the Data Source control and specify in your code which recordset should be displayed.

After adding a recordset definition, use the Data Source property to bind your web control (Spreadsheet, Chart, or PivotTable) to the Data Source control:

```
ChrtSpace1.DataSource = dsc1
```

Because you can add multiple recordsets to the Data Source control, you should use the DataMember property to specify the name of the recordset that the specified control will get its data from:

```
ChrtSpace1.DataMember = rstdef.Name
```

The above statement sets the DataMember property of the Chart control to the created recordset. To find information on using the Chart web component, refer to the previous section.

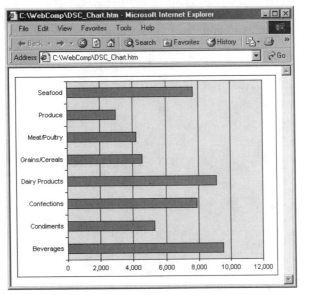

Figure D-6:
The Chart web component shown here requests its data from the invisible Data Source web component.

To prepare the web page shown in Figure D-6, open Notepad and enter the HTML and VBScript code shown below. Ensure that the path points to the Northwind database on your server. Save the file as Dsc_Chart.htm. You can find this file on the companion CD-ROM.

Dsc_Chart.htm

```
<HTML>
<BODY>
<object id=chrtSpace1 classid=CLSID:0002E500-0000-0000-C000-000000000046 _
      style="width:100%;height:340"></object>
<object id=dsc1 classid=CLSID:0002E530-0000-0000-C000-000000000046> _
      </object>

<SCRIPT Language="VBScript">

Sub Window_OnLoad()
```

```
        Dim strConnection
        Dim strSQL
        Dim c
        Dim rstdef

  ' Set the connection for the DataSource control
        strConnection="Provider=Microsoft.Jet.OleDB.4.0; data source=" & _
         "C:\Program Files\Microsoft Office\Office\Samples\Northwind.mdb"
        dsc1.ConnectionString = strConnection

  ' Define the SQL query string to obtain the data
        strSQL = "SELECT Categories.CategoryName, Sum(od.Quantity) AS [Total _
              Quantity] "
        strSQL = strSQL & "FROM Categories "
        strSQL = strSQL & "INNER JOIN (Products "
        strSQL = strSQL & "INNER JOIN [Order Details] as od "
        strSQL = strSQL & "ON Products.ProductID = od.ProductID) "
        strSQL = strSQL & "ON Categories.CategoryID = Products.CategoryID "
        strSQL = strSQL & "GROUP BY Categories.CategoryName;"

  ' Add a new Recordset definition to the DataSource control
        Set rstdef = dsc1.RecordsetDefs.AddNew(strSQL, dsc1.Constants. _
             dscCommandText)

  ' Get constants for the Chart component
        Set c = chrtSpace1.Constants

  ' Bind the chart space to the recordset definition in the
  ' DataSource control
          With chrtSpace1
            .DataSource = dsc1
               .DataMember = rstdef.Name
                 ' Create a new chart with CategoryName field for Categories
                     ' and Total Quantity field for Values
            .Charts.Add
               .Charts(0).Type = c.chChartTypeBarClustered
            .Charts(0).SetData c.chDimCategories, 0, "CategoryName"
               .Charts(0).SetData c.chDimValues, 0, "Total Quantity"
                .Charts(0).Axes(c.chAxisPositionBottom).Numberformat = "#,##0"
              .Charts(0).PlotArea.Interior.Color = "yellow"
          End With
  End Sub
  </SCRIPT>
  </BODY>
```

The PivotTable Web Component

The PivotTable web component brings the PivotTable report capability to your web page, Microsoft Access, or Visual Basic form. With this component, users can easily sort, filter, group, outline, and manipulate data. The PivotTable web component can get its data from a tabular data source (such as a Microsoft Excel spreadsheet, a database table, or an SQL query executed against the SQL Server, Oracle, or Microsoft Access database), an OLAP (multidimensional cube) data source, or an XML stream (see the second example in this section). You can also bind the PivotTable component to the Data Source component (DSC), as shown in the example that follows. To add a PivotTable web component to your web page, place the <OBJECT> tag and specify its class ID, as shown below:

```
<OBJECT classid="clsid:0002E520-0000-0000-C000-000000000046" id= _
    "Pivot1" height="200"  width="600"></OBJECT>
```

To use the Data Source web component for obtaining data for the PivotTable control, add a Data Source control to your web page, like this:

```
<OBJECT classid="clsid:0002E530-0000-0000-C000-000000000046" id="dsc1"> _
    </OBJECT>
```

Next, use the VBScript code to connect the PivotTable component to the data source:

```
strConnection="Provider=Microsoft.Jet.OleDB.4.0; data source=" & _
    "C:\Program Files\Microsoft Office\Office\Samples\Northwind.mdb"
dsc1.connectionstring = strConnection
```

Use the AddNew method of the RecordsetDefs collection to add a new recordset definition to the Data Source control and specify the query string that will provide the data:

```
dsc1.RecordsetDefs.AddNew strSQL, c.dscCommandText,"Pivot1Data"
```

Next, set the DataSource property of the PivotTable component to an instance of the Data Source control:

```
Pivot1.DataSource = dsc1
```

Finally, set the DataMember property of the PivotTable component to the name of the created recordset definition:

```
Pivot1.DataMember = "Pivot1Data"
```

Now that the PivotTable component knows how to obtain its data, you can quickly add all the fields in the dataset to the detail area by using the ActiveView.AutoLayout method of the PivotTable object:

```
Pivot1.ActiveView.AutoLayout
```

To prepare the web page shown in Figure D-7, open Notepad and enter the HTML and VBScript code shown below. Ensure that the path points to the Northwind database on your server. Save the file as Pivot.htm. You can find this file on the companion CD-ROM.

C:\WebComp\Pivot.htm

```
<HTML>
<BODY>
<object classid="clsid:0002E530-0000-0000-C000-000000000046" id="dsc1">
</object>
```

```
<OBJECT classid="clsid:0002E520-0000-0000-C000-000000000046" id=
    "Pivot1" height="200" width="600"></OBJECT>

<SCRIPT language=VBScript>
Sub Window_onLoad()
  Dim strSQL, strConnection, c

' SQL query
strSQL = "SELECT [Order Details].*, Orders.CustomerID, "
strSQL = strSQL & "Orders.EmployeeID, Employees.LastName "
strSQL = strSQL & "FROM Employees "
strSQL = strSQL & "INNER JOIN (Orders "
strSQL = strSQL & "INNER JOIN [Order Details] "
strSQL = strSQL & "ON Orders.OrderID = [Order Details].OrderID) "
strSQL = strSQL & "ON Employees.EmployeeID = Orders.EmployeeID;"
' Set the Connection string
    strConnection="Provider=Microsoft.Jet.OleDB.4.0; data source=" &
        "C:\Program Files\Microsoft Office\Office\Samples\Northwind.mdb"
' Set the connection string property
    dsc1.connectionstring = strConnection

 ' Get constants for the DataSource component
    Set c = dsc1.Constants

'Add the SQL statement to the Recordset definitions
    dsc1.RecordsetDefs.AddNew strSQL, c.dscCommandText,"Pivot1Data"

 ' Set the DataSource property of the PivotTable Component
    Pivot1.DataSource = dsc1
    Pivot1.DataMember = "Pivot1Data"

    With Pivot1.ActiveView
        .AutoLayout  ' automatically populate the PivotTable control
        .FilterAxis.label.visible = True
        .RowAxis.label.visible = True
        .ColumnAxis.label.visible = True
        .titlebar.visible = True
    End With
End Sub

</SCRIPT>
</BODY>
</HTML>
```

The next example demonstrates how to populate the PivotTable component with an XML file. Refer to Chapter 17 for an introduction on working with XML data in Excel. When loading the XML data, you must set the ConnectionString property of the PivotTable control to "Provider=MS-Persist" and indicate the full path to the XML file in the CommandText property, as illustrated in the following example procedure. Note that the VBScript code shown here demonstrates how to configure the PivotTable control at startup to only display information pertaining to a specific product. Use the InsertFieldset method to insert a field set on the specified axis

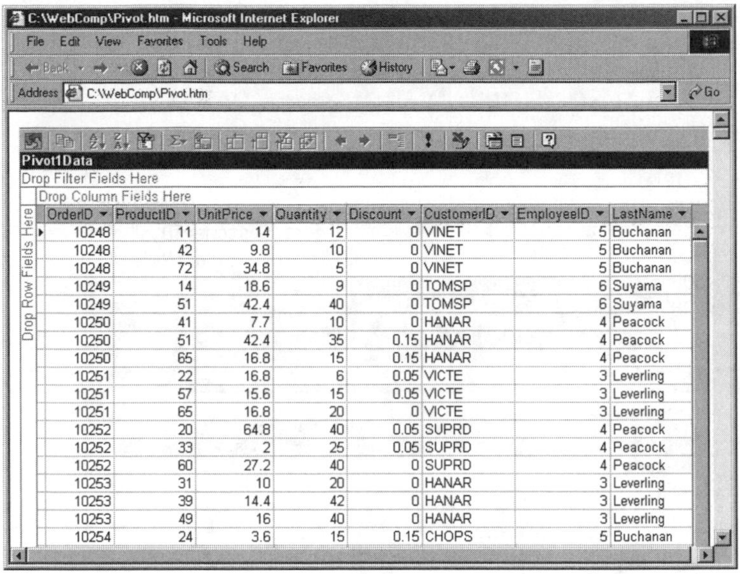

Figure D-7: As with the Spreadsheet and Chart components, the PivotTable component can be bound directly to the Data Source component.

(RowAxis, DataAxis, and FilterAxis). A Fieldset object represents a field or a set of fields in a data source. The following statement will place the ProductName field on the FilterAxis:

```
Pivot1.ActiveView.FilterAxis.InsertFieldSet
Pivot1.ActiveView.Fieldsets("ProductName")
```

Use the FilterMember property to set a default filter on the specified field:

```
Pivot1.ActiveView.FieldSets("ProductName").FilterMember = "Tofu"
```

To prepare the web page shown in Figure D-8, open Notepad and enter the HTML and VBScript code shown below. Ensure that the path points to the Northwind database on your server. Save the file as PivotXML.htm. You can find this file on the companion CD-ROM.

C:\WebComp\PivotXML.htm

```
<HTML>
<BODY>

<OBJECT classid="clsid:0002E520-0000-0000-C000-000000000046" id="Pivot1"
height="200"  width="600"></OBJECT>

<SCRIPT language=VBScript>
Sub Window_onLoad()
  Pivot1.ConnectionString = "Provider=MSPersist"
  Pivot1.CommandText = "C:\Inetpub\wwwroot\XMLTEST\Products.xml"
  Pivot1.DisplayFieldList = True
  With Pivot1.ActiveView
```

```
        .AutoLayout
        .TitleBar.Caption = "Northwind Products"
        .FilterAxis.InsertFieldSet .Fieldsets("ProductName")
        .FieldSets("ProductName").FilterMember = "Tofu"
      End With
    End Sub
    </SCRIPT>
    </BODY>
    </HTML>
```

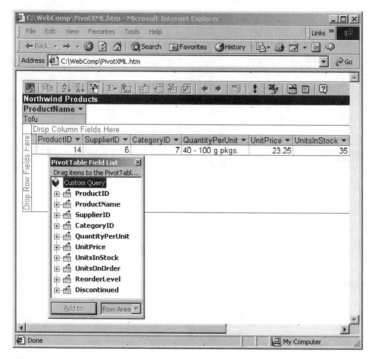

Figure D-8: This PivotTable control was populated with the data stored in an XML file.

This appendix introduced you to using Microsoft Office XP web components on a web page. These components can also be used on Microsoft Access and Visual Basic forms when you require data analysis features in your Windows applications. Creating solutions with Office web components is a complex topic and the subject of another book. Refer to *Programming Microsoft Office 2000 Web Components* by Dave Stearns (Microsoft Press, 1999) for more ideas and details on working with these ActiveX controls.

Index

Special Characters

! (exclamation point), 93
(number sign), 91, 93, 395
#Const, 394-395
#If...Then... #Else, 394-395
$ (dollar sign), 93
% (percent sign), 93
%>, 500
& (ampersand), 93
(+/–) (plus/minus), 541
* (asterisk), 569
.asa file extension, 512
.asp file extension, 500
.cpl (Control Panel Library file), 252-253, 257
.dll (Dynamic Link Library file), 252-253
.gif (file extension), 684
.iqy (file extension), 489
.jpg (file extension), 684
.lnk (file extension), 245
.mdb (file extension), 503
.png (file extension), 684
.tmp (file extension), 279
/ (slash), 539
: (colon), 72
? (question mark), 118, 537
@ (Currency type declaration character), 93
@*, 576, 580
@, 547
_ (underscore character), 128
{ } (curly brackets), 579
{TEXT}, 666
" ", empty string, 95
+ (plus sign), 92
< (less than operator), 148
<!--, 555-556
<% , 500
</Cell>, 539

<= (less than or equal to operator), 148
<> (not equal to operator), 148
<A Ref> </A>, 512
<AutoFilter>, 537
<BODY> </BODY>, 501

, 512
<Cell>, 537
<Data>, 537
<DIV>, 558, 567
<HR> <HR/>, 548
<HTML> </HTML>, 500
<INPUT TYPE>, 494
<NamedRange>, 537
<Names>, 537
<OBJECT>, 682, 692, 695
<OPTION>, 494
<Row> </Row>, 537
<rs:data>, 574
<s:AttributeType>, 575
<s:datatype>, 575
<s:Schema> </s:Schema>, 574
<SELECT>, 494
<TABLE> </TABLE>, 496, 501
<TD> </TD>, 496, 501
<TH> </TH>, 501
<Title> </Title>, 539
<TR> </TR>, 496, 501
<xsl:apply-templates>, 553
<xsl:attribute>, 553
<xsl:choose>, 553
<xsl:element>, 553
<xsl:for-each select>, 547-549, 553, 579
<xsl:if>, 553
<xsl:param>, 553
<xsl:template>, 553
<xsl:template match>, 579
<xsl:value-of>, 553
<xsl:variable>, 553
<z:row>, 575, 579-580

= (equal to operator), 148
> (greater than operator), 148
-->, 555-556
>= (greater than or equal to operator), 148

A

absolute cell addressing, 7-8
Access database, creating, 592
Activate event, 409, 415-416, 429
Activate method, 80-81
ActivateMicrosoftApp method, 253
Active Server Pages (ASP), 499, 600
   and XML, 586
   creating charts in, 525
   information lookups using, 667
ActiveX controls, 232, 285
Add method, 80-81, 326, 354, 470, 479, 490
Add Procedure dialog box, 113
AddInInstall event, 419
AddInUninstall event, 420
ADO (ActiveX Data Objects), 47
ADO Recordset, 573, 580-582, 590
ADODB, 441
AfterRefresh event, 436, 438
AllowMultiSelect property, 280
AND operator, 148, 152-153
AppActivate statement, 254-255
Append mode, 221
Application object, 45, 83
   events recognized by, 432-436
applications,
   controlling, 255-258
   controlling other, 258-260
   launching, 250
   running, 244
argument types, 120
arguments, 118
   for MsgBox function, 130
   optional, 123
   passing, 122
   versus parameters, 144
Arrange method, 82
Array function, 193
arrays,
   and looping statements, 187
   array element, 187
   array functions, 193
   declaring, 184
   dimensioning, 193

   dynamic, 190
   errors in, 196
   fixed-dimension, 191
   parameter, 198
   passing between procedures, 188
   static, 190
   two-dimensional, 189
   understanding,182
   upper and lower bounds, 185
As keyword, 123
ASP, *see* Active Server Pages
ASP script,
   creating, 501
   running, 508, 513
async property, 586
attribute, 536-537
Attributes property, 239-240
AutoCorrect object, 647
AutoFormat property, 630
AutoLayout property, 695
Automation, 258
   creating new document with, 266
AvailableSpace property, 241
Avg function, 123

B

BeforeClose event, 418
BeforeDoubleClick event, 411-412, 430
BeforePrint event, 418
BeforeRefresh event, 436, 438
BeforeRightClick event, 412, 430
BeforeSave event, 417
binary access files, 215
   advantages and disadvantages of, 232
   working with, 230
binding, 261-263
bookmarks, navigating with, 397
Boolean data type, 87
break mode, 377
   and Code window, 383
   and Immediate window, 381
breakpoint, 347
   using, 378-381
bugs, 52
built-in functions, locating, 125
ByRef keyword, 122-123
Byte data type, 87
ByVal keyword, 122-123

C

Calculate event, 411, 429
calculated field, 633
calculated item, 633
Call keyword, 143
Call Stack dialog box, 388, 390
Caption property, 82
carriage return, 215
cascading stylesheets (CSS), 579
Case clause,
    multiple expressions in, 165-166
    specifying range of values, 164
    using Is keyword in, 163-164
Case Else clause, 161-162
Catalog object, 455
CellFormat object, 645
cells,
    absolute addressing, 7
    copying, 80
    deleting, 80
    moving, 80
    recording a selection of, 76
    relative addressing, 7
    retrieving formatting of, 79
    selecting, 77
    working with, 73
Cells property, 73-74
Change event, 307-308, 316, 318, 411
Characters object, 646
Chart component, 484, 682
chart events, embedded, 431-432
Chart Menu Bar, 364
chart sheets, 82
ChartLayout property, 688
charts,
    creating an embedded chart from Access
      data, 470
    creating in ASP, 525
    events, 427
Charts collection, 470
ChartWrapCount property, 688
chChart object, 682
ChDir statement, 210
ChDrive statement, 210
check box control, 287
    versus option button, 294
Chr function, 128
chrtSpace object, 682
class, 324

creating, 330
    defining properties for, 331
class module, 324
    naming, 330
    versus standard module, 329
Clear method, 80
ClearComments method, 80
ClearContents method, 47, 80
ClearFormats method, 80
Click event, 309, 316-317
Close # statement, 402
Close method, 80-81
code,
    analyzing, 13
    breaking up long statements, 51
    cleaning up, 14-15
    executing, 16-17
    indenting, 154
Code window, 32-35
collection, 44, 324
    adding objects to, 326
    declaring custom, 326
    reindexing, 329
    removing objects from, 328
    working with, 324
collections
    CommandBars, 352, 354
    FileDialogFilters, 278-279
    FileDialogSelectedItems, 280
    PublishObjects, 483
    QueryTables, 490
    SelectedItems, 281
    SmartTags, 672
    WCDataSources, 684
columns, selecting, 77
COM, *see* Component Object Model
combo box control, 288
CommandBar object, 352
CommandBarComboBox object, 360
CommandBars collection, 352, 354
Comment Block button, 60
comments, 12, 556
    adding, 12
compilation, conditional, 394
Compile error: variable not defined, 96
Complete Word button, 59
Component Object Model (COM), 261
compound documents, 258
concatenation, 92

conditional compilation, 394
conditional statements
    If...Then, 149, 151-152
    If...Then...Else, 154-155
    If...Then...ElseIf, 158
    Select Case, 161-162
conditions, multiple, 152
ConnectionString property, 697
Const statement, 107, 138
constant, 57
    public, 107
    using, 107
ContentType property, 502
continuation character, 51, 128
Control Panel Library (CPL), 252-253, 257
Control Toolbox, 26, 596
control types, 286-289
controller, Automation, 258
controls,
    ActiveX, 26, 285
    adding to a CommandBar, 359
    adding to a worksheet, 26
    and CommandBar, 357-358
    changing names of, 296-297
    duplicating and moving, 293
    events of, 301-302
    methods of, 363
    properties of, 360
    setting properties of, 297
conversion, data type, 103, 137
Copy method, 80
CopyFile method, 235
CopyFolder method, 238
CopyFromRecordset method, 461-462, 581
Count property, 77-78
counters, 172
Create method, 455
CreateDatabase method, 450
CreateFolder method, 238
CreateObject function, 232, 234, 265, 444
CreateObject method, 503
CreateShortcut method, 245
CreateTextFile method, 238, 242, 681
CSng function, 103
CSS, *see* cascading stylesheets
CSV file format, 215
CSVURL property, 681
Ctrl
    with Shift, 21

    with Spacebar, 59
CurDir function, 202
Currency data type, 88
CurrentRegion method, 470
Customize dialog box, 22
CustomProperty object, 651
Cut method, 80

D
DAO, *see* Data Access Objects
DAO objects, 47
Data Access Objects (DAO), 440
data islands, 555-557
    transforming contents with VBScript, 557
Data Source web component, 692
data types, 87-88
    converting, 103, 137
    creating user-defined, 225
    of a variable, 92
DataMember property, 693, 695
DataRange property, 630
DataSource property, 693
Date data type, 88
DateCreated property, 239-240
DateLastAccessed property, 239
DateLastModified property, 239
DDE, *see* Dynamic Data Exchange
Deactivate event, 409, 416, 429
Decimal data type, 88
declaration, variable, 88-89
DELETE FROM statement, 520
Delete method, 81, 357
DeleteFile method, 235-236, 513
DeleteFolder method, 238
delimited text files, 220
Description property, 246
Diagram object, 651
dialog boxes
    Add Procedure, 113
    Call Stack, 388, 390
    Customize, 22, 352
    File Open, 277
    File Save, 277
    Format Cells, 79
    Function Arguments, 116
    Insert Function, 115
    Insert Hyperlink, 478
    Options, 35

PivotTable Layout, 617
Project Properties, 396
Publish as Web Page, 483, 642
Quick Watch, 387
References, 42, 263-264, 442
Save As, 483, 533
VBAProject – Project Properties, 40
dialog boxes in Excel, 274
digital signature, 30
Dim statement, 89-90
Dimension, *see* Dim statement
Dir function, 204
    attributes of, 204
directive, 394
directory, virtual, 505
DLL, *see* Dynamic-Link Library
Do…Until loop, 171
Do…While loop, 168-170
DoCmd object, 451
Document Object Model (DOM), 540, 561
Document Type Definition (DTD), 542
documents,
    compound, 258
    opening Word, 268
DOM, *see* Document Object Model
DOM object, 586
DOMDocument object, 561-563, 565, 584
Double data type, 88
DragOver event, 430
DragPlot event, 430
Drive object, 241
    properties of, 241
Drive property, 239-240
DriveExists method, 236
DriveLetter property, 241
Drives property, 239
DriveType property, 241
DropDownLines property, 360
DropDownWidth property, 360
DTD, *see* Document Type Definition
Dynamic Data Exchange (DDE), 258
Dynamic Link Library (DLL), 252-253
dynamic parameters, 495

E
early binding, 261-263, 265
ElseIf clause, 158
embedding, 258
empty string, 95

encoding, 576
End Function keyword, 112
End property, 77
End Property keyword, 332
End Select keyword, 161
End Sub keyword, 112
EOF function, 218
Erase function, 195
Err object, 402, 588
error messages
    Compile error, 53
    Object variable or With block variable
        not set, 104
    Overflow, 91
    Subscript out of range, 196-197
    Type mismatch, 92, 138
errors,
    capturing with Case Else, 162
    generating on purpose, 403
    in arrays, 196
    logic, 53-54
    run-time, 52-53
    syntax, 51-52
    trapping, 398
    understanding, 51
    versus mistakes, 399
event procedures, 301, 324, 406-407
    in class modules, 336
event, 324, 406
    sequences, 409
events
    Activate, 409, 415-416, 429
    AddInInstall, 419
    AddInUninstall, 420
    AfterRefresh, 436, 438
    BeforeClose, 418
    BeforeDoubleClick, 411-412, 430
    BeforePrint, 418
    BeforeRefesh, 436, 438
    BeforeRightClick, 412, 430
    BeforeSave, 417
    Calculate, 411, 429
    Change, 307-308, 316, 318, 411
    Click, 309, 316-317
    Deactivate, 410, 416, 429
    DragOver, 430
    DragPlot, 430
    FollowHyperlink, 413
    Initialize, 304, 336

MouseDown, 430
MouseMove, 430
MouseUp, 430
NewSheet, 424
NewWorkbook, 433
Open, 416
PivotTableCloseConnection, 427
PivotTableOpenConnection, 426
PivotTableUpdate, 413-414
Resize, 430
Select, 429
SelectionChange, 410
SeriesChange, 429
SheetActivate, 425, 434
SheetBeforeDoubleClick, 425, 435
SheetBeforeRightClick, 425, 435
SheetCalculate, 425, 435
SheetChange, 425, 435
SheetDeactivate, 425, 434
SheetPivotTableUpdate, 427
SheetSelectionChange, 425, 435
Terminate, 336
WindowActivate, 425, 435
WindowDeactivate, 425-426, 435
WindowResize, 426, 435
WorkbookActivate, 434
WorkbookAddInInstall, 435
WorkbookAddInUninstall, 435
WorkbookBeforeClose, 434
WorkbookBeforePrint, 434
WorkbookBeforeSave, 434
WorkbookDeactivate, 434
WorkbookNewSheet, 434
WorkbookOpen, 433-434
WorkbookPivotTableCloseConnection,
    435
WorkbookPivotTableOpenConnection,
    436
events, 301
    Application object, 432-436
    chart, 427
    embedded chart, 431-432
    enabling and disabling, 406
    form and control, 301-302
    new workbook events in Excel 2002,
        426-427
    query table, 436-438
    workbook, 415-427
    worksheet, 409-415

writing VBA procedures to respond to,
    303-304
Execute method, 281
Exit Do, 178
Exit For, 178
explicit variable declaration, 89
ExportPicture method, 684
Extensible Markup Language (XML), 532,
    662, *see also* XML *and* XML files
Extensible Stylesheet Language (XSL),
    534, 545, 552, *see also* XSL

F
F1, 78
F2, 61
F2 (with Shift), 106
F5, 17, 19-20
F7, 33
F8, 348
F8 (with Alt), 21
F9, 378
Fieldset object, 697
file attributes, retrieving, 209
file formats, 215
File object, 239
    properties of, 239
File Open dialog box, 277
File Save dialog box, 277
FileCopy statement, 212
FileDateTime function, 207
FileDialog object, 277-278
FileDialogFilter object, 279
FileDialogFilters collection, 278-279
FileDialogSelectedItems collection, 280
FileExists method, 235
FileLen function, 207-208
files,
    access types of, 215
    binary, 230-232
    finding information about, 234
    manipulating, 203-210, 212-215
    random access, 224-229
    sequential, 216-222
    Smart Tag list definition, 666
    working with, 232-239
Files property, 240
FileSearch object, 655
FileSystem property, 241
FileSystemObject, 235, 513

folder attributes, retrieving, 209
Folder object, 240
    properties of, 240
FolderExists method, 237
folders,
    manipulating, 202-207, 210-211
    working with, 232-234
FollowHyperlink event, 413
FollowHyperlink method, 480
For...Each...Next loop, 177
For...Next loop, 174-175
form module, 324
Format Cells dialog box, 79
Format function, 96
FormatCondition object, 649
forms,
    adding various controls to, 292
    creating, 283
    displaying custom, 300
    events of, 301-302
    placing controls on, 290
    sharing between applications, 284
Formula property, 78
frame control, 287
FreeSpace property, 241
Function Arguments dialog box, 116
Function keyword, 112
function procedures, 112
    testing, 125
functions
    Array, 193
    Avg, 123
    Chr, 128
    CreateObject, 232, 234, 265, 444
    CSng, 103
    CurDir, 202
    Dir, 204
    EOF, 218
    Erase, 195
    FileDateTime, 207
    FileLen, 207-208
    Format, 96
    GetAttr, 208
    GetObject, 267-268, 444-445
    Input, 218
    InputBox, 125
    IsArray, 194
    IsEmpty, 157
    IsObject, 105
    Lbound, 195-196
    Len, 119, 145, 228
    LOF, 218
    MsgBox, 119-120, 125
    Name, 203, 576
    RND, 228
    SetAttr, 208, 210
    Shell, 250-251
    Sum, 118
    Ubound, 195-196
    VarType, 107, 125, 137
functions,
    calling a Microsoft Access function, 459
    custom, 116
    executing, 115
    limitations, 120
    locating built-in functions, 125
    naming, 113
    passing arguments to, 118
    private, 116
    reasons for using, 114
    running from a worksheet, 115
    running from procedures, 117
    testing, 118, 125
    when to create, 142

G
GET method, 493-494
Get statement, using in binary files, 230
GetAtrr function, 208
GetBaseName method, 512
GetDrive method, 236
GetDriveName method, 236-237
getElementsByTagName method, 569
GetFile method, 235
GetFileName method, 235
GetFileVersion method, 235
GetFolder method, 237
GetObject function, 267-268, 444-445
GetOpenFilename method, 277, 281-282
GetRows method, 459-460
GetSaveAsFilename method, 277, 281-282
GetSpecialFolder method, 237
GetString method, 523-524
GetTempName method, 512
Global.asa, 512
Graphic object, 650
grid, setting grid options, 290

H

help, on-line, 54-55
hierarchy, Microsoft Excel Objects, 45-47
HotKey property, 246
HTML, *see also* Hypertext Markup
    Language
    creating files, 482
    document, 482
HTMLProject object, 657
HTMLProjectItem object, 658
HTMLURL property, 681
HTTP, 481
hyperlink, 259-260
Hyperlink object, 478-479
Hypertext Markup Language (HTML), 500,
    546-547

I

IconLocation property, 246
icons, 252
If...Then statement, 149, 151, 160
If...Then...Else statement, 154-155
If...Then...ElseIf statement, 158
image control, 288-289
Immediate window, 68-71
implicit variable declaration, 89
indentation, code, 154
Indent/Outdent button, 59
Initialize event, 304, 336
Input function, 218
Input statement, 221
input/output, 215
InputBox function, 125
    using, 134-135
InputBox method, 138-139
Insert Function dialog box, 115
Insert Hyperlink dialog box, 478
INSERT INTO statement, 519
InsertFieldset method, 697
instance, 267, 324
    creating, 335
instructions, 38
    processing instruction, 537
Integer data type, 87
interface, Automation, 261
Internet Explorer, 482
Is keyword, 163-164
IsArray function, 194
IsEmpty function, 157

IsObject function, 105
IsReady property, 241
IsRootFolder property, 240
IXMLDOMNode object, 567
IXMLDOMNodeList object, 569

J

JRO, 441
JScript, 500

K

keyboard, shortcuts, 21
keycodes, used with SendKeys statement,
    256
keyword, 59
keywords
    As, 123
    ByRef, 122-123
    ByVal, 122-123
    Call, 143
    End Property, 332
    End Sub, 112
    Me, 305
    New, 269-270, 335-336, 432-433
    Nothing, 336
    Optional, 198
    Public, 114, 333, 431
    Set, 140
    Sub, 112
    WithEvents, 432
Kill statement, 214

L

label control, 286
late binding, 261-263, 265
Lbound function, 195-196
Len function, 119, 145, 228
linefeed, 215
Line Input # statement, 217-218
linking, 472
    understanding, 258
list box control, 287
List Constants pop-up menu, 57
List Properties/Methods pop-up menu, 56
List property, 360
ListBox control, populating, 306
ListCount property, 360
ListIndex property, 305, 360
Load method, 562-563
LoadText method, 681

LoadXML method, 563
Loc statement, using in binary files, 230
local variables, 100
localhost, 508
Locals window, using, 388-390
LOF function, 218
logical operators, 148
Long data type, 87
loops, 168, 170
    avoiding infinite loops, 170
    exiting early, 178
    nesting, 179
loops
    Do...Until, 171
    Do...While loop, 168-170
    For...Each...Next, 177, 569-570
    For...Next, 174-175
    While...Wend loop, 174

M
macros, 2, 10
    analyzing code, 13
    cleaning up code, 14
    code execution, 16
    common uses, 2
    digital signature, 30
    disabling, 29
    enabling, 30
    improving, 17
    in Personal Macro Workbook, 27-29
    instructions, 20
    modifying, 8
    naming conventions, 6
    opening workbooks with, 29
    planning, 3
    printing, 27
    recording, 5
    renaming, 20
    running, 8, 20-26
    saving, 26
    security, 30
    storing, 6, 27-29
    testing, 15
MAPI, *see* Messaging Application
    Programming Interface
MapPath method, 511
master procedures, 142
MDAC, *see* Microsoft Data Access
    Components

Me keyword, 305
menus,
    creating a shortcut menu, 371-374
    creating a submenu, 368-369
    modifying a shortcut menu, 370-371
    programming, 365-368
    working with, 364-365
Messaging Application Programming
    Interface (MAPI), 271
method, 44
methods
    Activate, 80-81
    ActivateMicrosoftApp, 253
    Add, 80-81, 326, 354, 470, 479, 490
    Arrange, 82
    Clear, 80
    ClearComments, 80
    ClearContents, 47, 80
    ClearFormats, 80
    Close, 80-81
    Copy, 80
    CopyFile, 235
    CopyFolder, 238
    CopyFromRecordset, 461-462, 581
    Create, 455
    CreateDatabase, 450
    CreateFolder, 238
    CreateObject, 503
    CreateShortcut, 245
    CreateTextFile, 238, 242, 681
    CurrentRegion, 470
    Cut, 80
    Delete, 81, 357
    DeleteFile, 235-236, 513
    DeleteFolder, 238
    DriveExists, 236
    Execute, 281
    ExportPicture, 684
    FileExists, 235
    FolderExists, 237
    FollowHyperlink, 480
    GET, 493-494
    GetBaseName, 512
    GetDrive, 236
    GetDriveName, 236-237
    getElementsByTagName, 569
    GetFile, 235
    GetFileName, 235
    GetFileVersion, 235

GetFolder, 237
GetOpenFilename, 277, 281-282
GetRows, 459-460
GetSaveAsFilename, 277, 281-282
GetSpecialFolder, 237
GetString, 523-524
GetTempName, 512
InputBox, 138-139
InsertFieldset, 697
Load, 562-563
LoadText, 681
LoadXML, 563
MapPath, 511
MkDir, 66
MouseDown, 373
MouseUp, 373
Move, 81
MoveFile, 235
MoveFirst, 460
MoveFolder, 238
NewWindow, 82
OnKey, 159
Open, 503
OpenAsTextStream, 243-244
OpenDatabase, 464-465
OpenForm, 451
OpenRecordset, 460
OpenTextFile, 238, 242-243
OpenXML, 535
PivotTableWizard, 622
POST, 493-494, 600
Quit, 83
RecordCount, 460
Refresh, 492
Remove, 328
removeNamedItem, 584
RmDir, 67
Save, 246
SaveToFile, 582
Select, 81
SelectNodes, 570
SelectSingleNode, 571-572, 584
Server.MapPath, 588
SetData, 682-683
Show, 274
ShowPopup, 372, 374
TransferSpreadsheet, 463, 472
transformNode, 558
transformNodeToObject, 576

Unload, 309
WriteLine, 681
methods,
creating class, 334-335
for controls, 363
Microsoft Access,
calling a function, 459
connecting to, 443
connecting to using ADO, 448
connecting to using DAO, 447
creating a query table, 468
creating a text file, 466
creating a new database, 450
importing an Excel spreadsheet, 474
linking a worksheet, 472
opening a database, 443
opening a form, 451
opening a report, 454
opening a secured database, 447
performing Access tasks with Excel, 449
placing data in a table, 474
retrieving data into a spreadsheet, 459
running a query, 455
transferring a spreadsheet, 472
using Access data in Excel, 470
using Automation, 443
Microsoft Access DAO 3.6 Object Library, 440
Microsoft ActiveX Data Objects 2.5 Library (ADO), 441
Microsoft ADO Ext. 2.5 for DDL and Security (ADOX), 441
Microsoft Data Access Components (MDAC), 573
Microsoft Excel Object Library, 264
Microsoft Information Services (IIS) 5.0, 504
Microsoft Jet and Replication Objects 2.6 Library (JRO), 441
Microsoft Office Object Library, 277
Microsoft Office XP Web Components, 484, 675
Microsoft Outlook Object Library, 270
Microsoft Visual Basic for Applications Extensibility 5.3 Library, 653
Microsoft Visual InterDev 6.0, 500
Microsoft Word Object Library, 263-264, 266

Microsoft.Jet.OLEDB.4.0 provider, 448, 474, 589
MkDir method, 66
MkDir statement, 211
mode,
    Append mode, 221
    break mode, 377
    Output mode, 221
    step mode, 390
module, 10, 38, 324
    renaming, 40
    versus class module, 329
MouseDown event, 430
MouseDown method, 373
MouseMove event, 430
MouseUp event, 430
MouseUp method, 373
Move method, 81
MoveFile method, 235
MoveFirst method, 460
MoveFolder method, 238
MsgBox function, 119-120, 125
    button arguments, 130
    returning values from, 133
    using, 125
    using parentheses in, 134
MSPersist provider, 697
MSXML object library, 561-562
MultiPage control, 289, 311-313

N

Name function, 203, 576
Name property, 83, 239-240
namespace, 538
Namespace object (in Outlook), 271
NBSPACE, 525
nested statements, 160-161
nesting
    loops, 179
    If...Then statements, 160
Netscape Navigator, 482
New keyword, 335-336, 432-433
    using, 269-270
NewFile object, 656
NewSheet event, 424
NewWindow method, 82
NewWorkbook event, 433
Next statement, showing, 394
nodes,

in XML documents, 567
    retrieving information from, 569
nodeType property, 567
NOT logical operator, 148
Nothing keyword, 336
NumberFormat property, 79

O

Object Browser,
    locating procedures with, 68
    using, 61-64
Object data type, 88
object libraries, 440-442
object linking and embedding (OLE), 258-261
object variables, 104
    advantages of, 106
objects
    Application, 45, 83
    AutoCorrect, 647
    Catalog, 455
    CellFormat, 645
    Characters, 646
    chChart, 682
    chrtSpace, 682
    CommandBar, 352
    CommandBarComboBox, 360
    CustomProperty, 651
    Diagram, 651
    DoCmd, 451
    DOMDocument, 561-563, 565, 584
    Drive, 241
    Err, 402, 588
    Fieldset, 697
    File, 239
    FileDialog, 277-278
    FileDialogFilter, 279
    FileSearch, 655
    Folder, 240
    FormatCondition, 649
    Graphic, 650
    HTMLProject, 657
    HTMLProjectItem, 658
    Hyperlink, 478-479
    IXMLDOMNode, 567
    IXMLDOMNodeList, 569
    Namespace, 271
    NewFile, 656
    PageSetup, 648

PivotCache, 626
QueryDefs, 460
QueryTable, 468
Range, 45, 73
Reference, 653
Request, 611
ScopeFolder, 656
SearchScope, 656
Session, 512
Shape, 260
SmartTag, 672
SmartTagAction, 673
SmartTagOptions, 673
SmartTagRecognizer, 673
Speech, 644
Spelling Options, 644
Stream, 582, 590
Tab, 644
TextStream, 681
VBComponent, 653
VBProject, 653
XMLHTTP, 600
objects, 43
    Automation, 265
    creating custom objects, 329-330
    learning about, 72
    Microsoft Excel Object hierarchy, 45-47
    VBA Object Library, 66
ODBC, 491
Office XP objects, 655
Offset property, 75
OLE, *see* object linking and embedding
OLE DB, 491
On Error GoTo 0 statement, 398
On Error GoTo statement, 141, 398
On Error Resume Next statement, 308, 398
OnKey method, 159
Open event, 416
Open method, 503
Open statement, 216
OpenAsTextStream method, 243-244
OpenDatabase method, 464-465
OpenForm method, 451
OpenRecordset method, 460
OpenTextFile method, 238, 242-243
OpenXML method, 535
OperatingSystem property, 83
operators, 38, 148
Option Base statement, 185

option button control, 287
    controlling with VBA, 306-307
    versus check box, 294
Option Explicit statement, 96, 98-99
optional arguments, 123
Optional keyword, 198
Options dialog box, 35
OR operator, 148, 152
OrganizationName property, 83
Output mode, 221
overflow run-time error, 91

P
PageSetup object, 648
Parameter arrays, 198
Parameter Info window, 57-58
Parameter query, 457
parameters, 144
ParentFolder property, 239-240
ParseError property, 588
parser, 540
Path property, 83, 239-240, 242
Personal Macro Workbook, 6, 27
Personal Web Server 4.0, 504
PivotCache object, 626
PivotChart report,
    creating with VBA, 637
    saving as a web page, 640
PivotTable report,
    adding calculated fields and items, 631
    creating from external data, 623
    creating manually, 615-618
    creating with VBA, 621
    formatting/sorting/grouping, 628
    hiding items, 631
    saving as a web page, 640
    using PivotTableWizard method,
        623-627
PivotTable web component, 640, 695
PivotTableCloseConnection event, 427
PivotTableLayout dialog box, 617
PivotTableOpenConnection event, 426
PivotTableUpdate event, 413-414
PivotTableWizard method, 622
POST method, 493-494, 600
Preserve keyword, 193
Print # statement, 220-223
printing to Internet browser, 523-525
Private keyword, 331, 333

PRN file format, 215
procedures, 10, 38
    calling from another project, 41
    event, 303, 406
    exiting, 179
    for initializing a form, 304
    locating in Object Browser, 68
    passing arrays, 188
    property, 112
    stepping over, 392
    stepping through, 390-391
    stopping, 376-377
    stopping and resetting, 394
    subroutine, 112
    testing, 376, 401
    using arrays, 185
    watching execution of, 173
programming,
    menus, 365
    structured, 156
project, 39
Project Explorer, 31
Project Properties dialog box, 396
properties
    AllowMultiSelect, 280
    async, 586
    Attributes, 239-240
    AutoFormat, 630
    AutoLayout, 695
    AvailableSpace, 241
    Caption, 82
    Cells, 73-74
    ChartLayout, 688
    ChartWrapCount, 688
    ConnectionString, 697
    ContentType, 502
    Count, 77-78
    CSVURL, 681
    DataMember, 693, 695
    DataRange, 630
    DataSource, 693
    DateCreated, 239-240
    DateLastAccessed, 239
    DateLastModified, 239
    Description, 246
    Drive, 239-240
    DriveLetter, 241
    Drives, 239
    DriveType, 241

DropDownLines, 360
DropDownWidth, 360
End, 77
Files, 240
FileSystem, 241
Formula, 78
FreeSpace, 241
HotKey, 246
HTMLURL, 681
IconLocation, 246
IsReady, 241
IsRootFolder, 240
List, 360
ListCount, 360
ListIndex, 305, 360
Name, 83, 239-240
nodeType, 567
NumberFormat, 79
Offset, 75
OperatingSystem, 83
OrganizationName, 83
ParentFolder, 239-240
ParseError, 588
Path, 83, 239-240, 242
Range, 73
Resize, 76
SelectedItem, 281
SerialNumber, 242
SessionId, 511
SessionTimeOut, 513
Size, 239-240, 242
SpecialFolders, 247
SubFolders, 240
TargetPath, 245
Text, 360, 562
Type, 239-240, 354
Value, 78
WebTables, 492
WindowStyle, 246
WorkingDirectory, 246
XML, 562
XMLData, 681
property, 44
Property Get property procedure, 331,
    332-333
Property Let property procedure, 331,
    332-333
property procedures, 112, 331
    exiting from, 332

Property Set property procedure, 331
Public keyword, 114, 333, 431
Publish as Web Page dialog box, 483, 642
PublishObjects collection, 483
Put statement, using in binary files, 230

Q
queries,
   Parameter, 457
   Select, 455
   web, 488-489
query table events, 436-438
QueryDefs object, 460
QueryTable object, 468
QueryTables collection, 490
Quick Info button, 58
Quick Watch dialog box, 387
Quit method, 83

R
random access files, 215
   advantages and disadvantages of, 229
   working with, 224
Randomize statement, 189, 336
Range object, 45, 73
Range property, 73
range, saving as XML document, 559
RecordCount method, 460
Recordset object, 573
ReDim statement, 191-193
RefEdit control, 289
reference, establishing, 42, 263-264
Reference object, 653
References dialog box, 42, 263-264, 442
Refresh method, 492
relational operators, 148
relative cell addressing, 7
Remove method, 328
removeNamedItem method, 584
Request object, 611
Resize event, 430
Resize property, 76
Response.ContentType statement, 509
Response.Write statement, 503, 520
Resume Next statement, 213
RmDir method, 67
RmDir statement, 211
RND function, 228
root element, 545
rows, selecting, 77

RowSet schema, 574
RUN SUB, 17
run-time error, overflow, 91
run-time binding, 261

S
Save As dialog box, 483, 533
Save method, 246
SaveToFile method, 582
schema, 532
   for XML document, 542
   XML-SS, 543
scope, 333
   module-level, 99-100
   procedure-level, 99-100
   project-level, 99, 102
   variable, 99
ScopeFolder object, 656
scroll bar control, 288
SDK, 662
SearchScope object, 656
security, macro, 30
Seek statement, using in binary files, 230
Select Case statement, 161-162
Select event, 429
Select method, 81
SelectedItem property, 281
SelectedItems collection, 281
SelectionChange event, 410
SelectNodes method, 570
SelectSingleNode method, 571-572, 584
SendKeys statement, 255-257
sequential access files, 215-216
   advantages and disadvantages of, 222
   reading characters, 218
   reading data, 216
   reading lines, 217
   writing data to, 221
SerialNumber property, 242
SeriesChange event, 429
server, Automation, 258
Server.MapPath method, 588
Session object, 512
SessionId property, 511
SessionTimeOut property, 513
Set keyword, 140
SetAttr function, 208, 210
SetData method, 682-683
Shape object, 260

SheetActivate event, 425, 434
SheetBeforeDoubleClick event, 425, 435
SheetBeforeRightClick event, 425, 435
SheetCalculate event, 425, 435
SheetChange event, 425, 435
SheetDeactivate event, 425, 434
SheetPivotTableUpdate event, 427
sheets, chart, 82
SheetSelectionChange event, 425, 435
Shell function, 250-251
Shift (with Ctrl), 21
shortcuts, creating, 245
Show method, 274
ShowPopup method, 372, 374
Single data type, 87
single instance, 267
Size property, 239-240
smart tags, 661, 663, 667
    manipulating with VBA, 672
SmartTag object, 672
SmartTagAction object, 673
SmartTagOptions object, 673
SmartTagRecognizer object, 673
SmartTags collection, 672
SpecialFolders property, 247
Speech object, 644
Spelling Options object, 645
spin button control, 288
Spreadsheet component, 484
Spreadsheet web component, 677
SQL server, connecting to, 503
statements
    AppActivate, 254-255
    ChDir, 210
    ChDrive, 210
    Const, 107, 138
    DELETE FROM, 520
    Dim, 89-90
    FileCopy, 212
    Get, 230
    If...Then, 149, 151, 160
    If...Then...Else, 154-155
    If...Then...ElseIf, 158
    Input, 221
    INSERT INTO, 519
    Kill, 214
    Line Input #, 217-218
    Loc, 230
    MkDir, 211

Next, 394
On Error GoTo 0, 398
On Error GoTo, 141, 398
On Error Resume Next, 308, 398
Open, 216
Option Base, 185
Option Explicit, 96, 98-99
Print #, 220-223
Put, 230
Randomize, 189, 336
ReDim, 191-193
Response.ContentType, 509
Response.Write, 503, 520
Resume Next, 213
RmDir, 211
Seek, 230
Select Case, 161-162
SendKeys, 255-257
Stop, 383-384
Type...End Type, 225, 227
Write #, 220-223
statements,
    looping statements and arrays, 187
    paired, 176
Static keyword, 333
static parameters, 495
Step mode, 390
Stop statement, 383-384
Stream object, 582, 590
String data type, 88
string, empty, 95, 143-144
structured programming, 156
Sub keyword, 112
Subfolders property, 240
subprocedures, 142
    advantages, 145
subroutine procedures, 112
    when to create, 142
Sum function, 118
syntax,
    assistance, 55
    auto syntax check, 52
    VBA, 48

T
Tab object, 644
tab order, 300-301
tab-delimited files, generating, 509
TabStrip control, 289

using, 311-313
TargetPath property, 245
Terminate event, 336
text box control, 286
  synchronizing with spin button, 308
text files, 220
  creating with WSH, 242
Text Import Wizard, 468
Text property, 360, 562
TextStream object, 681
Toggle Bookmark button, 397
toggle button control, 287
Toggle Folders button, 32
toolbar, 352
  creating custom, 354
  deleting custom, 357
toolbars
  Edit, 55
  Standard, 32
  UserForm, 296
Toolbox, 596
  buttons, 285
TransferSpreadsheet method, 463, 472
transformNode method, 558
transformNodeToObject method, 576
TXT file format, 215
type conversion functions, 103
type declaration characters, 93
type mismatch error, 92, 138
Type property, 239-240, 354
Type...End Type statement, 225, 227
typed variables, 94

U

Ubound function, 195-196
Uncomment Block button, 60
Unicode (Big Endian), 576
Unicode (UTF-16), 576
Unified Resource Locator (URL), 484,
  490-491
Uniform Resource Identifier (URI), 538
Uniform Resource Name (URN), 538
Unload method, 309
URI, *see* Uniform Resource Identifier
URL, *see* Unified Resource Locator
URN, *see* Uniform Resource Name
user forms, 285
user interface, creating, 337
user-defined data type, 88

UserForm,
  closing with VBA, 308
  toolbar, 296
UserForm_Initialize procedure, 315
UTF-16, 576

V

validation in XML, 542
Value property, 78
variables, 86
  advantages of, 106
  array, 184
  assigning values to, 94-95
  creating, 88
  declaring, 88-90
  declaring typed variables, 94
  determining the type of, 107
  forcing declaration of, 98
  initialization of, 95
  lifetime of, 102
  local, 100
  locating definition of, 106
  module-level, 100
  naming, 87
  object, 104
  private, 101
  procedure-level, 100
  project-level, 101-102
  static, 102
  subscripted, 184
  types of, 92
  understanding the scope of, 99
Variant data type, 90
VarType function, 107, 125, 137
vb prefix, 109
VBA, *see also* Visual Basic for Applications
  creating and running web queries, 490
  creating hyperlinks, 478
  data types, 87-88
  debugging tools, 349
  grammar, 48
  Kill statement, 214
  locating help, 54-55
  logical operators, 148
  procedure testing, 376
  relational operators, 148
  stepping through procedures, 390-391
  stopping and resetting procedures, 394
  syntax, 48

understanding errors, 51
library, 442
VBA procedures,
scoping, 113
using constants, 107
watching execution, 346
VBAProject,
assigning a name, 39
naming conflicts, 40
VBAProject - Project Properties dialog box,
42
VBComponent object, 653
VBE, *see* Visual Basic Editor
VBIDE library, 653
VBProject object, 653
VBScript, 500, 557, 566
View Code button, 31
View Object button, 31-32
View objects, 456
virtual directory, creating, 505, 591
Visual Basic Editor (VBE), 9, 28, 31
Visual Basic for Applications (VBA), 2
Visual Basic for Applications Object
Library, 66, 442

W

watch expressions,
adding, 384
removing, 387
using Quick Watch, 387
WCDataSources collection, 684
web queries, 488-489
creating and running, 490
dynamic, 497
with parameters, 493
web server, 488
posting data to, 591
WebTables property, 492
Weekday function, returned values, 156
well-formed documents, 539
While...Wend loop, 174
WindowActivate event, 425, 435
WindowDeactivate event, 425-426, 435
WindowResize event, 426, 435
windows
Code, 32-34
Immediate, 68-70
Parameter Info, 57-58
Project Explorer, 31

Properties, 32
VBE, 31
Watches, 385
Windows Scripting Host (WSH), 232
creating a text file, 242
performing other operations with, 244
windows, working with, 82
WindowStyle property, 246
WithEvents keyword, 432
WorkbookActivate event, 434
WorkbookAddInInstall event, 435
WorkbookAddInUninstall event, 435
WorkbookBeforeClose event, 434
WorkbookBeforePrint event, 434
WorkbookBeforeSave event, 434
WorkbookDeactivate event, 434
WorkbookNewSheet event, 434
WorkbookOpen event, 433-434
WorkbookPivotTableCloseConnection
event, 435
WorkbookPivotTableOpenConnection
event, 436
workbooks,
disabling macros, 29
enabling macros, 30
events, 415
New Workbook, 6
Personal Macro Workbook, 6
This Workbook, 6
using macros with, 29
working with, 80
WorkingDirectory property, 246
worksheets,
entering data in, 78
events, 409
obtaining information, 78
returning information, 78-79
storing custom form data, 298
transferring form data, 309
working with, 80
Write # statement, 220-223
WriteLine method, 681
WSH, *see* Windows Scripting Host
WshShell object, 245

X

xl prefix, 109
XLStart folder, 27
XML, *see also* Extensible Markup Language

and ASP, 586
creating spreadsheet files, 534
data islands, 555-557
document nodes, 567
documents, 539
DOM (Document Object Model), 561
elements, 536-537
schemas, 532
unformatted (raw) XML, 541
validation types, 542
versus XSL, 535
via ADO, 573
XML files,
building outside Excel 2002, 542
changing the type of file, 575
element or attribute based, 574
formatting with stylesheets, 545
linking with a stylesheet, 550
transforming into HTML, 563
viewing files formatted with XSL,
550-551
viewing in Internet Explorer, 540
viewing source files in Notepad, 536

XML flattener, 543-545
XML Path Language (XPath), 548
XML property, 562
XML Spreadsheet Schema (SS), 605, 607
XMLData property, 681
XMLHTTP object, 600
xmlns (namespace), 538
XML-SS schema, 543, 605, 607
XPath, *see* XML Path Language
XPath expression, 572, 584
XSL, *see also* Extensible Stylesheet
Language
applying a stylesheet, 576
document, 545
versus XSLT, 552
XSL Transformations (XSLT), 548
formatting elements, 553
using XSLT template, 553
XSL-FO (Extensible Stylesheet Language
Formatting Objects), 552
XSLT, *see* XSL Transformations

Companion CD

The companion CD-ROM contains the example files discussed in the book. The files are organized into folders named for the chapters. Files for the appendixes are in the folder labeled Other.

Simply use Windows Explorer to browse the CD.

 Warning: Opening the CD package makes this book nonreturnable.

CD/Source Code Usage License Agreement

Please read the following CD/Source Code usage license agreement before opening the CD and using the contents therein:

1. By opening the accompanying software package, you are indicating that you have read and agree to be bound by all terms and conditions of this CD/Source Code usage license agreement.

2. The compilation of code and utilities contained on the CD and in the book are copyrighted and protected by both U.S. copyright law and international copyright treaties, and is owned by Wordware Publishing, Inc. Individual source code, example programs, help files, freeware, shareware, utilities, and evaluation packages, including their copyrights, are owned by the respective authors.

3. No part of the enclosed CD or this book, including all source code, help files, shareware, freeware, utilities, example programs, or evaluation programs, may be made available on a public forum (such as a World Wide Web page, FTP site, bulletin board, or Internet news group) without the express written permission of Wordware Publishing, Inc. or the author of the respective source code, help files, shareware, freeware, utilities, example programs, or evaluation programs.

4. You may not decompile, reverse engineer, disassemble, create a derivative work, or otherwise use the enclosed programs, help files, freeware, shareware, utilities, or evaluation programs except as stated in this agreement.

5. The software, contained on the CD and/or as source code in this book, is sold without warranty of any kind. Wordware Publishing, Inc. and the authors specifically disclaim all other warranties, express or implied, including but not limited to implied warranties of merchantability and fitness for a particular purpose with respect to defects in the disk, the program, source code, sample files, help files, freeware, shareware, utilities, and evaluation programs contained therein, and/or the techniques described in the book and implemented in the example programs. In no event shall Wordware Publishing, Inc., its dealers, its distributors, or the authors be liable or held responsible for any loss of profit or any other alleged or actual private or commercial damage, including but not limited to special, incidental, consequential, or other damages.

6. One (1) copy of the CD or any source code therein may be created for backup purposes. The CD and all accompanying source code, sample files, help files, freeware, shareware, utilities, and evaluation programs may be copied to your hard drive. With the exception of freeware and shareware programs, at no time can any part of the contents of this CD reside on more than one computer at one time. The contents of the CD can be copied to another computer, as long as the contents of the CD contained on the original computer are deleted.

7. You may not include any part of the CD contents, including all source code, example programs, shareware, freeware, help files, utilities, or evaluation programs in any compilation of source code, utilities, help files, example programs, freeware, shareware, or evaluation programs on any media, including but not limited to CD, disk, or Internet distribution, without the express written permission of Wordware Publishing, Inc. or the owner of the individual source code, utilities, help files, example programs, freeware, shareware, or evaluation programs.

8. You may use the source code, techniques, and example programs in your own commercial or private applications unless otherwise noted by additional usage agreements as found on the CD.

CL

[X] **Warning:** By opening the CD package, you accept the terms and conditions of the CD/Source Code Usage License Agreement.

Additionally, opening the CD package makes this book nonreturnable.

005 .
54
KOR

6000703010